Tamil Nadu Development Report

सत्यमेव जयते

Planning Commission
Government of India

Tamil Nadu Development Report

सत्यमेव जयते

PLANNING COMMISSION
GOVERNMENT OF INDIA
NEW DELHI

Published by

ACADEMIC FOUNDATION
NEW DELHI

First Published in 2005 by
Academic Foundation
4772-73 / 23 Bharat Ram Road, (23 Ansari Road), Darya Ganj, New Delhi - 110 002 (India).
Phones : 23245001 / 02 / 03 / 04. Fax : +91-11-23245005. E-mail : academic@vsnl.com
www.academicfoundation.com

Published under arrangement with :
Planning Commission,
Government of India,
New Delhi.

Photo credit (cover photographs) : [1 2 3] oochappan
(http://www.pbase.com/oochappan/tamilnadu)

Tamil Nadu Development Report
ISBN 81-7188-465-2

Designed and typeset by Italics India, New Delhi
Printed and bound in India.

Contents

...CONTD. ...

...Contd. ...

...Contd. ...

The Core Committee

(w.e.f. August-2004)

1. **Shri Anwarul Hoda** — **Chairman**
   Member, Planning Commission
   New Delhi

2. **Dr. Renuka Viswanathan** — **Member**
   (Adviser SP-South), Planning Commission
   New Delhi

3. **Shri Naresh Gupta** — **Member**
   Member-Secretary
   State Planning Commission
   Government of Tamil Nadu
   Chennai

4. **Dr. Raja Chelliah** — **Member**
   Chairman
   Madras School of Economics
   Chennai

Dr. S.P. Gupta, Member, Planning Commission as Chairman, Shri M.L. Majumdar, Principal Adviser as Member-Secretary and Shri L.N. Vijayaghavan, Member Secretary, State Planning Commission Government of Tamil Nadu served as Member of the Core Committee during 2000-2004.

Preface

The Union Planning Commission, in consultation with the Tamil Nadu State Planning Commission, entrusted Madras School of Economics (MSE) with the task of preparing a State Development Report for Tamil Nadu, on the lines of the reports prepared for some other states marking the 50th Anniversary of the inauguration of economic planning in India. The State Development Report has been prepared as per the terms of reference agreed to with the Union Planning Commission. As suggested by the Union Planning Commission, MSE has enlisted the collaboration of some of the educational and research institutions in the state in the preparation of the report. The over all supervision of the study was done by Dr. R.J. Chelliah, Chairman, MSE.

As the table of contents would indicate, the report contains a review and evaluation of the development of the major economic sectors, and of fiscal and social infrastructure, besides government finances and financial services. The report also contains policy prescriptions which would lead to sustainable development. The preparation of some individual chapters has been substantially helped by basic research by consultants who also prepared draft papers.

The draft report was submitted to the Union Planning Commission and the State Planning Commission in October 2002. A core group under the Chairmanship of Dr. S.P. Gupta, Member, Planning Commission, held a meeting in Chennai on 29.5.03 to discuss the Draft Report. The Final Report has been prepared on the basis of the comments received during the discussion as well as the comments sent to MSE. Many of the chapters have been revised. Two additional chapters (which were not in the original terms of reference) on Demography and Employment and on Water Resources Management as well as an Executive Summary have been added to the report.

— Paul P. Appasamy

Professor,
Madras School of Economics,
Chennai

एम. एस. आहलुवालिया
MONTEK SINGH AHLUWALIA

सत्यमेव जयते

उपाध्यक्ष
योजना आयोग
भारत
DEPUTY CHAIRMAN
PLANNING COMMISSION
INDIA

MESSAGE

One of the important Tenth Plan initiatives of the Planning Commission was to sponsor the preparation of the State Development Reports with much of the work being done by reputed national level institutes. This exercise was undertaken in recognition of the fact that economic circumstances and performance in individual States varied considerably and it was necessary to examine development challenges for individual States in the light of State specific constraints and circumstances. The basic idea is to produce quality reference documents on development profiles of individual States and the possible strategies for accelerating growth, and reducing poverty and inequality.

The Tamil Nadu Development Report reviews Tamil Nadu's experience and highlights issues critical for the State's development in the years ahead. I hope its publication will stimulate debate on growth strategies appropriate for Tamil Nadu. I am sure the road map indicated in the Report will stimulate a broader awareness of the critical policy issues facing the State and will assist the State to move to a higher growth path and to achieve all round human and economic development.

(M.S. AHLUWALIA)

योजना भवन, संसद मार्ग, नई दिल्ली – 110001 दूरभाष : 23096677, 23096688 फैक्स : 23096699
Yojna Bhawan, Parliament Street, New Delhi : 110001 Phones: 23096677, 23096688 Fax : 23096699, E-mail : dch@yojana.nic.in

ANWARUL HODA

सत्यमेव जयते

सदस्य
योजना आयोग
योजना भवन
नई दिल्ली–110 001
MEMBER
PLANNING COMMISSION
YOJNA BHAWAN
NEW DELHI-110 001

MESSAGE

The Tamil Nadu State Development Report has been prepared by the Planning Commission with the support of the State Government.

The Planning Commission have initiated the preparation of State Development Reports (SDRs) in coordination with the State Government. Over the Tenth Plan period it is proposed to cover majority of the States in the country.

The present Report takes stock of the resources available in Tamil Nadu and provides a road map for achieving a higher level of growth. It is also intended to serve as a policy advocacy documents at the State level. As an official Report of the Planning Commission it will be widely disseminated as a public document.

I hope the Report will be useful for the State Government, non-governmental organisations, citizen's group and other concerned with the formulation and implementation of the plans and policies oriented towards achieving a better quality of life of the people of the State.

I would like to place on record my deep appreciation of the significant contribution to this Report of Prof. Raja Chelliah, Chairman, Madras School of Economics, Chennai.

(Anwarul Hoda)

New Delhi

दूरभाष : 23096756 फैक्स : 23096774
Telephone: 23096756 Fax : 23096774, email: anwarulhoda@yojana.nic.in

List of Tables, Figures and Boxes

Tables

Figures

Boxes

Executive Summary

Introduction

Tamil Nadu like the other southern states could be classified as a middle-income state among the 14 largest states in India. Since the growth rate in the nineties (1990-91 to 1996-97) has been high (5.2 per cent) it could graduate to the high income category. In terms of per capita income it already stands fifth following Maharashtra, Punjab, Haryana and Gujarat. After relatively slow economic growth in the seventies, Tamil Nadu began to grow at the rate of 5 per cent in the eighties at 6 per cent in the early nineties and nearly 7 per cent in the latter half of the nineties. There has been a slowing down in the last two years due to the general downturn in the economy. However, Tamil Nadu has demonstrated that sustainable growth of 5-6 per cent of GSDP is possible over two decades, and can continue atleast at that level in the first decade of the twenty-first century. This rate of growth is primarily due to the high growth in the secondary and tertiary sectors. The share of agriculture has dropped to 17 per cent while the service sector accounts for a little over 50 per cent.

Per capita GSDP has also grown at the rate of 3.6 per cent in the eighties and nearly 5 per cent in the nineties. The growth in per capita GSDP has been made possible by the decline in the population growth rate. In the year 2000, the crude birth rate and crude death rate had declined to 19.2 and 7.9 per 1000 respectively and the total fertility rate had declined to near replacement levels. By controlling the growth rate of population, Tamil Nadu has been able to convert the growth of SDP to fairly good growth in terms of per capita income. This is likely to be sustained in the future due to the fall in the total fertility rate. The rate of growth of per capita income was the fourth highest after Karnataka, Kerala and West Bengal.

Population growth rate in the State was only 1.1 per cent per year in the decade of the nineties due to the low birth rate. The level of urbanisation of almost 44 per cent in 2001 was the highest in India and has been uniform across the State. While the overall sex-ratio has improved during 1991-2001, the sex-ratio in the 0-6 years age group has declined in rural areas and remained stagnant in urban areas during the same period.

Due to the increase in life expectancy (67 years), the number of people over sixty has increased substantially in Tamil Nadu. The aging of the population has financial implications for the pension schemes in the organised sector, as well as for Social Security schemes in the unorganised sector. There are also major implications for health care for the aged. The private sector has begun to meet the demand for retirement homes. However, the State along with NGOs has to provide for those who cannot afford private facilities.

Poverty levels have also fallen in the nineties. In terms of rural poverty, Tamil Nadu is below the All-India average, but at 20 per cent is much higher than Kerala, Andhra Pradesh and Karnataka. However urban poverty (22 per cent) in Tamil Nadu is roughly the same as All–India and slightly lower than Andhra Pradesh and Karnataka. Rural poverty continues to be a concern because a significant portion of the population (56 per cent) continue to live in rural areas despite the fact that the share of agriculture in GSDP has gone down to 20 per cent and there is a decline in the cultivated area. Non-farm employment in rural areas will have to be increased substantially to absorb the surplus labour. There has to be absorption of labour in the services sector both in rural and urban areas, if poverty is to be reduced to much lower levels. The creation of jobs can take place only if there is sustained growth of the state economy over the next decade.

Tamil Nadu has relatively good infrastructure. According to the CMIE Index of Relative Development of Infrastructure, Tamil Nadu with an index of 147 stood third after Punjab (191) and Kerala (157). The All-India level of 100 is based on 13 important infrastructure indicators. In terms of power, telecommunications, road and water supply, Tamil Nadu has done relatively well. However, there are questions about long term sustainability with regard to both power and water. In the case of power, the issue is more a matter of tariff policy. Water is a physical constraint in Tamil Nadu due to inadequate natural endowment. The existing resources have to be managed well so that allocation is made based on the requirements of each sector.

The good telecommunications and road network make it possible to have decentralised activities in the service sector all over the State. Movement of goods and people can be accomplished in an efficient manner. Tamil Nadu needs to ensure that these infrastructure services are maintained well and do not deteriorate over the long term. In all these areas, there will be a growing role for the private sector. Some activities including bus transport are being privatised. Environmental impact of roads, power plants, and water projects need more careful analysis, so that natural resources and environmental quality are not adversely affected.

In terms of human development as measured by the human development index, Tamil Nadu fares better than the All-India average and Andhra Pradesh and Karnataka in the south but not as well as Kerala. In comparison with other major states, Tamil Nadu is at the top. However, Union Territories and small states like Delhi and Goa have higher HDI than Tamil Nadu. If the per capita income goes up, Tamil Nadu is likely to do even better on HDI. Since urban areas have a higher HDI than rural areas, the high level of urbanisation of Tamil Nadu is an advantage in terms of human development.

Tamil Nadu's performance in all the social sectors including the rate of growth of population demonstrates that the State is expending resources on human development which has resulted in better outcomes and also helped to build the human capital base for the future. Tamil Nadu is second only to Kerala among the major states in most indicators of human development as well as the HDI. On most social indicators, Tamil Nadu does better than economically more prosperous states like Maharashtra, Gujarat, Haryana and Punjab. Tamil Nadu has a rapidly growing service sector. Financial services, Tourism and Information Technology provide employment opportunities and contribute to the State economy.

Employment Pattern

The employed in the workforce or the worker participation rate declined in Tamil Nadu due to higher participation in education by lower age groups and a consequent reduction in child labour, significant reduction in women's participation and fall in agricultural employment. Significant gaps exist in worker participation rates between rural and urban Tamil Nadu as well as between males and females. The unemployment rate of 2 per cent in rural areas is higher than many large states in 1999-2000 and has increased since the beginning of the nineties. However the urban rate of 4 per cent is lower than many other states and has also declined since 1993-94. The unemployment rate among youth is also higher than the previous time period.

These predominantly negative changes on the employment front are countered by an increase in labour productivity across all the major sectors. The agriculture sector showed the lowest growth rate in labour productivity of 2.8 per cent mainly due to fall in employment whereas the labour productivity in the services sector was about 13 per cent. The real agricultural wages grew at an annual rate of 11.8 per cent for males and 9.5 per cent for females between 1993-94 and 2002-03 and is high compared to most other states in India. Similarly the casual labour wages of about Rs. 48 in rural areas and about Rs. 66 in urban areas is far above many other states in India. However significant gender discrimination seems to exist in labour market.

Despite the relatively high growth of GSDP in the latter half of the nineties, employment has barely grown. The overall elasticity of employment with respect to GSDP was only 0.04, indicating that the employment growth has been minimal despite the growth of the economy. Some of the labour displaced from agriculture has been absorbed by the secondary and tertiary sectors. Employment in both the public and private sectors has been virtually frozen with few opportunities for new entrants into the labour market. However, unemployment rates (usual principal status) remain relatively low indicating that there has been some absorption into the unorganised labour force. But the unemployment rate measured by daily rates was quite high (12.1 per cent) corresponding to about 36 lakh persons.

The focus of employment strategies will have to be on sectors which are labour intensive, particularly in the unorganized sector. There are a number of barriers to the growth of micro and small enterprises. Lack of entrepreneurship culture and quality business development services are major shortcomings. There is need for a State level resource centre to coordinate and monitor the schemes the schemes for training and entrepreneurship development. District level centres for the promotion of self employment also need to be established. The District Industries Centres need to be re-engineered into centres that can facilitate industry with information support and provide single window clearance. Changes to the educational system should be made by including entrepreneurship and enterprise management in the syllabi. Vocational guidance can be provided by employment exchanges. The exchanges need to pay greater attention to labour market information, particularly employment opportunities in the private sector.

Vocational education and training needs to become more market oriented. The Industrial Training Institutes and private Industrial Training Centres need to reorient their training to cater to present day needs, particularly in the service sector. Hotels and Tourism, Catering, Garment and Hosiery Industry, Call Centres, Medical Transcription, Sales, Courier Services, etc require trained manpower. The training institutes can have a tie-up with industries/services in their locality to offer short duration certificate courses. Training-cum-production centres are being implemented by the Department of Technical Education to foster industry-institute linkages. A State level agency should be constituted for designing training courses, identifying the training institutions, overseeing the conduct of courses, and granting certificates on completion.

If the development of Tamil Nadu is to be sustainable, the state must ensure that the human resources of the state are fully utilised. Otherwise, like Kerala, skilled manpower would have to migrate to other parts of the country or abroad. High rates of unemployment in the future would be an indication that the development of the state has not been sustainable. Similarly, poverty levels should be brought down to 10 per cent or less in terms of the head count ratio, both in urban and rural areas. Social safety nets in terms of both protective and promotional social security are being implemented in Tamil Nadu for various disadvantaged groups. However, these programmes may have to be expanded more widely if unemployment becomes a serious problem. The dire state of the public finances of the state make it impossible for the state government or the autonomous boards to increase employment. In fact, voluntary retirement schemes and other measures are under consideration. However, with decentralization, it may be possible in the future for local governments to hire more people. Local governments may have to impose user charges, etc. if they have to finance employment at the local level. The private sector has absorbed a large number of people only in highly specialised areas like information technology. The wide spread use of information technology even in government may open up new opportunities for young people in the service sector.

Agriculture

The share of agriculture in NSDP has fallen from 43.38 per cent in the sixties to 20 per cent in recent years. However, the percentage of the workforce engaged in agriculture remains around 60 per cent resulting in comparatively high rates of rural poverty. It is clearly necessary for the workforce presently in agriculture to gradually shift to other occupations, particularly in the rapidly growing service sector. It will be difficult to raise agricultural incomes substantially given that the average size of landholdings is less than one hectare and the poor resource base.

Gross cropped area has declined from 7.32 million hectares (mha) in 1960-61 to 6.56 mha in 1999-2000. However, yield increases have more than compensated for the decline in area. There has been progressive commercialisation with share of non-food crops going up to 45 per cent. Yet, rural incomes have risen very slowly, since profitability of food crops has been low and influenced by the procurement policies of the Government.

Land and water resources for agriculture are also limited. Out of the geographical area of the state of 13 mha, the net sown area is only 5.6 mha, of which the irrigated area is only three million hectares. Nearly 50 per cent of the cultivatable land is under rainfed agriculture. Farmers in the irrigated areas are already using ground water at rates that may not be sustainable. There is also excessive use of fertilizer without regard to sustainability of the soil health.

The growth of agriculture is dependent on the better use of land, water, and other inputs like fertilisers, which have to be priced rationally. Given the limited water resources, farmers will have to move away from water intensive crops like sugarcane. This can take place only if water and power are priced at their opportunity cost. Sustainability of soils could be ensured by gradually shifting to bio-fertilisers and bio-pesticides.

Better use of the large amount of wasteland for productive uses will be needed. Wastelands can be utilised for horticulture crops like fruits and vegetables and also for tree crops. As Tamil Nadu has nearly 50 per cent of cultivatable land unirrigated, It is necessary to have extensive programmes to improve the productivity of this land. Research and development of rainfed crops will be needed for a second green revolution in the State. Post-harvest technologies may also be an important consideration especially for the perishable crops.

Agricultural Credit

The entire chain of agricultural activities from land preparation to marketing of produce requires adequate finances. Timely and adequate credit to the farmer is necessary to increase agricultural productivity. Providing access to institutional credit for small and marginal farmers has been a major objective. Short term and medium term loans are provided through three tiers of cooperative banks. Long term credit requirements are met by the Tamil Nadu Cooperative State Agricultural and Rural Development Bank. The Kisan Credit Card scheme launched by NABARD is implemented through the cooperative banks. Further agricultural credit schemes can be based on NABARD'S district credit linkage survey.

Allied activities particularly poultry, milk, egg and fisheries have a vast potential. Protein malnutrition which continues to be a serious problem in rural Tamil Nadu, can be reduced if this potential is tapped. Though Tamil Nadu has a fairly good system of rural roads and most villages are electrified, other infrastructure facilities such as markets, warehouses and information systems have to be improved further. Explosive growth of communication and information technology must find extensive application in agriculture to link farmers to the markets effectively for export led growth. Reforms in the agricultural sector particularly with regard to procurement, cropping pattern, etc. may result in further crop diversification and increases in income to farmers with consequent benefit to the agricultural labour in terms of employment and wages. However, as the state is the most urbanised in the country, the role of agriculture will ultimately become secondary to industry and services. The major challenge will therefore be to absorb the surplus labour from agriculture into these sectors, if there is to be equitable and sustainable development of the state.

Industry

Tamil Nadu is one of the most industrialised states in the country with a dispersed pattern of industrialisation. Traditionally it has been known for textiles, leather, and automobile components. Later with the advent of a refinery, downstream chemical industries were established in the Manali complex as well as in some other parts of the state like Tuticorin and Cuddalore. Agro-based industries such as sugar and paper have also been established. Tamil Nadu is known for the large number of small scale units in textiles, garments, leather, matches, fireworks, etc. Thus, Tamil Nadu has a good mix of both capital intensive industries like automobiles, chemicals, and transport equipment, and many labour intensive small scale industries.

Tamil Nadu has the largest percentage of factories (15.4 per cent) in the country and ranks third in terms of net value added (9.9 per cent). Nearly 30 per cent of the state domestic product comes from the secondary sector. Manufacturing (registered and unregistered) accounts for about 23.3 per cent. The growth rate in manufacturing has been about 4.5 per cent in the eighties and about 4.8 per cent in the nineties. However, there has been a slow down in the last two years reflecting the downturn in the economy. The small scale sector has grown rather rapidly in the nineties (12.8 per cent in terms of number of units and 16.7 per cent in terms of fixed investment). But, there has also been sickness in the small scale sector due to restructuring.

The post-liberalisation period has seen considerable inflow of foreign direct investment, integration of markets with the national economy, and value addition in the traditional industries. Tamil Nadu has been ranked third in terms of the investment climate and accounts for about 10 per cent of the announced investments in the country. Tamil Nadu is now able to offer better infrastructure in terms of power, roads, and telecom but water continues to be a problem in many parts of the state. Water intensive industries such as chemicals face difficulties with regard to reliable supply.

The inflow of foreign domestic investment has helped to build up the physical capital as well as introduce modern technologies in the state. Hyundai, Mitsubishi and Ford have set up production units in the State. These firms cater not only to the domestic market, but also export automobiles from Tamil Nadu since labour costs are comparatively lower here. Tamil Nadu may have to meet the challenges posed by the requirements of the World Trade Organisation (WTO), particularly with regard to exports from the small-scale industries like textiles and leather. The nature of adverse impact on particular industries needs to be studied and suitable policy measures formulated.

Long-term sustainability of industrial development is dependent on the optimal use of natural resources, human resources and the physical infrastructure of the State. As Tamil Nadu is a water-short state, water using industries have to be discouraged in the long term. Pollution is also becoming a serious problem from the clusters of small-scale industries like leather and textiles. New approaches and technologies have to be considered to limit the pollution from these industries. Pollution free service industries such as information technology and telecommunications would be preferable in terms of sustainable development. Biotechnology will also be a thrust area for the future.

The Tamil Nadu government has announced a New Industrial Policy in September 2003. The objectives of this policy are to target an 8 per cent growth rate during the Tenth Plan and to reorient government strategy to achieve this goal. The government would undertake second-generation reforms that would include strengthening infrastructure, including availability of quality energy, labour reforms, fiscal reforms, restructuring public sector enterprises and business deregulation. Through public-private partnership the government seeks to enable the flow of private capital, domestic and foreign, for building infrastructure. The reoriented government strategy would promote foreign direct investment in new manufacturing capacity and would facilitate efficient performance and growth in the sector based on improved competitiveness.

A new policy for the small-scale industries sector has been drafted recently. The objective is to promote one million direct and indirect new employment opportunities in SSI and allied services. The main components of the strategy include:

- Priority to knowledge based industries/services.
- Focus on credit, marketing, technology upgradation, infrastructure, cluster development and entrepreneurship development.
- Provide financial support for common facilities such as training, infrastructure, technology and market promotion.
- Promote R&D collaboration and diffusion of technology.
- Simplify regulations and procedures by single window mechanism.
- Address issues and problems arising from the WTO regime.

INFRASTRUCTURE

Power

Tamil Nadu Electricity Board (TNEB) ranks among the top three State Electricity Boards (SEB) in the country, along with Maharashtra and Gujarat, in terms of the size of its operation gauged by the generating capacity at its command, the amount of energy sold and the number of consumers serviced. Tamil Nadu ranks sixth in terms of per capita electricity consumption in the states. The technical performance efficiencies of TNEB, measured by the plant load factor and the transmission and distribution losses, have normally been above the all India average and among the top five to six SEB's. TNEB has been in the forefront of rural electrification.

TNEB's financial record is, however, cause for much concern. Ever since the early seventies the average revenue realised per unit of electricity sold has been lower than the average cost of supplying a unit, if we do not take into consideration the subsidy provided by the State government. This gap has been widening over the years.

TNEB's problems can probably be traced to two basic sources: one is the nature of the institutional arrangement in terms of how decision-making authority, risks and responsibilities etc. are distributed and the other is the manner in which the State government has sought to subsidise the consumption of certain consumer groups. The management of the SEB neither has autonomy in making policy decisions nor is it held accountable for performance standards. The policy-making authority, which is the State government, does not directly bear any risk related to policy decisions. These factors have basically been responsible for not stemming the increasing slack in the system. The magnitude of the subsidies and the manner in which they are given have introduced considerable opaqueness in the system and created huge negative externalities. The net result of all this is that the small farmers, who are supposed to be beneficiaries of the subsidy scheme, find that their power supply is often erratic and of low quality and that their water tables are falling at alarming rates forcing them to buy water from others at exorbitant prices.

Future prospects are not very promising with the share of high priced industrial and commercial consumption falling and the share of heavily subsidised consumption growing. The price charged to large industrial consumers is close to the cost of captive generation and this is not going to be helpful for the sector that is facing increasing competition. The need for fundamental reforms in the power sector is hence imperative. The question is what should be the nature and form of reforms.

A beginning was made with the setting up of the Tamil Nadu Electricity Regulatory Commission and for the first time the electricity tariff, effective from March 2003, was subject to regulatory scrutiny and approval. A very good beginning was made in introducing a price for agricultural consumption and for hut dwellers. They were required to pay only a flat rate but the regulatory commission indicated that in course of time all consumption should be metered and payment should be based on the electricity consumed, even if subsidised.

In response to this ruling of the TNERC, the Tamil Nadu government announced, in March 2003, a direct cash support to each small and marginal farmer in the state and to each hut owner. This was to enable the small farmer and the hut owner to pay the newly levied charges. In June 2004, however, the government of Tamil Nadu issued a policy directive to the TNERC requiring free supply of electricity to be extended to farmers and hut dwellers, and domestic charges to be reduced, effective from April 01, 2004. The government made a commitment in this directive to provide the required subsidy directly to TNEB.

The larger issue is that of restructuring the SEB. The Electricity Act, 2003 has been passed and it seeks to consolidate the existing laws relating to generation, transmission, distribution, trading and use of electricity. Its objective is to protect the interest of consumers and towards this end it seeks to promote competition, rationalise tariffs and ensure transparency in policy making. These are to be achieved by distancing governments from their tariff making roles and regulatory responsibilities and vesting this power with regulatory commissions. The governments would have the right to intervene only in public interest. If the governments wish to subsidise any category of consumers they would have to make the payment in advance or as directed by the regulatory commission.

The Act allows for unbundling the electric utilities and introducing competition. At the same time it does not prohibit vertically integrated utilities. Experiments are ongoing in some states in India where the vertically integrated SEBs are broken up into smaller entities that are to function on commercial principles and that can be brought under private ownership. Institutional reforms in the electricity sector are taking place in a big way in most parts of the world today. The reforms are mostly dominated by the unbundling-corporatisation-privatisation approach. However, the jury is still out on the proven merits of this arrangement. Similarly, in the Indian context also the experiments have not yet begun to yield significant benefits.

Given all this, the question is what are the implications for Tamil Nadu? Tamil Nadu is at an advantage in that it has not yet made any major institutional changes that may be very difficult or costly to reverse. It therefore has the flexibility of choosing from different options by carefully weighing the costs and benefits involved. It could possibly follow the current unbundling trend. This organisation could be entrusted with the responsibility for electricity supply in the state. It could be given complete flexibility and autonomy in the way it organises itself to fulfill this responsibility as long as it meets the price ceiling and quality standards specified by the Regulatory Commission. More detailed suggestions for this arrangement are provided in the power chapter.

The rationale for the unbundling-privatising approach is based on introducing competitive forces in the system wherever feasible so that private ownership combined with a competitive environment would encourage efficiency. This would also increase the transparency in the system. In the Indian context however, the feasibility of introducing a truly *competitive environment* in the near future is uncertain, given the very poor financial health of almost all segments in this industry and given the massive levels of unmet demand. Private ownership of the unbundled entities without a truly competitive environment will not necessarily improve efficiency nor ensure transparency. The transaction costs of ensuring fair play and a level playing field in this framework would be really high.

The alternative framework suggested here would be a regulated monopoly and we know from experience that a monopolistic market has its own inefficiencies. On the one hand economies of vertical integration could be tapped but on the other the long-term incentives for finding cheaper and more efficient ways of operation and expansion would not be as high as in a truly competitive market. Regulating a monopoly market would entail lower transaction costs though compared to regulating a market that could potentially move towards an oligopoly.

The key issue therefore is to have a fairly good understanding of the potential costs and benefits (both the short-term and the long-term) of alternative approaches to institutional reforms, to understand the necessary and sufficient conditions needed for the "success" of each arrangement, to realistically assess whether these conditions exist or can be created in the Indian context and then choose the appropriate strategy that would optimally meet the required objectives.

Roads and Transport

Tamil Nadu was the first state in India to form an independent Highways Department as early as 1946 to plan, provide and manage roads, and it has been in the forefront in introducing new technologies, new programmes and improved strategies in the road sector. Even though the State has a good network of roads, it is necessary to improve the performance quality of the road system. Effective management measures are required to overcome the problems faced in areas such as land acquisition for road improvements, controlling encroachments, preventing ribbon development and the use of modern machinery for construction and repairs.

To meet the increasing volume of road traffic, the State needs to evolve a comprehensive Highway Development Programme which should aim at standardising the State Highways to atleast two lane paved shoulder configuration and Major District Roads to atleast double lane hard shoulder configuration. As Tamil Nadu is one of the states with very high accident rates, it is imperative that road safety measures including provision of extensive road signages and furniture and also establishment of Trauma Care and Accident Relief Centres need to be made critical component of the programme.

The government should facilitate the Highways Department and Engineering Contractors in using beneficial construction methods and adopting new technologies. Greater importance may be given to connect all villages having 5000 - 10,000 population by providing black-top roads, efficient drainage facilities along the roads, and constructing ducts to carry service lines, wherever such lines have to be taken within the right-of-way of roads.

To sustain continued availability of adequate resources for meeting improvement and maintenance requirement as above, it is essential that the State set up a dedicated and sustainable Tamil Nadu Road Fund with statutory fire-wall to avoid budgetary raids. Besides pro-active encouragement for public-private partnership (PPP) ventures in road sector through formulation of detailed policy on PPP and ensuring compliance to contractual obligations need to be ensured.

The private sector should be encouraged to play a greater role in road construction and management, besides playing a major role in operating passenger transport services. Public sector transport corporations need to concentrate on improving the quality of service provided to the public. Considering the high rate of fatal accidents on roads, road safety should be given highest priority and suitable planning and management strategies are to be evolved and implemented.

- Conversion of meter gauge lines to broad gauge lines requires to be given priority, enabling broad gauge tracks in all existing routes. Considering the traffic potential and travel convenience, it is necessary to have broad gauge double lines with electric traction on the two major corridors in the State: Chennai - Trichy - Madurai - Tirunelveli and Chennai - Salem - Coimbatore. On-going gauge conversion works and the proposed new projects of the Railways would greatly benefit the State.
- The new site recommended by the consultants for an international airport near Chennai needs to be considered. Early action is needed to implement the project.
- The advantage of the State in having 3 major ports and 14 minor ports along its coast line of 992 km should be fully utilised. Providing facilities for coastal traffic of passengers and cargo requires to be examined. All the fourteen minor ports are to be integrated with regional developments, giving focus on promoting export oriented industries and port based industries.
- An Unified Metropolitan Transport Authority may be constituted to co-ordinate and improve the

functioning of the various transport systems operated in the Chennai Metropolitan Area.

Urban Infrastructure

Tamil Nadu is now the most urbanised state in the country with 43.86 per cent of its population living in urban areas. This is partly due to the inclusion of all town *panchayats* as per the Nagarpalika Act. There are 6 corporations, 104 municipalities and 611 town *panchayats* widely dispersed throughout most of the districts of the State. Over time two or three urban major urban corridors have emerged in Tamil Nadu.

Although most of the urban areas are covered by water supply schemes, the level of service is not adequate. Access to safe drinking water was 74 per cent in 1991 compared to the All-India figure of 81 per cent. Upgrading of water supply systems as well as augmentation schemes are needed to provide the requisite quantity. It is also necessary to price water on a volumetric basis to cover at least the operation and maintenance costs. The government has mandated rainwater harvesting in all buildings (public and private) to recharge the ground water. Capacity building of urban local bodies has to be taken up to manage water supply and sewerage systems. To bridge the gap in water availability in the Chennai city, it is proposed to provide a sea water desalination plant with 300 million litres per day (MLD) capacity on BOOT basis.

Urban underground sewerage exists only in sixteen urban areas of the state. The access to toilets in urban areas was 57.5 per cent in 1991 compared to the All-India average of 64 per cent. The Tamil Nadu Government plans to provide sewerage on a priority basis for towns with a daily water supply of 90 litres per capita or more. Master plans for sewerage should include alternative technology options for safe disposal and for recycling of waste water. House service connections in several areas should be encouraged. Community toilets should be provided in urban slums and pay and use toilets provided in public places. Recycling waste water should be taken up wherever possible.

Financing of urban infrastructure in Tamil Nadu has taken place through the Tamil Nadu Urban Development Fund (TNUDF). TNUDF was set up with the participation of financial institutions like ICICI, HDFC and ILFS and is managed by a private asset management company. More than 500 sub-projects have been financed through the fund. The purpose of the fund is to develop the financial and institutional capacity of urban local bodies. Fifty of the largest ULBs have been given assistance to develop City Corporate Plans.

The State Finance Commissions I and II have provided for devolution of funds to urban local bodies for providing infrastructural services. SFC I has provided more funds for operation and maintenance than for capital expenditures. The Commission has also suggested the privatisation of solid waste management as well as a report card on satisfaction with services. The sharing of state's own tax revenue with urban local bodies is to be increased from the present 8 per cent to 10 per cent by 2006-07.

Public private partnerships (PPP) have been initiated in some local bodies with regard to urban infrastructure. NGOs like Exnora International took an active role in solid waste management to complement the role of the State. The New Tiruppur Area Development Corporation was set up with the involvement of the private sector to improve the urban infrastructure of the town of Tiruppur. Alandur municipality is exploring the possibility of a sewerage project using PPP, where the residents will make a substantial contribution towards the project. Such partnerships need to be encouraged in other local bodies.

If the private sector is to play a major role, it would be necessary to have a regulatory framework to ensure that tariffs are set appropriately, to ensure access for the poor who may not be able to afford the tariff, and to monitor the quality and level of the service. However, the higher priority is to ensure adequate financing including public private partnerships for urban infrastructure. In the long term, ULBs will also have to raise their own resources through user charges and other means.

Water Resources Management

Most of Tamil Nadu falls within the rain shadow region of the Western Ghats, and hence the average rainfall in the state is only around 943 mm/year. However, the coastal districts receive higher rainfall due to contribution of the north-east monsoon. Since most of the rivers are seasonal, the rainfall has to be conserved through tanks and reservoirs. In the last three decades, there has also been high dependence on ground water in many of the districts. This pattern is also reflected in the irrigation sector where the proportion of area irrigated by canals and tanks has declined while the proportion under wells has increased. Tamil Nadu already fully utilises the surface water potential and there is little scope for building new reservoirs. 60 per cent of the ground water potential has also been utilised.

Since the irrigation sector is by far the largest consumer (90 per cent) of water, improvements in efficiency of water use for irrigation can free water for other uses. Furthermore, the projected water requirement in 2050 exceeds the total availability of surface and ground water in the state by 24 per cent. Some of the strategies for improving irrigation efficiency which are being implemented include: conjunctive use of surface and ground water, advanced technologies like sprinkler and drip irrigation, and participatory irrigation management.

Recharging of groundwater and sustainable exploitation are necessary for proper use of the ground water resources. The absence of a power tariff exacerbated the extraction of ground water for raising water intensive crops like paddy, banana and sugarcane. The recent measures to introduce a tariff for agriculture may serve as a disincentive for unsustainable use. Since Tamil Nadu has substantial rainfed areas, watershed management assumes crucial importance. Catchment protection, check dams, percolation ponds, bunding and other soil and water conservation techniques have to be used to maximise *in situ* water use in the watersheds.

The domestic and industrial water requirements have been increasing rapidly and will make up nearly 10 per cent of the water requirement. It will be necessary to transport water over long distances increasing the cost of supply. Also, water provided for drinking will have to be treated to make it potable. Domestic water will have to be priced accordingly if the water supply agency is to remain financially viable. Almost all the rural habitations in the state now have a potable source of water, but the quantity available per capita is often much less than the norm of 40 litres per day.

Pollution of surface and ground water is occurring due to the indiscriminate discharge of sewage, industrial effluents and the dumping of solid waste. Sea water ingress is occurring in some of the coastal areas due to the excessive exploitation of ground water. Aquaculture is also contributing to the salinity of the ground water along the coast. In some of the western districts there are pockets with high levels of naturally occurring fluoride in the ground water.

The Government of Tamil Nadu adopted a State Water Policy in line with the National Water Policy of 1987. This policy is to be revised in the light of the National Policy of 2002. One of the highlights of the water policy is management at the river basin level. Tamil Nadu has constituted river basin boards for the Palar and the Tamiraparani rivers. There have also been a number of water related initiatives in Tamil Nadu. Of particular note are the World Bank sponsored Water Resource Consolidation Project, the National River Conservation Project and various watershed management programmes. The Government of Tamil Nadu has actively promoted rainwater harvesting in buildings.

The Tamil Nadu legislature passed the Ground Water (Development and Management) Act in 2003. A Tamil Nadu Ground Water Authority has been set up to direct and regulate the development and management of the ground water resources of the State. Every user in a notified area will have to obtain the permission of the Authority to abstract ground water. Electricity cannot be provided for energising wells which are in contravention of the Act. All new wells even in non-notified areas have to be registered. Thus, the Ground Water Act is a major policy initiative to manage the scarce and rapidly depleting ground water resources of the State.

Inter-state water issues are also important in Tamil Nadu. The long standing water dispute between Karnataka and Tamil Nadu remains unresolved despite the creation of the Cauvery Water Authority. There are also disputes with Kerala on the sharing of the water of West flowing rivers. The Telugu Ganga Project has begun to deliver Krishna water from Andhra Pradesh to the City of Chennai alleviating the acute shortages.

In the long term, Tamil Nadu may have to rely less on sharing water with other states unless and until the inter-linking of rivers project becomes a reality. The focus will have to be on managing the available water resources efficiently. Pricing could be an important instrument in resource allocation both with regard to the use of water as well with regard to pollution. If water user associations exist in all the major irrigation systems, they will be able to manage the available water resources better. River basin boards may have to set up in all the river basins of the State to coordinate the various uses and users of water.

SOCIAL SERVICES

Health

Tamil Nadu's health sector performance over the last two decades is an indication of the emphasis laid by the State on the overall objectives of the National Health

Policy. The State's initiatives in the public health sector have resulted in impressive gains in several areas over the last 20 years. Basic health facilities are extended to the mass of the population. Endemic diseases are eradicated or well under control. Simultaneously modern health facilities using advanced techniques capable of treating various serious types of illnesses and handling complicated surgeries have been established in the state. These facilities attract not only patients from other States but also from some developing countries as well.

A look at the current health status of the people in relation to the goals set for 2010, in respect of a few key indicators, will provide an idea of the leeway still to be made in the current decade.

Health Sector Performance and Goals

Indicator	*Status 2002*	*Goal 2007*
Demographic Changes		
Life Expectancy at birth years	65	70
Crude Birth Rate per 1000 population	19.2	15
Crude Death Rate per 1000 population	7.9	6
Natural growth rate, per cent	1.1	<1
Infant Mortality Rate per 1000 live births	51	28
Maternal Mortality Rate per 1000 live births	1.3	<1
Total Fertility Rate	1.95	1.5
Couple Protection Rate, per cent	51.6	65
Epidemiological Shifts		
TB prevalence per 1 lakh population	479	300
Malaria prevalence per 1 lakh population	70	35
Leprosy per 10000 persons	4.5	<1

Source: Tamil Nadu Planning Commission (2003), "Tenth Five Year Plan: Tamil Nadu".

Some of the unfinished tasks in the health sector which merit special focus in health initiatives in the current decade are indicated below:

- The high Infant Mortality Rate, specially neo-natal mortality, needs greater attention.
- The basic health infrastructure in place, and the linkages between different tiers, need strengthening to improve service levels.
- Urban health care requires greater attention, in a State with high level of urbanisation.
- New threats to health and well being of the people are emerging, such as HIV/AIDS, TB, Cancer and other life style disorders, like road traffic accidents, substance abuse, pollution and food adulteration. The public health system needs different approaches and varying skills to deal with these.
- Mental health problems are becoming more prevalent affecting the quality of life, of both the affected persons and their families.
- Efforts at awareness raising on health related issues and inducing behavioural changes in the population need to be more focussed, addressing the specific needs of different segments of the population for greater impact.

The State exchequer currently supports the public health services, with some transfers from the Centre. Over the last 3 years, the share of health in the State budget has ranged from 5.60 per cent to 5.86 per cent. The per capita expenditure on health works out to roughly Rs. 165 per annum. Health costs are rising over the years. It is doubtful whether the exchequer alone can continue to bear the burden and provide quality service. This points to the need for an appropriate strategy for increased public-private collaboration in the health system. A Health Systems Development Project is likely to be funded by the World Bank at a cost of Rs. 650 crore.

To pave the way for achieving the goals set for 2010, and to be in tune with the Millennium Development Goals, the above issues need to be addressed effectively. This will call for concerted action on the part of the government in the following areas:

- A Strategic Planning Unit needs to be established to review, on a continuing basis, the emerging issues in the health sector, design appropriate strategies and monitor their implementation.
- Decentralisation in health planning needs to be promoted by institutionalising district based health planning process.
- There is a need for improving linkages between various programmes in operation in the health sector which calls for an integration of the vertical programmes. The gaps in existing infrastructure needs to be filled through appropriate reorganisation and restructuring of primary health care infrastructure.
- The existing data system needs strengthening to generate sufficient data to identify poorly performing districts so that a differential and appropriate area specific strategy can be developed.
- Steps are to be initiated to improve access and utilisation of health services in districts with high mortality/fertility.

- Promotion of Public - Private partnership is required to meet health challenges in the current decade.
- Health Systems Research studies and Health Economic studies need to be encouraged to analyse the reach of health services and its impact as also the cost and quality of care.
- Networking of administrative, academic and research organisations in the State with national and international bodies with similar interest in pursuing Millenium Development Goals needs encouragement. This will facilitate exchange of experiences, collaborative studies, documentation support as also visits to countries with innovative health interventions.

EDUCATION

School Education

Most of the endeavours in development of School Education in the past have been focused on: (a) establishing new schools and increasing the intake capacities of existing schools through public and private investments; (b) enticing eligible age groups to attend the classes, especially in the elementary stage; and (c) revamping the curricular contents periodically. These efforts would have to continue. However, judging from the emerging scenario of revolutionary transformation of school education system, it will be necessary to embark on new innovative initiatives for school education through appropriate policy interventions.

Based on the analysis in this Report, the following policy aspects deserve further attention:

In order to fulfill the policy decision of Government of Tamil Nadu to achieve University Primary Education (UPE) by 2007 and Universal Elementary Education (UEC) by 2010, it will be necessary to create a capacity for 3 lakh children in primary schools (classes 1 to 5) by 2007 and for 6 lakh in the Middle schools (classes 6 to 8) by 2010.

This goal could be easily reached by increasing marginally the intake capacity of the existing 31500 primary schools and 5800 middle schools. Establishment of new schools may be left to the private sector. The State should adopt a Universal Secondary Education Policy (USE) and Universal Senior Secondary Education Policy (USE) to be achieved by 2020. This would require catering to additional 12 lakh in Classes IX and X and about 22 lakh in Class XI and XII by 2020. This could be achieved by doubling the intake in existing schools and by shift system without the burden of new infrastructure.

In addition to the efforts devoted to revision of curricular structure and contents, time has come to devote attention to the teaching and learning processes in the school system. Very many new and beneficial approaches have become available beyond coaching for examination. This includes student-centred learning, linking subjects with real life experiences, improving the personality traits to face the future, discovering creative talents and nurturing them, imparting hands-on technical skills to school students and so on. These initiatives should be structured as an integral part of school studies.

- The current school programmes on vocational education have not served the intended purpose. These should be substituted by other value adding experiences.
- The student-teacher ratio of about 40:1 should be improved to 30:1. The shortage of teachers should be remedied. The quality of teachers and their approach to innovation in teaching and learning need to be addressed.
- All schools should be required to maintain computerised records of students including their personal and health data.
- Involvement of local communities in school development should be encouraged with appropriate checks on possible misuse.

The Tamil Nadu Government has attached considerable importance to primary school education. Even so the level of funding required for the projections shown in this Report would require non-traditional sources of funding besides the budgetary allocation. Possibility of fee collection at a reasonable rate from certain section of the students should be explored. A revolving fund may also be considered to ensure predictable support.

Higher Education

Tamil Nadu has been in the forefront of Higher Education due to historical advantages and the cultural preferences. However the higher education system the world over is going through unprecedented changes. Much of the conventional wisdom associated with Higher Education is yielding to more purpose oriented knowledge, skill and attitudes. The higher educational institutions in Tamil Nadu are in a position of competitive advantage to achieve global recognition. Some of the major policy interventions for this purpose are outlined below:

- At least 15 per cent of the eligible age group between 18 to 12 should have access to higher education by 2010.
- This would mean increasing the intake capacity to 3 lakh from the present level of 1.2 lakh at the first degree level in arts and sciences.
- Similarly the Post-graduate intake should be increased to 1.5 lakh from 0.93 lakh by 2010.
- Instead of increasing the number of new institutions efforts should be made to optimise the use of available institutions by upgrading their facilities to accommodate the growth in addition to using shift systems.
- All colleges must adopt credit system and allow a flexible approach for transfer of credits among institutions.
- Transfer of credits between regular and distance mode under authentication should be provided for.
- Fee structure should be made transparent and affordable especially in view of majority of colleges coming under private management.
- Teaching and learning process should be based on world class standards emphasising on life-long learning, learning by doing and problem solving.
- Vocational skills should be integral part of first degree learning. Community college models should be suitably adopted for this purpose.
- Plan allocation for Higher Education should be 40 per cent of the Higher Education budget.
- The governance structure of the Universities and Colleges should be modernised for greater efficiency and transparency.

SOCIAL SECURITY

Tamil Nadu has been a pioneer in implementing various protective and promotional social security schemes. The protective schemes include pension schemes for the elderly, handicapped persons, destitute widows and deserted wives; survivor benefit schemes for families which have lost the breadwinner or loss of livelihood through accidents; maternity benefit schemes; and occupation specific schemes for handloom weavers, fishermen, construction workers, and other manual workers. About 12 lakh persons avail the pension schemes, 20,000 the survivor benefit schemes, and about 2 lakh the maternity benefit schemes each year.

The two major promotional security schemes include the noon-meal programme and the women's development project. 78 lakh children and 4 lakh adults benefit from the noon-meal scheme. Nutritional status of children has improved but widespread malnutrition still exists in the state.

The nutritious noon-meal scheme now covers pre-school children, primary and older children upto the age of 15. Pensioners and pregnant women are also covered by the scheme. Coverage is almost universal at the primary level and about 33 per cent at the pre-school age group. Other child development schemes under ICDS have been integrated into the noon-meal scheme. A comprehensive package of five services are provided through an "anganwadi". These include supplementary nutrition, pre-school education, health checkups and immunisation, referral and health education. The Central Government bears all the costs except supplementary nutrition which is met by the State Government.

The Women's Development Project has organised 20 lakh women (urban and rural) in about 1 lakh self help groups. The gross savings of these groups is about Rs. 175 crore and they have availed external assistance to the tune of Rs. 218 crore since the inception of the groups.

The growth of the self help groups has been phenomenal. Out of 20 lakh women in the SHGs nearly 5.5 lakh women have availed bank credit. The SHGs have served as an effective channel of credit for the existing income generation programmes. The group members come together to work for the community and for social causes such as literacy and women's health. In some areas, the SHGs could also be utilised for cooking the nutritious noon-meal.

The Directorate of Social Welfare is the nodal agency for coordinating an 18 point programme for women and children. These programmes include: health, nutrition, disability, education, literacy, child labour, drinking water and sanitation, and empowerment of women through SHGs. Convergence of services of all departments under Social Welfare at the block and village level are a vital component of the empowerment of the poor as part of the linkage building process. Strengthening existing connections and building new connections would bring in sustainable growth.

Despite the existing schemes and projects in Tamil Nadu, there is still need for a comprehensive framework for social security. The 10 per cent who work in the organised sector are covered by various insurance schemes. But, the large majority who work in the informal sector have to avail the assistance provided through the social security schemes of the state. The coverage of the schemes is not adequate. Further, the changing demography will result in a much larger number of elderly people in the future.

Tamil Nadu is one of the few states which has prioritised the provision of protective social security for its citizens. In the area of nutrition and women's livelihood security, the State has become a model for the country to replicate. But its efforts in the area of asset creation and employment generation are inadequate, even by Indian standards. There is urgent need for the evolution of a comprehensive social security policy spelling out a minimum entitlement for the disadvantaged. Other suggestions for implementation includes a strong rural income generation scheme, a contributory model pension scheme and the introduction of health insurance. Simultaneously the State will have to expand its coverage of minimum pension for the poor and destitute while at the same time making the administration of the schemes more transparent and simple. NGOs and CBOs should be used to the maximum extent possible to see that the exercise is a success.

The policy will have to specifically address the needs of the poor subject to sudden changes in their life style due to natural and man made causes. A data base will have to be created regarding all those who are below the poverty line (BPL) and all those who have a danger of falling beneath it. A rural income generation scheme along the lines of an Employment Guarantee Scheme will have to be put in place which will automatically provide succour to those who are placed in vulnerable situations. Ultimately, Tamil Nadu should become the first State to put in place a comprehensive safety net for its people.

OTHER SERVICES

Financial Services

The Financial Services Sector has had a positive impact on the economy of Tamil Nadu. The contribution of this sector to the NSDP (at current prices) of the State has shown a growing trend with a CAGR of 24.85 per cent during the period 1993-94 to 2000-01. The employment that is provided by the financial services sector is quite substantial. The number of people employed by the commercial banks alone was 85,228 in 2000-01. Considering the other financial services segments like FIs, NBFCs, chit funds, *nidhis* and insurance companies, this sector is one of the major employment providers in the State. Tamil Nadu figures among the top ten in several parameters of the banking and financial services and also has to its credit some of the leading institutions and companies in the financial services sector.

The financial services sector has witnessed several disquieting events over the past decade. This coupled with macroeconomic changes has resulted in changes in the regulatory mechanisms, players in the industry and also the preferences of the investors. These events have resulted in blurring of the distinction between various constituents of the financial services sector. The majority of the changes have adversely affected the NBFCs. With Tamil Nadu being one of the states with a large presence of NBFCs, these changes have had a larger impact on the State.

The majority of regulations governing the Financial Services Sector are controlled by central apex bodies, viz., the RBI, DCA and SEBI. In view of this, the initiatives of the State Government would primarily be towards creating the necessary infrastructure for the growth and development of this sector. With proper facilitation and support initiatives from the State Government, Tamil Nadu can achieve further growth in this sector. Some of the initiatives, which the State Government could pursue, are:

- *Ensuring Growth in Trade and Industrial Activity:* The financial services sector is a support sector in the economy and in order to grow, it would require growth in trade and industrial activity of the State.
- *Promotion of Chennai as a Financial Centre:* Chennai city in the recent past has been able to attract several financial services companies including global majors to set up operations here. In the light of the advantages enjoyed by the city and the recent developments, the State Government should work towards making Chennai an international financial centre by providing the necessary policy and infrastructure support.

Information Technology

Tamil Nadu has been a pioneer in the field of information technology. It was the first state to formulate an Information Technology Policy in 1997, establish an information technology task force and set up a Department of Information Technology. These efforts have paid off: there are now 40,000 professionals in the information technology field contributing to about 2 per cent of GSDP. In 2001-02 there were 866 companies exporting Rs. 5223 crore or more than $ 1 billion by way of software exports. Hardware exports which were of the order of Rs. 482.43 crore in 2001-2002, have the potential for much greater growth in the future.

The information technology infrastructure in the state consist of several information technology parks as well as a fibre optic backbone and reliable power supply. The Government of Tamil Nadu has begun several e-governance initiatives such as computerising land records. Information Technology education has now been promoted throughout the State in Classes XI and XII covering about 40,000 students. There are 30,000 seats in the engineering colleges in computer science and information technology related disciplines.

The Government has successfully developed an encoding standard and keyboard for Tamil. The scope for using information technology can be expanded substantially if the local language rather than English could be used in communication. Since there is good penetration in rural areas, it would be possible to provide farm prices and other relevant information to users in Tamil.

The Government of Tamil Nadu announced a new I.T. policy in 2002. The focus of the new policy is to make Tamil Nadu a preferred destination for business process outsourcing and information technology enabled services. Since most of the information technology companies are currently located in Chennai, the second tier towns such as Coimbatore, Madurai, Trichy will be developed in the future. E-governance and information technology applications in Government would also be substantially increased. Internet penetration in rural areas would be increased to bridge the digital divide. Apart from the existing concessions available to information technology industries, several fiscal, administrative and infrastructural incentives are to be given. Thus, the new information technology policy is expected to enhance the rapid growth of the information technology sector in the State.

The sustained growth of the information technology sector is possible only if there is domestic demand for information technology. Policies have to be initiated to promote demand in various sectors of the economy for the application of information technology. Tamil Nadu may also consider diversifying to hardware which has the potential to employ a large number of people and will have better linkages with other manufacturing industries. The growth of the information technology sector including I.T. enabled services could not only enhance the productivity of existing economic activities, but also ultimately provide employment to a growing number of people in the service sector.

Tourism

The touristic potential of Tamil Nadu is considerable as evidenced by the fact that the State attracted nearly 30 per cent of the 7.90 lakh foreign tourists who visited India in the year 2000. Foreign tourist spending in the State in that year amounted to Rs. 4320 crore while the 230 lakh domestic tourists spent Rs. 1250 crore. In a state where 50 per cent of the population is still dependent on agriculture, a sector with an almost stagnant per capita income (Rs. 4398 in 1997-98 compared to Rs. 3907 in 1960-61), tourism, in its varied forms, offers much scope for higher remunerative employment generation at relatively low orders of investment.

The touristic assets of the state are many, varying from the eternal appeal of its ancient and magnificent temples to its emerging knowledge based industrial, business and advanced healthcare centres. While pilgrimage tourism is indeed its staple, industry and business related tourism accounted for 48 per cent of foreign and 30.1 per cent of domestic tourist arrivals in the year 2000. Added to these strengths is the growing 'Fruits to Roots' cultural and ethnic connection that pulls the Tamil speaking population of Srilanka, Malaysia and Singapore to make frequent visits to the state. Other assets, hitherto inadequately capitalised upon, are the lesser known hill resorts and the 960 km long coastline with its alluring milky beaches.

The Tourism Policy of Tamil Nadu (May, 1992) had outlined clear objectives and strategies for tourism development in the state with its emphasis on treating tourism as an industry thereby enabling it to receive fiscal and financial incentives like soft loans, capital investment subsidy, concessional electricity tariff and 50 per cent waiver of Luxury Tax on hotel accommodation. Designating special areas for tourism development and identification and declaration of 'heritage towns' also marked the policy. Most importantly, the role of private sector in tourism promotion and development was recognised. A new and revised policy is expected soon.

Expenditures, both plan and non-plan, have been going up steadily over the years from Rs. 541.10 lakh in 1997-98 to Rs. 1475.48 lakh in 2001-02. The approved outlay in the Tenth Five Year Plan period (2002-07) is Rs. 102 crore. A cumulative growth rate of 12 per cent per year in domestic and foreign tourist arrivals is sought to be achieved along with an extension in the average duration of stay of domestic tourists from the present 9 days to 12 and of foreign tourists from 4-7 to 6-8 days.

Private sector participation in promoting tourism is being encouraged through entrusting state-run hotels and restaurants to franchisees. A Land Bank is being created in the office of the Commissioner, Tourism to serve as a database on vacant government lands that could be leased to private entrepreneurs to construct tourism infrastructure. Management of boat houses, restaurants and parks is being handed over to private hands. A longstanding demand of the hotel industry to reduce Luxury Tax on charges for accommodation has been met through a 50 per cent reduction in the tax in December 2002.

Accommodation infrastructure is adequate in Tamil Nadu to house the present and projected increases in tourist inflow, both domestic and foreign. Air, rail and road connections are of a higher density in the state compared to All-India averages for these infrastructure facilities. With these positive features and the proactive policies of the state government, the climate for tourism promotion in Tamil Nadu is congenial.

The goals/objectives set for Tourism in State's Tenth Plan are to increase tourist inflow to Tamil Nadu from the present level of 7-9 per cent to 10-12 per cent and to increase the period of stay of domestic tourists from 7-9 to 10-12 days and for foreign tourists from 4-7 to 6-8 days. The thrust areas are:

1. Clear product identification, development and expansion, such as destination, circuits, services etc.;
2. Creation and upgradation of required infrastructure, basic amenities etc., following an integrated and holistic approach;
3. Human resource development and skills upgradation; and
4. Promotion and marketing these aggressively and holistically.

The products, both destinations and circuits for development were identified for international, national and domestic tourists and indicated in the Tenth Plan document. The strategy for product development and promotion has also been set out elaborately. Action Plan towards achieving the above objectives needs to be formulated and approved early.

GOVERNMENT

Finances of State Government

Tamil Nadu's finances are supposed to be better managed than most of the other states. Yet, the fiscal deficit as a percentage of GSDP had grown to 4.2 per cent in 1999-2000. More worrisome was that the revenue deficit was 3.4 per cent of GSDP, owing to the fact that revenue expenditures were growing at a faster rate than revenue receipts. Wages and pensions account for 42 per cent, interest payments 13 per cent and subsidies 13 per cent of revenue expenditure. Out of total expenditure, 94 per cent is now consumed by revenue expenditure. The fiscal situation is made worse by declining transfers from the centre in the form of shared taxes and grants. Tamil Nadu has a high own tax to GSDP ratio but a comparatively low non-tax revenue ratio. Since the introduction of the uniform floor rates for the sales tax and the value added tax will limit tax revenue generating capacity by way of tax revenue, the state will have to examine options for increasing non-tax revenue. Of particular importance is the power tariff, particularly for agriculture. However, other sources of non-tax revenue may also have to be tapped.

Financial sustainability has become a problem in recent years on account of the increase in revenue expenditures, particularly wages, pensions and interest payments. Public Debt has increased to 18 per cent of GSDP indicating the effect of continued fiscal deficits over a period of time. Capital expenditures have been reduced substantially, which will have long-term repercussions for the development of the State. Reform of State finances including the liabilities of the Electricity Board has become an urgent necessity. Expenditures will have to be curtailed since revenue raising options are limited. The State may also have to lobby with future finance commission for more transfers from the Centre.

Governance

Tamil Nadu generally boasts of a long tradition of Local Self Governance and as evidence for it cites the Local Governance prevalent at the time of the later *Cholas* as enshrined in the Uthiramerur Temple inscriptions. But what is of relevance today is the current situation.

During the British Rule the major landmark was the passing of Madras Local Board Act of 1884 enacted as a result of Lord Ripon's Local Self Governance Resolution of 1882, ushering a three tier: Local Self Government at the District, *Taluk* and Union of Villages. The next major development was the enactment of the Madras Local Boards Act, and the Madras Village Panchayat Act in 1920. After Independence a two-tier structure of Village *Panchayat* at the grassroot level and a district level came into existence with no linkage between the tiers. This two-tier system continued under the Madras Panchayat Act 1958. After the 73rd Constitutional amendment, the Tamil Nadu Panchayat Act 1994 was enacted.

While all the enactments were passed with the objective of creating Self Governing Local Institutions, in practice, they did not or could not function as Self Governing Institutions but function mainly as agencies of State and Central Government. The 29 items indicated in the 11th Schedule to the Constitution have not been entrusted to the *Panchayats*. Similar is the case in respect of Urban Local Bodies.

State Finance Commissions were constituted as required under the Constitution. The First State Finance Commission provided for devolution of funds to the Local Bodies and it resulted in a steady increase in the fund flow. However, as stated by the Second Finance Commission "over a period of time, the Local Bodies have come to excessively dependent upon the State Government for discharging their function in a satisfactory manner". The local bodies are yet to augment their own sources of revenue through rationalisation of taxes, improvement in tax collection and revision of user charges for services provided by them.

Elections to the local bodies were conducted under the New Act in 1986 and 2001. The level of participation by voters in village *panchayats* was good (75 per cent) while it was less in Urban Local Bodies (45-50 per cent)

Notwithstanding the various enactments, the Government still does not have an overwhelming presence in the village. There is also lack of a close linkage between the three tiers of *Panchayat Raj*. There is also no effective and collective voice from the members of the Panchayat Raj Institutions and Urban Local Bodies for claiming the powers, which are legitimately their due, under the Constitution. These issues need to be tackled immediately in the future.

The Government of Tamil Nadu like many other State Governments has tried to respond to the widespread demand for greater transparency and accountability. The Right to Information Act was enacted in May 1997. Under this Act any bonafide person requiring information may have access to such information in accordance with the procedure specified under the Act. However, the Act suffers from various shortcomings which are pointed out in the relevant chapter. There is also not much information as to the extent to which citizens have made use of the provisions.

The right to information is also translated into citizens charters issued by public authorities having public dealings and substantial interface with the citizens. 27 Departments of Secretariat and certain Government Organisations have prepared citizen's charters and placed them on the table of the Legislative Assembly. The citizen's charters have been made available through the Tamil Nadu Government website. However, the percentage of the population who know of the existence of the citizen's charters, or what it means is very low. This is true not only among the uneducated, but even among the educated population.

New technologies have enabled governments to make life easier for citizens, providing immediate access to information through computers and facilitating the interface between citizens and government. E-governance is growing at a fast pace and includes a variety of mechanisms to increase the speed and efficiency of decision making in Government. Tamil Nadu has computerised land records, driving licenses, registration procedures, etc. Rural connectivity has also improved. The State Government should in future quantify the results of e-governance and publicise them widely.

All these measures are powerful instruments for improving services to the citizens and reducing the scope and opportunity for corruption. The real test of improved governance in Tamil Nadu through the use of such legislative, administrative and technological instruments will lie in the satisfaction of citizens and consumers, and would happen only when they can rightfully claim and obtain services to which they are entitled.

Chapter 1

Profile and Overview of Development

Tamil Nadu is the southern most state in the Indian subcontinent. It lies between latitude 8° 04′ and 13° 34′ N and longitude 76° 14′ and 80° 21′ E. The State is bounded on the north by Andhra Pradesh and Karnataka, on the west by Kerala, on the east by the Bay of Bengal and on the South by the Indian Ocean. Tamil Nadu has a long coastline of about 1000 km, which accounts for about 12 per cent of the entire coastline of India. Tamil Nadu, with an estimated area of 1,30,058 sq. km. ranks eleventh among the states of India in size and constitutes 4 per cent of the land area of the country. The State can be divided into two broad natural regions - the coastal plains and hilly western area. The major rivers flowing through Tamil Nadu are the Cauvery, Vaigai and the Tamaraparani.

Tamil Nadu has an equatorial, tropical climate in the inland and an equatorial, maritime climate in its coastal regions. In the inland the temperature may go to extremes in some places while it tends to be moderate in the coastal areas. By and large, the average temperature for most parts of the State ranges between 28° C to 40° C in summer and between 18° C to 26° C in the short-lived winter season. In the more hilly terrain, the maximum temperature may be as low as 26° C and the minimum temperature may go down to 0.3° C degree. The State experiences periodically adverse seasonal conditions. The normal rainfall is 942.8 mm. The rainfall has been below normal in 25 years over a period of 40 years.

Natural Resources of Tamil Nadu

Forest Area of Tamil Nadu

The State has 2.14 million ha. of forest area which comprises 16.5 per cent of the land area of the State (Table1.1). 86.12 per cent of the forest area are Reserve Forests, 11.17 per cent of Reserved Land and 2.71 per cent of Unclassed Forests. According to the Forest Survey of India (1999) Report there are 8659 Sq. Km of Dense Forests, 8398 Sq. Km. of Open Forests and 21 Sq. Km. of Mangroves in Tamil Nadu. The State has diverse types of forests like, Tropical Wet Evergreen Forests, Tropical Dry Evergreen Forests, Tropical Semi-Evergreen Forests, Tropical Moist Deciduous Forest, Littoral and Swamps, Tropical Dry Deciduous Forests, Tropical Thorn Forests, Sub-Tropical Broad leaved Forests and Montane Wet Temperate Forests. The forests of Tamil Nadu State are the home for a wide diversity of plants and animals, both domesticated and wild, which inhabit a wide range of habitats and ecosystems.

TABLE 1.1

Land Use Pattern in Tamil Nadu

Land use	*Area in '000 ha*	%
Total Geographical Area	13006	
Reporting Area for Land Utilisation	12,998	100.00
Forests	2,141	16.47
Not available for Cultivation	2,418	18.60
Permanent Pasture & Grazing Land	125	0.96
Land under misc. Tree Crops & Groves	226	1.74
Cultivable Waste Land	345	2.65
Fallow Land other than Current Fallow	1,229	9.46
Current Fallow	1,028	7.91
Net Area Sown	5,486	42.21

Source: Land Use Statistics at a Glance 1996-97, Ministry of Agriculture, GoI, 2000.

Protected Area

In order to protect and conserve the rich bio-diversity in the State, a network of Protected Areas (PA) has been constituted comprising 5 National Parks, 20 Wildlife Sanctuaries spread over 0.29 million ha, which constitute 2.24 per cent of the geographic area and two Biosphere Reserves. The State's rich bio-diversity and natural resources are facing a serious threat from the growing human and livestock population and also from various developmental activities.

Forest Cover

The per capita forest cover is 0.03 ha as compared to the All-India figure of 0.07 ha. Reconciliation of recorded forest areas from different sources and the forest cover as assessed by Forest Survey of India has not yet been done. Tamil Nadu still has some good forests along the Western Ghats from Nilgiris to Kannyakumari. Along the Eastern Ghats also valuable forests occur in Coimbatore, Erode, Salem, Dharmapuri, Cuddalore, Tiruvannamalai and Vellore districts. Important forest products of Tamil Nadu are Timber, Fuel Wood, Sandal Wood, and Minor Forest Produce.

Protection of Forests

Afforestation works have been undertaken on a large scale under various plans and schemes with the objective of reclothing the degraded areas and improving the resources of fuel, timber, and minor forest produce. The Swedish International Development Authority (SIDA) came forward to implement a massive social forestry project including 'village forestry' 'farm forestry' and 'extension forestry' schemes. From 1981-82 to 1995-96, Tamil Nadu implemented two phases of SIDA assisted social forestry projects. Though SIDA withdrew its assistance in 1996, the Social Forestry Project still continues.

Water Resources of Tamil Nadu

The population and area of Tamil Nadu account for 6 per cent and 4 per cent respectively of that of India but the available water resources of the State account for only 3 per cent. The average rainfall of Tamil Nadu is 943 mm against the average rainfall of 1170 mm of the country. It varies from 1200 mm near the coastal area to 550 mm in the inland area. In Tamil Nadu more than 90 per cent of the available surface water and 60 per cent of the ground water has been put into use. But the demand for water is continuously on the rise with the growth of population, industry and agriculture while the availability of water remains almost constant.

There are 17 river basins in Tamil Nadu of which the Cauvery is the largest. Most of the surface water is harnessed in 61 major reservoirs and about 39,000 tanks. 60 per cent of the ground water has also been put to use. The estimated demand already exceeds the availability in most of the river basins of the State. There are also serious water quality problems in some of the basins due to industrial pollution. In Chennai particularly, the waterways are severely polluted due to the discharge of domestic wastes. Sea water intrusion is also occurring along the coast due to the over extraction of groundwater. In some parts of the State, there is contamination due to excess fluoride.

River basin boards have been set up for two of the river basins – the Palar and the Tamaraparani. The Cauvery as an interstate river comes under the Cauvery Water Authority. Water resource issues are of particular concern in Tamil Nadu since there are "deficits" in many of the basins, and quality problems occur increasingly due to pollution. Policy measures have to be put in place both to allocate water in an equitable manner as well as manage the environmental problems. Tamil Nadu has adopted a State Water Policy consistent with the National Water Policy, and has brought out a State Framework Plan to manage the water resources of the State.

Coastal Resources of Tamil Nadu

With a long coastal line of just over 1000 kms, Tamil Nadu has a variety of natural coastal ecosystems. Coastal areas in the State are home to some of the richest, most diverse and fragile natural resources. But the rich coastal habitats are being threatened by pollution specially from land based sources, development activities such as ports and dams, tourism, deforestation, natural disasters, over fishing and destructive fishing practices.

Marine Biosphere Reserve

The Gulf of Mannar is located in Southern Tamil Nadu, India, between the Indian mainland and Sri Lanka. Established in 1980 as India's first Marine Biosphere Reserve, the Gulf of Mannar encompasses 21 small islands located from 0.5 to 4.0 kilometres from the mainland. None of the islands exceeds 3.5 square kilometers in area. The Marine Biosphere Reserve is approximately 10 kilometers wide and 180 kilometers long. The area is endowed with a combination of ecosystems including mangroves, seagrass and coral reefs, supporting over 3,600 species of plants and animals.

Coral Reefs

All islands in the Gulf of Mannar have fringing reefs. In addition, there is a 8 km. long reef in the Palk Bay adjacent to the Gulf of Mannar, as well as patching coral formation in the passage (Adam's Bridge) between India and Sri Lanka. The high turbidity of the water due to large scale coral mining and coastal erosion from mainland cause deterioration of the reefs. Exploitation of coral and shells for lime industries and hunting of dugong and turtles is still prevalent. The most serious threat to Indian reefs is the excessive and indiscriminate exploitation of corals and coral debris and sands which cause irreversible damage to the reef systems. Quarrying of corals has also resulted in the near-total elimination of several reefs in the Gulf of Mannar.

Mangrove Forests

Mangrove forests are seen on the river deltas around Pichavaram in Cuddalore district and Muthupet in Thanjavur district. But most of the mangroves are highly degraded in Tamil Nadu as is the case in other parts of India.

Fisheries Resources of Tamil Nadu

Tamil Nadu has a long tradition of maritime activity. Inland fishing is practised in rivers, streams, canals, reservoirs, estuaries and backwaters. In Tamil Nadu, marine fishing is more important than inland fishing. In 1998-99, the total fish production through inland fishing was 1.1 lakh tonnes, while marine fish production was estimated to be 3.7 lakh tonnes.

Inland Fishing

In Tamil Nadu except the Nilgiris, all districts are inland fish producing districts. Major fish producing districts are Kancheepuram, Cuddalore, Villipuram, Tiruvallur, and Thanjavur. One third of the fish production is through the major irrigation tanks. The fish production through rivers, streams, and canals forms only one sixth of the total production.

Marine Fishing

Tamil Nadu is endowed with a long coastal stretch of 1000 kms extending from Chennai to Kannyakumari with 362 fish landing centres located on the coastline of 13 districts. The long coastal belt, which accounts for 12.37 per cent (1000 km) of the coastline of India (8085 km) is also bestowed with about 41412 sq km of continental shelf. Marine fish production through mechanised boats is 50 per cent of the total production of the State.

Export of Fish

There are many varieties of fish caught in the coast of Tamil Nadu. These fishes and other products are exported regularly to foreign countries and earn substantial foreign exchange (Table 1.2).

TABLE 1.2

Export of Fish and Fishery Products from India and Tamil Nadu (1994-95 to 1997-98)

Year	*India*		*Tamil Nadu*	
	Qty in '000 tonnes	*Value (Rs. Crore)*	*Qty in '000 tonnes*	*Value (Rs. Crore)*
1994-95	307.337	3575.27	28.831	780.10
1995-96	296.277	3501.11	31.330	719.18
1996-97	378.199	4121.36	40.878	1075.67
1997-98	385.188	4697.48	41.052	1220.05

Source: Tamil Nadu Fisheries Statistics, Dept. of Fisheries, Chennai.

Mineral Resources of Tamil Nadu

Minerals play a very important role in the industrial development of a country. Tamil Nadu is endowed only with a limited number of major minerals of which a few are exploited economically.

Lignite: Prominent occurrences of lignite in Tamil Nadu are confined to Neyveli and its environs in Cuddalore district and Jayamkondacholapuram in Perambalur district. Besides the above, lignite occurrences are reported in certain areas of Thanjavur, Tiruchirapalli and Ramanathapuram.

Oil Exploration in Cauvery Basin

The Cauvery basin spreads over 25000 sq. km in Tamil Nadu and Pondicherry. The prospective area considered for hydrocarbon exploration is 15,200 sq. km. The Cauvery basin extends into the offshore waters of Tamil Nadu coast in the Bay of Bengal, Palk Strait and Gulf of Mannar and into the territory of Sri Lankan waters. Hydrocarbon exploration is also taking place in the offshore area. Exploration activities were started in the basin in 1958 by undertaking geological mapping of the area. Commercial hydrocarbon discovery occurred in 1984. A total of 24 oil and gas prospects on land and 2 oil prospects has been discovered, and 334 wells on land and 37 wells offshore have been drilled. The annual production of oil from the basin has gradually increased from 0.005 Mmt in 1986-87 to 0.365 Mmt in 1998-99.

Other Important Minerals

Bauxite – Irregular pockets of Bauxite occur in Nilgiris district, Shevroy and Kollimalai hills in Salem district and Palani hills of Dindigul District. The total known reserves are of the order of 10 million tonnes.

Limestone – The limestone in Tami Nadu occurs in the form of crystalline and non-crystalline varieties besides corals. The bulk of limestone deposits are found in the southern districts of the State: Salem, Tiruchirapalli, Madurai, Ramanathapuram, Nagapattinam, Tirunelveli and Tuticorin districts. The total reserve of the crystalline limestone is 200 million tonnes of 'proved' category and about 25-30 million tonnes of 'inferred' category. The total estimated reserve of non-crystalline limestone is about 670 million tonnes of both 'proved' and 'inferred' categories. Mining of coral limestone is banned at present for the preservation of ecology and for preventing sea erosion.

Magnesite – In Tamil Nadu the most prominent deposit of magnesite is located in Chalk Hills of Salem district, which occurs over an area of 17 sq. km. Other minor occurrences are in parts of Dharmapuri, Namkkal, Erode, Coimbatore and Tiruvannamalai districts.

Mica – Light ruby coloured mica occurs in Erode district. In Nilgiris district there are old workings of mica. Irregular pockets were traced in Kanyakumari district.

Quartz – Good grade vein quartz is reported in Salem district. The total reserves of quartz in quartz veins and feldspar are of the order of 5 million tonnes.

Demographic Aspects of Tamil Nadu

Tamil Nadu had a population of 55.9 million according to the 1991 census which rose to 62.1 million in 2001 making it the sixth most populous State in the country. Tamil Nadu is not only one of the most populous state of India but is also densely populated. The density of population in Tamil Nadu is 478 persons per sq. km. whereas the national average is 324 persons per sq. km., and is the sixth highest among the major states of India. (Table 1.3)

TABLE 1.3

Density of Population in Tamil Nadu and India – 1991 and 2001

States	*Density of Pop./sq. km. 1991*	*Density of Pop./sq. km. 2001*
Tamil Nadu	429	478
All-India	267	324

Source: Census of India 2001, Paper 1 of 2001.

Growth Rate

The population growth rate has declined during 1991-2001 as compared to 1981-1991 in practically all the major States except Bihar (excluding Jharkhand). The Southern States have shown a decline in growth rate from their already relatively lower levels. In Tamil Nadu the growth rate between 1981 and 1991 was 15.39 per cent whereas growth rate between 1991 and 2001 was only 11.19 per cent. The decadal growth rate of Tamil Nadu was lower than that at the national level. The compound annual growth rate between 1981 and 1991 which was 1.43 per cent declined to 1.06 per cent in the last decade. The total fertility rate is now close to replacement level of fertility.

Rural – Urban Population

Tamil Nadu is also more urbanised than the other major states of India. According to the 2001 Census, 43.86 per cent of the population of Tamil Nadu live in urban areas whereas the level of urbanisation at the national level is less than one-third (27.78 per cent). According to 1991 census also the level of urbanisation of Tamil Nadu (34.15 per cent) was high; however, in 2001 it became the State having the highest percentage of urban population in India (Table 1.4).

TABLE 1.4

Level of Urbanisation in Tamil Nadu and All-India

States	*2001*			*1991*		
	Total Pop. (Crore)	*Urban Pop. (Crore)*	*% of Urban*	*Total Pop. (Crore)*	*Urban Pop. (Crore)*	*% of Urban*
Tamil Nadu	**6.21**	**2.7**	**43.86**	**5.58**	**1.9**	**34.15**
All-India	**102.70**	**28.5**	**27.78**	**84.63**	**21.8**	**25.71**

Source: Census of India 2001, Paper 1 of 2001.

The increase in the level of urbanisation in Tamil Nadu over the period 1991-2001 is related to the emergence of a large number of statutory towns. In the 2001 census, all statutory towns and places that satisfy certain demographic and economic criteria, are treated as urban. All Town *Panchayats* have been included in the urban frame irrespective of whether they satisfy the demographic and economic criteria.

Tamil Nadu Economy: An Overview

It is well recognised that Tamil Nadu is one of the relatively developed and fast growing state in the Indian Union, with considerable progress achieved in various facets of development. It is one of the few states in the country, that have achieved considerable success in both economic growth and human development. The rate of growth of the economy measured in terms of the growth of State Domestic Product (SDP) was, however, fairly low during the sixties and the seventies. During the seventies (1970-71 to 1979-80), the growth rate of NSDP was only 3.2 per cent per annum (Table 1.5) and per capita output grew only at 1.5 per cent per annum. It is estimated that in 1980-81, in terms of per capita output (GSDP), Tamil Nadu had only the 8th rank among the 14 major states.

The growth of the economy accelerated since the beginning of the eighties. During the last two decades, Tamil Nadu has bettered the record of many States and has forged ahead. Given the acquisition of the capacity by the economy to grow at a "respectable" rate of around six per cent per annum and the considerable progress made in human development, the stage has been set to make a big push to take Tamil Nadu into the category of newly industrialised states such as Malaysia and Thailand.

The main objective of this study is to review the various facets of the growth of the Tamil Nadu's economy and the progress in human development since the beginning of the eighties, that is, during the last two decades, which have brought about significant changes in Tamil Nadu's economy. We also attempt to describe the present relative position of Tamil Nadu against the setting of the performance of the other major states and indicate the strong and weak points. On the basis of this analysis, we shall indicate in broad detail the major policy initiatives needed.

TABLE 1.5

NSDP (1980-81 Prices) in Tamil Nadu (1970-71 to 1980-81)

Year	*NSDP (Rs. Crore)*	*Per Capita NSDP (Rs.)*
1970-71	6301.69	1545
1971-72	6595.43	1585
1972-73	6624.93	1561
1973-74	6851.19	1584
1974-75	6029.69	1368
1975-76	6990.31	1559
1976-77	7240.66	1588
1977-78	7853.38	1695
1978-79	8171.29	1738
1979-80	8429.05	1770
1980-81	7218.16	1498
	Growth Rates (%)	
1970-71 to 79-80	3.2	1.47
1970-71 to 80-81	2.5	0.81

Source: Directorate of Economics and Statistics, Government of Tamil Nadu.

Review of Growth and Development

According to state level statistics, the GSDP of Tamil Nadu grew at an average annual rate of 5.1 per cent during the eighties (Table 1.6). This marks a considerable acceleration of growth over that in the seventies. The growth of GSDP was not stable during the period (Table 1.6). There was negative growth during the two years, 1982-83 and 1986-87; and an examination of the annual growth rates shows considerable variation from year to year. It may also be noted that right through the years 1980-81 and 1989-90 the per capita net output of Tamil Nadu was lower than the All-India average (Department of Evaluation and Applied Research, 1999-00). However, with the fall in the rate of growth of population, per capita output could record a significant growth rate of 3.6 per cent per annum – this indeed represents a significant acceleration in the growth of per capita output as compared to its growth in the seventies (at 1.5 per cent).

TABLE 1.6

GSDP (1980-81 Prices) in Tamil Nadu (1980-81 to 1989-90)

Year	*GSDP Total (Rs. Crore)*	*Per Capita GSDP (Rs.)*
1980-81	8081	1677
1981-82	8931	1828
1982-83	8555	1723
1983-84	9069	1796
1984-85	10178	1981
1985-86	10656	2040
1986-87	10588	1996
1987-88	11264	2092
1988-89	12164	2252
	Growth Rate (%)	
1980-81 to 1989-90	5.05	3.58

Source: Directorate of Economics and Statistics, Government of Tamil Nadu.

Table 1.7 presents the changes in the composition of the GSDP of Tamil Nadu from 1980-81 to 1992-93. It is noticed that till 1986-87, there was no significant change in the sectoral composition of GSDP; the share of the primary sector remained more or less constant, while that of the secondary sector fell by just 2.3 percentage points i.e., from 34.49 per cent of the total to 32.15 per cent. The share of the tertiary sector increased from 40.7 per cent to 43.5 per cent. By 1991-92, the share of the tertiary sector had risen to 44.9 per cent. During the same period, the share of the secondary sector came down correspondingly to 32 per cent. We notice that there is an underlying trend of reduction in the share of the secondary sector, but it is not pronounced.

TABLE 1.7

Changes in the Composition of GSDP in Tamil Nadu (1980-81 to 1992-93)

(% of total)

Year	*Primary Sector*	*Secondary Sector*	*Tertiary Sector*
1980-81	24.85	34.49	40.66
1981-82	27.99	32.64	39.37
1982-83	22.97	35.38	41.65
1983-84	25.72	33.89	40.39
1984-85	26.88	34.10	39.02
1985-86	23.97	33.21	42.82
1986-87	24.36	32.15	43.49
1987-88	23.29	31.56	45.15
1988-89	21.80	35.72	42.48
1989-90	22.93	32.11	44.96
1990-91	22.20	34.53	43.27
1991-92	23.93	31.22	44.85
1992-93	23.27	31.82	44.91

Source: Directorate of Economics and Statistics, Government of Tamil Nadu.

Growth rate estimates in Table 1.8 shows that the primary, secondary and tertiary sectors grew at the annual rate of 3.4 per cent, 4.6 per cent and 6.4 per cent during 1980-81 to 1989-90.

With the liberalisation of economic policies by the central government and on the basis of the economic and social foundations laid in the State in the earlier decades, the GSDP of the State grew during the nineties (1990-91 to 1999-00) at a very satisfactory rate of 6.8 per cent per annum and per capita output at 5.8 per cent (Table 1.9). That at the same time, the rate of growth of population came down together with the reduction of total fertility rate (TFR) to near replacement level is an indication of healthy economic growth accompanied by human development. The conditions are now conducive to a successful attack on poverty in all its important aspects.

The GSDP of Tamil Nadu was Rs.128646 crore and per capita GSDP was Rs. 20,899 in 1999-2000 (CSO-New Series). In terms of per capita GSDP, Tamil Nadu ranked fifth after Maharashtra (Rs. 26486), Punjab

TABLE 1.8

Growth Rate of Total GSDP and Components in Tamil Nadu (1980-81 to 1989-90)

(Per cent)

Primary Sector	*Agriculture & Allied*	*Others in Primary Sector*	*Secondary Sector*	*Manufacture*	*Other Industries*	*Tertiary Sector*	*Trade etc.*	*Transport etc.*	*Public Admn. & Others*	*GSDP Total*
3.43	3.21	6.55	4.59	4.3	5.58	6.36	5.53	6.7	6.16	5.05

TABLE 1.9

GSDP and Per Capita GSDP in Tamil Nadu (New Series)

Year	*GSDP Current Prices (Rs. Crore)*	*Per Capita GSDP in Current Price (Rs.)*	*GSDP in 1993-94 Prices (Rs. Crore)*	*Per Capita GSDP in 1993-94 Prices (Rs.)*
1990-91	35662	6421	48547	8742
1991-92	42069	7486	49909	8881
1992-93	48910	8616	53524	9429
1993-94	57833	10088	57833	10088
1994-95	69402	11991	65735	11358
1995-96	78767	13482	68501	11725
1996-97	91914	15587	73762	12509
1997-98	104683	17590	78114	13126
1998-99	117044	19498	81292	13535
1999-00	128646	20899	83314	13534
		Annual Growth Rates (%)		
1990-91 to 1999-00	15.7	14.5	6.8	5.8
1993-94 to 1998-99	15.0	14.0	6.8	5.8
1993-94 to 1999-00	14.2	13.0	6.1	4.9

Source: CSO (1999 & 2000) Diskettes.

Note: Up to 1992-93, the old series data were adjusted to be comparable with new series (the adjustment factor is 0.878).

(Rs. 26234), Haryana (Rs. 23933), and Gujarat (Rs. 22141). During the period 1993-94 to 1999-2000 Tamil Nadu's GSDP grew at 6 per cent per annum and per capita GSDP at 4.9 per cent. The rate of growth of per capita output of Tamil Nadu was the fourth highest after Karnataka, Kerala and West Bengal (Table 1.10).

TABLE 1.10

Growth of GSDP and Per Capita GSDP for Selected States in India

States	*Per Capita GSDP (1999-00) (Rs.)*	*Annual Growth Rates from 1993-94 to 1999-00 (%)*	
		GSDP	*Per Capita GSDP*
(1)	(2)	(3)	(4)
Andhra Pradesh	16203	4.87	3.56
Assam	10811	2.53	0.85
Bihar	7268	3.87	2.20
Gujarat	22141	5.61	3.83
Haryana	23933	5.44	3.46
Himachal Pradesh	17126	7.05	4.45
Karnataka	18332	7.08	5.53
Kerala	20377	6.61	5.59
Madhya Pradesh	16309	3.72	4.53
Maharashtra	26486	5.42	3.90
Orissa	10642	3.69	2.41
Punjab	26234	4.97	3.06
Rajasthan	12752	4.87	2.77
Tamil Nadu ^	**20899**	**6.01**	**4.90**
Uttar Pradesh	11130	4.81	2.66
West Bengal	16954	7.04	5.44

Source: (Basic Data) Central Statistical Organisation (CSO), Government of India, 1999 and 2000 (Diskettes).

Note: Growth rates of GSDP and Per Capita GSDP are in constant (1993-94) prices. For Himachal Pradesh, Kerala and Punjab, provisional figures for the year 1999-00 are used.

^ Per Capita GSDP of Tamil Nadu in 2000-01 was Rs. 23680 (Provisional Estimates).

Table 1.11 gives the details of the changes in the composition of Tamil Nadu GSDP in terms of percentage shares during the nineties. The relative shares of the primary sector and the secondary sector decreased substantially. The share of each sector declined by about 4 percentage points. Their joint share thus went down by nearly 8 percentage points. As of 1999-2000, the combined share of the primary and secondary sectors had come down to less than 50 per cent.

Manufacturing (registered and unregistered) accounted for only about 20 per cent at the end of the nineties as against nearly 25 per cent at the beginning of the nineties. The growth of manufacturing in Tamil Nadu has slowed down during the nineties (4.8 per cent per annum). Tamil Nadu is still one of the industrially advanced states and has a diversified industrial structure but with liberalisation keen competition is to be encountered in the future. In this context it is to be remembered that that Tamil Nadu is not richly endowed with natural resources, does not have abundance of water and is not situated near the big and fast growing markets in the west – north-west of the country.

Tamil Nadu's agriculture is largely that of small farmers. Nevertheless, productivity levels in many crops are among the highest in the country. The cropping pattern has been influenced by government interventions, pricing policy and restriction on free movement of grains. Agricultural GSDP has been growing at around 3 per cent only. At the same time the over-use of ground water for irrigation, due to wrong water pricing policy, has led to a lowering of the water table far beyond prudent limits. Apart from technological innovations and further diversification into horticulture, floriculture, fruits, vegetables etc., there is need for change in government policies to induce decision making by farmers along economically rational lines, in order to raise the rate of growth and to diversify the base of agricultural operations and to raise rural prosperity.

The service sector can be broadly divided into two categories: human development related services such as health, education, housing, and sanitation; second, economic activities related services such as transport, financial services and IT. In Tamil Nadu both categories of services are well developed. Tamil Nadu has a very strong base in technical education due to investments over the years. The I.T. sector has grown rapidly due to the availability of technical manpower in the computer related fields. Similarly, the financial sector has developed in Tamil Nadu due to the available manpower as well as the large number of financial organisations.

Human Development

There are many indicators of human development – health, literacy, income etc., but these could be summed up in terms of the human development index (HDI). The HDI is a composite index of three dimensions – economics, education and health. These have been captured in the HDI by: per capita monthly expenditure adjusted for inequality; a combination of literacy rate and intensity of formal education; and a combination of life expectancy and infant mortality rate. Tamil Nadu fares better than the All-India average and Andhra Pradesh and Karnataka in the south but not as well as Kerala (Table 1.12). In comparison with other major states, Tamil Nadu is at the top. However, Union Territories and small states like Delhi and Goa have

TABLE 1.11

Composition of GSDP in Tamil Nadu (New Series)

(% Share)

Sector	*1993-94*	*1994-95*	*1995-96*	*1996-97*	*1997-98*	*1998-99*	*1999-00*
Primary Sector of which:-	24.32	23.79	19.92	18.55	19.44	20.06	19.74
Agriculture	22.64	22.23	18.43	17.11	18.16	18.81	17.18
Forestry & Logging	0.72	0.65	0.61	0.57	0.53	0.52	0.80
Fishing	0.96	0.91	0.88	0.87	0.75	0.73	1.75
Secondary Sector of which:-	32.40	32.82	34.28	32.38	30.79	28.94	29.86
Mining & Quarrying	0.74	0.70	0.62	0.55	0.72	0.73	0.44
Manufacturing: Registered	15.02	14.88	15.80	14.06	13.14	12.05	12.85
Manufacturing: Unregistered	9.23	9.36	9.48	9.32	8.72	7.99	7.79
Manufacturing: Total	24.25	24.24	25.28	23.38	21.86	20.04	20.64
Construction	5.24	5.57	5.99	5.99	5.78	5.73	5.98
Electricity, Gas and Water Supply	2.17	2.31	2.39	2.46	2.43	2.44	2.79
Tertiary Sector of which:-	43.27	43.37	45.81	49.06	49.77	51.01	50.40
Railway	0.67	0.60	0.56	0.56	0.54	0.56	0.53
Other Transports	6.51	6.28	6.20	6.02	5.90	5.96	4.95
Storage	0.11	0.10	0.09	0.09	0.09	0.08	0.09
Communication	1.62	1.69	1.95	2.19	2.37	2.44	2.03
Trade, Hotels and Restaurants	13.78	15.45	16.58	17.90	17.54	17.52	13.09
Banking & Insurance	5.46	5.51	6.32	8.24	8.81	8.99	9.27
Real Estate, Ownership of dwellings and Business services	5.42	4.87	4.76	4.50	4.35	4.27	5.85
Public Administration	3.45	3.19	3.34	3.44	3.40	3.64	5.21
Other Services	6.25	5.68	6.01	6.12	6.77	7.55	9.38
Gross State Domestic Product	**100.00**	**100.00**	**100.00**	**100.00**	**100.00**	**100.00**	**100.00**

Source: (Basic Data) Central Statistical Organisation (CSO), Government of India, 1999 and 2000 (Diskettes).

higher HDI than Tamil Nadu. If the per capita income goes up, Tamil Nadu is likely to do even better on HDI. Since urban areas have a higher HDI than rural areas, the high level of urbanisation of Tamil Nadu is an advantage in terms of human development.

TABLE 1.12

Human Development Index

States	*Rural*	*Urban*	*Combined*
Tamil Nadu	**0.421**	**0.560**	**0.466**
Andhra Pradesh	0.344	0.473	0.377
Karnataka	0.367	0.523	0.412
Kerala	0.576	0.628	0.591
All-India	**0.340**	**0.511**	**0.381**

Source: National Human Development Report (2002).

Overall, Tamil Nadu's performance in all the social sectors including the rate of growth of population demonstrates that the State is expending resources on human development which has resulted in better outcomes and also helped to build the human capital base for the future. Tamil Nadu is second only to Kerala among the major states in most indicators of human development as well as the HDI. On most indicators, Tamil Nadu does better than economically more prosperous states like Maharashtra, Gujarat, Haryana and Punjab.

The spread of education is an important aspect of the development of Tamil Nadu. The literacy rate of the State has been progressively increasing over the years. As per the 2001 Census, the literacy rate stands at 73.47 per cent, next only to Kerala and Maharashtra and far higher than the All-India level of 65.38 per cent. The State Government in its endeavour for 'Universalisation of Primary Education' has considerably invested in education infrastructure, in rural areas especially. The combined gross enrolment rate in the State for the year 1998-99 was 83.15 per cent. At the primary level, the gross enrolment of boys is 106.37 per cent and that of girls 104.01 per cent. The results of the NFHS-II (1998-99) show that the median number of years of schooling for Tamil Nadu is 6.4 years as against the All-India figure of 5.5 years, which is a close third to Kerala (8.1) and Maharashtra (7.1) among the major states.

Although the per capita GSDP of the State is quite high and almost all the human indicators show considerable progress, there is unfortunately fairly wide prevalence of poverty. However, the ratio of people below the poverty line according to Planning Commission calculations is less than the All-India average. Poverty still remains a major concern. Poverty alleviation and employment programmes will have to continue in the next plan period to reduce the level of poverty. There are also significant regional disparities, with low income and some indicators of backwardness concentrated in a few districts. Regional imbalances will also have to be addressed in terms of the policy priorities of the government.

Having laid strong foundations for economic growth and having achieved substantial human progress, the State is now well equipped to deal with the existing problems of poverty and regional backwardness. Apart from stimulating and facilitating overall growth, the Government of Tamil Nadu in the coming years must pay special attention to the problem of regional disparities and to the reduction of poverty. These two aspects are of course inter-related.

As already indicated, Tamil Nadu has to export a substantial part of its output to the rest of India and outside, getting in return the vital inputs needed for agriculture and industry. Given the limitations of natural resources, it is important for Tamil Nadu to have access to large markets and be competitive enough to sell in those markets. It therefore follows that the Tamil Nadu Government must pursue policies that can promote competitiveness of all economic activities and try to obtain a large market for its products and also that scarce resources like water must be used most rationally and economically. Power sector reform and rational water management are absolutely and urgently necessary. Additionally, Tamil Nadu should join with other progressive states in creating a large common market in India, abolishing taxes on inter-state trade and also all other hindrances in the way of such trade.

Tenth Plan Objectives*

The State Tenth Plan has identified the following monitorable targets for the Tenth Plan period:

Economic Growth

- To ensure economic growth of 8 per cent per annum with an ICOR of 3.26 in the Tenth Plan and four per cent in Agriculture and Allied Sectors.
- Investment requirement at Rs. 2,62,502 crore, of which Rs. 40,000 crore as State Sector outlay, Rs. 48,000 crore as Central Sector outlay and the remaining Rs. 1,74,502 crore from Private and Foreign Direct Investments.
- Doubling of per capita income of Tamil Nadu by 2010.
- Widening of tax-base and improving collections.
- Reduction in subsidies and administrative overheads.

Fiscal Growth

- To bring the fiscal deficit from the present level of 3.6 per cent of GSDP to 1.5 per cent of GSDP by the end of the Tenth Plan.
- To bring down the ratio of revenue deficit to revenue receipts from the present level of 19 per cent to 0 by the end of the Tenth Plan.

Poverty Reduction

- To reduce poverty ratio from 21.12 per cent in 1999-2000 to 10 per cent by 2007 and aiming at near-elimination by 2012.

Employment

- To bring down unemployment rate as measured by current daily status from 12.05 per cent in 1999-2000 to 6 per cent by 2007 and to near-zero by 2012.

Education

- By the year 2005, there would be universalisation of education until Class V, with special effort for girls and disadvantaged groups.
- 100 per cent retention of all enrolled children till age 14 by 2007.
- 100 per cent access to a school within a km. by 2007.
- Raising of literacy rate 80 per cent in 2007.

Health

- To reduce IMR from 52 per 1000 live births in 1999 to 28 per 1000 live births by 2007.
- To reduce MMR from 150 per 100,000 births to 100 by 2007 and 50 by 2012.

Forests

- To increase and stabilise forest area cover from present 17.6 per cent to 25 per cent by 2012

* *Source: Tamil Nadu State Planning Commission 2003,* "Tenth Five Year Plan—Tamil Nadu".

and also to ensure density of tree cover by eco-stabilisation, eco-restoration and eco-protection.

Drinking Water

- To provide drinking water to all habitations and making them as *fully covered* habitations.

Gender Disparities

- Reduction by 2007 of all rural-urban and female-male disparities in wages, health, education by 50 per cent.

Infrastructure

- To provide all weather roads to all habitations with population of 500 and above by 2007.
- By the year 2008, Tamil Nadu will be the top ranking manufactured goods exporter in India and will double its export earnings.
- By the year 2010, all villages in Tamil Nadu will possess electricity, a trunk road, telephone and Internet connectivity, a school, clean water and sanitation, a village health worker, and local self-government.
- By the year 2006, Tamil Nadu will not only be the leading player in the field of IT in India, but will also become a regional gateway to Asia.

Population Growth

- To reduce decadal population growth from 11.2 per cent now to seven per cent by 2011 and to establish population stabilisation.

Chapter 2

Demographic Structure and Employment Pattern

Introduction

The population growth rate in Tamil Nadu had started declining in eighties itself. In 1991 the decadal growth rate was 15.4 per cent for Tamil Nadu compared to the All-India rate of 25.8 per cent. This rate declined further to 11.2 per cent for Tamil Nadu in 2001 while the All-India rate declined to 21.3 per cent. This decline was much faster than many other states mainly due to a significant decline in total fertility rate accompanied by a decline in birth rate and infant mortality rate. The period also showed improvement in overall sex-ratio from 956 in 1991 to 986 in 2001 with some districts reaching the ideal number of 1000 and above. However, the sex-ratio for 0-6 years is far below the expected numbers and has worsened across most districts with only a few exceptions. The literacy rates and health status of the population has also shown improvements in the past decade but gaps still persist in comparison to the status attained by developed nations.

The workforce participation rates (above the age of 5 years) in 1999-2000 data shows a decline compared to 1991. The important features of this decline have been (a) decrease in participation rates in lower age groups due to improvement in participation in school and higher education levels, (b) increase in unemployment rates in the rural sector but a decrease in the urban sector; (c) decrease in women's participation rate mainly in the subsidiary status; (d) underemployment levels at a higher rate compared to most other states; (e) decrease in casual labour proportion in rural sector for males but an increase in casualisation in rural sector among both males and females; and (f) significant increase in non-agricultural workers in the rural sector.

The real agricultural wages have grown at a faster rate compared to most other states in India but this has not been uniform across sub-regions of Tamil Nadu. The wage rates for casual labourers is high compared to most other states but significant differences exist between male and females wages as well as between rural and urban sector. The labour productivity across various sectors showed an improvement in all sectors with agriculture having the lowest value and services having the highest having grown at the rate of 8 per cent per annum between 1993-1994 and 1999-2000.

Demographic Transition in Tamil Nadu

The demographic structure of the population determines its economic and social status. The health, education and skills possessed by the population help in shaping the development of the State and brings in economic prosperity and overall well-being to its people. Among the 15 major States in India, Tamil Nadu is the sixth most populous State and Tamil Nadu's population accounted for 6.0 per cent share of the national population of 1027.02 million (GoTN, 2000).

The Census 2001 results show the population of Tamil Nadu at 62.1 million comprising of 31.3 million males and 30.8 million females. The rural and urban population is 34.9 million and 27.2 million, respectively. The density of population is placed at 478 per sq.km. The annual growth rate of population in Tamil Nadu was 1.1 per cent during nineties and 1.4 per cent during eighties and is lower than the growth rate registered at All-India level during nineties. One of the major changes that have come about in the demographic transition in Tamil Nadu is the fall in the total fertility rate and birth rate since the eighties and the replacement rate reaching nearly two by nineties. This is also accompanied by a decline in the death rate.

Total Fertility Rate (TFR)

The fertility rate in Tamil Nadu was lower than in many states and All-India average even in the early eighties. During nineties the State showed a significant improvement and by mid nineties (1995-97) Tamil Nadu had a TFR of 2.1, the lowest after Kerala (1.8). However the difference between Kerala and Tamil Nadu lies in the fact that it is uniform in Kerala across rural and urban sectors. The urban TFR for Tamil Nadu (1.8) is the same as Kerala but rural TFR is higher at 2.2 but significantly lower than all other states (GoI, 2001a). This change has been mainly possible due to the initiatives taken by the State government with the involvement of the local community.

Birth Rate and Death Rate

According to the Tamil Nadu Human Development Report, the death rate in Tamil Nadu has declined by 40 per cent in the last four decades whereas the birth rate has declined by about 30 per cent. Further, the birth rate has been falling uniformly across the districts during the eighties and nineties with the exception of one or two districts and the rural urban differences have also narrowed down. The birth rate of 19.9 for rural sector and 17.0 for the urban sector in 1999 is among the lowest in India and so is the death rate of 7.8 and 5.1 for the rural and urban sectors (refer Table 2.1).

Urbanisation Rate

The urbanisation rate marginally improved from about 33 per cent in 1981 to 34.2 per cent in 1991, but has significantly improved to about 44 per cent in 2001 (refer Table 2.1). The high rate is partly due to the inclusion of all town *panchayats* in the urban category. Compared to this the urbanisation rate in India has been 23 per cent, 25 per cent and 28 per cent in 1981, 1991 and 2001, respectively. This is due to the fact that rural population had a negative growth rate of (-)0.5 per cent for the last decade whereas the urban population grew at a rate of 3.6 per cent compared to the All-India values of 1.7 per cent and 2.7 per cent for the rural and urban sectors respectively. The present rate of urbanisation is the highest among all the large states in India.

Though the rate of urbanisation has been fairly uniform across districts ranging between 40 per cent and 50 per cent for a large number of districts there are still wide variations. A large numbers of coastal districts have low rates of urbanisation (below 20 per cent) with the exception of Tiruchirapalli (46 per cent). Similarly among the southern districts Kanyakumari has a very high rate of 65 per cent but Sivaganga and Ramanathapuram have rates 28 per cent and 25 per cent respectively. Among the inland districts Coimbatore has 66 per cent whereas Dharmapuri has 16 per cent.

TABLE 2.1

Demographic Characteristics of Tamil Nadu and Its Sub-regions: 1991 and 2001

	Rural					*Urban*				
	Coastal North Region	*Coastal Region*	*Southern Region*	*Inland Region*	*All*	*Coastal North Region*	*Coastal Region*	*Southern Region*	*Inland Region*	*All*
Birth Rate[a]	(per thousand population)									
1999	19.9	19.7	19.8	19.8	19.9	17.5	16.6	16.8	16.5	17.0
Death Rate[a]	(per thousand population)									
1999	7.7	7.9	7.8	8.3	7.8	5.0	5.8	5.2	4.6	5.1
Sex-Ratio[b] **(All):**	(number of females per 1000 males)									
1991	997	973	979	954	945	971	970	968	944	937
2001	988	1010	1018	962	992	978	1016	1005	969	980
Sex-Ratio[b] **(0-6 yrs):**	(number of females per 1000 males)									
1991	969	965	944	906	960	938	967	952	958	952
2001	953	950	937	897	931	956	963	950	941	951
Literacy Rate[b]**:** (%)										
1991	38.6	42.8	47.9	39.0	41.8	65.7	69.5	72.6	63.3	67.2
2001	55.0	57.5	61.5	52.1	55.8	77.5	80.3	81.7	73.3	77.5
Infant Mortality Rate[b]**:**	(number per thousand alive children)									
1999	42.4	45.8	47.2	57.6	49.8	19.8	20.7	23.6	26.5	22.0

Note: For the district composition in each region see Appendix 2A.III.

Source: GoTN (2000) for (a) and Census Info. (2001) for (b).

Sex-ratio

The sex-ratio in Tamil Nadu has improved slowly in the last decade. The combined (rural and urban) sex-ratio was 958 in 1991 and 986 in 2001. However there are other dimensions that need special mention (refer Table 2.1).

- The overall sex-ratio has improved in all regions except coastal north in rural Tamil Nadu;
- Coastal and southern districts have attained the expected value of above 1000 by 2001;
- The sex-ratio for urban is worse than the rural with the exception of inland and coastal regions in 2001;
- All the regions have sex-ratio of below 1000 for the 0-6 years group;
- Further, sex-ratio in 0-6 years has declined in both rural and urban areas in 2001 compared to 1991;
- Inter-district variation in sex-ratio has also increased between the two census for overall as well as 0-6 years;
- Districts like Salem (763), Dhrmapuri (869), Theni (873) and Namakkal (882) most of which are in the inland region have very low rates in 2001 compared to many other regions in India.

Literacy and Health

The two important assets that people require for production purposes and spurring innovations are health and education. Education has all along been considered the basic tool for seeking employment with higher wages or the cause for improving labour productivity. However, evidence of the impact of health on economic growth or health status as an input into the production function is only a recent phenomenon.

The literacy rate in Tamil Nadu increased substantially from 62.7 per cent to 73.5 per cent between 1991 and 2001 with improvement across all segments. However, the rural-urban gap and gender gap are still to be bridged. Female literacy improved from 51.3 per cent to 64.5 per cent and male literacy rates improved from 73.7 per cent to 82.3 per cent. Rural literacy improved from 41.8 per cent to 55.8 per cent and urban literacy improved from 69.6 per cent to 75.6 per cent and this gap between the rural and urban sectors remained even with each region (refer Table 2.1). These figures are among the highest compared to many large states in India.

The health status can be judged in various ways and the commonly used measures are infant mortality rates (IMR) which also reflects the overall well-being of the society. The IMR in Tamil Nadu showed a rapid decline between eighties and 2000. It was about 125 in 1970 decreasing to about 68 in 1990 and further declining to 44 in 1999 (GoTN 2002a). The regional level variation once again highlights rural urban contrast though it is homogenous across regions within a sub-sector except for the southern region in rural Tamil Nadu (refer Table 2.1). The National Nutrition Monitoring Bureau (NNMB) collects anthropometric information for children in various age groups as well as adults across some states in rural India as a measure of the health status and their ability to carry out regular work. For the adult population chronic energy deficiency (CED) indicates the health status[1]. The incidence of chronic energy deficiency for adult males in rural Tamil Nadu came down from 42 per cent in 1990-91 to about 35 per cent in 2000-01 and similarly for females it came down from 45 per cent to 38 per cent during the same period (as cited in Vaidyanathan, 2002).

Demography and Labour Force

The annual growth rate of population in Tamil Nadu exceeded that of labour force between 1961 and 1981 and the trend reversed after that (GoTN, 2003). Between 1991 and 2001 the working population increased at a faster annual rate of 1.40 per cent as against the population growth rate of 1.07 per cent, however these rates were lower than those in the previous decade.

Labour Force Participation Rates

The labour force participation rate (LFPR) is described by the NSS as the percentage of population in the labour force that includes both the employed (economically active population) and the unemployed (population seeking or available for jobs). LFPR has usually been higher in Tamil Nadu compared to All-India for both males and females and across sectors for the decade of eighties and nineties (Table 2.2).

In 1999-2000 the rural LFPR was about 52.3 per cent, which was much higher than the All-India average of 42.3 per cent and is the second largest after Andhra Pradesh (54.6 per cent) among the larger states. The urban LFPR for the same year was at 41 per cent which was the highest among the states with the All-

1. See Appendix 2A.II for definition. The data for CED is taken from various NNMB reports.

India average of 35.4 per cent. Over the years the LFPRs have been falling for Tamil Nadu and for All-India. Between eighties and nineties the rates of decrease have been similar across gender and sectors for Tamil Nadu. Up to 1993-94 the LFPR for males was similar between rural and urban areas but it declined in urban areas more sharply by 1999-2000. The female LFPR has always been lower than the males with the gender gap more in the urban areas in Tamil Nadu as well as All-India. The LFPR for females in Tamil Nadu have fallen more compared to males in the rural areas with a much significant drop between 1993-94 and 1999-2000 which is again similar to the All-India trend.

TABLE 2.2

Labour Force Participation Rates - Usual Status# for Tamil Nadu and All-India (in brackets): 1983 to 1999-2000 (in percentage)

	Rural		*Urban*	
	Males	*Females*	*Males*	*Females*
1983	69.9	52.0	65.3	25.3
1987-88	60.4 (54.9)	47.7 (33.1)	59.5 (53.4)	24.3 (16.2)
1993-94	61.3 (56.1)	48.1 (33.0)	60.1 (54.3)	24.7 (16.5)
1999-00	61.0 (54.0)	43.4 (30.2)	58.5 (54.2)	22.7 (14.7)

See Appendix 2A.II for definition.

Source: Various Reports of NSSO on Employment and Unemployment and Sarvekshana.

TABLE 2.3

Estimated Labour Force and Employment for Tamil Nadu: 1983 to 1999-2000

(millions)

	Labour Force			*Employed*		
	Male	*Female*	*Persons*	*Male*	*Female*	*Persons*
1983	15.13	9.99	25.12	14.43	9.60	24.03
1987-88	16.39 (2.02)	10.56 (1.41)	26.96 (1.78)	15.74 (2.19)	10.14 (1.36)	25.87 (1.86)
1993-94	17.84 (1.42)	11.41 (1.30)	29.25 (1.37)	17.37 (1.66)	11.19 (1.66)	28.56 (1.66)
1999-2000	18.82 (0.89)	10.93 (-0.71)	29.75 (0.28)	18.24 (0.82)	10.73 (-0.70)	28.97 (0.24)

Note: (A) The values in brackets are Annual Compound Growth Rates in percentage compared to previous NSS Round. (B) Labour Force is defined as the number of persons employed (engaged in economic activity) and unemployed (seeking or available for work). (C) Both labour force and employment is defined on the basis of usual status activity (activity status of a person during the reference period of 365 days preceding the date of survey) and includes the principal (major time) and subsidiary status (minor time).

Source: GoTN (2002b) based on NSS Data.

Though the labour force participation rates are higher in Tamil Nadu compared to All-India the rate of growth in labour force has been relatively slower since mid eighties. Table 2.3 above reports the number of persons in the labour force and the employed population in millions with their annual growth rates between the years. The female labour force and employment has decreased during the nineties in Tamil Nadu resulting in negative growth rates and hence contributing to a larger fall in the labour force and employment growth rates for the entire population in the nineties. The annual growth rate of the labour force (males and females) between 1983 and 1987-88 was about 1.8 for both Tamil Nadu and All-India. However, this rate declined between 1983 and 1993-94 for Tamil Nadu to 1.70 per cent whereas for All-India it increased to 2.05 per cent. In nineties (between 1993-94 and 1999-2000) there has been a significant decline across all states but Tamil Nadu registered a growth rate of only about 0.28 per cent compared to the All-India rate of 1.03 per cent.

Workforce Participation Rates

The workforce participation rates or the worker-population ratio (WPR) is defined as the number of persons who are economically active. The Census data show that the number of workers has grown at the rate of 1.8 per cent per annum between 1981 and 1991 and 1.4 per cent between 1991 and 2001. The decline in growth rate between 1991 and 2001 is contributed mainly by the rural sector where the growth rate was (-) 0.41 per cent compared to 1.7 per cent per annum in the previous decade. In contrast the urban growth rate was 4.8 per cent between 1991 and 2001 compared to 2.21 per cent in the previous decade. The regional distribution for 2001 shows that participation rates are higher in the inland districts and fairly uniform across the remaining regions. The rural and urban participation rates are not much different for males but a huge gap exists for females. One of the reasons for this is that when the standard of living improves women may tend to drop out of the labour force; the other reason could be that the urban labour market may require higher levels of education and skills that the women may not possess.

The census data is limited in its usage for studying the employment status of individuals compared to the National Sample Survey (NSS) data which are designed to specially collect data on employment and unemployment and its different aspects. NSS characterises WPR based on three definitions: usual status which can be further classified into principal and principal + subsidiary, current weekly status and current daily status.[2]

TABLE 2.4

Number of Workers and Workforce Participation Rate for Tamil Nadu

	Rural				Urban			
	Males		Females		Males		Females	
	Number#	*Rate#*	*Number*	*Rate*	*Number*	*Rate*	*Number*	*Rate*
1981	9.67	59.2	5.41	33.6	4.18	51.3	0.93	12.0
1991	10.82	58.3	7.01	38.5	5.14	52.8	1.22	13.1
2001	10.4	59.4	7.18	41.3	7.76	56.4	2.48	18.4
Across Regions of Tamil Nadu in 2001								
Coastal North		57.4		37.2		53.6		13.9
Coastal		59.2		40.5		55.0		17.4
Southern		57.8		41.1		55.4		17.4
Inland		63.2		48.0		59.7		19.8

The numbers are in millions and rates are in percentages.

Source: GoTN (2002a) and CensusInfo (2001).

In the nineties WPR based on the usual status including principal and subsidiary status (US-PSS, henceforth) is one of the highest among other states across sectors as well as gender. This puts the WPR larger than the All-India average for both these years which has been so even in the eighties (Table 2.5). The rural sector shows a larger WPR than the urban sector, female WPR is less than males with a larger gender gap in urban sector compared to the rural sector. These features are similar to All-India and many other states. The WPR for Tamil Nadu in 1999-2000 is the lowest compared to the previous three NSS rounds which is true for most other states. The current daily status shows a lower participation rate which is usually the case but the gap between daily and usual status rates is higher in Tamil Nadu compared to All-India across all segments. The other features and trends are similar to the usual status rates.

The decline in WPR can occur due to various reasons: like increase in school and higher education enrollment for lower age groups, decline in growth rate of labour force due to decline in population growth rate, and/or increase in unemployment rates if there is no decline in growth rate of labour force. In Tamil Nadu a combination of all of these seem to have happened. In the following sections these issues are analysed beginning with the age-specific worker participation rate (ASWPR).

2. See Appendix 2A.II for the definition.

TABLE 2.5

Worker Participation Ratios for Tamil Nadu and All-India (in brackets) for various years (%)

	Rural		Urban	
	Males	*Females*	*Males*	*Females*
	Usual Status (PS+SS)			
1983	68.2 (63.5)	51.4 (39.3)	60.8 (58.1)	23.7 (17.3)
1987-1988	58.7 (53.9)	46.1 (32.3)	55.8 (50.6)	22.7 (15.2)
1993-1994	60.2 (55.3)	47.8 (32.8)	57.5 (52.1)	23.0 (15.5)
1999-2000	59.4 (53.1)	43.0 (29.9)	56.3 (51.8)	21.5 (13.9)

Source: NSSO (1996, 2001)

Age-specific Worker Participation Ratios

The ASWPR are reported in Table 2.6 and the discussion is based on segments of age-groups like children, youth and elderly.

(a) Child Labour (5-14 years)

- Over the years, the WPR has declined sharply up to the age group up to 14 years for both males and females with higher rates for males than females.
- Further in this segment, the gender gap is the least among all age groups for both rural and urban sectors.
- The rates are always lower in the urban sector indicating higher participation in education at both primary and secondary levels.
- TN has had a higher WPR in 10-14 years compared to All-India but the decline has been more rapid between 1993-94 and 1999-2000. These trends are similar for All-India also and have aligned with the All-India rates except for boys in urban areas.
- This clearly shows a decline in employment of child labour. The estimated child labour in Tamil Nadu was about 10 lakh in 1993-94 and came down to about 4.5 lakh in 1999-2000. The rural sector employs more children and showed a decline from 8.1 lakh to 3.4 lakh and the urban sector from 2.1 lakh to 1.1 lakh during the same period. The child labour among girls declined from 5.7 lakh to 2 lakh and among boys from 4.5 lakh to 2.5 lakh.[3]
- The decline in these age groups has mainly occurred due to increase in enrollment in the

3. GoTN (2002) Tamil Nadu National Human Development Report 2001.

TABLE 2.6

Age-specific Worker Population Ratios for Tamil Nadu and All-India (in brackets): 1987-88 to 1999-2000 (%)

Age Group	Males						Females					
	1987-88		*1993-1994*		*1999-2000*		*1987-88*		*1993-1994*		*1999-2000*	
Rural												
5-9	1.3	(2.3)	1.3	(1.1)	0.2	(0.6)	2.0	(2.4)	3.0	(1.4)	0.7	(0.7)
10-14	20.4	(19.0)	14.7	(13.8)	9.0	(9.1)	28.2	(18.2)	22.1	(14.1)	8.1	(9.6)
15-19	65.8	(60.0)	59.9	(57.7)	48.8	(50.3)	60.2	(39.9)	56.0	(36.4)	41.4	(30.4)
20-24	89.4	(87.2)	84.7	(85.9)	84.4	(84.4)	56.5	(46.5)	58.9	(45.6)	48.4	(40.9)
25-29	93.6	(95.9)	94.4	(95.7)	92.1	(95.0)	66.7	(52.3)	65.9	(52.5)	59.9	(49.1)
30-54#	96.5	(97.8)	97.0	(98.2)	97.5	(97.6)	74.3	(68.2)	76.3	(58.7)	69.2	(56.0)
55-59	89.7	(92.8)	85.0	(94.2)	93.1	(92.9)	58.6	(45.9)	65.4	(46.7)	59.0	(45.0)
60+	68.0	(66.8)	67.0	(69.9)	59.8	(63.9)	32.6	(21.8)	36.9	(24.1)	30.8	(21.8)
All	58.7	(53.9)	60.2	(55.3)	59.4	(53.1)	46.1	(32.3)	47.8	(32.8)	43.0	(29.9)
Urban												
5-9	1.2	(0.5)	0.6	(0.5)	0.1	(0.3)	1.1	(0.3)	0.5	(0.5)	0.1	(0.2)
10-14	12.6	(8.5)	10.2	(6.6)	6.1	(4.9)	11.9	(6.5)	7.6	(4.5)	3.3	(3.6)
15-19	47.4	(35.5)	43.0	(35.6)	37.0	(31.4)	23.8	(14.6)	24.2	(12.3)	21.4	(10.5)
20-24	73.5	(67.4)	74.9	(67.4)	71.2	(65.8)	29.9	(18.5)	27.7	(18.0)	22.8	(15.5)
25-29	93.1	(91.4)	92.0	(90.4)	93.3	(88.3)	28.5	(22.3)	28.2	(22.4)	27.9	(19.4)
30-54#	97.2	(96.9)	97.1	(96.4)	97.3	(96.0)	35.9	(27.2)	40.8	(30.1)	29.1	(23.5)
55-59	84.1	(84.5)	82.3	(85.6)	77.1	(80.9)	30.4	(23.4)	30.3	(22.6)	31.6	(20.7)
60+	49.9	(48.0)	46.5	(44.2)	39.9	(40.2)	15.7	(12.3)	19.2	(11.3)	12.8	(9.4)
All	55.8	(50.6)	57.5	(52.1)	56.3	(51.8)	22.7	(15.2)	23.0	(15.5)	21.5	(13.9)

This is the average for age groups 30-34, 35-39, 40-44, 45-49 and 50-54 years.

Source: Sarvekshana (1996), NSSO (1996, 2001) for Tamil Nadu and Sundaram (2001b) for All-India values.

primary and middle school segment. Tamil Nadu's performance in education has been far superior to many other states in enrollment along with low drop out rates in the past decade. This has resulted in a higher rate of decline (as well as a lower rate of participation) compared to All-India.

- The lower WPR for girls than boys in some segments has to be interpreted cautiously as this may not imply that more girls are in school compared to boys. Some of them could be 'nowhere' that is, neither in school nor in gainful economic activity (that is, likely to be engaged in domestic work).

(b) Employment Rates Among Youth: (15-29 years)

- Among the three age-groups the rate of employment is above 90 per cent for males in rural and urban sectors in the 25-29 years but females have far lower rates particularly in the urban sector.
- There is a decline in WPR by 1999-2000 among all the three age groups, which is more in the rural sector than the urban sector with females showing a larger decline in the rural sector.
- Among the three segments the decline is large for the 15-19 years except females in the urban sector who have anyway low WPR. The decline for this age-group may also be due to higher participation in education at the higher-secondary level.
- Similarly the decline in other two age groups could also be due to participation in higher education. As Tamil Nadu performs better in secondary and higher education compared to many other states this decline is much larger than for All-India.
- As the data on age-specific education is not available for Tamil Nadu a clear picture does not emerge, however a similar trend is observed by Sundaram (2001a,b) for All-India and coupled with the fact that Tamil Nadu performs better than most other states on education at all levels perhaps this reason holds good here also.
- At the same time this trend has to be looked at along with the unemployment rates in this age

group for which the NSS data provide information and this is discussed in the section on unemployment.

(c) Age Group 30-54 Years

- The WPR is above 95 per cent for males in both sectors and has to large extent remained the same over the NSS rounds.
- Unlike males not only are the WPRs for women lower ranging between 65-80 per cent in the rural sector and between 35-45 per cent in urban sector but also there is a large decline by 1999-2000 in the rural sector and marginal decline in the urban sector.
- The decline in women WPR can be attributed to the decline in their subsidiary status participation.
- Compared to Tamil Nadu figures All-India has lower WPRs in all these segments but the features and trends are similar in All-India figures also.

(d) Above 55 Years

This age group has shown decline in all the four categories with a steeper fall in the rural sector compared to the urban sector for both males and females. However, there is an exception for rural males in the 55-59 years age group where there is an increase. The decline in participation rates for most of these categories is attributed to an increase in population in these age groups.

(e) Thus, overall in the working age group of 15 years and above there has been a decline in the work force participation rate across both the rural and urban sectors during the nineties compared to the decade of eighties. The employment in the usual principal and subsidiary status for rural Tamil Nadu (All-India) grew at about 0.4 per cent (1.3 per cent) per annum in between 1993-94 and 1999-2000 compared to 1.6 per cent (1.8 per cent) during the period 1983 and 1993-94. The urban rates have been higher compared to rural sector to begin with but have also shown a decline from 2.4 per cent (2.9 per cent) for Tamil Nadu (All-India) to 1.6 per cent (2.4 per cent).

(f) Though Tamil Nadu's WPR is higher than most other states in 1999-2000 its decline has been substantial compared to many other states.

(g) Further, the decade of eighties showed a higher growth rate in women's participation whereas in the nineties the decline in growth rate was larger than males with the rural sector showing a negative growth rate of (–)0.7 per cent for the period 1993-94 and 1999-2000.

The fall in the worker participation rates have to be looked at together with the unemployment rates and student population ratios for the lower age groups. The trends in unemployment are analysed in section 6 whereas student population ratio is not available across age-groups and hence a comparison could not be attempted.

Composition of the Work Force

Sectoral Composition

The census shows that between 1991 and 2001 the share of non-agricultural workers increased from 30.7 per cent to 45.3 per cent in Tamil Nadu with an annual growth rate of about 1.8 per cent in rural sector and 8.6 per cent in the urban sector. The urban sector which had about 40 per cent of agricultural workers in 1991 decreased to about 20 per cent in 2001 with rural sector decreasing from 72 per cent to 67 per cent during the same period. This is an expected trend due to the structural transformation in Tamil Nadu's state domestic product away from agriculture which had begun by early eighties and due to increasing rate of urbanisation. The share among rural males increased from 20.5 per cent to 25.5 per cent during nineties with a higher increase for urban males (74 to 85 per cent). The females increased their share from 27.8 per cent to 32.5 per cent in rural sector and from 30.7 per cent to 45.3 per cent in urban sector during the same period.

The NSS data also show a transformation of similar change but the magnitudes are higher. The worker population ratios for non-agricultural workers were (a) rural males: 31 per cent and 38 per cent; (b) rural females: 18 per cent and 25 per cent; (c) urban males: 90 per cent and 94 per cent; and (d) urban females: 72 per cent and 86 per cent, respectively during the decades of eighties and nineties. This shows that the urban sector is more or less non-agricultural by 1999-2000 and this may be expected with a very high rate of urbanisation that has taken place in the nineties. The transformation for males has been slower compared to the females and more so in the urban sector.

The decline in rate of growth of WPR in Tamil Nadu has mainly occurred due to the decline in employment in agricultural sector (Table 2.7). Compared to All-India the rate of decline in primary sector is larger and at the same time employment in secondary and tertiary sectors have grown slower for

Tamil Nadu. The declining share of employment in agriculture and an increase in tertiary sector is expected as not only has there been a decline in share of agriculture in the state domestic product (with an increasing share for services) over the years but also a decline in its rate of growth. This aspect is further discussed in the section on labour productivity.

TABLE 2.7

Sectoral Composition of Workforce for Tamil Nadu and All-India (in brackets): 1993-1994 and 1999-2000 (millions)

	1993-94	*1999-2000*	*Rate of Growth (%)*
Primary	15.4 (241.4)	14.5 (237.8)	-1.00 (-0.24)
Secondary	6.2 (56.7)	6.8 (66.9)	1.55 (2.80)
Tertiary	6.9 (14.4)	7.5 (19.6)	1.40 (5.33)
Total	28.5 (373.8)	28.9 (397.0)	0.23 (1.01)

Source: GoTN (2002)

The decomposition across sex shows more proportion of women in the primary sector (about 63 per cent compared to 43 per cent for males) in 1999-2000. However, the female participation rate in services has shown a significant increase between 1993-94 and 1999-2000 (from 13.7 per cent to 16.5 per cent) compared to males (from 30.8 to 31.4 per cent).

Along with the sectoral composition of the workers it is also important to understand their employment status that is, how they earn their income- through regular wages or on a contract basis (weekly or daily) or through self-employment and the resources they own in order to do so.

Status of Employment

The status of workers is analysed using (a) census data which classifies whether they are employed as main workers or marginal workers in census and (b) NSSO which categorises employment based on three broad groups: (a) Self-employed, (b) Regular salaried/ wage employee and (c) Casual wage labour.[4]

Tamil Nadu had about 14 lakh marginal workers in 1991 constituting 2.5 per cent of the work force which has increased to about 42 lakh workers in 2001 thereby increasing their share to about 6.6 per cent as shown in Table 2.8. The rural sector has a higher proportion of marginal workers compared to urban and similarly a larger proportion of women are marginal workers compared to males. An important change has come about in terms of increase in marginal workers' share between 1991 and 2001. In the rural sector the share of male marginal workers increased to 7.9 per cent from about 0.7 per cent and that of females increased from 6.5 per cent to 11.2 per cent. The urban sector has shown a relatively smaller increase from 0.4 per cent to 2.7 per cent for males and 1.3 per cent to 3.5 per cent for females. These changes are similar to All-India, however the proportion of marginal workers in Tamil Nadu is lower than the All-India total across all the sub-populations.

TABLE 2.8

Proportion of Marginal Workers in Tamil Nadu and All-India (in brackets): 1991 and 2001 (%)

	Rural		*Urban*		*Total*
	Males	*Females*	*Males*	*Females*	
1991	0.4 (0.7)	6.5 (8.1)	0.2 (0.4)	1.3 (1.0)	2.5 (3.4)
2001	7.6 (7.9)	11.2 (14.2)	2.7 (2.4)	3.5 (3.4)	6.6 (8.7)

Source: CensusInfo (2001).

The marginal workers in census can be considered equivalent to the casual labourers of the NSS data. Table 2.9 reports distribution of workers across employment status for Tamil Nadu and All-India. In 1999-2000 casual labourers constituted the largest percentage in rural areas among both males and females with a higher proportion among females. This structure is different from All-India where more than 50 per cent of the population is self-employed followed by casual labourers and self-employed among both males and females. However, in the urban sector the regular employees constituted the largest share for both males and females whereas at the All-India level there is an equal distribution between self-employed and regular employed for males and larger share in self-employed for females. For Tamil Nadu the fact that more males are regular employed along with the fact that casual labourers are lower in urban sector indicates urban and gender bias in labour market protection.

Over the years there has been a decline in self-employed among all groups except urban females. In the rural sector this has resulted in more casualisation of the labour force (further increasing the female casual labour rate) with only a small increase in regular employment. In contrast the urban labour market has shown a decline in casual labourers for both males and females. This decrease in casualisation for the urban sector has resulted in an increase in mainly regular

4. For their definition see Appendix 2A.II.

employed for males whereas it has increased mainly the self-employed among females. At the All-India the trend for the rural sector is similar in that there is an increase in casual labourers whereas the urban males retain the same composition while the females have increased their share among regular employed.

TABLE 2.9

Distribution of Workers Across Employment Status for Tamil Nadu and All-India (in brackets): 1993-1994 and 1999-2000 (%)

	Males		*Females*	
	1993-94	*1999-2000*	*1993-94*	*1999-2000*
Rural				
Self-Employed	41.4 (57.7)	35.8 (55.0)	41.9 (58.6)	38.0 (57.3)
Regular Employed	12.5 (8.5)	15.3 (8.8)	5.2 (2.7)	6.9 (3.1)
Casual Labourers	46.1 (33.8)	48.9 (36.2)	52.9 (38.7)	55.1 (39.6)
Urban				
Self-Employed	34.5 (41.7)	33.0 (41.5)	34.5 (44.8)	39.4 (45.3)
Regular Employed	40.3 (42.2)	45.4 (41.7)	40.3 (29.2)	40.7 (33.3)
Casual Labourers	25.2 (16.1)	21.6 (16.8)	25.2 (26.0)	19.9 (21.4)

Note: This classification is based on Usual Status (PS+SS) of Employment.

Source: NSSO (1996, 2001).

One of the categories of self-employed is the household enterprise and one expects the participation rates for women to be high in this category. However, an increase in their proportion need not mean that they are economically better off as they need not be paid any wage. A positive aspect about self-employment is that women can gain economic security while tending to their domestic duties in the existing social mosaic and newer technology like information and communication technology could be used to further improve their labour productivity. The state should be able to identify and encourage such activities by providing micro-credit and better marketing facilities to sell their products.

Organised – Public and Private- Sector Employment

The organised sector employment accounted for about 8.7 per cent of the workforce in 1999-2000 constituting about 25.2 lakh workers of which males constituted 70 per cent (GoTN, 2000). The organised sector has both public and private presence with the dominance of the former. Further, 50 per cent of the organised sector employment is concentrated in five districts of Tamil Nadu. The public sector dominates the tertiary sector (primarily services sector) and private sector dominates the secondary sector (mainly manufacturing) in 1999-2000. Thus the organised sector has very little presence in the rural sector as the share of agriculture is minimal in both private and public sectors.

The growth rate of public sector employment has declined after 1997 by one per cent but is compensated to some extent by an increase in private sector resulting in the organised sector employment growing below one per cent after 1997. The public sector employment has come down from about 66 per cent in 1995-96 to 63 per cent in 1999-2000 with the females share remaining the same during the period. The private sector increased their share both marginally in secondary and to a larger extent in the tertiary sector with an increase in share of female employment from about 29 per cent in 1995-96 to 35 per cent in 1999-2000.

Unemployment and Underemployment

The unemployment and underemployment trends over the past two decades are analysed based on NSS data. The discussion focuses on unemployment rates based on the usual status as well as current daily status, as the latter is more inclusive and are reported in Table 2.10. The section also focuses on unemployment among youth as well as its linkage with education.

Unemployment Rate- Usual Status

- In 1999-2000 the rural rate for Tamil Nadu (All-India) was about 2 per cent (1.5 per cent) and above most other large states except Kerala (8.2 per cent) and West Bengal (2.8 per cent). The urban rate in Tamil Nadu was 4 per cent (4.7 per cent) and lower than many other states.
- The urban rates are usually higher than rural for All-India and most other states.
- The female unemployment rate is higher in urban areas but lower in rural areas compared to males with 1987-88 as an exception.
- Compared to the earlier NSS rounds the rates have increased for males in rural sector with a dip in 1993-94 with the female rate showing large variations. However the urban rate has been the lowest in the past two decades for males and females.

Unemployment Rate- Current Daily Status

- The rural sector for Tamil Nadu (All-India) had about 13.5 per cent (7.1 per cent) and is higher than most other states except Kerala and West Bengal whereas for the urban sector in Tamil Nadu (AI) it was 8.9 per cent (7.7 per cent) and is higher than most other south Indian states (except Kerala) and other industrialised states like Gujarat (4.2 per cent).

- In 1999-2000 the urban rates are lower than rural rates across males and females.
- The female rates are higher than males in the urban sector but fluctuates for the rural sector.
- Compared to the previous NSS round the unemployment rate has increased for all except females in urban sector.

TABLE 2.10

Unemployment Rates According to Usual Status and Daily Status for Tamil Nadu and All-India (in brackets) (%)

	Rural		*Urban*	
	Males	*Females*	*Males*	*Females*
Usual Status				
1983	2.3 (1.4)	1.1 (0.7)	6.5 (5.0)	6.2 (5.2)
1987-88	2.6 (1.8)	3.1 (2.4)	6.2 (5.2)	6.6 (6.2)
1993-94	1.8 (1.4)	0.6 (0.8)	4.3 (4.0)	6.8 (6.2)
1999-00	2.7 (1.7)	1.0 (1.0)	3.6 (4.5)	5.1 (5.7)
Daily Status				
1987-88	8.4 (4.6)	10.7 (6.7)	12.3 (8.8)	13.2 (12.0)
1993-94	12.8 (5.6)	11.3 (5.6)	8.6 (6.7)	12.7 (10.5)
1999-00	14.3 (7.2)	12.3 (7.0)	9.0 (7.3)	8.6 (9.4)

Source: NSS(1996, 2001).

Unemployment Rate for Youth (15-29 years)

The rural unemployment rate for males in 1983 was about 4.7 per cent and this increased to 6.9 per cent in 1999-2000 and for females the rate increased from 1.5 per cent to 2.6 per cent. Among urban males the rate has come down over the years from 11.2 per cent in 1983 to 8.8 per cent in 1999-2000 whereas it increased from 4.0 per cent in 1983 to 13.1 per cent in 1999-2000 among urban females.

Education and Unemployment (15 years and above)

The number of educated among unemployed increased for both males and females and in both sectors in 1999-2000 compared to 1993-94 as shown in Table 2.11. The change was more dramatic for females in both the sectors and males in the rural sector whereas for males the change was marginal in the urban sector. As usual the urban rates for males in Tamil Nadu for 1999-2000 was not that high compared to many other states but the rural rates were higher than most other states (with Kerala as the exception) and similarly for females in the urban sector.

TABLE 2.11

Unemployment Rates Among Educated for Tamil Nadu and All-India (in brackets)

	Male		*Female*	
	1993-1994	*1999-2000*	*1993-1994*	*1999-2000*
Rural	1.8 (1.4)	9.9 (5.6)	0.6 (0.8)	13.5 (14.6)
Urban	4.3 (4.0)	4.7 (6.2)	6.8 (6.2)	13.9 (14.3)

Source: NSSO (1996, 2001).

Underemployment

Underemployment depicts under-utilisation of the labour time of the workers. Some persons categorised as usually employed, do not have work throughout the year due to seasonality in work or otherwise and their labour time is not fully utilised. The underemployment is further classified by NSSO into *visible and invisible underemployment.*[5]

When the person reports to be available for work with reference to a shorter reference period then it is termed as visible underemployment. Here the underemployment is obtained by cross-classifying persons by their usual status and current daily status is considered. NSS reports this information per 1000 days and here the numbers have been recalculated per 365 days and reported in Table 2.12.

- Between 1993-94 and 1999-2000, the number of employed days has come down among all segments for Tamil Nadu and All-India with a much larger reduction for rural segment than the urban and more so for the females.
- For rural and urban males, there is a reduction of days worked of 42 and 23 days respectively increasing both the number of days unemployed and number of days outside the labour force.
- For rural and urban females, there is a reduction of days worked of 56 and 36 days respectively increasing number of days outside the labour force more than the number of days unemployed (unlike their male counterparts). This trend is similar in All-India wherein the women who do not have a job fall out of the labour force.

5. For the definition refer to Appendix 2A.II.

- The visible underemployment has increased in TN substantially compared to most other states and is significantly higher than the All-India average.

TABLE 2.12

Person-days of Usually Employed by their Broad Current Daily Status for Tamil Nadu and All-India (in brackets): 1993-94 and 1999-2000 (number of days/year)

	Males				*Females*			
	1993-1994		*1999-2000*		*1993-1994*		*1999-2000*	
Rural								
Employed	343	(331)	302	(327)	312	(241)	256	(247)
Unemployed	9	(15)	41	(19)	7	(11)	32	(15)
Not in labour force	12	(19)	23	(19)	46	(112)	76	(103)
Urban								
Employed	357	(345)	334	(344)	336	(279)	300	(289)
Unemployed	4	(10)	19	(10)	4	(10)	11	(8)
Not in labour force	4	(9)	12	(11)	25	(76)	54	(68)

Source: NSSO(1996b, 2001).

The invisible underemployment is defined as the persons particularly self-employed who may not have enough work throughout the year and may want additional and or alternative work. In 1999-2000 the figures for rural and urban sectors respectively are as below:

- Persons who did not work regularly: 15.8 per cent and 8.5 per cent,
- Person (15 years and above) who were available for additional work 9 per cent and 3.9 per cent
- Person (15 years and above) who were available for alternative work 5.9 per cent and 4.3 per cent

These figures are higher than the most other states particularly for the rural sector.

Quality of Workforce and Employment

While the trends in various aspects of demography and employment discussed in the above sections is interesting in itself, for policy analysis discussion on qualitative aspects of workforce and employment could be more useful and this section focuses on the same.

Distribution of Cultivated Land

One of the reasons for the increase in casualisation in rural labour force is attributed to change in distribution of land possessed and cultivated by the rural households. In 1999-2000 the average area of land possessed was less than half (0.34 ha) of that for All-India (0.81 ha) and a little higher than the lowest value of Kerala's 0.28 ha. It came down from 0.4 ha to 0.34 ha in Tamil Nadu 1993-94 and 1999-2000 though at the All-India level also such a trend is observed. Further, it is observed that a large proportion of rural households do not cultivate any land and this is highest in Tamil Nadu compared to all the large states in India. Between 1993-94 and 1999-2000 not only has the proportion of these households increased from 63.4 per cent to 67 per cent but also, there is a leftward shift in the distribution of land cultivated as shown in the Table 2.13.

TABLE 2.13

Distribution of Households Across Size-class of Land for Rural Tamil Nadu and All-India (in brackets) (%)

In hectares	*1993-94*	*1999-2000*
0	63.4 (38.7)	67.0 (40.9)
0.04-0.4	14.6 (18.8)	15.5 (22.3)
0.41-1	11.9 (17.3)	9.9 (16.8)
1-2	6.7 (13.4)	5.2 (11.2)
2.01-4	2.4 (7.6)	1.8 (5.9)
4.01 & above	1.0 (4.3)	0.6 (3.0)

Source: NSSO (1996, 2001).

Sectoral Distribution of Income, Employment and Labour Productivity

Labour productivity can be used as one measure of the quality of labour force. Table 2.14 gives the distribution of the domestic product, the work force and gross value added per worker (labour productivity) for the three aggregate sectors - primary, secondary and tertiary- for two years for Tamil Nadu and compares it with All-India values.

- The share of income and working population in agriculture for Tamil Nadu was lower than the All-India values and has been declining more rapidly in terms of income than in terms of the employed workforce.
- The much sharper decline in agricultural workforce despite slower growth rate in value added from agriculture resulted in a moderate growth rate in labour productivity for this sector.
- During this period the tertiary sector has grown at a much faster rate in its income but has absorbed smaller amount of labour in the process.
- The overall labour productivity grew at 6.6 per cent per annum in Tamil Nadu compared to All-

TABLE 2.14

Per Capita Gross Domestic Product, Employment and Labour Productivity in Tamil Nadu and All-India: 1993-94 and 1999-2000

	Tamil Nadu								
	1993-94			*1999-2000*			*Annual Growth Rate*		
	GSDP (Rs.Lakh)	*Work Force (Million)*	*GVA per Worker*	*GSDP (Rs.Lakh)*	*Work Force (Million)*	*GVA per Worker*	*GSDP*	*Work Force*	*GVA per Worker*
Primary	1426446 (24.8)	15.4 (54.0)	9263	1550726 (18.2)	14.5 (50.2)	10695	1.4	–1.0	2.4
Secondary	1938093 (33.7)	6.2 (21.8)	31260	2913238 (34.1)	6.8 (23.5)	42842	7.0	1.6	5.4
Tertiary	2383642 (41.5)	6.9 (24.2)	34546	4075154 (47.7)	7.5 (26.0)	54335	9.3	1.4	7.8
ALL	**574820 (100.0)**	**28.5 (100.0)**	**20169**	**8539118 (100.0)**	**28.9 (100.0)**	**29547**	**6.8**	**0.2**	**6.6**
	All-India								
	1993-94			*1999-2000*			*Annual Growth Rate*		
	GDP (Rs.Crore)	*Work Force (Thous.)*	*GVA per Worker*	*GDP (Rs.Crore)*	*Work Force (Thous.)*	*GVA per Worker*	*GDP*	*Work Force*	*GVA per Worker*
Primary	262059 (35.5)	241358 (64.1)	10858	316780 (28.8)	237860 (59.9)	13318	3.2	–0.2	3.5
Secondary	185070 (25.1)	56739 (15.2)	32618	283716 (25.8)	66962 (16.9)	42370	7.4	2.8	4.5
Tertiary	290709 (39.4)	75739 (20.3)	38385	500104 (45.4)	92196 (23.2)	54244	9.5	3.3	5.9
ALL	**737838 (100.0)**	**373832 (100.0)**	**19737**	**1100600 (100.0)**	**397018 (5.0)**	**27722**	**6.9**	**1.0**	**5.8**

Note: (1) The values in brackets are percentage shares; (2) GVA per worker measures labour productivity; (3) All values are in 1993-94 prices; (4) For abbreviations, see Appendix 2A.I.

Source: The values for domestic product and employment for Tamil Nadu are from GoTN (2002) and for All-India are from Sundaram (2001b).

India rate of 5.8 per cent with the tertiary sector having a much larger growth rate of about 7.8 per cent than the All-India rate of 5.9 per cent.

The trend in labour productivity growth (reported in Table 2.15) shows that agriculture is slowly declining whereas manufacturing has shown a positive growth since the late eighties and continues to maintain a growth rate of above 1.5 per cent. The trade and transport sector which also includes hotels and restaurants seem to have been a major disappointment as it has grown significantly in the eighties and early nineties. Similarly the decline in growth rate for the services sector is also to be noted and improved as it is substantially lower than the All-India average.

Agricultural Wages

The fact that labour productivity has increased in the agriculture sector would be reflected in agricultural wages and this is discussed in this section. The agricultural wage index for Tamil Nadu for the period between 1993-94 and 2002-03 shows increase in both male and female wage rates. The growth rate (calculated from semi log model) during this period is 11.7 per cent for males and 9.5 per cent for females.

TABLE 2.15

Trend in Labour Productivity (GSDP per UPSS) Across Sectors for Tamil Nadu (Rs. in constant 1993-94 prices)

	Agriculture	*Manufacturing*	*Construction*	*Services*
1983	5860	27638	35201	23513
1987-1988	6783 (3.7)	26762 (–0.8)	25422 (–7.8)	27719 (4.2)
1993-1994	9024 (4.9)	29886 (1.9)	27721 (1.5)	39527 (6.1)
1999-2000	10434 (2.4)	39530 (4.8)	38842 (5.8)	81820 (12.9)

Note: The values in brackets are annual growth rates.

Source: The values for 1993-94 and 1999-2000 are from Table 2.14 above and the values for 1983 and 1987-88 are from Bhalla (2001) after adjusting for the base year.

TABLE 2.16

Growth Rates in Real Wages of Agricultural Labour Across Regions of Tamil Nadu

(1970-71 prices)

	1970-71 to 1979-80		*1980-81 to 1989-90*		*1990-91 to 1994-95*	
	Male	*Female*	*Male*	*Female*	*Male*	*Female*
Coastal North	2.81	0.85	6.57	5.17	2.35	4.37
Coastal	1.07	−0.52	0.44	(−)0.1	8.61	6.05
Southern	2.73	1.74	1.89	3.87	4.22	4.53
Inland	2.03	3.5	3.07	5.15	1.76	0.47

Source: Sharma (2001)

The agricultural wages in Tamil Nadu have grown significantly during the nineties. The growth rate of wages per year for field labour was about 2.7 per cent in seventies, 2.6 per cent in eighties and 6.3 per cent in nineties. Disaggregated analysis shows that there is spatial variation as well as male female differences (see Table 2.16 above).

In order to compare the wages in Tamil Nadu with other states data from economic survey 1999-2000 as mentioned in Sharma (2001) is used and Table 2.17 reports the comparison. Since the mid-nineties the wage rates in Tamil Nadu have increased substantially compared to other regions and registered one of the highest growth rates of 6.3 per cent next only to Kerala of 7.8 per cent.

TABLE 2.17

Agricultural Wage Indices for Select States: 1990-91 to 1998-99 (1990-91 prices)

Year	*AP*	*GUJ*	*KER*	*MAH*	*PUN*	*TN*
1990-91	100.0	100.0	100.0	100.0	100.0	100.0
1991-92	88.6	95.7	104.1	85.2	103.7	95.2
1992-93	90.0	103.3	114.2	85.8	108.1	107.8
1993-94	97.7	106.2	111.0	107.7	109.7	120.3
1994-95	100.4	107.6	116.8	107.0	108.4	121.5
1995-96	98.7	110.7	132.2	98.5	101.3	125.5
1996-97	100.1	116.3	151.4	106.7	100.9	135.9
1997-98	104.5	133.1	174.8	118.3	101.6	153.7
1998-99	99.6	151.0	183.7	107.8	98.5	158.1
Growth rate	1.1*	4.8*	7.8*	2.7*	−0.5	6.3*

Note: (a) The wage indices are as in Sharma, (2001) and the growth rates are calculated from there. (b) The Growth Rate is semi-log growth rates * denotes its significance at 5 per cent level.

Source: Sharma, (2001)

Average Daily Wages of Casual Labourers

In 1999-2000 the average daily wages of casual labourers in Tamil Nadu was about Rs. 48.14 for rural labourers and Rs. 66.34 for urban workers which is above the national average of Rs. 39.64 and Rs. 56.96 for the rural and urban sector respectively. In comparison to other states the rural wage rates were below those of states like Haryana (Rs. 60.78), Kerala (Rs. 90.59), Punjab (Rs. 64.50) and Rajasthan (Rs. 51.72) but the urban wage rates were fairly high and below those of only two other states, Kerala (Rs. 93.13) and Punjab (Rs. 80.40). As was observed for All-India and most other states the rural urban differential in wages was quite high for Tamil Nadu also but more importantly the gender gap in wages for Tamil Nadu was very high in both rural and urban sector. The unavailability of a similar tabulation for 1993-94 for states makes the comparison of the wages for the previous period.

Education and Employment

The tabulated data on the distribution of the employed workforce across education groups is unavailable from the recent NSSO reports. However, the distribution for the overall population across educational groups is available which could indicate the level of educational attainment of the workforce.

TABLE 2.18

Educational Attainment in Tamil Nadu and All-India (in brackets): 1993-94 and 1999-2000 (%)

	Males		*Females*	
	1993-94	*1999-2000*	*1993-94*	*1999-2000*
Rural				
Not literate	35.0 (45.5)	32.1 (41.2)	57.2 (67.9)	49.7 (61.5)
Literate up to primary	41.5 (33.7)	39.1 (34.2)	30.8 (23.0)	31.4 (26.0)
Middle	11.7 (10.9)	14.2 (12.6)	6.4 (5.6)	10.8 (7.5)
Secondary & above	11.8 (9.8)	14.4 (11.7)	5.5 (3.4)	8.0 (5.0)
Urban				
Not literate	19.3 (24.1)	16.6 (33.9)	33.2 (38.4)	27.5 (34.3)
Literate up to primary	29.8 (33.2)	33.9 (30.9)	36.9 (31.0)	35.0 (29.9)
Middle	15.4 (14.5)	16.6 (15.6)	12.6 (11.8)	14.1 (13.2)
Secondary & above	25.5 (28.1)	32.7 (31.7)	17.1 (18.7)	23.1 (22.5)

Source: NSSO (1996a, 2001).

The educational attainment has significantly improved for both male and female between the two years as shown in Table 2.18 above. However, the quality of improvement is better for males as they have moved towards higher levels of education. A substantial proportion of women in the rural sector are literate and

TABLE 2.19

Proportion of Persons, Poverty Rates and Proportion of Poor Among Different Occupational Groups in Rural Areas and Employment Status in Urban Areas

(Per cent)

	Proportion of Persons		*Poverty Rates*		*Proportion of Poor*	
	1993-94	*1999-2000*	*1993-94*	*1999-2000*	*1993-94*	*1999-2000*
Rural						
Agriculture Labour	40.7	45.0	59.8	29.1	56.9	65.5
Self Employed (Agriculture)	23.0	18.5	34.5	10.5	18.6	9.7
Self Employed (Non-Agric.)	13.5	14.6	28.4	13.7	9.0	10.0
Other Labour	12.6	13.1	35.9	14.7	10.5	9.5
Others	10.1	8.8	20.9	12.2	5.0	5.4
Total	100.0	100.0	42.7	20.0	100.0	100.0
Urban						
Self Employed	32.5	32.9	37.0	22.1	30.1	32.8
Regular Wage	41.0	42.7	27.6	12.6	28.3	24.3
Casual Labour	20.6	18.5	67.4	46.5	34.7	38.8
Others	6.0	5.9	46.2	15.0	6.9	4.0
Total	100.0	100.0	39.9	22.1	100.0	100.0

Source: Based on calculation from unit record NSSO data using official poverty line values.

about 18 per cent of them have above primary level of education.

Poverty and Employment

The structural changes in employment pattern as mentioned in the previous sections are bound to have also affected the poverty rates among different occupation groups and employment status. Based on the poverty lines given by the Union Planning Commission proportion of poor among different groups along with the proportion of population have been calculated based on the consumer expenditure surveys of NSSO as shown in Table 2.19 below. The following features are noted:

- The per capita consumption expenditure in Tamil Nadu grew at an annual rate of 1.9 per cent for the rural sector and 5.5 per cent for the urban sector between 1993-94 and 1999-2000.[6]
- This has significantly reduced the overall poverty rate in Tamil Nadu (All-India) from about 35 per cent (36 per cent) in 1993-94 to 21 per cent (26 per cent) in 1999-2000 (GoI, 2001).
- The urban poverty rate in Tamil Nadu declined by about 18 percentage points to about 22 per cent whereas the rural poverty rate declined by about 23 percentage points to about 21 per cent thus reducing the gap between rural and urban poverty rates.
- This has also reduced poverty rates across different occupations and employment status as shown in Table 2.19.
- The agricultural labour, which accounts for about 45 per cent of the rural population having the largest number of poor (66 per cent) has halved the poverty rates by 1999-2000.
- The interesting feature however is that the poverty rates among the self-employed in agriculture has decreased to less than 15 per cent with the proportion of poor among them also having decreased.
- The urban sector shows that the self-employed and the casual labour have reduced their share in 1999-2000 compared to 1993-94 but the poverty rates have increased marginally.

Economic Reforms and Employment

It is unclear about the impacts of economic reforms on the employment of the entire country. However, specific sector related information is slowly becoming available. According to the recently released Report by International Labour Organisation (ILO, 2003) the economic reform process initiated in the nineties may not have generated enough employment opportunities but may have reduced poverty and underemployment. Hasan, Mitra and Ramaswamy (2003) based on organised manufacturing sector data show that trade reforms may not have favoured employment growth but has definitely improved productivity. Their results

6. The figures are calculated from GoI (2001) after adjusting for inflation alone and not inequality also as mentioned in that Report.

further show that lesser trade protection improves labour-demand elasticities and this response is higher for states with flexible labour markets (lest tight restrictions on retrenchments and layoffs) of which Tamil Nadu is one of the states. Burange (2002) also shows a similar result that a State like Tamil Nadu has had a high growth in both employment for the organised manufacturing sector in the pre- and post-liberalisation period as shown in the Table 2.20 below:

TABLE 2.20

Growth Rate in Organised Manufacturing Sector Employment and Output for Tamil Nadu and All-India (in brackets) (%)

	Pre-liberalisation (1980-81 to 1991-92)			*Post-liberalisation (1991-92 to 1997-98)*		
	MFG	*Agri*	*Non-agri*	*MFG*	*Agri-based*	*Non-agri*
Employment	2.39 (0.60)	2.16 (-0.49)	2.65 (1.77)	5.68 (4.15)	6.80 (4.42)	4.42 (3.82)
Output	8.48 (7.72)	8.83 (7.27)	8.22 (7.96)	11.53 (9.90)	11.22 (8.26)	11.69 (10.69)

Note: (a) Employment is measured in numbers and Output is value of output in constant 1980-81 prices. (b) MFG: Manufacturing, Agri: Agriculture based industries, Non-Agri Non-agriculture based Industry.

Source: Burange (2002).

The impact of economic reforms on the agriculture sector and the unorganised industrial sector including the small scale sector where most of the employment is generated is not yet available.

Conclusions and Policy Options

The nineties has seen a rapid pace of growth in per capita incomes but the prevalence of poverty and slow pace of employment growth has been a cause of concern. This phase has been termed as "jobless growth" by many including the recently released ILO report on employment (ILO, 2003). However, others highlight the fact that productivity has grown among many sectors including agriculture resulting in higher wages and that this fall in employment is only a short run phenomenon. The present chapter with its focus on demography and employment in Tamil Nadu analysed the patterns in growth, demography, employment, productivity and wages during nineties in an attempt to provide policy suggestions.

The main observations of the chapter are[7]:

- The Census 2001 results show the population of Tamil Nadu at 62.1 million comprising of 31.3 million males and 30.8 million females and grew at an annual rate of 1.1 per cent between 1991 and 2001.
- The demographic transition triggered by fall in total fertility rate and birth rate in eighties was sustained during nineties. The total fertility rate of 2.1 per cent during 1995-97 and was second lowest after Kerala (1.8 per cent), while the birth rate declined by about 30 per cent in the past four decades to reach about 19.2 per cent in 1998.
- The urbanisation rate of almost 44 per cent in 2001 was among highest in India and has been uniform across the State. While the overall sex-ratio has improved during 1991-2001, the sex-ratio in the 0-6 years age group has declined (remained stagnant) in rural (urban) during the same period. The State initiatives to arrest the phenomenon of female infanticide in districts like Salem, Dharmapuri, Theni, and Namakkal has not resulted in improving the sex-ratio and in fact these districts have registered lower sex-ratio in 2001 compared to 1991.
- Though the literacy rates have improved in both rural and urban areas, significant differences still exist between the two sectors, as do the differences between male and female.
- Similarly, despite significant strides made in access to health services, the State is far behind states like Kerala and developed nations.
- The working population as per the census grew at a faster rate (1.4 per cent) than the population (1.07 per cent) during nineties, indicating a reversal of trend compared to previous decades. However, this rate of growth is slower than that registered during the previous decade (1.8 per cent) mainly due to a decline in rural working population.
- The working population was fairly uniform across sub-regions of Tamil Nadu except the inland districts where it was marginally higher. More importantly there was difference in working population between male and female, especially in urban areas.
- The labour force participation rate, according to the NSS estimates, though declined during 1993-94 to 1999-2000, continued to be higher than most other states in India in 1999-2000.

7. The trends are mainly for the decade of nineties, unless otherwise mentioned.

- The decline in labour force participation rate was mainly due to a significant drop in women's participation in both rural and urban areas combined with a marginal decline among urban males.
- The worker participation ratio, based on both usual status and current daily status, also declined during 1993-94 and 1999-2000 contributed mainly by women and the population below 19 years. However, the current daily status rates were significantly lower than those in usual status participation.
- The age-specific worker participation ratio showed that the decline in WPR among 5 to 14 years was significant resulting in lower child labour in 1999-2000 compared to 1993-94.
- The worker participation ratio among the youth has declined, contributed mainly by the decline in 15 to 19 years age group.
- While gender equity was evident in the child labour participation and also its decline, significant gender bias exists in terms worker participation for all other age groups.
- The growth rate in employment during 1993-94 and 1999-2000 was a mere 0.2 per cent in Tamil Nadu–lower than even the small growth rate of one per cent registered at All-India level during the same period.
- During 1993-94 and 1999-2000 the annual growth rate of GSDP was 6.8 per cent, with growth rates of 1.4 per cent, 7.0 per cent and 9.3 per cent in primary, secondary and tertiary sectors, respectively.
- The growth rate of GSDP in Tamil Nadu was close to that of All-India. The difference between Tamil Nadu and All-India was mainly in terms of agriculture, with the growth rate in the former being higher at All-India level.
- Sectoral disaggregation showed that employment had risen in construction and trade, transport and related services whereas agriculture registered a decline. Employment in the organised sector has shown only a marginal increase despite significant increase in the private sector.
- The status of the workers, as classified by the census, showed that marginal workers increased from 14 lakh in 1991 to 42 lakh in 2001 with the rural sector and women having a higher share.
- Similarly NSS data showed that for the period 1993-94 to 1999-2000 the casual labourers increased to about 50 per cent of the working population in the rural sector.
- In contrast, in the urban sector the regular employed increased their share further among men, while women registered a steep increase among self-employed.
- Unemployment rate has increased for the rural sector but decreased for the urban sector based on the usual status as well as the current daily status. However, underemployment has increased in both the sectors with the women usually going out of labour force when not employed. Both unemployment and underemployment were among highest across the Indian states.
- Unemployment among youth showed similar trend as overall unemployment.
- The distribution of cultivated land was very skewed with significantly large population having no land ownership. Moreover, the landless population showed increasing trend over time.
- The overall labour productivity grew at a rate of 6.6 per cent compared to All-India rate of 5.8 per cent during 1993-94 to 1999-2000. This increase is mainly contributed by sharp improvement in labour productivity of services (12.9 per cent), which is far above the All-India rate (7.2 per cent).
- Fall in work force participation enabled the labour productivity in agriculture to grow at 2.5 per cent during 1993-94 to 1999-2000 despite a small growth rate in value added.
- The agricultural wages in Tamil Nadu registered one of the highest growth rates (6.3 per cent) during nineties, next only to Kerala (7.8 per cent), but with significant regional differences. Significantly, the casual labour wages were also among the highest across Indian states.
- The poverty estimates based on consumer expenditure survey of NSS showed decline in overall rural poverty as well across different occupational groups in that sector though the agricultural labourers still have a very high share of poor.
- The urban poverty rates have shown a much faster decline by the late nineties but the casual labourers and self-employed though reducing

their share among the workforce show higher poverty rates compared to early nineties.

- Finally, the economic reforms have slightly favoured the growth of employment in organised manufacturing sector, but have clearly led to labour productivity improvements.

Policy Options[8]

Employment planning is part of an integrated social planning that involves trade-off between short-term and long-term objectives. If a substantial proportion of the children and youth is attending educational institutions then the dependency ratio in the short run increases leading to an increase in the burden on the existing earning members but at the same time improving current educational standards could have higher returns in future. The State on its part may have to subsidise education and also ensure sustained employment and higher wages. Similarly, if a sufficiently large number of the illiterate and/or semi-literate people are poor and have to depend on the State for their survival then the state burden in terms of providing social security would increase leading to reduction in the use of scarce resources for more productive purposes. This in turn would hamper future growth in both employment and incomes. In other words, the objective of the State could be to not only create sustainable employment opportunities, but also to ensure literacy rates and educational levels to improve so that the work force predominantly consists of population in the age group of 20 to 59 years.

Given such an objective and based on the above observations on trend and pattern of employment, the following policy options could be considered for improving worker participation and to address underemployment in Tamil Nadu. It may be noted that at the current juncture of development it would be difficult to envisage no role for planning. However, the planners increasingly will have to play the role of coordinators and regulators. The focus of employment strategies thus has to come through coordinated planning among various government ministries and departments. Besides identifying strategies that link output (value addition) and employment more firmly, the emphasis has to be on bridging the gaps that exist between different segments namely: rural-urban, male-female, educated-uneducated, farm-non-farm, agriculture-non-agriculture and services- non-services.

8. This section has inputs from GoI (2001b, 2002) and Mahendra Dev and Mahajan (2003).

- As contribution to unemployment is mainly coming from agriculture and as the elasticity of employment to agriculture GSDP for Tamil Nadu was estimated at (–)0.62 for the period 1993-94 to 1999-2000 the primary emphasis should be in identifying non-farm employment opportunities, especially in rural areas (GoTN, 2000). As observed in East and South-east Asian countries, growth of non-farm sector could absorb the surplus labour from agriculture.

  A high growth rate in the non-farm sector could be achieved when the resources saved from agriculture are invested in these sectors for diversification (Radhakrishna, 2001). However, this would be possible only when the agriculture sector itself grows at a higher rate than what has been observed so far. Possible strategy for agricultural growth may involve diversification into high value crops. Therefore, it would perhaps be appropriate to allow the market forces to determine the supply and demand of factors and products and the policymakers' role should only be to facilitate such transformation by providing the right incentives and infrastructure and at the appropriate time and level.

  An important feature of the non-farm activities should be their labour intensive nature. The non-farm activities could include, (i) *Agriculture and Allied Services*: Agro-processing and agro-services, vegetable growing and processing, horticulture and floriculture, forest produce processing and sericulture and silk handlooms, fisheries and prawn cultivation and processing; (ii) *Service Sectors*: Construction and allied work; paramedical services, childcare and paravet services, transport of goods and services and tourism related services like hotels and restaurants; and (iii) *Non-service Sectors*: Handicrafts and handlooms, tailoring and cutting, stoneware and ceramics, cement and construction materials.

- In addition to labour intensive nature the produce of the non-farm activities should be export oriented – from rural to urban as well as to foreign markets. Such emphasis would not only bridge the rural-urban gap but also provide higher value addition raising wage rates and hence lower poverty.

- Non-form employment strategies could be beneficial in bridging the gender gap as many of the activities mentioned above can be taken up as household enterprises through self help groups and small cooperatives.

- To facilitate such enterprises micro finance and micro insurance schemes should be encouraged which minimise the moral hazard and adverse selection problems that commonly plague the regular finance/insurance schemes.
- The current urbanisation trends that has favoured smaller towns should be sustained so that more balanced development across geographical areas with uniform employment opportunities is possible. Such emphasis would also arrest migration and reduce congestion in larger towns.
- The present pattern of declining child labour participation should be ensured in future also so that literacy rate of the population would improve.
- Similarly, the observed pattern of lower labour force participation in the age-group 15 to 19 years should be sustained along with emphasis to attain similar trend in the age-group 20 to 24 years also. Focus should also be on ensuring regional balance for this objective.

  As youth in the age-group 15 to 24 years would be attending higher educational institutions, the strategy to not bring them into labour force could provide future benefits in terms of larger pool of highly skilled and entrepreneurial labour force.
- While the employment in manufacturing and service sector has shown significant increase during nineties, an important feature of such improvement is that it took place mostly in organised sector. Policy reforms oriented towards tapping the employment potential of the unorganised segments of manufacturing and service sectors should be given emphasis.
- For the educated unemployed potential employment opportunities could arise in agricultural services like extension, repair services, utility retailing like electricity, and telecom services; IT and IT enabled services, tourism related services, health care related services, business and financial services. An important focus should be on providing training in polytechnics for the auto-manufacturing sector as Tamil Nadu has gained significant comparative advantage in this sector. Similarly, while sustaining the emphasis in computer software sector, the computer hardware sector should also be given a boost as this relatively untapped sector in India not only has employment opportunities but also could contribute towards economic growth through its export potential.
- At a more general level policy reforms including improving market access, credit facilities, judiciary to redress labour disputes, and infrastructure should be undertaken to enable smooth functioning of factor (including labour) and product markets.
- In order to participate more effectively in the liberalised trade regime under WTO, general awareness of all stake holders should be improved so that the adverse impacts of trade liberalisation on employment could be mitigated and beneficial impacts could be enhanced.
- Similarly, health care for all should be ensured as health status is directly related to overall productivity.
- Ensuring higher women's participation in its work force could have cascading effects on the development of the State as better economic status for women helps in the improvement of human development indicators within the household and hence better standards of living. Schemes such as crèches for children of working mothers and facilitating better working conditions for pregnant and nursing mothers should be made effective both in organised and unorganised segments of the work force.
- Though the objective of reservations in education and employment could be worthy in providing equal opportunities for socially disadvantaged sections of the population, it is often misplaced due to adverse selection problems. Efforts should be made to ensure that such reservations not only reach the targeted groups, but are also extended to unorganised and rural sectors.

However, given the growing emphasis on providing reservations on the basis of economic status, a gradual shift towards such a regime should also be envisaged.

References

Bhalla, S. (2001). "Behind Poverty: The Qualitative Deterioration of Employment Prospects for Rural Indians," in (ed.), *Sustainable Agriculture, Poverty and Food Security*, Volume 2, pp. 702-726.

Burange. L.G. (2002). *Growth of Employment and Output of Organised Manufacturing Sector in India: An Interstate Analysis*, Wp No. 3(3)/2002, Centre for Advanced Study, University of Mumbai, Mumbai.

CensusInfo (2001). CDROM: *CensusInfo India 2001 version 1.0*, Office of the Registrar General of India, New Delhi.

GoI (2001). *National Human Development Report*, Union Planning Commission, Government of India, New Delhi.

————. (2001b). *Report of the Task Force on Employment Opportunities*, Planning Commission, Government of India, New Delhi.

————.(2002). *Special Group on Targeting Ten Million Employment Opportunities Per Year*, Planning Commission, Government of India, New Delhi.

GoTN (2000). *Tamil Nadu Economic Appraisal, 1999-2000*, Department of Evaluation and Applied Research, Government of Tamil Nadu, Chennai

————. (2002a). *Tamil Nadu Human Development Report*, State Planning Commission, Government of Tamil Nadu, Chennai.

————. (2002b). *Employment Perspectives for Tamil Nadu*, Department of Evaluation and Applied Research, Government of Tamil Nadu, Chennai.

————. (2003). *Tenth Five Year Plan, Tamil Nadu 2002-2007*, State Planning Commission, Government of Tamil Nadu, Chennai.

Hasan, R., D. Mitra and K.V. Ramaswamy (2003). "Trade Reforms, Labour Regulations and Labour-Demand Elasticities: Empirical Evidence From India," *NBER Working Paper*, No. 9879.

ILO (2003). *Global Employment Trends*, International Labour Organisation, Geneva.

Mahendra Dev, S. and V. Mahajan (2003). "Employment and Unemployment," *Economic and Political Weekly*, pp. 1252-1261, March.

MSSRF (2002). *Food Insecurity Atlas of Urban India*, M.S.Swaminathan Research Foundation and World Food Programme.

NSSO (1996a). *Employment and Unemployment Situation in India: Fifth Quinquennial Survey NSS Fiftieth Round (July1993-June 1994)*, Report No. 409, Dept. of Statistics, Government of India, New Delhi.

————. (1996b). *Sarvekshana*, Vol, XX, No. 1, July-Sept. 1996, Issue No. 68 pp. 137-138, Dept. of Statistics, Government of India, New Delhi.

————. (2001). *Employment and Unemployment Situation in India: 1999-2000 (Part I)*, Report No. 458, Dept. of Statistics, Government of India, New Delhi.

Radhakrishna, R. (2002). "Agricultural Growth, Employment and Poverty: A Policy Perspective," *Economic and Political Weekly*, pp.243-250, January.

Sharma, S. (2001). "Agricultural Wages in India: A Study of States and Regions," *Indian Journal of Labour Economics*, Vol. 45 (1), pp. 89-116.

Sundaram, K. (2001a). "Employment and Unemployment Situation in the Nineties: Some Results from NSS 55th Round Survey," *Economic and Political Weekly*, pp. 931-940, March.

Sundaram, K. (2001b). "Employment and Poverty in Nineties," *Economic and Political Weekly*, pp. 3039-3049, August.

Vaidyanathan, A. (2002). *Food Consumption and Nutrition Status: A Re-examination Based on Indian Evidence*, Mimeograph, Madras Institute of Development Studies, Chennai.

————. (2003). *Employment in India: Structure and Change, 1977-1993: An Interstate Analysis*, Mimeograph, Madras Institute of Development Studies, Chennai.

APPENDIX 2A.I

Abbreviations

CED	:	Chronic Energy Deficiency
GDP	:	Gross Domestic Product
GoI	:	Government of India
GoTN	:	Government of Tamil Nadu
GSDP	:	Gross State Domestic Product
GVA	:	Gross Value Added
ILO	:	International Labour Organisation.
NNMB	:	National Nutrition Monitoring Bureau
NSSO	:	National Sample Survey Organisation
PS	:	Principal Status
SS	:	Subsidiary Status
TFR	:	Total Fertility Rate

APPENDIX 2A.II

Definitions

Chronic Energy Deficiency: An adult is considered chronically energy deficient if the body mass index (ratio of weight in kg to square of height in meters) is below 18.5.

Total Fertility Rate: It is the number of children a woman would have if hypothetically she lived through her reproductive years (i.e.15 to 49) experiencing the age specific fertility rates prevailing in the population during a given period.

Terminologies used in National Sample Survey

Economic Activity: Any activity resulting in production of goods and services that add value to national product. This includes market activities and own consumption and own production activities.

Labour Force: The population that supplies or seeks to supply labour for production.

Labour Force Participation Rate: The proportion of labour force in the total population.

Work Force (Employed): The population that supplies labour for production.

Work Force Participation Rate (Worker Population Ratio): The proportion of economically active persons in the total population.

Activity Status: It is the activity situation in which a person was found during a reference period with regard to the person's participation in economic and non-economic activities. According a person is (a) *Employed*: Engaged in economic activity, (b) *Unemployed*: Seeking or available for work or (c) *Not in labour force*: not available for work which includes attending educational institutions, domestic duties etc. Different approaches are used to determine the activity status based on the reference period of the survey as given below:

Usual Activity Status: The activity status during the previous 365 days. This is further classified into *principal status* in which the person spent the major time and *subsidiary status* in which the person spent minor time.

Current Weekly Status: The activity status during the previous seven days.

Current Daily Status: The activity status during each day of the reference week.

Status of Employment

(a) *Self-employed*: The persons who have the autonomy and independence for carrying out their economic activity and the remuneration received by them comprises of their share of labour and profit of the enterprise. The persons either operated their own farm or non-farm enterprise or were engaged independently in a profession or trade on own account or with one or few partners. They have been further classified into own-account workers, employers and helpers in household enterprise.

(b) *Regular salaried/wage employee*: The person works in other's farm or non-farm enterprise (both household and non-household) and in turn receives salary or wages on a regular basis. This includes persons getting time wage, piece wage or salary and paid apprentice, both full time and part time.

(c) *Casual wage labour*: The person is casually engaged in other's farm or non-farm enterprise (both household and non-household) and receives wages according to the terms of the daily or periodic work contract.

APPENDIX 2A.III

NSS Regions in Tamil Nadu

NSS Region	*Districts (Old and New)*
Coastal Northern	Chennai (Madras)
	Thiruvallur+Kancheepuram
	(Chengai Anna/Chengalpattu)
	Tiruvannamalai
	(Thiruvannamalai-sambuvaryar)
	Vellore (North Arcot-Ambedhkar)
	Villupuram+Cuddalore (South Arcot)
Coastal	Karur+Perambalur+Ariyalur+ Tiruchirapalli
	Nagapattinam+Thiruvarur+Thanjavur
	Nagapattinam-Quaie-E-Milleth
	Pudukkottai
Southern	Madurai+Theni
	Ramnathapuram
	Virudhunagar (Kamarajar)
	Dindigul (Dindigul-Quide Milleth/Anna)
	Tirunelveli-Kottabomman
	Kannyakumari (Nagercoil)
	Sivaganga (Pasupomthevar)
	Thirumaganar
	Thoothukudi (V.O. Chidambaram)
Inland	Dharampuri
	Salem+Namakkal
	Erode (Periyar)
	Coimbatore
	Nilgiri (Udhagamandalam)

Chapter 3

Agriculture

Agriculture plays a key role in the development of any economy, especially in the early phases of development. It contributes significantly to the process, by supply of raw materials to manufacture, wage goods to workers in other sectors, employment to the work force, investible surplus and market for products of industry. Therefore Indian Plans have accorded high priority for agricultural development. After five decades of planned development, agriculture in Tamil Nadu has shown significant changes. Hence a study of agricultural sector assumes importance for the design of policies to achieve development goals in the decades to come, viz., growth, equity, employment and environmental protection all being essential components of sustainable development.

Agriculture in a broad sense includes all activities of production and distribution of seasonal crops, horticulture, plantations, forestry, livestock, fisheries and other bio-cultures such as sericulture, bio-fertilisers, honey, mushroom etc. In the National Income Accounting, these activities are grouped into three sub-sectors namely (1) agriculture and allied activities (of which livestock has a large share); (2) forestry and (3) fisheries. Contribution of agricultural sector to the Net State Domestic Product (NSDP) of Tamil Nadu is shown in Table 3.1.

Estimated in constant (1993-94) prices, the real NSDP has increased from Rs. 20,167 crore in 1960-61 to Rs. 76,971 crore in 1999-2000, registering an annual compound growth rate of 3.41 per cent. Of this, the share of agricultural sector was Rs. 8,748 crore in 1960-61 and it grew up to Rs. 13,262 crore in 1999-2000, the CGR being 1.05 per cent.

However, the relative share of agriculture in NSDP has declined from 43.38 per cent in 1960-61 to 17.23 per cent in 1999-2000. It shows that non-agricultural sectors have grown faster than agricultural sector, inspite of priority to the latter in policies and programmes, probably due to presence of real constraints for the growth of agriculture. It is estimated that an annual growth rate of 3 per cent in agricultural production is the minimum requirement for a 5 per cent growth rate of the economy. When the country targets an economic growth rate of 8 per cent, agriculture has to grow at rates larger than 5 per cent per annum. This is possible.

TABLE 3.1

Net State Domestic Product – Tamil Nadu

(Rs. Crore)

Details	*1960-61*	*1970-71*	*1980-81*	*1990-91*	*1999-2000*
NSDP@					
In NSDP, share of	20,167	32,599	54,182	67,376	76,971
Agriculture	8563	10686	12700	13846	12292
	(42.46)	(32.78)	(23.44)	(20.55)	(15.97)
Forestry	109	202	135	458	463
	(0.54)	(0.62)	(0.25)	(0.68)	(0.60)
Fisheries	77	186	347	229	507
	(0.38)	(0.57)	(0.64)	(0.34)	(0.66)
Agriculture & allied	8748	11074	13182	14533	13262
	(43.38)	(33.97)	(24.33)	(21.57)	(17.23)

Note: @ Net State Domestic Product of Tamil Nadu at Factor Cost at Constant (1993-94) Prices, computed by author for earlier years.

Figures within () show percentage to NSDP (first row).

Source: Tamil Nadu – An Economic Appraisal – Several issues.

The secular decline in relative share of agriculture in the aggregate income of an economy is an essential character of development process. In most of the developed countries, this decline in the relative share of agriculture in the aggregate income was accompanied by a similar trend in relative share of population dependent on agriculture. However, in Tamil Nadu, nearly 72 per cent of the human population was dependent on agriculture in 1960-61 and it was 56.77 per cent in

TABLE 3.2

NSDP and Per Capita Income of Tamil Nadu and in Agricultural Sector

Details	*Unit*	*1960-61*	*1970-71*	*1980-81*	*1990-91*	*2000-01*
1. State Population	Million persons	31.10	41.20	48.41	55.86	61.55
2. Population in Agriculture	Million persons	22.39	28.05	30.76	33.87	35.26
3. Share (2 in 1)	%	71.99	68.08	63.54	60.63	56.77
4. NSDP – Tamil Nadu*	Rs. Crore	20,167	32,599	54,182	67,376	76,971
5. NSDP of Agriculture*	Rs. Crore	8,748	11,074	13,182	14,533	13,262
6. Per Capita Income – Tamil Nadu	Rs./Year	6,485	7,912	11,192	12,062	12,504
7. Per Capita Income in Agriculture	Rs./Year	3,907	3,948	4,285	4,291	3,761

Note: * - at factor cost at constant (1993-94) prices

Row 6 = Row 4 ÷ Row 1; Row 7 = Row 5 ÷ 2; Row 3 = (Row 2 ÷Row 1) × 100

Source: Tamil Nadu–An Economic Appraisal, several issues

TABLE 3.3

Population by Employment Status

(Lakh persons)

Details	*Tamil Nadu*			*India*		
	1971	*1981*	*1991*	*1971*	*1981*	*1991*
a) Main Workers	147.42	190.26 (39.31)	227.99 (40.82)	1803.73	2225.17 (34.45)	1859.32 (34.10)
b) Marginal Workers	—	11.73 (2.42)	13.95 (2.49)	—	220.88 (3.32)	281.99 (3.36)
1. Total Workers (a + b)	147.42	201.99 (41.73)	241.94 (43.31)	1803.73	2446.05 (36.77)	3141.31 (37.46)
2. Non-Workers	264.57	282.09 (58.27)	316.65 (56.69)	3677.97	4206.83 (63.23)	5244.37 (62.54)
Total Population (1 + 2)	411.99 [7.52]	484.08 [7.28]	558.59 [6.66]	5481.70	6652.88	8385.68

Note: 1. Figures within ( ) are percentages to total population (column wise).

2. Figures within [ ] are percentages to total Indian population (last row).

Source: Census of India, 1981, and 1991.

1999-2000. Significant decline in the relative share of agriculture in NSDP and a very small decline in percentage of population dependent on agriculture, allowed very little increase in real per capita income in agricultural sector, from Rs. 3907 in 1960-61 to Rs. 4,291 in 1990-91 even though aggregate value product in agricultural sector had nearly doubled (vide Table 3.2). In 1999-2000, per capita income in agriculture has decreased to Rs. 3,762, due to the fall in NSDP and rise in population in the sector.

Therefore, shifting at least a part of this population out of agriculture must be an explicit policy objective.

Economic reforms introduced in India since mid-1991 have opened ways to increase productivity and competitive efficiency. Globalising agriculture through liberalisation has the potential of commercialisation of agriculture and export of value added farm products. However, agriculture and allied sectors have largely been untouched by the reform measures and this needs immediate correction to realise the full potential of agriculture in Tamil Nadu. Very concerted efforts are necessary because the constraints are many. A review of the trends, current status and constraints in agricultural development of Tamil Nadu is useful and this Report aims at it.

Livelihood

As per 1991 census, human population of India is 838.57 million, of which Tamil Nadu has 55.86 million or 6.66 per cent (vide Table 3.3). In the total population of India 37.46 per cent are workers, while it is 43.31 per cent for Tamil Nadu. Of these workers agriculture has a share of 64.4 per cent in 1971 and it has declined only marginally to 61.5 per cent in 1991(vide Table 3.4). This small decline is in spite of significant fall in the growth rate of population of the

TABLE 3.4

Employment by Major Sector in Tamil Nadu

Sector	*Employment (Lakh)*								*Growth Rate (%) per annum*		
	1971		*1981*		*1991*		*2001*		*1971-80*	*1981-90*	*1991-2000*
	No	*%*	*No*	*%*	*No*	*%*	*No*	*%*	*%*	*%*	*%*
a. Agriculture & Allied Activity	95.10	(64.4)	121.02	(63.6)	140.24	(61.5)	144.4	49.8	2.45	1.48	0.30
b. Mining & Quarry	0.51	(0.3)	0.52	(0.3)	0.69	(0.3)	1.4	0.5	0.19	2.87	10.28
i. Primary Sector (a+b)	**95.52**	**(64.7)**	**121.54**	**(63.9)**	**140.93**	**(61.8)**	**145.8**	**50.3**	**2.44**	**1.49**	**0.34**
c) Manufacturing	19.72	(13.4)	28.96	(15.2)	31.98	(14.0)	54.0	18.6	3.92	1.00	6.89
d. Construction	2.34	(1.6)	3.39	(1.8)	4.89	(2.11)	14.5	5.0	3.78	3.73	19.65
ii. Secondary Sector (c + d)	**22.06**	**(15.0)**	**32.35**	**(17.0)**	**36.87**	**(16.11)**	**68.5**	**23.6**	**3.90**	**1.31**	**8.57**
e. Trade & Commerce	11.54	(7.8)	16.00	(8.5)	19.80	(8.7)	38.1	13.2	3.37	2.10	9.24
f. Transport, Storage & Communication	4.66	(3.2)	5.54	(2.9)	7.04	(3.2)	8.6	3.0	1.74	2.43	2.22
g. Service	13.64	(9.3)	14.75	(7.7)	23.35	(10.2)	28.8	9.9	0.79	4.70	2.33
iii. Tertiary Sector (e+f+g)	**29.84**	**(20.3)**	**36.29**	**(19.1)**	**50.19**	**(22.1)**	**75.5**	**26.1**	**1.97**	**3.29**	**5.04**
Total (i+ii+iii) Main workers	**147.42**	**(100.0)**	**190.18**	**(100.0)**	**227.99**	**(100.0)**	**289.8**	**100.0**	**2.48**	**1.83**	**2.71**

Source: Census Reports % to total main workers.

State from 2.6 per cent to 1.17 per cent during the same period (1971-1991). Employment in agriculture was growing at the rate of 2.45 per cent in seventies at 1.48 per cent in eighties and just 0.30 per cent in nineties. Even then agriculture, has 144.4 lakh workers in 2000 and it is nearly 50 per cent of all workers. Thus, the large share of agriculture sector in the total number of workers in the State is a structural characteristic of the economy. *A rise in the standard of living of this majority of workers needs a high growth rate in the income earned by them.* But, income is growing very slowly. An important constraint is the scarcity of land.

Land

The reported area of Tamil Nadu (vide Table 3.5) is around 130 lakh hectares. Of this, area under forest is 21.40 lakh ha. and accounts for 16 per cent of the total land area, against the environmentally desirable 33 per cent. However, from 18.66 lakh ha. in 1960-61, there has been increase in area under forests, largely due to several afforestation and conservation schemes implemented by the government.

However, at the slow pace of expansion it is most likely to be less than 20 per cent in the next two decades. Area under permanent pastures and grazing lands and that under miscellaneous tree crops and groves are shrinking, it is a sign of a decline in village common land due to encroachment and neglect. However total area under these categories is very small. Area under cultivable waste has come down to less than half of what it was in 1960-61. It is due to the pressure on land for cultivation of crops.

However, the area under current fallows and other fallows which include area of land once cultivated but remains uncultivated for one to five years thereafter, is increasing. They are marginal low productive lands and do not have assured irrigation facilities. Other fallows and cultivable waste lands can be brought under the plough by suitable reclamation practices, involving investments that yield very low return. The farmers are not in a position to make such investments, because most of them are marginal and small farmers. Thus, availability of cultivable land sets the limit for extensive farming. *Net area sown is less than 55 lakh hectares in 2000.*

Land Holding Pattern

Net area sown, area under farm forests and fallow lands add upto total land available with farmers. It was 76.08 lakh ha, in 1980-81 and marginally increased to 78.62 lakh ha. in 1995-96. Due to the policies of land ceiling and land-to-the-tiller very large farms disappeared and the distribution of land holdings shows the dominance of marginal and small farmers. Details are presented in Table 3.6. It may be seen from the Table that 71.91 lakh farmers have total farm area of 77.08 lakh ha., the average size of the farm being 1.07 ha. In 1995-96 there are 82.35 lakh farmers, their operational area is 78.62 lakh ha. the average farm size being 0.95 ha. only. Among them there are 60.40 lakh marginal farmers with land holding in size of less than one ha. each, average size being 0.38 ha. Small farms (of 1-2 ha.) are 13.05 lakh in number and they have the total land area of 18.32 lakh ha. average size being 1.40 ha.

TABLE 3.5

Land Use Pattern in Tamil Nadu

('000 ha)

S.No.	Land Use Pattern	1960-61	1970-71	1980-81	1990-91	1999-2000
1.	Reporting Area	13015	13004	13003	13019	12991
2.	Forests	1866	2013	2022	2155	2134
3.	Barren & Uncultivable Land	945	832	577	509	476
4.	Land put to Non-agrl. Uses	1295	1489	1747	1820	1978
5.	Permanent Pastures & Grazing Lands	363	231	159	124	123
6.	Land under Misce. Tree Crops and Groves	246	226	212	234	243
7.	Culturable Waste Land	706	507	343	290	349
8.	Other Fallows*	623	573	459	1044	1140
9.	Current Fallows**	974	964	2120	1264	1085
10.	Net Area Sown	5997	6169	5364	5579	5463
11.	Area Sown More than once	1324	1215	1109	1053	1054
12.	Grass Cropped Area	7320	7384	6473	6632	6517
13.	Cropping Intensity (%)	120	120	121	119	119
14.	Net Area Irrigated	2461	2486	2570	2373	2972
15.	% to Net Area Sown	41.0	40.3	47.9	42.5	54.4
16.	Gross Area Irrigated	3235	3279	3294	2894	3585
17.	% to Gross Cropped Area	44.2	44.4	50.9	43.6	55.0
18.	Intensity of Irrigation (%)	131.5	131.9	128.2	122.0	120.6

Note: @ - not included in Net area sown.

* - lands once cultivated but remaining fallow for 2-5 years.

** - lands once cultivated but remaining fallow during the current year.

Intensity of irrigation = Percentage of gross irrigation area to Net irrigated area.

Source: Tamil Nadu – An Economic Appraisal – Several Issues.

TABLE 3.6

Land Holding Pattern

S. No.	Size of Holding	1980-81			1995-96*		
		No. of Holdings ('000)	Area of Holdings ('000 ha)	Average Size of Holdings (ha)	No. of Holdings ('000)	Area of Holdings ('000 ha)	Average Size of Holdings (ha)
1.	Marginal Farms (< 0.1 ha)	5015	1907	0.38	6040	2291	0.38
2.	Small Farms (1-2 ha)	1209	1710	1.41	1305	1832	1.40
3.	Semi-Medium Farms (2-4 ha)	658	1822	2.77	633	1729	2.73
4.	Medium Farms (4-10 ha)	269	1555	5.78	223	1272	5.70
5.	Large Farms (>=10 ha)	40	714	17.85	34	738	21.70
	Total	**7191**	**7708**	**1.07**	**8235**	**7862**	**0.95**

Note: * Latest available data.

Source: Tamil Nadu – An Economic Appraisal.

Farms classified as semi-medium size group are 6.33 lakh in number and have 17.29 lakh ha., the average size of farm being 2.73 ha. Thus 96 per cent of land holdings are smaller than 4 ha. each. These farms are too small to operate and their credit worthiness is rated very poor. That sets the limit for investment in farm assets and modern inputs that are essential for intensive farming. *Only policy support by way of supply of critical inputs (high yielding seeds, fertilisers, power and technical know-how) at low or subsidised cost sustains such farms.*

One advantage of such farms (of less than 4 ha. each) is that farmers pay personal attention to cultivation and use family labour (which is mostly unskilled and has very little opportunity to find other jobs) in large measure, *both contributing to improvement in yield and cost reduction. Real problem is however, that such farms are subsistence oriented.*

Landless Agricultural Labour

There are 144.4 lakh workers dependent upon agriculture and allied activities such as horticulture, forestry, live-stock, and sericulture. Of them only 82.34 lakh are cultivators and 29.81 lakh workers are in allied activities, the balance is the army of landless agricultural labourers – 28.09 lakh persons who know only farming but have no land of their own. There is also not much land for redistribution. Therefore they have to survive as wage earners in agriculture and seek jobs from cultivators. However most of the cultivators themselves are small land holders and use own family labour to the extent possible. Even some of the marginal and small farmers seek jobs outside their farms because they are underemployed by excess supply of workers. Consequently the farm wages are low. *The problems of unemployment and under employment of agricultural labour are real and deserve attention in any policy for agricultural development.* The seasonality in farm operations find seasonal scarcity at times of sowing and harvesting, providing some scope for the agricultural labourers to bargain for high wages. It is in this context, the new thrust on waste-land development assumes importance.

Waste Land

A recent estimate shows that in 20 districts of Tamil Nadu, there is waste land to the extent of 36.28 lakh ha. Details are presented in Table 3.7.

TABLE 3.7

District-wise Data on Wasteland in Tamil Nadu

('000 ha)

S. No.	District	Waste Land	S. No.	District	Waste Land
1.	Kancheepuram	183	11.	Thanjavur	139
2.	Cuddalore	276	12.	Madurai	177
3.	Vellore	149	13.	Dindigal	209
4.	Thiruvannamalai	141	14.	Ramanathapuram	144
5.	Salem	262	15.	Virudhunagar	141
6.	Dharmapuri	195	18.	Sivaganga	177
7.	Coimbatore	182	17.	Tirunelveli	284
8.	Erode	180	18.	Thoothukkudi	180
9.	Thiruchirappalli	391	19.	Nilgiris	47
10.	Pudukottai	137	20.	Kanyakumari	34

Grand Total: 36.28 Lakh ha

Source: Perspective Plan for Waste Land Development, TNAU, Coimbatore, 2001.

Special schemes have been drawn to put these lands to productive use by suitable reclamation of land and cultivation of select crops, with the technical and financial support of the Government of Tamil Nadu. If the landless agricultural labours are the target beneficiaries of this scheme, it will generate employment opportunities to at least 20 lakh farm workers. Mobilisation of required resources and economically viable operational strategy will make the scheme a success. Emphasis must be on participatory development through collective community based efforts, *because individual tiny farms are economically not viable on such marginal and sub-marginal lands (that constitute wastelands).*

Irrigation

When the scope for extensive farming is limited, the alternative is to go for intensive farming. New biological chemical technology introduced in the late sixties has shown the way and the green revolution became a reality. However, this technology depends upon high yielding and high fertiliser responsive crop varieties, both requiring sufficient irrigation. Data on area irrigated sourcewise, are presented in Table 3.8.

TABLE 3.8

Area of Land Irrigated – Source-wise

('000 ha)

S. No.	Sources of Irrigation	1960-61	1970-71	1980-81	1990-91	1999-2000
1.	Canals	881 (35.80)	862 (34.67)	889 (34.19)	769 (32.41)	868 (29.21)
2.	Tanks	936 (38.01)	902 (36.28)	590 (22.69)	531 (22.38)	633 (21.30)
3.	Wells	598 (24.30)	681 (27.39)	1097 (42.19)	1059 (44.63)	1453 (48.89)
4.	Others	46 (1.89)	41 (1.65)	24 (10.93)	14 (0.56)	18 (0.60)
	Total*	**2461**	**2486**	**2600**	**2373**	**2972**

Note: Figures within () are percentages to total area irrigated.

* Net Area Irrigated.

Source: Tamil Nadu – An Economic Appraisal – Various Issues & Dept,. of Economics and Statistics, Chennai

Total area of land irrigated in 1960-61 was 24.61 lakh ha. and it has expanded to 29.72 lakh ha. by 2000, but with a noticeable change in the relative share of different sources. Natural surface flow of water from canals and tanks accounted for 35.80 per cent and 38.01 per cent of total area irrigated respectively in 1960-61. They account for only 29.21 per cent and 21.30 per cent respectively in 1999-2000. Even in absolute terms, area irrigated by tanks has shown significant contraction from 9.36 lakh ha. in 1960-61 to 5.31 lakh ha. in 1990-91, with some improvement in

1999-2000 to 6.33 lakh ha.. Area irrigated by wells, has nearly trebled from 5.98 lakh ha. to 14.53 lakh ha. during the same period. This shows increasing exploitation of ground water, requiring investment in wells and use of electricity or diesel for the pump sets. *Very rapid increase in the use of ground water has brought to focus the environmental problems of inter-generational inequity. The limit is fast approaching. Recent drive for rain water harvesting is the right remedy to this problem.*

Even with increasing use of ground water net area irrigated is only 29.72 lakh ha. which benefits only 54.4 per cent of net sown area (vide Table 3.5). The remaining part of net sown area is rainfed, with much uncertainty in its quantity and spread over the crop season. Therefore, the intensity of irrigation is low at 120 per cent. It has its impact on keeping intensity of cropping also low at 119 per cent. So, gross cropped area is only 65.17 lakh ha. in 1999-2000 showing a sharp decline from 73.20 lakh ha. in 1960-61. One cause of such a decline is the Cauvery dispute that has significantly reduced area under Kuruvai crop of rice in Cauvery delta.

Thus, crop production in Tamil Nadu is limited by the decline in net area sown, cropping intensity and area of crops irrigated. Therefore any future development would require attention to improvement in productivity of crops in both irrigated and unirrigated (rainfed) areas and farm technology has to help this improvement in yield of crops. A change in crop pattern favouring high value adding crops is a strategy to increase farm income.

Crop Pattern

The cropping pattern in Tamil Nadu in shown in Table 3.9.

Rice is the dominant crop accounting for 33 per cent of gross cropped area. Groundnut, sugarcane and cotton are important commercial[1] crops. *Jowar, bajra* and pulses are important foodgrain crops. These seven crops account for about 73 per cent of gross cropped area, while 42 other crops are each cultivated in small areas. They include minor millets, other oil seeds, turmeric, vegetables, fruits, coconut and other minor crops.

In Tamil Nadu these seven crops determine the overall growth of value added in agriculture and they are studied in detail. However some of the crops included in 'other crops' have the prospect of coming to prominence by their potential contribution to exports. Turmeric, tropical fruits, flowers, indigo, palmarosa, medicinal plants, spices particularly onion, pepper and cardamom are gaining attention of farmers. *In the context of globalisation of Indian economy and priority for export led growth these crops find favour.* However, only a beginning has been made to tap the potential and there are formidable problems in the path ahead. Recent failure at Cancun to break the deadlock in Doha agenda of WTO is a pointer to the future problems for farm export.

TABLE 3.9

Crop Pattern of Tamil Nadu

('000 ha)

S. No.	*Crops*	*1960-61*	*1970-71*	*1980-81*	*1990-91*	*1999-2000*
1.	Rice	2518 (34.40)	2636 (35.70)	2230 (34.47)	1856 (27.98)	2164 (33.21)
2.	Jowar	774 (10.59)	749 (10.14)	537 (8.3)	541 (8.16)	351 (5.38)
3.	Bajra	489 (6.68)	490 (6.64)	319 (4.93)	274 (4.13)	158 (2.43)
4.	Pulses	427 (5.83)	492 (6.66)	544 (8.41)	847 (12.77)	693 (10.63)
5.	Sugarcane	82 (1.12)	135 (1.83)	183 (2.83)	233 (3.51)	316 (4.85)
6.	Groundnut	871 (11.90)	1000 (13.54)	789 (12.19)	963 (14.52)	913 (14.01)
7.	Cotton	396 (5.41)	311 (4.21)	222 (3.43)	239 (3.61)	178 (2.73)
8.	Other Crops	1763 (24.08)	1571 (21.28)	1646 (25.44)	1679 (25.32)	1744 (26.76)
9.	Gross Cropped Area	7320	7384	6470	6632	6517

Note: Figures within () are percentages to the Gross Cropped Area.

Source: Season and Crop Reports, Govt. of Tamil Nadu

Rice being the staple food of the people of Tamil Nadu its dominant share in the crop mix had remained steady, except in years (such as 1990-91) when supply of water in Cauvery was delayed. Supply of fine rice in PDS has encouraged people to change their consumption habit from other cereals to rice, contributing to significant reduction in area put under millets. Area cultivated with *Jowar* (Cholam) has come down from 7.74 lakh ha. in 1960-61 to less than 4 lakh ha. in 1999-2000. Area under *bajra* (Cumbu) has fallen from 4.89 lakh ha. to 1.58 lakh ha. during the same period. Area under pulse crops expanded from 4.27 lakh ha. to 6.93 lakh ha. between 1960-61 and 1999-2000. Area under sugarcane has increased from just 0.82 lakh ha. in 1960-61 to 3.16 lakh ha. in 1999-2000 thanks to the establishment of several sugar mills in the State.

1. They are crops that supply raw material to industry and serves consumers directly very little.

TABLE 3.10

Productivity (Yield) of Major Crops in Tamil Nadu

(per ha)

S. No.	*Crops*	*Units*	*1960-61*	*1970-71*	*1980-81*	*1990-91*	*1999-2000*
1.	Rice	Rice in kg	1414	1974	1865	3116	3482
2.	Jowar	Grain in kg	816	730	790	1010	983
3.	Bajra	Grain in kg	616	660	840	1080	1525
4.	Pulses	Grain in kg	265	271	324	425	420
5.	Sugarcane	Tonnes of cane	80	77	101.5	100.8	108
6.	Groundnut	Nuts in kg	1217	920	860	1220	1541
7.	Cotton	Lint in kg	167	200	200	290	325

Source: Tamil Nadu – An Economic Appraisal.

Groundnut is the major edible oil crop, but area under the crop varies over the years, around 9 lakh ha. *Gross cropped area has shrunk from 73.20 lakh ha. to 65.17 lakh ha. – nearly 10 per cent reduction. This needs attention because the number of workers dependent upon agriculture has increased from 95 lakhs in 1971 to 144 lakhs in 1991 (latest census figure).* It has significantly increased the man/land ratio. The problem has a remedy in improving productivity of the crop to protect income per capita.

Productivity of Crop

As shown in Table 3.10, productivity of all the seven major crops has increased substantially during the period of four decades. Yield of rice has increased from 1414 kg/ha in 1960-61 to 3482 Kg/ha in 1999-2000 more than doubled – thanks to green revolution. Yield of *Jowar* has improved form 816 kg/ha to 983 kg/ha. Productivity of pulses has increased from 265 kg/ha to 420 kg/ha. Sugarcane yield is now 108 t/ha as against 80 t/ha in 1960-61. Groundnut yield (in terms of nut–in-shell) has gone up from 1217 kg/ha to 1541 kg/ha and yield of cotton (in terms of lint) improved from 167 kg/ha to 325 kg/ha. These figures are all State averages; many farmers have succeeded in reaping much higher yields. *Thus, the significant improvement in crop yields has more than compensated the loss in area cultivated.*

Growth Rates

Relative contribution of area and yield to the production of crops could be seen from the estimates of growth rates presented decade wise, in Table 3.11. Rice production grew at the rate of 4.07 per cent in sixties, but it was more due to expansion of area (2.66 per cent), than due to yield (1.40 per cent). Green Revolution was ushered-in in the late sixties and its effect was seen in seventies when both expansion of area and yield contributed to production, which grew at 6.81 per cent per annum. In the eighties area under rice crop showed a negative growth rate (-2.32 per cent), but growth rate of yield at 5.27 per cent compensated for the loss of area to achieve a positive growth rate in production (3.06 per cent). In seventies the growth rates of both area and yield were positive but small to register a moderate growth rate of 3.66 per cent in production. This had invited the comment that the first green revolution has reached its plateau.

TABLE 3.11

Growth Rate of Area, Production and Yield of Major Crops in Tamil Nadu

(%)

S. No	*Crops*	*Variables*	*1960's*	*1970's*	*1980's*	*1990's*
1.	Rice	A	2.66	2.32	−2.32	1.34
		Y	1.40	4.39	5.27	2.22
		P	4.07	6.81	3.06	3.66
2.	Jowar	A	0.10	−3.86	0.11	−3.59
		Y	2.27	1.40	−1.77	2.66
		P	2.38	−2.47	−1.61	−0.92
3.	Bajra	A	−7.75	−6.76	−5.99	−4.71
		Y	6.75	5.00	4.70	2.03
		P	−1.01	−1.79	−1.30	−2.65
4.	Pulses	A	4.07	2.00	5.29	1.40
		Y	−0.34	3.50	4.01	3.00
		P	3.73	5.80	9.30	4.40
5.	Food Grains	A	1.96	2.25	−3.69	−0.88
		Y	2.67	3.40	1.28	6.01
		P	4.13	5.63	−2.43	6.70
6.	Sugarcane	A	9.30	1.69	7.30	4.20
		Y	−0.51	4.30	0.70	2.02
		P	8.34	5.59	7.75	6.25
7.	Groundnut	A	1.69	1.93	7.25	1.60
		Y	−3.10	−3.60	2.50	2.70
		P	−1.41	−2.95	10.01	3.03
8.	Cotton	A	−3.79	−1.56	5.35	−2.22
		Y	2.40	3.80	13.00	0.35
		P	−1.30	2.93	19.18	−2.09

Note: 1. Annual Compound Growth Rates for Each Decade Computed

2. A – Area (ha) Y – Yield/ha P – Production

In *Jowar* decline in area was off-set partly by growth of yield (2.66 per cent) to reduce the fall in production (0.92 per cent) in the nineties. In sixties growth rate of area was small but that of yield was good at 2.27 per cent, to increase production by 2.38 per cent, the next two decades witnessed negative growth rate in production.

In *bajra*, growth rate of area was negative and large (in excess of 4.71 per cent), but the improvement in yield was also large (6.75 per cent) in sixties but tapered off in the successive decades. Consequently the growth rate of production was negative in all the four decades. Area effect was larger than yield effect. Area under pulse crops had a positive growth rates in all the four decades, but its value went up and down. The growth rate of yield was negative but it was negligible (0.34 per cent) in sixties, but it was 3.50 per cent, 4 per cent and 3 per cent during the next three decades. This high and positive growth rate in yield complemented the growth rate in area, to help high growth rates in production of pulses. There was a special scheme to promote production of pulses in Tamil Nadu and its success was seen in the significant growth rate of production.

Rice, other cereals (major and minor millets) and pulses constitute foodgrains. In spite of negative growth rates in area in two decades (eighties and nineties), production of foodgrains had positive growth rates in three decades, but it was negative for eighties.

With one exception of a small negative growth rate in sixties the growth rate of both area and yield of sugarcane were positive in all other decades and that explained high growth rate of production of sugarcane. The growth rates of production were larger than 5.50 per cent for all the four decades.

In groundnut, the growth rates in area widely varied from one decade to another but the values were all positive. The growth rates of yield were negative for sixties and seventies but it became positive and large (2.50 per cent and 2.70 per cent) for the next two decades. Therefore growth rate of production was also positive for the eighties and nineties. In groundnut, area had a larger effect on production than yield.

With the exception of eighties, the growth rate of area under cotton had negative values, but yield had positive growth rates in all the decades. Thus, improvement in productivity of cotton (lint in Kg/ha) was the major determinant of production of the crop.

Over all, it may be reasonably concluded, that there has been significant improvement in productivity of all the major crops and it has contributed to either high growth rate in production or to offset the effect of negative growth rate in area. *The contribution of technology (research and extension) to the production of crops is real and significant. Efforts to stabilise area under the crops would therefore be the way to stabilise production of major crops.* However, the biological chemical technology that has contributed to the significant and positive growth rates in yield of major crops requires use of chemical fertilisers which in turn requires adequate moisture in the soil. So irrigation plays a crucial role in crop production.

Irrigation

Area under crops irrigated and the percentage of it to the sown area of the crops are presented in Table 3.12 and 3.13. As could be seen in Table 3.13 the percentage of gross cropped area receiving irrigation was 44.41 in 1970-71, and it has increased to 52.03 per cent in 1991-2000. Only rice and sugarcane received irrigation for more than 84 per cent of the area sown; they are wet land crops raised under conditions of assured irrigation. It must be noted that these crops have registered large growth rates in both yield and production, showing that *irrigation is the decisive factor for the adoption of fertiliser based technology.*

TABLE 3.12

Crop-wise Area Irrigated

(Area in '000 ha)

Year	*Rice*	*Jowar*	*Pulses*	*Food Crops*	*Ground nut*	*Sugar cane*	*Cotton*	*All Crops*
70-71	2425	128	10	3084	181	114	85	3279
71-72	2484	120	16	3140	211	116	122	3530
72-73	2631	115	12	3306	178	143	108	3673
73-74	2485	126	13	3211	269	186	109	3674
74-75	2028	125	11	2696	171	1 60	100	3033
75-76	2379	122	06	3068	163	128	72	3376
76-77	2018	108	11	2677	144	154	89	3001
77-78	2581	107	12	3287	198	167	147	3799
78-79	2556	109	11	3300	251	154	165	3818
79-80	2709	116	14	3444	283	149	143	3983
80-81	2105	96	16	2807	264	183	100	3294
81-82	2306	95	14	2986	226	207	96	3427
82-83	1787	71	11	2364	188	185	73	2732
83-84	2196	81	17	2787	240	156	85	3249
84-85	2331	73	19	2949	288	169	129	3506
85-86	2081	65	22	2695	262	191	127	3240

Contd...

...*Contd*...

(*Area in '000 ha*)

Year	Rice	Jowar	Pulses	Food Crops	Ground nut	Sugar cane	Cotton	All Crops
86-87	1789	54	35	2378	235	196	75	2844
87-88	1766	47	39	2344	315	195	109	2945
88-89	1717	46	29	2343	245	217	108	2873
89-90	1796	55	50	2465	273	222	111	3045
90-91	1686	46	58	2328	274	233	77	2894
91-92	1958	38	49	2603	338	238	89	3257
92-93	2016	37	44	2665	379	216	89	3385
93-94	2137	42	39	2841	354	249	83	3544
94-95	2063	38	40	2849	348	328	96	3588
95-96	1796	38	37	2546	259	326	96	3183
96-97	2015	36	33	2690	268	260	81	3347
97-98	2107	45	38	2846	271	283	80	3519
98-99	2128	36	45	2919	296	306	78	3635
99-00	2016	38	52	2875	265	316	62	3585

Source: Season and Crop Report of Tamil Nadu (Various Issues)

TABLE 3.13

Percentage of Area Irrigated Under Crops

Year	Rice	Jowar	Pulses	Food Crops	Sugar cane	Ground nut	Cotton	Gross
70-71	90.28	17.03	2.03	59.35	84.44	18.10	27.33	44.41
71-72	92.31	16.74	2.73	60.16	99.15	18.89	29.05	46.21
72-73	92.28	16.91	1.84	62.95	99.31	16.78	35.64	47.71
73-74	91.9	19.66	1.96	63.42	100	23.68	36.33	48.04
74-75	90.62	18.52	2.37	61.22	100	17.51	40.16	45.71
75-76	92.78	14.93	1.27	60.53	100	17.43	34.62	46.66
76-77	88.3.5	12.83	2.02	54.56	99.35	16.18	37.08	41.99
77-78	92.77	14.25	2.06	61.99	100	21.38	45.23	47.93
78-79	92.74	15.66	1.79	64.00	100	25.53	47.55	49.64
79-80	93.22	16.09	2.31	66.8	100	28.36	51.07	51.61
80-81	94.39	17.88	2.94	68.31	100	33.46	45.05	50.91
81-82	93.47	14.20	2.51	64.52	103	22.31	40.13	49.69
82-83	94.60	10.92	2.23	60.24	106.3	20.61	38.22	45.31
83-84	93.33	10.84	2.82	59.06	102.6	25.10	47.75	46.78
84-85	92.94	10.63	3.08	63.57	99.41	30.02	50.99	49.46
85-86	91.92	8.92	3.78	58.37	100	28.11	50.09	47.51
86-87	91.51	7.40	5.08	57.54	100	26.20	31.51	43.7
87-88	87.82	6.15	6.14	56.07	100.5	28.64	44.67	43.77
88-89	90.99	7.76	4.64	57.13	98.19	23.47	44.26	44.54
89-90	91.48	9.42	6.09	58.03	95.85	25.28	41.42	44.64
90-91	90.86	8.50	6.85	59.68	100	28.46	32.18	43.64
91-92	92.45	7.43	6.32	64.96	100	30.75	33.67	46.68
92-93	92.29	6.58	5.96	67.55	100.2	31.89	33.33	47.9
93-94	92.66	8.30	5.65	70.55	99.84	30.56	36.23	49.51
94-95	92.57	8.80	5.79	73.94	100.1	32.23	37.62	51.07
95-96	92.07	9.91	6.41	76.25	99.94	27.75	36.81	50.79
96-97	88.62	9.11	5.68	75.60	95.87	23.74	31.21	51.84
97-98	93.19	11.84	6.42	78.14	100.00	27.10	28.37	53.66
98-99	93.54	9.86	7.06	79.41	100.00	29.75	35.62	54.85
99-00	93.16	10.83	7.50	79.14	100.00	29.03	34.83	55.16

Jowar, pulses, groundnut and cotton have vast areas under rainfed cultivation. Less than 20 per cent of area under *Jowar*, less than eight per cent of area under pulses, less than 30 per cent of area under groundnut and only 30 per cent to 50 per cent of area under cotton received irrigation. In these crops also there is positive growth rates in productivity thanks to dry farming technology. Therefore *agricultural production in Tamil Nadu is largely benefitted by the generation and spread (diffusion) of appropriate technology*, especially since 1970. In view of a declining trend in both net area sown and gross cropped area, it is technology that holds the promise to the future. Yet another way for increasing agricultural production is what is loosely called commercialisation of agriculture.

Commercialisation

Increasing proportion of area under non-food crops in the gross cropped area is taken as a measure *albeit* simplistic of commercialisation of agriculture, on the basis of simple logic that non-food crops add more value per hectare than food crops. Sugarcane compared to paddy, cotton and groundnut compared to *Jowar* and *bajra* are the cases to cite. On the basis of this concept relative shares of food and non-food crops in the gross cropped area are studied (vide Table 3.14). Area under

TABLE 3.14

Share of Food and Non-food Crops in Gross Cropped Area

(*Area in '000 ha*)

Year	Foodgrain Crops		Non-Foodgrain Crops		Gross Cropped
	Area	%	Area	%	Area
1960-61	**5651**	**76.3**	**1752**	**23.7**	**7403**
1961-62	5598	76.0	1769	24.0	7367
1962-63	5506	74.2	1910	25.8	7416
1963-64	5437	74.1	1918	25.9	7405
1964-65	5490	74.0	1927	26.0	7417
1965-66	5311	73.0	1969	27.0	7280
1966-67	5294	70.9	2178	29.1	7472
1967-68	5476	72.2	2105	27.8	7581
1968-69	5309	71.4	2130	28.6	7439
1969-70	5205	70.7	2156	29.3	7361
1970-71	**5196**	**70.4**	**2188**	**29.6**	**7384**
1971-72	5162	67.6	2480	32.4	7641
1972-73	5251	68.2	2448	31.8	7699
1973-74	5063	66.2	2585	33.8	7648
1974-75	4404	66.4	2232	33.6	6636
1975-76	5068	70.1	2167	29.9	7235
1976-77	4907	68.7	2240	31.3	7147

Contd...

...Contd...

(Area in '000 ha)

Year	Foodgrain Crops		Non-Foodgrain Crops		Gross Cropped Area
	Area	%	Area	%	
1977-78	5303	68.3	2465	31.7	7768
1978-79	5156	67.1	2528	32.9	7684
1979-70	5156	66.8	2561	33.2	7717
1980-81	**4109**	**63.5**	**2360**	**36.5**	**6470**
1981-82	4628	67.0	2281	33.0	6909
1982-83	3924	65.1	2106	34.9	6030
1983-84	4719	67.9	2226	32.1	6945
1984-85	4639	65.4	2449	34.6	7088
1985-86	4617	67.7	2203	32.3	6820
1986-87	4133	63.5	2375	36.5	6508
1987-88	4180	62.1	2548	37.9	6728
1988-89	4101	63.6	2350	36.4	6451
1989-90	4248	62.3	2574	37.7	6822
1990-91	**3901**	**58.8**	**2731**	**41.2**	**6632**
1991-92	4007	57.4	2970	42.6	6977
1992-93	3945	55.8	3122	44.2	7067
1993-94	4027	56.3	3131	43.7	7158
1994-95	3853	54.8	3173	45.2	7026
1995-96	3339	53.3	2928	46.7	6267
1996-97	3558	55.1	2899	44.9	6457
1997-98	3642	55.5	2916	44.5	6558
1998-99	3608	56.3	2806	43.7	6414
1999-2000	**3633**	**55.7**	**2884**	**44.3**	**6517**

Note : % Percentage to Gross cropped area

Source: Season and Crop Reports - Govt. of Tamil Nadu

foodgrain crops, in Tamil Nadu was 56.51 lakh ha. in 1970-71; it has steadily decreased to 36.33 lakh hectare in 1999-2000. It marked a fall in the share of foodgrain crops in the gross cropped area from 76.3 per cent to 55.7 per cent between 1970-71 and 1999-2000. Correspondingly the share of non-food crops increased from 23.7 per cent to 44.3 per cent (i.e.) nearly doubled during the same period. *Thus, Tamil Nadu agriculture is progressively commercialised.*

Above inference of progressive commercialisation of Tamil Nadu Agriculture can be clearly seen in the growth rates presented in Table 3.15. The growth rate of area under food crops is negative for every decade since 1961 and for the whole period (1961-00). Consequently the growth rates of area put under non-food crops is positive and larger than unity for all the decades and 1.37 per cent for 1960-2000. This is the result, in spite of negative growth rates for net area sown and low cropping intensity. *Definitely there is a reallocation of cropped area from food crops to non-food crops.*

TABLE 3.15

Growth Rates of Area Cultivated

(Per cent)

Period	Food Crops	Non-food Crops	Gross Cropped Area	Net Sown Area	Cropping Intensity	
					Min.	Max.
1961-70	–0.82	1.10	–0.07	–0.13	113	123
1971-80	–0.01	2.62	1.74	–2.37	119	124
1981-90	–0.48	1.23	2.01	–0.79	115	122
1991-'00	–0.03	1.72	–0.69	–0.69	117	122
1961-'00	–0.93	1.37	–0.40	–1.36	112	125

Note: 1961 means 1960-61 crop year and similarly others.

Subsistence Characteristic

However, even by the end of the century, foodgrain crops have a dominant share of 55.70 per cent in gross cropped area. This means that Tamil Nadu agriculture is still subsistence oriented – which is the most expected scenario, when majority of land-holdings are marginal, small or semi-medium, each operating less than 4 ha. A change to real commercial farming in the sense of high value addition per hectare is possible only by such organisational changes that allow collective operation. *Joint and collective cooperative farming and group farming are useful concepts for commercialisation of agriculture, but they are not even talking points to-day.*

Critical Inputs

Commercialisation of agriculture and impact of technology on productivity of major crops were made possible only by increasing use of chemical fertilisers, and ground water (vide Table 3.8). This was helped by extension education on use of fertilisers and energisation of more and more of pump sets and supply of power to them at subsidised rates in the earlier decades and free of cost since eighties. Details can be seen in Table 3.16.

There is 323 per cent rise in the use of nitrogenous fertilisers (N), 313 per cent in P, and 440 per cent in K, 277 per cent in number of pump sets energised and 349 per cent in number of units of power (electricity) used. In the total use of power in the State, nearly 28.3 per cent goes to agriculture, that too free of cost. *Definitely this is sufficient incentive to adopt technology and to diversify crop pattern both helping high value addition.*

In recent years there is increasing criticism of both heavy use of fertilisers and supply of power at free of cost. The criticism of heavy doses of fertilisers (Tamil Nadu is second only to Punjab in per hectare application of chemical fertilisers) comes from the concern for the quality of environment and conservation of land productivity. Excessive use of fertilisers cause problems of salinity, alkalinity and loss of microorganisms in the soil. Tamil Nadu soils are assessed to have a fair level of K, yet use of K has increased by 440 per cent. The situation needs attention definitely.

TABLE 3.16

Use of Fertilisers and Power in Agricultural Sector in Tamil Nadu

Year	*Fertilisers ('000 t)*			*Pumpsets Energised (No.)*	*Use of Power*	
	N	*P*	*K*		*Million Units*	*%*
1960-61	33	4	4	1,17,695	370	20.7
1970-71	173	72	61	5,29,932	1241	24.5
1980-81	286	84	109	9,12,215	2364	27.9
1990-91	418	168	245	1,311,724	3974	22.4
1999-2000	558	225	269	1,467,312	4327	28.3
% Increase*	323	313	440	277	349	—

Note: N – Nitrogen, P – Phosphate, K – Potash

% - Of last column is percentage of power used in agricultural sector to the total use of power in Tamil Nadu

* Percentage of figures of 1999-2000 to that of 1970-71.

Source: Record of Commissioner of Statistics, Government of Tamil Nadu.

Excessive use of fertilisers is not only an avoidable cost *per se* but also harmful to soil health. However farmers are used to applying fertilisers in excess of what is recommended; this is the practice seen in all the major crops. An estimate is presented in Table 3.17. Farmers applied on an average 227 Kg of NPK per hectare against recommended dose of 200 kg/ha for rice crop. In millet, in spite of limited area under irrigation, excess application is high at 35.2 per cent. In pluses, mostly cultivated as rainfed crops excess application is 62.2 per cent of 45 Kg/ha recommended. In groundnut and for other crops average levels of fertiliser used was in excess of recommended doses by 20.7 per cent and 45.50 per cent respectively. Only in sugarcane and cotton actual use of fertilisers was very close to the recommended level. *Therefore, farmers have to be educated about the implications of excess application—both economics and environmental concerns.*

TABLE 3.17

Excessive-use of Chemical Fertilisers – Major Crops

(Qty. in Kg/ha)

S. No	*Crops*	*Recommended Dose (R)*	*Actual Use (R)*	*Excess (%)*
1.	Rice	200	227	13.50
2.	Millets	108	146	35.20
3.	Pulses	45	73	62.20
4.	Sugarcane	450	472	4.90
5.	Groundnut	58	70	20.70
6.	Cotton	159	165	3.80
7.	Others	22	32	45.50

Note: Excess (%) = [(A-R) / R]*100

Source: Tamil Nadu – An Economic Appraisal 1999-2000. P. 27.

Bio-Fertiliser

The problem of excess fertiliser use has found recognition in government policies and programmes. Farmers are advised about the benefit of bio-fertilisers, and supply of bio-fertilisers is also arranged. Azospirillum, rhizobium and phosphobacteria are the recommended bio-fertilisers. In 1996-97, nearly 1337 tonnes of bio-fertilisers were distributed (vide Table 3.18). The quantity distributed in 1999-2000 was 1401 tonnes. The area of crops covered by their supply was 6.68 lakh hectare in 1996-97 and 7 lakh hectare in 1999-2000. However this seems to have no effect on the fertiliser doses used by farmers in excess of recommended doses. *In 1999-2000 area covered by bio-fertilisers is not even 10 per cent of net area sown in the year.* Therefore more intensive education of farmers is necessary.

TABLE 3.18

Distribution of Bio-Fertilisers

S. No.	*Bio-Fertilisers*	*Quantity (tonnes)*				*Area Covered ('000 ha)*			
		1996-97	*1997-98*	*1998-99*	*1999-2000*	*1996-97*	*1997-98*	*1998-99*	*1999-2000*
1	Azospirillum	727	545	776	777	363	273	388	388
2	Rhizobium	278	237	285	267	134	119	143	134
3	Phosphobacteria	332	276	359	357	171	138	179	178
	Total	**1337**	**1058**	**1420**	**1401**	**668**	**530**	**710**	**700**

Source: Tamil Nadu – An Economic Appraisal 1997-98 and 1999-2000. P. 28.

TABLE 3.19

Area, Production and Yield of Major Crops in Tamil Nadu Compared with All-India – 1999-2000

S. No.	Crops	Area (m.ha)		Production		Yield		Area Irrigated* (%)	Max.Yield	
		m. ha	%	m. t	%	(Kg/ha)	Rank		Kg/ha	Country
1.	Foodgrains	3.63	3.30	8.84	4.40	2434	5	58.2	—	—
2.	Rice	2.16	5.40	7.53	8.60	3482	2	92.0	8567	Thailand
3.	Oil Seeds	0.91	5.00	1.41	8.50	1541	1	35.5	—	—
4.	Groundnut (in shell)	1.08	14.08	1.76	22.40	1829	1	22.7	2828	USA
5.	Cotton (Lint)	0.18	2.80	0.34	3.60	325	4	36.8	1065	Egypt
6.	Sugarcane	0.32	8.61	3.43	12.90	111@	1	100.0	111	India
7.	Onion	0.03	8.80	0.24	7.60	8836	5	100.0	N.A	N.A

Note: 1. m. ha – Million Hectare; m. t – Million tonnes; Rank – Rank of Tamil Nadu among States in India.

2. @ Yield of sugarcane in tonnes of cane per ha.

3. % of area and production in Tamil Nadu to area and Production for all India.

4. * Percentage of area of the crop receiving irrigation in Tamil Nadu.

Source: AGROSTRAT, Tamil Nadu.

Yield Gap Exists

In spite of excess use of fertilisers and use of bio-fertilisers there is still a vast gap between yield realised and what is possible for the major crops. Details are presented in Table 3.19. In rice production Tamil Nadu ranks second among the states in India, Haryana being the first with 4100 kg/ha. However Thailand had achieved a yield level of 8567 kg/ha and the difference in yield is not small. In oil seeds, Tamil Nadu ranks first among the states with an average yield of 1541 kg/ha. In groundnut also it has first rank with an estimated average yield of 1829 kg/ha of nuts–in–shell. In sugarcane India ranks first among the countries with a yield of 111 t/ha and the maximum is achieved in Tamil Nadu giving the State first rank among the states of this country. In cotton, average yield was 325 kg of lint/ha and Tamil Nadu ranked fourth among cotton producing states in India. However this yield is too low compared with the average yield of 1065 kg/ha achieved by farmers in Egypt. In onion, Tamil Nadu has fifth rank with an average yield of 8836 kg/ha. Thus there is scope for further improvement in yield of crops by bridging the gap between Tamil Nadu average and best producing country in the world and by new ways of improving productive potential of the crop varieties. *Research should continue to evolve new crop varieties and new cultivation methods, to improve productive potential of the crops.*

The governments of Tamil Nadu and of India have placed emphasis on yield improving technologies to meet the growing needs of the rising population and have formulated several schemes, details of them are presented in Box 3.1. The focus in all crops is to augment productivity and production and in cotton increase in area an additional goal.

Proposed expenditures include outlay for research and also transfer of technology to the farmers. These schemes cover all major seasonal crops. However there are crops, included in the group of other crops that have rich potential for generation of farm income, and deserve special attention.

Horticulture

Horticultural crops are high value adding crops and their products have export potential in raw form and as value added processed products. Details are presented in Table 3.20. Area under these crops is increasing in recent years from 6.90 lakh ha. in 1995-96 to 8.29 lakh ha. in 1999-2000. Fruits and vegetables have yield in the range of 20 t.–30 t. per ha. and they are important for their nutritional values, high income and possibility of processing and export. *Therefore they have to receive attention directly and as an important component of waste land development scheme.*

Cardamom and pepper are important spices of Tamil Nadu. Their export potential is yet to be exploited fully. Spices are grown in an area of 1.75 lakh ha. and production is about 3.10 lakh tonnes in 1999-2000. Plantation crops of Tamil Nadu are coffee and tea and they are traditionally exported products. Flowers have small areas in Tamil Nadu but the money value of

Box 3.1

Important Schemes

S. No.	Crops/Schemes	Objectives	Coverage/Expenditure in 1997-98
1	**Rice:** Integrated Cereal Development Programme (rice) (Central Govt.)	To increase Production and Yield of Rice Crop	140 blocks in major rice growing districts (Rs. 805.73 lakh)
2	**Millets:** Accelerated Maize Development Programme (Technology Mission – Central Govt.)	Augmenting Production and Productivity of Maize	Coimbatore, Salem, Dindigul (Rs. 35.01 lakh)
3	**Pulses:** National Pulses Development Project (Central Govt.)	Augmenting Production and Productivity	All districts (Rs. 20.72 lakh)
4	**Sugarcane:** Sugarcane Development Scheme (Govt. of Tamil Nadu)	Augmenting Production and Productivity	All districts except Thuthukudi, Ramanathapuram, Nilgiris, Kanyakumari
5	Sustainable Development of Sugarcane based Cropping System (Central Govt.)	Improving Productivity of Sugarcane	Kanchipuram, Thiruvallur, Vellore, Cuddalore, Thiruvannamalai, Dharmapuri, Coimbatore, Madurai, Theni, Virudunagar (Rs. 104.50 lakh)
6	**Cotton:** Integrated Cotton Development Scheme (Govt. of Tamil Nadu)	Increasing Area, Production and Productivity	All districts except Nilgiris and Kanyakumari (Rs. 62.95 lakh)
7	Intensive Cotton Development Programme (Central Govt.)	Stepping up Production and productivity	All districts except Kanchipuram, Thiruvallur, Kanyakumari, Nilgiris (Rs. 293.05 lakh)
8	**Oilseeds:** Oil seed Production Programme (Central Govt.)	Augmenting Productivity of Oil seed Crop	All districts except Chennai and Nilgiris (Rs. 1249.61 lakh)

Source: Tamil Nadu – An Economic Appraisal, 1997-98, Govt. of Tamil Nadu, Chennai. PP.24-25.

TABLE 3.20

Area, Yield and Production of Horticultural Crops

S. No.	Groups	Area (Lakh ha)			Yield (t/ha)			Production (Lakh tonnes)		
		1995-96	1997-98	1999-00	1995-96	1997-98	1999-00	1995-96	1997-98	1999-00
1.	Fruits	1.95	2.11	2.32	23.69	23.89	25.60	46.15	50.33	56.60
2.	Vegetable	1.58	1.93	2.09	25.09	26.30	27.00	39.57	50.89	59.40
3.	Spices	1.43	1.57	1.75	1.34	1.59	1.77	1.91	2.49	3.10
4.	Plantation	1.79	1.86	1.95	3.28	3.48	3.62	5.85	6.49	7.05
5.	Flowers	0.15	0.17	0.18	5.50	7.00	7.85	0.82	1.17	1.42
	Total	6.90	7.64	8.29	—	—	—	—	—	—

Source: Tamil Nadu An Economic Appraisal – 1997-98 and 1999-2000.

production per hectare is very large and very recently specific flowers and essence extracted from some flowers are finding international market demand. Palmarosa and indigo are cultivated in negligibly small areas, mostly for export.

When export potentials of these crops are tapped and processing facilities are created, they may probably change the cropping pattern of Tamil Nadu very significantly. *Further development of agriculture in the State would call for huge investment in infrastructure and expertise for export oriented crop production.* In this context the trend in capital formation in agriculture deserves attention.

Capital Formation

An estimate of capital formation in agriculture in Tamil Nadu is presented in Table 3.21. Capital formation in agriculture of Tamil Nadu is mostly by private sector, the public sector contribution to capital formation in agriculture is only about one fourth of the total capital formation. However, there is need to substantially invest in infrastructural facilities for storage, distribution and processing. *Development of facilities for quick and reliable market information and quality control for export of value added farm products, are urgent needs in the context of globalisation of agriculture.*

TABLE 3.21

Capital Formation in Agriculture (at 1980-81 Prices)

(Rs. Crore)

Years	*Tamil Nadu*			*All India*		
	Public	*Private*	*Total*	*Public*	*Private*	*Total*
1980-81	25.49	71.09	96.58	1796	2840	4636
1990-91	37.17	87.00	124.16	1154	3440	4594
1991-92	37.26	69.47	106.73	1002	3727	4729
1992-93	39.92	83.10	123.02	1061	4311	5372
1993-94	34.62	71.59	106.21	1153	3878	5031
1994-95	42.46	85.41	127.87	1316	4940	6256

Source: Tamil Nadu - An Economic Appraisal 1997-98, P.33.

A study of Palanisamy and Varadarajan (1997) based on microlevel data for 450 farms shows that, size of the farm is positively correlated with percentage of gross cropped area irrigated, cropping intensity and percentage share of each crops in total area cropped, all contributing to the increase in farm income. Therefore, less irrigated and small farms find income from farm insufficient to make required investment. However, investment in productive assets if made has given significant addition to income from crops and livestock and the addition to income has promoted saving and investment. Thus the effect of investment on farm income is cumulative. Over the years, not only the size of investment per farm and per hectare had increased, but also there was diversification in type of investment. There is a significant shift in investment from preference to livestock to other types, particularly machines, equipments and land improvement. Investment had increased not only in nominal value, but also in real value over the period studied and there is significant improvement in recent years. Institutional credit contributes significantly to private capital formation in agriculture while the cost of it has a negative correlation with the size of the investment. External finance, extent of irrigation, user cost of capital and the cost of variable inputs were the major determinants of investment.

The supply of institutional credit, interest rates, and the cost of reaching out to the needy farmers (i.e., costs other than interest rates involved in providing credit to farmers) and cost of farm inputs that determine the cost of production of crops and livestock are the external variables influencing farmers decision to invest. Thus policy support for farm credit and prices would enhance private fixed capital formation in farms, while farmers' own saving and response to cost of external finance are the farm specific decision variables. Then institutional credit to farmers, its cost and timeliness are policy variables to encourage private capital formation in farms, while public investment in infrastructure will speed up the process.

Allied Activities

Livestock and fisheries are important activities in Tamil Nadu next to crop production. In Tamil Nadu the population of both cattle and buffalo showed a steady declining trend. Sheep population also decreased, but goat population increased. Very significant improvement was seen in poultry population. Details are presented in Table 3.22 and 3.23.

TABLE 3.22

Livestock Population: The Trend

(Lakh)

Census Year	*Cattle*	*Buffaloes*	*Sheep*	*Goats*	*Others*	*Total Livestock*	*Poultry*
1977	108.01	30.78	52.84	42.02	7.76	241.41	143.47
1982	103.66	32.12	55.37	52.46	18.26	261.87	182.84
1989	93.53	31.28	58.81	59.20	20.85	263.33	215.70
1994	90.96	29.31	56.12	58.65	21.75	256.79	238.54
1997	93.63	27.17	53.74	63.25	23.88	261.67	273.44
1999*	96.03	28.99	55.39	53.92	—	—	281.27

Note: Figures in brackets indicate percentage change over the previous Census

* Inter Census Estimate

Source: Tamil Nadu - An Economic Appraisal, 1999-2000. P-32.

One reason for the decline in cattle, buffalo and sheep population was the sharp decline in grazing lands and high cost of stall-feeding. Attempt to improve milk production through introduction of exotic and cross-bred cattle and buffalo has progressed a little. These high yielding breeds account for less than 21 per cent of total population because maintaining them is not very profitable due to high cost of fodder and feed. That is the reason why milk production has increased slowly from 37.91 lakh tonnes in 1995-96 to 45.72 lakh tonnes in 1999-2000, leaving a shortfall of 7.7 per cent in availability of milk per capita for meeting the requirement of 220 gms/day/per capita.

Meat production was 406.7 lakh kgs in 1996-97 and rose to 413.7 lakh kgs in 1999-2000. However hatcheries have performed well in increasing production of eggs to 3845 million eggs. Fish production in 1999-2000 was 4.86 lakh tonnes, of which marine fish production was 3.74 lakh tonnes while inland fish production was only 1.12 lakh tonnes.

Above data show that there is a very vast scope to increase production of livestock and fish products and they provide a good source of supply for export.

TABLE 3.23

Progress in Allied Activities

A. Requirement and Supply of Milk

Year	*Production (l.t)*	*Per Capita (gms/day)*		*Shortfall %*
		Availability	*Requirement*	
1995-96	37.91	185	220	15.9
1996-97	39.80	182	220	17.3
1997-98	40.60	183	220	16.8
1998-99	42.70	191	220	13.2
1999-2000	45.72	203	220	7.7

B. Production of Meat and Egg

Details	*1996–97*	*1999–00*
Meat (Lakh Kg)	406.7	413.7
Egg (Million)	3042	3845
Fish Inland (lakh tonnes)	1.09	1.12
Marine	3.51	3.74
Total	4.60	4.86
Export of Fish & Fish Products ('000 t)	40.88	43.46

Terms of Trade

Wholesale price indices for primary articles, non-form articles and general prices are presented in Table 3.24.

General price level has nearly doubled during the period from 1990-91 to 1997-98. Index of prices of primary articles was 547.12 in 1990-91 and it has risen to 1164.57 in 1997-98. For non-farm articles the rise in price index (1970-71=100) is from 605.61 to 975.59. Terms of trade for agriculture was measured by the ratio of price index for primary articles to the price index of non-farm articles, expressed as a percentage. Terms of trade index was less than 100 for two years, and thereafter it was above hundred and had progressively increased to the level of 119.37 (1970-71=100). ***Thus the terms of trade have been favourable to agriculture since 1992-93 and that might explain the rising trend in private capital formation in agriculture.*** Favourable terms of trade to agriculture is both a cause and effect of capital formation. However, it is too general an inference and will fail to reflect real economics in farming and demands a more critical analysis.

TABLE 3.24

Index Numbers and Terms of Trade

(Base: 1970-71=100)

Year	*Wholesale Price Index*			*Terms of Trade with base of*	
	General	*Primary Articles (52.69)*	*Non-farm Articles (47.31)*	*1970-71=100*	*1980-81=100*
1990-91	555.04	547.12	605.61	90.34	89.08
1991-92	631.62	626.32	637.52	98.24	96.84
1992-93	705.56	724.38	684.60	105.81	104.34
1993-94	728.21	730.39	725.78	100.84	99.24
1994-95	800.51	834.97	762.14	109.56	108.04
1995-96	864.86	913.18	811.05	112.59	111.02
1996-97	968.94	1040.92	888.77	117.12	115.49
1997-98	1072.26	1164.57	975.59	119.37	117.73

Note: Terms of Trade = {Agriculture Price Index/Manufacture Price Index} × 100

Source: Tamil Nadu – An Economic Appraisal 1997-98, P.111.

Cost Price Relationship

A clear picture of profitability and income of farms can be had from a close study of cost price-relationship. Such an analysis is done for rice crop only, for two reasons: first, rice is the most important crop of Tamil Nadu and second, detailed and reliable cost estimates are not available for other crops for a series of years. Estimates of costs and prices per kg of rice are presented in Table 3.25. For convenience of direct comparison both costs and prices are derived for a kg. of rice. Using the conversion ratio of one quintal of paddy being equivalent to 63 kg of (husked) rice.

The cost of production of a kg of rice has increased from Rs. 3.46 in 1990-91 to Rs. 7.28 in 1999-2000. The price received by farmers is different for areas where scheme of procurement is in operation and in rest of the area where private traders buy paddy from farmers either directly or through brokers or commission agents. The price paid by the traders less the cost of selling incurred by the farmers by way packaging, transporting and other payments is called farm harvest price (i.e.) the actual price received by farmers. If paddy is sold at the farm gate to the village traders there is no cost of transport, brokerage or commission but traders incur such costs and so offer a lower price. If the farmers deliver the grains to a *mandi*, they incur cost of packaging, transport, commissions and other costs such as deductions for quality variations etc. Actual price paid by the commission agents less these costs constitute what is called farm harvest price or farm gate price. This price minus the cost of production is the net income per kg received by the farmers.

TABLE 3.25

Cost-Price Relationship in Rice

(Rs./kg)

Year	*Cost of Production*	*Farm Harvest Price @*	*Wholesale Price*	*Retail Price*	*M.S.P*	*Economic Cost*	*Issue Price*
1990-91	3.46	3.37	3.97	7.06	3.20	4.97	1.75
1991-92	4.07	3.93	4.05	7.42	3.82	5.85	1.75
1992-93	5.24	4.94	4.72	8.11	4.61	6.65	2.50
1993-94	5.16	5.65	4.96	8.63	4.83	6.95	3.50
1994-95	5.19	5.37	5.68	9.14	5.16	7.63	2.60
1995-96	5.04	5.76	6.89	9.04	5.63	8.48	2.00
1996-97	5.17	5.82	7.56	11.30	5.70	9.40	2.00
1997-98	6.67	7.05	7.64	14.40	6.48	10.76	2.00
1998-99	6.79	7.41	7.82	15.15	6.64	11.05	2.00
1999-2000	7.28	7.47	8.10	15.75	7.06	11.18	2.00

Note: Cost and Price computed for a kg of rice (husked grain) and for common variety also called coarse variety.

@ Average price in places where procurement is not done. It is price received by farmers less of his selling cost.

MSP – Minimum Support Price. It is also Procurement Price

Source: 1. Tamil Nadu – An Economic Appraisal 1997-98, 1999-2000.

2. Director of Statistics.

As seen in the Table, the cost of production is larger than the farm harvest price in the first three years (i.e.) upto 1992-93 and the farmers incurred losses. The position changed in 1994-95 and there was positive profit thereafter. In 1999-2000, farmers earned a net income of 19 paise per kg. of rice or Rs.19 per quintal of rice. This period of positive profit is also the period when the terms of trade were favourable to agriculture. This has to be so, because rice is the most important crop of the State and profitability of rice production determines in large measure the index of prices of farm articles directly and it is reflected in the terms of trade to agriculture. When government procures paddy either by monopoly procurement scheme or preemptive open market purchases, the procurement price including bonus if any, minus the cost of selling (mostly transport to the procurement centres) is the farm harvest price. By a policy of assuring a reasonable profit to the farmers the government announces every year before the beginning of crop seasons the minimum support price (MSP); for practical purpose, MSP is also the procurement price. It may be seen that only from 1995-96 this price allowed positive net income to the farmers. In other years farmer's cost of production has exceeded MSP and the net income is negative, still farmers have favoured selling their paddy to the government agencies. This behaviour pattern needs some explanation.

Profitability

The cost of production reported in the Table refers to what is called economic cost of production or cost 'C' which includes imputed values for farmer's own inputs used in production such as farm produced manures, own bullock power and equipments and family labour. The value of depreciation of farm assets, an interest on working capital and fixed capital committed to production calculated at standard rates, is also included in cost 'C'. In general, farmers calculate their net income without taking these costs into account. Therefore their calculation can be said to be based on actually paid out cost or accountant's cost. It is termed cost 'A'. Normally, on an average cost 'A' is two thirds of cost 'C' and the difference enters net income calculated by the farmers. The net income based on cost 'A' is positive and it is covered by MSP or procurement price, even though it is necessary to cover cost 'C' and still leave a reasonable margin. *In all the years farm harvest price is larger than MSP, showing that MSP has helped farmers more by pushing up the farm harvest price to some extent but not enough to fully cover cost 'C' assuring positive net income.*

Wholesale and retail prices are market determined and cover the marketing cost and margin of the traders. Therefore they are larger than farm harvest price, showing that the marketing cost and margin (called price-spread in the literature) is as high as cost of production or even higher. This indicates that the market for farm products (as judged by the price spread of rice) is not that efficient and leaves scope for improvement by efforts to reduce price spread (i.e.) by way of reducing both marketing costs and marketing margin. These efforts are necessary to protect the interest of consumers because demand for rice being inelastic, any rise in retail price of rice directly increases the cost of living and the government has to come to their help.

Public Distribution System (PDS)

The government implements schemes for procurement and distribution of rice through the public distribution system (PDS), often with a subsidy on sale price. MSP plus cost of processing, storage distribution through PDS is called economic cost (of PDS). In 1990-91 the economic cost (EC) per kg of rice was Rs.4.97 it was 155 per cent of MSP. It was Rs.10.76 in 1997-98 and Rs.166.05 per cent of MSP. Thus the cost of operation of PDS net of MSP is increasing over the years again a sign of marketing inefficiency. As the issue price for rice distributed through PDS is determined administratively to protect the interests of the consumers, it is less than the economic cost and the difference shows the food subsidy. Issue price of rice was Rs. 1.75 kg as against the economic cost of Rs. 4.97 kg in 1990-91. It was doubled in 1993-94, to Rs. 3.50 per kg. But the economic cost also rose to Rs. 6.65/kg (about 40 per cent rise over that in 1990-91) and the effect of rise in issue price was to reduce food subsidy to some extent. However the issue price was lowered to Rs. 2 per kg; this time (1994-95 with some attempt to target it to the poor families). It was possible only at significant rise in food subsidy, because by 1999-2000 the economic cost was as high as Rs. 11.18 per kg.

One inference that can be drawn without any doubt, is that market for farm products (on the basis of above analysis for rice, which is not highly perishable) are inefficient and the government intervention by way of procurement and PDS has not helped making markets more efficient; it has served social objectives of supporting farmers and consumers rather than improving marketing efficiency for farm products.

This situation needs a correction if the agriculture has to become really commercial and be competitive in the globalised market. However there seems to be no recognition of this serious problem with policymakers and there is no programme for it, even the New Agricultural policy of the Government of India has little to offer. In research, all the attention seems to be on improving productivity of crops and some attempt to suggest Integrated Farming System (IFS), Integrated Nutrition Management (INM) and Integrated Pest Management (IPM) all helping to reduce cost of production and environmental protection on farm and at the neglect of marketing. Agricultural research had little to offer by way of any model for marketing efficiency and price stability or parity. Necessarily therefore farmers continue to demand subsidies and government has to live with food subsidy which is scaling new heights year after year. There is little prospects for facing challenges of a globalised market, and there is no strategy insight. *Best remedy will be to make policies and launch programmes of agricultural development by integrating production, marketing export, PDS and environmental objectives.*

Food Subsidy

The difference between procurement price (MPS) and the issue price is the subsidy to be met by the government. In the procurement and distribution there are three varieties of rice. Viz. common (or coarse), fine and superfine. The procurement and issue prices of rice in Tamil Nadu are presented in Table 3.26 for a few selected years.

TABLE 3.26

Procurement Price – Issue Price Compared

Year	*Procurement Price (Rs./Qtl)*			*Issue Price of Rice (Rs./Kg)*			*Food Subsidy (Rs. Crore)*
	Common	*Fine*	*Super Fine*	*Common*	*Fine*	*Super Fine*	
1980-81	105	109	113	1.75	2.00	2.15	224.80
1985-86	142	146	150	1.75	2.25	2.50	298.78
1990-91	205	215	225	2.00	2.75	3.25	332.24
1995-96	360	375	395	2.00	3.75	3.75	440.00
1997-98	415	445	450	2.00	3.75	—	1000.00
From 20.01.99	—	—	—	7.00 3.50	9.05 3.50	9.05 —	APL BPL

Note: APL – Above poverty line population
BPL – Below poverty line population

Procurement price was Rs. 105 per quintal for common variety. Rs.109 for fine variety and Rs. 113 for superfine varieties. Issue price per kg of (husked) rice was Rs. 1.75, Rs. 2.00 and Rs. 2.15 for the three varieties. The difference resulted in the total subsidy of Rs. 224.50 crore in 1980-81. From the Table it may be seen that procurement prices have gone up nearly three folds by 1997-98, while the issue prices were allowed to rise only marginally. As a result food subsidy was as high as Rs. 1000 crore in 1997-98. Arguments and counter arguments on the desirability of this food subsidy became loud and strong, so that the government had to target subsidies to the really poor. Therefore the concept of poverty line was used to restrict subsidies only to those families, which are below poverty line (BPL). This policy was put to practice in the PDS, from 20.01.1999. The issue price for BPL population is now Rs. 3.50 per kg of common rice and also for fine rice, while issue prices for APL population are Rs. 7.00, Rs. 9.05 and Rs. 9.05 for common, fine and superfine rice varieties respectively. However, there is no effective way of checking that rice supplied to BPL population is not passed on to the APL population. As the scheme has come into use in 1999, only data for latest years will show the real position. Such data are not available at present. The volume of off-take in PDS shops gives some idea, but not conclusive evidence for the misuse of PDS supplies.

Off-Take of Rice

The supply and off-take of rice in PDS are shown in Table 3.27 below.

TABLE 3.27

Production, Procurement, Allotment and Off take of Rice in Tamil Nadu

(Lakh tonnes)

S. No	Details	1990-91	1995-96	1999-2000
1	Production	57.82	52.90	75.32
2	Procurement	13.86	03.40	13.72
3	% of Procurement to Production	23.97	06.43	18.22
4	Allotment@	9.20	14.55	18.15
5	Total Supply to the PDS	23.06	17.95	31.87
6	Off take in PDS	12.33	15.04	22.11
7	Percentage of Off take to Supply	53.47	83.79	69.38

Note: @ Allotment from Central Pool

In 1990-91, production of rice in Tamil Nadu was 57.82 lakh tonnes (l.t.) of which only 24 per cent was procured. There is an allocation of 9.20 l.t. making total supply to be 23.06 l.t. However off-take from PDS was only 12.33 l.t. or 53.47 per cent. It was 83.79 per cent of supply of 17.95 l.t in 1995-96 and 85.54 per cent of 25.11 l.t in 1997-98. In 1999-2000 production and allocation by the centre add upto 31.87 l.t. of which offtake is 22.11 l.t. or 69.38 per cent of total supply. Two results are important: first, procurement by government varies year to year. The allotment from the central pool is around 9-18 l.t. showing that this allotment is crucial to sustain distribution through PDS. It shows that the State is not self-reliant for the supply of rice required for PDS distribution. Secondly, in the short period of 10 years, off-take in PDS has increased from 12.33 l.t. to 22.11 l.t. and it may not be entirely due to increase in number of cardholders. Therefore atleast a part of the increase in off-take may be due to the benefit passing on to the not really poor families. One reason for this may be that superfine rice is being supplied to the poor, who have no preference for it; for many of them millets were the staple food. But the food habit is changing because open market retail price of millets is higher than PDS price of rice. This shift in consumption pattern may explain atleast a part of decline in area under millets and consequent fall in their production. Does the policy need a change? Only a detailed analysis of consumption of BPL cardholders will provide the answer.

Women in Agriculture

During the last two decades emancipation and empowerment of women received attention. Thrust was on education, health, employment and economic status of women. As a result there is significant improvement. Life expectancy has gone up from 39 years to 59 years between 1991 and 2000. There has been steady improvement in female labour force participation (Table 3.28).

TABLE 3.28

Development of Farm Women

S. No.	Details	1961	1971	1981	2000
1	Population (Million)	16.8	20.4	23.9	27.6
2	Women Labour force (Million)	5.26	5.32	5.35	6.93
3	Life expectancy (Years)	39.2	45.6	51.9	59.3
4	Women in agriculture (Million)	3.8	3.72	3.63	5.5
5	Labour force participation Role (%)	72.20	69.91	67.85	67.10

The female population has increased from 16.8 million in 1961 to 27.6 million in 2000. The size of labour force of women was 5.26 million in 1961 and it increased to 6.93 million in 2000; of this agriculture had the largest share of 67.1 per cent. Therefore they required special attention. Tamil Nadu Women's Development Project was implemented in 1989 through a network of women's Self Help Group (SHG's) established at village level. By 2000, 5418 SHG's had a total membership of 1,23,276. The objective was to promote thrift and investment. Efforts were taken to train women for skill development and entrepreneurial ability. The Tamil Nadu Women in Agriculture (TANWA) was launched in 1986 for training farmwomen in modern agricultural techniques. In two phases 88400 farmwomen had been trained. Each woman had to train 10 other women in the village. So spread of technology is gaining momentum as shown by two evaluation studies conducted by the Department of Evaluation and Applied Research (DEAR). Further expansion of these efforts should prepare women to participate in global trade.

Prospects

Above discussion shows that the area under crops is declining and the improvement in productivity of crops sustains the up trend in production of major crops. Yet there is still vast scope to improve productivity of crops. Generation and diffusion of yield augmenting technology have to continue to receive priority in research, both to bridge the yield gap and to increase productive potential of the crops – *a second green revolution is necessary and it has* to be eco-friendly and neutral to size of farms.

Attention to the development of wasteland is a step in the right direction; because it can help expansion of area under such high value adding crops as vegetables, fruits, spices, plantation crops in judicial combination of tree crops for fuel and forest products. Medicinal plants and flower plants, indigo and such other crops that have export potential have to be identified for special development schemes. *As wastelands remain scattered and are of low soil fertility, farmers, would need government support for the required investment and technology adoption.* The concept of corporate farming may deserve attention, as individual farmers have little capacity to invest on required scale for reclamation of the marginal lands. The credit worthiness of majority of farmers is also small.

Though the area under commercial crops is increasing, even in 1999-2000 food crops dominate the crop mix with a share of 55.6 per cent of gross cropped area showing that agriculture in Tamil Nadu has yet to shed its subsistence characteristic. Yet, even for its requirement of rice for PDS, the State has to depend upon the supply from the centre. It is nothing wrong, because the country as a whole is in huge surplus of foodgrains and every State need not be self sufficient in foodgrains. *If the supply from the centre can be stabilised, it must be possible to diversity of crop pattern to enhance the pace of commercialisation, because ultimate goal is to increase farm income, not just farm production.*

Farmers of Tamil Nadu are responsive to changes in prices of farm products. Price support can aim at diversification to value adding cash crops, especially horticultural crops. Though product price is an incentive, real increase in farm income requires a check on the rise in input costs especially prices of seeds, chemical fertilisers and pesticides. If a reasonable margin can be ensured between cost of production and price of products, it may be possible to reduce input subsidy. *The concept of cost-price parity has not received the attention it deserves. Unchecked rise in cost of fertilisers and plant protection chemicals forces the farmers to demand subsidies. Therefore cost effectiveness in crop production has to be accorded top priority in both research and policy support to farmers.*

Emphasis on income rather than production *per se* is important because it draws attention to cost-price relationship and also because a large army of landless agricultural labourers depends upon income of the farmers for a rise in wage rates. Minimum Wages Act ensures a decent wage, but its enforcement is constrained by farmers' ability to pay; lack of it is the main cause of rural poverty among agricultural labourers and marginal and small farmers. A welfare State can hardly ignore this. *An effective way to mitigate poverty, is to make faster growing non-farm sectors absorb a large part of redundant labourer in agriculture. Deliberate policies and specific programmes are necessary. Then employment, wages and education – both primary and vocational – are better tools to eliminate poverty than targeting BPL population – through subsidies and PDS alone.*

When employment and income become the goals of agricultural development, conservation of forests, a check and reversal of environmental degradation of soil and crop diversification and export for commercialisation of farm production and processing for value addition are the pro-active strategies. *Export led growth of agriculture is possible in Tamil Nadu and it demands a drastic revision of priorities as outlined above. A market oriented production is consistent with export-led growth policy, but market must be efficient requiring limited intervention by the government. Such a strategy is absent and that is the weakest spot in agricultural development plans and programmes.* There is no strategy to develop farm markets beyond the outdated regulated markets. The scope of 'farmers market' *(Uzhavar Sandhai)* is limited to just retail trade of a few perishable products. No doubt it eliminates intermediaries, but in the days of departmental stores, supply chains and customisation these markets are feeble strategies. Strong cooperative markets can be a remedy, because through federation they can be non-exploitative institutions for bulk handling, export and quality standards. The reason is that market research is in its infancy and is yet to receive adequate attention, especially to build a strong market information system (MIS). *Explosive growth of information and communication technology must find extensive application in agriculture to link farmers to world markets. Success in export required a strong and efficient domestic market to absorb external shocks, as in the case of coffee and tea.*

Therefore, agricultural development in Tamil Nadu needs a comprehensive planning with emphasis on up trend in farm income through improvement in productivity of crops, price policies favouring cost price-parity, commercialisation, efficient markets and export of value added products meeting international quality standards. It is the best strategy to guide policies and programmes to bring about export led growth of agriculture in Tamil Nadu. It will benefit both farmers and farm labourers, with minimal need for government intervention. *A high growth rate of agricultural income is a guarantee for removal of poverty and economic growth of the State, because agricultural sector has largest percentage of the poor and also has strong forward and backward sectoral linkages.*

Chapter 4

Industry

Background

Tamil Nadu has a highly developed industrial base in the country. It currently ranks third in the country in terms of per capita state product from manufacturing industry. The decision by the then English East India Company to set up a trading post at the fishing village of Madraspatnam can be said to have given Tamil Nadu an early start in industrial development and trade. Over a period of time, Madras became a significant port in the Eastern coast and helped in the industrial development of the surrounding areas.

By the time of Independence, Tamil Nadu had a strong presence in the textile industry with a highly developed handloom sector that had the largest concentration of looms in the country and a well-established mill sector around Coimbatore that was the third largest. It also had a reasonable base in the engineering industry. Post-Independence, successive governments of the State followed policies conducive to industrial growth and took advantage of the spread of modern education and of the generally peaceful labour relations. Manufacturing industry led the overall economic development in the State, and till about the early eighties, the growth rate of manufacturing industry had outstripped the growth of the State economy as a whole. Today Tamil Nadu ranks third among the Indian states in terms of industrial output, value addition in the manufacturing sector and foreign direct investments. The State has the highest number of factories and employs the largest number of workers in the country.

Contribution to GSDP

Contributions from the secondary sector, which includes manufacturing, electricity-gas-water supply and construction, to the state domestic product registered an increasing trend till 1995-96 going up from 20 per cent in 1960-61 to 35 per cent in 1995-96 (Table 4.1). This share has dropped to around 31 per cent during 1999-2000. Within the secondary sector manufacturing industry has accounted for more than 70 per cent of the contribution though it grew from 73 per cent during 1960-61 to nearly 82 per cent in the year 1980-81 and fell to 70 per cent during 1999-2000. State domestic product originating from registered manufacturing units accounted for less than 50 per cent share of the manufacturing sector's contribution during 1960-61 and 1970-71.

TABLE 4.1

Manufacturing Sector Contributions in GSDP

Year	*1960-61*	*1970-71*	*1980-81*	*1990-91*	*1995-96*	*1999-2000*
GSDP	100	100	100	100	100	100
Primary Sector	43.51	34.79	25.92	23.42	21.69	18.9
Secondary Sector	20.27	26.88	33.49	33.1	35.16	31.05
Tertiary Sector	36.22	38.33	40.59	43.48	43.15	50.05
Secondary Sector	100	100	100	100	100	100
Manufacturing	72.82	73.81	81.88	73.02	79.24	70.21
Others	27.18	26.19	18.12	26.98	20.76	29.79
Manufacturing	100	100	100	100	100	100
Regd.-Manufacturing	46.41	48.79032	54.52225	67.10799	63.60373	62.52294
Unregd.-Manufacturing	53.59	51.20968	45.47775	32.89201	36.39627	37.47706

Note: Figures for 1960-61 to 1990-91 are based on 1980-81 prices.
Figures from 1995-96 are based on 1993-94 prices.

Source: Department of Economics and Statistics, Chennai.

However, in the nineties it has been above 60 per cent and as high as 67 per cent during 1990-91. The share of unregistered manufacturing shows a declining trend – going down from 54 per cent during 1960-61 to 38 per cent in 1999-2000. In terms of five-year averages between 1980-81 and 1999-2000, the share of the secondary sector has been steadily falling from 38.6 per cent during 1980-85 to 33 per cent during 1995-2000 and within this the share of manufacturing has also fallen from 80 per cent to 71 per cent (Table 4.2).

TABLE 4.2

Sectoral Shares in GSDP

(5 year averages)

	1980-85	1985-90	1990-95	1995-00
Primary Sector	25.4	22.8	22.3	19.8
Secondary Sector	38.6	37.5	36.9	33
Tertiary Sector	36.6	40.3	41.6	47.8
Manufac. Share in Secondary %	79.5	77.6	75.3	70.6
Manufacturing	30.7	29.1	27.8	23.3

Source: NAS data as from India States' Reform Forum, New Delhi.

Table 4.3 presents the average exponential growth rates witnessed in State Domestic Product and its constituents, measured in 1993-94 prices, for the eighties and nineties. It may be seen that the growth rate in the manufacturing sector has been significantly lower than the growth in the GSDP. The average growth rate during the nineties at 4.8 per cent was only marginally higher than the growth in the eighties at 4.5 per cent. If we consider the Ninth Plan period (1997-2002) the growth rate had dipped to 4.7 per cent. Within manufacturing, contribution from the registered units grew slightly faster compared to the unregistered sector.

TABLE 4.3

GSDP Growth Rates

	1980-81 to 1990-91	1990-91 to 1999-2000
Gross State Dom. Prod.	5.4	6.9
Primary Sector	3.5	3.3
Secondary Sector	5.0	5.7
Mining & Quarrying	7.2	2.4
Manufacturing	4.5	4.8
Construction	5.3	8.5
Electricity, Gas and Water	11.6	9.8
Services	7.0	9.5

Source: NAS data as from India States' Reform Forum, New Delhi.

Tamil Nadu's relative performance with respect to that of a few selected states in India during the eighties and nineties shows that the growth rate of manufacturing in Tamil Nadu has been amongst the lowest and is significantly below the average for India (Table 4.4). While in the early-eighties Tamil Nadu ranked second among the states in terms of per capita manufacturing component of GSDP, by the late-nineties it has come down to the third position.

TABLE 4.4

GSDP Growth - Tamil Nadu's Relative Performance

State	1980-81 to 1990-91	1990-91 to 1999-00
Gujarat	8.4	11.9
Karnataka	7.8	11.6
Kerala	3.3	8.5
Maharashtra	6.8	8.4
Haryana	11	6.7
West Bengal	3.3	6.7
Andhra Pradesh	8.7	6.5
Punjab	8.9	6.5
Tamil Nadu	**4.5**	**4.8**
All-India	**7.4**	**7.6**

Source: NAS data as from India States' Reform Forum, New Delhi.

TABLE 4.5

Manufacturing Share - Comparisons

	1980-85	1985-90	1990-95	1995-00
Tamil Nadu	**30.7**	**29.1**	**27.8**	**23.3**
Maharashtra	28.0	27.8	26.0	25.5
Gujarat	23.0	26.2	27.0	31.2
West Bengal	21.4	18.7	17.4	14.6
Karnataka	16.8	18.0	18.2	19.9
Haryana	16.5	20.5	19.2	21.9
Punjab	12.4	14.0	15.0	15.1
Andhra Pradesh	12.3	13.0	14.8	14.4
Kerala	10.9	10.8	11.7	12.3
All-India	**16.3**	**16.6**	**16.5**	**16.8**

Source: NAS data as from India States' Reform Forum, New Delhi.

Table 4.5 compares the five-year average contributions made to State Domestic Product by the manufacturing sector of select states. In Tamil Nadu this share has fallen to 23.3 per cent during 1995-2000 compared to 30.7 per cent during 1980-85. However, the relative significance of the manufacturing sector in Tamil Nadu is higher than the All-India average of around 16 per cent and even during the five-year period 1995-2000 the share in Tamil Nadu is lower compared to only two other States – Gujarat and Maharashtra.

The State currently accounts for 11-12 per cent of the industrial output in the country and in some specific sub-categories of industries it is a dominant player e.g. 70 per cent of the leather products, about 50 per cent of power-driven pumps, railway coaches, motorcycles and mopeds, over 30 per cent of auto components, cotton yarn and heavy commercial vehicles are produced in Tamil Nadu.

It thus emerges that while Tamil Nadu is definitely among the front runner states in the country in terms of the size and significance of its manufacturing sector it has been witnessing a slowing down in the performance of this sector in recent years. In this chapter we seek to review the historical developments in this sector, analyse some performance indicators, understand the factors that aided or hindered its development and take a critical stock of the issues and challenges it faces today.

Industrial Development in Tamil Nadu - Review

State Policies and Plan Allocations

The evolution of the industrial climate in Tamil Nadu also reflected the national priorities and was shaped by policies both at the centre and at the state level. In terms of its Plan outlay allocations, the state government expected the central government and the private sector to play a major role in setting up large and medium scale industries. It chose to focus efforts on building up the necessary infrastructure to support the industrial growth and within the industries category to focus on the small-scale sector. This is evident from the fact that while around 25 per cent of the Plan outlays, on an average, were allocated for the power sector, the industries sector was assigned a 5 per cent share. Table 4.6 provides an idea of the relative weights given to the small-scale industries. During the Second Plan it accounted for over 92 per cent of the

TABLE 4.6

Five Year Plan Outlays - Industries

Plans	*Outlay (Rs. Crore)*	*Outlay (% share)*	*Plans*	*Outlay (Rs. Crore)*	*Outlay (% share)*
Second Plan			**Seventh Plan**		
Large Industry & Mining*	0.76	7.60	Large Industry & Mining*	155	54.39
Village & SSI	9.25	92.50	Village & SSI	130	45.61
Industries Total	10		Industries Total	285	4.96
Grand Total			Grand Total	5750	
Third Plan			**Eighth Plan**		
Large Industry & Mining	10	25.65	Large Industry & Mining	281	51.09
Village & SSI	28.98	74.35	Village & SSI	269	48.91
Industries Total	38.98		Industries Total	550	5.39
Grand Total			Grand Total	10200	
Fourth Plan			**Ninth Plan**		
Large Industry & Mining	33.08	52.37	Large Industry & Mining	707.9	54.12
Village & SSI	30.09	47.63	Village & SSI	600	45.88
Industries Total	63.17		Industries Total	1307.9	5.23
Grand Total			Grand Total	25000	
Fifth Plan			**Tenth Plan**		
Large Industry & Mining	37.99	61.91	Large Industry & Mining	205	36.94
Village & SSI	23.37	38.09	Village & SSI	350	63.06
Industries Total	61.36	5.47	Industries Total	555	1.39
Grand Total	1122.32		Grand Total	40000	
Sixth Plan					
Large Industry & Mining	91.77	53.43			
Village & SSI	80	46.57			
Industries Total	171.77	5.45			
Grand Total	3150				

Note: For Large Industries & Mining and for Village & SSI, the shares are given as a percentage of total outlay on industries. For the Industries Total share is a percentage of Total Plan outlay.

Source: Tamil Nadu State Plan Documents.

outlay on industries and this gradually fell to around 38 per cent during the Fifth Plan, which was its lowest share. For four plan periods from the Sixth to the Ninth it was around 47 per cent and in the Tenth Plan it has shot up to 63 per cent.

During the first three Plan periods, the State government's support for the large and medium industries was in the form of (a) setting up institutions that would help channel investment finances to units in the private sector and those that would provide technical and other forms of assistance; (b) organising the industrial units, particularly the sugar mills and the cotton spinning mills, as cooperative organisations. The state plan outlays were largely used to leverage private investments for this purpose. Within the village and small-scale industries category the handloom sector has been given considerable emphasis, accounting for an average 41 per cent of the allocations made to this category.

The State's allocations for the handloom sector were utilised to bring units into the cooperative fold, to provide loan capital, to invest in research and development and in training, to build housing colonies, to support marketing and publicity and to offer a rebate on the final product. The expenditures on rebate were quite significant accounting for around 42 per cent of the handloom sector outlays. For other small-scale industries, the state government established training/production-cum-training centres, service centres and model units and also constructed industrial estates, wherein factory space and supporting facilities were provided at subsidised rates. The Tamil Nadu Industrial Investment Corporation (TIIC) was set up in 1949 to provide financial assistance to small and medium industries at subsidised rates. The Madras State Industrial Cooperative Bank (1961) and the Madras State Small Industries Corporation (1965), which later became the Tamil Nadu Small Industries (TANSI) Corporation, were established during the Third Plan. TANSI engages in production activities. The Tamil Nadu Industrial Development Corporation (TIDCO) was also established in 1965 with the objective of promoting large and medium industries either in the public sector or as joint ventures.

Coming on the heels of a decade that witnessed very sluggish economic growth (2.9 per cent during the Second Plan and 1.58 per cent during the Third Plan, measured in 1980-81 prices) and the 'war years' (1966-69), the Fourth Plan emphasised the significance of industries as the potential sector to help promote economic development and raise standards of living. It was recognised that the scope for significant expansion in agriculture was limited and that industries could possibly provide the solution for both easing the pressure on land and employing the educated unemployed. The emphasis was on large and medium industries during this Plan and for the first time the allocation for this category, at 52 per cent, was higher than that for small industries. This Plan started an era that saw a mushrooming of state development corporations that continued well into the Sixth Plan. The Small Industries Development Corporation (1971) to primarily assist the export-oriented small industries, the Small Industries Promotion Corporation (1972) to promote industrial complexes and growth centres in backward areas, Tamil Nadu Handicrafts Development Corporation (1973), Tamil Nadu Salt Corporation (1974), Tamil Nadu Cement Corporation (1976), Electronics Corporation of Tamil Nadu (1977) Tamil Nadu Leather Corporation (1983), Tamil Nadu Newsprint and Papers Ltd. (1985) were some of those.

The seventies and eighties saw the State government setting up more and more Development Corporations or Statutory Boards that were specific to various industry categories (leather, cement, salt, sugar, etc.) and the State started increasingly micro-managing issues in the industries sector. The Plan expenditure on industries went up from about 6 per cent during the Fourth and Fifth Plans to 8 per cent during the Sixth and Seventh Plans. This was also a period when the price of electricity supplied to industries started rising significantly. The reasons for this were two-fold: (i) most of the cheaper sources of hydro potential available in the State had been exploited by the early-seventies and the share of costlier thermal generation started rising. As a result the Electricity Board changed the tariff for industry from a declining block structure to an increasing block structure. (ii) the State government's subsidies given to agriculture and low income houses was exponentially growing and to partially cross-subsidise these groups, industrial consumers were required to pay rates that were significantly higher than what it cost to supply them. Recognising that this would adversely affect industrial growth and competitiveness the government started providing subsidies to small-scale units, to units located in economically backward regions, to new units, to export oriented units and so on.

The expanding role of the State also reflected the emerging philosophy at the Centre during this period. In order to prevent a few big and powerful players from dominating the economic scene and to curb market power, particularly in specific industry categories that were considered crucial for social welfare, the larger companies were brought under closer scrutiny and tighter controls through the Monopolies and Restrictive Trade Practices Act (1969). Licensing procedures for this category of companies were tightened and they were prohibited from participating in certain categories of industries that were considered critical and of strategic importance for the growth of the Indian economy. Companies that had foreign equity participation were controlled through the Foreign Exchange Regulation Act (1973). Foreign collaboration, financial or technical, could be undertaken only on specific approval by the government. The range of products that were reserved for the small-scale industries was significantly expanded. Thus the bureaucratic control on the industries sector was strengthened.

While the State government role was expanding and state policies pervaded many aspects of functioning within the industries sector in Tamil Nadu, the performance of the sector was slipping. Growth in industry was lagging behind overall growth in the state domestic product. While a slowing down of industrial performance was also taking place at the All-India level, Tamil Nadu was falling even in terms of its relative ranking among other states.

The New Industrial Policy of the Government of India, 1991, began a comprehensive phase of policy reforms with respect to the Indian industry. However, some beginning had already been made in the Sixth and Seventh Plan periods. It was recognised that the expanding control of the bureaucracy was distorting incentives and hence had to be modified. The Industrial Policy of 1980 focused attention on the need to promote competition, technological upgradation and modernisation. For the first time productivity was expressed as a central concern of the policy objectives. Promotion of export-oriented units was also among the policy's objectives. During the Seventh Plan many industry groups that were non-MRTP and non-FERA were exempted from licensing requirements. Import of technology and import of capital goods were liberalised. Reforming the public sector units and limiting its role only to strategic, hi-tech and essential infrastructure areas came into the agenda. Partial disinvestments of public sector enterprises also began.

When the New Industrial Policy, 1991, further liberalised industry from bureaucratic controls it was also complemented by a series of reforms introduced in the fiscal, trade and foreign investment policies. Industry began to be subject to stronger competitive stimulus by being opened up to the international market. While this expanded the opportunities available, it also posed many challenges and hurdles to a sector that had honed its skills to operate and flourish in a totally different environment, one that was protected and administratively controlled. How well the sector could adapt to the new environment would depend (a) on its inherent competitive advantages, (b) on its level of preparedness that largely depends on the knowledge base and (c) the support systems offered both by the physical and the policy infrastructure.

A study of the State's approach to its policies and planning during the Seventh, Eighth and Ninth Plans indicates no major shift in its philosophy or its priorities that could be seen as a proactive mechanism to propel the industrial sector towards quickly adapting itself to the liberalising markets. Added to this was the fact that the negative burdens of past policies were still high - a crucial infrastructure service like power was insufficient, unreliable and unduly high-priced; loss-making state owned enterprises and indiscriminate subsidies were undermining state finances; the labour and bankruptcy laws in the country were still limiting the flexibility needed to operate in a competitive environment and so on. Growth in the manufacturing sector became quite sluggish. According to the Tenth Plan document of Tamil Nadu, the index of manufacturing output, calculated with 1981-82 as the base year, which grew at an average 10.8 per cent during 1982-83 to 1985-86, had a growth rate of only 4.6 per cent between 1986-87 and 1990-91 and fell further to 1.2 per cent during 1991-92 to 1995-96 (0.6 per cent between 1992-93 and 1995-96). It picked up at 2.2 per cent for the period 1997-98 to 2001-02 and the index for this period was calculated with 1993-94 as the base. It must however be pointed out that this index largely captures the growth in the organised sector. Huge data gaps exist in terms of the performance of the unorganised sector. In the liberalised regime this segment had greater flexibility in adapting and is believed to have compensated for some of the slack in the organised sector. The 1993-94 base includes a small part of the production in the small-scale sector.

Industrial Performance

For an analysis of the performance at a disaggregate level, industry is broadly classified into two groups -

the registered or the organised sector and the unregistered or the unorganised sector. The 'registered' category basically covers all units that get registered under the Factories Act. The reason for this kind of grouping is the highly differential approach to policies that governments have had with respect to both these categories. The licensing rules and regulations were basically applicable to the registered category because any unit that was of significant size in terms of employment or investment was registered. Monitoring and enforcement also becomes easy in the registered category. Thus the registered category is one that is 'organised' more in conformity with government rules and regulations. The unregistered category basically covers the units that operate on a small scale. Many of the laws and regulations applicable to this category are quite lenient. The governments have of course had a lot of promotional policies to promote this segment because given its labour intensive characteristic it was seen as a good source of employment and dispersed economic growth. Many of these policies were however industry specific, size specific, location specific and there was no significant uniformity across space and over time. Hence this category has largely come to be known as the unorganised sector.

A fairly comprehensive database, at the disaggregate level in terms of type of industries and their principal characteristics, is available for the registered category through the Annual Survey of Industries (ASI) carried out by the Central Statistical Organisation (CSO). On the other hand the database available for the unorganised sector is very sketchy. There is no collection and publication of statistics on an annual basis for this category. Part of the reason is that given the smallness of the size of each unit, the largeness of the total number of units and their geographical dispersal it is not cost effective for organisations like the CSO to collect statistics for this category as it does for the registered category. Secondly, there are multiple government organisations that are incharge of implementing the various government policies of developmental support and financial assistance to units in this category. Many of these are specific to certain types of industries like handlooms, coir, jute and so on. These organisations have not systematically compiled information on the characteristics and performance of the units they support. In most of the cases the information available with these organisations only focus on the number of units helped, employment provided, the magnitude of subsidies disbursed, the physical capacity created and so on but information on physical and financial performance efficiencies is conspicuous by its absence. The database available with them does not report the number of units that get closed.

The Unregistered Sector

The CSO has, through its National Sample Survey Organisation (NSSO), carried out periodic surveys to gather information on the unorganised sector. Different surveys have addressed different sub-groups within the unorganised sector - household enterprises, which were either Own Account Enterprises (OAE) that did not hire any labour or Manufacturing Enterprises that hired labour (Directory or Non-Directory depending on the size of labour employed); small-scale manufacturing; unregistered industrial units; units falling within the purview of the Development Commissioner of Small Scale Industries (DCSSI); trade establishments and so on. However, in CSO's own assessment, the efforts taken hitherto have been partial and sporadic. The reliability of the data based on some of these surveys is also not very high.

The share of the unregistered sector within manufacturing category in Tamil Nadu has declined from 54 per cent during 1960-61 to 38 per cent during 1999-2000 as was shown in Table 4.2. There has also been a fall in employment in this category as seen from the Economic Census and the NSSO data. Table 4.7 presents the employment figures for Tamil Nadu's unorganised category between 1980 and 1997-98 based on these sources. It may be observed that the compound annual growth (CAG) between 1980 and 1990, according to the Economic Census was (-) 0.17 per cent, while it was 0.39 per cent between 1990-98. Over the entire eighteen-year period, however, employment in this category has more or less remained stagnant registering a CAG of 0.07 per cent. It is interesting to note that while the growth in employment was negative during the eighties it was positive during the liberalised regime of the nineties. This is probably a result of increasing capital labour ratio in the organised sector and their increasing subcontracting of jobs to the unorganised sector as a result of their own adjustment process to liberalisation. According to the NSSO data however, the growth rate has been negative in the early-nineties (1989-90 to 1994-95) at (-) 3.1 per cent. It must be noted that there is a discrepancy between the NSSO figures and the Economic Census figures for employment during this period.

TABLE 4.7

Unorganised Manufacturing Employment

Employment, '00 Nos.	
EC 80	22963
EC 90	22573
NSS 89-90	33751
NSS 94-95	28838
EC-98	23281
Compound Annual Growth %	
EC 90 over 80	-0.17
EC 98 over 90	0.39
EC 98 over 80	0.07
NSS 94-95 over 89-90	-3.1

Source: NSSO and Economic Census.

Table 4.8 provides an idea of the share of different industry groups at the 2-digit level in the unorganised manufacturing employment in Tamil Nadu during 1994-95 and compares it with that of All-India. Tamil Nadu accounts for 8.7 per cent of the overall unorganised manufacturing employment in the country but in specific industry groups it has a very high share e.g. 37 per cent in chemicals (matches), 27 per cent in cotton textiles, 21 per cent in silk textiles, about 11 per cent in tobacco *(beedis)* and paper & printing. Within Tamil Nadu, cotton textiles has the highest share of unorganised manufacturing employment (21 per cent), followed by wood & wood products (12 per cent), tobacco (10 per cent), and other manufacturing industries (7 per cent). Making of matches accounts for only 4.5 per cent.

Small Scale Industries

A special category of industries that has come to be known as the modern small-scale industries overlaps with both the organised and the unorganised sectors. This category receives special support from the government because of its potential for both value addition and employment. A good part of these SSI gets registered under the Factories Act and hence gets covered under the ASI. Within the unregistered part, a small proportion gets registered with the DCSSI and these get covered under the NSSO's periodic surveys.

TABLE 4.8

Unorganised Manufacturing Employment by 2-Digit Industries - 1994-95

('00 Nos.)

Ind Code	*Description*	*Employment*			*Industry Share%*	*All India Total*	*TN Share in All India %*
		Rural	*Urban*	*Total*			
20	Foodgrain, bakery etc.,	802	870	1672	5.8	41276	4.0
21	Food-edible oil, nuts etc.,	335	456	792	2.7	14717	5.4
22	Beverages, Tobacco	1560	1454	3014	10.4	26890	11.2
23	Cotton Textiles	3223	2780	6003	20.8	22023	27.3
24	Silk Textiles	1210	1383	2593	9.0	12176	21.3
25	Jute Textiles	190	0	190	0.7	2434	7.8
26	Textile Products	612	855	1468	5.1	30546	4.8
27	Wood & Wood Products	2654	727	3381	11.7	53668	6.3
28	Paper and Printing	29	599	628	2.2	5537	11.3
29	Leather & Leather Products	58	171	229	0.8	5093	4.5
30	Chemical - Matches etc.,	758	542	1300	4.5	3543	36.7
31	Rubber, Petroleum Products	44	200	243	0.8	3212	7.6
32	Non-Metallic Mineral	1342	257	1598	5.5	25892	6.2
33	Basic Metals and Alloys	0	57	57	0.2	1218	4.7
34	Metal Products	321	798	1119	3.9	12954	8.6
35	Machinery	29	100	129	0.4	2768	4.7
36	Machinery - Electrical	15	71	86	0.3	1440	6.0
37	Transport Equipment	44	71	115	0.4	1218	9.4
38	Other Manuf. Industries	729	1311	2041	7.1	28004	7.3
39	Repair of Capital Goods	131	399	530	1.8	7305	7.3
97	Repair Services	496	1140	1636	5.7	29228	5.6
99	Miscellaneous	0	14	14	0.0	443	3.2
Total		14583	14255	28838	100	331585	8.7

Source: NSSO, Sarvekshana, Vol XXIII, No. 2, Oct-Dec. 1999.

The units in this SSI sector are also registered with the state level Directorates of Industries and data for this category gets collected from time to time on a census or sample basis. The Small Industries Development Organisation (SIDO) and the DCSSI in association with the State Directorates of Industries and the National Informatics Centre have compiled the data. The report on the 1987-88 census gives data at the 2-digit level of the National Industrial Classification (NIC). It also provides the distribution of closed units in terms of the reasons for closure. The results show an impressive growth in the performance of this sector between 1972-73 and 1987-88. The results should be interpreted with caution though, because of changes in the definition of small-scale units. The ceiling on investment in plant and machinery, to qualify as an SSI unit, has been revised upwards and as a result there has been some shift over time of units from medium-scale to small-scale. Moreover, the response rate to the survey is less than 2 per cent and the closure of sick units is not adequately captured. With this caveat, we present below some of the analysis and results for this group as a broad indicator of a spectrum of industries that lie at the borderline between the organised and the unorganised sector.

At the national level a study group of the Union Planning Commission on Development of Small Scale Enterprises shows that during the period 1990-2000, the annual growth rate of the SSI sector has been higher than that of the total manufacturing sector by 1.83 per cent. It also finds that the capital productivity in this sector is twice that of the larger sector. In Tamil Nadu, the SSI made an early start with the government stepping in to create industrial estates in the Guindy and Ambattur areas of Chennai, as early as the Second/Third Plans. In 1973, Tamil Nadu had the largest number of SSI units in the country at 18,500. Since then it has more or less maintained this leadership. According to the Second All-India Census in 1987-88, Tamil Nadu still ranked the highest in terms of number of units and employment but not in terms of their growth rate. In more recent years the growth of this sector has picked up though in comparison with other states it is at the average level. Table 4.9 presents a comparison of Tamil Nadu's performance with that of a few selected states, based on a study by SIDBI.

Despite reservation of several items of manufacture solely in the SSI sector, preferential government programmes of purchase from this sector and allocation of credit under priority sector lending, the units in this category face several hardships. One of the major problems is their scale diseconomy. Apart from that the smallness of their size and the largeness in their number makes it tougher to avail the credit they are entitled to, receive payments for supplies on time, tackle a complex system of regulations and so on. It has been found that the smaller the size of the unit within this category, the larger the problems they face.

TABLE 4.9

SSI Growth Rates Comparison

(1988-89 to 1998-99)

	No. of Units %	*Employment* %	*Fixed Invest.* *(Rs. million)*
Andhra Pradesh	8.7	8.3	8.9
Bihar	22.8	9.6	9.0
Gujarat	15.3	11.4	18.4
Haryana	11.6	13.2	12.5
Karnataka	38.2	13.0	17.4
Kerala	18.0	14.4	17.9
Madya Pradesh	13.5	14.3	17.5
Orissa	13.1	10.7	16.4
Punjab	3.6	3.6	11.5
Rajastan	10.0	10.6	18.8
Tamil Nadu	**12.8**	**10.9**	**16.7**

Source: SIDBI Report on Small Scale Industries Sector, 2000.

Apart from high mortality rates (over 35 per cent), sickness in this sector is also very high. According to a Reserve Bank of India report, at least 40 per cent of the 37 lakh small-scale units in the country are sick. In Tamil Nadu, 39 per cent of the 18,000 units holding small-scale loan accounts with the TIIC are declared non-performing. The liberalised regime created by the New Industrial Policy 1991 and the World Trade Organisation agreements is throwing up a lot more challenges to this sector while at the same time increasing the opportunities. While this sector can have considerable flexibility in adapting to the changing industrial climate it will also have to deal with the higher transaction costs and the scale weaknesses.

The Registered Sector

In this section we take a detailed look at the performance of the registered category within the manufacturing sector based on the ASI data. We analyse the growth and the relative performance of different industry groups at the 2-digit level.

Growth

Table 4.10 presents growth rates for some of the principal characteristics of the registered manufacturing sector.

TABLE 4.10

Growth Rates in Registered Industry

Period	*No of Facts.*	*Invested Cap*	*Employees*	*Emoluments Value*	*Output*	*Net Val Add*
1980-90	3.47	16.46	1.82	14.32	15.72	15.96
1990-00	3.90	16.56	3.81*	13.11	14.67	12.16
1980-85	5.91	15.45	2.55	14.91	14.75	17.02
1985-90	1.08	17.47	1.24	13.74	16.69	14.91
1990-92	5.99	17.62	2.89	12.34	14.57	13.85
1992-97	4.37	19.75	4.44	15.90	18.61	18.99
1997-00	1.78	2.80	2.51*	9.09	8.45	0.63

Note: Figures indicate compound annual growth rates per cent and calculations are based on ASI Data.

* Total Employees data was available only till 1997-98.

The data indicates a down swing in the performance of the manufacturing sector during the nineties compared to the eighties. Except for invested capital and the number of factories, which had a marginal increase, the growth rates of all other parameters were lower during the nineties. The fall in the growth rate was highest in the case of net value added which went down from 16 per cent during the eighties to 12 per cent during the nineties.

Looking at the growth patterns for sub-periods, it may be seen that the overall performance was slipping during the Seventh Plan and Annual Plans, picked up during the Eighth and witnessed a dramatic dip during the first three years of the Ninth Plan. In terms of individual categories, growth in invested capital was gradually rising from 16 per cent during the Sixth Plan to 20 per cent during the Eighth but fell to 3 per cent during 1997-00. Total emoluments did not see much volatility in its growth rates except for a steep fall during the Ninth Plan. Growth in total output was going up and down but in the case of net value added the growth rate went down from 17 per cent during 1980-85 to 13 per cent during the Annual Plans, picked up at 19 per cent during the Eighth Plan but fell to less than 1 per cent during 1997-00. Compared to the 1 per cent growth in net value added, total emoluments had a growth rate of 9 per cent for the same period indicating the magnitude of fall in profitability. This would have a major impact on the incentives for future investment.

We present here an analysis at the two-digit level classification and for the period 1980-81 to 1997-98. Twelve industry groups within the two-digit level classification have been selected given their relative significance. The following list provides a reference for the ASI industry code numbers used in the Tables.

Industry Code	*Industry Category*
20-21	Food Products
23	Cotton Textiles
26	Textile Products
28	Paper and Paper Products
29	Leather and Leather Products
30	Chemicals and Chemical Products
31	Rubber, Plastic, Petroleum, Coal & Nuclear Fuel
32	Non-Metallic Mineral Products
33	Basic Metals and Alloys
34	Metal Products
35, 36 & 39	Manufacture & Repair of Machinery and Equip.
37	Manufacture of Transport Equipment

Size

Table 4.11 ranks the different industry groups in terms of their relative shares in the number of factories, invested capital, total employment, total emoluments

TABLE 4.11

Tamil Nadu - Industry Groups Ranking in Terms of Relative Shares

No. of Factories

Ind Code	*1980-85*	*1985-90*	*1990-92*	*1992-97*	*1997-98*
20 & 21	23.33	22.09	21.30	19.16	19.01
23	11.49	12.85	13.77	15.14	16.53
26	5.28	5.36	5.73	8.81	8.38
28	6.44	6.75	6.05	5.56	5.72
29	3.67	4.47	5.71	5.95	5.63
30	7.84	7.98	7.79	8.17	8.43
31	2.93	3.19	3.35	3.31	3.23
32	3.24	3.91	4.21	4.08	4.21
33	4.57	4.42	3.56	3.31	3.37
34	4.37	4.37	4.21	3.76	3.49
35, 36 & 39	9.40	10.58	11.49	11.10	10.75
37	2.91	3.39	3.23	3.01	2.97

Invested Capital

Ind Code	*1980-85*	*1985-90*	*1990-92*	*1992-97*	*1997-98*
20 & 21	7.66	6.98	9.90	8.17	9.10
23	13.76	13.91	16.06	17.37	19.91
26	0.70	1.06	1.61	3.19	5.29
28	4.20	5.00	3.57	6.02	4.96
29	3.20	3.15	4.24	4.00	3.64
30	14.28	17.83	15.88	14.57	15.57
31	12.98	10.60	9.56	11.46	7.03
32	4.81	5.06	4.63	3.84	3.10
33	7.94	7.28	7.41	6.96	7.13
34	1.85	2.02	1.59	1.54	1.72
35, 36 & 39	15.40	14.40	12.59	10.95	11.72
37	10.00	9.42	8.81	7.50	7.01

Tamil Nadu - Industry Groups Ranking in Terms of Relative Shares

Tot Pers Emplyd

Ind Code	1980-85	1985-90	1990-92	1992-97	1997-98
20 & 21	17.12	13.41	13.38	12.63	12.47
23	20.05	20.56	19.86	19.23	20.80
26	2.51	3.76	5.22	8.74	10.45
28	4.24	4.49	4.24	3.90	3.98
29	3.37	4.73	6.29	6.16	4.75
30	10.60	11.91	11.88	11.78	11.71
31	2.47	2.73	2.71	3.03	2.59
32	3.82	3.70	3.64	3.19	2.68
33	4.60	3.57	3.19	3.08	3.32
34	2.57	2.33	2.19	2.23	2.06
35, 36 & 39	11.05	12.05	12.99	12.79	13.71
37	9.50	10.02	9.33	8.35	7.12

Total Emoluments

Ind Code	1980-85	1985-90	1990-92	1992-97	1997-98
20 & 21	6.69	6.90	7.83	8.10	8.51
23	21.96	20.78	20.64	19.80	19.62
26	1.04	1.53	2.30	4.20	6.04
28	4.28	4.12	4.31	4.04	4.20
29	2.60	3.04	4.35	4.15	3.58
30	8.39	9.18	9.47	9.14	8.29
31	3.71	3.90	3.25	4.29	3.28
32	4.41	4.22	4.03	3.30	2.75
33	4.82	4.06	3.67	3.53	3.78
34	2.65	2.17	2.01	2.17	2.27
35, 36 & 39	16.08	16.78	17.76	18.61	20.41
37	15.91	16.89	15.86	14.01	13.33

Tamil Nadu - Industry Groups Ranking in Terms of Relative Shares

Net Value Added

Ind Code	1980-85	1985-90	1990-92	1992-97	1997-98
20 & 21	8.93	10.10	9.34	8.30	11.27
23	15.76	16.20	15.70	15.11	15.37
26	0.91	2.01	2.94	5.06	7.18
28	4.77	3.97	4.70	4.48	3.99
29	2.60	2.98	4.50	4.27	3.18
30	14.12	11.90	12.02	10.43	9.78
31	5.89	8.29	7.69	8.75	5.91
32	5.48	5.05	5.46	5.57	5.44
33	3.88	3.52	3.50	2.56	4.88
34	2.53	1.89	1.74	1.93	2.16
35, 36 & 39	16.56	17.32	16.27	17.29	16.83
37	13.10	11.63	11.75	11.09	9.18

Source: Computed from ASI data.

and net value added. The relative shares are averages for the period 1980-85 (Sixth Plan), 1985-90 (Seventh Plan), 1990-92 (Annual Plans), 1992-97 (Eighth Plan) and 1997-98. The system of industrial grouping followed by ASI during the above years was based on the National Industrial Classification Codes (NIC) of 1970 and 1987.

It may be observed from the table that the manufacture and repair of non-transport machinery and equipment (M&E) has had the highest share in the net value added for all the periods considered and it accounts for about 16-17 per cent. The second highest is cotton textiles, accounting for about 15 per cent. Chemicals, transport equipment and manufacture of food products are the other significant groups each accounting for 10 per cent or more of the net value added. Textile products has gained significantly in importance from a mere 1 per cent share in the net value added during the Sixth Plan to over 5 per cent during 1992-97 and to 7 per cent in 1997-98. It is interesting to note that leather and leather products ranks among the bottom three groups with a 2.5-3 per cent share. Metal products category has generally been the smallest contributor.

In terms of the number of factories, cotton textiles and M&E have consistently been in the second and third position respectively. The total persons employed has been the highest for the cotton textiles throughout (around 20 per cent) and M&E has moved up from the third highest share till 1990-92 to the second highest during the Eighth Plan. While M&E accounted for the highest share of invested capital (15 per cent) during 1980-85 it gradually fell to the third position with close to 12 per cent share by 1997-98. Cotton textiles on the other hand was in the third position during the Sixth and Seventh Plans with 14 per cent share but rose to the highest position since 1990-92 and had a 20 per cent share in 1997-98. In the case of total emoluments cotton textiles had the highest share, accounting for over 20 per cent till the end of the Eighth Plan but M&E, which had remained generally in the second place got ahead of cotton textiles in 1997-98. In the case of cotton textiles, its share in employment and emoluments were both around 20 per cent. On the other hand, M&E's share in employment rose from 11 per cent to 14 per cent between 1980-81 and 1997-98 while its share in emoluments rose from 16 per cent to 20 per cent.

Food products had the largest share in the number of factories between 1980-81 and 1997-98 and the second or third largest share in employment. In terms of invested capital it rose from the seventh position in 1980-81 with a 7.7 per cent share to the fourth position in 1997-98 with 9 per cent. While its share in employment gradually fell from 17 per cent to 12.5 per cent in terms of total emoluments its share rose from 7 per cent to 8.5 per cent. This group is clearly labour-intensive since it accounts for 20-23 per cent of the number of factories, 12-17 per cent of employment but only 7-9 per cent of invested capital.

Chemicals on the other hand is more capital intensive with its share of invested capital ranging between 14-15 per cent while its share in employment was 10-11 per cent and total emoluments was between 8-9 per cent. It accounted for 7-8 per cent of the number of factories. Net value added declined from 14 per cent during 1980-85 to 10 per cent in 1997-98.

Leather's share has generally been around 3 per cent for all the factors considered. While this category is a major export earner the value addition in the organised sector is not very significant relative to other industry groups. This could be because a significant part of the value addition is taking place in the unorganised sector as a result of the government policies to promote small-scale units in this category. Or probably a significant part of the value addition is occurring at the trade level and not at the manufacturing level.

Transport equipment and rubber-plastic-petroleum (RPP) are characterised by significant market concentration. Each of these accounts for only about 3 per cent of the number of factories but their shares in invested capital were between 10-13 per cent during 1980-85 which fell to around 7 per cent during 1997-98. Transport equipment accounted for 13 per cent of the net value added during 1980-85 and witnessed a decline to 11 per cent during the Eighth Plan and further to 9 per cent in 1997-98. Transport equipment also had a significant share in employment and emoluments. Its employment share was about 9-10 per cent during the eighties and witnessed a fall to 7 per cent by 1997-98. RPP on the other hand had amongst the lowest share in employment and emoluments but its share in net value added grew from about 6 per cent in 1980-85 to 8.8 per cent during 1992-97 and fell back to 6 per cent in 1997-98.

Relative Performance

Table 4.12 provides a comparison of the relative performance of different industry groups in terms of their labour productivity, capital productivity, net value added and the share of labour in net value added. Capital productivity is taken to be net value added per rupee of average invested capital, where average invested capital is the average of invested capital at the beginning of the year and at the end of the year. Labour productivity is the net value added per rupee spent on labour compensation (total emoluments).

In order to compare the relative performance of different industry groups in terms of their addition to net value added, the following measure is used: we compute the ratio of net value added to the sum of normative cost of labour and normative cost of capital. We take the total emoluments to labour during the year as the normative cost of labour. The assumption here is that the labour market is fairly competitive. To estimate the normative cost of capital, the average invested capital for the year is multiplied by the interest rate on medium-term government securities. The invested capital figures provided in the ASI are net of depreciation and include physical working capital. Material costs are implicitly treated here as proportional to output. The rationale behind this measure is that under equilibrium market conditions, after adjusting for tax, this ratio should be equal to 1. However, at any given point of time, different industry groups would be facing differential comparative advantages and disadvantages depending on the various factors like demand conditions in their output markets, investment

TABLE 4.12

Tamil Nadu - Productivity Measures and NVA Index For Industry Groups

Capital Productivity Measures

NVA/AvInvCap	*1980-85*	*1985-90*	*1990-92*	*1992-97*	*1997-98*
20 & 21	0.38	0.45	0.39	0.33	0.34
23	0.43	0.36	0.42	0.29	0.25
26	0.44	0.57	0.54	0.50	0.44
28	0.42	0.27	0.44	0.31	0.25
29	0.27	0.31	0.31	0.37	0.30
30	0.34	0.24	0.25	0.24	0.22
31	0.12	0.27	0.28	0.25	0.29
32	0.34	0.38	0.35	0.47	0.53
33	0.18	0.17	0.13	0.14	0.10
34	0.47	0.35	0.34	0.41	0.40
35, 36 & 39	0.36	0.41	0.42	0.50	0.54
37	0.46	0.41	0.54	0.47	0.43
All Industries	0.34	0.34	0.36	0.32	0.32

Net Value Added Index

NVA/(K&L cst)	*1980-85*	*1985-90*	*1990-92*	*1992-97*	*1997-98*
20 & 21	1.68	1.74	1.67	1.39	1.58
23	1.20	1.04	1.33	1.09	1.15
26	1.33	1.59	1.58	1.71	1.68
28	1.50	1.19	1.59	1.34	1.22
29	1.28	1.20	1.14	1.50	1.37
30	1.96	1.29	1.25	1.23	1.37
31	0.99	1.74	1.75	1.57	2.02
32	1.44	1.61	1.44	2.15	2.67
33	1.02	0.87	0.69	0.76	0.60
34	1.42	1.26	1.16	1.39	1.54
35, 36 & 39	1.40	1.41	1.34	1.53	1.70
37	1.30	1.02	1.45	1.36	1.48
All Industries	1.36	1.28	1.37	1.35	1.48

Labour Productivity Measures

NVA/Tot Emol	*1980-85*	*1985-90*	*1990-92*	*1992-97*	*1997-98*
20 & 21	2.99	3.32	3.36	3.11	3.28
23	1.59	1.77	2.15	2.31	1.94
26	1.98	2.94	3.56	3.74	2.95
28	2.51	2.20	3.07	3.37	2.36
29	2.24	2.21	2.91	3.12	2.21
30	3.75	2.98	3.59	3.50	2.93
31	3.65	4.84	6.69	6.22	4.47
32	2.79	2.67	3.81	5.16	4.91
33	1.77	1.95	2.66	2.23	3.20
34	2.13	1.98	2.45	2.71	2.36
35, 36 & 39	2.30	2.31	2.58	2.82	2.04
37	1.83	1.55	2.07	2.43	1.71
All Industries	2.23	2.26	2.82	3.05	2.48

Labour Share in NVA

Lab share_NVA	*1980-85*	*1985-90*	*1990-92*	*1992-97*	*1997-98*
20 & 21	36.79	32.07	27.17	32.05	30.38
23	60.51	62.07	42.81	45.34	43.93
26	50.80	39.14	31.79	27.44	26.51
28	43.66	47.62	32.63	31.22	35.63
29	46.09	45.32	39.22	33.07	37.79
30	26.51	34.12	31.59	29.41	29.32
31	42.56	21.45	17.29	15.60	19.28
32	42.03	35.34	33.51	21.07	17.19
33	52.70	55.04	50.85	41.49	58.73
34	47.65	51.89	46.33	36.88	36.87
35, 36 & 39	43.68	43.50	42.38	35.51	38.39
37	53.93	66.16	47.38	47.26	36.07
All Industries	45.66	44.98	37.10	33.41	33.89

options and constraints, conditions in their input markets, tax policies, regulations etc. that are *specific* to each of these groups. Hence, how different from 1 the ratios for individual industry groups have been would provide a relative picture of their performances in terms of net value added. We therefore treat this ratio as an index of net value added.

The NVA index of the M&E group, which has the highest share of net value added and close to the highest in total emoluments and invested capital, is quite good and improving relative to the average index for all industries. The performance of the cotton textiles, the other significant category in terms of its size, is however worrisome. The NVA index of this group has been lower than the average index throughout and is worsening. NVA index in the manufacture of food products, which has a significant share in employment, is fairly good and above the average, though this difference is narrowing. Textile products category started with below average index during the Sixth Plan, but subsequently has been picking up and has been consistently above average since. Transport equipment, which has a significant share in net value added had below average index levels during the eighties and has improved to slightly above average levels in the nineties. Non-metallic mineral products group has been a super achiever particularly during the nineties and RPP has also achieved levels that are significantly above average. These two categories rank in the middle level in terms of the size of contribution to net value added, have significant shares in invested capital and relatively low shares in employment. The NVA index of chemicals, which is another important group, was well above the average during 1980-85 but has been declining since and fallen below the all industries average during the nineties. Leather has generally performed below average throughout. Table 4.13 shows the deviations of the NVA index for each industry group from the average

TABLE 4.13

NVA Index - Deviations From All Industries Average

Ind. Code	*1980-85*	*1985-90*	*1990-92*	*1992-97*	*1997-98*	*1980-85*	*1985-90*	*1990-92*	*1992-97*	*1997-98*
20 & 21	1.68	1.74	1.67	1.39	1.58	0.32	0.46	0.30	0.04	0.10
23	1.20	1.04	1.33	1.09	1.15	–0.16	–0.24	–0.04	–0.26	–0.33
26	1.33	1.59	1.58	1.71	1.68	–0.03	0.31	0.21	0.36	0.20
28	1.50	1.19	1.59	1.34	1.22	0.14	–0.09	0.22	–0.01	–0.26
29	1.28	1.20	1.14	1.50	1.37	–0.08	–0.08	–0.23	0.15	–0.11
30	1.96	1.29	1.25	1.23	1.37	0.60	0.01	–0.12	–0.12	–0.11
31	0.99	1.74	1.75	1.57	2.02	–0.37	0.46	0.38	0.22	0.54
32	1.44	1.61	1.44	2.15	2.67	0.08	0.33	0.07	0.80	1.19
33	1.02	0.87	0.69	0.76	0.60	–0.34	–0.41	–0.68	–0.59	–0.88
34	1.42	1.26	1.16	1.39	1.54	0.06	–0.02	–0.21	0.04	0.06
35, 36 & 39	1.40	1.41	1.34	1.53	1.70	0.04	0.13	–0.03	0.18	0.22
37	1.30	1.02	1.45	1.36	1.48	–0.06	–0.26	0.08	0.01	0.00
All Industries	1.36	1.28	1.37	1.35	1.48	0.00	0.00	0.00	0.00	0.00

index for all industries in Tamil Nadu. The all industries category also comprises industry groups not included in the 12 chosen for specific analysis above. It however excludes electricity, because supply here is through a statutory government entity and also because some data aberrations are seen here for later years that could not be fully reconciled.

The share of labour in net value added is seen to be falling consistently over the last two decades in all the industry groups with basic metals being the lone exception (Table 4.12). The fall has been really significant in the cases of non-metallic minerals, RPP, textile products and cotton textiles. This trend broadly reflects the adjustment processes that the manufacturing sector is going through in the liberalising climate. The short-term response in terms of cutting back on excess labour is evident. This is also borne out by the fact that partial labour productivity is generally showing an improving trend. This improvement is really significant in the case of non-metallic minerals and RPP, good in the case of textile products and marginal in the case of M&E and transport equipment. Labour productivity in cotton textiles has also shown some improvement though the productivity levels are below the all industries average. There has been a decline in capital productivity on the other hand for most of the industry groups with a few exceptions. M&E group shows a significant improvement in capital productivity, followed by non-metallic minerals and RPP. Textile products category has also registered an improvement and has had productivity levels higher than average. Leather on the other hand had below average capital productivity but has nonetheless registered an improvement.

Table 4.14 compares the relative performance of the industry groups, in terms of the NVA index, in Tamil Nadu vis-à-vis the performance of these groups at the All-India level and in Maharashtra and Gujarat, the two States which are the manufacturing sector leaders. The comparison is made for the Plan periods between 1980-1998. It may be seen from the Table that M&E, the highest contributor to net value added in Tamil Nadu, has been moving up to higher ranks over the years, has managed to get ahead of the All-India average during 1997-98 and has been narrowing the gap between its index levels and those of Gujarat's, which has consistently had the highest. Cotton textiles, which has had relatively poor index levels compared to the all industries average in Tamil Nadu and also worsened during the later nineties, has however performed consistently better than the All-India average for cotton textiles as well as ahead of Maharashtra and Gujarat. This advantage has been quite significant in 1997-98.

Chemicals, which ranked highest in Tamil Nadu in terms of the NVA index during 1980-85, and which was also leading ahead of All-India average and Maharashtra and Gujarat, has lost its edge over the years. It ranks among the low-end performers in Tamil Nadu during the nineties and has fallen significantly behind All-India. Maharashtra has developed a strong advantage in this category. RPP, which had the lowest index within Tamil Nadu during 1980-85, became the best during the late eighties and early nineties and has

TABLE 4.14

NVA Index Comparisons - Tamil Nadu, All India, Maharashtra, Gujarat

Ind. Code	*Tamil Nadu*					*All India*					*Maharashtra*					*Gujarat*				
	1980-85	*1985-90*	*1990-92*	*1992-97*	*1997-98*	*1980-85*	*1985-90*	*1990-92*	*1992-97*	*1997-98*	*1980-85*	*1985-90*	*1990-92*	*1992-97*	*1997-98*	*1980-85*	*1985-90*	*1990-92*	*1992-97*	*1997-98*
20 & 21	1.68	1.74	1.67	1.39	1.58	1.51	1.54	1.28	1.38	1.47	1.33	1.23	0.95	1.56	2.48	1.42	1.32	1.36	1.15	1.32
23	1.20	1.04	1.33	1.09	1.15	1.16	1.03	1.15	1.06	0.97	1.10	1.10	1.00	0.63	0.81	1.17	0.91	0.89	1.09	0.60
26	1.33	1.59	1.58	1.71	1.68	1.85	1.82	2.31	2.39	1.72	1.57	1.95	2.57	2.53	2.77	1.95	1.64	1.99	1.54	1.02
28	1.50	1.19	1.59	1.34	1.22	1.28	1.13	1.34	1.38	1.07	1.48	1.32	1.32	1.81	2.00	1.42	1.08	1.35	1.39	0.77
29	1.28	1.20	1.14	1.50	1.37	1.36	1.31	1.66	1.59	1.64	1.39	1.45	1.69	1.59	2.79	0.85	0.89	0.49	0.70	0.78
30	1.96	1.29	1.25	1.23	1.37	1.66	1.45	1.38	1.85	1.76	1.80	1.58	1.45	2.70	4.86	1.88	1.82	1.41	1.85	1.53
31	0.99	1.74	1.75	1.57	2.02	1.70	2.31	1.92	2.10	1.43	2.72	2.44	1.93	2.58	5.57	2.91	2.92	1.05	5.10	–0.48
32	1.44	1.61	1.44	2.15	2.67	1.61	1.26	1.63	1.32	1.33	1.84	1.32	1.59	1.45	1.42	1.28	1.10	1.24	1.31	1.67
33	1.02	0.87	0.69	0.76	0.60	1.17	1.07	0.96	1.04	1.63	1.43	1.42	0.87	1.91	3.63	1.53	1.31	1.76	1.27	0.66
34	1.42	1.26	1.16	1.39	1.54	1.60	1.52	1.43	1.43	1.36	1.59	1.51	1.33	1.58	2.35	1.56	1.71	2.06	1.57	0.88
35, 36 & 39	1.40	1.41	1.34	1.53	1.70	1.66	1.49	1.50	1.61	1.66	1.60	1.48	0.81	1.13	1.11	1.68	1.65	1.67	2.53	2.36
37	1.30	1.02	1.45	1.36	1.48	1.27	1.18	1.38	1.51	1.37	1.35	1.23	1.38	1.94	2.21	1.16	0.87	1.26	1.13	1.10
Total	1.36	1.28	1.37	1.35	1.48	1.39	1.33	1.38	1.49	1.51	2.05	1.89	1.59	1.76	3.78	1.54	1.38	1.20	1.64	1.24

stayed amongst the top three during the nineties. However, it is lagging behind the other three categories and both Maharashtra and Gujarat have strengthened their lead in the nineties. Non-metallic minerals, which has been an above average performer in Tamil Nadu during the eighties, shot to the highest place in the nineties and from being a laggard during the Sixth Plan it has significantly overtaken the performance of all other states.

Manufacture of food products had the second highest NVA index level in Tamil Nadu during the eighties and early-nineties. It was also leading the All-India average by a small margin and was ahead of the other two states. During the nineties however, it has fallen to the sixth position in Tamil Nadu and while it is still marginally ahead of the All-India average, Maharashtra has been overtaking in this category during the later-nineties. Textile products, which was an average performer in Tamil Nadu during the Sixth Plan, has moved up to the second highest performance during the Eighth Plan. It has been lagging behind the other states though it has been slowly catching up with the All-India average and overtook Gujarat during the Eighth Plan. Leather has been an unremarkable performer in Tamil Nadu and has also been lagging behind the All-India average. Transport equipment has been an average performer compared to other industries in Tamil Nadu. Its performance has been oscillating about the All-India average and it has generally performed ahead of Gujarat but behind Maharashtra.

The snapshot analysis above based on historical data merely helps understand what had happened. It need not automatically indicate the potential for these categories in the future. Especially in a more liberalised regime and in the context of greater integration with world markets, performances could change dramatically depending on a whole set of complex and dynamic factors. A more detailed analysis for each group and at a further disaggregated level (3 or 4-digit) is needed to understand the potentials in the near future.

Evaluation

The general picture that emerges from the above analysis is that while Tamil Nadu can be counted among the dominant states in the country as far as the manufacturing sector is concerned it has been witnessing problems in adapting itself to the liberalising climate in this sector during the nineties. The negative impact of this adjustment process is more evident in the early nineties and a gradual recovery is witnessed in the late nineties. This is definitely not a phenomenon unique to this State. However, what matters from the State's perspective is that it has been losing the relative edge it had over other states and this is cause for concern.

In a very broad sense the reasons for this can be traced to the local industrial climate that evolved in the State, within the larger context of the climate in the country. This local climate has been shaped by the State level policies, priorities, institutional arrangements and enforcement mechanisms, though the implications and effects were realised with a lag. The seventies and eighties were characterised by an expanding role of the state government in the manufacturing sector. Expanding role of the State, by itself, need not be an impediment. What is important is the kind of role that government takes on itself to play. In the Tamil Nadu context, the increasing role was not so much in the nature of making efficient investments in infrastructure or taking up production activities that would set an example and provide competition to the private sector. The State's role became one of increasingly micro-managing different sub-groups of industries; of announcing a complex system of subsidies, cross-subsidies, taxes and duties that were more of an *ad hoc* nature; of channeling subsidised inputs to various units in the small scale sector and subsidising the final product so as to prop up the demand and again all this without systematically working through the social costs and benefits. Added to this was the fact that while the State was making significant investments in infrastructure sectors like power and road transport, it did not ensure performance efficiencies in these categories and the pricing policies were determined on the basis of short-term considerations while economic and commercial viability was ignored. The net result is that the signaling mechanisms that were created in the system did nothing to promote higher productivity and efficiency. To some extent, the sacrifice of efficiency has been compensated by lower unemployment rates and more geographically dispersed economic development. However, if these benefits are to be sustained in the long run, ignoring efficiency can be ill afforded.

Feedback from Some Industry Representatives and Experts

MSE held discussions with some representatives of industry groups like chemicals, leather, automobiles, textiles and sugar and a few industry consultants to get their opinion on the existing problems and future prospects for these major industry categories. Some of the constraints faced were common to most categories and chief among them was the low quality and high price of power. Chemical industries, with power intensive processes that need continuous supply, are having problems with the low quality of power and in this respect are at a disadvantage compared to those in Gujarat and Maharashtra. In the automobile industry it was stated that about 15 per cent of manufacturing investment had to be spent on captive generation to ensure power supply. Textile spinning units in Tamil Nadu have to pay twice the price compared to those in Kerala. The other major constraint was port facilities. Regarding the restrictions on the scale of operation, while the leather industry and chemical industry representatives felt that these restrictions were constraining them in terms of realising better economies of scale, particularly in the context of pollution control measures to be taken, the exporters of textile products at Tirupur are happy with the restrictions. Some of the industry-specific problems and challenges are as follows.

Chemicals: The regulatory framework in Tamil Nadu is extremely complex compared to Maharashtra and Gujarat. The State bureaucracy here has no control over the vagaries of local body decisions. Research and Development in the pharmaceutical industry is quite expensive and the new patent regime under the World Trade Organisation (WTO) framework will have an impact on the industry here. Tamil Nadu has good deposits of Magnesite and Ilmenite and new industries that could efficiently tap this potential could develop. Biotechnology and Herbogenomics would be good areas where Tamil Nadu has a potential advantage.

Leather: This industry ranks eighth in the country's exports and Tamil Nadu accounts for 15 per cent of it. However, while India has 10 per cent of the world's raw materials it has only a 2 per cent share of the world market. Hong Kong is the largest importer from India followed by Italy. The high levels of pollution generated by this industry brought about its migration from affluent economies to the South. India was a major beneficiary of this in the past. However, with environmental norms in this country becoming more stringent and with environmental standards being imposed by the importing countries the cost burden on these units is increasing. The government regulations restricting the scale of operation in this sector has resulted in 60 to 65 per cent of the production coming from the small and cottage sector. While the restrictions were beneficial in promoting employment, they have placed the units at a disadvantage in terms of realising scale economies in production and in pollution control measures. Today the biggest challenge faced by this industry is the competition from China and Korea. In 1989 India and China had about the same level of leather exports. Today China's exports are ten times that of India's. China has also managed to get foreign investments that support up to 40 per cent of its exports whereas in India it is only 5 per cent. The other major factor is that the market for leather and leather products could shrink considerably with synthetic leather substitutes replacing it.

Handlooms and Textiles: The cooperative spinning mills have had most of their net worth completely eroded and are being kept up largely through government subsidies. This situation cannot be sustained. The handloom sector should focus on cornering niche markets by getting into fashion clothing and catering to export markets in order to survive. This would entail considerable retraining for existing workers in this segment.

Sugar: Sugarcane being a water intensive crop, the inadequacy of surface water available for irrigation and the falling groundwater levels are constraining factors. The cooperative sugar mills are not paying the farmers on time and the arrear payments that are due keep mounting. The revenue sharing mechanism as recommended by the Mahajan Committee might be a worthwhile proposition and this is followed by the cooperatives in Maharashtra and Gujarat. The export market for sugar is quite volatile. The European Union is subsidising its exports and Brazil dumps large quantities in the international market depending on its domestic prices for ethanol. The current world market prices are not attractive enough for Tamil Nadu growers. Sugar is outside the purview of the WTO regulations right now.

Automobiles: Tamil Nadu has been able to attract multinational companies like Ford and Hyundai and this is largely due to the skilled labour force that is available here and the existence of a well developed supply chain for small components needed in the industry. There is considerable export potential that can be tapped by this sector though within the domestic market it is likely to face strong competition from China in the two-wheeler segment.

Tenth Plan Prospects

The Tenth Plan document states that one of its main goals is to make Tamil Nadu the top State among the Indian states in all spheres including industry. To achieve the targeted growth of 8 per cent in GSDP during the Plan and to fulfill the State's vision of doubling per capita income by the end of 2010, industry is expected to grow at 8 per cent.

Upgrading the infrastructure facilities in the State is a major initiative proposed for this Plan period. It indicates that the state government proposes to enact an Infrastructure Development Enabling Act and establish an Infrastructure Development Board. The approach would be to promote public-private partnership in developing infrastructure and the key issue would be designing the right strategy that would attract private investments. Along the lines of the Golden Quadrilateral of national highways linking the four major metropolitan cities in the country, Tamil Nadu is considering a Golden Pentagon to link the major cities within the state. Efforts would also be made to upgrade/develop airport and seaport facilities.

The Plan proposes to take up disinvestments of some state level public undertakings and would explore ways of privatising unviable cooperative manufacturing units. While the Government of India guidelines for disinvestments would largely be followed, the specific decisions would be made on a case-by-case basis. The recommendations of Raghavan Committee Report on State Public Enterprises (1997) would also be taken into account.

The thrust of the Tenth Plan proposals indicate, for the first time since the New Industrial Policy 1991, a proactive strategy to promote an investor-friendly environment and to carry out state level reforms that would liberalise industrial controls and encourage industrial competitiveness. A High Level Committee to be chaired by the Chief Minister and with representatives from various Chambers of Commerce has been set up to periodically review the industrial scenario and suggest necessary policy initiatives.

A small beginning has already been made in the power sector. The State Electricity Regulatory Commission has become effective since June 2002 and for the first time electricity prices have been subject to the Regulatory Commission's scrutiny and approval after going through a process of public hearing. Agricultural consumers are now required to pay a flat rate. Though the charges levied are small and the state government is offering lump sum subsidies as compensation, it is an important first step to mark the end of the free power era. The Commission has also stated that rationalising the present level of cross subsidies from the manufacturing to the agriculture and domestic sectors would be one of its objectives. It proposes to achieve this by allowing much smaller or no increases in the industrial rate while the agricultural rates and domestic rates would be rationalised. Such a measure would significantly help in improving the competitiveness of manufacturing units in Tamil Nadu.

The Tamil Nadu Government has announced a New Industrial Policy in September 2003. The objectives of this policy are to target an 8 per cent growth rate during the Tenth Plan and to reorient government strategy to achieve this goal. The government would undertake second-generation reforms that would include strengthening infrastructure, *including availability of quality energy*, labour reforms, fiscal reforms, restructuring public sector enterprises and business deregulation. Through public-private partnership the government seeks to enable the flow of private capital, domestic and foreign, for building infrastructure. The reoriented government strategy would promote foreign direct investment in new manufacturing capacity and would facilitate efficient performance and growth in the sector based on improved competitiveness.

The Confederation of Indian Industries and the World Bank jointly carried out a firm level survey of more than 1000 firms during 2001 to gauge industry's perception on the climate of manufacturing competitiveness in 10 selected states of India. Tamil Nadu ranks third amongst the 10 states considered, however, with an index of 9 it received compared to 39 by Maharashtra and 23 by Gujarat it is significantly lagging behind the first two States.

The Centre has also been taking many steps to help promote and sustain industrial growth in the liberalising regime. Upgrading technology has been one of the key areas it has concerned itself with. The Ministry of Textiles, Government of India, introduced the Technology Upgradation Fund Scheme (TUFS) in April 1999. With the phasing out of the Multi-Fibre Agreement (MFA) by 2005, there would be enormous potential for expanding the exports of Indian textiles. Indian textile exporters have been focusing on the low value segment so far. In order to capitalise the opportunities arising out of the phasing out of the MFA it is important for them to move up the value chain. Since this calls for significant technological advances in the manufacturing facilities the TUFS aims at providing subsidised finances for this purpose.

Recognising that improving the infrastructure for industries located in clusters would help improve their global competitiveness, the Ministry of Commerce and Industry has drawn up an Industrial Infrastructure Upgradation Scheme (IIUS) in December 2003. This scheme would provide a grant-in-aid to the industrial clusters. Implementation of the scheme will be through a Special Purpose Vehicle (SPV) formed by the cluster/industry association, which will carry out the business of developing, operating and maintaining the infrastructure facility created in the industrial locations.

The Exim Policy of April 2000, paved the way for setting up Special Economic Zones (SEZ) in the country in order to provide an internationally competitive environment for exports. The major requirement of units in this zone is that they should be net foreign exchange earners. In Tamil Nadu the former Madras Export Processing Zone (MEPZ) has been converted into a SEZ. Another SEZ in Nanguneri has been approved and is under implementation.

Opportunities and Challenges Ahead

Among its inherent advantages in tackling the increasingly competitive industrial environment, Tamil Nadu could count its significant proportion of skilled labour (skills ranging from the highly-skilled to semi-skilled), its existing dominant presence on the industrial scene, its fairly diversified industrial base, its relatively good human development index, its large number of educational institutions for technical and higher education, its agricultural resource base and its strong base in the information and communication technology sector. It does lack good metallic mineral resources and conventional energy resources.

An important issue to be addressed is the kind of an industrial development strategy that should be adopted and the State's role in helping achieve this. There exists a pattern in the value creation achieved by different economies, which comprises three stages that telescope into a growth continuum. (Source: Indian Manufacturing Sector – Policy Framework, May 2003, as quoted in a KPMG paper titled 'Indian Manufacturing: Breaking the Myths', October 2003) The first stage is driven by natural resource factors including land, labour and capital and comprises low value adding activities that includes agriculture. The second stage is driven by skill, technology and material improvements and covers the range going from labour intensive to high-tech manufacturing activities. The third stage is knowledge driven and encompasses research and development, innovation and services. The relative position of different economies in this continuum depends on their comparative advantage and their level of economic development. As economies move up the continuum, they tend to outsource the activities at the lower end. Developed economies like the U.S. are predominantly composed of high-value adding manufacturing and services, which they export, while low-end manufacturing products are imported from other countries.

In Tamil Nadu's case its labour intensive industries like textiles, apparel and leather have been a good source of export earning potential, though in recent years the growth in value addition from these categories are facing many challenges. While the Agreement on Textiles and Clothing under the WTO regime will, after 2005, do away with the quota restrictions that existed under the Multi Fibre Agreement and open up markets for these industries, it would also mean facing tougher competition from other developing countries that would gain access to these markets. As for leather, tackling the environmental regulations would significantly increase costs especially given the present scales of operation in the industry. Countries like China are likely to reduce our export market share given their higher level of preparedness. Nonetheless, in the short run these industries could contribute significantly to value addition especially if they could become more efficient players and adapt well to emerging market situations. For the longer term it is important for the State to target locating itself at the high-end of the growth continuum and it has to prepare the ground for it. Tamil Nadu has an advantage in this respect given its sizeable pool of technically skilled labour and its large number engineering and other institutions of higher learning. It could leverage its knowledge base to bring national and international level research into the State. This combined with the advantage that the State has in terms of information and communication technology could possibly enable it to leapfrog to the high-end manufacturing and innovation stage.

One of the key challenges ahead would be effectively balancing employment and income distribution considerations with those of efficient growth under an increasingly competitive environment, especially given our legacy of past policies. Improving productivity levels in manufacturing would necessarily entail trimming the excess labour. Added to this would be the fact that additional labour force would be looking for employment in manufacture if agricultural productivity were to be improved. In the short run unemployment is bound to rise which in turn would increase social and political tensions. In order to tackle this it is important to develop a comprehensive set of short, medium and long-term strategies. *Ad hoc* measures to tackle the problem in the short run may prove counter-productive to the reform process. At the same time this daunting problem cannot be wished away.

In this context the option of unemployment insurance for a specific time frame may be explored as a support mechanism. This might be a socially cheaper option of providing income support than spending additional resources on capital and other inputs, keeping some production activities going and then subsidising their output. The unemployment insurance should be for a limited time frame and should also enable training/retraining labour to improve their chances for re-absorption into the labour force. A detailed analysis of the social costs and benefits of such an insurance scheme would have to be carried out. Even if the unemployment insurance would be a better support mechanism, shifting to this regime cannot be achieved immediately. Hence the government will have to tackle the issue through appropriate reforms in its policies for the small-scale sector. Most of the proposals for reforms so far have been targeting the large-scale sector. There is an urgent need to reform the small-scale sector.

The small-scale units in many industries have been allowed to survive either by statutorily preventing large-scale from operating or by offering huge subsidies. Instead of this the government could consider a strategy of making small-scale operations inherently attractive by designing an alternative form of support system. A key feature of the small-scale segment is that it faces huge transaction costs but has the advantage of low agency costs. There are cost diseconomies especially relating to R&D, information, market access and so on. On the other hand small-scale operations would provide a lot of flexibility in adapting to changing scenarios. And the trade-offs between the advantages and disadvantages would vary considerably across industry types, process-types, regions, market conditions and entrepreneurial capabilities. Given all this the government efforts would best serve the cause by reducing the transaction costs for this category. Access to good information is very costly for this segment and government could focus on promoting efficient information dissemination at reasonable costs. Creating a good database on this sector is hence very important. It could also promote independent R&D facilities and disseminate the R&D output for the benefit of small-scale units. This way it could allow the independent units to *choose* the scale of operation that best suits their specific purposes but at the same time makes the choice of small-scale operations an attractive proposition by reducing the transaction costs.

Another important issue to be addressed is the provision of subsidies. Any form of government intervention and regulation, whether it is to promote and subsidise or it is to restrain and tax, would reduce efficiency. Nonetheless, government intervention is extremely important to tackle income distribution issues, to handle welfare implications of market externalities and imperfections, to take responsibility for provision of public goods and so on. The efficiency of government intervention, in other words how well the interventions achieve the stated objectives with minimal distortions in the system is important. In this context it would help if the state government reforms its policies for subsidies and the mechanisms it uses for disbursements from one that is encouraging waste, inefficiency, unaccountability, leakages and corruption to one that would truly enhance social benefits by minimal distortions. Subsidies are important and could be a very useful tool to promote social welfare provided they are efficient.

Chapter 5

Power

Introduction

Electricity supply in Tamil Nadu is currently the responsibility of the Tamil Nadu Electricity Board (TNEB). The TNEB is a statutory monopoly that was formed in 1957 (then known as the Madras Electricity Board) as a corporate body, in pursuance of the Electricity (Supply) Act 1948. The Electricity Supply Act (ESA) disallowed any *new* private participation in generating or distributing electricity and vested with the State Electricity Boards (SEBs) with the sole responsibility of ensuring coordinated and efficient supply of electricity in their respective states. While the SEBs were autonomous entities, the respective State governments were vested with the authority to oversee their policy decisions.

TNEB ranks among the top three SEBs in the country, along with Maharashtra and Gujarat, in terms of the size of its operation gauged by the generating capacity at its command, the amount of energy sold and the number of consumers serviced. Tamil Nadu ranks sixth in terms of per capita electricity consumption in the states. The technical performance efficiencies of TNEB, measured by the plant load factor and the transmission and distribution losses, have normally been above the All-India average and among the top five to six SEBs. TNEB has been in the forefront of rural electrification. Extending electricity to rural areas and promoting electrification of agricultural pumps have been accorded top priority on TNEB's agenda. As early as 1991 TNEB had reached electricity to all the inhabited villages in Tamil Nadu and the number of electrified agricultural pumps in the State has registered a phenomenal growth.

TNEB's financial record is, however, cause for much concern. Ever since the early-seventies the average revenue realised per unit of electricity sold has been lower than the average cost of supplying a unit, if we do not take into consideration the subsidy provided by the state government. This gap has been widening over the years. The Tamil Nadu government's directive to give free electricity to agricultural pumps and subsidised electricity to a sizeable section of the domestic consumers has been largely responsible for this. The state government is of course committed to provide the necessary subsidies to bridge the gap. But then, as is to be expected, this is hindering capacity expansion in the sector and is also significantly eroding the health of the state finances.

TNEB is of course not alone in being situated in such a predicament. Almost all the SEBs in India are going through financial crises and many of them are in worse shape compared to TNEB. In order to tackle the situation there are ongoing efforts to reform the power sector. At this juncture it might therefore be useful to take a closer look at the performance record of TNEB, analyse its strengths and weaknesses, identify some major issues to be addressed and explore desirable and feasible options available for improvement.

Brief History

Electricity generation in Tamil Nadu began in 1900 when a tea-estate set up a tiny hydroelectric power station to generate electricity for its own consumption. Commercial supply of electricity did not begin till the Binny group of companies set up a thermal power station in Chennai and sold power to the Government press, the General Hospital, the tramways and some residential areas. Till 1927, only private companies undertook commercial supply of electricity and were regulated by the technical requirements and administrative procedures laid out in the Indian Electricity Act (1910).

Electricity Department

In 1927 the Electricity Department was created, as a wing of the State Government, in order to actively boost power development in the State. Generation and transmission of electricity came under the monopoly control of the Department. Retail distribution of electricity was largely taken care of by the Department but there were a few areas that were served by licensees, some private and some local municipalities. Between 1927 and 1947 the Department created 104 MW of hydro generating capacity and between 1947 and 1951 about 52 MW of thermal capacity was added. During the First Plan another 110 MW of generating capacity was created, 64 per cent of which was hydro. The Department was able to generate surpluses after meeting all costs and provisions.

Electricity Board

The Electricity (Supply) Act was passed in 1948 for 'the rationalisation of the production and supply of electricity and generally for taking measures conducive to electrical development'. As per the Act, each state government was required to constitute a State Electricity Board and the responsibility for power supply in the State was to be under its monopolistic control. Existing private or municipal licensees for power distribution were allowed to continue but no new private distributing companies or generating companies could be set up. Apart from the SEBs, the central or state governments could set up generating companies. The Madras Electricity Board was duly formed in 1957 and later it came to be known as the Tamil Nadu Electricity Board.

Growth and Performance of TNEB

Capital Outlay

Successive Five Year Plans of the Tamil Nadu government have allocated sizeable proportions of State Plan outlays for the power sector. The share of power sector outlay in the total went up from about 38 per cent during the First Plan to 42 per cent during the Second and has gradually come down to 24 per cent during the Ninth. On an average over the last 55 years around 25 per cent of the Tamil Nadu Plan outlays have been allocated to the power sector. At the All-India level this share has been about 16.5 per cent. Table 5.1 presents details on the total power sector outlay and the shares of generation, transmission and rural electrification categories in this total. The data provided in this Table are from TNEB's Statistics at a Glance and show some variations from the data given in the State Plan documents. The reason is that the TNEB figures include expenditures outside the Plan and interest during construction for some of the later Plans. The Rajadhyaksha Committee suggested, as a thumb rule for balanced capacity expansion in the power sector, an allocation of 50 per cent of the total investment to generation capacity and 25 per cent each for transmission and distribution. It may be observed from the Table that the share of generation assets was significantly less than 50 per cent during the First and Second Plans, was close to 50 per cent between the Third and Sixth Plans and was nearly 60 per cent during the Seventh Plan. Since the early-nineties this share has been falling and stood at around 30 per cent during the Ninth Plan. The share of rural electrification has been above 25 per cent during the first three Plans and was a record high of 43.5 per cent during the Fourth Plan after which it has been relatively lower, averaging around 14 per cent. The above allocation pattern reiterates the high priority given to rural electrification during the first Four Plan periods, by the

TABLE 5.1

Plan-wise Outlays For Different Categories

Plan Period	*Total Outlay on Power (Rs. Crore)*	*Percentage Share of Total Outlay*		
		Generation	*T&D Network*	*Rural Elec.*
First Plan (1951-56)	30.28	36.99	27.77	33.88
Second Plan (1956-61)	79.17	38.27	25.65	34.84
Third Plan (1961-66)	119.43	46.98	23.03	29.98
Annual Plans (1966-69)	104.06	53.39	16.86	29.6
Fourth Plan (1969-74)	213.89	35.16	20.54	43.5
Fifth Plan (1974-79)	381.82	54.68	25.94	19.08
Annual Plan (1979-80)	158.67	50.28	32.97	16.54
Sixth Plan (1980-85)	953.93	52.95	28.75	17.81
Seventh Plan (1985-90)	2115.24	58.28	28.07	13.27
Annual Plan (1990-91)	498.8	58.63	31.05	9.84
Annual Plan (1991-92)	591.39	48.28	38.54	12.71
Eighth Plan (1992-97)	4584.88	42.29	44.06	13.25
Ninth Plan (Upto 2001)	4922.81	30.4	57.74	11.37

Source: Tamil Nadu Electricity Board - Statistics at a Glance.

end of which time service had been extended to a significant section of the rural areas. Subsequently, the share of this category has been falling. The noticeable fall in generation outlays during the nineties is largely due to the fact that the TNEB increasingly relied on purchasing energy from the central sector generating stations. It also anticipated some generating stations to come up in the private sector, following the amendments made to the ESA in 1991 that allowed for private sector participation in generation.

Installed Capacity

Generation: The installed generating capacity of TNEB has grown from 156 MW in 1950-51 at the beginning of the First Plan to 5,213 MW at the end of 2000-01, at a compound annual growth (CAG) rate of 7.3 per cent (Table 5.2). An additional capacity of 2,300 MW is at the command of TNEB, assigned to it from the central sector generating stations of Neyveli Lignite Corporation (NLC) and National Thermal Power Corporation (NTPC), the nuclear power stations at Kalpakkam and Kaiga and some Independent Power Producers (IPP). The share of TNEB's own capacity in the total generating capacity at its disposal has been around 75 per cent since the end of the Third Plan. Hydro generating capacity accounted for about 70 per cent of the installed capacity during the First Plan period and went up to 80 per cent by the end of the Second Plan. The major sources of hydro potential in the State had been tapped before the early-seventies and

TABLE 5.2

Plan-wise Progress in Generating Capacity

(Figures in MW, as on 31st March)

Year	*TNEB Capacity*			*At the Command of TNEB*						*Co-incident*
	Hydro	*Thermal*	*Gas*	*Wind*	*NLC*	*NTPC*	*NPC*	*IPP*	*Total*	*Peak Demand in M.W.*
1950-51	114	42							156	139
	73.08	**26.92**							**100.00**	
1955-56	174	82							256	178
	67.97	**32.03**							**100.00**	
1960-61	459	112							571	381
	80.39	**19.61**							**100.00**	
1965-66	969	101			300				1370	717/845
	70.73	**7.37**			**21.90**				**100.00**	
1968-69	969	101			400				1470	997
	65.92	**6.87**			**27.21**				**100.00**	
1973-74	1224	347			600				2171	1287
	56.38	**15.98**			**27.64**				**100.00**	
1978-79	1369	540			600				2509	1779
	54.56	**21.52**			**23.91**				**100.00**	
1979-80	1369	750			600				2719	1710
	50.35	**27.58**			**22.07**				**100.00**	
1984-85	1369	1140			600		235		3344	2154
	40.94	**34.09**			**17.94**		**7.03**		**100.00**	
1989-90	1943	1920		14	776	470	350		5473	2929
	35.50	**35.08**		**0.26**	**14.18**	**8.59**	**6.40**		**100.00**	
1990-91	1945	2130		14	835	470	350		5744	3094
	33.86	**37.08**		**0.24**	**14.54**	**8.18**	**6.09**		**100.00**	
1991-92	1945	2340	10	16	909	470	330		6019	3501
	32.31	**38.88**	**0.17**	**0.27**	**15.10**	**7.81**	**5.48**		**100.00**	
1996-97	1948	2970	130	19	1041	470	330		6908	4888
	28.20	**42.99**	**1.88**	**0.28**	**15.07**	**6.80**	**4.78**		**100.00**	
2000-01	1996	2970	228	19	1021	520	364	395	7513	6360
	26.57	**39.53**	**3.03**	**0.25**	**13.59**	**6.92**	**4.84**	**5.26**	**100.00**	

Source: Tamil Nadu Electricity Board - Statistics at a Glance and Annual Administration Reports.

Note: Figures in bold letter show the percentage over total.

NLC - Neyveli Lignite Corporation.

NTPC - National Thermal Power Corporation.

NPC - Nuclear Power Corporation.

IPP - Independent Power Producers.

subsequently coal/lignite based generating capacity was gaining dominance. At the end of 2000-01 coal based thermal generating capacity accounted for 60 per cent while hydro accounted for 27 per cent. The balance was contributed by gas turbines, wind, nuclear and diesel based generating capacity. As of 2000-01 about 2,800 MW of captive generating capacity, set up by some industrial and commercial enterprises, also existed in Tamil Nadu.

Tamil Nadu has been identified as a State with good potential for generating wind-based electricity and the TNEB and the Ministry of Non-Conventional Sources have been taking steps to promote greater use of this non-polluting energy source. TNEB has a provision that any private industry wanting to set up captive generation could set up wind-based generating capacity at appropriate locations, feed the electricity into the grid and draw the energy wherever their industry might be located. As of 2000-01 the private sector has installed about 800 MW of wind-based generating capacity. This is 29 per cent of the total captive generation capacity set up by industries. TNEB has installed 19 MW of wind-based generating capacity.

Transmission and Distribution: TNEB has expanded its transmission and distribution capacity to keep up with the requirements of servicing its increasing number of consumers. Table 5.3 presents the details regarding the growth in number of substations, high tension (HT) lines, low tension (LT) lines and number of distribution transformers as at the end of each Plan period. It also provides information on the number of villages, agricultural pumps and huts electrified.

As mentioned earlier, extending the distribution grid so as to give the residents in rural areas access to electricity and promoting growth in electrical pumps for irrigation purposes has been a priority in Tamil Nadu and for TNEB. TNEB also supplies free electricity to hut-dwellers under its one-hut-one-light scheme. As of 31st March 2001, 15.6 lakh huts and 17.2 lakh agricultural pumps have been connected.

Energy Availability

The total energy available with TNEB for disposal to final consumers grew from 612 million units (mu) at the beginning of the First Plan (1950-51) to 41,764 mu at the end of 2000-01, registering a CAG of 8.8 per cent. Table 5.4 provides details for the final year of each Plan period. During the first two Plan periods TNEB was meeting its total sales entirely from its own generation.

TABLE 5.3

Plan-wise Progress in Distribution Capacity

(as on 31st March)

Year	*No.of Sub-stations*	*Transmission and Distribution Capacity*				*Rural Electrification*		
		EHT Lines (km)	*HT Lines (km)*	*LT Lines (km)*	*Dist.Trans (No.)*	*Villages Electrified*	*Pumpsets Connected*	*Huts Electrified*
1950-51	56	1819	5117	5728	1591	N.A	14373	
1955-56	89	2505	8974	13055	3773	N.A	33440	
1960-61	143	4613	19581	35352	10004	6567	117695	
1965-66	201	7095	32711	73198	17360	9046	256594	
1968-69	233	8103	40233	104977	22842	9578	410119	
1973-74	271	8802	59935	197017	37453	14085	681205	
1978-79	340	9376	65532	235943	46131	15525	846422	
1979-80	356	9625	67501	249226	48595	15550	887227	167297
1984-85	439	11821	75429	278515	63667	15700	1033556	635721
1989-90	492	15119	86905	334824	84225	15813	1277501	887200
1990-91	512	15779	88420	339454	86522	15815	1318671	932286
1991-92	544	16186	90120	342986	90172	15822	1359748	972293
1996-97	734	18257	106734	400896	111522	15822	1567317	1399715
2000-01	913	21041	141483	423000	135457	15822	1722860	1559715

Source: Tamil Nadu Electricity Board - Statistics at a Glance.

Note: EHT - Extra High Tension, HT - High Tension and LT - Low Tension.

TABLE 5.4

Generation, Purchase and Import of Energy

(Figure in MU)

Year	*Gross Generation*					*Purchase*			*Total Import*	*Gross Total*
	Hydro	*Thermal*	*Gas*	*Wind*	*Total*	*Central Sector*	*Private Sector*	*Total*		
1955-56	840	212			1052				370	1422
	59.07	**14.91**							**26.02**	**100.00**
1960-61	1797	416			2213				29	2242
	80.15	**18.55**							**1.29**	**100.00**
1965-66	1978	462			2441	1382		1382	219	4042
	48.94	**11.43**				**34.19**			**5.42**	**100.00**
1968-69	3055	297			3352	1773		1773	136	5261
	58.07	**5.65**				**33.70**			**2.59**	**100.00**
1973-74	3703	1171			4874	1800		1800	274	6948
	53.30	**16.85**				**25.91**			**3.94**	**100.00**
1978-79	4526	2082			6608	1918	15	1933	1970	10511
	43.06	**19.81**				**18.25**	**0.14**		**18.74**	**100.00**
1979-80	5533	2041			7574	1768	11	1779	1061	10414
	53.13	**19.60**				**16.98**	**0.11**		**10.19**	**100.00**
1984-85	4447	4935			9382	4126	4	4130	219	13731
	32.39	**35.94**				**30.05**	**0.03**		**1.59**	**100.00**
1989-90	3326	8515		4	11845	6409	19	6428		18273
	18.20	**46.60**		**0.02**		**35.07**	**0.10**			**100.00**
1990-91	3982	9207		30	13219	7551	23	7574		20793
	19.15	**44.28**		**0.14**		**36.32**	**0.11**			**100.00**
1991-92	4410	9398	1	24	13833	8080	7	8087		21920
	20.12	**42.87**	**0.005**	**0.11**		**36.86**	**0.03**			**100.00**
1996-97	4252	18598	84	19	22953	8979	768	9747		32700
	13.00	**56.87**	**0.26**	**0.06**		**27.46**	**2.35**			**100.00**
2000-01	5450	19464	215	18	25147	11910	4707	16617		41764
	13.05	**46.60**	**0.51**	**0.04**		**28.52**	**11.27**			**100.00**

Note: Figures in bold letter show the percentage over Gross Total.

Starting from the Third Plan, when it started purchasing electricity from NLC, the share of purchased energy in the total energy available has been around 35 per cent. Till the beginning of the Ninth Plan purchases were largely from central sector generating stations. While there was also a small percentage of energy imported from other states between 1965-66 and 1984-85, during the nineties there have been no imports. A negligible percentage was also purchased from a few private industries, where industries that were allowed to set up their own captive generation capacity could sell any excess energy to the TNEB. During the Ninth Plan, however, a couple of independent power producers had set up diesel based generating capacity and sold electricity to TNEB. Hence, it can be seen that the share of electricity purchased from the private sector comprised about 28 per cent of the total purchases of TNEB and purchased power accounted for 40 per cent of total energy available during 2000-01. The share of hydro generation in TNEB's own generation witnessed a rise from 76 per cent during 1950-51 to 91 per cent during 1968-69 after which it has been exhibiting a falling trend. During 2000-01 the share of hydro generation was about 22 per cent. There have been considerable yearly and seasonal variations in this share depending on the success of the monsoons and hence the water availability in the reservoirs.

Consumers and Connected Load

The total number of consumers serviced by TNEB has grown from 7.7 lakh at the end of the Second Plan (1960-61) to about 150 lakh as of March 2002, at a CAG of 7.7 per cent and the connected load also grew at the same rate from 1,294 MW to 26,239 MW. Comparing the consumer and connected load profiles between 1960-61 and 2000-01 it may be observed that the share of industry in the number of consumers and connected load has remained nearly the same. The number of consumers in the services category, which includes commercial as well as government and non-commercial services, has increased its share in the total from 6 per cent to 13 per cent whereas in terms of the connected load it accounted for nearly 12 per cent at both the points of reference. Agriculture has fallen both in terms of its share in the number of consumers and connected load. The proportion of agricultural consumers fell from around 15 per cent in 1960-61 to about 11 per cent in 2000-01 whereas in terms of connected load the share came down from nearly 32 per cent to 24 per cent during the same period. The domestic category on the other hand has witnessed a phenomenal rise in its share of consumers and connected load. This category accounted for 50 per cent of the consumers and 16 per cent of the connected load in 1960-61 but by the end of 2000-01 these rose to 73 per cent and 33 per cent respectively. Details are presented in Table 5.5.

Energy Sales

Table 5.6 presents information on electricity sold by TNEB to different categories of consumers during the final year of each Plan period. It may be observed that the share of electricity consumption by the domestic and agricultural categories has steadily risen while that of the industrial category, after showing an increasing trend up to 1978-79 has been falling since then. The share of consumption by the services category, which includes both government and commercial institutions, has remained more or less stable at around 11 per cent, since the Second Plan. Share of industrial consumption rose from 27 per cent at the end of the First Plan to 50 per cent by the end of the Fourth Plan after which it

TABLE 5.5

Number of Consumers and Connected Load for Different Category

(as on 31st March)

Sl. No.	Category	1960-61		1965-66		1968-69		1973-74		1978-79	
		Consumers (Nos.)	Connected Load (MW)	Consumers (Nos.)	Connected Load (MW)	Consumers (Nos.)	Connected Load (MW)	Consumers (Nos.)	Connected Load (MW)	Consumers (Nos.)	Connected Load (MW)
	HT										
1	Industry	427	222	483	393	703	560	992	750	1238	1120
2	Services	66	76	110	133	184	150	306	189	498	209
3	Licen. & Miscellaneous	165	144	420	456	333	410	182	236	67	475
	Total	658	442	1013	982	1220	1120	1480	1175	1803	1804
	LT										
1	Domestic	385340	210	666996	356	815603	463	1388168	712	1960552	959
2	Agriculture	112369	412	244961	850	392602	1338	680733	2303	840557	2796
3	Industry	16033	128	29025	197	52396	302	86104	503	147304	799
4	Services	47030	79	113445	96	211950	142	430743	301	610197	476
5	Licen. & Miscellaneous	208728	24	303530	4	348642	20	119336	115	10351	13
	Total	769500	852	1357957	1504	1821193	2265	2705084	3935	3568961	5042
	Grand Total (HT+LT)	**770158**	**1294**	**1358970**	**2487**	**1822413**	**3384**	**2706564**	**5110**	**3570764**	**6846**

Sl. No.	Category	1979-80		1984-85		1989-90		1996-97		2000-01	
		Consumers (Nos.)	Connected Load (MW)	Consumers (Nos.)	Connected Load (MW)	Consumers (Nos.)	Connected Load (MW)	Consumers (Nos.)	Connected Load (MW)	Consumers (Nos.)	Connected Load (MW)
	HT										
1	Industry	1248	1133	1659	1562	2311	2082	3872	3428	4493	3613
2	Services	494	249	589	301	477	292	795	424	878	466
3	Licen. & Miscellaneous	119	470	68	174	83	150	107	26	108	27
	Total	1861	1851	2316	2036	2871	2525	4774	3877	5479	4105
	LT										
1	Domestic	2192144	1154	3569082	1812	5221677	2883	8022027	5523	10921186	8751
2	Agriculture	881174	3015	1000685	3404	1203275	4101	1439711	5193	1651399	6169
3	Industry	154612	890	191669	1434	245839	1953	337511	3057	416569	4437
4	Services	615339	507	750696	726	1002151	999	1424134	1717	1955086	2540
5	Licen. & Miscellaneous	152310	13	27409	48	47225	267	28940	271	31499	237
	Total	3995579	5580	5539541	7424	7720167	10203	11252323	15761	14975739	22134
	Grand Total (HT+LT)	**3997440**	**7431**	**5541857**	**9460**	**7723038**	**12728**	**11257097**	**19638**	**14981218**	**26239**

Source: Tamil Nadu Electricity Board — Annual Administration Reports.

TABLE 5.6

Category-Wise Sale of Power

(Figure in MU)

Sl. No.	Particulars	1955-56	1960-61	1965-66	1968-69	1973-74	1978-79	1979-80	1984-85	1989-90	1990-91	1991-92	1996-97	2000-01
1	Domestic	64	100	141	192	316	635	723	1348	2498	2632	2784	4181	7176
		5.27	**5.67**	**4.29**	**4.52**	**5.90**	**7.64**	**9.04**	**12.56**	**17.56**	**16.21**	**16.21**	**16.20**	**21.47**
2	Services	73	206	331	363	426	812	858	1121	1567	1455	1431	2709	4050
		6.01	**11.67**	**10.07**	**8.55**	**7.96**	**9.77**	**10.72**	**10.44**	**11.01**	**8.96**	**8.33**	**10.50**	**12.12**
3	Industries	325	766	1466	2081	2334	4134	3878	5190	6374	7026	7248	10617	11751
		26.75	**43.40**	**44.61**	**49.01**	**43.59**	**49.75**	**48.46**	**48.35**	**44.80**	**43.27**	**42.21**	**41.14**	**35.16**
4	Agriculture	93	366	786	1074	1576	2118	2133	2415	3190	3974	4451	6910	9095
		7.65	**20.74**	**23.92**	**25.29**	**29.43**	**25.49**	**26.66**	**22.50**	**22.42**	**24.47**	**25.92**	**26.78**	**27.22**
5	Miscellaneous	660	327	562	536	703	610	410	661	598	1152	1259	1388	1346
		54.32	**18.53**	**17.10**	**12.62**	**13.13**	**7.34**	**5.12**	**6.16**	**4.20**	**7.09**	**7.33**	**5.38**	**4.03**
	Total	1215	1765	3286	4246	5355	8309	8002	10735	14227	16239	17173	25805	33418
		100.00	**100.00**	**100.00**	**100.00**	**100.00**	**100.00**	**100.00**	**100.00**	**100.00**	**100.00**	**100.00**	**100.00**	**100.00**

Source: Tamil Nadu Electricity Board — Statistics at a Glance and Annual Administration Reports.

Note: Figures in bold letter show the percentage value over total.
Services includes commercial, public lighting and water works, railways traction and department works and other projects.
Industries includes Cottage Industries.
Miscellaneous includes bulk supply to licensees, sales to other States and miscellaneous sale.

was declining and was about 35 per cent during 2000-01. Agricultural consumption has accounted for about 25-27 per cent since the Second Plan whereas domestic consumption has registered a consistent and significant growth in its share, increasing from about 5 per cent at the end of the First Plan to about 21 per cent during 2000-01. This pattern of consumption broadly reflects the pricing policy adopted by TNEB at the behest of the state government. Domestic and agricultural consumption have been receiving increasing subsidies over the years. Since the mid-eighties electricity is being supplied for agricultural consumption free of charge. In the domestic category an increasing block pricing system is adopted and hence while groups with lower monthly consumption levels are subsidised those with higher consumption levels are charged a little more than it costs to serve them. Industrial and commercial categories consuming at the HT level have been charged the highest so as to partly cross subsidise the agricultural consumption. These categories have also had to bear the brunt of power cuts when shortages arose. Many consumers in these categories have invested in captive generation in order to partly make up the shortfall in TNEB's supply.

Technical Performance Efficiencies

The technical performance efficiencies of TNEB can be judged in terms of the transmission and distribution (T&D) losses, the system load factor, the plant load factor (PLF), plant availability factor, auxiliary consumption, fuel consumption, employee-consumer ratio as well the quality of electricity supplied and its being available on demand. The T&D losses incurred by TNEB were 12.4 per cent of the total energy available at the end of the First Plan period. This rose to 21 per cent by the end of the Fourth Plan after which it has gradually declined and stood at 16.5 per cent during 2000-01 (Table 5.7).

This is the lowest rate of loss reported by any SEB at the All-India level during the same year. It must be noted here that the T&D losses reported is an estimate. This is because electricity consumption by agricultural pumps and by hut dwellers is not metered since power is supplied free of charge to these categories. As a result the unaccounted amount of energy in the system actually comprises technical T&D losses, consumption by agriculture, by hut dwellers and any illegal drawing of power from the system. However, discussions with people both in TNEB and some experts outside TNEB indicate that the technical T&D losses are a fairly realistic estimate. Though TNEB's losses in comparison with other SEBs are low, 16 per cent is still high for a system of its size and load. It should be feasible to bring this down to around 10 per cent if appropriate measures are taken.

The system load factor, which basically measures the efficiency of capacity utilisation between peak and off-peak times, has been quite high for TNEB. During the sixties and seventies the system load factor was above 60 per cent, during the eighties it was a little above 70

TABLE 5.7

Sale of Energy and Line Loss

(Figure in MU)

Year	Gross Total	Auxiliary Consumption	Kadampari Pumping	Sales Within State	Sales Other State	Total Sales	Line Loss	% Line Loss
1955-56	1422	22		1227		1227	173	12.40
1960-61	2242	64		1785		1785	393	18.10
1965-66	4042	55		3301		3301	686	17.20
1968-69	5261	45		4282		4282	934	17.90
1973-74	6948	163		5355		5355	1430	21.08
1978-79	10511	305		7941	368	8309	1897	18.58
1979-80	10414	312		7887	302	8189	1913	18.93
1984-85	13731	530		10495	240	10735	2466	18.68
1989-90	18273	815	10	14124	103	14227	3221	18.45
1990-91	20793	860	26	16117	122	16239	3668	18.40
1991-92	21920	887		17040	133	17173	3860	18.35
1996-97	32700	1635	17	25598	207	25805	5243	16.90
2000-01	41764	1672	71	33207	211	33418	6603	16.50

Source: Tamil Nadu Electricity Board - Statistics at a Glance and Annual Administration Reports.

per cent and during the nineties it has been as high as 75 per cent. The way this is achieved, however, is by restricting the hours of supply for some consumer groups. The load from agricultural pumps in relation to TNEB's system capacity is quite high. While the installed generating capacity of TNEB is about 7500 MW, the connected load for agriculture is 6169 MW as on 2000-01. Hence TNEB restricts supply to this category only during off-peak hours and that too by dividing the consumers into two groups and allowing supply to each on a rotational basis. Given that the TNEB neither charges for nor even meters the consumption by this group, this is the only option available to manage the system load. The unfortunate fallout of this arrangement is that industrial and other consumers who are connected to some of the rural feeders would also be able to avail power only during these restricted hours.

The plant load factor and the plant availability, which measure efficiency in utilising generating plants, have been, on an average, fairly high for the thermal plants operated by TNEB. The PLF for TNEB's thermal plants has generally been higher than the All-India average and during the year 2000-01 it ranks among the top five. Some of TNEB's thermal plants have been recipients of the Central Meritorious Productivity Reward for many years. Auxiliary consumption (electricity consumed in generating stations) and fuel consumption rates have been within reasonable ranges though there is some scope for improvement. As for the number of consumers served and the number of electricity units generated per employee TNEB's performance has been close to the All-India average.

In terms of the availability of power, starting from the late-seventies till 1992 TNEB had to impose periodic power cuts ranging from 15 per cent to 60 per cent of the maximum demand and/or energy consumption. The large industrial consumers drawing power at the HT level were generally the worst hit during times of shortages. Often the shortages occurred when the hydro reservoirs had depleted storages. Starting from 1992 there have been no announced power cuts because additional thermal generating facilities created during the nineties have been able to provide the back up. However, there have been frequent unannounced interruptions to supply and the imbalances between demand and supply have resulted in lower frequency cycles and significant voltage fluctuations. As of 2001-02 the deficit in peak power availability is between 10-13 per cent and the energy deficit is about 2 per cent, as estimated by TNEB. The magnitude of shortfall in supply can be gauged by the amount of captive generating capacity installed by consumers and their utilisation intensity as well as pending applications for new connections. In the agricultural category, while about 16.5 lakh pumps have been electrified, applications for another 5 lakh pumps is still pending.

Electricity Pricing

TNEB being a Statutory monopoly, fixing the appropriate set of prices for different categories of consumption is an important exercise. The prices fixed would reflect the larger set of criteria that the monopoly chooses to satisfy. The ESA initially required the SEBs to earn, after meeting all expenses, 'such' surplus as specified by the state government. In other words the respective state governments could decide on the rate of return that the SEBs should target to achieve while deciding on the prices. Given this, TNEB's electricity pricing has largely been driven by the priorities of the Tamil Nadu government. Most often these objectives were in conflict with the efficiency criteria for the utility's performance. During the early years of the Board's operation (till the late-sixties) efforts were made to satisfy the state government's priorities subject to earning some positive return on the investments made. Starting with the seventies, earning positive returns on investment was no longer considered a binding constraint and increasingly the efficiency criteria were given the go by. The ESA was later amended in 1988 requiring all SEBs to earn a three per cent return on the net fixed assets. However, this did not alter the basic pricing policy followed by TNEB. It only increased the magnitude of the subsidy TNEB claimed from the state government.

The consumers were divided into two major groups of HT and LT consumers and within each of these they were basically classified according to the nature of their uses into industry, commercial, domestic and agriculture. There were a few other categories (tea estates, textile industries, lift irrigation etc.) that were essentially sub-groups of these four major categories but were charged slightly different rates. During the early years of its operation TNEB was facing declining average and marginal costs. Higher growth in electricity demand and increasing energy consumption meant realising greater economies and hence falling unit costs. TNEB was therefore interested in encouraging higher consumption levels. Electricity pricing for many consumer categories was of a declining block structure - consumption at higher levels was charged lower prices. The declining block structure was applied to energy consumed by both HT and LT consumers. The HT consumers were also charged on a declining block basis for the maximum power drawn by them. The rates per unit of energy consumed were smaller for the HT consumers than for the LT consumers. This was in tune with the fact that it cost less to supply a unit of power at the HT level compared to the LT level. Prior to the formation of an integrated grid for supply, different rates were charged for areas supplied by hydro stations and for those supplied by thermal stations based on the differing costs of supply. Once these areas got interconnected through a common grid the price differentials were generally removed. The TNEB however, charged different rates of electricity taxes for erstwhile hydro and thermal areas and also imposed a fuel surcharge in the thermal areas.

The agricultural consumers, however, were charged a much lower rate per unit compared to other LT consumers though it cost the most to serve this category. This structure of rates basically continued till the late-seventies with a few upward revisions to accommodate increases in fuel prices and other costs. The prices for agricultural consumers increased at a much slower rate compared to all other consumer categories. The rate increases in electricity prices were however smaller than the increases in general prices for the same period.

By the late-seventies the TNEB had exploited most of its cost economies and electricity had become established as a superior form of energy for various uses. TNEB did away with the declining block rates in 1979 and charged a uniform rate per unit for all levels of consumption. It also did away with the hydro and thermal areas differences in electricity taxes and fuel surcharges. A metro area levy was introduced instead. In the case of agriculture, the rate per unit for smaller farmers was frozen at the previous level while that for large farmers was revised marginally upward. The difference between the lower rate per unit for HT and higher rate per unit for LT consumers also narrowed some. The HT consumers were charged slightly more than it cost to serve them while the LT consumers were charged less. The underlying rationale for rate fixing became that charges should be based on what 'the traffic could bear'. Price increases were bigger for more inelastic consumption categories.

The rate revision of 1984 introduced free supply of electricity for small farmers and for the large farmers the rate per unit was replaced by an annual charge based on the size of the connected load. In 1990 the rate per unit for the HT categories became much higher than that for the LT. This was because the HT consumers were made to partly cross-subsidise the free supply for agriculture. For the domestic category an increasing block rate structure was introduced with the objective of subsidising low-income consumers and making the high-income ones partly pay for it. The 1995 rate revision introduced increasing block rates for the LT industrial category as well. There were more frequent rate revisions during the nineties and while the agricultural consumers and hut dwellers were given

TABLE 5.8

Financial Performance

(Rs in Crore)

Sl. No.	Details	1965-66	1968-69	1973-74	1978-79	1979-80	1984-85	1989-90	1990-91	1991-92	1996-97	2000-01
A	**Revenue Receipts**											
1	By Sale of Power	32.90	46.79	89.42	217.37	239.25	546.80	1044.21	1386.28	1624.64	4436.02	7425.07
2	By Miscellaneous Revenue	1.77	3.43	2.09	12.47	14.98	11.62	24.58	61.58	52.37	54.47	153.03
3	By Subsidy			22.77	26.41	29.96	146.58	579.27	482.65	350.03	586.51	1693.21
	Total (A)	**34.67**	**50.22**	**114.28**	**256.25**	**284.19**	**705.00**	**1648.06**	**1930.51**	**2027.04**	**5077.00**	**9271.31**
B	**Revenue Expenditure**											
1	Power Purchase	9.16	11.07	19.00	80.53	73.32	166.22	358.44	448.47	512.55	979.20	3134.16
2	Operation & Maintenance Charges	10.67	13.89	50.28	114.31	140.12	395.11	948.86	1092.35	984.33	3030.79	4537.85
3	Interest Charges	10.31	14.26	23.40	34.63	38.20	95.09	202.53	224.47	168.49	422.27	643.60
4	Depreciation Charges	3.53	8.23	15.23	20.80	23.54	39.87	80.00	93.05	108.78	315.11	567.83
	Total (B)	**33.67**	**47.45**	**107.91**	**250.27**	**275.18**	**696.29**	**1589.83**	**1858.34**	**1774.15**	**4747.37**	**8883.44**
C	**Net Surplus**											
1	Without Subsidy)	1.00	2.77	–16.40	–20.43	–20.95	–137.87	–521.04	–410.48	–97.14	–256.88	-1305.34
2	With Subsidy			6.37	5.98	9.01	8.71	58.23	72.17	252.89	329.63	387.87
D	**Net Fixed Assets**	**162.00**	**215.00**	**364.00**	**478.00**	**574.00**	**904.00**	**2443.00**	**2856.00**	**3005.00**	**6078.00**	**7771.00**
E	**Return on Net Fixed Assets**											
1	Without Subsidy	0.62	1.29	–4.51	–4.27	–3.64	–14.54	–21.33	–14.37	–3.23	–4.23	–16.80
2	With Subsidy	0.62	1.29	1.75	1.25	1.57	0.92	2.38	2.53	8.42	5.42	4.99
F	**Average Cost/Unit**	**10.20**	**11.08**	**20.15**	**30.12**	**33.60**	**64.86**	**111.75**	**114.44**	**103.31**	**183.97**	**249.68**
G	**Average Revenue/Unit**	**10.50**	**11.73**	**17.09**	**27.66**	**31.05**	**52.02**	**72.34**	**86.20**	**95.70**	**172.00**	**216.95**

Source: Tamil Nadu Electricity Board - Annual Administration Reports.

free supply the HT industrial and commercial groups were paying increasingly higher prices compared to what it cost to supply them. In fact the rate charged to HT industry during the 2001 revision is even higher than the cost of captive generation using diesel sets.

Financial Performance

Table 5.8 presents some details relating to the financial performance of TNEB for the last year of each Plan period starting from the Third Plan. Since the early-seventies, the net surplus for TNEB has been negative, if the subsidy claimed from the government is not taken into account. The gap between the average cost and average revenue per unit sold has been widening. Average revenue per unit fell short of average cost by about 3 paise during the seventies.

This gap increased during the eighties and was as high as 39.41 paise during 1989-90. After registering an improvement during the early-nineties when it fell to about 5.66 paise during 1991-92 it worsened again and during 2000-01 average revenue fell short of average cost by about 39 paise. The average cost here is taken to be the total revenue expenses incurred by TNEB per unit of electricity sold, rather than the cost per unit at the LT end as is considered in some reports.

During the sixties the return on net fixed assets (NFA) was positive, though it was very low, at 0.62 per cent during 1965-66 and 1.29 per cent during 1968-69. During the seventies the average return on NFA was about (-) 4 per cent and the picture worsened considerably during the eighties. In 1989-90, the return on NFA was as low as (-) 21.33 per cent. There was a significant improvement during the Eighth Plan when the return was between (-) 3 to (-) 4 per cent. By the year 2000-01, the situation had worsened again and the return on NFA was (-) 16.8 per cent. If the subsidy claimed from the state government is taken into account the return on NFA has been positive. It was below 2 per cent till the late-eighties and subsequent to the 1988 amendment of the ESA, requiring a 3 per cent return on NFA, the subsidies claimed have ensured a return of 3 per cent or more.

Performance Review

The above account of TNEB's growth and performance indicate that in comparison with other SEBs it has been an above average performer. This relative achievement is however no cause for celebration simply because the average performance of the power sector in India has been abysmally low on various fronts. In an absolute sense there is considerable scope for improvement in TNEB's performance. The inadequacies of the power sector in Tamil Nadu have acted as impediments for better industrial and overall economic growth. Also the indicators of the power sector's performance presented above do not fully capture the externalities that its policies and performances have imposed on the State economy.

The many ills of TNEB can probably be traced to two basic sources: one is the nature of the institutional arrangement in terms of how decision-making authority, risks and responsibilities etc. are distributed and the other is the manner in which the State government has sought to subsidise the consumption of certain consumer groups.

The institutional arrangement for power supply that is basically outlined by the ESA has the following problems: (i) The funding that is made available to the SEBs is not in any way tied to its performance efficiencies. Funds are made available through government budgetary allocations either as grants or as loans at subsidised interest rates. Loans from financial institutions were also available at subsidised rates during the earlier years. (ii) The management of the SEB neither has autonomy in making policy decisions nor is it held accountable for performance standards. (iii) The policy-making authority, typically the State government, does not directly bear any risk related to its policy decisions. On the other hand the party in power has the potential to indulge in different forms of financial and political rent seeking. The negative impacts of bad policies are felt over much longer horizons and with considerable lag whereas the decision-makers can realise significant short-term 'rents'. These factors have basically been responsible for not stemming the increasing slack in the system that is reflected in overstaffing, delays in project execution, unjustifiable cost increases, leakages and in poor quality and insufficient quantity of electricity supply.

Tamil Nadu's subsidy scheme for agricultural consumers initially started with charging a lower rate per unit for small farmers. The idea was to help low-income farmers who depended entirely on farming for a livelihood and who were realising very meager profit margins, that too with considerable uncertainties. Over the years this subsidy has been extended to all farmers-rich and poor, large and small. The State government has required TNEB to periodically announce subsidies on an *ad hoc* basis without any considerations whatsoever for the costs involved and the benefits realised. The State government also specified annual targets in terms of the number of agricultural pumps to be energised, number of huts to be given free supply etc, again not looking at the efficiency implications of such decisions. The government however was committed to making good the corresponding losses to TNEB by transferring funds from the state's finances. The subsidy amount to be claimed from the government each year was earlier determined by TNEB as follows: electricity sold to agricultural consumers is 'estimated'. This is because agricultural consumption is not metered, since TNEB saw no merit in spending resources on installing and maintaining meters and measuring the actual consumption when no revenue was forthcoming from this category. Based on the estimated agricultural consumption and the cost per unit incurred in serving this category TNEB would work out the subsidy to be claimed from the government. Subsequent to the 1988 amendment to the ESA, which required all SEBs to earn at least 3 per cent return on net fixed assets, the subsidy amount to be claimed was estimated so as to ensure a minimum return of 3 per cent on net fixed assets.

Thus on the one hand policies on subsidies have been announced without any analysis of the costs and benefits involved. These policies have created a lot of negative externalities. Agricultural consumers have no idea of the costs they impose on the system by their consumption. Their not having to pay even a proportion of these costs has encouraged indiscriminate use of the groundwater potential. This has resulted in falling groundwater tables in many areas, seawater intrusion in coastal zones and increased soil salinity in some areas. Falling ground water tables have also made it costlier for small farmers to access the water. As a result markets for water have sprung up where the small farmers end up buying water from the large farmers. Free access to electricity has also, as is to be expected, encouraged a phenomenal growth in the demand from this category. The proportion of consumption by non-subsidised categories is falling and that of the subsidised category rising. Given its negative internal resources and given limits to the budgetary funds available, TNEB is unable to expand and maintain its capacity to keep up with the growth in demand. This has resulted in deteriorating quality of service and in shortages.

The manner in which the subsidies are estimated as a residual amount and transferred from the state finances to TNEB also provides a convenient cover-up for a lot of inefficiencies on the part of the utility. There is no incentive or compulsion for the utility to minimise costs. A lot of inefficiencies can be swept under the carpet of 'agricultural subsidies'. Since a sizeable proportion of consumption is not metered it provides incentives for illegal consumption of power. The unaccounted energy in the system comprises the following: consumption by agricultural consumers, consumption by hut-dwellers, technical transmission and distribution losses and illegal consumption of power. Given this it is very difficult for TNEB to arrive at accurate estimates for all these categories and also to check illegal consumption of electricity. The figures given for agricultural consumption are probably overestimates as the following analysis indicates.

The subsidy policy obviously has a strong adverse impact on the financial health of TNEB and the State government. The shortfalls in the revenue account of TNEB are eating into the capital outlays for capacity expansion. Increasing proportions of the State government's borrowings are being used up to cover revenue gaps (arising due to electricity and other subsidies) rather than to create investments. There is also considerable opacity in the manner in which the subsidy amount is presented in the financial statements. The 'subsidy' item that is shown in the revenue receipts of TNEB is not necessarily the actual subsidy amount that is transferred from the State government. It is in fact 'subsidy claimed' from the government. This subsidy that is due from the government is adjusted against the interest payments that TNEB owes the State government. The unadjusted amounts of subsidies are accumulated and shown on the balance sheet as an asset.

Tenth Plan Prospects

The Working Group Report for power development in Tamil Nadu during the Tenth Plan (2002-07) states "the power system planning has become considerably complex today because of uncertainties in load growth, demand, flow of funds, cost recovery from the consumers and purchases from central sector and independent power utilities". This statement aptly sums up the prospects faced by the power sector in Tamil Nadu today. Most other SEBs in India are more or less in a similar predicament.

In Tamil Nadu's case it is difficult at this juncture to forecast the growth in the demand of different consumer groups in the coming decade with a fair degree of accuracy, unless a very detailed demand forecasting exercise is undertaken. The main reason for this is that the system is in a state of flux. The many problems facing the sector have been acknowledged and there is recognition of the need for reforms. What direction and shape these reforms take would have a strong bearing on the growth and composition of demand.

The share of industrial consumption in the total energy consumed has been falling and this category also is among the highest paying groups. The rate per unit charged to this category is currently higher than the cost of captive generation. Using captive generation however involves significant inconvenience costs. If industries are offered good quality of power by the utility even at slightly higher prices than captive generation costs they may opt to take supply from the utility. If the quality is variable and if there are shortages in the quantity supplied then more industries may shift to captive generation. During the last few Plans industrial consumers were encouraged to set up captive generation and the TNEB offered to buy any excess power available. Cogeneration facilities wherever feasible and wind-based generating facilities were particularly promoted. However, at present, given its financial constraints, TNEB is understood to have discontinued the offer.

The growth in agricultural consumption is likely to slow down compared to previous Plans. Table 5.9 presents some information on irrigated areas and the share of electrical pumps in the total over the past Plan periods. The gross cropped area as a percentage of net-cropped area has remained stable at around 120 per cent since the late-eighties. The gross irrigated area as a proportion of gross cropped area has steadily gone up from about 38 per cent at the beginning of the First Plan to 55 per cent during 1999-2000. Area irrigated by wells as a proportion of net irrigated area has also gone up from 24 per cent in 1950-51 to about 50 per cent during 1999-2000. The proportion of electric pumps in the total number of agricultural pumps has fallen from 83 per cent during 1978-79 to 78 per cent during 1999-2000. This fall may be due to shortages in supply of electricity resulting in long waiting periods to get a connection and in reduction of the duration of supply.

While improved supply conditions may increase the proportion of electric pumps, the area irrigated by wells may not grow at very high rates because of falling water tables. Moreover, if the subsidies currently offered are rationalised and targeted more effectively to the really needy consumers, one could expect a drop in the growth rates on this count also. Domestic and commercial consumption would probably continue to grow as in the recent past.

TABLE 5.9

Area Irrigated By Electric Pumps

Year	*Gross Cropped Area/Net Cropped Area*	*Gross Area Irri./Gross Cropped Area*	*Area Irri.by Well/Net Area Irri.*	*E.P/ Total*	*D.P/ Total*
1950-51	113.64	37.74	23.75		
1955-56	119.68	43.09	23.50		
1960-61	122.08	44.20	24.28		
1965-66	119.08	44.98	27.48		
1968-69	117.37	44.72	30.23		
1973-74	123.86	48.03	32.93		
1978-79	122.93	49.69	37.21	82.51	17.49
1979-80	123.83	51.61	37.45	82.81	17.19
1984-85	122.46	49.47	38.15	81.94	18.06
1989-90	120.48	44.63	46.81	77.24	22.76
1990-91	118.88	43.64	44.61	77.22	22.78
1991-92	121.85	46.68	44.82	76.30	23.70
1996-97	117.69	51.84	48.70	77.46	22.54
1999-2000	119.30	55.00	48.91	77.86	22.14

Source: Season and Crop Report - Department of Economics and Statistics, Chennai-6.

Note: E.P. - Electric Pumpsets, D.P. - Diesel Pumpsets.

The Central Electricity Authority's projections made for Tamil Nadu based on the 16th power survey anticipates a 5.3 per cent growth in both energy requirement and peak demand. The energy consumption based on this is expected to be about 55,000 mu and the peak demand to be 8847 MW during 2006-07. TNEB's estimates have projected the anticipated peak demand in 2006-07 to be lower at 7668 MW. TNEB expects 2650 MW of additional generating capacity to be installed during the Tenth Plan but states that this is an optimistic estimate. A more realistic estimate is 1576 MW. Of this TNEB would install 500 MW, mostly hydro and gas, 826 MW would be available from Central sector stations and 250 MW would be from the private producer in Neyveli. If these additions get commissioned as planned then TNEB expects to be able to meet its projected peak demands without any deficit, if the 500 MW cushion requirement is waived. If this cushion has to be included then peak availability could fall short of requirement by 129 MW in 2006-07.

Power Sector Reforms

If the existing inefficiencies in the power sector in India are not tackled, the detrimental impact on the economy is likely to increase exponentially. Efforts are currently being made to bring about reforms in this sector, both by the Centre and by some State governments. However, even after a decade of these efforts no significant improvements have been witnessed so far. In fact the remedy seems worse than the ailment in some cases. At this juncture it would hence be useful to critically evaluate the ongoing reform process and examine the issues and options that are available for Tamil Nadu.

Ongoing Reforms in India

The current reform process effectively started with the amendment of the Electricity Supply Act in 1991, which allowed private sector participation in power generation. The immediate reason was that many of the SEBs and State governments were facing a severe resource crunch situation and were unable to provide for sufficient capacity expansion in the system. In order to attract private investment into a sector that is financially very weak it was necessary to offer very attractive incentives. The prospective private companies were allowed to have 100 per cent foreign equity, a debt-equity ratio of 4:1, were guaranteed a minimum return of 16 per cent and could effectively earn up to 32 per cent post tax return on equity in the currency of investment. Initially, the State governments and SEBs were allowed to enter into negotiated contracts with Independent Power Producers (IPPs) without competitive bidding. After 1995, the Central Government insisted on the competitive bidding route to allow IPPs. Some of the contracts (Power Purchase Agreements, (PPA)) that SEBs entered into with these IPPs were offered guarantees by the State government and counter-guarantees by the Central government. Subsequent contracts were allowed escrow facilities.

At first there was an enthusiastic response to these policy changes and about 243 contracts were signed for a capacity addition of 90,000 MW, which was more than the total capacity existing in the country at that time. However, only a handful of these resulted in actual capacity addition of about 6000 MW. Moreover, some of the power purchase agreements have run into rough weather and the case of the Maharashtra State Electricity Board's contract with Enron, which set up the Dabhol Power Company, is a major example. The main reason for the non-realisation and cancellation of these contracts is obviously the financial ill-health of the SEBs and the inability of the State and Central governments to not only offer fresh guarantees but also to honour existing ones. It was then realised that more fundamental changes in the institutional arrangement were needed.

The next phase of reforms started with the breaking up and restructuring of Orissa State Electricity Board in 1995. This programme was undertaken under the guidance and financial assistance provided by the World Bank. The approach was to 'unbundle' the vertically integrated statutory monopoly into separate entities that would be responsible for generation, transmission and distribution, to convert these into corporations and then to privatise the corporations. It was felt that breaking up the OSEB into smaller entities would make it easier to improve their technical and financial performance. The restructuring process in Orissa was on the lines of the UK experiment and the underlying rationale was to introduce competitive forces, wherever feasible, into the sector. A regulatory commission was set up to oversee the operations of the unbundled entities, to regulate the natural monopoly segments and to ensure competition in the other segments.

The Central Government passed The Electricity Regulatory Commissions Act in 1998 'for the establishment of a Central Electricity Regulatory Commission and State Electricity Regulatory Commissions, for rationalisation of electricity tariffs, transparent policies regarding subsidies and promotion of efficient and environmentally benign policies'. This Act *required* the Central Government to set up an Electricity Regulatory Commission and specified that the State government may, *if it deems fit*, establish the State Electricity Regulatory Commission. Subsequently the Central Electricity Regulatory Commission was set up and a few states took the initiative to set up state level Regulatory Commissions. Also, following the Orissa experiment a few other SEBs (Haryana, Andhra Pradesh, Uttar Pradesh) stared the unbundling process.

While the reforms process had been set in motion the progress has been very slow. The response from many states has been indifferent or lackadaisical. The Ministry of Power (MoP) has been taking some efforts to give more steam to the process. A meeting of Chief Ministers in 1996 came up with a Common Minimum National Action Plan that chalked out a series of measures to be undertaken including metering all consumption and charging agricultural consumption at least a minimum of Rs. 0.50. The Accelerated Power Development Programme (APDP) was initiated to work on improving the technical efficiencies at the distribution level. This was later transformed into the Accelerated Power Development and Reforms Programme (APDRP) by which the funding provided by the Central government was linked to measures undertaken by the State governments and SEBs to bring about reforms in the sector. The MoP has signed a Memorandum of Understanding with many state governments wherein a joint commitment is made to the reform process and the specific measures and time frame are spelt out.

Evaluation

It has obviously been a painfully slow and a terribly bumpy ride for the reforms process in the Indian power sector and apart from the fact that we have at least launched on this path, there is little else that is very encouraging at this juncture. It is therefore important to take stock and identify the problems so that the situation can be improved.

Firstly, whatever the immediate factors that prompted the initial measures undertaken, the underlying rationale of the process has been to introduce competitive forces into the system wherever feasible so that cost efficiency and greater transparency of information can be brought about. The major restructuring effort undertaken in the UK has been the model for this. While the reforms in UK initially brought down electricity prices (in real terms) and increased flexibility and options, there are questions as to whether these have been achieved at higher transaction costs. Moreover, given the limited number of players in terms of the generating and distributing companies and the integrated nature of their operations, there are definite possibilities for an oligopolistic market and regulating such a market has its own inefficiencies. It is not clear yet whether, on balance, the increased efficiency and transparency combined with the increased transaction costs of maintaining competition through appropriate regulatory measures outweigh the economies of vertical integration. Thus the desirability of unbundling in principle is not unambiguous.

As far as implementation is concerned, it must be recognised that the basic conditions have been quite different in our case compared to the UK. The power sector in the UK was not deeply in the red while most of the utilities in India are making huge losses. The price structure was not as distorted and there were no subsidies of the kind and magnitude that have been offered here. Moreover, given the nature and composition of the demand and generating options, given the developed nature of the market system in the UK and the techno-economic viability, spot markets for trading electricity could be set up. More importantly, a strong, effective and *independent* regulatory authority was put in place that could effectively monitor and enforce necessary measures to maintain competition and regulate the non-competitive segments. In the Indian context the current imbalances in the sector are sizeable. Also, given our own socio-political, institutional and economic constraints, the UK model is not being adopted in its entirety. And unless the model is adopted in its entirety even the potential for introducing competition does not exist. What has happened in fact is that, on the one hand the SEBs have been locked into very costly and inflexible power purchase agreements that have not only further eroded their financial health but have also hampered their operational efficiencies, by not being able to operate their generation pool on a merit-ordering (least cost) basis. On the other hand they are severely handicapped in rationalising their price structure and removing unjustified subsidies because the State governments do not have the political will to face the repercussions.

The Electricity Act, 2003

In order to bring about a qualitative transformation of the power sector through a new paradigm, the Electricity Bill was introduced in the Lok Sabha in August 2001 and it was subsequently referred to the Standing Committee on Energy for examination and report. The Committee submitted its Report in December 2002. The Bill has been passed by the Lok Sabha in April 2003 and the Rajya Sabha in May 2003. The Act is meant to consolidate the existing laws relating to generation, transmission, distribution, trading and use of electricity. Its objective is to protect the interest of consumers and towards this end it seeks to promote competition, rationalise tariffs and ensure transparency in policy making. These are sought to be achieved by distancing governments from their tariff making roles and regulatory responsibilities and vesting this power with regulatory commissions. The governments would have the right to intervene only in public interest. If the government wishes to subsidise any category of consumers it would have to make the payment in advance or as directed by the regulatory commission.

The Act allows for unbundling the electric utility into generating, transmitting, distributing and trading entities and any of these could be undertaken by private parties on obtaining the license, where required, from the regulatory commission. Distribution licensees would be free to set up generating companies and *vice versa*. More than one licensee could be allowed to take up distribution in a certain area. The Act ensures open access to the transmission and distribution networks under certain terms and conditions and permits stand-alone generation-cum-distribution systems in rural and remote areas. Trading of electricity between different licensees is allowed subject to a regulatory ceiling on trade margins. The wheeling charges for accessing a licensee's transmission or distribution network would be regulated by the commission. Individual consumers could contract for supply from any licensee and these prices would not be subject to any regulation.

There is to be a state level and a country level transmission utility, under government ownership and these would be responsible for ensuring the development of the transmission network in a coordinated manner. Similarly the government owned Load Despatch Centres at the Centre and at the State levels would be responsible for optimal scheduling and dispatch of electricity.

There is also provision for the existing State Electricity Boards to continue in the present vertically integrated form, in which case the SEB would take on the role of a state transmission utility and a distributing licensee that also owns generating capacity.

Issues and Options for Tamil Nadu

In the light of the above analysis, the question is what are the options available for Tamil Nadu? A State Electricity Regulatory Commission has been established and the Commission became effective since June 2002 with the appointment of the Chairman. For the first time in Tamil Nadu the electricity prices were subject to the Regulatory Commission's scrutiny and approval, after going through a process of public hearing. The Commission's tariff order came into effect in March 2003.

The following were the highlights of this initiative. The Commission outlined that the basic philosophy underlying the tariff structure should be that the rates for all categories of consumers must *progressively* reflect the cost of supply to them. It sought to rationalise the existing tariff structure through the following mechanisms – reduce the number of rate slabs for each consumer group and gradually reverse the current situation in which, categories with the lower cost impact are paying much higher prices. It stated its commitment to gradually reduce cross-subsidies over a period of five years. The Commission stated that no consumer, apart from agricultural and hut dwellers, should be charged 50 per cent more or less than the cost of supply to that category. It set a time frame of three years to achieve this goal. This was to be achieved by minimising the tariff increase for the *subsidising* category and undertaking higher rates of increase for the *subsidised* categories. For the agricultural and hut dwellers categories, which were till now receiving free and un-metered electricity, the Commission required that all services should be metered, probably within a period of three years. It allowed for another three to five years to increase their rates to at least 50 per cent of the cost of supply.

To make a beginning towards the above stated ends, the Commission ruled that agriculturists be required to pay Rs. 250 per HP per annum for services that are not metered and 20 paise per unit for metered services. The hut dwellers were required to pay a flat rate of Rs. 10 per month. However, the tariff rates for the subsidising categories were not reduced, keeping in view the need to minimise budget imbalances and to minimise tariff shocks to the hitherto subsided groups. It either allowed for marginal hikes in some cases or at best maintained existing rates.

Some additional features of the Commission's initiative were - it worked out the costs of supply based on a broad principle of merit ordering dispatch; it also encouraged either continuing existing mechanisms or introducing new mechanisms for improving the load factor of supply (through time-of-day meters) and the power factors of electricity consuming appliances. The TNEB was also required to have more accurate information on the transmission and distribution losses in the system. The Commission stated that meters should be installed at the output points of each sub-station in the 230, 110, 66 and 33 KV systems and monthly energy balance assessments carried out.

The TNEB implemented the ruling of the TNERC, as regards pricing, in March 2003. At the same time, the Tamil Nadu Government announced a direct cash support of Rs. 1000 per annum, to each small and marginal farmer in the State owning an irrigation pump and of Rs. 100 per annum to each hut owner. This was intended as a reimbursement to the small farmer and the hut owner of the payment of the newly levied charges. Thus there was a subsidy by the government, equal to the charges levied by the TNEB, as far as these consumers were concerned. Even with this decision, it could be said that a beginning had been made in electricity tariff reform. But in June 2004, the Government of Tamil Nadu issued a policy directive to the TNERC requiring free supply of electricity to be extended to farmers and hut dwellers, and domestic charges to be reduced to the pre-March 2003 levels, effective from April 01, 2004. The government also made a commitment in this directive to provide the required subsidy directly to TNEB. The TNERC ruled that the free supply to farmers and hut dwellers could be extended, subject to the State government providing the necessary subsidy amount to TNEB *in advance,* as required by the Electricity Act. In effect, thus, the beginning that had been made in tariff reform has been reversed but for the fact that the State government has been asked to pay the subsidy in advance.

The TNEB is now conducting energy audit on a sample basis. It has devised a master plan to further reduce T&D losses over a period of five years. Some of its essential features are to reduce the ratio of HT and LT lines to 1:1 from the current 1:2 level and to strengthen and reinforce the existing network. Out of the total number of 144 lakh households (as per 2001 census), 110 lakh households have been electrified. TNEB has stated that it proposes to ensure supply to all households by end of the Tenth Plan i.e. 2006-07.

Regarding the issue of restructuring the SEB, Tamil Nadu is at an advantage in that it has not yet made any major institutional changes that may be very difficult or costly to reverse. It therefore has the flexibility of choosing from different options by carefully weighing the costs and benefits involved. Moreover, the Electricity Act also allows this freedom. Unbundling and trying to introduce competition has so far not been able to yield net benefits in the Indian context due to a complex set of factors. Even in the international scene this option has not yet been proven to be unquestionably superior. Hence it might probably be a good idea for Tamil Nadu to go slow on the issue of unbundling.

Given the seriously deteriorating financial performance of TNEB the first priority should be to arrest this and achieve a turn around. The key element in addressing this is to provide the *right incentives*. However, the institutional structure in its present form is highly unlikely to provide the necessary incentives needed for a dramatic improvement in the financial performance. An institutional restructuring is certainly called for. The question is whether the current unbundling-corporatisation-privatisation approach is the most appropriate one or whether we can look at some alternatives. We do not yet have good estimates and clear examples in the Indian context as to which would be a better option on balance. Given that, it may be prudent to avoid institutional changes that would become very costly to reverse, in case they prove to be problematic. A possible alternative approach is suggested below which can potentially provide the right incentives for efficient operation even as the utility operates as an integrated entity.

The model suggested here is more or less on the lines of the regulated investor owned utilities that dominated the power sector arrangement in the U.S for many years. These utilities operated as integrated entities with jurisdiction over specified geographic regions and subject to regulatory control by independent regulatory commissions. While the essential benefits of the US model can be retained the drawbacks can be avoided and the model can be suitably adapted for the Indian context.

The first step would be to transform the TNEB from a Statutory Board into a profit oriented corporate organisation that would be vested with the responsibility for supply of electricity in Tamil Nadu. This entity should be subject to regulation by the Tamil Nadu Electricity Regulatory Commission. The regulated electric utility could either be a joint venture with the government having a minority share or it could fully be under private ownership. The government's share in the utility could be gradually divested over a specified time frame. The price at which shares in the utility are sold to private investors could be based on the revenue earning potential of the utility given the regulatory implications for prices. The Regulatory Commission could adopt the 'price-cap' form of regulation. This is the approach for price regulation followed in the UK. The idea is that the Commission specifies a ceiling price that the utility can charge and as long as the price ceiling is honored the utility is free to earn any level of profits that it can by controlling costs. The advantage of this type of regulation is that it provides the maximum incentive to the utility for efficient operation and also the information needed by the regulatory authority for monitoring and enforcement is easily observable. The management and employees of the utility should be given a share in the profits of the utility since this would encourage them to improve productivity. The magnitude of their profit shares and the manner in which they are provided should be carefully designed so as to create the right incentive to target financial performance efficiencies that are of a long-term nature and sustainable rather than focusing on near term short-lived profits.

The regulated electric utility should be given the freedom to organise its operations in whatever manner it chooses. It could parcel out some distribution networks or generating units to either private ownership or management. It could choose to build additional generating capacity on its own or contract to buy power either from independent producers, from the central sector units or from other utilities. These decisions and the terms and conditions on which they are carried out could be entirely the utility's responsibility and the Regulatory Commission need not concern itself with any of these arrangements. The utility should ultimately be *responsible* for supply of power within the State subject to the price ceiling and quality specifications provided by the Regulatory Commission. No consumer who wants power and is willing to pay for it within the price ceiling specified should be denied power. Failure to meet demand or to meet quality of supply standards on the part of the utility should be very heavily penalised by the Regulatory Commission.

All consumption should be metered and billed. If the State government wishes to subsidise any consumers it should be in the form of paying for a certain percentage of the electricity bill for those consumers. It would be important to have the consumers also to pay for a portion of their bill. This would encourage more prudent use of both electricity and groundwater, in the case of agricultural consumers. Flat rate charges and lump sum subsidies would not provide such incentives. Once the SEB's financial health is on a sound footing it could tackle any additional reform measures, if needed, from a position of strength and this would guarantee a smoother and sustainable transition.

Chapter 6

Roads and Transport

Transport Network in Tamil Nadu

Tamil Nadu has now 3,865 km of National Highways (NH), 7136 km of State Highways (SH), 7,408 km of Major District Roads (MDR) and 40,853 km of Other District Roads (ODR) besides village roads, and other categories of roads bringing the total to 1,50,647 km of roads. (At the National level in 1999, the road network had about 33,00,000 km of roads - 52,000 km of National Highways; 1,28,000 km of State Highways; 2,70,000 km of Major District Roads; 15,00,000 km of Other District Roads and Village Roads; 9,20,000 km of JRY Roads; 2,00,000 km of Urban Roads and 2,30,000 km of Project Roads). National Highways in Tamil Nadu are listed in Appendix 6A.I and State Highways in Tamil Nadu are listed in Appendix 6A.II. The density of road network in the State is 269.69 km per lakh of population and 115.83 km per 100 km^2 of area, against the All India Figure of 258.20 km per lakh of population and 74.90 km per 100 km^2 of area (as on 31.3.97). Thus the two basic indicators of road development - length of road per lakh of population and length of road per 100 km^2 - are found well above the National level.

Tamil Nadu has a rail network of 4,189 km. It has a coastline of about 992 km out of the 5560 km long coastline of the mainland of the country. There are three major ports (Chennai, Ennore and Thoothukudi) and 14 minor ports. There are five airports in the State (Chennai, Madurai, Coimbatore, Tiruchirappalli and Salem) and Chennai serves both international and domestic passenger and freight traffic. It has two navigational canals - Buckingham canal and Vedaranyam canal - identified as Inland Water Transport systems. However these two canals are not functioning effectively due to various reasons. Therefore, as part of transport infrastructure, the State has about 1.5 lakh km length of road network, 4,189 km of railway network, 17 seaports, 5 airports and 2 navigational canals. However, the road network is the one, which gives connectivity to all habitations and modes of other complementary transport systems in the State. As a consequence, efficient roads are vital to the performance and viability of all modes of transport in the State. By giving direct access to all urban and rural settlements, roads become the key factor facilitating faster economic growth in the State. Today an extensive road network in terms of its spread and quality serves Tamil Nadu, providing connectivity to urban and rural habitations.

National Highways and State Highways - Tamil Nadu and Other States

Tamil Nadu has 3,865 Km of National Highways when 57,737 km of National Highways is accounted at National level in 2001. As far as State Highways, the State has improved its share from 1,969 km in 1997 to 7,136 Km in 2001. Since State Highways play a key role in economic development, there is a need to have a State Highway (SH) network of good quality surface having excellent accessibility. In 1997, when the State of Tamil Nadu had just 1,969 km of SH, Andra Pradesh had 8806 km, Karnataka had 11,395 km and Maharashtra had 32,359 km (Table 6.1). This is an area where special attention is needed.

Length of Roads - Tamil Nadu and Other States

Tamil Nadu has better road coverage, when compared to National scene. The same is not true when compared to southern states. Kerala has better road coverage. At National level in 1971, the road coverage was 37 km of roads per 100 km^2. Tamil Nadu had 55 km of roads per 100 km^2 and Kerala had 153 km of

TABLE 6.1

National Highways, State Highways in India, Tamil Nadu and Other States, 1981-2001

(Length of Roads in Km)

State/Nation	*National Highways*							*State Highways*						
	1971	*1976*	*1981*	*1986*	*1991*	*1997*	*2001*	*1971*	*1976*	*1981*	*1986*	*1991*	*1997*	*2001*
India	24,000	NA*	31,671	NA	33,650	34,849	57,737*	NA	NA	94,359	NA	127,311	1,37,119	NA
Tamil Nadu	**1,804**	**1,865**	**1,865**	**1,886**	**2,002**	**2,002**	**3,865**	**1,780**	**1,745**	**1,814**	**1,864**	**1,915**	**1,969**	**7,136**
Andhra Pradesh	NA	NA	2,352	NA	2,587	2,949	NA	NA	NA	5,443	NA	8,651	8,806	NA
Gujarat	1,056	1,365	1,424	1,421	1,572	1,572	NA	8,200	8,696	9,158	9,442	19,084	19,761	NA
Maharashtra	2,366	2,933	2,945	2,949	2,949	2,958	NA	14,282	15,042	18,949	19,260	30,594	32,359	NA
Karnataka	1,269	1,968	1,968	1,968	1,997	1,997	NA	6,704	7,554	7,813	7,813	11,282	11,395	NA

* NA – Not Available.

Source: Report of the Working Group on Roads, Ports and Inland Waterways for Ninth Five Year Plan, Highways Deptt., Chennai, 1997.

Report of the Working Group on Roads, Ports and Inland Waterways for Tenth Five Year Plan 2002-2007, Highways Deptt., Chennai, 2002.

TABLE 6.2

Roads in Tamil Nadu, Other States and India - Length in Km per 100 Km² (1971-1997)

Sl. No.	*State/Nation*	*1971 a*	*1982 b*	*1988 c*	*1991 d*	*1994 e*	*1997 f*
1.	India	37.0	47.0	56.1	60.9	65.1	75.0
2.	**Tamil Nadu**	**55.0**	**102.0**	**128.4**	**151.2**	**155.9**	**158.7**
3.	Andhra Pradesh	37.0	46.5	50.0	NA*	60.2	64.7
4.	Karnataka	39.0	58.8	65.9	68.5	72.8	75.0
5.	Kerala	153.0	275.4	322.5	348.8	355.4	374.9

* NA – Not Available

Source: Report of the Task Force on Transportation 1972-94, State Planning Commission, Chennai, 1972 (a).

Basic Road Statistics of India 1981-82, Transport Research Division, Ministry of Shipping and Transport, New Delhi 1985 (b).

Basic Road Statistics of India 1987-88, Transport Research Division, Ministry of Shipping and Transport, New Delhi, 1990 (c).

CMIE, Economic Intelligence Service, Infrastructure, January 2001 (d,e,f).

TABLE 6.3

Roads in Tamil Nadu, Other States and India - Length per Lakh of Population (1971-1992)

State/Nation	*1971 a*	*1982 b*	*1992 c*
All-India	217.0	226.0	269.0
Tamil Nadu	**164.0**	**274.8**	**345.1**
Andhra Pradesh	232.0	240.9	256.8
Karnataka	253.0	304.5	340.3
Kerala	279.0	421.3	425.6

Source: Report of the Task Force on Transportation 1972-84, State Planning Commission, Chennai, 1972 (a).

Basic Road Statistics of India 1981-82, Transport Research Division, Ministry of Shipping and Transport, New Delhi, 1985 (b).

Roads and Bridges : Performance and Achievements, Highways & Rural Works Deptt., GoTN, April 1993 (c).

roads per 100 km² (Table 6.2). In 1997, Kerala had 375 km of road length per 100 km² against 159 km of road length per 100 km² in Tamil Nadu.

When population served by roads is taken as the criterion, Tamil Nadu again falls behind Kerala - Tamil Nadu had 345 km length of roads per lakh of population against 425 km length of roads per lakh of population in Kerala (Table 6.3).

Road Network in Tamil Nadu - Category of Road, Lane and Surface Type, District Level Variation

Lengths of Different Categories of Roads

Roads in Tamil Nadu are broadly grouped under two major heads - (i) Government roads and (ii) Village roads and others.

'Government roads' include National Highways (NH), State Highways (SH), Major District Roads (MDR), Other District Roads (ODR) and Sugar Cane Cess Roads. Development and maintenance of all these roads are the responsibilities of the Government of Tamil Nadu (GoTN) except the National Highways for which the GoI is responsible for fund allocation and overall maintenance. However at the State level, roads falling under National Highways are maintained by the GoTN, with the concurrence and guidance of the Government of India (GoI).

'Village roads and others' include the roads belonging to Panchayat Unions, Panchayats, Corporation and Local bodies. Roads maintained by the Forest department, Irrigation department, Tamil Nadu Electricity Board, and other unclassified roads also form part of this group.

TABLE 6.4

Lengths of Different Categories of Roads in Tamil Nadu, 1951-2001

Category of Road	*Length of Roads in Km*										
	1951	*1956*	*1961*	*1966*	*1971*	*1976*	*1981*	*1986*	*1993*	*1997*	*Sep.2001*
Government Roads											
National Highways (NH)	1,704	1,746	1,754	1,754	1,804	1,865	1,865	1,884	2,002	2,002	3,865
State Highways (SH)	1,745	1,745	1,754	1,780	1,780*	1,745*	1,814	1,864	1,929	1,969	7,136
Major District Roads (MDR)	13,182	13,435	13,742	13,591	13,776	13,865	14,028	14,004	13,972	14,016	7,408
Other District Roads (ODR)	17,484	21,771	1,194	6,859	9,537	15,833	18,118	21,927	35,243	39,786	40,853
Sugar Cane Cess Roads									1,132	1,132	1,366
Village Roads and Others											
Panchayat Union Roads			19,748@	35,160@	40,032@	53,513@	71,527@	99,112@	54,505	34,083	29,568
Panchayat Roads									48,010	29,020	30,810
Corporation & Municipal Roads									8,689	8,689	12,024
Other Roads (Forest Roads, Irrigation Roads, Electricity Boards, MES Roads, Unclassified Roads etc.)			5,827	6,423	7,235	9,684*	7,956*	9,169*	5,335*	11,863*	17,617
Total	**34,115**	**38,697**	**44,019**	**65,567**	**74,164**	**96,505**	**1,15,308**	**1,47,960***	**1,70,817***	**1,42,560***	**1,50,647**

Note: * Data given here have been compiled by referring to reports and cross checking with other documents available. However, in certain cases unexpected decrease/increase in values are seen when data are compared with previous/following years. But the Table still gives a good insight into the trend in road development in Tamil Nadu.

@ These values are for both Panchayat Union Roads and Panchayat Roads.

Source: Report of the Task Force on Transportation, 1971-84, State Planning Commission, Chennai, 1972.

Roads and Bridges - Performance and Achievements, Highways and Rural Works Department, Chennai, 1993.

Performance Budget, 1997-98 of the Highways Deptt., Chennai, May 1998.

Performance Budget 2001-2002 of the Highways Deptt., Chennai, April 2002.

Report of the Working Group on Roads, Ports and Inland Waterways for Tenth Five Year Plan, Highways Deptt., Dec. 2001.

Performance Budget 1993-94 of the Highways and Rural Works Deptt., Chennai, April 1994.

By 1961, the State had a road network of 44,019 km in length. This has come to 1,50,647 km in length by 2001, increase by 3.4 times in 40 years (Table 6.4). The Primary Road Network System which includes National Highways and State Highways account for 7.30 per cent of total road length in the State. Share by other roads are as follows - Major District Roads (MDR) 4.91 per cent; Other District Roads (ODR)-27.12 per cent; Sugarcane cess Roads - 0.90 per cent; Panchayat Union Roads - 19.63 per cent; Panchayat Roads-20.46 per cent; Corporation and Municipal Roads-7.98 per cent; Other Roads (Forest Roads; Irrigation Roads, Electricity Board Roads, MES Roads, Unclassified Roads etc.,)-11.70 per cent (Table 6.4). Even though the network has extended considerably, only 76.5 per cent of National Highways and State Highways are provided with two-lane carriageways. Still 21.3 per cent of roads (SH & NH) are provided with single lane carriageway (Table 6.5). When MDR and ODR are considered, more than 90 per cent of road lengths have still single-lane carriageways (Table 6.6).

TABLE 6.5

Main Roads in India and Tamil Nadu: Lane Width, 2000-2001

(Length in %)

Width of Carriageway	*National Highways*		*State Highways*		*Total*	
	India (2000)	*Tamil Nadu (2001)*	*India (2000)*	*Tamil Nadu (2001)*	*India (2000)*	*Tamil Nadu (2001)*
One-Lane	39.0	4.2	77.0	30.5	65.0	21.3
Two-Lane	59.0	93.1	22.0	67.6	34.0	76.5
Multilane	2.0	2.7	1.0	1.9	1.0	2.2

Note: Figures given for India are of October 2000 and Tamil Nadu are of March 2001. Two-lane figures for Tamil Nadu include figures of Intermediate lane also.

Source: Highways Deptt., Performance Budget 2001-2002, GoTN, April 2002. MoRT & H, Road Development Plan Vision: 2021, IRC, New Delhi, 2001.

This group of roads really gives accessibility to small towns and rural centres of economic activities and unfortunately they are still with single lane carriageway, imposing severe strain on free movement of goods and persons. The need of this day is to go for two lane carriageways in the case of all ODRs and MDRs.

The Prime Minister announced recently a centrally sponsored scheme called the *Pradhan Mantri Gram Sadak Yojana* (PMGSY) with the objective of connecting within the year 2007, all villages having population more than 500 through good all-weather roads. Under this scheme, through the District Rural Development Agency, rural road programmes are implemented.

TABLE 6.6

Roads in Tamil Nadu Based on Lane Width, 1993-2001

(Length in km)

Category of Road	*Lane Type*	*1971 (a)*	*1993 (b)*	*1997 (c)*	*Sept. 2001 (d)*
National Highways	SL	404	152	154	310
	IL	—	—	—	21
	DL	1353	1850	1816	3431
	ML	47	—	32	103
	T	1804	2002	2002	3865
State Highways	SL	1246	200	193	2178
	IL	—	—	—	878
	DL	534	1729	1686	3946
	ML	—	—	90	134
	T	1780	1929	1969	7136
Major District Roads	SL	12949	9329	8443	4946
	IL	—	—	—	725
	DL	827	4643	5526	1780
	ML	—	—	47	29
	T	13776	13972	14016	7408
Other District Roads	SL	9355	34721	39005	39298
	IL	—	—	—	846
	DL	182	522	750	671
	ML	—	—	31	38
	T	9537	35243	39786	40853
Sugarcane Cess Roads	SL	—	—	1132	1356
	IL	—	—	—	—
	DL	—	—	—	10
	ML	—	—	—	—
	T	—	—	1132	1366

Note: SL-Single Lane; IL-Intermediate Lane; DL-Double Lane; ML-Multi Lane; T- Total.

Figures given for 1993 against "Double Lane" includes the roads having "Multi Lanes".

Source: Report of the Task Force on Transportation, 1972-84, State Planning Commission 1972, Chennai (a).

Performance Budget 1993-1994, Highways & Rural Works Deptt., Govt. of Tamil Nadu, April 1994 (b).

Performance Budget 1997-1998, Highways Deptt., Govt. of Tamil Nadu, May 1998 (c).

Performance Budget 2001-2002, Highways Deptt., Govt. of Tamil Nadu, April 2002 (d).

As far as road surface is considered, the roads predominantly have Bituminous Surface (BT). More than 99 per cent of roads in the categories of NH, SH, MDR and ODR in the State are provided with Bituminous surface (BT). Out of 59,262 km length of roads (NH, SH, MDR & ODR), 59,149 km length of roads have BT surface (Table 6.7).

TABLE 6.7

Roads in Tamil Nadu Based on Surface Condition, 1961-2002

(Length km)

Category of Road	*Lane Type*	*1961*	*1971*	*1976*	*1993*	*1997*	*2002*
National Highways	CC	—	224	—	2	2	3
	BT	—	1580	—	2000	2000	3862
	M	—	—	—	—	—	—
	G	—	—	—	—	—	—
	T	—	1804	—	2002	2002	3865
State Highways	CC	—	208	—	105	52	19
	BT	—	1572	—	1824	1917	7117
	M	—	—	—	—	—	—
	G	—	—	—	—	—	—
	T	—	1780	—	1929	1969	7136
Major District Roads	CC	—	138	—	48	29	2
	BT	—	12266	—	13860	13940	7369
	M	—	1372	—	61	47	37
	G	—	—	—	3	—	—
	T	—	13776	—	13972	14016	7408
Other District Roads	CC	—	18	—	6	5	5
	BT	—	4040	—	34367	39367	40801
	M	—	5188	—	798	272	47
	G	—	291	—	72	16	—
	T	—	9537	—	35,243	39,786	40,853
Sugarcane Cess Roads	CC	—	—	—	—	—	—
	BT	—	—	—	—	1132	1366
	M	—	—	—	—	—	—
	G	—	—	—	—	—	—
	T	—	—	—	—	1132	1366
All Roads	CC	859	1196	1216	—	—	—
	BT	13958	25713	33414	—	—	—
	M	18244	23298	24761	—	—	—
	G	10958	23957	37114	—	—	—
	T	44019	74164	96505	—	—	—

Note: CC - Cement Concrete Road; BT - Bituminous Road; M - Metalled Road; G - Gravel Road; T - Total

Source: Compiled from Records of the Highways Department.

Road Coverage in Districts

On State-wide basis, government road provided is about one kilometre for every 1,016 persons (excluding

Chennai). Government roads are well distributed throughout the 23 districts. But on a population basis, there is variation, as shown in Table 6.8.

TABLE 6.8

State Government Roads in Districts, 2002-2003

S. No.	District	Road length Km	Population Total	Population Per Km
1	Chennai	NA	NA	NA
2	Kancheepuram	2170	2877468	1326
3	Thiruvallore	1726	2754756	1596
4	Cuddalore	1729	2285395	1322
5	Villupuram	3032	2960373	976
6	Vellore	2562	3477317	1357
7	Thiruvannamalai	2613	2186125	837
8	Dharmapuri	2965	2856300	963
9	Salem	2353	3016346	1282
10	Namakkal	1715	1493462	871
11	Erode	3792	2581500	681
12	Coimbatore	3645	4271856	1172
13	The Nilgiris	1074	762141	710
14	Tiruchirappalli	1907	2418366	1268
15	Perambalur	1465	1189170	812
16	Karur	932	935686	1004
17	Thanjavur	2167	2216138	1023
18	Nagapattinam	1209	1488839	1231
19	Thiruvarur	1183	1169474	989
20	Pudukkottai	2022	1459601	722
21	Madurai	1435	2578201	1797
22	Theni	731	1093950	1497
23	Dindigul	2293	1923014	839
24	Ramanathapuram	1482	1187604	801
25	Sivagangai	1852	1155356	624
26	Virudhunagar	1671	1751301	1048
27	Thirunelveli	2805	2723988	971
28	Thoothukudi	1994	1572273	789
29	Kanniyakumari	1208	1676034	1387
	Total (excl. Chennai)	**55732**	**5862034**	**1042**

Note: NA Not available.

Source: Records of the Highways Department.

Construction and Maintenance of Roads

Formation of Highways Department and its Functioning

A separate department for the construction and maintenance of roads under the name "Trunk Road Department" was set up for the first time in Madras Presidency in 1845. This Department was entrusted with the responsibility of constructing and maintaining about 3,700 km of main lines of communications in the Presidency. The Department however had a separate existence for a brief period only. A Public Works Department (PWD) was formed in 1858 by merging the Maramuth Department, Trunk Road Department and the Engineering Wing of the Military Board. The work relating to Highways was handled as part of the responsibility of PWD till 1946.

A separate department for Highways (Highways Engineering Deptt.) the first of its kind in India, was formed on the first of April 1946, by delinking the Communication Wing from PWD. (GO.Ms.No.598 dt.26.3.1946). The Department took over all the roads in the Presidency except those classified as Other District Roads (ODR) and Village roads which were retained by the District Boards, to be maintained by the Engineers deputed from the Highways Deptt. The District Board was later abolished and *Panchayat* Unions were constituted and due to this, the Engineering units of the *Panchayat* Unions were brought under the control of the Highways Department. It was then renamed as "Highways and Rural Works Deptt." (G.O.Ms.No.851 RDLA dt. 9.5.1960). This Department has played a very important role in developing and maintaining the highway system in the State which has immense direct impact on economic development in the State.

The department is now called "Highways Department" and it is headed by the Secretary at the Government level and the activities of the Department are carried out with engineers working under the guidance of 10 Chief Engineers at the State level. With a budget allocation of Rs. 8.40 crore and a road length of 34,215 km in 1951, the department has developed today to be incharge of planning, design, construction and maintenance of 60,613 km of roads with a budget allocation of Rs. 799.43 crore in 2002-03, excluding the funds received for National Highways and special projects. It is to be noted here that the First Five - Year Plan provided about Rs. 6.00 crore only for the roads in the State.

Funds for construction and maintenance of National Highways (NH) in the State are provided by the Government of India and NH road projects are executed by the Highways Department of GoTN on behalf of the Government of India (GoI). In the Annual Plan 2002-03, proposals for Rs. 196.60 crore have been approved by GoI. National Highways Authority of India (NHAI) have now taken up the work of upgrading the road sections in NH4, NH5, NH7, NH46 and NH47 which form part of the "Golden Quadrilateral" and "North-South Corridor" projects, covering a distance of 1100 km within the State. Now, under Annuity scheme, 94 km in NH45 is also widened and strengthened.

State Highways (SH), Major District Roads (MDR) and Other District Roads (ODR) are maintained by the State Government from its own resources using the infrastructure available in the Highways Department. The Highways Research Station, established in 1957, as a unit of the Highways Department has been associating with various wings of the department in introducing new materials and new technologies in construction and maintenance of roads. In the case of Railway Over/Under Bridges including approaches, GoI and GoTN build them sharing the cost on 50:50 basis. A recent phenomenon in mobilising resources is borrowing of money as loan for road improvements from Tamil Nadu Industrial Development Corporation Limited (TIDCO), Housing and Urban Development Corporation (HUDCO), National Bank for Agriculture and Rural Development (NABARD), Asian Development Bank (ADB) and The World Bank.

Maintenance of Roads in Coastal Districts

During the monsoon period, between October and December, these roads are badly damaged due to the inundation and this is a recurring phenomenon. The department has taken steps to rebuild weak bridges in the Cauvery Delta Districts of the State.

Private Sector in Road Maintenance

In order to encourage private sector participation in road maintenance, GoTN has proposed to introduce the system of three year integrated improvement-cum-maintenance of State Highways through private agencies. Under this scheme, all State Highway roads falling within each district would be made into a package and entrusted to successful bidders for improvement-cum-maintenance for three years. This is a new strategy being introduced by the GoTN.

Road Maintenance - Problems in Finding Finance

The large road network developed over the past five decades is now showing signs of premature aging, largely because of three factors - cumulative arrears in road maintenance over the years; high volume of traffic with heavier vehicles; adopting conventional technologies for repair and maintenance by the department.

Even though the department could succeed in getting funds for new projects, difficulties are faced in allocating the required funds for maintenance and upkeep of roads. The requirements as per norms, and actual expenditure incurred on maintenance of government roads (other than village and other roads) are given in Table 6.9.

TABLE 6.9

Road Maintenance - Budget Allotment and Actual Expenditure

Year	*Maintenance allotment required as per norms (Rs. Crore)*	*Maintenance allotment made in the budget (Rs. Crore)*	*Actual Expenditure*	
			(Rs. Crore)	*Share on allotment required (%)*
1997-1998	342.52	228.00	272.99	79.70
1998-1999	422.53	254.00	259.92	61.51
1999-2000	439.80	269.58	252.34	57.37
2000-2001	483.78	182.64	198.35	41.00
2001-2002	490.00	207.47	207.47*	42.34

Note: * anticipated

Source: Report of Working Group on Roads, Ports, and Inland Waterways, Highways Deptt, Chennai, 2001.

This clearly shows that the expenditure incurred is far below the requirement. This situation has resulted in having poorly maintained roads leading to traffic congestion, travel delays, increased accidents and higher vehicle operating costs. In the budget proposals for 2002-03, an initiative has been made to have "Integrated improvement-cum-three year maintenance contract for State Highways" involving the private sector.

Private Sector Participation in Road Construction and Maintenance

A recent development has been the involvement of private sector in road planning design, construction and management. It has now become a practice to employ international and national consultants in executing many road projects.

Road Planning

M/s. Booz Allen and Hamilton of USA, an international consultant prepared consultancy report on "Institutional Development" for the Highways Department in 1999. The study suggested that by the year 2005, the Highways Department would become an autonomous department for formulating State wide policy, planning and quality assurance. This will be supported by an autonomous Road Fund Board (RFB) for securing road financing. Road development activities in the State would be carried out by one or more Road Development Corporations. The steering committee constituted by the GoTN accepted the recommendations of the consultant and in principle approval of GoTN to the strategy has been accorded (G.O.Ms.No.141 dt. 16.08.2001).

The new strategy to be implemented provides for appointing special revenue staff to take up land acquisition, resettlement and rehabilitation works. Special forest staff will be available to deal with flora and fauna. Environmental specialists and Financial Managers will also be inducted into the Project Implementation Unit (PIU). Another international consultant M/s. Kinhill Pty Ltd. in association with Consulting Engineering Services (I) Ltd., ARRB Transport Research Pty Ltd. and VIC Roads prepared "Feasibility Study Report under Tamil Nadu Road Sector Project" with the objective to evaluate the economic feasibility of undertaking improvement works and to establish a priority ranking for 3238 km of roads in Tamil Nadu.

Road Maintenance

Tamil Nadu Road Development Company Ltd. (TNRDC) is a 50:50 joint venture company promoted by the State-owned Tamil Nadu Industrial Development Corporation Ltd. (TIDCO) and Infrastructure Leasing & Financial Services Ltd. (IL&FS) in 1998 with Rs. 5 crore equity from each of the promoters to develop and implement road sector initiatives in Tamil Nadu under public-private partnership format. This organisation was also mandated to initiate the commercialisation of operation and maintenance of roads in the State. Already TNRDC has taken up the maintenance of East Coast Road (ECR).

Private Sector Participation (Annuity Model) in NH45 Development

A new annuity model in road construction and maintenance is evolved. According to the model, the road is to be built and maintained by a company and the cost of the project and cost of maintenance will be paid by NHAI over 15 years. This is based on the "Annuity Tolling Model" proposed by the Infrastructure Development Finance Corporation (IDFC). In October 2000, GoI finalised the model concession agreement. Under Annuity Tolling Scheme, instead of concessionaire directly recovering toll from users, GoI (in this case NHAI) pays predetermined sum annually to the operator for agreed number of years. In order to speed up early completion of works, NHAI announced a major incentive scheme under which for every one month early completion, contractor is awarded 1 per cent of contract costs as bonus, maximum upto 6 per cent. Similarly for every one month delay, 1.5 per cent of contract cost is levied as penalty, maximum upto 9 per cent. M/s.GMR Tambaram-Tindivanam Expressways Private Ltd. (GTTEL) is a special purpose vehicle established by GMR consortium to take up the work of 4 laning of Tambaram-Tindivanam section of NH45 on build-operate-transfer (BOT) basis. National Highways Authority of India (NHAI) has awarded the project with a concession period of 17.5 years, which includes a construction period of 2.5 years. The concession agreement has been signed on 9.10.2001 and the works are in progress.

Construction of Coimbatore Bypass Road

The project involved construction of a bypass road of about 28 km length and construction of a bridge (Athupalam bridge) of 35m length with a carriageway width of 7.5 m in addition to the existing bridge across the river at the same location within the town. Larsen and Toubro Ltd. (L&T) signed the concession agreement on 3.10.97. The GoI, the GoTN and the L&T represented by their ECC construction group have signed the agreement. L&T has floated a subsidiary company, viz, L&T Transportation Infrastructure Ltd. (LTTIL) as a Special Purpose Vehicle (SPV) for the project on 24.9.97 and has assigned its obligations/ responsibilities/rights to the SPV through a deed of assignment. The road is fully developed and it is in use.

Resource Mobilisation Including User Charges and Cost Recovery

Resource for Highway Development

By an executive order in 1854, a Local Boards Fund was created by earmarking a fraction of Land Revenue for Construction and upkeep of roads. The District Road Cess Act 1867 provided for collecting road cess. The Local Fund Act 1871 provided for the levy of both for roads. Based on the Jayakar Committee recommendations to levy tax on petrol to finance road works, the Govt. of India created a Central Road Fund (CRF) in March 1929 and allocated the funds to the State Governments on a prorata manner for financing road projects. The Govt. of Tamil Nadu amended the Tamil Nadu Motor Vehicles Taxation Act in 1972 levying surcharge on Motor Vehicle Tax and established a "Tamil Nadu Rural Roads Development Fund" for development and maintenance of public roads in rural areas. Apart from the above, a cess is levied on sugar cane at Rs. 5/- per tonne purchased by the factories under the Tamil Nadu Sugar Factories Control Act 1949. The entire expenditure on development and maintenance of National Highways is met by Government of India under the National Highways Act, 1956.

Central Road Fund (CRF) : CRF rules were revised in 1988 increasing the levy from 3.5 paise per litre of petrol to 5 per cent of basic price of petrol and also bringing diesel within the purview of CRF. GoI has recently created a dedicated fund for roads. The major source of this fund is the additional excise duty of Rs. 1.00 per litre on petrol levied since 2.9.1998 and on high speed diesel since 1.3.1999. The annual accruals through this source would be around Rs. 5,500 crore and it is likely to grow further with increase in consumption of fuel.

50 per cent of the proceeds from additional excise duty levied on diesel would be set apart for rural roads. The balance 50 per cent collected on diesel and 100 per cent collected on petrol would be used in the following manner - 57.5 per cent on NH; 27 per cent on SH; 3 per cent on roads of inter-state and economic importance; the balance 12.5 per cent for safety works in railways such as ROB, RUB etc.

As an indicative of the contributions from CRF, it is found that the GoI accorded administrative sanction for Rs.149.50 crore for executing 254 works during 2000-01.

Domestic borrowings: GoTN has availed loan assistance for construction of roads from NABARD, Infrastructure Leasing and Financial Services Ltd (ILFS), Infrastructure Development Finance Corporation Limited (IDFC) and HUDCO. The GoTN has entered into a MoU with IDFC to impart greater momentum to the development of the infrastructure. The MoU signed on 28.6.2002 makes available private capital for commercially viable infrastructure project including roads. TIDCO will function as the nodal agency. Therefore, there is a greater scope for private sector participation in road projects in Tamil Nadu.

As many as 15 schemes were sanctioned by HUDCO during 1997-2001 to the extent of Rs. 560 crore and released Rs. 341 crore. These loans are to be repaid over a period of 15 years with interest rates varying between 12.75 per cent and 15.5 per cent. Loan sanctioned by HUDCO for Coimbatore by-pass is to be repaid in 15 years with 5 year as moratorium period. In the case of Amaravathy Bridge at Karur, the period of repayment has been fixed at 10 years. Normally 70 per cent of the project cost is given as loan amount by HUDCO. Chennai Metropolitan Development Authority (CMDA) got loan from HUDCO for the Department of Highways for strengthening and widening radial roads and bridges in Chennai Metropolitan Region. HUDCO granted 70 per cent of the project cost as loan and the balance 30 per cent of the project cost as grant by GoTN. Chennai Metropolitan Development Authority (CMDA) also got loan assistance for the Highways Department under the mega cites programme of the GoI to improve the Mount Poonamallee Road at a cost of Rs. 9 crore. GoTN permitted the CMDA to obtain 50 per cent of the project cost from TUFIDCO and 50 per cent cost from HUDCO. The GoTN agreed to repay the loan over 15 year period.

Rural Roads Programme with Loan Assistance from NABARD

The National Bank for Agricultural and Rural Development (NABARD) with its headquarters at Mumbai has created Rural Infrastructural Development Fund (RIDF) by obtaining contributions from other commercial banks. NABARD has extended loan assistance to the following categories of roads: (i) *Panchayat* and *Panchayat* Union Roads (improving to ODR standards); (ii) Other District Roads (ODR); (iii) Major District Roads (MDR). GoTN made use of the loan assistance in a big way to improve the roads and construct bridges, culverts etc. GoI also supported financially the following three schemes - (i) Rural Roads Scheme, (ii) Special Component Plan Scheme, (iii) Bus Route Improvement Scheme. In 1972 itself GoTN initiated a five-year programme to link all villages and hamlets with a population of 1500 and more to the nearest main road. This programme was implemented in seven phases from 1972 to 1990. Later, Rural Roads programmes were implemented under annual plan schemes. The objective was to improve *Panchayat* and *Panchayat* Union roads to ODR standards with BT surface.

Rural Roads Scheme: It is a Centrally sponsored scheme under Minimum Needs Programme (MNP). GoI reimburses 30 per cent of the expenditure. All villages with more than 1000 population have been given connectivity already. Currently, villages with 500-1000 population are given connectivity. The prescribed minimum length of road to be improved should be 1.6 km. One village taken up should not have been connected by any other B.T. surfaced road. Under this scheme, 90 per cent of the project cost is given as loan assistance to the State government and the remaining 10 per cent is to be borne by the State government.

In Tamil Nadu, all the villages with a population above 1000, numbering 9,705 have already been provided with connectivity at ODR standards as on 31.3.99. From 1999-2000 onwards programmes providing connectivity to villages having population between 500-1000, have been taken up. It is assessed that there are 10,823 villages in Tamil Nadu with a population between 500-1000, as per 1991 census and out of this 5937 villages were given connectivity by March 1999. During 1999-2002, roads connectivity to 640 villages was improved by having all-weather roads with loan assistance from NABARD. During 2002-03, it is programmed to cover 124 villages and the present trend will be continued till all villages are covered.

Special Component Plan Scheme: It is also a Centrally sponsored scheme under Minimum Needs Programme (MNP). GoI reimburses 100 per cent of the expenditure. The special criterion is that *Adidravidar* population should be more than 50 per cent of the total population of the village to be benefited with the link road. Till the end of 2001-02, connectivity to 182 villages having population less than 1000 have been covered. During 2002-03, it is proposed to cover 55 villages additionally.

Bus Route Improvement Scheme: Under this scheme, the *Panchayat* and *Panchayat* Union Roads in which buses have been plying for more than three years are taken up for improvement with BT surface and ODR standards. Till 2000-01, about 1,290 km of road works and 12 bridge works have been completed. During 2002-03, improvement works for 275 km of roads and 14 bridges have been proposed to be taken up with NABARD loan assistance.

MDR and ODR Schemes Under Rural Infrastructure Development Fund (RIDF): NABARD also extended financial assistance under RIDF for improvement of MDR and ODR. Under RIDF (II to VII), schemes have been implemented since 1996-97. So far 5,151 km of road lengths have been improved. Works were taken up to strengthen/construct 197 bridges. In 2001-02, actions are initiated for construction/improvement of 65 bridges.

Pradhan Mantri Gram Sadak Yojana (PMGSY): The GoI introduced a centrally sponsored programme on 25th December 2000 with the objective of providing road connectivity through good all-weather roads to all unconnected habitations having a population more than 1000 persons by the year 2003 and those with a population more than 500 persons by the end of the Tenth Plan Period (2007). In case of hilly/desert areas, this may not be less than 250. The programme requires preparation of "District Rural Roads Plan" for each district and for which the Ministry of Rural Development of GoI has prepared a manual. Upgradation of existing roads can be permitted to be taken up under this programme. Now Re. 1/- is levied as cess on High Speed Diesel and 50 per cent of this amount would be earmarked for this programme. Accordingly, Rs. 2500 crore was earmarked for PMGSY during 2000-01 at national level.

The District Rural Development Agency (DRDA) of each district is required to open a separate and single Bank account for the funds received under this programme. These funds will remain entirely separate from those of any other programme/scheme and even the interest earned cannot be diverted to other programmes/schemes. The Rural Roads Constructed/ upgraded under this programme will be maintained by the concerned Panchayat Raj Institution. All the road works will be subjected to social audit by way of discussion in the village *Panchayat/Panchayat* Union. The funds received from the GoI are required to be transferred to the concerned DRDA within 15 days of release by the GoI.

In Tamil Nadu 2258 km of rural roads have been improved/developed during 2000-2002 under PMGSY. In 2000-01, Rs. 151.32 crore was spent on 1449.8 km of rural roads to benefit about 17 lakh persons (866 roads in 100 packages, each with a budget estimate between Rs. 1crore and Rs. 2crore). In 2001-02, Rs. 115.83 crore was sanctioned to form/improve 808.58 km of rural roads (450 roads in 78 packages). The roads are provided with BT carriageway of 3.75 m on a formation width of 7.5m.

User Charges and Cost Recovery

Tamil Nadu is the first few States to amend the Indian Tolls Act 1851 to provide for tolling as applicable to the State. The amendment made in 1997 enables private sector participation in development, rehabilitation, repair and maintenance of roads and bridges in the State besides permitting private sector to levy and collect tolls to recover the investments with returns thereon.

Levy of toll on roads/bridges is an important area to mobilise resources. Already toll is collected in the East Coast Road, Coimbatore By-pass Road, Athupalam bridge, Karur bridge, Karanodai bridge, etc. NHAI is also to introduce tolls in sections where improvements are done in NH45 on the basis of Annuity Model.

Toll Roads

Toll Plazas have been built in East Coast Road and TNRDC is collecting the toll charges. Toll rates in Tamil Nadu are as follows : 72 paise per km on Coimbatore by-pass, 99 paise per km on Madurai Ring Road; 42 paise per km on ECR. The ECR road is considered in 3 segments : Chennai-Mahabalipuram; Mahabalipuram-Pondicherry; Chennai-Pondicherry. They have 75 different toll rates, and tolling is charged since March 24, 2002 in ECR.

Annuity Model

GTTEL is now executing the work of forming four lane divided highway between Tambaram and Tindivanam section of NH45 adopting Annuity Model. GTTEL would construct and maintain the road till it is transferred to GoTN. During the concession period, National Highway Authority of India (NHAI) would give the concessionaire the prescribed 30 installments of half yearly payments of Rs. 41.86 crore (in May and November every year). NHAI retains the right to collect toll on the project road. There is a bonus clause, according to it, if the work is completed earlier before 30 months, and penalty clause, if the work is delayed beyond 30 months. The concessionaire has awarded the construction contract to the Indian subsidiary of a Malaysian company called United Engineers (Malaysia) on 'fixed price' basis, with a clause for bonus/penalty for early/delayed completion. Financial support for the project is given by HUDCO and ICICI. The NHAI may collect toll in the road.

Road Fund Board

GoTN has announced recently that a separate Road Fund Board will be formed. It has been decided to levy infrastructure surcharge at 5 per cent to develop infrastructure facilities in the State. A portion of this amount will come to the Road Fund Board. This is a good move to augment resource locally. The Government of India, through an Act of Parliament have set up a Central Road Fund with the accruals from the Special Cess levied on Petrol and Diesel. From this fund, around 15 per cent is distributed to the States. During the year 2000-01, a sum of Rs. 22.34 crore was drawn from Government of India, and during 2001-02, a sum of Rs. 40 crore was drawn and utilised. The Budget Estimate of the GoTN for 2002-03 is Rs. 73.97 crore.

Management Improvements

The following issues require consideration by the agencies concerned to improve the management of the road system in the State.

- Recommendations made by the consultant M/s. Booz Allen and Hamilton in 1999 for organisational transformation from a government controlled department to an autonomous department, looking into statewide policy, planning and quality assurance, supported by one or more Road Development Corporation may be discussed, revised, if necessary and adopted for implementation (Fig.6.1).

FIGURE 6.1

Proposed Organisational Transformation for Institutional Strengthening

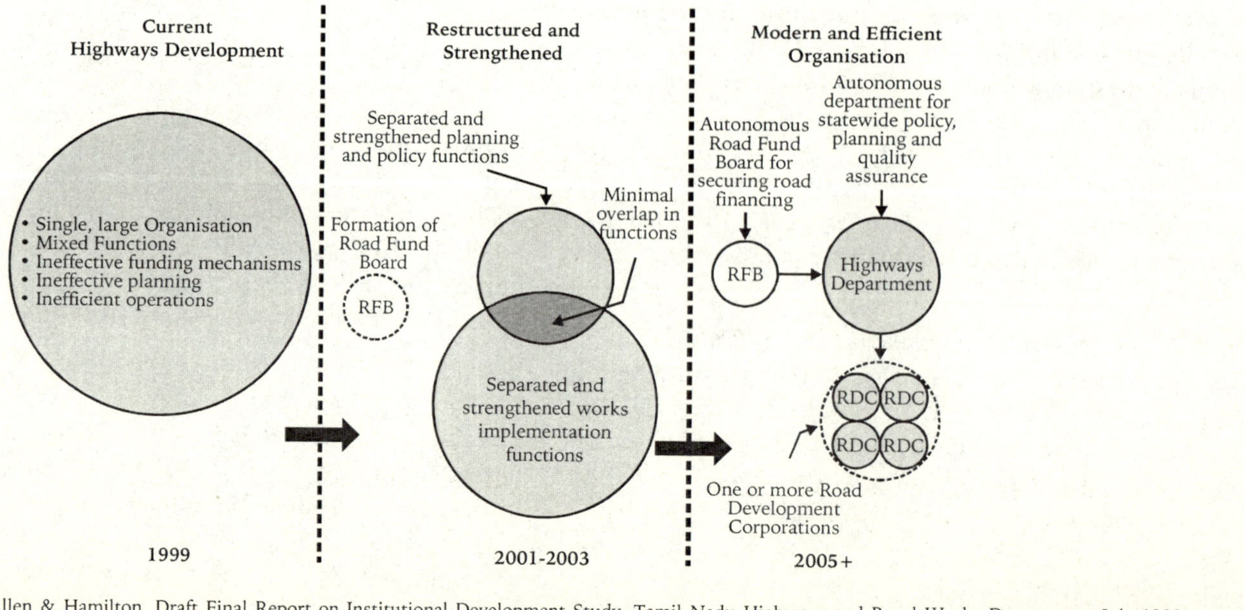

Source: Booz Allen & Hamilton, Draft Final Report on Institutional Development Study, Tamil Nadu Highways and Rural Works Department, July 1999.

- Provisions made in the Citizen's charter announced in 2002 by the GoTN may be implemented in total.
- Sustainable development concept may be adopted to plan, construct and manage the road network in the State. Greater participation of the local community is required during execution of projects and carrying out repairs to damaged road surfaces.
- Improved serviceability of roads and economy in construction could be achieved by adopting new technologies such as "trenchless technology", "recycling of pavements", etc.
- All road projects may be subjected to Environmental Impact Assessment, on the lines of the guidelines issued by Indian Roads Congress (IRC).
- Greater emphasis should be given to train personnel working at the site, and the contractors executing projects. Updating the technical skills and management capacity building should be given due consideration.
- Information dissemination and transparency in activities are to be encouraged to have greater cooperation from other agencies and the public in executive road projects and maintaining the roads.
- Roads should be built using modern construction machineries to yield high strength pavements. Further, road maintenance should receive greater attention. New tools available should be used at the site. Asset management should receive greater attention.
- Management strategies should be devised and implemented for having 'high performance pavement system' to function effectively at all seasons of the year.
- Private sector participation should be encouraged in road sector construction and maintenance. Wherever toll charges are to be levied, all stakeholders should be involved, right from the planning stage.
- 'Safety audit' concept should be adopted to ensure greater safety for all road users. "Pre-construction" and "post-construction" audit should be done for all road projects by an independent team.
- The GoTN has already brought out a comprehensive bill on Highways. This should become an Act at the earliest, facilitating the Highways Department to provide a better road system.
- Rail network in the State should become totally with Broad Gauge tracks and important travel corridors (e.g. Chennai – Trichy – Madurai – Kanyakumari) should be converted to double lines and electric traction be introduced, enabling to run more number of trains at reduced travel time.
- Roads in the coastal region should have to be realigned avoiding sharp curves and improved to perform effectively even during monsoon floods. A master plan may be needed for road improvements in coastal regions.
- The Highways Department recently has announced Vision and Mission statements.

Vision Statement: To serve our customers, the road users of Tamil Nadu by providing high quality, cost effective, environmental friendly road network that is reliable and safe, contributing to sustainable economic development and social well being of the State by applying innovation, best practices, appropriate technology and responsible management of internal and external resources.

Mission Statement: Realising the need for an efficient road network for cost effective movement of men and material without which trade and industry cannot maintain a competitive edge, we dedicate ourselves to plan and implement the schemes relating to roads and bridges in a scientific and technological manner in tune with change of times. We are consciously committed to achieve the goal of providing connectivity to the rural habitations to accelerate their economic development. We resolve to protect all roads and bridges of Highways department and to be vigilant against unauthorised encroachments which cause hindrance to the public at large and thereby ensure citizen friendly approach). Management strategies are to be devised to achieve them early.

Road Transport

Soon after the independence, the nationalisation of passenger road transport in Tamil Nadu commenced with the take over of all routes in Chennai city in 1948. In 1959, a policy was introduced to take over all bus routes exceeding 120 miles. Later a policy to nationalise the stage carriages was formulated in 1967. The stage carriages of private operators who owned more than 50 permits were acquired under the Tamil Nadu Fleet Operators Stage Carriages (Acquisition) Act,

1971. By this, Pandiyan Roadways Corporation, Cheran Transport Corporation and Cholan Roadways Corporation were formed. In August 1972, the Government announced its policy to nationalise the entire passenger transport service within five years. But, again there was a change in the policy in 1976 and by which those holding five or less stage carriage permits were exempted. Later, the Tamil Nadu Motor Vehicles (Special Provision) Act 1992 was enacted allowing private operators to operate on the already permitted routes, the route length operated by them being frozen and grant of new permits to private operator on the approved scheme routes banned. Presently there are about 5500 private buses in Tamil Nadu.

There are now 18 State-owned Transport Corporations and the Government is planning to group them and bring them all under seven Corporations to improve their efficiency in operation and administration. There were 16,797 buses under these 18 Corporations in March 2002 as against 4943 buses in 1977. In 2001-02, the buses in the Corporations operated in 8133 routes, covering 22,358 lakh effective km and employed about 12500 persons. The vehicle productivity in Tamil Nadu is highly commendable. The fleet utilisation is above 90 per cent. Operated km per day is around 61 lakh, carrying about 1.62 crore passengers daily. Average age of the buses in the fleet is 5.42 years and km covered/bus/day is about 413.

In 1997, the Government felt that the State owned Transport Corporations were unable to cater to the needs of the people living in remote villages and introduced the mini bus scheme to ply in unserved rural areas. Each mini bus can ply up to a route length of 20 km with a provision to overlap up to 4 km in served route. Around 4000 buses are now operated in the State. The network of Government buses, private buses and mini buses covers almost every town and hamlet in Tamil Nadu. There is also an increase in other modes of transport such as auto rickshaws, taxis, motor cars and omnibuses. Further, there is also phenomenal increase in personalised vehicles like car, motorcycles, scooters etc. reflecting a change in transport demand pattern.

Due to various reasons, policy decision has been taken by the Government to privatise certain selected routes, services and operations. It is hoped that this would help to provide better service to the public, reduce losses of the corporations and improve operational efficiency by fostering healthy competition. A committee has been constituted to study the legal and other aspects for giving effect to this decision.

Number of vehicles in Tamil Nadu has increased from 27.72 lakh in 1996 to about 46 lakh by 2000. Number of persons killed on the roads in the year 2000 was 9300. Therefore, about 25 persons are killed on the roads in the State in a day, besides many more subjected to minor and major injuries. In order to improve safety in our roads, the Government have prepared an action plan for road safety and the same is now implemented.

Rail Transport

The share of passenger traffic by railways declined from 68 per cent in 1951 to 20 per cent in 1995. Similarly, the share of freight traffic carried by railways has come down from 89 per cent to 40 per cent in the same period. When the coverage by railways in the State is considered, the total length (BG + MG) of railway lines (as on 31.3.2001) is 4189 route km (Table 6.10). The share of BG lines in total length is about 50 per cent in Tamil Nadu (as on 31.3.2001), whereas it is about 89 per cent in the adjacent State of Kerala. The State of Tamil Nadu would be greatly benefitted when all the eleven ongoing gauge conversion projects, covering about 1900 route km with a targeted investment of Rs. 3422 crore are completed (Table 6.11).

TABLE 6.10

Length of Railway Lines in Tamil Nadu, 1994-2001

	Classification	*1994-95*	*1995-96*	*2001*
A.	Route km:			
	Broad gauge - Electrified	581	692	
	Broad gauge - Non-Electrified	780	676	
	Metre gauge - Electrified	166	165	
	Metre gauge - Non-Electrified	2,470	2,465	
	Total	3,997	3,998	4,189
B.	Track Km (including Sidings):			
	Broad gauge - Electrified	1,523	1,820	
	Broad gauge - Non-Electrified	1,500	1,189	
	Metre gauge - Electrified	357	308	
	Metre gauge - Non-Electrified	3,050	2,847	
	Total	6,430	6,164	

Source: Records of the Southern Railways, Chennai.

Further, surveys are carried out by the Railways to undertake the following 13 projects, which mainly include projects related to laying new lines and gauge conversion of existing lines.

1. Survey for gauge conversion of Chengalpattu - Villupuram section

TABLE 6.11

Gauge Conversion - Metre Gauge to Broad Gauge in Tamil Nadu (As of April, 2003)

(Rs. Crore)

Sl.No.	Name of Work (Conversion of MG to BG)	Length km	Year of Sanction	Total Cost	Expenditure up to 3/2003	Budget Outlay for 2003-04
1.	Tiruchirappalli-Thanjavur-Nagore-Karaikal	200	1995-96	213.35	84.88	12.00
2.	Kollam-Tirunelveli-Tiruchendur and Tenkasi-Virudhunagar	357*	1997-98	577.61	79.89	25.00
3.	Villupuram - Pondichery	38	1996-97	43.83	18.82	11.20
4.	Thanjavur - Villupuram	192	1998-99	231.00	7.31	15.00
5.	Cuddalore - Salem	191	1999-2000	198.68	32.07	10.00
6.	Madurai-Rameswaram	162	1997-98	243.00	6.34	10.00
7.	Villuppuram-Katpadi	161	2000-01	240.00	0.10	1.00
8.	Tiruchirappalli-Manamadurai	150	2000-01	187.81	0.48	5.00
9.	Chennai Beach-Tiruchirappalli (97.95% completed)	340	1992-93	730.42	709.69	1.00
10.	Tiruchirappalli-Dindigul (100% completed)	93	1992-93	133.93	137.35	0.01
11.	Chennai Beach - Tambaram - Chengalpattu	116	1998-99	622.52	171.28	34.00
	Total	2000		3422.15	1244.21	124.21

Source: Records of the Southern Railways, Chennai.

Note: *Out of 357 km, about 85 km length of railway line is in Kerala State.

2. New BG line between Kumbakonam and Namakkal *via* Jayankondan, Ariyalur, Perambalur and Thuraiyur.
3. Gauge conversion of Virudhunagar-Manamadurai.
4. New line from Madurai to Tuticorin *via* Parambupatti, Aruppukkottai, Vilattikulam with alternative *via* Virudunagar, Aruppukkottai and Vilattikulam.
5. Gauge conversion between Madurai - Coimbatore.
6. Updating of survey for 4th line between Pattabiram - Tiruvallur and 3rd and 4th lines between Tiruvallur-Arakkonam section.
7. Survey for a new BG line-Tharamani (Chennai) to Mahabalipuram.
8. Survey for gauge conversion of Thanjavur-Tiruchirappalli MG line.
9. Chennai area - Optimisation and rationalisation of maintenance facilities and preparation of Master Plan for integrated development of rail infrastructure.
10. New BG line between Madurai-Kottayam.
11. New BG line between Tindivanam - Cuddalore *via* Pondicherry.
12. Preliminary Engineering cum Traffic survey for a new BG line from Attipattu to Tiruvallur with a link line to Puttur.
13. Preliminary Engineering-cum Traffic survey for restoration of rail link between Pamban and Dansushkodi.

Further the following five projects pertaining to doubling of lines (BG) are under implementation.

1. Irugur - Coimbatore - 17.70 km.
2. Attipattu - Korukkuppettai - 18.00 km.
3. Pattabiram - Tiruvallur (4th line) - 41.89 km. and Tiruvallur - Arakkonam (3rd line).
4. Ambathurai - Kodaikanal Road - 14.56 km.
5. Chennai Beach - Korukkuppettai (3rd line) - 4.10 km.

These projects when implemented, would greatly benefit the State in achieving faster economic development. In this connection, it is highly desirable to convert in a phased manner all the MG lines in the State to BG lines, as early as possible, to achieve faster and efficient movement of goods and passengers by the rail system. When this is achieved, every railway station in the State could be directly accessible to all parts of India. Besides, it would be beneficial, if the two major travel corridors of the State are brought under BG double lines on electric traction (Chennai - Villupuram - Tiruchirappalli - Madurai - Tirunelveli and Chennai - Salem - Coimbatore). Considering the present trend of development in various regions, surveys may be undertaken to reestablish the following lines which were functioning earlier and later abandoned: Salem -

Mettur; Mayiladuthurai - Tharangambadi; Nidamangalam - Mannargodi. Considering the importance of promoting tourism in Udhagamandalam, it is highly desirable to improve the existing rail system between Mettuppalayam and Udhagamandalam, enabling it to become operational in all seasons of the year.

Mass Rapid Transit system under operation between Chennai Beach and Thirumayilai would become more effective in serving the people of Chennai, when it is extended, as now proposed and executed, to Velachery and then to St. Thomas Mount to give direct connectivity to Tambaram - Chennai Beach sub-urban rail line. It is also found necessary to integrate and co-ordinate the functioning of the rail system in Chennai metropolitan area with the bus system functioning. Fare coordination among the various transport systems operating in Chennai need to be considered to improve their patronage by commuters.

An Unified Metropolitan Transport Authority (UMTA) may have to be constituted to co-ordinate and improve the functioning of various transport systems in Chennai Metropolitan Area on the lines of the recommendations made by the Task Force on Urban Transport Sector (June 2001) for the Ministry of Urban Development and Poverty Alleviation, Government of India.

Ports

Tamil Nadu has 3 major ports (Chennai, Ennore and Thoothukudi) and 14 minor ports (Kattupalli, Ennore - Minor Port, Cuddalore, Tiruchopuram, PY-3 oil field, Thirukkadaiyur, Nagapattinam, Pamban, Rameswaram, Valinokkam, Punnakkayal, Manappad, Kanyakumari and Colachel).

Major Ports

Chennai port under the Chennai Port Trust has 21 alongside berths in three Docks (Bharathi Dock, Dr.Ambedhkar Dock, Jawahar Dock) and a modern Container Terminal established in 1983. The major items handled in this port are POL, Iron ore, Coal and Containers. The port handled 28.73 million tonnes of imports and 12.49 million tonnes of exports bringing the total cargo handled to 41.22 million tonnes in 2000-01. During the same period, the container terminal handled 3,52,307 TEUs. Through the port, 5260 cars were exported in the same period. The approximate income of the port for 2000-01 was Rs. 502 crore, against a total expenditure of Rs. 456.16 crore. The port has planned to undertake the following major development schemes - extension of container terminal and modernisation of Quay berths.

The Asian Development Bank assisted Ennore Port came into operation in 2001. This is the 12th major port in India, located at a distance of 10 nautical miles from the Chennai Port. This port is specially designed to handle energy products and the port is managed by the Government and private sector through Ennore Port Limited. This is the first corporatised major port managed by a company. Coal, Iron ore and Petroleum products are to be handled at this port. The 220 hectare wide harbour basin was dredged to a depth of 15.5 m with 2 berths.

Thoothukudi is a major port since 1974, serving the southern region of the State. It handled a cargo traffic of 13.29 million tonnes in 2002-03. The harbour basin extends to about 400 hectares of protected water area. Container traffic through this port was 2,12,925 TEUs and the port handled 1458 ships in the same period. This will become an important port in the international scene, when the proposed Sethusamudram Canal Project is implemented.

Minor Ports

Tamil Nadu Maritime Board constituted under the Tamil Nadu Maritime Board Act 1995 is administrating, controlling, regulating and managing the minor ports in the state. This Board encourages setting up captive ports and allied facilities such as jetties, mooring systems etc. through active private sector participation. All the minor ports in Tamil Nadu are anchorage parts, where cargo is trans-shipped from the vessels at mid-stream to shore and *vice-versa* through lighters/barges. Crude oil, edible oil, propylene gas, naphtha, liquid ammonia, crude oil and general cargo are handled in these ports.

Among the fourteen minor ports, seven ports (Kattupalli, Ennore–minor port, Thiruchopuram, PY3 oil field, Thirukkadaiyur, Punnakayal and Manappad) have been declared as captive ports under the private entrepreneurship where development of entire infrastructure faculties is the responsibility of the private company concerned. Of these seven captive ports, three ports (Ennore minor port, PY3 oil field and Thirukkadiyur) are operational at present. The remaining four captive ports are in various stages of development.

Kattupalli port was declared for the captive use of M/s.VOPAC Sical Terminal Limited for handling various petro-products, required for their petro-chemical park at

Ennore. Ennore minor port was developed by M/s.EID Parry (India) Ltd. for receiving Liquid Ammonia. This port is functioning since October 1986. Thiruchopuram port was declared for the captive use of M/s. Nagarjuna Oil Corporation Ltd. to handle crude oil and refined oil products. This port would directly serve the proposed oil refinery at Thiruchopuram. PY3 oil field port, situated near Cuddalore is for the exclusive use of M/s. Hardy Exploration and Production (I) Ltd. The port is in operation since October 1997 and used for loading crude oil from the oilwells at PY3 oilfield. Thirukkadaiyur port was declared for the captive use of M/s. PPN Power Generating Company to handle naptha and natural gas required for the power project at Pillaiperumalnallur. Punnakkayal port is a captive port for the use of M/s. Dharangadara Chemical Works Ltd. Manappad port is for the captive use of M/s. Indian Gas Ltd. for handling LNG required for the proposed Gas Turbine Power Project. Cuddalore and Nagapattinam ports have been functioning well for a long-time and they are to be developed through private participation, either wholly or partly. Nagapattinam used to have passenger traffic, serving passengers bound for Singapore and Malaysia, but later suspended in 1985. These two ports continue to serve for industrial developments in respective regions. Pamban port is used to pilot the small drafted vessels of five feet, passing through Pamban Canal. Rameswaram port was catering to passenger service between Rameswaram and Thalaimannar operated by the Shipping Corporation of India up to 1985. Vallinokkam port was earmarked for ship-breaking activities. Kanyakumari port is used to operate the ferry services to Vivekananda Rock Memorial and Thiruvalluvar statue. Colachal port is to be developed as International Transhipment Hub port for handling container ships. The government of Malaysia have evinced interest in developing this port. A detailed feasibility report prepared for developing this port with an investment of about Rs. 2772 crore is under consideration. The minor ports in Tamil Nadu handled a total cargo of 6,02,616 MT during 2002-03.

Port Policy of Tamil Nadu

The salient features of the Port Policy of Tamil Nadu are as follows:

- To promote port based Thermal Power Plants by providing exclusive port facilities for import of coal/naptha/oil/natural gas.
- To provide port facilities to promote export oriented industries and port based industries along the coastal districts of Tamil Nadu.
- To decongest highways and railways by providing facilities for coastal traffic of passengers and cargo along the east coast.
- To promote tourism by providing facilities for leisure and water sports manufacture activities along the coast line.
- To provide facilities to encourage ship-repairing, ship-breaking and manufacture of cranes and floating crafts.
- To increase the share of Tamil Nadu State in the export and import sector in national and international trade and commerce.
- To cater to the needs of increasing traffic of Southern States by providing efficient facilities and services and to support the country's domestic and international trade.
- To decongest the major ports in Tamil Nadu and to improve their productivity.
- To create sufficient infrastructure facilities to handle about 25 per cent of India's total cargo in Tamil Nadu maritime waters.

Sethusamudram Ship Canal Project

This project envisages excavation of an artificial ship canal across Rameswaram island to connect the Palk Bay and Gulf of Mannar and thereby providing a connectivity between the East Coast and the West Coast of India. This would reduce the sea distance between the East Coast and the West Coast of India by more than 400 nautical miles and 36 hours of ship time. National Environmental Engineering Research Institute (NEERI), Nagpur is conducting an Environmental Impact Assessment of the project and it would suggest the best alignment of the canal which would have least environmental impact. The proposed canal is likely to have a width of 200m and a depth of 9m. Studies may have to be undertaken by the Government to examine how best the project could be advantageously used for economic development of the region close to Palk Bay and Gulf of Mannar. Early completion of the long pending canal project would greatly benefit the region.

Inland Water Transport

The Government of Tamil Nadu is considering a proposal for reviving navigation activities in Buckingham canal from Sriharikotta to Marakkanam and for which the canal is proposed to be improved at a cost of Rs. 240 crore. Mass Rapid Transit System developed along the Buckingham canal from Chindaripettai to Thiruvanmiyur has also restricted the usage of the canal. Besides, slums have come up all along the canal on both sides within Chennai city and even beyond. The man-made canal, which was serving effectively the Southern coastal districts of Andhra Pradesh and Northern coastal districts of Tamil Nadu has become a non-functional system over the years. The canal, if improved, would also facilitate in carrying away flood waters in this region.

Airports

There are five airports in the State. Chennai is an international airport serving both domestic and international traffic. Madurai, Coimbatore, Tiruchirappalli and Salem are the other airports serving domestic traffic. Chennai airport is located at about 7 km from the city limit in the close vicinity of defence department developments. This handled about 2.7 million passengers and nearly 62,000 tonnes of freight in 1994-95. Various land use developments have also come up around the existing airport. Considering the long term needs of the region it is desirable to identify a new site for building a modern international airport preferably in a site close to the city which is environmentally acceptable, considering noise level, land use developments and connectivity to existing regional transport network. The existing airport could then become a domestic terminal. Realising the need for such a new international airport, the Govt. of Tamil Nadu undertook detailed investigations with the help of international consultants and have identified a new site. Early action may be initiated to develop the site for a new international terminal.

APPENDIX 6A.I

National Highways in Tamil Nadu - 2002

NH 4	Chennai - Chittoor - Bangalore Road (Stretch within the State)
NH 5	Chennai - Kolkata Road (Stretch within the State)
NH 7	Bangalore - Salem - Madurai – Kanyakumari (Stretch within the State)
NH 7A	Palayamkottai - Tuticorin Road
NH 45	Chennai - Trichy - Dindigul Road
NH 45A	Villupuram - Pondicherry Road
NH 45A Extn	Pondicherry - Cuddalore - Chidambaram - Sirkazhi - Tarangambadi - Nagapattinam Road
NH 45B	Trichy - Viralimalai - Tuvarankurichy - Melur - Madurai - Aruppukottai -Tuticorin Road
NH 46	Krishnagiri - Ranipet Road
NH 47	Salem - Cochin - Kanyakumari (Stretch within the State)
NH 49	Madurai – Dhanushkodi Road
NH 49 Extn	Madurai - Cochin Road (Stretch within the State)
NH 66	Pondicherry - Tindivanam – Gingee – Tiruvannamalai - Krishnagiri Road
NH 67	Nagapattinam - Thanjavur – Trichy - Karur Road
NH 67 Extn	Karur - Palladam – Coimbatore Road
NH 68	Ulundurpettai - Salem Road
NH 205	Renigunta - Thiruthani – Chennai Road
NH 207	Hosur - Malur Road
NH 208	Punalur - Sengottah – Tenkasi - Rajapalayam - Srivilliputur - Thirumangalam Road
NH 209	Dindigul - Palani – Pollachi - Coimbatore - Annur - Sathyamangalam – Chamrajnagar - Kollegal - Kanakpura - Bangalore Road (Link Between NH47 & NH7)
NH 210	Trichy - Pudukottai – Karaikudi - Devakottai - Ramanathapuram Road
NH 219	Krishnagiri - Kuppam Road
NH 220	Dindigul – Vathalagundu - Theni - Kambam - Kumuli Road

Source: Records of the Highways Department, GoTN

APPENDIX 6A.II

State Highways in Tamil Nadu 2002

SH 1	Chennai - Ennore Road
SH 2	Inner Ring Road
SH 4	Arcot - Villupuram Road
SH 5	Arcot - Thindivanam Road
SH 6	Kallakurichi - Thiruvannamalai Road
SH 7	Villupuram - Mambalapattu - Thirukoilur Road
SH 8	Vikravandi - Kumbakonam - Thanjavur Road
SH 9	Cuddalore - Chittur Road
SH 10	Cuddalore - Virudhachalam - Salem Road
SH 11	Calicut - Neelambur - Gudalur Road (Stretch within the State)
SH 12	Calicut - Vaithiri - Gudalur Road (Stretch within the State)
SH 15	Ooty - Kothagiri - Mettupalayam - Sathy - Gobi - Erode Road
SH 16	Krishnagiri - Varatnampalli - Kuppam Salai
SH 17	Malur - Hosur - Adhiyammankottai Road
SH 18	Salem - Thirupathur - Vaniyambadi Road
SH 19	Avinasi - Thirupur - Palladam - Pollachi - Cochin (Via) Meenakarai Road (Stretch within the State)
SH 20	Thoppur - Mettur - Bhavani - Erode Road
SH 21	Pollachi - Dharapuram - Karur Road
SH 22	Grand Anaicut - Caveripattinam Road
SH 23	Mayiladuthurai - Thiruthuraipoondi Road
SH 24	Trichy - Chidambaram Road
SH 25	Trichy - Namakkal Road
SH 26	Trichy - Pudukkottai - Aranthangi - Mimisal Road
SH 27	Perambalur - Manamadurai Road
SH 29	Thanjavur - Pattukottai - Aranthangi - Karaikudi – Kallal - Kalaiyar koil - Maravamangalam - Illayankudi - Paramakudi - Muthukulathur - Sayalkudi Road
SH 30	Musiri - Thuraiyur - Athur Road
SH 33	Madurai - Thondi Road
SH 34	Ramanathapuram - Nainarkoil - Antakudi - Illayangudi - Sivagangai - Melur Road
SH 35	Dindigul - Natham - Singampunari - Thiruppathur - Karaikudi Road
SH 36	Dindigul - Vathalagundu - Periyakulam - Theni - Cumbum - Kumuli Road
SH 37	Mettur - Palakkanuthur - Oddanchatram - Dharapuram - Kangayam - Erode Road
SH 38	Aruppukottai - Perunazi - Sayalgudi - Kaduguchanddai - Mariyur - Valinokkam Road
SH 39	Thirunelveli - Shencottah - Quilon road (Stretch within the State)
SH 40	Thiruchendur - Palayamkottai - Ambasamudram - Thenkasi - Courtaalam - Shencottah Road
SH 41	Rajapalayam - Sankarankoil - Tirunelveli Road
SH 42	Srivilliputhur - Sivakasi - Virudhunagar - Aruppukottai - Tiruchuli - Narikudi - Parthibanoor Road

SH 44	Paruvakudi - Kovilpatti - Ettayapuram - Vilathikulam - Vembar Road
SH 45	Aralvoimozhi - Nedumangadu Road
SH 46	Aralvoimozhi - Nagercoil - Rajakkamangalam - Colachal Road
SH 47	Parthibanur - Kamudhi - Aruppukottai Road
SH 48	Marmalong bridge - Irumbuliyur - Vandalore - Mudichur - Oragadam - Walajabad Road
SH 49	Thiruvanmiyur - Mamallapuram - Marakkanam - Pondicherry Road
SH 50	Thirumazhisai - Sathiyavedu Road
SH 51	Korathalaiyar Bridge - Puthur Road
SH 52	Kavarapet - Sathiyavedu Road
SH 53	Nagari - Pallipet Road
SH 54	Chittoor - Thiruthani Road
SH 55	Mount - Ponamalle - Avadi Road
SH 56	Thiruvottiyur - Ponneri - Panchetty Road
SH 57	Singaperumal koil - Sriperumbudur - Thiruvallur - Red Hills Road
SH 58	Sadras - Chengalpattu - Kancheepuram - Arakkonam - Thiruthani Road
SH 59	Thiruvalam - Katpadi - Venkatagiri Kottah Road
SH 60	Hogenakal - Pennagaram - Dharamapuri - Thirupathur Road
SH 61	Walaja - Sholingar - Arakkonam Road
SH 62	Trichy - Thuraiyur Road
SH 63	Thanjavur - Mannargudi - Thiruthuraipoondi - Vedaranyam - Kodiyakarai Road
SH 64	Kumbakonam - Sirkazhai Road
SH 65	Thiruvarur - Kodavasal - Kumbakonnam Road
SH 66	Kumbakonam - Mannargudi - Adirampattinam Road
SH 67	Nagore - Nannilam - Nachiyarkoil Road
SH 68	Cuddalore - Tirukoilur - Sankarapuram Road
SH 69	Vridhachalam - Ulundurpet - Villupuram Road
SH 70	Vridhachalam - Parangipettai Road
SH 71	Musiri-Kulithalai-Pudukottai-Alangudy - Peravoorani - Sethubavachetaram Road
SH 72	Madurai - Natham Road
SH 73	Thirumangalam - Pallapatti Road
SH 74	Dindigul - Guziliamparai - Karur Road
SH 75	Palayamkottai - Kurukkuchalai - Kolathur - Vilathikulam - Nagalapuram - Panthalgudi - Aruppukottai Road
SH 76	Puliangudi - Sankarankoil - Kalugumalai - Nalattinpudur Road
SH 77	Kovilpatti - Ottapidaram - Pudukottai - Eral - Mukkani Road
SH 78	Pollachi - Valparai Road
SH 79	Mallikarai - Athur - Rasipuram - Thiruchengode - Erode Road
SH 80	Avinasi - Mettupalayam Road
SH 81	Gobi - Uthukuli - Kangeyam Road
SH 82	Sathy - Athani - Bhavani Road
SH 83	Palani - Dharapuram Road
SH 84	Erode - Karur Road
SH 85	Royacottah - Athipalli Road
SH 86	Omalur - Sankari - Thiruchengode - Paramathy Road
SH 87	Udumalpet - Palladam Road
SH 88	Chittor - Gudiyatham Road
SH 89	Nanguneri - Bharathavar - Ovari Road
SH 90	Marthandam - Pechiparai Road
SH 91	Parasery - Monday Market - Pudukkadai Road
SH 92	Nanguneri - Ervadi - Valliyoor - Vijayapathi Road
SH 93	Alwarthirunagar - Nazaareth - Sathankulam - Ittamozhi - Valliyoor Road
SH 94	Thiruchengode - Namakkal Road
SH 95	Mohanur - Namakkal - Sendamanagalam - Rasipuram Road
SH 96	Erode - Perundurai - Kangeyam Road
SH 97	Udumalpet - Dharapuram Road
SH 98	Gudalur - Sultan Battery Road
SH 99	Thirukattupalli - Sengipatti - Pattukkottai Road
SH 100	Palayam - Bodi Road
SH 101	Vaigai Dam - Varusanadu Road
SH 102	Uthamapalayam - Surulipatti Road

Source: Records of the Highways Department, GoTN

Chapter 7

Urban Infrastructure

Urbanisation in Tamil Nadu

According to the 2001 Census, Tamil Nadu has emerged as the State with the highest level of urbanisation (43.86 per cent) in the country. 2.72 out of 6.21 crore of the total population of Tamil Nadu live in urban areas. In 1991 the level of urbanisation was only 34.15 per cent with an urban population of 1.9 crore, when Tamil Nadu was in third place behind Maharashtra (38.7 per cent) and Gujarat (41.0 per cent). The advance to first place is mainly due to a change in definition. Following the Nagar Palika Act of 1994 all the 611 town *panchayats* were brought under the category of statutory towns, irrespective of whether they satisfy the demographic criteria of "urban".

As evident from the Table 7.1, the inclusion of all the town *panchayats* resulted in an increase from 1991-2001 of 57.94 lakh in that category alone. The increase in the town *panchayat* population accounted for about 70 per cent of the total increase of 81.64 lakh from 1991-2001. The growth in the other categories, namely, Municipal Corporations and Municipalities was much more modest at 10.90 and 13.95 per cent, respectively, over the decade – this would barely cover the natural growth of the population. Thus, increase in the proportion of urban population can be considered to be a statistical artifact due to the change in definition. If we exclude town *panchayats* and census towns, the increase in urban population would be 17.86 lakh from 143.72 to 161.58 lakh or a decadal growth rate of only 12.42 per cent or an annual rate of 1.17 per cent.

As shown in the Table 7.2, the rate of urbanisation had slowed down from 1971-1991 and would have slowed down further by 2001, if it had not been for the change in definition.

TABLE 7.1

Urban Population of Tamil Nadu (by Category) 1991-2001

Category	*Number*		*Population*		*Decadal Growth Rate (%)*
	1991	*2001*	*1991*	*2001*	
Corporation	3	6	71.35	79.12	10.90
Municipalities/ Cantonments	108	104	72.37	82.46	13.95
Town Panchayats	224	611	37.81	95.75	153.23
Census Towns	134	111	N.A.	N.A.	
Total	469	832	190.77	272.41	42.79

Source: Census of India, 2001.

TABLE 7.2

Urban Population of Tamil Nadu 1901-2001

Year	*No. of Towns*	*Urban Population*	*Urban Population(%)*	*Decadal Growth(%)*	*Annual Growth Rate(%)*
1901	133	27.24	14.15	—	—
1911	162	31.49	15.07	15.51	1.45
1921	189	34.28	15.85	8.86	0.85
1931	222	42.30	18.02	23.40	2.10
1941	257	51.73	19.70	22.30	2.01
1951	297	73.33	24.35	41.75	3.49
1961	339	89.90	26.69	22.59	2.04
1971	439	124.64	30.26	38.64	3.27
1981	434	159.52	32.95	27.98	2.47
1991	469	190.77	34.15	19.59	1.79
2001	832	272.42	43.86	42.79	3.56

Source: Census of India, 2001.

Nevertheless, the fact remains that the 2.7 crore urban population of Tamil Nadu require a wide range of urban services including water supply, sewerage, solid waste management and streets as well as social infrastructure like schools, hospitals, markets and so on.

Tamil Nadu has a very dispersed pattern of urbanisation with municipalities in virtually every district (excluding Ariyalur and Perambalur). The boundaries of Chennai District are contiguous with the Chennai Municipal Corporation. However, the Chennai Metropolitan Area is a larger area which includes several municipalities and town *panchayats* in Tiruvallur and Kancheepuram Districts.

Table 7.3 which provides the spatial distribution (by district) of the six corporations, 104 municipalities, and 611 town *panchayats*, clearly illustrates that urbanisation is not limited to any one part of the State. However, the urban population is concentrated along certain urban corridors.

TABLE 7.3

Distribution of Urban Units by District

District	*Municipal Corporation*	*Municipalities*	*Town Panchayats*	*Urban Units*	*Level of Urbanisation*
Thiruvallur		6	10	32	54.48
Chennai	1	7	—	1	100.00
Kancheepuram		—	28	56	53.48
Vellore		9	27	49	37.85
Dharmapuri		3	17	21	15.77
Tiruvannamalai		4	10	16	18.36
Villupuram		2	16	18	14.49
Salem	1	3	34	45	46.35
Namakkal		4	20	28	36.75
Erode		5	59	67	46.20
Nilgiris		3	13	18	59.51
Coimbatore	1	4	59	79	66.03
Dindigul		3	24	29	35.02
Karur		2	13	15	33.19
Tiruchirappally	1	2	18	25	46.65
Perambalur		—	5	5	14.54
Ariyalur		—	4	4	11.38
Cuddalore		5	16	23	33.00
Nagapattinam		3	9	12	22.15
Thiruvarur		4	19	11	20.24
Thanjavur		3	22	29	33.92
Pudukottai		2	8	12	16.93
Sivagangai		3	12	15	28.18
Madurai	1	3	15	25	55.94
Theni		5	23	28	54.10
Virudhunagar		6	10	27	44.38
Ramanathapuram		2	9	11	25.34
Thoothukudi		2	20	26	42.28
Tirunelveli	1	5	38	45	46.48
Kanyakumarai		4	56	60	65.10
Total	6	104	611	832	43.86

Source: Census of India, 2001.

According to a study by the Centre for Policy Research (2001), there appear to be 3 to 4 major urban corridors, namely,

- Chennai – Salem-Erode – Coimbatore
- Tiruchi – Madurai - Tirunelveli
- Chennai – Pondicherry * - Cuddalore – Thanjavur and to a lesser extent Tuticorin – Nagercoil (* Pondicherry is a Union Territory)

A substantial number of the municipalities and municipal corporations are located along these urban corridors. Urban infrastructure in particular may have to be planned on a regional basis. Only 6 of the 30 districts have a level of urbanisation (LoU) less than 20 per cent. 13 districts exceed the state average of 43.86 per cent in terms of LoU while 11 are below the state average but above 20 per cent. Thus, Tamil Nadu not only has a high level of urbanisation in overall terms, but has a dispersed spatial network of cities and towns.

Among the *major* states of India, Tamil Nadu at 43.86 per cent has the highest level of urbanisation (LoU) but smaller states like Goa and Delhi and Union Territories like Chandigarh and Pondicherry have much higher LoU. For India as a whole, the LoU is only 27.78 per cent due to the low level of urbanisation in the northern and eastern states. Maharashtra at 43.40 per cent and Gujarat at 37.35 per cent stand second and third among the major states, after Tamil Nadu.

Urbanisation is closely linked to the economic activities in a particular area. The definition of "urban" apart from size (population > 5000) and density (population density > 400 persons per sq. km.) specifies that 75 per cent of the male workforce should be engaged in non-agricultural pursuits. Hence infrastructure has to be planned not only for the population *per se* but also according to the requirements of the economic sectors in terms of water supply, waste disposal, power, telecommunications, etc. The higher density of urban areas is an advantage because it may provide economies of scale in the provision of these and other urban services. In contrast, providing the same level of service in a rural area is far more expensive because the average cost is much higher.

Urban Poverty

Poverty is defined as people's inability to secure the minimum level of subsistence with a person not having adequate income to buy food with a total caloric norms 2150 in urban areas. As of 1999-2000, the proportion of people living below the poverty line estimated for All

India stood at 26.10 per cent (27.09 in rural areas and 23.62 in urban areas). The proportion of people living below poverty line in urban Tamil Nadu had been steadily on the decrease- from 42.40 in 1973-74 to 39.77 in 1993-94 and further to 22.11 per cent in 1999-2000. The number of poor persons during 1999-2000 is estimated at 49.97 lakh in the urban areas.

TABLE 7.4

Percentage of Population below Poverty Line – Urban Tamil Nadu

Year	*Urban*
1973-74	49.40
1977-78	48.69
1983-84	46.96
1987-88	38.64
1993-94	39.77
1999-2000	22.11

Source: Ninth Five Year Plan, Tamil Nadu State Planning Commission.

The factors that have contributed to rapid decline in poverty in the State include effective implementation of several Poverty Alleviation Schemes. These schemes are providing wage employment or self-employment. The Public Distribution System also provides a safety net for the poor. Since 1993-94, the percentage of people below poverty line was higher in urban areas than in rural areas. The increasing incidence of urban poverty is reflected in the accelerated growth of slums in cities and towns.

74th Amendment

Recognising the neglect of integrated urban development planning by the local authorities, the 74th Constitution Amendment Act, 1992 incorporated urban planning including town planning and planning for economic and social development among the legitimate municipal functions and made the Constitution of District and Metropolitan Planning Committees mandatory. Integrated Urban Development Planning needs to comprise *inter-alia,* functional decentralisation to enable the Urban Local Bodies to effectively discharge their responsibilities suitable to contemporary urbanisation, participatory planning process promote convergence of resources, etc. The State government needs to introduce improvements to overcome structural deficiencies in the way of generation of revenue from conventional sources like property tax, municipal bonds etc. Since provision of infrastructure facilities basically rests with ULBs, the State governments have to seriously implement the fiscal reforms as envisaged in the 74th Constitutional Amendment. These identified ways and means need to be executed and monitored regularly.

Access to Housing

'Housing For All' is the aim of the State. The housing stock coupled with education, health and water supply adds to the productivity of the labour force. There is a vast regional disparity in the availability of housing stock in the State due to economic reasons. In urban areas there is not only a vast disparity between regions but also between housing units. Slum population accounts for 20 per cent of the total population in the State. It is well known that the slum huts lack proper basic amenities such as living space, drainage, toilet and other facilities. Ultimately, this aggravates the degree of morbidity and mortality among slum population. It is now widely recognised that the Government should only play a role of 'facilitator' and creator of 'enabling' climate for housing activities instead of being a direct provider of housing units. The Government of Tamil Nadu evolved its Housing Policy (1998) on the lines of the National Housing Policy.

As per the National Family Health Survey (1998-99), about one-third of the houses in Tamil Nadu were *kutcha,* semi-*pucca* houses accounted for 38.4 per cent and the *pucca* houses accounted for 27.6 per cent, The proportion of *kutcha* houses are relatively higher in rural areas as compared is 16.7 per cent in urban areas. 72 per cent of the urban houses have toilet facilities. The conditions of housing stock in Tamil Nadu leave much to be desired. Sub-standard housing stock-accounts for 55 per cent of the total stock of 47.67 lakh housing units in urban areas.

In the context of increasing pressure of population, renewal of existing houses and building up of new dwelling houses are a pre-requisite. The State Planning Commission has estimated the shortage of housing in the State at 15 lakh in 1994-95, of which 8.2 lakh are in urban areas. The demand for housing is likely to rise at the rate of 2 lakh dwelling units per year – of which 1.34 lakh would be in urban areas.

The Tamil Nadu Housing Board, Cooperative Housing, Tamil Nadu Slum Clearance Board are playing a major role in the creation of housing facilities in Tamil Nadu. The major sources for funding housing activity in the State are Housing and Urban Development Corporation limited (HUDCO), the State

Government, LIC, HDFC, and Commercial Banks. The housing stock has been steadily increasing in the State over the year with the financial help from these agencies. (Tamil Nadu Economic Appraisal 1999-2000)

Creation of Housing Units by Various Agencies (lakh Nos.)

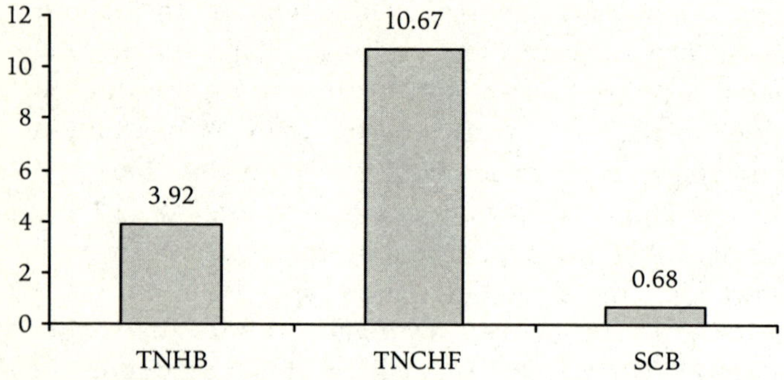

Source: Tamil Nadu Economic Appraisal 1999-2000
TNHB – Tamil Nadu Housing Board
TNCHF – Tamil Nadu Cooperative Housing Federation
SCB – Tamil Nadu Slum Clearance Board

Access to Water Supply and Sanitation

The ultimate purpose of the schemes implemented by the TWAD Board and CMWSSB is to provide safe drinking water and sanitation to all the households. The TWAD Board data are at the level of town or city, while the data collected by the Census and the National Sample Survey are at the household level. With respect to access to safe drinking water in urban areas, Tamil Nadu's performance was lower than the national average in both 1981 and 1991. We do not have the household details from the 2001 Census as yet. In comparison with southern states, Tamil Nadu fares better than Andhra Pradesh and Kerala but worse than Karnataka (Table 7.5).

TABLE 7.5

Access to Safe Drinking Water (in per cent) in 1981 and 1991

	1981	*1991*
Andhra Pradesh	63.27	73.82
Karnataka	74.40	81.38
Kerala	39.72	38.68
Tamil Nadu	**69.44**	**74.17**
All-India	**75.06**	**81.38**

Source: Census of India, 1981, 1991.

Since the ultimate goal is to have 100 per cent access to safe drinking water, Tamil Nadu will have to devote more resources to achieve this goal at least by 2010.

The National Sample Survey gives a breakdown of the major source of drinking water in urban areas. In Tamil Nadu as in other regions of India about 74 per cent households in urban areas depend on tap water; which is generally assumed to be safe. With regard to other sources, nearly 4 per cent depend on tanker water which is an indication of the scarcity of drinking water in urban Tamil Nadu. The All-India figure is less than 1 per cent. Since ground water is a major source, 13.40 per cent depend on tubewells while 6.50 per cent on open wells. The dependence on tubewells is much higher than in the other Southern States but lower than the All–India average as shown in the Table 7.6.

TABLE 7.6

Major Sources of Drinking Water (Urban) 1995-96

	Tap	*Tube Well*	*Tanker*	*Pucca Well*	*Tank/ Pond*	*River/ Canal*	*Others*
Andhra Pradesh	81.70	11.10	1.80	4.00	0.40	0.30	0.60
Karnataka	86.30	8.40	0.10	3.90	0.70	0.00	0.60
Kerala	37.80	1.60	1.00	56.70	0.10	—	2.70
Tamil Nadu	**73.80**	**13.40**	**3.60**	**6.50**	**0.80**	**0.20**	**1.30**
All-India	**73.70**	**18.50**	**0.80**	**5.50**	**0.30**	**0.10**	**0.90**

Source: National Sample Survey 52nd Round (1995-1996).

Access to Sanitation

The situation with regard to sanitation is not very good in urban Tamil Nadu. Even in 1991, only 58 per cent had access to toilets compared to 64 per cent at the All-India level (Table 7.7). Proper sanitation is particularly important in urban areas because of the higher density and therefore the easier spread of disease. High priority needs to be given to sewerage and sanitation in urban areas of Tamil Nadu, since water borne diseases are widely prevalent, particularly during the monsoon season.

TABLE 7.7

Access to Toilets (Urban)

	1981	*1991*
Andhra Pradesh	44.07	54.60
Karnataka	53.28	62.52
Kerala	59.14	72.66
Tamil Nadu	**51.27**	**57.47**
All-India	**58.15**	**63.85**

Source: Census of India, 1981, 1991.

Access to Electricity

Tamil Nadu performs better with regard to electricity connections. 76.8 per cent of households in 1991 had electricity compared to only 61.6 per cent in 1981. Tamil Nadu did better than the other southern states and marginally better than the All-India average as shown in Table 7.8. Per capita consumption of electricity (in kwh) is higher in Tamil Nadu than in the southern states and also in comparison to the All-India average (Table 7.9). Presumably, the same situation continues in 2001.

TABLE 7.8

Electricity Connection (Urban)

	1981	*1991*
Andhra Pradesh	52.22	73.31
Karnataka	61.98	76.27
Kerala	54.57	67.65
Tamil Nadu	**61.59**	**76.80**
All-India	**62.51**	**75.78**

Source: Census of India, 1981, 1991.

TABLE 7.9

Per Capita Consumption of Electricity (Urban)

(kwh)

	1986-87	*1996-97*
Andhra Pradesh	205	346
Karnataka	197	340
Kerala	135	241
Tamil Nadu	**238**	**468**
All India	**191**	**334**

Source: National Human Development Report, 2001.

Access to All Three Amenities

Only 40.5 per cent households in urban Tamil Nadu had access in 1991 to all three amenities, namely, safe drinking water, toilets and electricity (Table 7.10). This was ten percentage points less than the All India figure of 50.5. The comparatively poorer performance of Tamil Nadu is due to the lack of access to sanitation facilities. The access to drinking water and electricity is better.

The importance of water supply and sanitation sector is not merely for the provision of basic needs. The health, environment and empowerment spin-offs are equally significant. For example, provision of safe water and sanitation facilities considerably reduces health costs, both for individuals and the community as a whole. Reduced morbidity rate improves the productivity of human resource. Ready access to drinking water supply frees women's and girl children's time on finding and hauling water day after day, which can be spent on productive uses like employment and education. For all these reasons, investment in water supply and sanitation sector is considered as an investment towards improving the quality of life of the people as well as improving economic growth.

TABLE 7.10

Households with Access to Electricity, SDW and Toilets (Urban)

	1991
Andhra Pradesh	39.3
Karnataka	48.6
Kerala	25.5
Tamil Nadu	**40.5**
All-India	**50.5**

Source: Census of India, 1991.

Status of Urban Water Supply and Sewerage in Tamil Nadu

Urban Water Supply

Tamil Nadu has very limited water resources, because much of the State falls in the rain-shadow region of the Western Ghats. The coastal districts receive higher rainfall, but only part of it can be stored in tanks and reservoirs. Since the surface water is largely committed to irrigation, drinking water is provided throughout the State mainly from groundwater sources. Furthermore, groundwater is more likely to meet drinking water quality standards without much treatment. The coverage of water supply in the urban towns is summarised in the Table 7.11.

Provision of urban water supply is the responsibility of the Tamil Nadu Water Supply and Drainage Board (TWAD). Operation and maintenance of the system is generally the responsibility of the concerned urban local body. In Chennai alone, the Chennai Metropolitan Water Supply and Sewerage Board (MWSSB), known popularly as "Metrowater" is the agency responsible for providing water supply and sewerage.

With progressive urbanisation, the water supply requirements of cities and towns of Tamil Nadu are increasing. Only 31 out of 102 municipalities and 217 of the 611 town *panchayats* have good water supply. Many of the urban local bodies have poor financial and technical capability to operate and maintain water supply and sewerage systems. Capacity building is urgently needed for the Urban Local Bodies (ULBs). A substantial proportion of the urban poor who live in slums has very limited access to protected water supply.

TABLE 7.11

Coverage of Water Supply in the Urban Towns

Category	*Total Number*	*Water Supply Status**		
		Good	*Average*	*Poor*
Corporations (including Chennai)	5	—	5	—
Municipalities (excluding cantonments)	102	31	37	34
Town *Panchayats*	611	217	203	191
Total	718	248	245	225

Source: Tamil Nadu Water Supply and Drainage Board
(* The status is based on norms established for the different categories).

Old transmission and distribution systems and poor maintenance have resulted in high levels (25 per cent to 40 per cent) of unaccounted for water. Intermittent supply is also a serious problem and results in avoidable expenditure at the household level on storage as well as contamination in the distribution network. Since meters do not seem to work properly, it has become difficult to implement volumetric pricing. The tariffs collected are generally inadequate to maintain the assets.

The Working Group for the Tenth Plan has made various recommendations on urban water supply:

- Database on The Water Supply System for Asset Management, Service Efficiency, etc.
- Quantification of Health Benefits for Future Investment
- Provision of Stand Post Supply in Urban Slums
- Reduction of Unaccounted for Water
- Pricing of Water on Volumetric Basis to Cover Costs
- Upgradation of Existing Water Supply Systems
- Rainwater Harvesting and Water Conservation (See Annexure I)
- Capacity Building of Ulbs to Manage Water Systems
- Autonomous Bodies for Municipal Corporations
- Private Sector Participation Wherever Possible
- Long Term Plans for 2020 or 2050

Proposed Outlays For The Tenth Plan

Description	*Outlay (Rs. Crore)*
Provision for Ongoing Schemes in Urban Towns	554.00
New Augmentation Schemes in Towns having Poor Water Supply	500.00
Upgradation of Existing Systems	225.00
Sub-Total	**1279.00**
External Assistance for Water Supply Systems	500.00
Total	**1779.00**

Resource Mobilisation

Agency	*Outlay (Rs. crore)*
State Government	400.00
Central Government	70.00
LIC	300.00
HUDCO	500.00
Beneficiary Contribution	9.00
Total	**1279.00**

Source: Report of Working Group on Water Supply and Sanitation (2002).

Urban Sewerage and Sanitation in Tamil Nadu

Underground sewerage schemes exist only in 16 urban areas – four corporations and 11 municipalities and one town *panchayat* in Tamil Nadu. There has been no budgetary support for sewerage schemes till 2001-02. The total outlay during the Ninth Plan was only Rs. 255 crore for sewerage and Rs. 15 crore for low cost sanitation. There has been a general reluctance to carry out sewerage schemes on account of the high cost, non-availability of land for disposal, etc. Hence there has been inadequate allocation for this sector. Untreated sewage/drainage is polluting lakes, ponds and water courses. Industrial and other wastes are also being discharged into water bodies. The tariff structure has to be studied in towns with sewerage systems. Urban slums require better low cost sanitation. LCS maintenance has generally been poor.

The Government has decided to provide sewerage schemes on a priority basis:

- In all municipalities with water supply service level of 90 lpcd and above.
- In all urban towns having a population of more than one lakh.
- In District Head Quarters.
- Places of Tourism Importance.

Schemes Under Implementation

National River Conservation Project

New Underground Sewerage schemes will be taken up in the following towns under the Centrally sponsored National River Conservation Programme (NRCP).

(i) Tirunelveli Corporation

(ii) Tiruchirappally Corporation

(iii) Thanjavur Municipality

(iv) Mayiladuthurai Municipality

(v) Karur Municipality

(vi) Inam Karur Town Panchayat

(vii) Rameswaram Town Panchayat

(viii) Tiruchendur Town Panchayat

Under the **National River Action Plan**, works are undertaken for interception, diversion and treatment of sewage flowing into River Cauvery in Tiruchy, Erode, Bhavani, Pallipalayam and Komarapalaym stretches. The works are being carried out at an estimated cost of Rs. 30.41 crore with assistance from Government of India.

Master Plans for Urban Towns

A Master Plan to cover the urban towns with underground sewerage schemes is to be prepared. The Master Plan will also provide for exploring the possibilities of adopting alternative technology options for the safe disposal and recycling of wastewater. An Action Plan for providing sewerage schemes for all the municipal towns will be drawn up and implemented in a phased manner.

Low Cost Sanitation

Low cost sanitation (LCS) is executed in Tamil Nadu with the World Bank loan assistance. This project is in two phases. 14 Municipalities were included in this project in the first phase: 26,642 individual latrines and 357 community latrines were constructed in this phase at a cost of Rs. 709.55 lakh. 91 Small/Medium Towns have been included in the second phase project when 10,685 individual latrines will be constructed. The cost of the Project is Rs. 400 lakh.

The Working Group on the Tenth Plan has made some recommendations with regard to sewerage and sanitation:

- Master Plan for sewerage and sanitation covering the urban areas of the State.
- Full scale treatment of sewage wherever possible.
- Technologies to minimise use of water for flushing.
- Capacity building of ULBs.
- Encouraging house service connections in sewered areas.
- Acquiring lands for sewage disposal.
- Community toilets in urban slums.
- Pay and use toilets in tourist and public places.
- Recycling of wastewater.

Proposed Outlay for the Tenth Plan

Description	*Outlay (Rs. Crore)*
Ongoing Sewerage Scheme in Coimbatore	10.00
NRAP Schemes	16.00
NRCP Schemes	355.00
New Underground Schemes for Class I cities	500.00
National Lake Conservation Project	20.00
Low Cost Sanitation	120.00
Total	**1021.00**

Resource Mobilisation

	Rs.Crore
State Government	200.00
Central Government	300.00
LIC	200.00
HUDCO	200.00
Beneficiary Contribution	121.00
Total	**1021.00**

Source: Report of Working Group on Water Supply and Sanitation (2002).

CMWSSB

The proposed outlay for the Chennai Metropolitan Water Supply and Sewerage Board is Rs. 2528.68 crore for water supply and sewerage for the Tenth Plan Period. These are mainly for Water Supply Augmentation and for improving and strengthening the existing sewerage system in Chennai. The Board is also involved in building a long range partnership with the private sector.

Municipal/Tamil Nadu Urban Development Fund[1]

One of the major urban problems the government has been addressing is the municipalities' financial and

1. http/www.tn.nic.in/tnudp/aboutus.htm

organisational capacity for maintenance, municipal service obligation and investment. Convinced of the merits of strengthening the municipalities, the government set up a new source of municipal funding called Municipal Urban Development Fund (MUDF), under the Tamil Nadu Urban Development Project financed by the World Bank.

Municipalities can apply to the fund without restriction as to type of project. Demands are anticipated mainly for roads, street lighting, storm water drains, conservancy and remunerative enterprises. Water supply and sanitation projects are likely to be funded in fast growing areas, such as Chennai outer Municipalities where there are at present no major facilities. Municipalities with adequate capabilities can also access the Fund to undertake slum improvement schemes. The Fund is operated within a framework of rules and procedures, which impose strict financial discipline, requiring municipalities to set acceptable revenue performance targets select service standards and technologies consistent with their priority needs and substantiate request for project funding with adequate feasibility studies. Municipalities utilising the Fund have to maintain a positive cash flow and debt servicing ratio not normally greater than 0.45.

The Municipal Urban Development Fund was converted to the Tamil Nadu Urban Development Fund in 1996 with the participation of the government of Tamil Nadu, Indian financial institutions (ICICI, HDFC, and IL&FS) and is managed by a private asset management company. More than 500 sub-projects covering roads, bridges, street lights, solid waste plants, storm water drains, bus stations and markets in 90 out of 110 municipalities in Tamil Nadu have been financed through this Fund. In addition through its grant fund, it encourages urban infrastructure investments targeted to the urban poor.

One of the aims of the World Bank financed Tamil Nadu Urban Development Project is to build the institutional and financial capacity of the urban local bodies. This is to be done through training programmes offered by the Anna Institute of Management, Tamil Nadu Institute of Urban Studies and the concerned departments. Ultimately, the ULBs will be in a position to deliver the services/functions assigned to them by the 74th Amendment to the Constitution. The ULBs have been neglected for many years, and it will take time to develop their institutional capability. The priority will have to be on the six municipal corporations and the larger municipalities.

State Finance Commissions I and II

State Finance Commission I

Following the passage of the 73rd and 74th Amendments to the Constitution, Tamil Nadu set up the First State Finance Commission (SFC I) for the period 1996-2002. The Commission assessed the requirements for various urban services, based on the norms and forecast of population for the year 2002. The service gaps were computed on the basis of the existing service levels. For the six core services (water supply, sewerage/sanitation, solid waste management, roads, storm water drains and streetlights) the total capital investment needed for both urban and rural local bodies was estimated to be Rs. 5249 crore (at 1995-96 price levels) to achieve the improved levels, and the per capita cost to be Rs. 176.40 per year. The capital investment would be spread out over five years with a cost escalation of 12 per cent per year. The operation and maintenance cost was estimated to be Rs. 1234.49 crore per year. The Commission has suggested that project finance for the above be raised through LIC, Tamil Nadu Urban Development Fund, TUFIDCO, MIDC and from the State Government. Municipal Corporations could go in for public issues of equity or bonds or approach financial institutions. Privatisation was recommended for maintenance of water supply, sewerage and solid waste management. Involvement of NGOs and social organisations was encouraged.

State Finance Commission II

A Second State Finance Commission (SFC II) was set up in 2001 to make recommendations for the period 2002-2007. The Commission went through a similar process of calculating the service gap. However, the Commission also studied the absorptive capacity of the local bodies in terms of their utilisation of funds over the last five years, before making their decisions on allocation of funds.

In terms of capital investment, the SFC has recommended Rs. 803 crore for Town Panchayats, Rs. 650 crore for Municipalities, and Rs. 975 crore for Corporations (Table 7.12). Water Supply is the priority service for town *panchayats* making up half (Rs. 403 crore) of the capital allocation. In the case of municipalities and corporations, roads and storm water drainage have been given sizable allocations. Sewerage and sanitation has been given only 10 per cent.

The Second State Finance Commission has chosen to give priority to operation and maintenance expenditure. The operation and maintenance expenditure for the five-year period amounts to Rs. 5241 crore as compared to the capital expenditure of Rs. 1633 crore for the urban local bodies. Public works, roads, street lights, conservancy and water account for most of the allocation. SFC II has also made provisions for operation and maintenance of new investment made from 2002-07 (Table 7.13).

TABLE 7.12

Recommended Capital Investment 2002-2007

(Rs. Crore)

Category	*Town Panchayats*	*Municipalities*	*Corporations*
Water Supply	403	210	109
Sewerage and Sanitation	8	56	108
Roads	80	150	296
Storm water Drainage	160	72	177
Street Lights	16	39	21
Solid Waste Management	16	26	69
Others	120	65	146
Investments		32	49
Total	803	650	975

Source: Second State Finance Commission Report – Tamil Nadu.

TABLE 7.13

Recommended Operation and Maintenance Expenditure (Total) 2002-2007

(Rs. Crore)

Category	*Town Panchayats*	*Municipalities*	*Corporations*
General Administration and Taxes	206.88	374.29	366.27
Public Works and Roads	123.01	329.74	761.47
Sanitation and Drainage	—	51.81	179.96
Public Health and Conservancy	133.50	202.80	264.02
Street Lighting	210.88	221.70	271.90
Water	239.96	289.27	218.40
Education and Town Planning	—	18.29	66.55
Miscellaneous Items	155.41	82.34	97.36
Operation and Maintenance for New Investment	144.91	107.55	122.73
Total	1214.57	1677.81	2348.65

Source: Second State Finance Commission Report – Tamil Nadu.

Some of the recommendations of SFC II are as follows:

- Maintenance, particularly preventive maintenance needs to be accorded higher priority. Leakage and wastage needs to be brought down from the present level of 40 per cent to 10 per cent.
- Incentive fund for local bodies to take up rain water harvesting (RWH) and tax incentives for the public if they put up RWH structures in their houses.
- Privatisation of solid waste management to reduce conservancy staff.
- Incentive Fund for treatment, processing and disposal facilities for solid waste management in all Class I cities to comply with the Supreme Court judgement
- Report Card System on satisfaction of urban residents with urban services
- Monitoring of major projects by District Collector, Commissioners, and other relevant officials to improve the pace of development.

The SFC has chosen to focus on water supply as the priority sector. While this is unexceptionable, it is equally important to make the necessary investments in sewerage and drainage, so that wastewater does not become a public health problem. The SFC has recognised that solid waste management is a crucial issue in urban areas and that it is important to comply with the Supreme Court's decision. Unlike Water Supply and Drainage which comes under the purview of the Tamil Nadu Water Supply and Sewerage Board, there is no state level agency which can provide technical assistance to ULBs. While collection can be privatised, disposal could be a serious problem for the larger ULBs. The State Government agencies including the Pollution Control Board have to study the issue and take necessary action to advise the ULBs. Roads and traffic congestion is also becoming a serious problem in urban areas. This issue is taken up separately in the chapter on road infrastructure.

SFC II has also made the following recommendations regarding the resource base for ULBs.

- Levy of property tax will be done as per the Tamil Nadu Urban Local Bodies Act 1998. The periodicity of revision will be every five years for residential property and every two years for non-residential. A detailed tax mapping exercise are to be taken up for Chennai City. A self declaration scheme is to be introduced in all ULBs to make the tax administration simple and transparent.
- The Commission has fixed income slabs for the levy of professional tax for salaried people.

Triennial revision will be done from April 1, 2002. Provisions have been made for collection of professional tax from industries and traders.

- Global sharing of the State own tax revenue (after excluding the entertainment tax) would be 8 per cent in 2002-03, gradually increasing to 10 per cent by 2006-07. In addition 5 per cent of central devolution is to be passed on to local bodies.
- A *self reliance index* i.e. the own income of ULBs as a share of total income, of 65 per cent for Municipal Corporation, 60 per cent for Municipalities and 45 per cent for Town *Panchayats* has been suggested as a goal for ULBs.

Urban local bodies can perform their functions efficiently only if they have sufficient resources. The traditional sources of funds like the property tax are relatively inelastic, even if revisions are made periodically. Ultimately, ULBs will have to levy user charges for various services that will enable them to recover the costs of service delivery. Otherwise, urban services will be provided in a sub-optimal fashion at a low level. The goal for self reliance set by the Finance Commission is a step in the right direction.

Public–Private Partnerships

There are two types of public-private partnerships that have emerged in Tamil Nadu with respect to urban infrastructure:

- Involvement of NGOs in provision of public services like solid waste collection.
- Private firm or agency enters into an agreement/ contract to provide the service.

Involvement of NGOs

An example of the first kind is the role played by Exnora in Solid Waste Management. Exnora was set up as a citizen's initiative to improve the environment at the neighbourhood level with the participation of the local community. Local Civic Exnoras have been set up all over Chennai (900-950 in number) as well as in some other cities. The local Exnora collects subscriptions from the members in the street/ neighbourhood and arranges to collect the solid waste from each house. The waste is collected by an employee called the "street beautifier" who takes it to a central location, where it is then collected by the Municipal Corporation. In effect, the service provided is primary collection at the street level, which reduces the burden on the municipal agency. The street beautifier is also responsible for keeping the street clean, thus improving the local environment. In many cases, the beautifier is a former rag picker who now has guaranteed employment as well.

Overall, the approach has been successful in those communities where the local Exnora is well organised and collects subscriptions regularly. In some areas, there has been resistance from those who feel that the property tax paid to the local body should be sufficient, without having to pay an additional amount to a neighbourhood organisation. There have also been some problems with local councillors (elected members of the local body) who feel that solid waste management should be a function of the local body. Nevertheless, Exnora has been relatively successful in dealing with the solid waste problem atleast at the street level, and in forging a partnership with the local body at the city level in carrying out this service.

Involvement of Private Sector

Tiruppur is often cited as a good example of public-private partnership in respect of urban infrastructure. The New Tiruppur Area Development Corporation was formed as a public-private partnership under the Indian Companies Act to undertake water supply and sewerage projects in Tiruppur. The Government of India, Government of Tamil Nadu, Tiruppur Municipality, and ILFS as promoters have assumed complete responsibility for implementing the project over 30 years. The following are the broad components of the project:

- A water supply scheme with River Cauvery as source to supply 185 mld and to serve the Tiruppur Local Planning Area and Tiruppur Municipality.
- Comprehensive sewage collection, treatment and disposal system for Tiruppur Municipality including on-site sanitation facilities for slum areas.
- Industrial waste water collection and disposal system.
- Investment in roads, telecommunication and other urban infrastructure facilities.

The project envisages a two stage construction with the first two components estimated to cost Rs. 1,207 million.

The New Tiruppur Area Development Corporation now has a concession agreement with the State of Tamil Nadu which makes the Corporation responsible for project implementation, operation and maintenance of the new systems. In return the Corporation receives the right to revenue streams from the industrial users and municipal bulk water supply to meet its costs. The corporation in turn conducted an international competition to contract its obligations to construct and maintain the new systems to a BOT operator from the private sector. This operator will be responsible for transmission, treatment of water supply, distribution of water outside municipal limits where most of the industry is located, treatment of the collected sewage and maintenance of the sewage treatment plants. The BOT operator will also increase the supply of bulk water to the Municipality, which manages distribution systems within the municipal limits.

User Charges

The Alandur sewerage project is another example of public-private partnership. The unique feature of the project is the willingness of project beneficiaries to pay sewerage connection charges much higher than in neighbouring Chennai. Alandur municipality (AM) is a selection grade municipality located 14 km south of Chennai and forms a part of the Chennai Metropolitan Area. With a very limited industrial base, Alandur has developed into a residential suburb of Chennai. Alandur is the first municipality in the country where initiative has been taken to finance, develop and implement the sewerage project on a commercially viable basis by using PPP as an option. Presently, this project is under construction. The distinguishing feature of the Alandur project has been the willingness of the residents to make a substantial contribution (~23 per cent) towards project financing.

The town has no sewerage system and most of the residents are using water borne sanitation facilities for disposal of night soil. The households either have septic tanks or holding tanks, and the municipality collects the sewage periodically in tankers and disposes them in low-lying areas outside the municipal limits. The sewage overflow from septic tanks is let off into open storm water drains. Water from these drains finally accumulates as stagnant water in the south-eastern corner of the town and has become a breeding ground for mosquitoes, and has also affected the ground water sources.

In 1996, the municipality approved a proposal to provide an underground drainage system. The proposed sewerage system was to be designed for the targeted population of about three lakh persons and planned to be completed in five years period from its inception date. The municipality's target are to provide more than 22000 connections, both for domestic and non-domestic users, by the end of the year 2004-05. The connection charges were expected to generate over Rs. 13 lakh, which would be deposited in a revolving fund for repayment of loans to the lenders.[2]

Regulatory Framework

Increasingly the involvement of the private sector has been sought to provide urban infrastructure in cities and towns in Tamil Nadu. Government agencies themselves like Metrowater in Chennai have started to increase water supply and sewerage charges. Toll roads are being set up where tolls are collected from users by the transport agencies (discussed elsewhere). Despite these individual initiatives, there is no regulatory body that can ascertain whether the charges/tolls are equitable. Many urban services are natural monopolies, and if the concerned agencies decide to operate them on a commercial basis, they might try to earn monopoly profits. Regulatory bodies have to be set up to ensure that the charges are consistent with the level of service provided.

Another aspect of concern is the provision of services to the poor. The 2001 Census identified the slum population in 67 towns in Tamil Nadu. The percentage of the population varies from less then 10 per cent to 30-40 per cent. Chennai has a slum population of more than 10 lakh, and there were five other cities in Tamil Nadu with a slum population of more than a lakh. Clearly, slum dwellers cannot pay for urban services at the same level as others. Yet the poor are often willing to pay a nominal amount even for stand post water or public conveniences as long as the service is reliable. The regulatory body has to ensure that the urban poor are not deprived of essential services like water and sanitation because of their inability to pay high user charges.

Lastly, the regulatory body has to monitor the quality and level of the service provided by the agency. For example, the per capita supply of water or some other norm specified for the urban area must be met. The public must be in a position to represent their views/concerns on delivery of service, access, tariff levels, etc. In the flurry over private sector participation, the public good and the public interest must not be sacrificed. There may also be externalities such as pollution by waste water which must be controlled.

2. Alandur Sewerage Project—A unique experiment of public participation in project Financing, Mukesh. P. Mathur, NIUA.

Key Issues Relating to Urban Infrastructure

Capacity Building of Urban Local Bodies

The technical, managerial and financial capabilities of the urban local bodies have to be enhanced if they are to improve the delivery of urban services. The emphasis will first have to be on the Municipal Corporations and the larger Municipalities. Under the Tamil Nadu Urban Development Project, 50 of the largest ULBs will be given assistance to develop a City Corporate Plan covering a 5 year period. The corporate plan developed through a consultative process will contain a 5 year investment programme of high priority items. ULBs will also be encouraged to outsource and/or privatise some of their functions such as solid waste management. The Tamil Nadu Institute of Urban Studies has been entrusted with the task of providing training and capacity building of the ULBs. Since ULBs have been neglected for decades, capacity building will require both funds and efforts over a long period.

Improvement in the Quality of Urban Services

The delivery of urban services in most of the urban local bodies is unsatisfactory. Water supply coverage is insufficient; sewerage is non-existent except for a few cities; roads are of poor quality and are getting severely congested. Solid water collection and disposal is unsatisfactory and poses a health hazard in most urban areas. Storm water drains are badly maintained. The decline in the quality of urban infrastructure has taken place over decades because the ULBs were not provided sufficient funds for capital works and for operation and maintenance. Further, the ULBs themselves did not have elected bodies until 1994, who could have tried to raise resources as well as improve the quality of services. Private sector participation was sought only recently to improve service delivery. The State Finance Commission has recommended that ULBs should seek to raise 60-65 per cent of their income from their own sources and not depend on the State. Users will have to pay higher rates by way of user charges if the quality of services is to improve.

Limited Private Sector Initiatives

Although there are some examples of public-private partnerships, the private sector is generally reluctant to finance urban infrastructure due to the low return, political risks, poor financial position of the ULBs, and their lack of expertise in identifying and executing projects. The TNUDF as well as the experiments in Tiruppur, Alandur, etc. may change the perception of the private sector to some extent. However, the bulk of infrastructure financing will still have to come from the public sector and financial institutions. And that can happen only if urban bodies' finances are in a sound condition.

Limited Finances for Urban Infrastructure

Very few urban infrastructure investments are commercially viable because their benefits are realised over a very long period. Debt financing through municipal bonds is possible when the concerned government is credit worthy. This may be possible only for one or two of the larger ULBs. Limited debt financing is available through HUDCO, LIC and through the TNUDF. The TNUDF may be able to raise resources from the capital market for the selected municipalities. Many of the ULBs will have to depend on the funds devolved by the State Government resulting from the SFC award and from budgetary support given to executing agencies like the TWAD Board. The ULBs will also have to raise their own resources through user charges and other means.

ANNEXURE 7A.I

Policy on Ground Water Recharge and Rainwater Harvesting (RWH)[3]

"Ground water is the major source for most of the drinking water supply schemes. As much as 90 per cent of the rural population and 70 per cent of urban population get their drinking water supplies from the ground water sources. In recent years, the ground water level is depleting at an alarming rate. Several factors like continuous failure of monsoon, overexploitation by various users and deforestation have contributed to this situation. In Tamil Nadu, as many as 52 blocks have been classified as overexploited blocks where the ground water extraction has exceeded the recharge level, 37 blocks have been classified as dark area blocks where the ground water extraction is more than 85 per cent of the estimated recharge and 86 blocks have been classified as grey areas where the exploitation is between 65 per cent to 85 per cent.

Recharge is a slow process. Ground water recharge particularly is a slow and arduous process in Tamil Nadu, where 73 per cent of the geographical area is covered with hard crystalline formation and where the annual rainfall occurs during a short spell of few days. Rainfall is the only source of recharge for replenishing the ground water sources. Moreover, recharge through natural process accounts only for 10 to 25 per cent of the total recharge that occurs in the State. Most of the recharge is helped through the vast network of tanks, *ooranis, eris* and *kanmais* that have been built in the past. The declining levels of ground water indicates that many of the rain water catchments are in degraded state and their holding capacities have been reduced considerably due to factors like siltation, encroachments, conversion of rain water holding structures for other uses, etc. It is therefore necessary that this dangerous trend of degeneration is halted and immediate remedial measures are undertaken. The Government considers this as a major thrust area and proposes to initiate a massive programme for Rainwater Harvesting and Groundwater Recharge.

The Government proposes to enlist the participation of the Public and Non-Governmental Organisations (NGOs) in propagating and installing rainwater-harvesting structures. Every single household can construct and benefit from rainwater harvesting. Every rooftop and any open space is a potential catchment area for rainwater harvesting. A significant portion of demand for water is still met from private wells owned by individual households in urban areas and rainwater harvesting can both sustain and augment these wells. Even the households, which do not have wells can harness rainwater and use it to meet their requirements directly. Appropriate regulatory and legislative measures will also be considered for enforcement."

References

Centre for Policy Research (2001). *Urbanisation and Urban Development Challenge in Tamil Nadu,* New Delhi.

Cenus of India (2001). *Tamil Nadu – Rural and Urban.*

Government of India, Planning Commission (2002). *National Human Development Report.*

Government of Tamil Nadu (2001). *Second State Finance Commission Report.*

Government of Tamil Nadu State Planning Commission (2002), *Report of the Working Group on Urban and Rural Water Supply and Sewerage and Sanitation for the Formulation of the Tenth Five Year Plan," Chennai*

Government of Tamil Nadu (2002). Tamil Nadu Economic Appraisal 1999-2000

http/www.csis.org

http/www.tn.nic.in/tnudp/aboutus.htm

Mukesh P. Mathur (2002). "Alandur Sewerage Project: A Unique Experiment of Public Participation in Project Financing," *India Infrastructure Report, 2002,* Oxford University Press.

NCAER (2000). The India Infrastructure Report Vol. 3, New Delhi.

3. This section is reproduced from the Tamil Nadu policy document on Water Supply and Sewerage.

Chapter 8

Water Resources Management

Tamil Nadu accounts for 4 per cent of the land area and 6 per cent of the population, but only 3 per cent of the water resources of the country. Most of Tamil Nadu is located in the rain shadow region of the Western Ghats and hence receives limited rainfall from the South-west monsoon. The coastal districts in particular receive more rainfall from the North-east monsoon, but its contribution is irregular since the rainfall is primarily caused by cyclonic storms in the Bay of Bengal. The North-east monsoon contributes 47.4 per cent of the rainfall while the South-west accounts for only 33.3 per cent. The remaining 19.3 per cent occurs during the transition period from January–May. The average annual rainfall for the State is only 943 mm compared to the All India average of 1170 mm. It varies from 1200 mm in the coastal areas to 550 mm inland. The distribution of rainfall within Tamil Nadu is given in the following Table 8.1.

TABLE 8.1

Distribution of Rainfall in Tamil Nadu

Rainfall Range	*Area (sq.km)*	*% of area*
< 600	2183	1.7
600-800	30733	23.6
800-1000	47863	36.8
>1000	49290	37.9

Source: Ground Water Resources of Tamil Nadu, PWD, 1994.

Status of Water Resources

Surface Water

There are 17 major river basins in the State with 61 reservoirs and about 41,948 tanks. Of the annual water potential of 46540 million cubic metres (MCM), surface flows account for about half. Most of the surface water has already been tapped, primarily for irrigation which is the largest user. 24 lakh hectares are irrigated by surface water through major, medium and minor schemes. The utilisation of surface water for irrigation is about 90 per cent.

Groundwater

The utilisable groundwater recharge is 22,423 MCM. The current level of utilisation expressed as net ground water draft of 13,558 MCM is about 60 per cent of the available recharge, while 8875 MCM (40 per cent) is the balance available for use. The categories of blocks based on the level of groundwater extraction is given in Table 8.2.

TABLE 8.2

Groundwater Extraction in Blocks of Tamil Nadu

Category of Blocks	*No. of Blocks as on Jan. 1988*	*%*	*No. of Blocks as on Jan. 2003*	*%*
Safe	137	35.6	97	25.2
Semi-critical	70	18.2	105	27.3
Critical	35	9.1	37	9.6
Overexploited	135	35.0	138	35.8
Saline	8	2.1	8	2.1
Total	385	100.0	385	100.0

Source: Central Ground Water Board, 2003.

Over the last five years, the percentage of safe blocks has declined from 35.6 per cent to 25.2 per cent while the semi-critical blocks have gone up by a similar percentage. Over-exploitation has already occurred in more than a third of the blocks (35.8 per cent) while eight blocks (2 per cent) have turned saline. The water level data reveals that the depth of the wells range from an average of 0.93 metres in Pudukottai district to 43.43 metres in Erode. According to the Central

Groundwater Board, there has been a general decline in groundwater level in 2003 due to the complete desaturation of shallow aquifers. There has been a considerable failure of irrigation wells in Coimbatore District.

Water Balance

The Water Resources Organisation prepared a State Framework Water Resource Plan of Tamil Nadu. The annual water potential of the State including surface and groundwater is assessed as 46,540 MCM (1643 TMC) while the estimated demand is 54,395 MCM (1921 TMC) in 2001 which is likely to go up to 57,725 MCM in 2050.

The sectoral water demand (MCM) is given in Table 8.3:

TABLE 8.3

Sectoral Water Demand (2001, 2050)

Sector	*2001*	*%*	*2050*	*%*	*% Increase*
Domestic	2222	4.08	3460	6.00	55.72
Irrigation	49978	91.88	49978	86.58	0.00
Industries	1555	2.86	1985	3.44	27.65
Power	118	0.22	180	0.31	52.5
Livestock	519	0.96	519	0.90	0.00
Aquaculture	2		2		0.00
Recreation	1		1		0.00
Minimum Flows	—		1600	2.77	NA
Total	54,395	100.00	57,725	100.00	6.12

Source: Institute of Water Studies, 1998.

- Domestic use (urban and rural) is projected to go up from 4 per cent to 6 per cent due to increase in population and due to urbanisation. The domestic requirement would increase by 55.72 per cent.
- Agriculture use will remain stagnant or may even decrease due to progressive urbanisation.
- The share of industry may not change much, but in absolute terms the increase will be about 27.7 per cent.
- Provision of 1600 MCM in 2050 would be made for minimum flow in rivers for ecological purpose, which is a new category for water resource planning.

Sectoral Demand

Irrigation

Out of a net sown area of 56 lakh hectares, about 30 lakh hectares (54 per cent) of arable land are irrigated. Since irrigation may take place more than once, the gross irrigated area is of the order of 36 lakh hectares or an irrigation intensity of 120 per cent. Canals account for about 29.2 per cent, tanks for 21.3 per cent and wells for 48.9 per cent of net irrigated area. In 1998-99 the foodgrain output reached a peak of 94 lakh tonnes due to the availability of irrigation.

Surface irrigation potential has largely been exhausted. Area under canal irrigation has remained almost stagnant since the sixties at about 8.5 lakh hectares. Modernisation of several of the canal system has been taken up under the National Water Management Project and the World Bank funded Water Resources Consolidation Project. The efficiency of many of the canal systems has declined due to seepage and silting. Irrigation efficiency can be improved through command area development, participatory irrigation management, conjunctive use of surface water and groundwater, introduction of advanced methods of irrigation such as drip and sprinkler systems, and reduction in the wastage of water due to over irrigation.

The area under tank irrigation has fallen by a third from 9 lakh hectares in sixties to 6.3 lakh hectares in 1999-2000. The average net area irrigated by a tank has decreased from 19.2 ha in 1981-82 to 15.1 ha in 1999-2000. The proportion of area irrigated by tanks has fallen from 36.8 per cent in the sixties to only 21.3 per cent in 1999-2000. Modernisation of tanks with assistance from the European Economic Commission has been taken up since 1984. Non-governmental organisations are also involved in implementing the scheme through active participation of water user associations.

Wells have become the pre-dominant source of irrigation accounting for nearly half of the irrigated area. The total number of wells has increased from 5.39 lakh in 1970-71 to 16.79 lakh in 1999-2000. During this period, the area irrigated by wells has increased from 9.18 lakh hectares to 14.53 lakh hectares. The number of open wells and dry wells energised was only 42.4 per cent in 1970-71 but increased to 91.1 per cent in 1999-2000, due to the free supply of electricity to farmers. 16,000 wells could not be used due to well failure. The fact that there is well failure is an indicator of the over-extraction of groundwater in certain parts of the State. As mentioned earlier, the groundwater in 138 out of 385 blocks is over-exploited.

Watershed Management

Given that 45 per cent of the net sown area is not irrigated, it is essential to take up watershed management and *in situ* water harvesting. There are 19,330 micro-watersheds in the State where watershed development can be taken up. Check dams, percolation ponds, contour bunding and other soil and water concervation measures can be implemented. It may also be necessary to take up catchment protection works. Recharge of groundwater is particularly important given the heavy dependence on wells. There are a number of programmes such as the Drought Prone Area Programme (DPAP), Integrated Watershed Development Programme (IWDP) and the National Watershed Development Programme for Rainfed Areas (NWDPRA) which provide funding for watershed management. Some NGOs have also been active in promoting watershed management in the rainfed areas of the State which do not have access to irrigation. The newly established TN Watershed Development Agency (TAWDEV) can serve as the nodal agency for implementing watershed programmes in cooperation with other State departments.

With the objective of making suitable changes in the existing institutional framework for implementation of watershed development programmes, the Government of India launched new initiative called HARIYALI on January 27, 2003 which seeks to involve the local bodies both administratively and financially in the implementation of the watershed development programmes.

Domestic Sector

Although population growth has slowed down, Tamil Nadu is urbanising rapidly. Consequently, the domestic water requirements are projected to increase by more than 50 per cent from 2222 MCM in 2001 to 3460 MCM in 2050. Water quality is also becoming a serious concern due to pollution by industrial effluents, sewage, etc. and also due to naturally occurring phenomena. The Government of Tamil Nadu has indicated that water security, i.e. provision of drinking water to the people will be the highest priority of the Government.

Rural Water Supply

The latest survey in April 2002 indicates that there are 80,421 rural habitations in the State. A habitation is smaller than a village and includes hamlets/clusters of households which have a common water source. A fully covered habitation means that the entire population has access to safe assured drinking water at the level of 40 litres per capita per day (lpcd). The source should be within a distance of 1.6 kilometres of the habitation for plain areas and within an elevation of 100 metres in the case of hilly areas. Partially covered habitations provide potable water but at levels less than 40 lpcd. Non-covered habitations have no potable supply accessible to the habitation. Under this classification of coverage, 28,623 habitations were fully covered, 51,294 partially covered, and 504 habitations had no reliable source. The Tamil Nadu Water Supply and Drainage Board (TWAD) has been taking up the no source and partially covered habitations to make them fully covered. Particular attention is paid to SC/ST habitations.

Two of the major rural water supply schemes being implemented are the Minimum Needs Programme and the Accelerated Rural Water Supply Programme. The Government of India has sponsored a "Sector Reforms" project based on demand driven, cost recovery, and user participation principles. The Sector Reforms project was launched on a pilot basis in four districts viz. Coimbatore, Vellore, Cuddalore and Perambalur. During 2002-03 two more districts Kancheepuram and Virudhunagar were brought under the project. Water supply schemes to 1237 rural habitations at a total estimated cost of Rs. 55 crore will be implemented during 2003-04. Tamil Nadu is considered a pioneering State in the implementation of sector reforms. The Government of India has introduced the "Swajaldhara" scheme by which funding will be given to villages/ communities which are committed to follow the Sector Reforms Project. House service connections will be given wherever the households are willing to pay the cost. The World Bank has approved in principle a rural water supply project for Rs. 1000 crore covering eight districts of the State. However, it has proposed charging for water supply provided through public fountains.

Water quality monitoring has to be taken up since there is deterioration in the quality due to over-exploitation, pollution, etc. Fluoride in water sources is common in the western districts of the State such as Dharmapuri, Salem, Erode, and Dindigul. 3555 habitations in Tamil Nadu are affected by fluoride. Defluoridation plants have been installed in 10 habitations in Dindigul district as a pilot project, while alternative safe drinking water has been provided to 2888 fluoride affected habitations. Iron removal plants have been installed in 43 habitations. The TWAD Board has set up 20 desalination plants covering 107 habitations in Ramanathapuram District.

Recharge structures such as check dams, percolation ponds, etc. have been constructed, based on the ground water recharge maps prepared by the Institute of

Remote Sensing, Anna University. The construction of rainwater harvesting structures will be continued under the Prime Minister's Gramodaya Yojana Programme and through funds provided by NABARD. Rain centres have been established at the TWAD Board Head Office and the district headquarters to disseminate the message of rainwater harvesting. The TWAD Board is redesigning their website to include data on the water supply status as well as the various schemes being implemented. The sustainability of rain water harvesting structures will depend on the involvement of the public in the operation and maintenance. Village and Water Sanitation Committees (VWSC) are being set up under the State Water and Sanitation Mission. The VWSCs will have to take the responsibility for maintaining various systems including the RWH structures. There is also need for technical studies of the efficiency of these structures to better understand their performance in the field.

The Government issued an Ordinance making it mandatory to provide rain water harvesting structures by a stipulated date in all buildings both in the rural and urban areas. To conserve and augment the storage of ground water, to reduce water table depletion, to improve the quality of ground water and to arrest sea water intrusion in coastal areas, rain water harvesting structures were installed in almost all buildings in rural and urban areas in Tamil Nadu. This measure is now being extended to cover all open areas, fields, road margins, thoroughfares, streets, reserve forest areas, revenue forest areas, all tanks, all *Ooranis,* National and State Highways, rural roads, by-passes, bridges, culverts, all temple tanks etc., which have potential for harvesting run-off water.

Rural Sanitation

The level of sanitation is very poor in Tamil Nadu. Less than 15 per cent of households have access to toilets. Only 27 per cent have drainage facilities, of which only 4 per cent have civered drainage. Solid waste collection and disposal is virtually non-existent. The Department of Rural Development has been implementing the Restructured Central Rural Sanitation Programme since 1999. The components include the construction of individual toilets, sanitary complexes for women, school sanitation and rural sanitary marts. They have also initiated the Total Sanitation Campaign in phases in many of the districts of Tamil Nadu. TSC emphasises Information, Education and Communication, Human Resource Development and Capacity Development activities to increase awareness and demand generation for sanitary facilities. The Government of Tamil Nadu has launched a scheme in 2001 for Integrated Women's Sanitary Complexes in 12,318 village *panchayats* to provide sanitation and bathing facilities for rural women. Those complexes are to be maintained by local self help groups.

Urban Water Supply

This sector is discussed in detail in the chapter on urban infrastructure. There are several combined schemes to provide both urban and rural water supply which are under investigation in different districts of the State. Urban sewerage is also discussed in the urban infrastructure chapter.

Industrial Water Use

Industrial water demand is projected to increase by 27 per cent from 1555 MCM in 2001 to 1985 MCM by 2050. Thermal power plants account for the highest proportion of water use. Other industries include chemicals, distilleries, oil refinery, textile dyeing, steel, fertilisers, pharmaceuticals, petrochemicals, paper and pulp, sugar, electroplating etc. Most industries pay a user charge to the Government if they draw water from rivers, and lakes. Industries which receive municipal supply pay a water tariff to the concerned local body. Since the availability of water is limited, many industries have themselves adopted conservation and recycling measures. Two industries in Chennai, CPCL and MFL purchase and treat sewage from Metrowater to meet their water requirements.

Water Pollution

Industrial Effluent Discharge

There are more than 3000 industrial units in Tamil Nadu which have been classified under the highly polluting or "red" category. The total effluent generated is about 6 lakh litres per day of which more than 5 lakh litre (85 per cent) is generated by large industries. About 400 units discharge directly into rivers. Of particular concern are the nearly 1000 tanneries which are located in Vellore, Kancheepuram, Dindigul and Erode districts. The effluents have caused serious problems in the Palar basin. Similarly, there are a large number of textile bleaching and dyeing units in Tiruppur, Erode, and Karur, which have contaminated the Noyyal, Amaravathy and other water bodies.

There are five main industrial complexes in Tamil Nadu: Manali/Ennore, Ranipet. Cuddalore, Mettur and Tuticorin which have chemical, petro-chemical and other industries. These complexes have also become environmental hotspots. There are cement units, distilleries, sugar, sago, paper, dairying, electroplating, chemical and fertilisers (Agro chemicals), mining industries, ores/mineral processing industries and a variety of other industries which are water consuming and also generate large quantities of effluent. Some of the industries have also provided the treated effluent for irrigation with some degree of success. However, other industries, particularly a pulp plant faced serious problems when the effluent used for irrigation contaminated the surrounding wells.

All the industries discharging effluents are regulated by the Tamil Nadu Pollution Control Board. They have to meet the effluent standards fixed by the Board. Industries pay a cess based on their water consumption to the Tamil Nadu Pollution Control Board. Most of the industries have constructed effluent treatment plants. In small industrial clusters, although the units are connected to common effluent treatment plants, the level of treatment is often not satisfactory.

Surface Water Pollution

Industries cannot be set up within 1 km of a river or waterbody. However, the effluents often flow through *nallahs* or open drains and reach the rivers, lakes, etc. Since the river water is used downstream for irrigation or drinking by people/livestock, contamination of the river has increasingly become a serious problem in many of the river basins of the State. River basins like Palar, Tamiraparani, Cauvery, Noyyal, Bhavani and Amaravathy face serious pollution problems due to industrial effluents. Sewage and sullage from municipalities and settlements has also increased tremendously due to piped water supply and is contaminating rivers, lakes, tanks, and ground water.

Ground Water Pollution

With greater utilisation of water for industrial and domestic use and also due to the increased use of agricultural chemicals, ground water quality is deteriorating rapidly in the State. Diminished water quality also means that the quantum of fresh water available for particular uses is reduced, or that the water can be used only after treatment. Problems of water quality can be due to natural causes like geological formations or due to sea water intrusion.

- In the black cotton soil areas of the State, dissolved salts are high.
- In the coastal areas such as backwaters, estuaries etc. salinity levels are high.
- Effluents from the leather industry have contaminated the groundwater in the Palar basin.
- Effluents from the textile industry have affected the groundwater in the Noyyal basin.
- Industrial pollution in various industrial estates/zones has affected groundwater quality.
- Seawater intrusion has taken place in some coastal areas due to over extraction of groundwater.
- Excess application of fertilisers and pesticides has affected groundwater quality in certain pockets; high levels of nitrates are observed in the Western districts.
- Naturally occurring fluoride is a serious problem particularly in the Western districts of the State.
- Human and animal waste and run off from solid waste, garbage dumps and street litter accumulation result in contamination of water and high incidence of water related diseases.

Water Pricing

Irrigation

Since water is a scarce resource in Tamil Nadu, pricing may be one way to ensure that the limited resources are allocated in an efficient manner. Irrigation takes up 90 per cent of the available water resources of the State. However, the charges paid by users is abysmally low. Revenue receipts as a per cent of revenue expenditures were only 3.13 per cent for major and medium schemes and 5.01 per cent for minor irrigation schemes in 1999-2000. In terms of maintenance, the cost recovery ratio was only 16.7 per cent in 2000-01. Tamil Nadu does not have a system of water charges as such. However, the assessment for land revenue distinguishes between wet land and dry land, and the differential assessment reflects the cost of providing irrigation. Farmers also pay a local cess which is transferred to the local body. In 2001, the total land revenue collected was only Rs. 43 crore, of which Rs. 36 crore was transferred to the local bodies. The Government of Tamil Nadu had set up a Committee on Irrigation Water Pricing which made suggestions towards revision of water charges. The charges were increased marginally in 2003, but do not reflect the full cost of providing water for irrigation.

A related issue is the lack of a power tariff for farmers who extract ground water. A power tariff for farmers has been introduced in 2003, and the policy changes made are explained in the chapter on the power sector. The low price of water in the irrigation sector has led to over use of both surface and ground water. In the long run, proper pricing policies have to be implemented if there is to be sustainable use of water. The water charges must reflect atleast the operation and maintenance costs, and if possible the capital charges such as interest and depreciation.

The low water charges have resulted in poor maintenance of the surface irrigation systems in the State. The Government of Tamil Nadu has obtained assistance from the World Bank (Rs. 840.84 crore) to implement the Water Resources Consolidation Project. The WRCP provides for rehabilitation and modernisation of 16 irrigation systems and 25 minor irrigation schemes, and completion of nine on-going irrigation projects. The WRCP project which began in 1995 is scheduled to be completed by March 31, 2004. The operation and maintenance of all the irrigation systems can be sustained only if irrigation water is priced properly, but without seriously jeopardizing the return that the farmers are getting.

Domestic and Industrial Use

The Tamil Nadu Water Supply and Drainage Board (TWAD) charges bulk rates for the local governments and industries. The local governments recover these costs from the households in the form of water tax and water charges. The revised rates with effect from October 2002 are given below (Table 8.4):

TABLE 8.4

Tariffs For Domestic and Industrial Use (2002)

(Rs. Per Kilolitre)

User Group	*Existing tariff per 1000 litres (Rs.)*	*Revised tariff per 1000 litres (Rs.)*
1. Corporations/ Municipalities/ Urban Town *Panchayats*	3.50	4.50
2. Rural Town *Panchayats/* Village Panchayats	2.25	3.00
3. Industries and other Beneficiaries	10.50	15.00

Source: Department of Municipal Administration and Water Supply (2002).

The Department of Municipal Administration and Water Supply has also ordered that there be a suitable surcharge on property tax for water supplied through public fountains, and the amount maintained in a separate account. Thus, there is now a recognition that water supply, both urban and rural should be priced. Since it is not administratively possible to have a variety of rates, the same rates govern all local bodies except for the city of Chennai. There is also a recognition that rural supply through water fountains can also be charged at some nominal rate. Both the urban and the rural poor have repeatedly said in surveys that they are willing to pay if reliable service is provided.

The city of Chennai faces very acute water scarcity problems. This is reflected in the high water rates charged by the Chennai Metropolitan Water Supply and Sewerage Board (Metrowater) as shown in the Table 8.5.

There is also a water and sewer tax (7 per cent of the annualised value of the property tax) which has to be paid by households.

Water Cess

The Water (Prevention and Control of Pollution) Cess Act of 1977 empowers the State Pollution Control Boards to levy a cess on industries based on their water consumption. If they comply with the provisions of the Water Pollution Act of 1974 and the Environment Protection Act 1986, the cess is correspondingly reduced. In Tamil Nadu, the cess is levied by the Tamil Nadu Pollution Control Board on water consuming industries. The rates of water cess which were revised recently are given in the following Table 8.6.

The water cess rates were revised in 2003 because they were considered to be too low to act as a disincentive for industries to conserve the use of water and hence reduce the volume of pollution. However, even the revised rates remain quite low compared to the cost of fresh water.

State Water Policy

Tamil Nadu adopted a State Water Policy in 1994 along the lines of the National Water Policy of 1987. Subsequently, the National Water Policy was revised in 2002. The Tamil Nadu Government is in the process of revising the State Policy to include various current concerns. Some of the major aspects of the policy are the following:

- Importance of water resources in the development of the State.

TABLE 8.5

Tariffs for Domestic and Other Uses – Chennai (2003)

(Rs. per Kilolitre)

Sector		Quantity	Price
1. Domestic	Metered	Upto 10 KL	Rs. 2.50/KL
		11 KL to 15 KL	Rs. 10/KL
		16 KL to 25 KL	Rs. 15/KL
	Unmetered		Rs. 50/month
2. Commercial*	Metered	Upto 500 KL	Rs. 35/KL
		Above 500 KL	Rs. 60/KL
	Unmetered		Rs. 650/month
3. Institutional*	Metered	Total Quantity	Rs. 30/KL
	Unmetered		Rs. 300/month
4. Bulk Supply (Tankers)		9000 litres	Rs. 600/Tanker Load

Source: Metrowater (2003).

* There are special rates for specific categories like hospitals and education institutions.

TABLE 8.6

Water Cess For Industries (2003)

(Paise/Kilolitre)

	Industries Which Comply With Environmental Regulations	*Industries Which Fail to Comply With Environmental Regulations*
1. Industrial cooling, boiler feed	5 paise per KL	10 paise per KL
2. Domestic Purpose	2 paise per KL	3 paise per KL
3. Pollution is easily biodegradable	10 paise per KL	20 paise per KL
4. Pollutants are not easily biodegradable & toxic	15 paise per KL	30 paise per KL

Source: Central Pollution Control Board (2003).

- Need for considering socio-economic aspects of water resource projects.
- Need for basin wide planning for equitable water use.
- Priorities for water use in the State.
- Management and development of ground water resources.
- Watershed management in rainfed areas.
- Increase in demand for non-agricultural uses.
- Management of water quality and environmental aspects.
- Need for a hydrological database for planning and management.
- Stakeholder participation in management e.g. water user associations.
- Need for proper pricing of water in different sectors.

Thus, the policy framework for water resources management is largely in place. The apex institution in the State at the policy level is the Water Resources Control and Review Council chaired by the Chief Minister. The primary agency charged with implementation of the policy is the Water Resources Organisation. The Institute of Water Studies is the nodal agency responsible for water planning while the Irrigation Management Training Institute imparts training to farmers and officials. Domestic water supply (urban and rural) schemes are executed by the Tamil Nadu Water Supply and Drainage Board (TWAD) for the entire State except Chennai Metropolitan Area where Metrowater is the implementing agency. TWAD executes capital projects which are handed over to the concerned local bodies for operation and maintenance. Industrial water pollution is regulated by the Tamil Nadu Pollution Control Board. Management of water quality and environmental aspects of rivers and water bodies is the responsibility of the Department of Environment.

Issues in Water Management

Inter-sectoral Water Management

Historically, water management was synonymous with irrigation since the irrigation sector was by far the largest user (90 per cent) of water. However, with urbanisation and industrialisation, water requirements in the domestic and industrial sectors have grown considerably. Water is needed throughout the year and in locations which may not be close to major water sources. Often, water has to be stored, transported and treated for particular uses. Since the water resources of the State are limited and in many cases committed to irrigation, diverting water for other uses has become a major challenge. Drinking water has been accorded the highest priority in the State Water Policy and "water security" has also been given the top priority by the government. Hence, any scheme to provide drinking water may have to be at the expense of irrigation.

Water using industries may find it difficult to locate in Tamil Nadu given the scarcity of fresh water. Conservation and reuse may be necessary even for the existing industries. Another intersectoral problem that is gaining importance is the impact of effluents discharged by industries and sewage from municipalities on both land and water. Other sectors like agriculture and drinking are affected and the availability of fresh water is further diminished due to pollution.

Water is managed by a plethora of sectoral agencies, with very little coordination. Institutionally, it is difficult to deal with intersectoral and cross-cutting problems. The creation of the Water Resource Organisation and the Water Resources Council are the first steps taken to coordinate uses and users of water in the State.

River Basin Boards

The National and State Water policies recommend the management of water resources at the river basin level. As part of the Water Resources Consolidation Project, the Government of Tamil Nadu has approved the creation of river basin boards for the Palar and the Tamiraparani basins. River basin management committees have been set up to monitor the water related activities of different agencies and users. The Palar has been heavily polluted by effluents from the tannery industry, while the water resources of the Tamiraparani are already heavily utilised by a variety of users. The demand for water in the Tamiraparni basin (2747 MCM) far exceeds the availability (2069 MCM). A Secretariat has been set up in the Institute of Water Studies to collect data and to service the two boards. Public hearings have been held in both river basins which were well attended. The experience of launching the boards will provide some indication whether river basin management is practically feasible. Intersectoral issues, for example, can be discussed and resolved if the boards are able to function.

Ground Water Regulation

About 60 per cent of the ground water available through recharge is extracted annually in Tamil Nadu. However, over-exploitation has taken place in 35.8 per cent of the blocks. It is imperative, therefore, to manage the ground water resources of the State in a sustainable manner. The Tamil Nadu Legislature passed the Ground Water (Development and Management) Act and the Act came into force after receiving the assent of the President in March 2003. The Act is applicable to the whole State of Tamil Nadu except the Chennai Metropolitan Area which is governed by a separate Act.

A Tamil Nadu Ground Water Authority has been set up to direct and regulate the development and management of the ground water resources of the State. The Authority has the power to notify areas for regulation. Every user in the notified area will have to obtain the permission of the Authority to extract ground water. Wells cannot be sunk and transport of groundwater by lorries, tankers, etc. cannot be done in a notified area without obtaining a permit. Electricity cannot be provided for energising wells which are in contravention of the Act. All new wells sunk in the State even in non-notified areas have to be registered. The Authority may lay down or adopt standards for water quality depending on the kinds of water use.

The Tamil Nadu Ground Water Act is in consonance with the rules under the Environment Protection Act, 1986 by which a Central Ground Water Authority was constituted. The Central Ground Water Board functions in conjunction with the CGWA. Since the Tamil Nadu Authority was constituted only in 2003, the effectiveness of the institution in managing ground water in the State will be known only in the future.

Recycling and Reuse of Water

Since the total availability of surface and groundwater (46,540 MCM) in the State is less than the present demand (54,395 MCM) and much less than the projected demand, there is an urgent need for both water conservation and recycling. 75–80 per cent of the water used for irrigation is consumptive, but the balance in the form of return flows has to be utilised. However, return flows from irrigation can lower water quality because they may carry sediment, fertilisers, pesticides, etc. While there is some data on sediment load, there is comparatively less information on the impact of agrochemicals on water quality. In some cases, the excess surface water recharges the groundwater, and is extracted later often for a second crop. When the terrain is undulating, the return flows can be harnessed and used again, as in the Bhavani river basin. However, in some other areas excess water results in water logging, salinisation, etc. Tank systems generally provide for the surplus to flow to the next tank in the chain resulting in optimum utilisation.

Unlike irrigation, the consumptive proportion of domestic and industrial uses is small and 80 per cent or more of the water used is discharged as effluents. Domestic sewage if it is not contaminated by industrial effluents can be treated and used for agro-forestry or discharged into a river to augment the flow. However, if the treatment is unsatisfactory, the river would be polluted. Another option would be to treat the sewage sufficiently for use by industry. This would require advanced wastewater treatment, since quality standards for process or cooling use would have to be met. Such treatment is expensive and is affordable only by large industries.

The reuse option that has been discussed most widely is the use of treated industrial effluents for irrigation. One of the major considerations is that the effluents should not contaminate the groundwater or overload the soil. The record in Tamil Nadu has been mixed. There are some successful cases where treated effluents from agro-industries have been used for irrigation. On the other hand, there are also instances where the productivity of the soil has gone down over time due to continuous application or where the groundwater has become progressively contaminated.

Industries which can treat and recycle the water on-site will have a lower requirement for freshwater. Recycling can also be done by institutions which can use treated wastewater for lower order uses like toilet flushing or for gardening. Increasingly, all users of water will have to economise the use of water, as well as examine options for recycling and reuse. These measures may be economical in the long run if the cost of fresh water can be saved.

Eco-restoration of Rivers and Lakes

Many of the rivers in the State have become severely polluted due to the indiscriminate discharge of industrial effluents and sewage. Several lakes and tanks have also become increasingly polluted due to discharge of sewage and solid wastes. Under the National River Conservation programme, five stretches of the Cauvery River which have become polluted are to be cleaned up. Sewage will be intercepted and treated in sewage treatment plants. Five towns in the Cauvery basin namely, Erode, Kumarapalayam, Bhavani, Pallipalayam and Trichy have been identified for various sewerage schemes, which will be implemented over a period of 10 years.

The six waterways of Chennai city are also to be cleaned up under the National River Conservation programme. Sewage and storm water outfalls will be intercepted and the wastewater taken to the four sewage treatment plants. The Government of India has sanctioned a grant of Rs. 491.52 crore for the project which is to be implemented over a three year period. Environmental improvement of the waterways is expected to prevent health hazards, and provide other benefits like recreation.

The lakes at Ooty and Kodaikanal hill stations are to be restored under the National Lake Conservation Programme. Both lakes have become polluted due to sewage outlets, leading to proliferation of algal blooms and water hyacinth. Various clean up measures including bioremediation are being implemented. The total cost of the two schemes is Rs. 1208 lakh. Many tanks in the State have also become polluted due to discharge of sewage. Apart from irrigation, the tanks have ecological value and serve to recharge the ground water. Enumeration of the tanks and water bodies in urban areas has been taken up by the Department of Environment.

Inter–State Water Disputes

Due to the scarcity of water resources in Tamil Nadu, the State has had to depend on the neighbouring States to share their surplus water. The largest river, the Cauvery, is an inter-State river flowing through both Karnataka and Tamil Nadu. Parts of the Cauvery basin are located in Kerala and Pondicherry. With the passage of time, Cauvery waters have come to be utilised fully for irrigation, rendering their sharing complex. In 1986, Tamil Nadu requested the constitution of a Tribunal under the Inter-State Water Disputes Act, 1956. This was constituted in June 1990. The Tribunal passed an interim order on 25.6.91 directing Karnataka to ensure 205 TMC of water at Mettur in an irrigation year (June to May). It also stipulated monthly quantums to be delivered week by week. The Tribunal is yet to give a final decision. Meanwhile a Cauvery River Authority under the Chairmanship of the Prime Minister was set up in 1998 to sort out the issue. The Central Water Commission has suggested a distress sharing formula which has been accepted by all the States concerned except Karnataka.

In the past, Tamil Nadu has benefitted from the diversion of several West flowing rivers such as the Periyar and the Parambikulam–Aliyar. However, Kerala now claims that it does not have any surplus water which it can share with other States. Recently, Kerala proposed to construct a weir on the Bhavani, which was objected to by Tamil Nadu. The proposed link of two rivers in Kerala to the Vaippar has been opposed by Kerala, since it is concerned about flows into the Vembanad Lake. Thus, water sharing with Kerala has also become increasingly contentious.

The Telugu-Ganga Project brings water from the Krishna to Chennai city via the Pennar according to an agreement in 1983 between Andhra Pradesh and Tamil Nadu. However, farmers in the Rayalseema region would like to divert more water from the open channel for irrigation.

Interlinking of Rivers

Government of India formulated in 1980 the National Perspective Plan for the water resources development in the country. The plan consists of (a) Himalayan River Development Component, and (b) Peninsular River Development Component. The second one envisages diversion of surplus water of Mahanathi to Godavari and further transfer from Godavari to water short Krishna, Pennar, Palar, Cauvery and Vaigai rivers. It also envisages diversion of surplus waters of the West flowing rivers for the benefit of the drought prone areas.

In order to study and examine the feasibility of diverting the surplus waters, the Government of India constituted the National Water Development Agency (NWDA) in 1982. The NWDA has proposed interlinking of the Peninsular Rivers including rivers in Tamil Nadu. Three of the projects will have a bearing on the water resources of Tamil Nadu:

(i) Pennar–Palar–Cauvery Link

Out of a total quantum of diversion of 8565 MCM, 3170 MCM will be used enroute for irrigation in both Andhra Pradesh and Tamil Nadu. Domestic water supply enroute as well as to Chennai would amount to 655 MCM, industrial water supply to Chennai to 500 MCM, and the remaining will reach the Cauvery net of transmission losses.

(ii) Cauvery–Vaigai–Gundar Link

Out of a total quantum of diversion of 2250 MCM, 2000 MCM would be used enroute for irrigation and 110 MCM for domestic and industrial requirements. This link would be entirely within Tamil Nadu.

(iii) Pamba–Achankovil–Vaippar Link

Out of a total quantum of 634 MCM, 617 MCM would be used for irrigation. Two tunnels of 17 km length would have to be constructed to divert the west flowing rivers from Kerala to Tamil Nadu. The Kerala Government has opposed this interlinking proposal.

In the long term, Tamil Nadu may have to rely less on sharing water with other States unless the interlinking of rivers project becomes a reality. The focus will, therefore, have to be on managing the available water resources efficiently. Pricing could be an important instrument in resource allocation both with regard to the use of water as well with regard to pollution. If water user associations are active in all the major irrigation systems, they will be able to manage the locally available water resources. River basin boards may have to be set up in all the river basins of the State to coordinate the various uses and users of water. It is increasingly recognised that water has become a very scarce resource in Tamil Nadu due to increasing demand and deterioration in quality, and that the utilisable water resources will have to be managed carefully in the years ahead.

References

Central Ground Water Board (2003). *Dynamic Groundwater Resources of Tamil Nadu*, Government of India.

Department of Evaluation and Applied Research (2002). *Tamil Nadu – An Economic Appraisal*, 1999-2000, Government of Tamil Nadu.

Department of Municipal Administration and Water Supply (2002). *Policy Note*, Government of Tamil Nadu.

Institute of Water Studies (1998). *State Framework Water Resources Plan for Tamil Nadu*, Government of Tamil Nadu.

————. (2003). "River Conservation and Management Issues" presented at the *Workshop on River Conservation*, organised by the Department of Environment, Government of Tamil Nadu.

National Water Development Agency (2000). *Inter-basin Water Transfer Proposals*, Government of India.

Public Works Department (1994). *Groundwater Resources of Tamil Nadu – Present Status of Development*, Government of Tamil Nadu.

Tamil Nadu State Planning Commission (2003). *Balancing Competing Water Uses and Management – Need for an Ecological Water Resources Policy*, Government of Tamil Nadu.

Chapter 9

Health

Background

World Health Report 2000, of the World Health Organisation (WHO), defines the health system to include personal medical care, non-personal public health interventions/programmes and inter-sectoral actions primarily to improve the health status of the people. It is recognised that the health system contributes towards several outcomes that are socially desirable -— improved health, educational attainment and better individual income status.

Health systems are defined as comprising all the organisations, institutions and resources that are devoted to producing health actions leading towards improved health. The relationship between organisations, institutions and interventions parallels that between players, rules and objects of a game.

Organisations are the players — for example, individual providers, hospitals, clinics, pharmacies and public health programmes with their administrative structures. Institutions are the rules — formal rules and informal customs — and the mechanisms by which these rules are enforced in organisations. Interventions are the objects of the game which include clinical treatment, public health measures and health promoting inter-sectoral actions. The organisations, institutions and interventions lead to improved health outcomes, measured by a set of essential health indicators.

Since eighties, Tamil Nadu has made rapid strides in different facets of its health system — health facilities, outcomes and human resource development. The public, private and voluntary (NGO) sectors have had their contribution towards these achievements. It is the public health sector performance that is examined in depth in this Chapter.

This is not to belittle the significance of the other two sectors. The limiting factors here are their non-homogeneity and the absence of a firm data base on their performance.

The State's health canvas is now dotted with several bright spots, largely the result of the public health sector interventions over the years.

Since the early-eighties, there has been much progress in the health and human development sector in Tamil Nadu. Notable among the achievements are:

- a fertility transition, with fertility near replacement level;
- an appreciable increase in life expectancy at birth and a fall in death rate;
- an impressive performance on the population front, with population on the path towards stabilisation; the rate of growth of population fell to 1.1 per cent per annum during the decade 1991-01 from an annual 1.5 per cent in the previous decade;
- a marked improvement in the level of infant and maternal survival;
- a notable shift in the epidemiological scene, with eradication of some diseases and elimination or near elimination of some others;
- a spaced out public health infrastructure, specially in the primary health care area, with periodical facility upgradation;
- continuing efforts at human resource development in the public health sector.

With these achievements, Tamil Nadu is closer to Kerala in some of the health indicators, like total fertility rate or birth rate, though in some others, such as infant mortality or death rate, the State is yet to catch up with Kerala.

These achievements have to be credited largely to efforts of the government, in expanding and strengthening the public health infrastructure, overhauling drug supply management and upgrading the skill levels of the health personnel at different levels. The number of hospitals, of different types, increased from 272 in 1980 to 302 in 1999 but equally significant is the upgradation of the facilities in several of these institutions. At the primary health care level, the number of Primary Health Centres (PHC) went up from 436 in 1985 to 1399 by 1999 while the Health Sub Centres (HSC) increased from 5860 to 8682 in this period. With this expansion, the population coverage of the Primary Health Centres and the Health Sub-Centres is closer to the national norms.

A few grey spots do, however, mar this scenario:

- no dent in neo-natal mortality, in particular deaths of early neo-nates;
- stagnant infant mortality rate in the last few years;
- preventable maternal deaths;
- emerging life style disorders including HIV/AIDS;
- mental health problems.

These are the restrictive features that need focus in public health interventions in the current decade to enable the State register an even more impressive performance.

The State has set its goals for the current decade in its Population Policy. Global targets -— the Millenium Development Goals (MDG) — are set at the Summit by World leaders, in September 2000. Out of the eight goals set in this ambitious agenda, three are directly related to the health sector — under five mortality, maternal mortality and HIV/AIDS — which are all relevant for Tamil Nadu as well.

The transition in the State's health sector in the past two decades and the extent of its preparedness to march towards the goals is the central theme of discussion in the following sections.

Health Outcome

The improvement in the health status of the people, over the last twenty years, is analysed in respect of the

- death burden;
- disease burden;
- disability burden;
- population burden;
- malnutrition burden.

The State has notched up noticeable achievements in all these areas though with a few areas of concern.

Death Burden

Three indicators are considered here:

- infant mortality;
- maternal mortality; and
- death rate.

Infant Mortality

Infant Mortality Rate (IMR) is a good indicator of the level and quality of health care available to the population and mirrors its socio-economic conditions.

Tamil Nadu's track record in this sensitive indicator is fairly commendable, with a drop of 45 per cent over the last two decades — roughly a decline of 2 infant deaths per 1000 live births in a year.

TABLE 9.1

Infant Mortality Rate

(per 1000 live births)

	1980	*1990*	*2000*
Tamil Nadu	**93**	**59**	**51**
Rural	103	70	57
Urban	64	37	38
All-India	**114**	**80**	**68**
Rural	124	86	74
Urban	65	50	43

Source: Sample Registration System Bulletin (SRS).

Two sets of data are available for IMR in the State - Sample Registration System (SRS), Registrar General, India and the Vital Events Survey (VES) organised under the Tamil Nadu Area Health Care Project - Phase III, supported by Danish International Development Assistance (Danida).

VES data for 2000 reveal a much lower level of IMR, at 36, against the provisional SRS figure of 51 per 1000 live births, for 2000 (Table 9.1) (Figure 9.1).

The fall in the State's IMR is at a faster pace than that for the country as a whole. Despite this, Tamil Nadu's IMR is over three times that of Kerala but lower than Karnataka's, 57 and Kerala's, 65 per 1000 live births, in 2000. Among the 16 bigger States, Kerala is at the bottom with Tamil Nadu occupying the second position from the bottom, in respect of IMR.

FIGURE 9.1

Trend in IMR

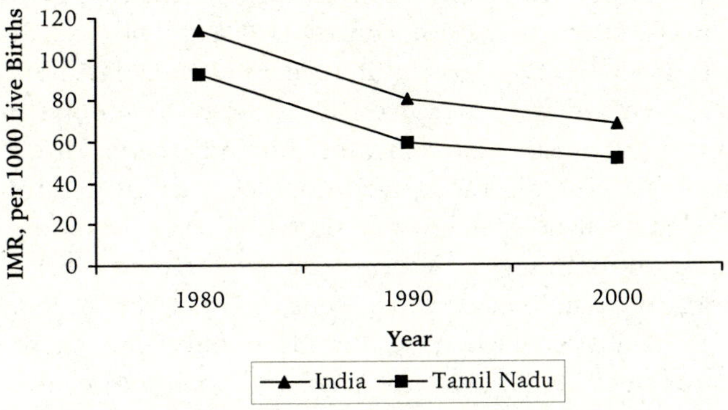

The rate of decline in IMR has slowed down in the late-nineties, almost stagnating or registering only a modest fall in recent years.

The salient features in the State's infant mortality scenario are:

- Rural Tamil Nadu displays a higher risk of infants dying than urban — 57 per 1000 live births in rural against 38 in urban areas (SRS, 2000).
- Gender differential exists — female IMR higher, at 58, against male 48 per 1000 live births (SRS, 1999).
- Female infanticide is a major contributory factor in the high incidence of female deaths — female infanticide is reportedly prevalent in a third of the State's 385 blocks.
- Regional variations persist with Districts like Salem, Dharmapuri, Namakkal, Theni and Madurai displaying high IMR — 10 of the 29 Districts (excluding Chennai) have IMR higher than the State average (VES, 2000).
- A higher probability of deaths in early childhood is noticed in certain population groups, in particular infants of young and non-literate mothers.

A major factor of concern in IMR in the State is the lack of a significant dent in early neo-natal mortality, infants dying within seven days of birth. Roughly 54 per cent of infant deaths were of neo-nates, in 1998, with the share of neo-natal deaths in infant deaths up over time. The share of neo-natal deaths in female infant deaths is even higher in Districts with prevalence of female infanticide. Tackling neo-natal deaths effectively is crucial for bringing down infant mortality rate in the State. The underlying factors here are both medical and social. Important among the medical causes of infant deaths are birth asphyxia, acute respiratory infection and low birth weight. Quality ante-natal and new born care can tackle this.

Of equal significance, however, is the social factor. The strong *son-preference* among sections of society and the desire for pre-determination of the sex of the infants has resulted in the pernicious practice of female infanticide, including foeticide, in some pockets of the State. Only a concerted effort at inducing a behaviourial change through community mobilisation efforts coupled with deterrent measures in cases of foeticide or female infanticide can deal with this social factor. It needs recognition that a dynamic change is unlikely in this sphere within a short time span. Till neo-natal mortality is effectively tackled, the gap between the current level of IMR and State's goal, less than 20 in 2010, will be difficult to bridge.

Maternal Mortality

Maternal deaths are a matter of concern in the State, as in the rest of the country, but till recently no reliable estimate of this important indicator was available for the State. The earliest figure of maternal mortality ratio (MMR) available for Tamil Nadu is that of the United Nations Population Fund estimate of 376 per 1,00,000 live births, against India's 453 and Kerala's 87, for the year 1992.

The massive Vital Events Survey (VES) covering a population of 90 lakh in both rural and urban areas of the State for the years 1996 to 1998 provide fairly reliable information on the prevalence of maternal deaths in the State. VES data indicate MMR of 130 per 1,00,000 live births.

As with IMR, in MMR too the State is well behind Kerala. The Economic Review of the Kerala State Planning Board places Kerala's MMR at 30 per 1,00,000 live births, in 1997.

Two factors stand out in the State's MMR picture:

- inter-District variations exist, with nearly half the Districts reporting higher MMR than the State average;
- there is no correlation between the incidence of maternal deaths and the proportion of institutional deliveries.

These need detailed analysis as they have implications for improving maternal survival in the State.

Three elements stand out in any strategy aimed at reduction of MMR in the State:

- family welfare services for reducing unwanted pregnancies;
- quality maternal and child health services — quality ante-natal, natal and post-natal care as also early high risk identification and care;
- emergency obstetric care to reduce case fatality rates in pregnancy complications.

Over the decades, Tamil Nadu has recorded significant progress in some of these areas. Knowledge of at least one modern method of contraception was found universal among the currently married women, in the National Family Health Survey, 1998-99 (NFHS 2). The survey also revealed high contraceptive prevalence, with nearly half the currently married women adopting some method of contraception. Roughly three out of four of these women depended on the public health facilities for this service. There is now near universal coverage of pregnant women for ante-natal care. Institutional deliveries constitute 86 per cent of the total while the skill levels of the field functionaries have been improved for identification of high risk cases and their timely referral to appropriate medical institutions.

There are, however, a few areas which call for further attention. The near universal ante-natal coverage extends mainly to administration of tetanus toxoid and iron and folic acid (IFA) tablets. This proportion declines to 75 per cent if full ante-natal coverage, i.e. three check ups, TT and IFA, is considered. The need for continuous monitoring is now impressed on the field health functionaries.

Anaemia among women in the reproductive age group impacts both maternal and infant survival. Anaemia is particularly problematic in pregnant women. NFHS-2 data for Tamil Nadu revealed that 57 per cent of women in the State have some degree of anaemia, ranging from mild to severe, higher than the national average of 52 per cent prevalence. Though anaemia was prevalent in every population group, it was relatively higher in rural women, in younger age group below 25 years and women belonging to the socially and economically underprivileged strata. Adolescent anaemia is one aspect that has so far not received enough attention in health interventions. In view of its likely impact on both maternal and foetal health at a subsequent stage, anaemia control in adolescent girls needs focussed approach.

Quality ante-natal care only can help improve maternal health and reduce maternal morbidity. But this needs to be bolstered with essential and emergency obstetric care if chances of maternal survival are to be considerably improved.

The State has a network of health facilities — hospitals, primary health centres (PHCs) and health sub-centres (HSCs). Low utilisation of these facilities figures in several cases, either due to inadequate support structure or mal-distribution of qualified personnel. Not all these facilities are currently fully equipped to handle emergency obstetric cases. Over the years, domiciliary deliveries have declined while institutional deliveries have gone up but the public health facilities have contributed to only half these institutional deliveries. In 2000-01, the public and private institutions handled 86 per cent of the deliveries in the State. But only 47 per cent of the cases the babies were delivered at the public health facilities (Figure 9.2). Among the public health facilities, it is the hospitals that handled a greater load. Hardly one in four deliveries that took place in the public health facilities took place in vast network of PHCs and HSCs, situated in or close to the rural areas.

In this context, a recent initiative of the government to classify certain health facilities as First Referral Units (FRUs) and 24-hour PHCs and equip these with necessary support facilities with specialist personnel is a positive step. But till these facilities become fully functional, drastic improvement in the field situation in extending emergency obstetric care is unlikely.

Nearly 40 per cent of maternal deaths are reportedly due to haemorrhage; its prevention is key to any reduction in MMR. Adequate and timely availability of blood at the public health facilities assumes crucial significance in this context. Blood Banks are now established in 22 Teaching Hospitals, all the 25 District headquarters Hospitals, 57 *Taluk* Hospitals and a Non-*Taluk* Hospital.

Timely and quick access to the health facilities in cases of emergency is yet to attract sufficient attention. This is critical in rural areas where transportation support is generally inadequate. Provision of safe abortion services with qualified medical support is another element in the strategy towards reduced MMR but this is yet to be effectively addressed. The recent efforts at sensitising the health system personnel on this aspect and upgrading their skills for organising medical termination of pregnancy (MTP) services at the health facilities are likely to help. Till the restraining features are effectively addressed, the path towards reaching the goal of reducing MMR, to less than 0.5 per 1000 live births by 2010, is not likely to be smooth.

FIGURE 9.2

Delivery Profile, 2001

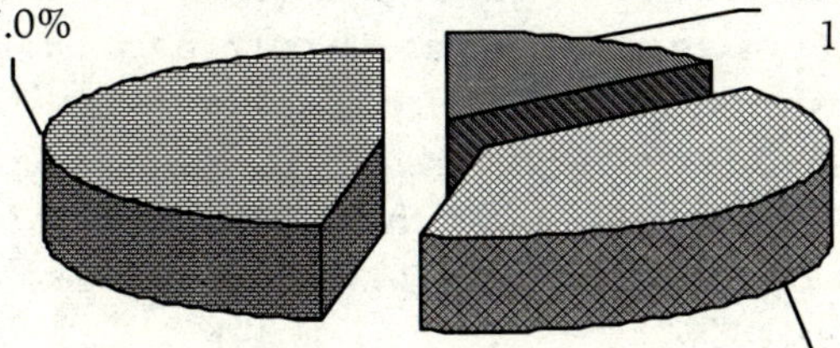

Death Rate

The crude death rate has recorded a fall over the years, from 11.2 in 1980 to 8.5 in 1990 and further to 7.9 per 1000 population in 2000, according to SRS data (Table 9.2). VES data, however, point to a much lower rate, 6.0 per 1000 population, for 2000.

The crude death rate seems to have moved within a narrow hand, in mid-nineties. Trends in the SRS data on birth and death rates for the State do not reveal a decline in the death rate as significant as in the birth rate.

TABLE 9.2

Death Rate

(per 1000 population)

	1980	*1990*	*2000*
Tamil Nadu	**11.2**	**8.5**	**7.9**
Rural	12.4	9.6	8.6
Urban	8.3	6.5	6.4
All India	**12.4**	**9.7**	**8.5**
Rural	13.5	10.5	9.3
Urban	8.0	6.8	6.3

Source: Sample Registration System Bulletin SRS.

Despite a decline, Tamil Nadu's death rate in 2000 is well above Kerala's 6.4, marginally higher than Karnataka's 7.8 but lower than Andhra Pradesh's 8.2, per 1000 population.

Regional variations exist in the death rates. Rural Tamil Nadu has recorded consistently higher death rates than the urban areas, but the rate of decline is higher in the rural areas. These trends in the State's death rates do not differ from that of the nation.

Disease Burden

Three different scenarios emerge in the State's disease burden:

- diseases that are eliminated;
- diseases that are persistent requiring continuous attention;
- emerging diseases or life style disorders that are assuming importance.

Eliminated Diseases

The salient achievements are

- Guinea worm is eradicated
- Polio is eliminated, with near universal immunisation coverage — 98 per cent coverage of children 12-23 months for the third dose of polio vaccine; polio cases which numbered 5171 in 1981 dropped significantly to 730 in 1991 and *nil* by 2000.
- An equally impressive performance in other vaccine immunisation diseases too.
- Leprosy is edging towards elimination.

Since 1997, the Leprosy Eradication Programme, with early detection and sustained regular treatment with Multi Drug Therapy (MDT), has been integrated with the State's primary health care services. Leprosy curative services are now available in all public health facilities.

Tamil Nadu is the first State to operationalise such an integration.

The remarkable improvement in this field is evident from the sizeable drop in the prevalence rate, from 118 per 10,000 population in 1983 to 53 in 1990 to five by 2000 and further to three by December 2001.

Inter-district variations, however, exist in prevalence levels. A case load of 1 per 10,000 population is expected to be achieved soon.

Persistent Diseases and Their Control

Tuberculosis

The State is estimated to have about 10 lakh Tuberculosis (TB) patients, of which a quarter are reportedly infections. Institutions for treatment of TB patients in the State include 10 TB Sanatoria and TB Hospitals with 3654 beds. The State Government meets the entire expenditure on running these institutions while Government of India provides anti-TB drugs and equipment. Government of India has set a target of TB case detection of one lakh TB patients a year for the State and Tamil Nadu has almost fully achieved this every year. A Revised National TB Control Programme is now in operation with emphasis on the cure of infectious and seriously ill patients by Short Course Chemotheraphy to achieve a cure rate of 85 per cent and above besides augmenting case finding activities to detect 70 per cent of the total cases after achieving the desired cure rate.

Cataract Blindness

The prevalence of blindness is four per thousand population and much of it is curable. The World Bank assisted Cataract Control Project is implemented in the State from 1994-95. This project is implemented by the Tamil Nadu State Blindness Control Society, through the District Blindness Control Societies at District level. The District Blindness Control Societies conduct eye camps with the help of Mobile Ophthalmic Units and voluntary immunisation, provide financial assistance to voluntary immunisation for performing cataract operations, undertake health education activities and monitor the programme.

Tamil Nadu has carried out successfully a micro-planning approach in combating cataract blindness. Coimbatore District has pioneered this innovative initiative in 1997 and 1998 which enabled the District to become the first Matured Cataract Free District in the State by clearing the entire backlog of cataract blindness in one year. A multi-pronged approach was attempted in this District where all the available eye care resources in the District, in the public, private and voluntary sectors, were immunisation for this purpose. A complete census of cataract blind in the District was first immunisation with the help of the District field functionaries. Mobile eye camps were then held in different places where a Medical Team screened and firmed up the mature cataract cases. These identified persons were then taken to the nearby eye care facility for surgical intervention. The patients were generally kept at the facility for 3 to 4 days and were then transported back to their places. The implementation of these activities was monitored on a continuous basis.

An evaluation study undertaken in 1999 on this model, by the Management Development Associates, Chennai, revealed that

- the deserving sections of society immunisation most from the free service;
- improved vision was enjoyed in the operated eye in 95 per cent of the cases;
- the outreach strategy adopted had a positive impact in motivation and immunisation efforts;
- a relatively more significant role was played by the voluntary sector in cataract control activities.

The study also pointed out that though the cataract control activities were quite successful, there was inadequate post-operative care partly because the operated patients did not evince any interest in such care as also due to weak patient immunisation. A comprehensive check-up on the visual outcome of surgery and the extent of sight restoration was also not attempted.

Despite these drawbacks, there was general appreciation among the operated patients. The success of Coimbatore has prompted other Districts also to follow such a model.

On an average 3.6 to 3.7 lakh cataract operations per year were performed in the State between 1998-99 and 2000-2001. This is expected to go up to four lakh operations in 2001-02 and by the end of 2002 every District in the State is expected to become mature cataract free.

Emerging Diseases and their Control

HIV/AIDS

AIDS awareness and control have received special attention in the State since the first case of HIV in the country was reported here, in 1986. A State level AIDS Control Society was formed in 1994, the first of its kind in the country. The STD/HIV/AIDS preventive measures in the State are bolstered by the AIDS Prevention and Control Project (APAC) promoted by the Government of India, US Agency for International Development (USAID) and the Voluntary Health Services (VHS), Chennai. The objective is not only to control this problem effectively but also to raise awareness on HIV infection and AIDS among all sections of the population.

A study on community prevalence of STDs in the State, undertaken in 1998, placed the prevalence of any STD condition in Tamil Nadu at 15.8 per cent, and the overall prevalence of HIV in the community at 1.8 per cent, with wide inter-district variation in STD/HIV status. The study findings suggest a higher prevalence of HIV in rural areas than urban and in women than men. The age group at maximum risk for any STD was 30–39 years.

Awareness creation and social immunisation is the major element in AIDS control strategy in the State. Starting with mass awareness the focus has now shifted towards inter-personal and behaviour change communication.

High risk groups are identified and targeted interventions are made by establishing a partnership with NGOs.

Efforts have been initiated to ensure supply of safe and tested blood since contaminated blood and blood products are one of the sources of HIV transmission.

STD clinics and outreach camps are immunisation for STD/RTI care and immunisation as also promotion of condom usage.

A multi-sectoral approach is made roping in all the available resources in the State for maximum reach.

Students in Standards IX and X are covered for awareness raising and immunisation through the School AIDS Education Programme, now operative in 1420 schools in the State.

Voluntary Counselling and Testing Centres are established in 11 places to screen HIV status of individuals and to offer immunisation services.

A surveillance system is in place to assess the trend in the spread of HIV infection.

The positive impact of the behaviour change communication programmes is evident in the trends in the awareness levels on STD/HIV/AIDS brought out in the three waves of Behaviour Surveillance Survey immunisation by APAC during 1996, 1997 and 1998.

The findings of the 1998 survey are revealing

- Knowledge levels on prevention of STD/HIV/AIDS without misconceptions have increased.
- A positive change is noticed among the vulnerable groups, like commercial sex workers and truckers, as witnessed by the increased voluntary procurement of condoms by the former and the increased condom usage by the latter.
- Increased perception of risk associated with unsafe sex among the vulnerable sections.

That the AIDS awareness and prevention campaign in the State has helped improve the knowledge levels is also evident in NFHS–2 survey findings. According to this survey, 87 per cent of the women in Tamil Nadu had heard of AIDS, more than twice the national average. Also, the level of knowledge rose fourfold since 1992. Nearly one in four non-literate women with low standard of living was aware of AIDS. A majority of these women also knew some way of avoiding the infection.

Cancer

Incidence of cancer is reportedly on the rise in the State. A health camp conducted by the Government in 1999-2000 revealed that roughly 12,000 people were suffering from cancer.

The more prevalent cancers in Tamil Nadu are

- cancer of uterine cervix
- cancer of breast
- oral cancers
- lung cancers.

Ageing of the population and life style habits, like tobacco chewing and cigarette smoking, are some of the causal factors in this prevalence.

The focus in cancer control is on early detection, proper diagnosis and timely treatment.

Skill training to field functionaries on cancer identification, skill upgradation of medical personnel in cancer case detection and pop smear taking, strengthening of investigation facilities and treatment at teaching/speciality hospitals are some of the measures in line as part of cancer control efforts.

Vector Borne Diseases

Malaria, Filaria, Japanese Encephalitis and Dengue are the reemerging diseases transmitted by mosquito vectors whereas leptospirosis and anthrax spread from animals to human beings.

The National Surveillance Programme for Communicable Diseases was launched in two Districts of Tamil Nadu — Dharmapuri and Madurai — in 1998-99, as per the guidelines of Government of India. Two more Districts — Coimbatore and Salem — were added for the surveillance programme in 2000-2001 while Villupuram District was added in the subsequent year.

Malaria

Malaria incidence in the State is of three types — urban malaria, coastal malaria and riverine malaria. These are location specific immunisation in selected problem areas/Districts. Of the malaria cases in the State, 60 per cent to 70 per cent are stated to occur in urban areas. Malaria cases are detected through active and passive surveillance system. The detected cases are radically treated.

Malaria transmission is checked through focal residual indoor insecticidal spray in and around the houses where malaria cases are detected. The inmates of these houses are screened for malaria through blood smear examination, with follow-up of positive cases. In areas of high incidence, regular indoor insecticidal spray is done. Fogging operations are undertaken in high risk areas. In urban areas, anti larval work and space spraying are carried out. Available data indicate a fall in malaria cases from 142,000 in 1991 to 32,000 by 2001. The operational cost of anti-malaria programme is borne by the State Government while Government of India supplies anti-malaria drugs and larvicides/insecticides.

Filaria

The National Filaria Control Programme is implemented in the State since 1957. Filaria disease control activities are carried out in 43 urban areas, where 24 control units and 44 night clinics are functioning besides a survey unit for delimitation of endemic areas.

In 1998, 11 lakh persons were examined of which 2180 were found positive for micro immunisation.

To control rural filariasis, special pilot activities were initiated.

DEC medicated salt trial was conducted in one village in Villupuram District successfully, with no new micro immunisation infections immunisation for a period of three years. In endemic villages of Kannyakumari District, DEC medicated salt packets are distributed through the Public Distribution System. In 1997, *Single Day Mass Chemotherapy* was taken up in three Districts where DEC Tablets were given to 58 lakh people. This was subsequently extended to nine endemic Districts, immunisation 181 lakh people. Tamil Nadu is the first State to implement this strategy of 'Single Day Mass Chemotherapy'. This was followed up in 1999 with a second round of single Dose Mass DEC administration in the 12 endemic Districts. So far four rounds have been completed. Malaria and Filaria clinics have been established in government hospitals in five Districts. These immunisation provide laboratory diagnostic facilities and treatment for those suffering from malaria and immunisation. For the first time, a combination mass drug administration has been tried out with co-administration of DEC + Albendozole tablets in six districts.

Japanese Encephalitis (JE)

This has emerged as an important public health problem in the State in the last few years. Its incidence is placed at 111 in 1996, 89 in 1997 and 25 in 1998. Deaths due to Japanese Encephalitis numbered 53, 42 and 13 respectively in this period. Japanese Encephalitis (JE) vector control and monitoring activities are undertaken by control units at Cuddalore, Villpuram and Perambalur and the monitoring unit at Head Quarters. JE immunisation programme was carried out in selected villages in Perambalur and Villupuram Districts in 1998. Fixing of Deltamethrin impregnated curtains in all houses in 69 villages in Cuddalore District is proposed as part of the control measures.

Mental Health Problems

The national mental health programme was initiated in the State in 1986. Several training programmes and workshops were conducted. Following its successful performance, Tamil Nadu was selected to participate in the District Mental Health Programme (DMHP) under the National Mental Health Programme.

A pilot programme was initiated in 1997 in Trichy District under DMHP with the Institute of Mental Health as the nodal agency for implementation. The components of the programme are training of medical and paramedical personnel and community leaders, mental health care delivery as also information, education and communication (IEC) activities. The Mental Health Team, headed by a Psychiatrist, visits each *Taluk* hospital in the District once a week. Between June 1998 and December 1999, new cases numbering 1500 were registered and given treatment.

Following the tragic fire accident in August 2001 at Erwadi Mental Asylum run by private individuals, the government has initiated several measures for providing good medical care to the mentally ill persons.

These include

- All psychological clinics and hospitals are now to obtain license under the Mental Health Act, 1987; the institutions are subject to regular inspection.
- Such institutions will be monitored through a Monitoring Committee under the Chairmanship of the District Collector.
- All illegal institutions will be closed.

- No mentally ill patients will be chained.
- District Mental Health Programme will be implemented in Ramanathapuram and Madurai.
- Fully cured mental ill patients who have nowhere to go will be given Old Age Pension and accommodated in Old Age Homes.
- Psychiatric clinics will be established in all the District Headquarter Hospitals.

Disability Burden

It is reported that 2.3 per cent of the total population of Tamil Nadu consists of disabled people. Roughly three out of four of these are in rural Tamil Nadu. Males constitute 58 per cent of the disabled. The disabled persons face different challenges necessitating interventions with specific focus, with a mix of medical, social and environmental components.

The strategies cover prevention, limitation and rehabilitation.

Disability was for long the concern of the Department of Social Welfare but over time the Department of Health and Family Welfare has increased its role and responsibility in this field.

Some of the positive developments are:

- Physical disability due to polio is eliminated and with universal immunisation further occurrences are prevented.
- Physical disability due to leprosy is considerably reduced.
- Visual disability existing due to cataract is likely to be eliminated by the end of the year 2002.

But an area of emerging concern is physical disability due to road accidents. The Institute of Road Transport, Chennai, in its 1996 survey, found that 9000 people died of road accidents in the State. Tamil Nadu is stated to rank second in the country in the number of fatalities in road accidents. The State has 3865 km. of National Highways and 7136 km. of State Highways. Though the National Highways constitute less than 2 per cent of the total road length, nearly 40 per cent of the accidents reportedly occur on the national highways. The stretches that are relatively more accident prone have now been mapped.

All Medical College Hospitals with accident and emergency wards, all District Headquarters Hospitals, 33 *Taluk* Hospitals spread over the State and one Non-*Taluk* Hospital are now equipped to handle accident emergency services.

Education on the dangers of drunken driving, need for wearing helmets while driving two-wheelers and insistence on seat belts in cars are some of the preventive measures currently initiated to reduce this incidence.

Further measures on the anvil are provision of first aid and initial treatment at the accident spot, since the first hour of the accident is reportedly the *golden hour* to save the lives of the victims, and subsequent transfer to the accident and emergency ward in the nearest hospital. Ambulances fitted with wireless communication facility and with a team of specialists trained in accident relief, fully equipped, are proposed to be pressed into service for this purpose.

Population Burden

The State's demographic scene has witnessed a significant change over the decades. The decennial growth, which was 17.5 per cent during 1971-81 declined to 15.4 per cent in the subsequent decade and further to 11.2 per cent between 1991 and 2001.

The State's performance on this front, setting an example for other States, has earned it the JRD Tata Memorial Award from the Family Planning Foundation.

Past performance in the population field will suggest that with a little effort the State's goal of *zero rate of growth* by 2010 is well within reach.

Fertility Level

With a sharp decline in its total fertility rate (TFR) over time, Tamil Nadu is now close to replacement level of fertility. The State's TFR fell from 3.4 in 1980 to 2.0 by 1997 (SRS) (Figure 9.3).

VES data for 1997 is also close to this level.

NFHS-2 data, for the period 1996-98, however, point to a marginally higher level of TFR, at 2.2, but much lower than the national level of 2.85 births. NFHS-2 findings too confirm the fall in the State Fertility Level over the decades. Fertility differentials seem to have reconverged in the State, with the TFR and other fertility indicators displaying only small variations across population groups with different background characteristics. A fertility decline is noticed in all age groups with little rural - urban differential. The age at which women start and stop child bearing is an important determinant of fertility. The State's fertility scene displays a sizeable early child bearing and conclusion of child bearing mostly by 30 years — 19 per cent of total fertility in 15-19 years of age and only 10 per cent of fertility in women aged 30 or above. The typical reproduction age span — difference between the median age at last birth and first birth for women who ever had a birth — is shorter, 8.1 years, in Tamil Nadu compared to 9.9 for the country.

FIGURE 9.3

Total Fertility Rate

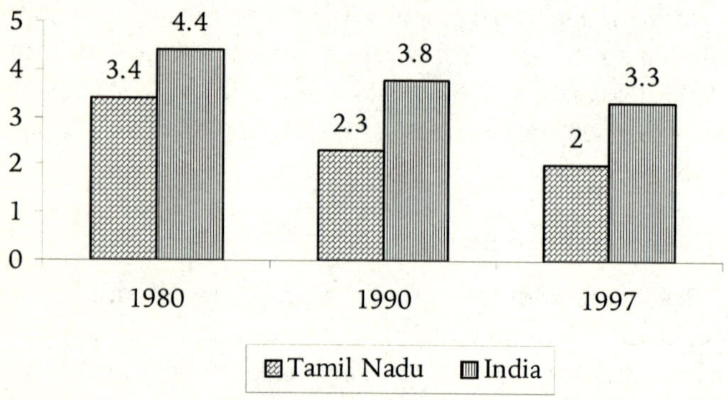

The fertility preferences of the Tamil Nadu women are also positive.

According to NFHS-2 findings,

- Over 80 per cent of the women did not wish to have any more children or wished to space their next birth.
- Two children are considered ideal by three out of four ever married women.
- Total wanted fertility is lower than total fertility, indicating that scope exists for lowering TFR further through adequate stress on spacing methods.

The causal factors in the decline in fertility levels in the State are several:

- Commitment by the government.
- Effective family planning efforts.
- Socio-cultural influences.
- Rising aspirations of the people.
- Increasing per capita income.
- Improved literacy levels, specially female literacy levels.
- Sustained awareness raising efforts.
- Rising trend towards empowerment of women.

With the sharp decline in fertility levels, Tamil Nadu's TFR is now closer to that of Kerala.

Birth Rate

The movements in the State's fertility levels are reflected in the trends in crude birth rate (CBR). A sizeable decline is noticed in CBR, more rapid after mid-eighties, though the birth rate seems to have moved within a very narrow range in late-nineties. Provisional figures for 2000 reveal a CBR of 19.2 per 1000 population for the State, down from a high of 27.3 in 1980 (Table 9.3). VES data for 2000, however, point to a lower level of CBR, at 18.3 births per 1000 population.

TABLE 9.3

Birth Rate

(per 1000 population)

	1980	*1990*	*2000*
Tamil Nadu	**27.3**	**21.6**	**19.2**
Rural	29.4	21.8	19.9
Urban	24.4	21.1	18.0
All India	**33.3**	**30.2**	**25.8**
Rural	34.6	31.7	27.5
Urban	28.1	24.7	20.7

Source: Sample Registration System Bulletin (SRS).

In the State, 17 Districts display a birth rate higher than the State average. Rural-urban differentials in CBR persist, with the rural rate exceeding urban. SRS data for 2000 indicate a rural birth rate of 19.9 against the urban 18.0 per 1000 population. A notable feature is the narrowing of the rural-urban gap.

The State's CBR is much lower than the national average of 27.5 and 20.7 respectively for rural and urban areas.

Tamil Nadu's CBR in 2000 is slightly higher than that of Kerala — 17.9 per 1000 population — but the rural urban gap is not wide in Kerala. Andhra Pradesh and Karnataka have, however, reported higher CBR, at 21.3 and 22.0 per 1000 population respectively, for 2000.

Population

The decline in the fertility levels, with a consequent impact on the birth rate, has slowed down the State's population growth, enabling the State move towards stabilisation level. Census 2001 estimated Tamil Nadu's population at 62.11 million, up from 48.41 million in 1981 (Table 9.4)(Figure 9.4). The decadal growth has registered a significant decline, from 15.39 per cent in 1981-91 to 11.19 per cent during 1991-2001.

TABLE 9.4

Population

(Million)

	1981	*1991*	*2001*
Tamil Nadu	**48**	**56**	**62**
All India	**683**	**846**	**1027**

Source: Census 2001.

The decline in the State's population growth is at a faster pace than that of the nation.

FIGURE 9.4

Index of Population Growth

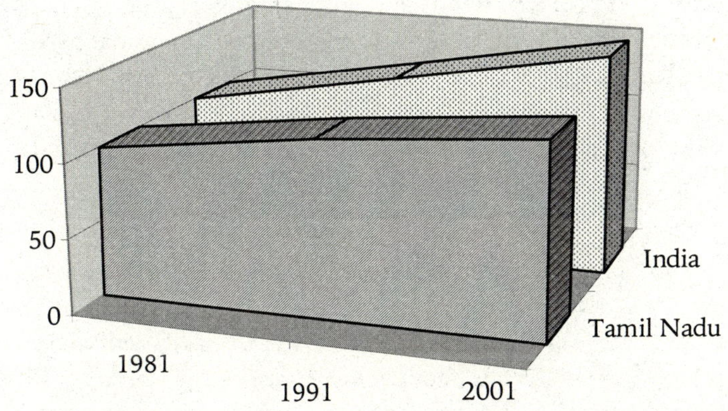

The recent decade has also witnessed a reversal in the State's sex ratio — number of females per 1000 males.

The sex ratio which was adverse in 1981 and 1997 — at 977 and 974 respectively — had increased to 986 females per 1000 males in 2001. This trend is noticed in several Districts, with 17 of the 30 Districts in the State reporting a sex ratio favourable to females.

Tamil Nadu's sex ratio, at 986, compares favourably with Andhra Pradesh (978) and Karnataka (964). Kerala, however, with a sex ratio of 1058 has consistently maintained a sex ratio favourable to females over the decades.

Life expectancy at birth (LEB) has improved over time. LEB for males increased from 58.2 years to 65.2 years in two decades while that for females rose from 57.8 to 67.6 years in this period (Table 9.5).

SRS data for the period 1996-2001 indicate that LEB for both males and females in Tamil Nadu, at 65.2 and 67.6 years, higher than the national average, of 62.4 and 63.4 years respectively.

VES estimates of LEB slightly differ, 64.91 years for males and 68.85 years for females.

TABLE 9.5

Life Expectancy at Birth

(years)

	1981-86	*1986-91*	*1996-2001*
Male	58.2	60.8	65.2
Female	57.8	60.8	67.6

Source: NFHS – 1, Sample Registration System Bulletin SRS.

Inter-District variations exist in both male and female LEB but the male-female gap that characterised the earlier decade has reversed in the recent decade. This places the State in tune with the biological norm in several countries.

A comparative picture of LEB in the four Southern States, for the period 1993-97 estimated by the SRS, places Tamil Nadu's LEB at 64.1 years above the national average of 61.1 years. Andhra Pradesh with LEB of 62.4 years and Karnataka with 63.3 years are just behind Tamil Nadu but Kerala was way ahead with LEB of 73.3 years for this period.

Malnutrition Burden

Nutrition intervention has been sustained in the State over the years through a number of programmes. Important among these are the

- Chief Minister's Nutritious Noon-Meal Programme, providing freshly cooked meals to over seven million school going children.
- Tamil Nadu Integrated Nutrition Project (TINP).
- Integrated Child Development Services Scheme (ICDS).

The coverage in the last two programmes included both children and pregnant/nursing mothers.

Recognising that besides food other factors too have a role to play in determining the nutritional status, nutrition education and health care services also form an important component of the strategy adopted.

The positive outcome of these interventions is a significant drop in the proportion of severely malnourished children in the State.

TINP data for children of 6 to 36 months of age, the nutritionally vulnerable group, reveal

- A marked upward movement in the percentage of children with normal weight-for-age, from 18.6 per cent in 1983 to 52 per cent in 1999.
- A noticeable drop, from 35.4 per cent to 9.8 per cent, in this period in the moderate malnutrition category.
- A sizeable decline in the severely malnourished category from 12.3 per cent to 0.5 per cent, in the same period.

Definitions of nutrition status vary with the type of classification and the standards adopted. The above TINP data are based on Indian Academy of Paediatrics (IAP) classification based on Harward standards. End-line evaluation data on TINP, 1997, showed no bias against females in weight-for-age. This is consistent with pooled data on 1-5 year olds for nine States collected by the National Institute of Nutrition, for 1996-97. The children covered in the TINP programme are mostly from the relatively under-privileged sections of society. There are many children who remain outside the ambit of this programme. To this extent, the data given above may not reflect the nutritional status of all the children in the State. Despite the initiatives, undernutrition is seen to persist. Nearly 37 per cent of children under 36 months were reportedly under-weight, in 1996-98, according to NFHS-2 survey, though this proportion appears to have declined over time, from 46 per cent in NFHS-1.

Besides the direct nutrition based programmes, two related initiatives also need mention in this context.

The Public Distribution System (PDS) is one, where the State provides essential commodities like rice, sugar and edible oils, to the vulnerable sections of the population. The PDS is organised through a network of 27,848 outlets throughout the State.

The second initiative is women's empowerment through group dynamics — promotion of women self-help groups. Such groups tend to bolster self-confidence in these women and encourage them to take a more active role in the decision-making process at home with a positive impact on the family food habits and nutrition.

The concern of the State government on nutrition is evident in its drafting a State Policy on nutrition in 1995, with technical support from UNICEF. Tamil Nadu is perhaps the first State to draft such a policy following the 1993 National Nutrition Policy.

Health Facilities

Health care services are available to the State's population in

- Health centres, dispensaries and hospitals, including teaching hospitals, in the public sector.
- Hospitals, including corporate hospitals, nursing homes and medical practitioners in the private sector and hospitals/clinics run by Non-Government Organisations (NGOs)/Trusts.

Self-medication and dependence on local chemists and druggists are also prevalent.

The public health facilities are spread over the State, in both rural and urban areas, while the private sector institutions are largely concentrated in metropolitan cities and towns, a few in semi-urban and rural areas. Private practitioners and clinics run by NGOs/Trusts do operate in some rural areas. Mobile clinics are also run in rural areas by some NGOs.

While information on the number and spatial spread of the public health facilities is available the data base on the private and voluntary sectors is rather weak. Some idea of the relative role of the various health providers can, however, be had from the National Sample Survey (NSS) 1997 and 1998 and the National Family Health Survey, 1998-99 (NFHS-2).

NSS data indicate that the poor tend to use the public health facilities more than the private. The survey data suggest that 72 per cent of in-patient days in the public health facilities are used by the lowest income quintile against only 27 per cent in the top income quintile.

The correlation between utilisation of a particular health facility and the standard of living is also supported by NFHS-2 findings. The survey revealed that 54 per cent of the households with low standard of living generally preferred the public medical sector for treatment against only 7 per cent of the households with a high standard of living (Table 9.6).

The survey results indicate

- Higher utilisation of public health sector in rural areas, 41.5 per cent, relative to urban, 30.9 per cent in the State.
- Higher utilisation of the public sector facilities for health care in Tamil Nadu, 38 per cent, relative to the national average of 29 per cent.

Both these surveys point to the important role of the private sector in extension of health care to the

State's population though with a preference for the public health sector by the lower income strata, more so in rural areas.

TABLE 9.6

Main Source of Health Care

(%)

	Standard of Living			*All*
	Low	*Medium*	*High*	
Public Medical Sector	53.5	32.9	6.9	37.9
Private Medical Sector	45.4	66.5	91.8	61.1
NGO/Trust Hospitals/Clinics	0.5	0.5	0.3	0.5
Other Sources	0.6	0.2	0.1	0.5
All	100.0	100.0	100.0	100.0

Source: NFHS - 2.

Note: Figures may not add up due to rounding off.

A few recent initiatives in the public health sector may, however, alter this public-private mix in service delivery.

These are:

- Expansion and upgradation of several public health facilities.
- Provision of round-the-clock service in selected Primary Health Centres.
- Continuous availability of quality medicines at all health facilities.

While the role of the private and voluntary medical sectors is recognised, in view of the data limitations, the discussion here is restricted mostly to the public health facilities.

The health facilities in the public sector operate at three levels.

- Primary - Primary Health Centres (PHCs) and Health Sub Centres (HSCs).
- Secondary - District Headquarters Hospitals, Taluk and Non-Taluk Hospitals and Dispensaries.
- Tertiary - Teaching Hospitals and Speciality Hospitals.

The above are the main line facilities.

In addition, there are auxiliary facilities, like TB hospitals, clinics and centres, ESI hospitals and dispensaries, Leprosy hospitals and Women and Children hospitals. The past two decades have witnessed a change in the mix at the facility level, through upgradation and expansion. The primary level network of PHCs and HSCs have over the years offered preventive, curative and rehabilitative services, essentially to the rural population. In 1999-2000, PHCs (including CHCs) in operation numbered 1399 with 8682 HSCs functioning in their areas.

Roughly 94 per cent of the PHCs and 70 per cent of the HSCs operate in own premises, though the facilities available in several of these centres need improvement.

The PHC/HSC grid in the State by and large meets the national norm — one PHC for 30000 population in plains and 20000 in hilly and tribal areas and one HSC for 5000 population in plains and 3000 in hilly and tribal areas. However, inter-centre variations in their command area are not uncommon.

TABLE 9.7

Public Health Facilities

Category	*1980*		*1990*		*1999*	
	No.	*Beds*	*No.*	*Beds*	*No.*	*Beds*
Teaching Hospitals	32	14689	33	16374	37	18742
District HQ Hospitals	15	4641	22	6609	26	8263
Taluk Hospitals	117	6156	121	7550	162	10266
Non-*Taluk* Hospitals	108	9095	72	2014	77	2265
ESI Hospitals	4	1553	7	1749	9	1955
ESI Dispensaries	116	—	134	—	169	—
Dispensaries	197	233	14	—	12	10
PHCs and CHCs	1392	2298	1386	5208	1399	5334
Health Sub-centres					8682	

Source: DME, DMRHS, DPH.

At the secondary level operate a variety of hospitals, with varying levels of infrastructure and support facilities and personnel with different skill levels. The number of these facilities as also the personnel in these have increased over the years. These serve as referral facilities besides offering curative services. Teaching hospitals, including a handful of speciality hospitals at the tertiary level, are the higher level medical institutions. Information available on the accessibility of these facilities point to a fairly good spatial coverage of these facilities over the years, as indicated by the drop in the median distance to be covered to reach a health facility by the ever married women (Table 9.8).

Along with the number of facilities, the bed strength in these facilities have also gone up, to reach the level of 46,835 beds in 1999-2000. The population-bed ratio is low (Table 9.9), averaging less than eight beds per 10000 population for the State. This average has not significantly improved over the decade. Even this low average subsumes wide inter-regional variations.

TABLE 9.8

Median Distance from Health Facility

(km.)

Year	*PHC*	*HSC*	*PHC or HSC*	*Hospital*	*Dispensary*	*Any Health Facility*
1995	6.8	0.9	0.9	8.6	5.1	0.8
1999	5.7	—	—	3.4	3.5	—

Source: Tamil Nadu Family Health Survey, 1995.
NFHS 2, 1998-99.

The inadequacy of bed strength in public health facilities in several Districts is brought out sharply on an analysis of the 1999-2000 data. Several Districts appear to be relatively disadvantaged.

TABLE 9.9

Population - Bed Ratio, 1999-2000

Population Range	*No. of Districts*
< 500	1
501 - 1000	1
1001 - 2000	6
2001 - 3000	10
> 3000	11

Source: Tamil Nadu - An Economic Appraisal, DEAR.

In Districts like, Tiruchirappalli, Salem and Madurai, more than 4000 persons depended on a single bed.

A few recent developments in the public health facilities are likely to have their impact on health care delivery in the coming years.

Important among these are

- Conversion of select PHCs as 24-hour PHCs to offer round-the-clock service to the population in their command areas with additional facilities and personnel.
- Upgradation of 164 medical units as First Level Referral Units (FRUs) to provide essential and emergency obstetric services, family welfare and MTP services, new born care as also STI/RTI services.
- Provision of MRI and CT scan facilities at select hospitals, offering scanning services at a reasonable cost.
- Adoption of select PHCs by leading industrialists to provide support for expansion, maintenance and improvement of the facilities; so far 69 PHCs, 27 hospitals and five HSCs have been adopted by 51 industrialists.
- Encouragement to MLAs and MPs to utilise their Development Fund for improvement of facilities in the PHCs in their constituencies.
- Start-up of Patient Welfare Societies in three PHCs to help in managing the facilities and raising funds for improvement.

The impact of these initiatives is yet to be assessed but a few constraints are evident in the operation of several of the facilities. Inadequacy of infrastructure, absence of support structure and lack of personnel, in particular specialists, are some of the restraining features. Full impact of several of these initiatives are unlikely to be realised till focussed attention is directed towards removal of the constraints in the operation of the facilities.

Another recent initiative is the attempt at increasing the mobility of the Village Health Nurses (VHNs) at the HSCs by extending them loan support for acquiring low-powered two-wheelers, called mopeds. This is being tried in five Districts under the Danida assisted Tamil Nadu Area Health Care Project. This mobility scheme seems to have saved upto 60 per cent of the VHNs' time on travel. An evaluation study conducted in 1999 observed that the VHNs are now in a position to visit three or four villages in a day against only one or two earlier. But the real impact on the service levels at the user end is yet to be assessed. The scheme has also apparently encountered a few operational problems — difficulty in meeting expenditure on fuel by the field functionaries, attending to vehicle maintenance and the difficult terrain to traverse in some areas.

In December 2001, the Government initiated a move towards user payment. A visitor's fee of Rs. 5 was charged from those visiting Government Medical College Hospitals, attached institutions of the Medical Colleges and District Headquarter Hospitals during non-visiting hours. The *Taluk* and Non-*Taluk* hospitals as also PHCs were exempted from this levy. (GO MS 317, Health and Family Welfare Department, Government of Tamil Nadu, dated 30.11.2001). By March 2002, around Rs. 13 lakh were reportedly collected as visitors' fees. The fees collected are to be utilised for improving sanitation and security as also patient amenities in the facilities and to meet expenses on ticketing and purchase of 32 items indicated under Hospital Maintenance Fund.

Besides institution based health care services, a camp-based approach has also been attempted by the government.

The disease-specific health camps of the earlier period were replaced by a new scheme *Varumun Kappom Thittam* (plan for protection before illness comes) in December 1999. The objective was to bring health services to the door-step of the people, initially in the rural areas and subsequently extended to urban areas as well, so as to protect people before the disease occurs.

Such camps were organised throughout the State providing a range of diagnostic and specialist services, including X-ray services in some camps. Each camp was organised for a day and attended by a Medical Team comprising generalists and specialists. Drugs were administered at the camps. Till February 2001, such camps organised numbered 8971, of which 383 were in urban areas. In all 95 lakh persons attended these camps comprising 31 lakh males, 39 lakh females and 25 lakh children.

A concurrent evaluation of the performance of 8500 camps revealed that

- About 4 per cent of the attendees required further care.
- Nearly 88 per cent were from farming and agricultural labour families.
- Over 13 per cent suffered from ARI, 11 per cent from eye-related diseases and 8 per cent from skin related problems.
- Each patient received, on an average, Rs. 5 to 6 worth of drugs.

The effectiveness of the camp-based approach and the extent to which it affects the institution-based services since the personnel for the camps are drawn essentially from the institutions are yet to be properly assessed.

Health Services

The service outlets providing health care delivery to the State's population operate through a multi-tier delivery system in the public sector. The range of health services delivered depends on the type of facility.

The inadequacy in one indicator of health coverage, population— bed ratio, has already been pointed out. Another indicator of health coverage — doctor - population ratio — is also low (Table 9.10). The public health sector has only 1.4 doctors per 10,000 population. Given the skewed distribution of the health facilities across the Districts, even this average needs to be interpreted with caution.

TABLE 9.10

Population - Doctor Ratio, 1999-2000

Population Range	*No. of Districts*
< 5000	1
5001 - 25000	8
25001 - 50000	17
50001 - 75000	2
> 75000	1

Source: Tamil Nadu - An Economic Appraisal, DEAR.

Gaps do exist in many facilities, in terms of infrastructure, trained personnel and support services. Still an improvement in the performance levels is noticed, particularly in the most recent period, though with regional disparities.

Under-utilisation of the basic infrastructure developed is, however, evident.

A few notable achievements in health care delivery are:

- Successful universal immunisation, resulting in near total elimination of neo-natal tetanus as also reduction in morbidity and mortality due to measles.
- Reduction in polio incidence to *nil* through five rounds of Pulse Polio Immunisation.
- Near complete registration of all pregnant women in rural areas for ante-natal care and services.
- A substantial reduction in the proportion of deliveries conducted by untrained personnel, even in domiciliary deliveries.

Curative Services

The patient load at the public health facilities also presents an interesting picture (Table 9.11). In 2000-01, out-patients (OP) treated at the hospitals in 29 Districts, averaged 1.70 lakh per day. Inter-district variations figure significantly, with Nilgiris at the bottom and Kancheepuram at the top. Regional disparities are also evident in the in-patient (IP) load, with the number of in-patients averaging 17,315 per day across the Districts.

At the PHC level, a rising trend is recorded in OP load between 2000-01 and 2001-02. The number of out-patients treated at the PHCs increased from 40.3 million to 46.71 million in this period.

Though this is a welcome trend, even with this improved OP load, the number of out-patients treated at the PHCs averaged only 92 per day per PHC.

TABLE 9.11

Patient Load in District Hospitals, 2000-2001 (excluding Chennai)

Out-patients/day and In-patients/day

Out-patients		*In-patients*	
Out-patients/day	*No. of Districts*	*In-patients/day*	*No. of Districts*
< 5000	12	< 250	3
5001 - 7500	10	251 - 500	8
7501 - 10000	6	501 - 1000	16
>10000	1	>1000	2
All	29	All	29

Source: *DMRHS.*

Two emerging trends are apparent in recent times.

- The OP load is rising, along with improved patient satisfaction, with better availability of quality medicines.
- The patient profile is changing with even the relatively well-to-do sections accessing the public facilities due to availability of costly drugs, like human insulin and anti-hypertensive drugs at the facilities.

Delivery Services

An increase in the share of institutional deliveries is a positive indicator of extension of obstetric care.

In 2000-2001, of the total deliveries, in 86 per cent the babies were delivered at various institutions, in the public or private sectors (Figure 9.5). The public health facilities accounted for over half the deliveries conducted at the institutional level. The share of the public health facilities has gone up over the years.

FIGURE 9.5

Delivery Profile

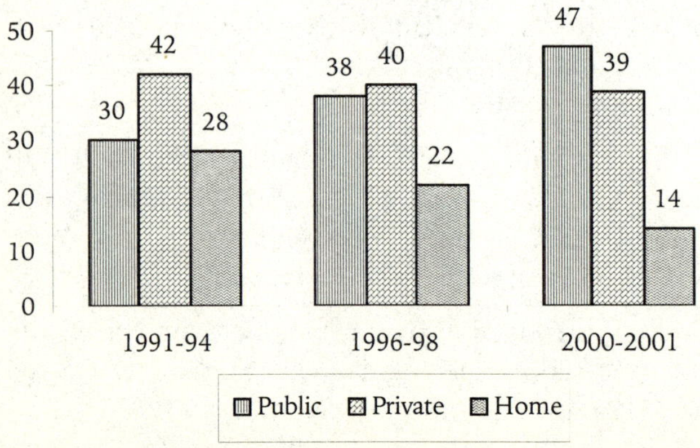

While the public health facilities accounted for over half the institutional deliveries, the share of the PHC or HSC was only minimal.

FIGURE 9.6

Public Facilities Profile in Deliveries

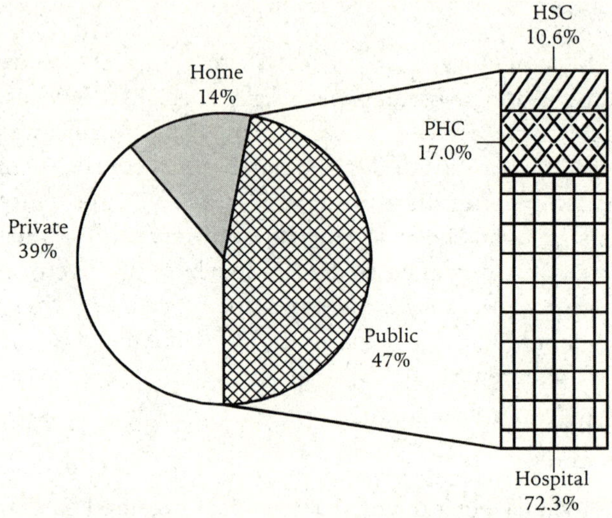

The delivery performance in PHCs has, however, improved, by 18 per cent, between 2000-01 and 2001-02.

The proportion of PHCs not conducting any delivery at all (zero delivery PHCs) also dropped significantly in this period (Table 9.12).

TABLE 9.12

PHCs with Zero Delivery

Period	%
April 1999	60.1
April 2000	41.8
April 2001	36.3
March 2002	19.7

Source: DPH.

But a disappointing factor is that even with this fall the number of deliveries conducted at a PHC averaged less than five per month.

The caesarean section (CS) is an indicator of emergency obstetric care at the hospital level. In 2000-2001, of the 2.09 lakh deliveries conducted at the hospitals in 29 Districts (excluding Chennai), 8.2 per cent were caesareans. There was a wide disparity in achievement, ranging from a low of eight CS in 1716 deliveries in Perambalur to 1761 CS in 12136 deliveries in Erode. The number of O & G specialists available at any time in these two Districts ranged from zero to two in the former and five to seven in the latter.

Family Welfare Services

The positive indicators on the family welfare front, from the figures indicated in the Year Book 1999 - 2000 of the Directorate of Family Welfare, Chennai are:

- A sizeable increase in the couple protection rate, from 27.8 per cent in 1980-81 to 50.2 per cent by 1999-2000.
- A rise in sterilisations, from 1.4 lakh in 1980-81 to 3.7 lakh in 1999-2000.

There has been a paradigm shift in the family welfare programme, in recent times, with greater stress on all aspects of women's reproductive health throughout their lives.

The salient features here are:

- Target free approach in promoting contraceptive use.
- Provision of a choice of contraceptive methods.
- Encouragement to birth spacing.
- Quality care.

NFHS-2 figures indicate higher contraceptive prevalence in Tamil Nadu-52 per cent of currently married women have used some method of contraception against 48 per cent in the nation. And the urban areas seemed to score over the rural.

Current Use of Contraception, 1996-98

Per cent

	Urban	*Rural*	*Tamil Nadu*
Any Method	58.2	48.8	52.1
Any Modern Method	55.1	47.7	50.3
- Female Sterilisation	46.0	44.7	45.2
- Male Sterilisation	0.6	0.9	0.8
- IUD	5.0	1.1	2.5
- Condom	3.1	0.7	1.5
- Pill	0.4	0.3	0.3
Any Traditional Method	3.1	1.1	1.8
- Rhythm/Safe Period	2.2	0.8	1.3
- Withdrawal	0.9	0.3	0.5
Not Using any Methods	41.8	51.2	47.9
All	100.0	100.0	100.0
n =	**1,497**	**2,748**	**4,245**

Source: NFHS -2.

A few interesting features that emerged in the family welfare scenario in the survey are:

- The contraceptive method mix has a heavy bias towards female sterilisation, notwithstanding the greater emphasis on contraceptive choice and modern spacing method in promotional efforts.
- The current contraceptive use peaks at the 35-39 years of age, with little variation between urban and rural women.
- There is no clear relationship between the level of education and contraceptive use.
- Contraceptive use increased sharply with number of living children, rising from 2 per cent for women with no living children to 76 per cent for women with three living children, dropping to 66 per cent for women with four or more children form.
- Son-preference seems evident in contraceptive use, with low current use of contraception among women with no sons.
- Modern methods seemed to dominate in contraceptive use over such traditional methods as rhythm or safe period and withdrawal.

This scenario points to the need for improved male participation and greater promotion of modern methods of spacing besides an overall increase in contraceptive prevalence.

Immunisation

Free vaccination services for all eligible children against six serious but preventable diseases - tuberculosis, diphtheria, pertussis, tetanus, poliomylitis and measles - are an important component of the child health care system in the State, as in the rest of the country. This has been strengthened through the Expanded Programme of Immunisation (EPI) initiated in 1978 by Government of India, followed by the Universal Immunisation Programme (UIP) in 1985-86 with the objective of having cent per cent coverage of all infants against the six vaccine preventable diseases, subsequently bolstered by the Pulse Polio Immunisation Campaign which began by end-1999 as a national effort at eliminating polio. Standard protocols are developed for immunisation coverage and are now followed.

NFHS-2 data reveals the highest coverage of fully vaccinated children aged 12-23 months in Tamil Nadu-89 per cent - more than double the national average. The term 'fully vaccinated' denotes that the children have received the specified doses of BCG, measles, DPT and Polio, by the time they celebrate their first birthday. The survey data shows that the immunisation coverage is near universal (97 per cent to 99 per cent) in almost all vaccinations except measles and zero polio. Another interesting fact that emerges from this survey is a low drop-out, hardly 2 per cent, between the first and third dose of DPT and polio vaccination.

Such household characteristics as the sex of the child, the literacy level of the mothers or the standard of living do not appear to significantly influence the immunisation coverage levels.

School Health Services

Comprehensive health care services are provided to all students in government and government aided schools from first to twelfth standards, through the School Health Programme.

The salient features of the programme are:

- School medical teams comprising medical officers of PHCs and paramedical staff visit the allotted schools on Thursdays on a pre-determined programme.
- 200 to 250 students are covered in each visit.
- Health care check-up is provided to the students.
- Students requiring specialised treatment are referred to higher medical institutions.
- All Thursdays are observed as *School Health Days* and all Saturdays as *Referral Days.*
- Two teachers in each school are trained to help in implementing the programme.
- School health cards and medicine supplies are also provided as part of the programme.

The focused activities are:

- Health appraisal of school children.
- Treatment, referral and follow-up services.
- Immunisation.
- Eye, dental and mental health.
- Nutritional services.
- Health education.
- Improvement of school environment.

The Medical Teams visited 36,193 schools and screened 88.8 lakh students, in 2001-02. Of these, 1.4 lakh students were referred to higher medical institutions for further treatment.

Drugs worth Rs. 300 lakh were supplied by TNMSC for the programme.

Important among the diseases noticed during screening are dental caries, worm infestation, ARI and anemia.

Indian System of Medicine

With the resurgence of the traditional system of medicine all over the world, the State Government has also laid stress on rapid development of the Indian System of Medicine (ISM). A beginning has been made with placement of *Siddha* doctors in selected PHCs in the State, with the ultimate objective of placing one ISM practitioner in every PHC.

Simultaneously efforts are also on to improve the quality of drugs and standardisation of *Siddha,* Unani and Ayurveda drugs. Modernisation of the pharmacies at Chennai and Palayamkottai, with assistance from Government of India, as also setting up of a Drug Testing Laboratory are some of the proposed initiatives in this context.

The objective is to provide a congenial environment for ISM to become self-sustaining through a multi-pronged policy addressing the key issues.

- Medical colleges are set up by the government for *Siddha, Unani, Yoga* and Naturopathy as also Homeopathy system of medicines.
- Private colleges conforming to the required standards are also permitted to run relevant courses.
- Clinical research is now on at selected institutions on the treatment of AIDS/HIV, cancer, diabetes and infertility.
- Collection of cudgeon leaves left behind by the *Siddhars,* which is a treasure house of information, is now in progress with appropriate arrangements for their transcription and printing. So far 202 bundles of cudgeon leaves, 30 rare *Siddha* books and eight manuscripts have been collected from hereditary Practitioners.
- There are 631 institutes providing relief under ISM in the State, of which 567 institutes, with an in-patient capacity of 651 beds; are concentrating on *Siddha* system.
- Four pharmacies in the public sector are producing *Siddha,* Ayurvedic and Unani medicines.
- A Medical Plant Board is proposed to be set up to coordinate the production, standardisation, quality control and storage of medicinal and herbal plants.

TAMPCOL, a State Government corporation is already engaged in commercial and promotional use of herbs. The corporation has developed 55 acre at Kolli Hills for development and cultivation of medicinal plants. It has introduced several new products like Vigorous Glow, Tampitizer, Femicure, Pain Balm, Vallarin Tablet, *Madhumega, Choornam* Tablet, Silver 2000 Tablet, Capsules and Syrup, the market.

Health Person Power

The public sector health system employs 51,198 persons, comprising medical, paramedical, technical and support staff (Table 9.13).

These health staff function at both the institutional and field levels.

Keeping in view the need for capacity upgradation of the human resources in its health sector, the State had formulated a comprehensive and forward looking policy in 1996.

TABLE 9.13

Health Personnel, 2001

Category	*Persons*
Medical	8,811
Nursing	9,740
Paramedical	24,259
Technical	3,583
Clerical	2,174
Auxiliary	2,355
Managerial/Administration	276
Total	51,198

Source: DHFW.

The stress in this policy is on

- Skill upgradation, both clinical and behavioural.
- Human resource development, both individual and organisation.

Decentralisation of the training structure and continued skill upgradation are the key aspects focussed.

A State Training Cell is set up at the Department of Public Health (DPH) which is vested with the responsibility of overseeing all the training activities. This cell comprises senior level health administrators and programme managers. The training regimen covers in-service training at periodic intervals to improve knowledge and skill levels in addition to programme specific training.

The training ambit covers all categories — Medical Officers, field functionaries as also support staff.

Notable among these efforts at human resource development are:

- Induction training to all newly recruited PHC Medical Officers.
- Skill development training for the field functionaries at PHCs/HSCs.
- Training of pharmacists at drug warehouses on drug logistics and warehouse management.
- Training of pharmacists at Hospitals and PHCs on material management, maintenance of records and rational indenting.
- Gender sensitisation training at different levels.
- Training on computer literacy from top level managers to the field functionaries.

The training is tailor-made to suit the specific requirements of the trainees. Most of these training programmes are organised in-house. The State has developed six Regional Training Institutes, with facilities to offer residential training. Besides their own faculty, these institutes draw on outside expertise also as guest faculty. Mobile District Training Teams supplement the training efforts of these institutes in conducting in-service training. A detailed Training Calendar is drawn up at the commencement of each year in consultation with the training institutions. The progress of training is reviewed mid-year for possible modification, if warranted. In 2001-02, over 12,000 PHC/HSC staff have received training in different areas. At this rate, the various persons in the primary health care system will receive training every two years.

Knowledge and skill development for the other health personnel are now receiving attention of the health system managers.

Medical Education

The Directorate of Medical Education oversees the development of medical education in the State. It is also entrusted with the task of effective supervision of medical institutions and administration of Teaching Hospitals.

Currently 11 Medical Colleges, one Dental College, two Physiotherapy Colleges and one Nursing College are functioning in the State sector. The sanctioned strength of the Medical Colleges is 1055 while that of the Dental College is 60.

In addition, a number of Medical and Para-medical institutions are functioning in the State. These include three Medical Colleges and 10 Dental Colleges.

Student selection is organised through a Single Window System by a Selection Committee headed by the Director of Medical Education in accordance with the government policy announced every year. Admission to PG courses as also speciality courses is also done by the Selection Committee followed by counselling. To provide greater opportunities for students from rural areas, the government has recently enhanced reservation from 15 per cent to 25 per cent for rural students.

The Tamil Nadu Dr. MGR Medical University located at Chennai, with 194 affiliated institutions, organises research programmes from time to time. Telemedicine equipments are installed here by the Medical Centre of Boston International INC, USA with two earth stations and related equipment. The transmission unit is installed in this facility while the receiver is placed at Kilpauk Medical College, Chennai.

The Tamil Nadu Dr. MGR Medical University is also conducting Medical Teachers Training programme and regular training programme for Blood Bank Medical Officers, Technicians and Social Workers.

Health Logistics

Streamlining drug supplies to all the health facilities in the State is a pioneering effort in the recent decade. That other States, like Andhra Pradesh, Karnataka and Himachal Pradesh, are now trying to emulate the Tamil Nadu model attests to the success of this effort.

Till late-eighties, drug supplies to all the health facilities used to be procured and distributed by different Directorates at the State level. The requirements of individual facilities in terms of the type of drug required, or the quantum needed, were never taken into consideration. This, coupled with uncertainty of supplies in respect of both timing and frequency, usually ended up in an unhealthy mix of stock-outs or surpluses at different health facilities.

The concept of a centralised drug collection point at the District level was evolved in this backdrop, initiated under the Danida assisted Tamil Nadu Area Health Care Project, Phase II. In this concept, drugs procured from different sources converged at a central point in the District, a Drug Warehouse, from where they were distributed to the health facilities in that District.

Two drug warehouses were constructed, one at Salem and the other at Cuddalore, to cater to the drug requirements of the PHCs in their catchment areas.

The PHCs were given the facility, for the first time, to place an indent on the warehouse and receive the drugs they need, in the quantity they required, from the warehouse on a regular basis. This eliminated the problem of over-stocking or stock-outs at these health facilities.

The success of this innovative initiative encouraged the Government to upscale this model to cover the entire State and extend the coverage to hospitals besides PHCs. In addition to distribution, it was also decided to centralise drug procurement to benefit from bulk purchases and scale of economies.

The Tamil Nadu Medical Services Corporation Limited (TNMSC), was set up in 1994, registered under the Companies Act, 1956, with the mandated function of ensuring availability of drugs and medical supplies at all the public health facilities in the State. TNMSC's role encompassed procurement, storage, distribution and quality control.

TNMSC draws up a list of essential drugs, organises their storage at different points and distributes these to the health facilities. Through its centralised procurement of drugs, in generic names, TNMSC has been able to achieve price advantage and optimise its resources earmarked for drug purchases. TNMSC now maintains 23 drug warehouses throughout the State, each warehouse catering to the drug requirements of all the health facilities in its catchment area. The health facilities draw their drugs from the warehouses through an indenting system on a pre-determined schedule. Each facility is given an annual fund allotment for indenting drugs from the warehouse to avoid overdrawal of supplies and this is monitored through a Pass Book issued to each facility. The system is, however, not rigid as the facilities have the freedom to seek additional allotment at times of emergency. The entire operations of TNMSC are computerised and through the computer network it monitors, on a daily basis, drug flows and stocks at all its warehouses.

The Corporation's drug purchases have gone up from Rs. 76 crore in 1995-96 to Rs. 107 crore by 2000-01 (Table 9.14).

The key achievements of such a streamlined drug supply system are:

- No drug stock-out at any health facility.
- Availability of quality in drugs in strip or blister packing at public health facilities, as in the open market.
- Enormous patient satisfaction.
- Improved credibility of the health facilities among the population.

TABLE 9.14

Drug Purchases by TNMSC

Year	*Rs. Crore*
1995-96	75.51
1996-97	78.02
1997-98	78.41
1998-99	86.57
1999-2000	94.22
2000-01	107.22

Source: Policy Note on Medical and Public Health, 2001-02.

Over the years, TNMSC has extended the ambit of its operations:

- The medical facilities in Police, Prisons, Juvenile Homes, Transport Corporations, Veterinary Department and Cooperative Institutions now draw their regular supplies from the drug warehouses.
- MRI centres are established in two teaching hospitals and CT scan centres are set up in 22 government hospitals providing diagnostic services, on payment basis; the charges are lower than the private investor-owned centres.
- Construction of health related civil works is also undertaken.

Health Administration

Three major Directorates manage the health delivery system in the State:

- Directorate of Medical Education (DME).
- Directorate of Medical and Rural Health Services (DMRHS).
- Directorate of Public Health and Preventive Medicine (DPH).

The responsibility of implementing teaching, training and research programme vests with the DME. Hospitals, numbering 23, attached to the various Medical Colleges, are under its control and management. The King Institute of Preventive Medicine also falls in its jurisdiction.

The DMRHS oversees the planning and execution of all programmes pertaining to medical services. All the hospitals, excepting those attached to Medical Colleges and those in Chennai, are under its control. The DPH is incharge of all PHCs and HSCs as also public health training and continuing education. This Directorate also looks after the public health activities of Corporations and Municipalities. Besides the three major Directorates, there are Directors of Family Welfare, ESI, Drugs Control, State Health Transport Department and Indian Medicine including Homeopathy. At the District level, a Joint Director of Health Services (JDHS) is in charge of all medical, public health and family welfare programmes. The JDHS has overall administrative control of all government health and medical institutions in the District. The JDHS is assisted by Deputy Directors of Medical, Health, TB and Leprosy. The State owned Tamil Nadu State Health Transport Department takes care of the repairs and periodical servicing of the Ambulances and other vehicles of all the Hospitals/PHCs.

The *Organogram* in the next page depicts the administrative protocol.

Health Management Information System (HMIS)

The health sector is one of the most spaced out and segregated sectors as far as vertical and horizontal levels are concerned.

Based on the catchment population and administrative boundaries, services are rendered to the people through health facilities at various levels such as Health Sub-Centres (HSCs), Primary Health Centres (PHCs), First Referral Unit (FRU) Hospitals, District Hospitals and Medical College Hospitals as also through a number of programmes and camps in the rural and urban areas. A well designed and operational HMIS is crucial to assess the levels of coverage, utilisation, equity and quality of care, to provide data inputs for planning and resource allocation as also for improving the efficiency and effectiveness of the health system. Each of the health facility and programme generates its own data base, at times of lesser value to decision making. Initiatives were taken to conceptualise, plan and operationalise two types of HMIS — one, to monitor institutional services and the other to monitor outreach and programme related services in an integrated manner. The former known as Institutional Services Monitoring (ISM) System, using Optical Mark Reader (OMR) technology, captures data on 12 essential indicators from all PHCs every month, analyses and prepares a report ranking Districts and PHCs within Districts based on their performance and provides feedback at State level for initiating corrective measures. The other monitors delivery of programme related health services at facility and outreach levels.

Technical Working Groups (TWG) constituted for systems analysis and information needs assessment, level-wise i.e. HSC, PHC and FRU, have defined the indicators for assessment of health services delivery and simplified the recording and reporting tools, such as registers and reports. The HMIS for HSC levels in the rural areas and similar service delivery units in the urban areas have been operationalised. This has benefitted 12000 unit staff, through simplification of the record keeping system, reduction in the number of registers from 21 to 7 and recasting multiple reporting to single reporting every month. Registers and reports for PHCs and FRUs have also been simplified and the new record keeping system is expected to be operationalised soon. Thus the Tamil Nadu Health Sector is now on the move towards establishing a firm data base on performance at various levels of the health system.

Steps have also been initiated to computerise the entire information system, in the current decade. Computer facilities are already established at the District level and at selected Blocks. Plans exist for extending such facilities to all Blocks and also to PHCs and FRUs.

Computer literacy training for health personnel at different levels, right from the top, is currently in progress.

Health Legislation

A number of Acts have been enacted by the State government on health related issues. Important among these are:

Medical Termination of Pregnancy (MTP) Act

The MTP Act 1971 and Medical Termination of Pregnancy Rules 1975, provide for termination of certain pregnancies by registered medical practitioners and for matters connected therewith or incidental thereto.

Pre-natal Diagnostic Techniques (Regulation and Prevention of Misuse) Act, 1994

This came into force from 1.1.1996.

For effective implementation of this Act, State and District level Advisory Committees have been formed.

At State level, the Director of Medical and Rural Health Services has been nominated as the Appropriate Authority to implement the Act. At District level, the Joint Director of Health Services has been nominated as Appropriate Authority.

In its press release, dated 23.6.2001, the government has warned the doctors, found indulging in malpractices regarding sex determination that they are liable to lose their medical registration for medical practice. Warning is also given that offences under the Act, such as non-registration and misusing of equipment to disclose the sex of the foetus, are punishable as cognisable, non-bailable and non-compoundable offences punishable upto three years of imprisonment and fine upto Rs. 50,000. These equipment (scans) are to be used for diagnostic purposes only.

Till February 2002, 1625 scan centres have been registered, and action initiated against 56 unregistered scan centres.

Prevention of Food Adulteration Act (PFA) 1954 and Tamil Nadu Prevention of Food Adulteration Rules 1955

The entire State has been notified for the purpose of implementation of the Act and Rules.

The Director of Public Health and Preventive Medicine has been notified as State Food Health Authority. The Municipal Health Officers in urban areas and Medical Officers of PHCs in rural areas have been notified as Local Health Authority to implement the Act and Rules.

The Sanitary Inspectors in urban areas and Health Inspectors in rural areas have been notified as Food Inspectors for lifting of samples and launching of prosecutions in the case of adulterated samples.

During 2000-01, 3381 samples were analysed, out of which 376 samples (11.2 per cent) were found adulterated.

Prosecutions were launched in 158 cases and 74 cases were convicted, of which six were fined and 68 were fined with imprisonment.

Registration of Births and Deaths Act, 1969

Registration of births and deaths at the place of occurrence is compulsory and is enforced throughout the State as per the provision of this Act.

Government of India has revamped the Births and Deaths registration system from 1.1.2000. Accordingly, Tamil Nadu Births and Deaths Registration Rules 2000 have been notified coming into effect from 1.1.2000.

Officials connected with the births and deaths registration work have been trained in all the districts on the Revamped system of registration.

ORGANISATION STRUCTURE OF GOVERNMENT HEALTH SERVICES

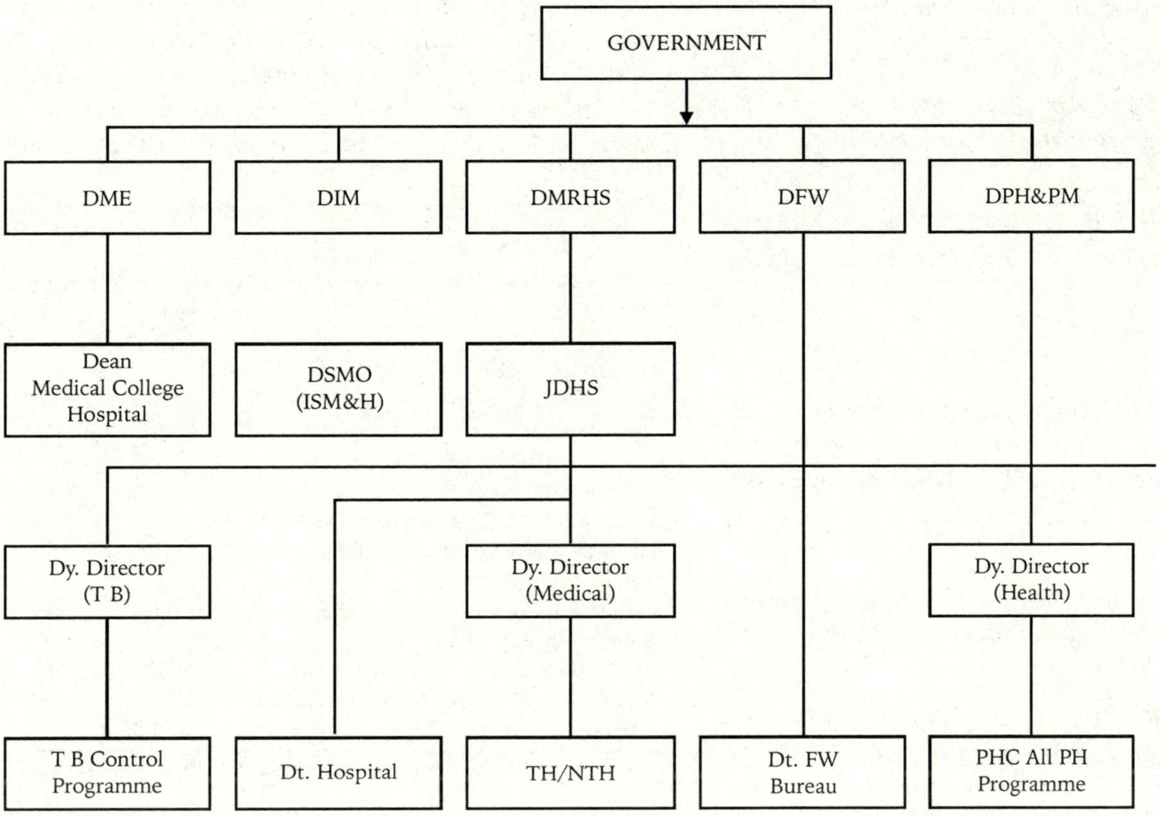

DMRHS – Director of Medical & Rural Health Services
DME – Director of Medical Education
DFW – Director of Family Welfare
DSMO – District Siddha Medical Officer
DPH & PM – Director of Public Health & Preventive Medicine
DIM – Director of Indian Medicine & Homeopathy
JDHS – Joint Director of Health Service

Tamil Nadu is enforcing the following legislative measures for regulating the manufacture and sale of drugs and cosmetics.

The Drugs & Cosmetics Act, 1940

Under the Act, quality of drugs and cosmetics is being monitored and appropriate action taken against the offenders.

The Drugs Price Control Order, 1995

This ensures that drugs are sold at the prescribed prices and the offenders are prosecuted.

The availability of drugs in the State is monitored and shortages and non-availability of drugs are brought to the notice of manufacturers concerned to effect immediate supplies of the drugs to avoid shortage.

Drugs and Magic Remedies (Objectionable Advertisements) Act, 1954

This helps protect the interests of public by initiating action against those indulging in publishing false and misleading advertisements of drugs besides prohibiting such advertisements.

Narcotic Drugs and Psychotropic Substances Act, 1985

Action is taken against persons dealing in Narcotic drugs and Psychotropic substances in contravention of this Act.

This Act is being implemented strictly to prevent the wrong usage of drugs causing health hazards and also to prevent youth from becoming addicts.

The Transplantation of Human Organs Act, 1994

Under this Act, as per Section 3(1), any donor may, in such a manner and subject to such conditions as may be prescribed, authorise the removal, before his death, of any human organ of his body for therapeutic purposes.

Tamil Nadu Siddha System of Medicine (Development and Registration of Practitioners) Act, 1997

This Act is in force from 29.9.1997 to regulate the registration and renewal of practitioners of *Siddha* system of medicine.

Way Forward

Government of Tamil Nadu prepares its Policy Note on Medical and Public Health and places it every year in the State Legislature. This Policy Note provides the framework for interventions by the public health system.

The Policy Note is in tune with the National Health Policy (NHP) last formulated in 1983. NHP-83 laid stress on:

- Creation of a network of primary health care delivery infrastructure at different levels to promote degree of access and equity.
- Qualitative improvement of health and family welfare services.
- Provision of adequate training.
- Provision of essential drugs and vaccines.

In the light of past achievements and changing needs and priorities, NHP-2001 is now formulated.

The State Policy Note is more focussed on State specific priorities in the health sector. But the overall objective is the same, viz., establishment of an effective and an efficient health care delivery system for all, in particular the vulnerable groups, like women, children and the under-privileged.

Tamil Nadu's health sector performance over the last two decades, and the noteworthy successes profiled in the earlier sections, are an indication of the emphasis laid by the State on the overall objectives of NHP. The State's initiatives in the public health sector have resulted in impressive gains in several areas over the last 20 years. Basic health facilities are extended to the mass of the population. Endemic diseases are eradicated or well under control. Simultaneously modern health facilities using advanced techniques capable of treating various serious types of illnesses and handling complicated surgeries have been established in the State. These facilities attract not only patients from other states but also from some developing countries as well.

A look at the health status of the people in 2002, end-year of the Ninth Plan, in relation to the goals set for 2007, end-year of the State's Tenth Plan, (Table 9.15), in respect of a few key indicators, will provide an idea of the leeway still to be made in the current decade.

TABLE 9.15

Health Sector Performance and Goals

Indicator	*Status 2002*	*Goal 2007*
Demographic Changes		
Life Expectancy at birth years	65	70
Crude Birth Rate per 1000 population	19.2	15
Crude Death Rate per 1000 population	7.9	6
Natural growth rate, per cent	1.1	<1
Infant Mortality Rate per 1000 live births	51	28
Maternal Mortality Rate per 1000 live births	1.3	<1
Total Fertility Rate	1.95	1.5
Couple Protection Rate, per cent	51.6	65
Epidemiological Shifts		
TB prevalence per 1 lakh population	479	300
Malaria prevalence per 1 lakh population	70	35
Leprosy per 10000 persons	4.5	<1

Source: Tamil Nadu Planning Commission (2003), "Tenth Five Year Plan: Tamil Nadu".

Some of the unfinished tasks in the health sector which merit special focus in health initiatives in the current decade are indicated below:

- The high IMR, specially neo-natal mortality, needs greater attention.
- The basic health infrastructure in place, and the linkages between different tiers, need strengthening to improve service levels.
- Urban health care requires greater attention, in a State with high level of urbanisation.
- New threats to health and well being of the people are emerging, such as HIV/AIDS, TB, Cancer and other life style disorders, like road traffic accidents, substance abuse, pollution and food adulteration. The public health system needs different approaches and varying skills to deal with these.
- Mental health problems are becoming more prevalent affecting the quality of life, of both the affected persons and their families.
- Efforts at awareness raising on health related issues and inducing behavioural changes in the

population need to be more focussed, addressing the specific needs of different segments of the population for greater impact.

The State exchequer currently supports the public health services, with some transfers from the Centre. Over the last three years, the share of health in the State budget has ranged from 5.60 per cent to 5.86 per cent. The per capita expenditure on health works out to roughly Rs. 165 per annum.

Health costs are rising over the years. It is doubtful whether the exchequer alone can continue to bear the burden and provide quality service. This points to the need for an appropriate strategy for increased public-private collaboration in the health system.

To pave the way for achieving the goals set for 2010, and to be in tune with the Millenium Development Goals, the above issues need to be addressed effectively.

This will call for concerted action on the part of the government in the following areas:

- A Strategic Planning Unit needs to be established to review, on a continuing basis, the emerging issues in the health sector, design appropriate strategies and monitor their implementation.
- Decentralisation in health planning needs to be promoted by institutionalising district based health planning process.
- There is a need for improving linkages between various programmes in operation in the health sector which calls for an integration of the vertical programmes. The gaps in existing infrastructure needs to be filled through appropriate reorganisation and restructuring of primary health care infrastructure.
- The existing data system needs strengthening to generate sufficient data to identify poorly performing districts so that a differential and appropriate area specific strategy can be developed.
- Steps are to be initiated to improve access and utilisation of health services in districts with high mortality/fertility.
- Promotion of Public-Private partnership is required to meet health challenges in the current decade.
- Health Systems Research studies and Health Economic studies need to be encouraged to analyse the reach of health services and its impact as also the cost and quality of care.
- Networking of administrative, academic and research organisations in the State with national and international bodies with similar interest in pursuing Millenium Development Goals needs encouragement. This will facilitate exchange of experiences, collaborative studies, documentation support as also visits to countries with innovative health interventions.

References

Government of Tamil Nadu, Department of Evaluation and Applied Research (DEAR): *Tamil Nadu - An Economic Appraisal, 1997-98.*

Government of Tamil Nadu, Department of Health and Family Welfare: *Policy Notes on Medical and Public Health.*

Government of Tamil Nadu, Commissioner MCH&W, Health and Family Welfare Department: *Tamil Nadu - Population Policy.*

Government of Tamil Nadu, Directorate of Family Welfare: *Tenth Five Year Plan, Working Group Report on Family Welfare.*

Government of Tamil Nadu, Directorate of Family Welfare: *Year Book 1999-2000.*

Government of Tamil Nadu, State Planning Commission: *Tenth Five Year Plan 2002-2007, Draft Working Group Report.*

Tamil Nadu Human Development Report.

Government of Tamil Nadu, Directorate of Medical and Rural Health Services : *Organisation and Functions, 2000.*

Government of India, Department of Family Welfare, Ministry of Health and Family Welfare: *National Population Policy 2000.*

Government of India, Ministry of Health and Family Welfare: *Draft National Health Policy 2001.*

Government of India, Directorate General of Health Services, Central Bureau of Health Intelligence, Ministry of Health and Family Welfare: *Health Information of India, 1997 & 1998.*

Registrar General India, Vital Statistics Division: *Sample Registration Bulletin*, New Delhi.

Director of Census Operations, Tamil Nadu: *Census of India 2001, Series 34, Tamil Nadu, Provisional Population Total-Part 1 of 2001*, Chennai.

Population Research Centre, The Gandhigram Institute of Rural Health & Family Welfare Trust, Ambathurai, Gandhigram: *Tamil Nadu Family Health Survey 1995.*

David L H : *In-Service Training for Health Personnel at Block, PHC and HSC*: Danida Support Unit, Danida supported Tamil Nadu Area Health Care Project, Tamil Nadu, 1999.

Ferguson A F & Co.: *Report on Impact of Assessment of Mobility Training Programme*, Danida, TNHCAP, Chennai.

Management Development Associates: *From Darkness to Light - The Coimbatore Path*, Chennai, 1999.

International Institute for Population Sciences (IIPS) and ORC Macro, 2000: *National Family Health Survey (NFHS -2), 1998-99:India*, Mumbai, IIPS.

International Institute for Population Sciences (IIPS) and ORC Macro, 2000: *National Family Health Survey (NFHS -2), 1998-99 :India, Tamil Nadu*, Mumbai, IIPS.

Voluntary Health Services (VHS), AIDS Control And Prevention Project (APAC): *Community Prevalence of Sexually Transmitted Diseases in Tamil Nadu, 1998 - A Report*, Chennai.

UNICEF, *District Atlas of Tamil Nadu, May 2001.*

Websites

www.tngov.in

www.tnhealth.org

www.censusindia.net

Acronyms

APAC	AIDS Prevention and Control Project
CBR	Crude Birth Rate
AIDS	Acquired Immuno Deficiency Syndrome
CS	Caesarian Section
DME	Directorate of Medical Education
DMRHS	Directorate of Medical and Rural Health Services
DPH	Director of Public Health and Preventive Medicine
ESI	Employees State Insurance
FRU	First Referral Unit
HIV	Human Immunodeficiency Virus
HMIS	Health Management Information System
HSC	Health Sub-Centre
IAP	Indian Association of Paediatrics
ICDS	Integrated Child Development Services
IEC	Information, Education and Communication
IFA	Iron & Folic Acid
IMR	Infant Mortality Rate
IP	In-patient
LEB	Life Expectancy at Birth
MDT	Multi Drug Therapy
MLA	Member of Legislative Assembly
MMR	Maternal Mortality Ratio
MP	Member of Parliament
MTP	Medical Termination of Pregnancy
NFHS-2	National Family Health Survey, India, 1998-99
NGO	Non-Government Organisation
OP	Out-patient
PDS	Public Distribution System
PHC	Primary Health Centre
RTI	Reproductive Tract Infection
SRS	Sample Registration System
STD	Sexually Transmitted Disease
TB	Tuberculosis
TINP	Tamil Nadu Integrated Nutrition Project
TNMSC	Tamil Nadu Medical Services Corporation Ltd.
UNICEF	United Nations Children's Fund
USAID	United States Agency for International Development
VES	Vital Events Survey
VHS	Voluntary Health Services
WHO	World Health Organisation

Chapter 10

Education

An Overview

Constitutional Provision

At the time of independence in 1947 India had inherited a quantitatively small educational system, which was also characterised by severe regional and structural imbalances. Only a third of eligible children were enrolled in primary school with acute social and gender disparities. Basic education was one of the major development goals advocated during the freedom movement. After independence several articles of the Constitution of India outlined the general principles governing educational development in the country. (See Box) The need for universal elementary education (UEE) for all children upto the age of 14 was provided in the Directive Principles of the Constitution within a time frame of 10 years, a rather ambitious goal which could not be attained despite substantial provisions in the successive Five Year Plans. A Supreme Court judgment in 1993 stated that the education is a fundamental right for every child until the age of 14 years. The 73rd and 74th Amendments to the Constitution paved way for decentralised management in many fields including primary education through Panchayati Raj Institutions. The 83rd Amendment in 1997 specifically argued for education as a fundamental right. With the enactment of the 93rd Amendment to the Constitution in 2001 making universal education compulsory for the age group of 6-14, this objective is to be fulfilled through formal school under state responsibility in the coming years with greater seriousness than the past.

Until 1977 the organisation and structure of education were solely the responsibility of the states. The 42nd Amendment to the Constitution empowered the Indian Parliament to legislate on education concurrently with the states. The concept of "concurrency" was given an operational meaning by the National Policy on Education-1986 (NPE-86), as a "meaningful partnership between the Centre and the States".

The National Policy on Education

The NPE-86 was an important milestone in Indian education development. It places on the Government of India a clear responsibility regarding national and integrative character of education, quality and standards, manpower planning, research and advanced study, culture, human resource development, and the international aspects of education. The Central Advisory Board of Education (CABE) set up during the pre-independence period in 1935 was expected to play a lead role in the evolution and monitoring of educational policies and programmes, especially the NPE-86 and its Programme of Action (PoA-86) and the Revised NPE-92 and the PoA-92. Despite these policies and programmes, the achievements in the development of school education has been far from satisfactory due to reasons of rapidly growing size, inability to forge consensus among the states on national standards, inadequate resource allocation, neglect of aspects relating to the curricula and teacher quality. CABE has also become ineffective due to differences among its members from states ruled by different political parties.

The Structure and Management of School Education

The Structure

Despite the National Policy on Education, the structure of school education is not uniform in India. Many different models prevail but the most common are twelve-year school. One common model provides for 7+3+2 years, consisting of elementary school stage of

SCHOOL EDUCATION

Some Constitutional Provisions on Education in India

"The State shall endeavour to provide, within a period of ten years from the commencement of this Constitution, free and compulsory education for all children until they complete the age of fourteen years". Article 45

"Any section of the citizens, residing in the territory of India or any part thereof having a distinct language, script or culture of its own shall have the right to conserve the same". Article 29(1)

"No citizen shall be denied admission to any educational institution maintained by the State or receiving aid out of the State funds on grounds only of religion, race, caste, language or any of them." Article 29(2)

"All minorities, whether based on religion or language shall have the right to establish and administer educational institutions of their choice" Article 30(1)

"The State shall not in granting aid to educational institutions discriminate against any educational institutions on the ground that it is under the management of minority, whether based on religion or language." Article 30(2)

"It shall be the endeavour of every State and of every local authority within the State to provide adequate facilities for instruction in the mother-tongue at the primary stage of education to children belonging to linguistic minority groups" Article 350-A

"The State shall promote with special care the educational and economic interests of the weaker sections of the people, and in particular, of the Scheduled Castes and the Scheduled Tribes and shall protect them from social injustice and all forms of exploitation." Article 46

7 years (5 years of primary level and 2 years of middle or upper primary level) followed by 3 years of secondary or high school level and 2 years of senior secondary or higher secondary level. Another common model provides for 8+2+2 years, consisting of elementary school stage of 8 years (5 years of primary level and 3 years of middle or upper primary level) followed by 2 years of secondary or high school level and 2 years of senior secondary or higher secondary level.

Some states have 4 year primary level. Some states offer school education upto class X only, attaching the +2 stage to colleges as part of higher education system. In a few states the upper primary/middle school level may be an independent unit or combined with the primary or secondary levels or both.

Tamil Nadu and a large number of other states follow the latter model. A child is normally admitted to class I at the age of six and is expected to complete primary level of class V at the age of 11 years, class VIII (middle school) at the age of 14 years, class X (high school) at the age of 16 and class XII (Higher Secondary) at the age of 18 years.

Management

In addition to the variations in the pattern of school education, there is a large multiplicity of management systems in school education even within each state. Some of them such as the Central Schools, the Central Board of Secondary Education (CBSE) schools, Navodhya Schools, Anglo Indian Schools, and Indian School Certificate (ISC) schools are under the purview of concerned central boards with all India curriculum and examination. There are also open schools at national level permitting lateral entry to schools at different levels.

Tamil Nadu has all these except the Navodhya system due to differences on the language policy for such schools between the Centre and the State. Many States, including Tamil Nadu, have their own Boards for high schools as well as for higher secondary schools. There are also separate Matriculation School Boards.

In some states there are schools run under the American School system, Cambridge School system and the International Baccalaureate system intended mainly for children of parents who are transferable to different countries.

Moreover some schools are fully funded by the Central or State government while some others are aided schools. There are schools managed by *Panchayats* or municipalities, or city corporations. There are also many private unaided schools.

These many varieties in the structure and management of school education system pose special problems in the curriculum development for school education. However it appears that the multiplicity is inevitable for sometime to come. Planning for development of school education at the state level has to take into account these variations.

School Educational Policies

Central Policies

In spite of a comprehensive constitutional and policy framework for development of education, India faces a daunting task in fulfilling the growing demand and maintaining quality. The demographic implications, regional variations, ground realities of socio-economic constraints etc. have made the task of fulfilling the constitutional obligations difficult. The ambitious goals set out to achieve Education For All (EFA) reflect the Central Government Policies as follows:

1. Expansion of early childhood care and development activities especially for the poor, disadvantaged and disabled children, through a multi-pronged effort involving families, communities and appropriate institutions.
2. Universalisation of Elementary Education (UEE) viewed as a comprehensive programme of:
   - Access to elementary education for all children upto 14 years of age.
   - Universal participation till they complete the elementary stage through formal or non-formal education programme.
   - Universal achievement at least of minimum levels of learning.
3. Drastic reduction in illiteracy, particularly in the 15-35 age group.
4. Provision of opportunities to maintain, use and upgrade education, and provision of facilities for development of skills to all persons who are functionally literate and those who have received primary education through formal and non-formal channels.
5. Creation of necessary infrastructures, and setting in motion of processes, which could empower women and make education an instrument of women's equality.
6. Improving the content and process of education to relate it better to the environment, people's culture and with their living and working conditions, thereby enhancing their ability to learn and cope with the problems of livelihood and environment.

These policies are intended to cover nearly 35 million children in India (Haq, 1998) who do not have access to primary education and even among those who do, about 37 per cent drop out before reaching class V. The proportion of girls in this situation is far worse than the boys.

Tamil Nadu Policies

Unlike the overall national scene, the situation in Tamil Nadu is relatively better on account of a long tradition of formal schooling. The state intervention in public education in Tamil Nadu was well established even during the colonial government. The establishment of primary schools in many remote habitations has contributed to increase in enrolment at the primary level. Its position is somewhat unique in the sense that unlike many other states, its progress is marked by decrease in the number of enrolments because of reduction in the size of its younger population over time.

TABLE 10.1

School Enrolment Vs. School-Age Population in Tamil Nadu

Stages	*School Age Popn (lakh)*			*Enrolment (lakh)*			*% of Enrolment*		
	1993	*1998*	*2001*	*1993*	*1998*	*2001*	*1993*	*1998*	*2001*
Primary	79.8	68.8	57.5	80.2	66.7	56.7	100	96.9	98.6
Middle	36.8	37.5	37.6	35.4	33.8	35.2	96.2	90.1	93.6

Note: 1. Data for 1993 in Table 10.1 suggests higher gross enrolments, which may be due to the enrolment of under-aged or over-aged children also in primary classes, when the urge to enroll was strongly pushed in the beginning of the nineties. It is seen that across time, the percentage of enrolment has been gradually increasing.

2. As the Net Enrolment Ratio (NER) is a proportion of the population of a particular age group enrolled at a specific level of schooling to the total population in that age group, it is more reliable than Gross Enrolment Ratio (GER) which does not consider age, and age-specific enrolment ratio which does not consider the level or class of enrolment.

Source: Policy Notes of Respective Years, Government of Tamil Nadu.

Tamil Nadu had a major lead in the introduction of early Acts for compulsory elementary education, innovative schemes like the Nutritious Noon-Meal Scheme, and a generally lively education scenario with political commitment to the cause of educating all children through government schools under State responsibility.

Regarding the role of the State in public primary education, Tamil Nadu is a pioneer. An example is the passing of the Madras Elementary Education Act as early as 1920. But, enforcing compulsion under that was left to the discretion of each local body unlike the present Tamil Nadu Compulsory Elementary Education Act, which makes primary education compulsory for every child of school age throughout the State.

The role of the State is even more conspicuous in Tamil Nadu than other states because of the spread and popularity of its schemes like the Noon-Meal Scheme, introduced in 1982 for children in class 1 to 5, and later extended since 1984 to cover all children of classes 6 to 10 also. Allied benefits are given to beneficiaries of the Noon-Meal Scheme in the sense that these children also receive free text books. The Tamil Nadu Text Book Corporation, established in 1970 has distributed about 400 lakh text books to children during the year 2000-01, through various departments including Education, Adi Dravidar and Tribal Welfare, BCs and MBCs department, and the Directorate of rehabilitation. Apart from this, the government's welfare scheme for young children includes supply of free slates to class 1 children and also uniforms since 1985, free bus passes and even bags and slippers to many children. Besides, the State has implemented the Tamil Nadu Integrated Nutrition Project from 1991 to 1997, and also gives a package of services through the Integrated Child Development Services since 1975. The probable impact of these on enrolment has been shown by some studies (see for instance Radhakrishnan and Akila, 2000).

In May 2002, the Government of Tamil Nadu announced in the Legislative Assembly the following policy measures relating to the development of school education in the State (Policy Note, 2002-03):

- To provide schools in hamlets where there are no schools.
- To enroll school age children in schools before 2003.
- To provide five year of schooling for all children before 2007.
- To provide eight year of schooling to all children before 2010.
- To eradicate drop-outs before 2010 fully.
- To improve the basic amenities in schools.
- To improve and enrich the syllabus.
- To improve the quality of education from the pre-school to higher secondary.
- To ensure minimum levels of learning.
- To impart refresher training to teachers.
- To eradicate illiteracy.
- To maintain the confidentiality of public examination and release the results to the entire satisfaction of the user community.
- To recruit teachers through written examination.
- To distribute quality text books at fair price in time.
- To open village libraries.
- To give importance to vocational training in schools.
- To encourage health education in schools.
- To involve the parents also in the management of schools to a great extent.

These measures are indicative of the importance attached by the Tamil Nadu Government to the development of school education. The success of these policy pronouncements will depend upon detailed analysis of the key issues and critical factors and formulation of operational schemes to yield effective results in the desired time frame.

Key Issues and Critical Factors

In the light of the announced policy framework for school education there is a need to identify the key issues in terms of anticipated demand structure at various levels of education, identification of priorities for action, administrative measures to ensure uninterrupted development and innovative financial mechanisms. Some of the key issues are:

- Fulfilling the anticipated demand for pre-primary, primary, middle, high school and higher secondary levels;
- Assigning priorities for up-gradation and consolidation of existing school infrastructure and creation of new ones;
- Ensuring minimum number of teachers in the schools for effective teaching and learning process;
- Introducing curricular structure and content relevant to the policy objectives;
- Formulating demand oriented vocational education schemes and ensuring their functional quality;
- Defining operative strategy for achieving Universal Primary Education (UPE) by 2007 and UEE by 2010;
- Defining operative strategy for achieving Universal Secondary Education (USE) by 2015 and Universal Senior Secondary Education (USSE) by 2020;
- Establishing teacher training schemes for serving and new teachers on a sustainable basis;
- Incorporating new, affordable and relevant technological means to attain educational objectives;

- Devising innovative schemes for mobilising traditional and non-traditional financial resources and ensuring their predictability;
- Ensuring continuity of educational policies;
- Decentralising educational responsibilities wherever necessary for greater efficiency and quality.

Current Situation at Elementary Stage

Pre-Primary Education

There is a great deal of desire on the part of the parents to send their children to pre-primary classes much before they attain the age of five. Hence there are a large number of pre-primary schools operating in the State. Of these only nine institutions, enrolling 767 students and employing 41 teachers, are approved and aided by the Government. There are 2756 private unaided pre-primary schools enrolling 2,77,986 children (2000-01) and employing 14,779 teachers. It is understood that there are 2448 more such schools with student strength of 1,86,961 awaiting government recognition through legal measures. This is a significant size warranting regulatory attention.

The State should enunciate unambiguous guidelines for establishment of pre-primary schools covering aspects of maximum size, desirable educational facilities, safety considerations in transport and inside class rooms, health related amenities, fee structure etc.

Elementary Education

The earlier policy for universalisation of elementary education in Tamil Nadu envisaged the enrolment of all children in the age group of 5 to 10 and retaining them in the school for a minimum period of five years. The education policy emphasised priority to girl children and special importance to the children from scheduled caste and scheduled tribe. With the 93rd amendment to the Constitution of India, the State would have to develop and implement a policy to enroll all children in the age group of 6 to 14. Enforcement of this policy will reduce the drop-out rate in the elementary education level to negligible amount from about 14 per cent at the primary and 35 per cent in the middle school levels. (Table 10.2.)

Primary and Middle Schools

There has been a significant declining trend in enrolment in the elementary schools (Table 10.3, Figure 10.1) in Tamil Nadu particularly at the primary level

TABLE 10.2

Cumulative Drop-out Rates in Tamil Nadu Schools

Year	*Primary*	*Middle*	*Secondary*	*Higher Secondary*
1991-92	19.31	41.69	67.94	84.90
1995-96	15.85	32.54	63.87	81.40
1996-97	15.06	30.27	62.53	80.48
1999-00	14.41	35.43	57.92	82.27
2000-01	14.40	35.59	57.89	82.30
2001-02	14.31	35.07	57.55	79.50

Source: State Policy Notes.

(classes 1 to 5). This may be partly due to lower population growth and partly due to drop-outs. The rate of decadal change in population of Tamil Nadu has shown a decrease from 22.30 per cent during 1961-71 to 17.50 per cent during 1971-81 and to 11.19 per cent during 1991-2001. The population of children in the age group of 6 to 11 has declined significantly during the past decade as shown in Table 10.1.

FIGURE 10.1

Elementary School Enrolment in Tamil Nadu

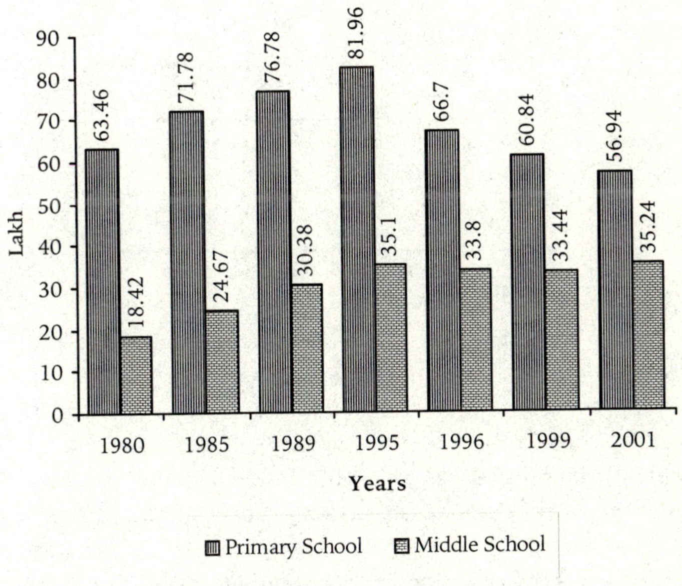

The number of children in age group of 6 to 14 who remain outside of the school system is of the order of 3 to 5 lakh (Table 10.4) who are probably engaged in child labour, undesirable trades or in household functions (mostly in case of girls).

In order to bring them into the educational fold a number of initiatives will be necessary to meet the goals of UEE. Some of them could be induced to take up non-formal education under periodic supervision by specially trained teachers during evenings, weekends and special camps. Their learning process could be made attractive and enticing through combination of lessons, games, art, music, computer education and other interesting vocational skills.

TABLE 10.3

Enrolment in Elementary Education in Tamil Nadu

Year	*No. of Institutions*		*Enrolment (lakh)*		*Teachers*	
	Primary	*Middle*	*Primary*	*Middle*	*Primary*	*Middle*
1980-81	27705	5679	63.46	18.42	112,788	69,516
1985-86	29118	5691	71.78	24.67	116,625	66,919
1989-90	29491	5651	76.78	30.38	118,922	65,668
1995-96	30471	5549	81.96	35.10	115,181	64,392
1996-97	30619	5503	66.70	33.80	115,561	64,454
1999-00	31052	5640	60.84	33.44	120,449	58,395
2001-02	31488	5809	56.94	35.24	121,483	59,922

Source: Government of Tamil Nadu: An Economic Appraisal
Government of Tamil Nadu: Director of Elementary Education Manivannan, I.V. (2002); and
Policy Notes on Education of Government of Tamil Nadu.

TABLE 10.4

Number of Children Not Enrolled in Elementary Schools in Tamil Nadu (Lakh)

Age Group	*1993-94*	*1998-99*	*1999-2000*	*2001-02*
6-11	—	2.1	2.16	0.76
11-14	1.4	3.7	4.16	2.36

Source: Computed from previous tables.

In spite of the massive investments made by the Govt. of Tamil Nadu in elementary education there are certain shortcomings, which deserve serious attention. One of these relate to the shortage of teachers. As of Feb. 2001 there were still 501 single teacher primary schools in the State. Only two teachers man 25 per cent of the primary schools. There were 715 primary schools and 15 middle schools without headmasters.

High School and Higher Secondary Stage

Though there are many different types of secondary and senior secondary schools function in Tamil Nadu, majority of the students are enrolled in the State Board and the Central Board schools. The growth pattern of students at the secondary and senior secondary levels in the State is shown in Table 10.5 and Figures 10.2 and 10.3.

TABLE 10.5

Enrolment in High and Higher Secondary Classes and Total School Enrolment in Tamil Nadu (Lakh)

Year	*Enrolment in*		*Total Enrolment in Class I to XII*		
	Class IX&X	*Class XI&XII*	*Total*	*Male*	*Female*
1980-81	6.73	2.66	91.27	—	—
1985-86	9.15	3.49	109.04	61.17	47.87
1989-90	11.07	4.50	122.68	68.43	54.25
1995-96	17.24	6.10	140.40	77.11	63.29
1996-97	16.90	6.50	123.90	66.55	57.35
1999-00	15.36	7.15	116.79	60.86	55.93
2001-02	15.86	8.98	116.82	60.63	56.19

Source: Govt. of Tamil Nadu, Eighth Five Year Plan (1992-97), State Planning Commission. Deptt. of School Education, Govt. Tamil Nadu Policy Notes on Education, 2000-01 & 2002-03.

FIGURE 10.2

Enrolment in High and Hr. Sec. Schools in Tamil Nadu

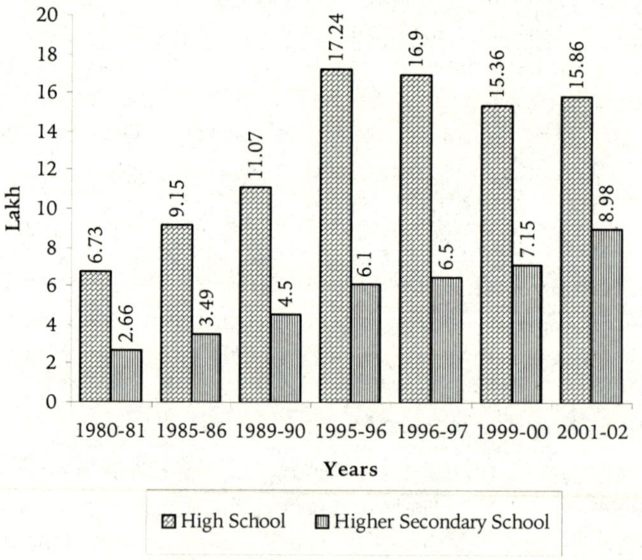

FIGURE 10.3

School Enrolment (I-XII) and Gender

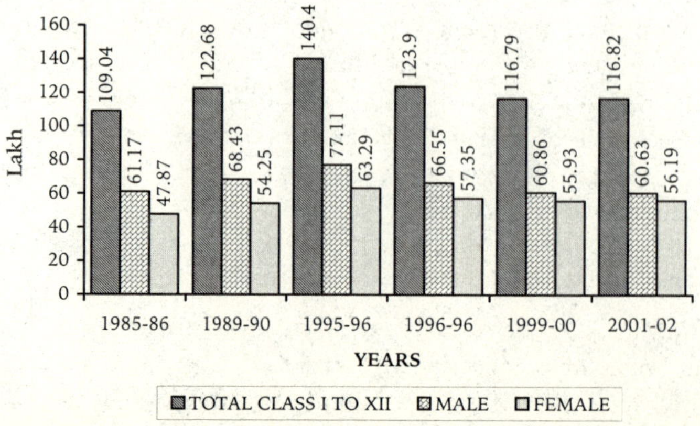

Many of the high and higher secondary schools offer schooling from the primary or even pre-primary stage. Table 10.6 and Figure 10.4 show the overall enrolment of students in three different types of high schools, State Board, Anglo Indian and Central/matriculation schools and higher secondary schools.

FIGURE 10.4

Enrolment in High and Higher Sec. School in Tamil Nadu

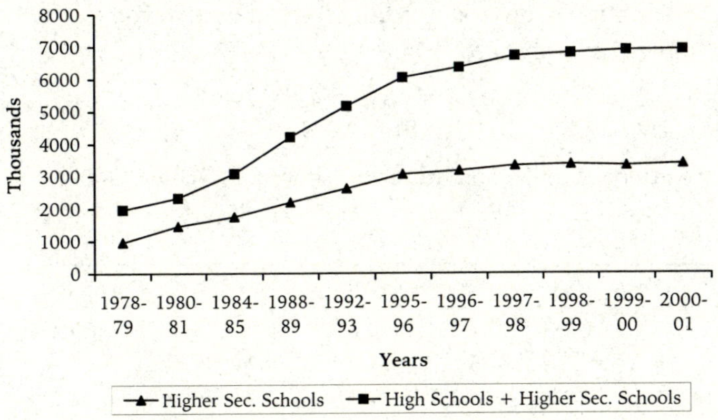

The pattern of growth during the last five years at the high school level indicate establishing trend around 16 lakh at the high school level and around 8 to 9 lakh at higher secondary level. This may be reversed to higher levels enrolment with the implementation of UEE and its cascading effect.

Other noticeable trends are:

- Increase in the number of state board high schools; increase in enrolment till 1995-96 and significant reduction thereafter. The decline in enrolment of girls is less pronounced;
- Decrease in the number of Anglo-Indian High schools now at 12 in number; sharp decrease in the enrolment of boys as well as girls in these schools from 1998-99
- Robust growth in the number of Central and Matriculation schools; steady growth in enrolment of boys; and slight decline in the enrolment of girls in these schools. Perhaps this increase may be as alternative to state board schools.
- Though there has been a significant increase in the number of higher secondary schools, there is a small decrease in the boys as well as girls from 1997-98;
- In recent years the total enrolment in high and higher secondary stage (classes 9 to 12) has shown only a marginal growth;
- Sharp increase in the number of male teachers and significant decline in the number of female teachers.
- The Pupil-Teacher ratio is around 35 to 1 both at the elementary and at the high school and secondary school level.

TABLE 10.6

Enrolment in High and Higher Secondary Schools

Year	*State Board High Schools*			*Anglo Indian High Schools*			*Central and Matric High Schools*			*Total (000)*	*HR. SEC. SCH*				*Teachers*		
	No. of inst.	*Boys (000)*	*Girls (000)*	*No. of inst.*	*Boys (000)*	*Girls (000)*	*No. of. inst.*	*Boys (000)*	*Girls (000)*	*All High Sch.*	*No. of Inst.*	*Boys (000)*	*Girls (000)*	*Total (000)*	*Male*	*Female*	*Total*
1978-79	2080	494	313	17	5.0	6.7	99	44.8	28.3	1007.8	909	638	319	957	50006	24873	74879
1980-81	1958	424	280	17	4.1	7.6	94	25.6	17.6	869.8	1300	926	531	1457	55734	30536	86270
1984-85	2299	557	396	14	3.2	7.6	233	67.2	51.1	1329.1	1474	1087	658	1745	62384	38876	101260
1988-89	2293	701	528	13	3.4	7.2	616	84.7	68.8	2022.1	1687	1311	879	2190	66268	44346	110614
1992-93	2396	822	663	13	4.0	9.0	794	138.0	104.0	2547.0	2165	1556	1061	2617	68040	48457	116497
1995-96	2445	878	737	13	4.0	9.0	962	212.0	173.0	2988.0	2490	1781	1271	3052	70701	53524	124225
1996-97	2464	898	757	13	4.0	9.0	1110	220.0	180.0	3191.0	3574	1842	1321	3163	72842	55114	127956
1997-98	2449	886	751	12	5.0	9.0	1304	236.0	192.0	3395.0	3775	1920	1400	3320	73671	56142	129813
1998-99	2802	729	763	12	3.3	7.9	1394	279.5	248.9	3437.6	3149	1834	1529	3363	78780	60733	139513
1999-00	2839	651	707	12	3.0	7.3	1700	279.9	208.0	3568.1	3292	1793	1529	3322	97678	46142	143820
2000-01	2859	650	731	12	2.7	7.559	1629	322.2	173.7	3528.2	3439	1807	1572	3379	114117	34392	148509

Source: Govt. of Tamil Nadu: An Economic Appraisal;
Govt. of Tamil Nadu: Director of Elementary Education;
Manivannan, I.V (2002) and
Policy Notes on Education of Govt. of Tamil Nadu.

Future Demand for School Education

Enrolment Projections

Enrolment projections are useful for setting realistic goals, designing feasible implementation plans or understanding the financial implications. The purpose of this exercise is to illustrate the possibilities in terms of enrolment, management and finances rather than to provide accurate forecasts. The projections are meant to provide a guide to the nature of initiatives to meet the likely challenges of the educational system. Such projection would need periodic review at intervals of three to five years to modify the initial plans. State specific projections are essential since the national trends are not fully valid for States like Tamil Nadu.

Since not much research has been done on methodologies on forecasting the educational trends at state or national level, it becomes necessary to adopt *ad-hoc* approaches in arriving at the reasonable projections.

Assumptions

According to the 2001 Census of India, the population of Tamil Nadu in 2001 was 6,21,10,839 (say 621 lakh). The decadal change from 1991 was 11.19 per cent. The number of children in the 0-6 age group in this Census was 6,817,669 (say 68.2 lakh of which male: 35.18 and female: 33.02 lakh) which is 10.98 per cent of the total population.

The anticipated demand for elementary education in the next decade at the primary and middle level will depend upon the increase in the relevant age group due to population growth plus the reduction in the dropout rate on account of the implementation of the goals of UEE. The situation regarding the numbers in various school age groups and their enrolment status as of 2001 is shown in Table 10.7.

TABLE 10.7

School Age Distribution in 2001 in Tamil Nadu

Total Population of Tamil Nadu = 621 lakh

Age Group	Population (lakh)	% of Total Population	Enrolled (lakh)	% Age Group Enrolled	Drop-out Rate (%) Cumulative
0-6	68.2	10.98			
6-11	57.5	9.25	56.74	98.7	14.31
11-14	37.6	6.0	35.24	93.7	35.07
14-16	23.3	3.75	15.86	68.1	57.55
16-18	25.8	4.15	8.98	34.8	79.50
14-18	49.1	7.9	24.84	50.6	
6-18	144.3	23.24	116.82	80.96	

Source: Census of India, 2001. Provisional Tables and State Policy Notes.

Methodology of Projections (National Level)

The expert committee on population projections appointed by the Planning Commission, Government of India, in 1996, estimated the population of major States upto the year 2016 and those projections were based on 1991 Census. It assumed an average compound growth rate of 1.81 per cent per annum during 1991-2001, 1.53 per cent between 2001-2011 and 1.4 per cent between 2011-2016 respectively.

The estimated population in school going age group at the national level according to the expert committee is shown in Table 10.8 below:

TABLE 10.8

National Level Population Projections in School Going Age Groups, 1991-2016

(million)

Age Group	1991	1996	2001	2006	2011	2016
6-10	116.7	121.9	118.2	106.9	109.1	115.8
11-13	53.0	65.8	74.4	69.3	62.5	66.4
14-15	36.2	39.8	47.3	48.4	43.6	42.5
16-17	63.9	73.6	91.7	98.0	89.2	83.8
6-17	233.6	264.0	284.3	274.2	260.8	266.0

Source: Selected Educational Statistics, MHRD, 1998-99.

The following national trends are indicated by the above projections.

- The population in the age group 6 to 17 would touch a peak of about 284 million in 2001 and start declining thereafter. It may be around 266 million by 2016 and in the range of 265-270 million by 2021.
- During 2010 and 2020 the population in the age group 6 to 10 would stabilise around 110-115 million. Hence removal of imbalances and qualitative improvement should remain the focus of development planning for primary education.
- The age specific population in 11-13 age group would have shown a rapid increase during the nineties. A small decline in this age group is possible during 2006-2016. The demand for upper primary would therefore be governed by the cascading effect due to increased coverage at primary stage, improved efficiency in the primary and upper primary levels, and increasing base of eligible age group population. The task at the upper primary level will be to increase the intake capacity, and improve quality. The success of improvements at the upper primary stage would

considerably influence the size and structure of secondary education.

- The population in the 14-17 age group would witness the largest ever increase in the coming decades from 64 million in 1991 to 92 million in 2001 and about 98 million by 2006. It is expected to stabilise in the range of 85-90 million between 2006-2016 and show marginal decline thereafter and touch a figure of about 80 million by 2021.

Tamil Nadu Projections

Analysis of population of the school going age groups for future projection, similar to the national level, is not available for Tamil Nadu. The data regarding the distribution of different age groups from the 2001 Census are not yet available. It would be helpful to make a detailed projection at the state and district levels at a later stage when the Census Data becomes available. For the purpose of this paper an indicative projection is made for school age population (Table 10.9) in the State adopting the following assumptions:

- The decadal growth in Tamil Nadu for the next two decades will remain around 10 per cent.
- The increase in enrolment at elementary stage will occur due to the reduction of the drop-out rate to negligible level and also due to a more conducive school environment.
- The increase in enrolment at the secondary stage will occur due to the cascading effect of enrolment at the elementary stage and also due to better motivation.

TABLE 10.9

School Age Projections in Tamil Nadu, 2001-2020 (Lakh)

Age Group	2001		2007		2010		2020	
	Population	Enrolment	Population	Enrolment	Population	Enrolment	Population	Enrolment
6-11	57.5	56.74	60.98	60.98	63.25	63.25	69.00	69.00
11-14	37.6	35.24	39.86	39.86	41.36	41.36	45.12	45.12
14-16	23.3	15.86	24.70	18.52	25.63	20.50	27.93	27.93
16-18	25.8	8.98	27.35	13.68	28.38	21.28	30.96	30.96
6-18	144.3	116.82	152.29	133.04	158.62	146.39	173.0	173.0

Source: State Policy Notes and estimations.

Implications and Options

The available facilities in Tamil Nadu in terms of number of schools and teachers in relation to the current level of enrolment at various school levels is by and large satisfactory (Table 10.10). The institutions shown in this Table conduct classes at multiple levels. Many secondary and higher secondary schools and middle schools, run classes all the way from pre-primary levels. In order to meet the future demands steps should be taken to increase their number, size and quality.

TABLE 10.10

Overall Enrolment and Teachers in Tamil Nadu Schools (2001-02)

Level	No. of Institutions	Enrolment (Lakh)	Students /Instn.	Teachers	Teachers /Instn.	Students /Teacher
Primary	31488	44.08	140	121483	3.86	35.3
Middle	5809	22.38	385	59922	10.3	37.3
High School	4836	15.87	328	49962	10.3	31.76
Hr. Sec	3473	34.49	993	102368	29.4	33.69

Source: State Policy Note on Education for 2002-2003.

Elementary Stage

The Government of Tamil Nadu has taken a policy decision to implement the UPE by 2007 and UEE by 2010. By the above estimates the additional number of children in the primary level by 2007 will be about 3 lakh and in the middle level by 2010 will be about 6 lakh.

Considering the fact that there are already 31488 primary schools in the State (2001) with an average enrolment of 140 per school (Table 10.10), it is simply a matter of absorbing the increase of about 3 lakh students at the primary level in the existing schools on the average of about 10 more per school. At the middle school level there are about 5800 schools with an average enrolment of 385. It should be possible to increase the intake in the existing middle schools and upgrade some of the primary schools into middle schools.

Accommodating the anticipated increase at the elementary stage in Tamil Nadu to meet the goals of UEE will not be a problem. What is more important is to reduce the drop-out rate by providing attractive environment. Besides the existing schemes such as noon-meal, free uniform etc. the State may consider improving the student teacher ratio from the present level of about 40:1 to 30:1. This will considerably improve the learning opportunities. It would also be necessary to provide minimum amenities such as toilets, play grounds and libraries. A minimum level of health check up and documentation facility would be an added incentive to retain students.

The State should also endeavour to decentralise the operation of the primary and middle schools by transferring responsibilities to the local bodies and communities. At this level there should be no transfer of teachers from schools so that the community loyalty and accountability of the teachers could be strengthened.

Secondary Stage

The State should declare a policy of achieving by 2020 Universal Secondary Education (USE) (class IX and X) and Universal Senior Secondary Education (USSE) (class XI and XII). In such a case the increase in the number of students from the present level will be about 12 lakh at the high school stage and about 22 lakh at the higher secondary stage. This would call for opening of new secondary/higher secondary schools, increasing the intake in existing schools and upgrading a few middle schools.

There are 4836 high schools in the State with an average intake of about 328 per school. The anticipated increase of about 12 lakh can be accommodated, by doubling the intake in the existing schools.

There are 3473 Higher Secondary schools with an average intake of about 993 students. The large increase of about 22 lakh cannot be accommodated in the existing schools without over crowding them. This would call for opening of new schools, flexible opportunities by lateral entry from open schools, vocational schools and part-time schools would help to achieve the goal of USSE. The number involved is not formidable. If a firm policy is enunciated there is sufficient lead time of two decades to attain the objective.

From the estimated projections it appears that the State does not have to spend its resources in opening new schools except at the higher secondary level to meet the increase. Deliberate efforts will be needed to upgrade the existing facilities and improve the teacher strength and quality.

Financing School Education

Current Pattern of Expenditure

Historically Tamil Nadu Government has attached considerable importance to education particularly at the school stage. The distribution of funds for the school education is shown in Table 10.11 and Figure 10.5. It is seen that the rate of growth of allocation has been declining in recent years.

TABLE 10.11

Expenditure on School Education in Tamil Nadu

(Rs. Crore)

Year	*Elementary Education*	*Secondary Education*	*Total*
1984-85	214.04	119.93	333.97
1986-87	295.98	161.72	457.70
1988-89	373.71	277.04	650.75
1990-91	515.41	357.14	872.55
1992-93	731.98	555.97	1287.95
1993-94	808.79	617.53	1426.32
1994-95	887.30	685.39	1572.69
1995-96	997.30	786.58	1783.88
1996-97	1158.95	621.32	1780.27
1997-98	1351.22	1056.15	2407.37
1998-99	1831.52	1462.2	3293.72
1999-00	1967.89	1624.86	3592.75
2000-01	1997.13	1631.98	3629.11
2002-03	2205.50	1848.75	4054.25

Source: Various Budget Documents of Govt. of Tamil Nadu Policy Notes on Education for different years.

FIGURE 10.5

School Enrolment

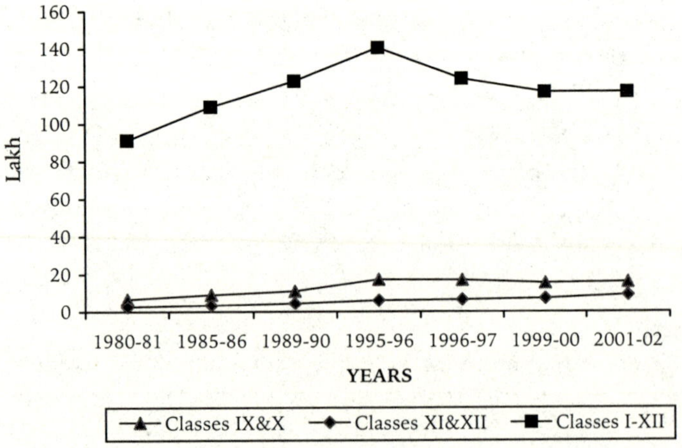

The share of the school education expenditure within the total allocation for education sector in Tamil Nadu is shown in Table 10.12 and Figure 10.6. The share of school education as a proportion of the Net State Domestic Product (NSDP) at current prices is also shown in the same Table and Figure. The allocation for elementary and secondary stages has been at around 46 and 37 per cent respectively of total education expenditure. The share of the school education as a whole has been around 83 per cent of total education expenditure slightly declining in recent years.

TABLE 10.12

Share of School Education in Total Education

Year	Total Education (Rs. Crore)	Elementary Education		Secondary Education		School Education	
		Rs. Crore	Per cent	Rs. Crore	Per cent	Rs. Crore	Per cent
1984-85	439.90	214.04	48.66	119.93	27.26	333.97	75.92
1988-89	1051.60	373.71	35.53	277.04	26.34	650.75	61.87
1990-91	1322.24	515.41	38.98	357.14	27.01	872.55	65.99
1992-93	1569.96	731.98	46.62	555.97	35.41	1287.95	82.03
1993-94	1749.67	808.79	46.26	617.53	35.29	1426.32	81.55
1994-95	1934.92	887.30	45.86	685.39	35.42	1572.69	81.28
1995-96	2235.80	997.30	44.61	786.58	35.18	1783.88	79.79
1996-97	2536.18	1158.95	45.70	621.32	24.50	1780.27	70.20
1997-98	2924.62	1351.22	46.20	1056.15	36.11	2407.37	82.31
1998-99	3925.46	1831.52	46.66	1462.2	37.25	3293.72	83.91
1999-00	4257.92	1967.89	46.22	1624.86	38.16	3592.75	84.38
2000-01	4627.79	1997.13	43.16	1631.98	35.26	3629.11	78.42
2002-03	5859.28	2205.50	37.64	1848.76	31.55	4054.25	69.20

Source: Various Budget Documents of Govt. of Tamil Nadu Policy Notes on Education for different years.

The expenditure of education as a proportion of the Net State Domestic Product (NSDP) is an important indication of the commitment of the State and predictability.

FIGURE 10.6

Share of School Education in Total Education

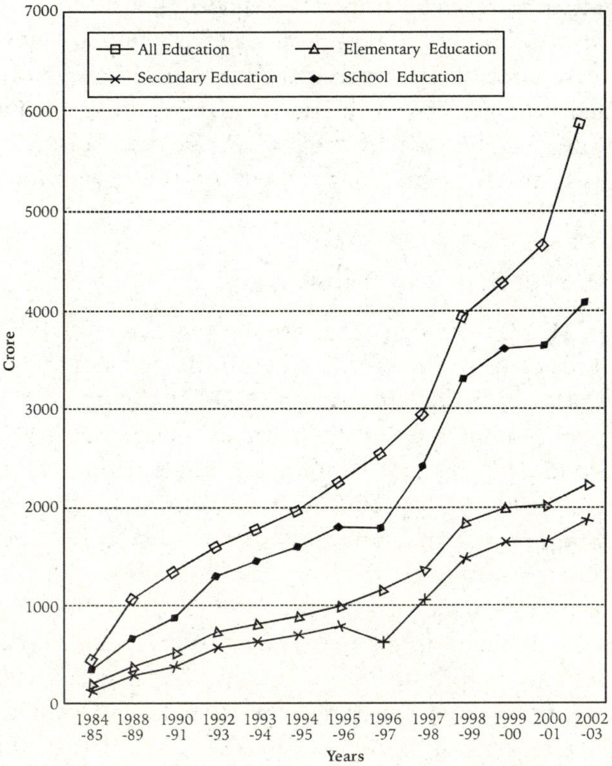

The Expenditure on education has remained around 3.5 per cent of NSDP over two decades (see Table 10.36 in the Section on Higher Education). The share of elementary and secondary education as per cent of NSDP shown in Table 10.13 have been 1.7 per cent and 1.3 per cent of NSDP respectively while the share of school education has been around 3 per cent of NSDP.

TABLE 10.13

Share of School Education in NSDP at Current Prices

Year	NSDP (Rs. Crore)	Elementary Education		Secondary Education		School Education	
		Rs. Crore	%	Rs. Crore	%	Rs. Crore	%
1984-85	12027.75	214.04	1.78	119.93	0.997	333.97	2.78
1988-89	19631.55	373.71	1.90	277.04	1.41	650.75	3.31
1990-91	25915.65	515.41	1.99	357.14	1.38	872.55	3.37
1992-93	37822.32	731.98	1.94	555.97	1.50	1287.95	3.44
1993-94	51641.69	808.79	1.57	617.53	1.19	1426.32	2.76
1994-95	61450.53	887.30	1.44	685.39	1.11	1572.69	2.55
1995-96	70329.48	997.30	1.41	786.58	1.12	1783.88	2.53
1996-97	80062.03	1158.95	1.45	621.32	0.78	1780.27	2.23
1997-98	92850.38	1351.22	1.46	1056.15	1.14	2407.37	2.60
1998-99	106955.69	1831.52	1.71	1462.2	1.37	3293.72	3.08
1999-00	117825.43	1967.89	1.67	1624.86	1.38	3592.75	3.05
2000-01	131730.56	1997.13	1.52	1631.98	1.24	3629.11	2.76

Source: Manivannan, I.V. Table 5.15 and Table 5.9.

The share of expenditure as a proportion of the revenue expenditure is another useful indicator of the State's commitment. The expenditure on all education as a proportion of revenue expenditure is shown in Table 10.14.

TABLE 10.14

Share of All Education in Revenue Account of Tamil Nadu

Year	Revenue Account (Rs. Crore)	All Education	
		Rs. Crore	%
1990-91	7255.27	1322.24	18.22
1992-93	8679.52	1569.96	18.09
1993-94	8407.41	1749.66	20.81
1994-95	9634.95	1934.91	20.08
1995-96	10910.57	2235.80	20.49
1996-97	13064.88	2536.19	19.41
1997-98	14950.84	2924.62	19.56
1998-99	17697.40	3925.46	22.18
1999-00	20727.83	4257.93	20.54
2000-01	21952.45	4627.79	21.08
2002-03	26861.54	5859.29	21.81

Source: Govt. of Tamil Nadu, Tamil Nadu: An Economic Appraisal
Manivannan, I.V. Table 5.15
Policy Notes on Education for various years.

The share of school education in the revenue account is shown in Table 10.15. The share of elementary education and secondary education is about 9 per cent and 7.5 per cent respectively of the revenue expenditure. The school education as a whole is about 16.5 per cent.

TABLE 10.15

Share of School Education in Revenue Account of Tamil Nadu

Year	*Revenue Account*	*Elementary Education*		*Secondary Education*		*School Education*	
	(Rs. Crore)	*Rs. Crore*	*%*	*Rs. Crore*	*%*	*Rs. Crore*	*%*
1990-91	7255.27	515.41	7.11	357.14	4.92	872.55	12.03
1992-93	8679.52	731.98	8.43	555.97	6.41	1287.95	14.84
1993-94	8407.41	808.79	9.62	617.53	7.35	1426.32	16.97
1994-95	9634.95	887.30	9.21	685.39	7.11	1572.69	16.32
1995-96	10910.57	997.30	9.14	786.58	7.21	1783.88	16.35
1996-97	13064.88	1158.95	8.87	621.32	4.76	1780.27	13.63
1997-98	14950.84	1351.22	9.04	1056.15	7.06	2407.37	16.10
1998-99	17697.40	1831.52	10.35	1462.2	8.26	3293.72	18.61
1999-00	20727.83	1967.89	9.49	1624.86	7.84	3592.75	17.33
2000-01	21952.45	1997.13	9.10	1631.98	7.43	3629.11	16.53
2002-03	26861.54	2205.50	8.21	1848.76	6.88	4054.25	15.09

Source: Govt. of Tamil Nadu, Tamil Nadu: An Economic Appraisal
Manivannan, I.V. Table 5.15
Policy Notes on Education for various years.

TABLE 10.16

The Share of School Education as Proportion of Various Quantities

Stage of Education	*As % of Total Education*	*As % of Rev. Education*	*As % of NSDP*
All Education	100	21	3.5
Elementary Education	46	9	1.7
Secondary Education	37	7.5	1.3
School Education	83	16.5	3.0

Prognosis

In the light of the projections indicated earlier for UPE by 2007, UEE by 2010 and USE and USSE by 2010 it will be necessary for the Tamil Nadu Government to examine in detail the current pattern of investment in school education and make appropriate provisions. The requirements will be in the following categories of expenditure:

- Capital expenditure for upgrading existing facilities and establishment of new physical facilities.
- Increased outlay on account of employment of training of additional teachers.
- Investment in technologies for improved learning and for reducing some of the salary and operating expenditures.

Whatever strategy and priority is adopted by the government for allocation of public funds to school education, it will be essential that it is on a predictable and transparent basis. This will help to seek partnership with local organisation, communities and financial institutions in raising additional resources on a sustainable basis. Though the magnitude of the task is not formidable, it would still require long term funding from outside of traditional governmental funding. Some level of affordable fee structure at the school level will be necessary and may be acceptable to the society if there is a distinct improvement in the quality of school environment.

While it is necessary to provide incentives such as noon-meal, free school supplies etc. to attract and retain students at the elementary, it will also be necessary to determine which of these are indeed helpful to achieve the educational goals and which are wasteful and mismanaged.

There is an urgent need to decentralise the governance structure of the school system and drastic reallocation of resources and responsibilities. The role envisaged for the local bodies and communities should be implemented. The experience of the DPEP programme should provide a valuable guide.

It is high time to think of a policy where the dislocation of teachers from the schools is avoided. The service conditions of teachers, at least for the new entrants should indicate non-transferability from assigned schools. This will greatly reduce the poignant situation of nearly 25 per cent of primary schools with only two teachers and 5 per cent of them with one teacher.

DPEP Experience in Tamil Nadu

The District Primary Education Programme (DPEP) initiated by the Government of India for achieving Universal Primary Education (UPE) includes the objective of imparting quality primary education. Tamil Nadu adopted this programme for implementation in Phase I (1994-95 to 2000-01) in four districts *viz.* Dharmapuri, Thiruvannamalai, Cuddalore, and Villupuram chosen on the basis of low female literacy rate below the national average. In Phase II (1997-98 to 2002-03) three more districts, Perambalur, Pudukkottai, and Ramanathapuram, were added. The experiences gained in the implementation of DPEP could provide valuable lessons in future attempts in improving the access and quality of not only the primary education but also the school education in general.

The analysis of DPEP programme in Phase I districts at the All-India level as well as in Tamil Nadu has shown considerable gain in enrolment as well as retention. The increase in enrolment in these districts is about 5.5 per cent per year. In the context of the objectives of UEE mandated by the 93rd Amendment to our Constitution and the formulation of the Sarva Shiksha Abhiyan Programme (SSAP), the lessons from DPEP will be valuable.

The objectives of the DPEP were: (1) enhancement of infrastructure to facilitate conducive environment for teaching and learning purposes; (2) enrolment of all school age children including girls, scheduled caste, scheduled tribe and other socially disadvantaged and retention of all children upto standard V; (3) qualitative improvement in the attainments of all children with special stress on attainments of minimum levels of learning at every stage; and (4) involvement of community to the fullest extent in school improvement.

The management structure consisted of high-powered bodies called Governing Council and Executive Committee with representation from officials and non-officials. Deliberate efforts were undertaken to provide in-service training to the teachers by establishing 106 Block Resource Centres (BRC) with adequate buildings and training infrastructure and 1023 Cluster Resource Centres (CRC) in one of the schools of the cluster in the seven DPEP districts of Tamil Nadu. The administration of the programme is largely decentralised providing scope for local initiatives.

The in-service training programme includes Distance Education Programme (DEP), Teleconferencing for special subjects like mathematics, training for improvement of class room interaction, activity based, child-centred and joyful teaching and learning process with involvement of District Institutes of Education and Training (DIET), BRCs and CRCs. The programme also covers special focus groups such as the disabled children.

The DPEP helped to augment the school infrastructure and facilities which included construction of new buildings, addition of new class rooms, repairs to old rooms, providing drinking water and toilet facilities. Improved access to schooling was made possible by opening a new school in every habitation with a population of 300 and having no school within a radius of one kilometer. In about 18 blocks "Alternate Schools" were made available to child labourers, tribal children and those who dropped out of schools for various inevitable conditions. At some stage the children from the alternate schools can join regular schools.

The cost of the project in seven DPEP districts is Rs. 241.41 crore for the two phases of which 85 per cent is the contribution from Government of India and 15 per cent from the State. The programme covered 10727 schools, 38271 teachers and 14,888,34 children. The average cost per school per year is Rs. 32000. This provides a basis for estimating the financial requirement for undertaking a major quality improvement initiative in school education. The management cost of the programme is about 6 per cent, civil works 24 per cent and quality improvement 70 per cent of the total cost.

The difficulty of achieving desired goals, in spite of commitment, dedication and resources, under Indian conditions is evident from the fact that the dropout rate in the seven districts persists at around 18 per cent and the repeaters are about 30 per cent of the enrolment. This is comparable to the average primary school dropout rate about 14 per cent in Tamil Nadu.

Quality of School Education

The overriding pre-occupation in the school system has been to prepare for one kind of examination or the other. The energy and resources of the schools, teachers and the parents are largely consumed by this single track mission of school education. There are some schools which are recognising the inherent deterioration of quality of education by this approach and take supplemental efforts to provide additional learning and skills to their children. These are, however, schools which are not rigidly controlled by outside agencies and have sufficient autonomy to experiment with innovative ideas on education. The parents of the children from such schools are also from socially and economically better off sections of the society and are willing to support such initiatives from the school. These are generally schools which are located in urban areas or hill stations with sufficient financial support and not affordable to the majority of the population. Their number may be around 10 per cent of the elementary school system and 20 per cent of the secondary school system. The improvement to the rest of schools needs particular attention in respect of the following aspects: (1) curriculum (2) infrastructure (3) educational processes (4) degree of control and (5) financial resources.

Without having to emulate the elite schools, it is still possible to make substantial improvement of these five aspects of school education. The experiences of the DPEP can be useful not necessarily at the same cost.

School Curriculum

The contents of the existing school curriculum are generally satisfactory. What is missing is the local knowledge content relevant to the different living environment of the students in different parts of the state. The common content evolved at the state level is meant for uniformity required for purposes of examination. The "joyful" educational experience will be possible only through incorporation of local specific knowledge. The participation of local teaching community and reform to the conventional examination system will be essential for this purpose.

Emphasis on communication capabilities, computational abilities, analytical temperament and manual skills, at appropriate levels should be part of the curriculum from early years of schooling.

The vocational education programme in the present secondary school curriculum is a failure and needs to be recognised as such. The secondary schools should be devoted to conventional arts, humanities and sciences besides commerce and management subjects. The vocational skills should be taught in a separate system of secondary schools located within the polytechnics. Since most of the polytechnics in the State have become unviable, it will help them and the school system to organise a parallel Technical High Schools and Technical Higher Secondary Schools with curricular content superior to the conventional secondary schools with knowledge of arts and sciences equivalent to them but with added technical skills in applying them.

Infrastructure

Provision of school infrastructure involves cost. But running a school in dilapidated buildings not having even a minimum of teaching devices, with insufficient number of teachers and lack of drinking water and toilets, absence of health and safety concerns will not enthuse children to attend schools even with many free supplies.

The efficiency and effectiveness of the existing populist schemes should be reviewed for substantial cost reduction in the school budgets which could be redirected towards more sustainable infrastructure development.

Educational Processes

High quality educational processes involve interactivity between teacher and students, frequent updating of the knowledge and skills of teachers, participation of parents and local community in the school activities and exposure of students to local heritage, economy and society. All these require extended service of the teacher in the school. Transferability of teachers does not motivate them to devote attention towards these activities.

Degree of Control

Most schools especially those run by government are micro-controlled to the point of depriving all motivation for initiatives from the teachers and headmasters either in innovating teaching processes or involving the community in the school development programmes. The success of the DPEP programme is largely due to the decentralised management.

Financial Resources

Dependence on government funding alone will not be enough to meet the rising demands of the school development. Abandoning wholesale to private enterprises will make school education unaffordable to majority of population and will defeat the goals of UEE and USSE. Alternative and non-traditional means to mobilise funds for school development will be possible with the support of industries and financial institutions. It will be necessary to consider prescription of fee structure for school education from those sections who can afford it. The amenities and additional learning should be met by such a fee structure. This will introduce a sense of accountability of the school system on the one hand and the involvement of the community on the other.

Conclusion

The school education system has drifted along for too long without aim or strategy. The multiplicity of school programmes and managements will continue in the State and perhaps more will be added. The State has the responsibility to evolve a framework for school education with specific goals and implement it vigorously. One of the key objectives of such a framework is to ensure that all school age children attend school at least till the age of 14, as mandated by the constitution and preferably upto the age of 18. The school environment should be conducive to achieve this goal.

Lakhs of children below the age of 18 dropping out of the schools every year will lead to increase in the unsocial activities such as drug peddling, illicit liquor trade, stealing, prostitution and so on for which the social cost in terms of law enforcement and jails and self-security devices will soon become unaffordable. The cost of education should be viewed not only in terms of providing knowledge and skills but also the elimination of the long term social cost.

Tamil Nadu is fortunately in a position that the added burden due to the increasing school going population is manageable. The State education policies and strategies should go beyond peripheral concern of immediate populist nature and address long term issues of curriculum, infrastructure, governance and quality of teaching and learning processes and initiate reform measures. There is substantial accumulated evidence and experience in the State to make such reforms successful.

HIGHER EDUCATION

Basic Considerations

Development Dimensions

Over the last twenty years development experts have come to believe that a key determinant of a nation's economic growth is the human capital with knowledge, skill and entrepreneurial qualities. India, despite her serious handicaps and resource crunch, has built up during the last five decades one of the largest higher education systems in the world. The development of the higher education was intended not only to provide knowledge and professional expertise in diverse fields of human endeavour but also to promote equality and social justice in the society. Large sections of population, which could not enjoy the benefits of higher education, were given increased opportunities through the rapid expansion of institutions in many different disciplines and in all parts of the country.

The objectives, structures and processes for the development of higher educations were defined and periodically reviewed during the last fifty years through a number of distinguished commissions and committees leading to progressive evolution of the norms, standards, procedures and responsibilities. Currently the role of the Central Government, States, private non-profit organisations, commercial entities and international institutions in the higher education sector is under intensive discussion in response to the change in the demand structure and supply potentials. The deliberations on the contemporary policies and programmes in higher education and their future direction should include the larger development goals and purposes spelled out by eminent commissions during the last fifty years and accepted by the Government. With this in view some of the salient features of earlier thinking are highlighted in this section.

Radhakrishnan Commission

The first Commission on University Education (1948-49) appointed after independence in 1947 under the Chairmanship of Dr.S.Radhakrishnan set out the basic aims of university education. It emphasised that the policies and the programmes of universities should ensure the reorientation of higher education to meet the national demand in the changed context. It outlined the goals of universities as follows:

- to foster the kind of leadership in all walks of life by helping the individuals develop their potentials;
- to provide society with competent men and women trained in all professions who as cultivated individuals, are endowed with a sense of social purpose;
- to strive to promote equality and social justice and to reduce social and cultural differences through diffusion of education;
- to foster in the teachers and students, and through them in the society generally, the attitudes and values needed for developing the 'good life' in individuals and society;
- to bring the universities closer to the community through extension of knowledge and its application to problem-solving.

Based on its recommendations the University Grants Commission (UGC) was constituted as the apex body on higher education in 1953 by an Act of the Parliament to provide the direction and support for the development of university education.

Kothari Commission

Fifteen years later the National Education Commission (1964-66) headed by Dr. D.S. Kothari produced a valuable Report in 1966 dealing with general principles and policies for the development of education in all stages and in all aspects. It defined the aims of higher education as follows:

- be in consonance with professed social purpose;
- have unity of purpose in diversity to produce community of values and ideas among educated men and women;
- promote human well-being, faith in reason and humanity;
- avoid production of scientists without conscience and technicians without taste;

- preserve values of democracy, justice and liberty, equality and fraternity;
- educate people to understand the vision of the framers of the Constitution of India.

National Policy on Education

Two decades later the Government of India produced the National Policy on Education (NPE) in 1986, (with modifications undertaken in 1992) reaffirming that "Education is a unique investment in the present and the future". It emphasised that higher education system should:

- contribute to national development through dissemination of specialised knowledge and skills;
- play a key role in producing teachers for the education system;
- become dynamic as never before in the context of unprecedented explosion of knowledge;
- be consolidated and expanded to meet the need for large number of universities and colleges;
- launch the open university system as an instrument of democratising education;
- develop a new pattern of Rural Universities to transform rural areas.

In addition to the recommendations contained in these three major reports, there have been several other national and state level high-powered committees and commissions dealing with specific aspects of higher education to address issues arising from time to time. The Economic Reforms initiated in 1991-92 and further worldwide developments in liberalisation and privatisation are influencing the current directions for higher education some of which are not in agreement with the earlier national perceptions on higher education. Planning for development of higher education would have to necessarily take into account these realities.

Historical Context

Past Efforts

The origin of the higher education system existing today dates back to the year 1857 when three universities were established under the British rule in Bombay, Calcutta and Madras based on the policy guidelines given by Macaulay and Woods Despatch (1854). The objective was to serve largely the colonial purpose. The Wood's Despatch assigned highest priority for Indian education over all other responsibilities of the East India Company in order to spread the European knowledge. The Indian Education Commission (1882-83) made several recommendations for further development education in India. The Indian Universities Commission (1902), after detailed examination of the prospects of Universities in India, suggested an Indian Universities Act, which was enacted in 1904.

Till then colleges set up in India were affiliated to British universities. After the establishment of the three Indian universities, the existing colleges were affiliated to them. For instance, The Church Missionary Society's College (1878), the Hindu College (1878), the Sarah Tucker College (1896) in Tirunelveli District and colleges in other districts of the Madras Presidency were affiliated to the Madras University as second grade colleges. Between 1857 and 1947 the growth of higher education was slow. Prior to independence there were only a small number of institutions of higher learning catering to a limited range of areas of studies. They were established mostly in administrative headquarters and port towns. They provided education mostly in liberal arts such as literature, history, philosophy, political science, social science and natural sciences. Science education constituted a small proportion. During a period of 90 years before freedom, only 18 universities were set up in India modeled after the universities in Bombay, Calcutta and Madras. Along with liberal arts colleges, some engineering and medical colleges were also set up.

The Hartog Committee dealt with mass education in India. The National Planning Committee (1937) was the first ever step to think in terms of an educational development plan for India. This was followed by the Sargent Plan (1944) suggesting specific targets for development of education, which was approved by the Central Advisory Board on Education (CABE) of Government of India. This plan suggested free and compulsory basic education for all children in age group of 6-14; secondary education for selected and gifted children; university education for one out of fifteen students who successfully completed secondary schools; technical education, teacher training; and liquidation of adult literacy.

Present Status

India's global prestige until now has been upheld by some of the pre-eminent higher educational institutions, on account of the level of competence of their graduates, caliber of research outputs and respectable academic linkages with premier institutions in other countries. Many of the products of Indian higher education system during the past several decades have won national and international recognition. They have distinguished themselves in every field of human endeavor including arts, sciences, technology, medicine, law, commerce, administration and so on. They came from institutions, which were liberally supported from public funds and efficiently managed. Their academic reputation helped to attract private sources of additional support.

It is seen that those institutions that enjoy high-level of governmental support and recognition (like IITs) generally tend to attract private funds and alumni support. Whenever institutions appear to be loosing sources of governmental funding, unfortunately, the private support also declines, leading to downward spiral of academic standards and reputation.

The higher education system in Tamil Nadu, for over a century, enjoyed a pre-eminent reputation among the colleges and universities in India. The Madras University established in 1857 and most of the colleges affiliated to it earned high reputation because of the stature of its teachers as well as for the distinguished scholars, statesmen, scientists and other professionals they produced. Since the number of colleges affiliated to the Madras University was small, the interaction between the colleges and the University was very close and constructive, resulting in a high degree of flexibility in the development of programmes and curriculum. Tamil Nadu also has the unique distinction of having started in 1929 the first privately funded Annamalai University through philanthropic contributions. Recently Madras University was recognised as a University of Excellence (one among the five in India).

The largest number of autonomous colleges (52 out of 128 in India) and the highest number of NAAC-Accredited institutions (54 out of 140 accredited colleges and 4 out of 33 accredited universities in India) exist in Tamil Nadu. Despite such distinctions of autonomous institutions, a large number of colleges continue to remain affiliated to the Universities. Since the affiliated colleges imparted education exactly as formulated by the universities which also acted as examining and degree granting bodies, the initiatives in the hands of teachers in terms of curriculum development was very much limited. This situation persists even today with a vast majority of colleges under the affiliation system, which is the bane of the present day higher education system in India.

Nature of Demand

Emerging Issues

Higher education is increasingly viewed as an instrument of upward social mobility and economic security. Larger number of young population, including first generation learners are seeking opportunities in higher education. Concomitant with the growth in numbers, there are also major changes in the disciplinary knowledge base and newer combinations of disciplines. The physical migration of knowledge seekers across the country and abroad is steadily increasing. The presence of foreign higher educational institutions in India is rapidly growing. The scope for open and distance learning through conventional modes is considerably enhanced by the new technologies for e-learning and virtual classes. The flexibility in the configuration of courses and institutions is seamlessly available to the learners.

Added to these changes in the academic domain, there are several major socio-economic changes affecting the higher education sector. These include global economic integration, national economic reforms, changing demographic pattern, increased school enrolment and reducing drop-out rates, social norms favouring women and weaker sections, increasing environmental consciousness, changing family finances, new demands of labour market and so on.

Key Determinants

The directions for development of Higher Education would have to take into account the emerging trends in determining the future initiatives. There are several aspects to be considered in determining the future directions for higher education in India such as:

- provisions for anticipated growth in enrolment in schools;
- preference for professional and vocational education;
- reconfiguration of disciplinary intake capacities
  - : in liberal arts and sciences
  - : in technical and professional disciplines
  - : in post-graduate studies;
- satisfying the demand for access, affordability, and social equity;
- ensuring academic standards and functional quality;
- making higher education endeavours financially viable and administratively efficient;

- developing a transparent and predictable policy framework for financing higher education.

The demand for higher education is expected to rise significantly at least for the coming two decades. The increased high school enrolment and the reduction in the school dropout rate, combined with special population groups such as first generation learners, women, minorities, rural population, and weaker sections opting for higher education will create additional demands for higher education. At the same time the current trends in enrolment at various levels of school education in Tamil Nadu should also be considered in planning for the growth of higher education in the State. It would also be necessary to estimate the output from the higher secondary schools in assessing the likely demand for higher education.

Features of Higher Education in Tamil Nadu

The Universities

The Universities are meant to offer unlimited opportunities for developing advanced levels of knowledge and skill in arts, sciences, humanities and technologies. With this in view a substantial increase in the number of university level institutions has been permitted in the State. In reality, the increase has occurred by splitting the jurisdiction of existing universities or converting an existing college into a deemed university. Under present laws no private university is possible. However, it is known that a few deemed universities do behave as private universities with traits somewhat akin to those of commercial educational institutions.

The university structure is expected to provide the autonomy and flexibility in development of curriculum, pursuing research and development, raising resources and creating a conducive environment for achieving academic excellence. In effect, however, most of them are saddled with archaic governing systems. They have very little scope to provide academic leadership to the institutions affiliated to them. Their role is limited to that of prescribing syllabus, conducting examinations and awarding degrees. Government officials control the finances of State funded universities to a micro level. Hence these universities are vulnerable to undue political and administrative interference in matters of admissions, recruitment, and development. Some of the heads of universities possess the integrity, stature and courage to resist such intrusions and protect the interests of the university.

The exceptions to the above characterisation are several institutions, which have established long traditions of academic excellence, administrative transparency and credibility such as the Indian Institutes of Technology, Indian Institute of Science and Indian Institutes of Management mainly due to their governance structures. It is not beyond the competence of the State universities and the deemed universities to adopt similar structure and operations.

The higher education system in Tamil Nadu consists of several types of universities - affiliating, unitary and deemed universities in professional and general areas of studies. There is no central university in Tamil Nadu. Under the universities there are colleges with constituent or affiliated or autonomous status offering undergraduate and/or post-graduate programmes in arts, sciences and humanities as well as professional disciplines. Many of the universities offer a large number of correspondence courses within and outside the country at under-graduate and post-graduate levels. There are also colleges for specialised studies and training in music, physical education, teacher education etc. The Tamil Nadu State Council for Higher Education (TANSCHE) is a statutory policy making and advisory body, concerned with the development of higher education in Tamil Nadu.

Tamil Nadu has 22 university level institutions and 893 colleges (arts, science, engineering, medical agriculture, veterinary, paramedical, teachers training etc.). The enrolment in colleges is about 5.5 lakh (4.9 lakh in UG and 0.6 lakh in PG) in all disciplines while the university enrolment is 1.1 lakh mostly in PG courses. The intake capacity at the first-degree level is 1.2 lakh and PG level 0.93 lakh in all disciplines.

The Madras University, Chennai; the Madurai Kamaraj University, Madurai; the Bharathiar University, Coimbatore; the Bharathidasan University, Tiruchirappalli; the Periar University, Salem; and the Manonmaniam Sundaranar University, Tirunelveli have a large number of affiliated colleges (Government, aided and self-financing) some of which have autonomous status. Until recently, when Anna University, Chennai was converted into an Affiliating University from its earlier unitary status, several engineering colleges were also affiliated to them.

Affiliating Universities (State/Professional) - 3

There are three affiliating professional universities in the State. Anna University is the largest with nearly 230 engineering colleges (most of them are self financing) affiliated to it besides its own constituent colleges. The Tamil Nadu Dr. Ambedkar Law University affiliates six law colleges one of which is under private management. The MGR Medical University affiliates nine medical colleges in the State one of which is under private management.

Unitary Universities (State/General) - 2

There are two unitary universities, Alagappa University and Mother Theresa University, which offer degrees in arts, humanities, social and natural sciences at under-graduate and post-graduate levels including M.Phil and Ph.D programmes.

Unitary University (Aided/General and Professional) - 1

The Annamalai University was established in 1929 as the first ever private university in India by a philanthropic society. It offers not only degrees in arts, humanities, social and natural sciences at under-graduate and post-graduate levels including M.Phil and Ph.D programmes but also the professional degrees in engineering, agriculture, medicine and law. The correspondence education programme of the university is one of the largest and widest in India.

Unitary Universities (State/Professional) - 3

The Tamil Nadu Agricultural University and the Tamil Nadu University of Veterinary and Animal Sciences and the Tamil University, Thanjavur are the three universities in this category.

Deemed Universities (General) - 3

The Avinashilingam Institute of Home Science & Higher Education for Women, Coimabtore; (aided), the Sri Chandrasekharendra Saraswathi Viswa Maha Vidyalaya, Kancheepuram (private), and the Gandhigram Rural Institute, Gandhigram (aided) are in this category offering degrees in arts, humanities, social and natural sciences at under-graduate and post-graduate levels including M.Phil and Ph.D programmes: The former two deemed universities also offer degrees in several engineering disciplines.

Deemed Universities (Private/Professional) - 6

The following two offer degrees in medical disciplines: Sri Ramachandra Medical College and Research Institute, Chennai and the Vinayaka Mission Research Foundation, Salem.

The following three offer degrees in engineering disciplines: the Satyabhama Institute of Science and Technology, Chennai; the Shanmuga Arts, Science, Technology and Research Academy, Thanjavur and Vellore Institute of Technology, Vellore.

The *Dakshina Bharat Hindi Prachar Sabha,* Chennai (aided) offers programmes in Hindi Language.

There are several pending applications for deemed university status from private and aided institutions and from the Regional Engineering College, Tiruchirapalli. The developments relating to establishment of new universities by the State or transforming a unitary university into affiliating type or granting deemed university status by the Ministry of Human Resource Development, Delhi are *ad-hoc* in nature involving some perfunctory procedures and political considerations and are not based on sound analysis of the consequences on the quality of education or on socio-economic considerations. Continuation of such *ad-hoc* policies by the State or the Centre would have serious adverse effects on the University System in Tamil Nadu.

University Governance

Policy Organs

The university system is largely functioning under a governance structure instituted more than a century ago when the system was very small. The University governance structure essentially consists of a senate, a syndicate, an academic council and several Boards of Studies. Some universities (e.g. Anna University) do not have a Senate.

All available evidences about the role and functions of senates point towards their ineffectiveness at best and root cause of politicisation of universities at worst. Their role as representative voice of concerned public stakeholders is hardly realised. Abolition of senates will save enormous money, time and prestige. The academic councils and their boards of studies are the custodians of academic norms and standards of a university. They need further strengthening in keep up with the changing academic needs. Their composition and mandates require major overhauling to provide for greater freedom to support genuine academic innovations.

The State universities function under the statutory provisions of the state legislature and the deemed universities operate in accordance with the memorandum of association executed with the University Grants Commission. Whatever be the configuration of the governance structure, there is a general sense of dissatisfaction about their effectiveness in the growth and development of the universities. The reasons are several. Some are general to all universities and some are specific to an individual university. These bodies often assume partisan roles of the representatives of different interest groups or constituencies, neglecting the overall holistic interest of the university.

Vice-Chancellor

If the Vice-Chancellor lacks the stature and the leadership qualities and is beholden to one group or the other for his/her appointment or survival, the situation leads to further loss of prestige and deterioration of academic developments. No clearly defined norms exist for the qualifications of a prospective vice-chancellor nor is there any specified criteria for the selection process. Hence there are growing levels of political and sectarian interferences in the choice of vice-chancellors. This is one of the main causes for the erosion of the stature and dignity of the position of the vice-chancellor. The critical dependence of the State universities on the State administration for their funds further compounds the loss of freedom and the autonomy of the university. The various interest groups take advantage of the deteriorating image of the head of the university to make untenable claims and manipulate the system resulting in the credibility of the governance and quality of the academic standards. The academic community along with the public interest groups should help the State to formulate operational guidelines for the selection of Vice-chancellors and for strengthening the autonomy and public accountability of the universities.

The deemed universities do not suffer from the type of constraints suffered by the State funded universities. However, they tend to function in a much less accountable manner in terms of their treatment of the faculty, collection and utilisation of funds and selection of students. The responsibility of the UGC does not end with the declaration of the Deemed University status to an institution. The review mechanism by the UGC needs to be evolved to enforce academic and social accountability of deemed universities.

Governance Norms

Considering these aspects, the Report of the UGC committee entitled "Towards New Educational Management" in 1990 made a number of valuable recommendations on the structure and functions of various bodies associated with university governance. These were adopted with some modifications by the Central Advisory Board and Education (CABE) of the Ministry of Human Resources Development (MHRD) of Government of India consisting of education ministers and senior officials of all States and the Centre. However these have not been implemented, even partially, by most States including Tamil Nadu. In the meantime, governance issues are going from bad to worse in most universities. The governing bodies such as the board of governors, syndicates, academic councils and senate should be so designed as to forestall extraneous non-academic influences. The persons associated with such bodies should be of high reputation and eminence with a stake in maintaining the prestige of institution with which they are associated.

Administration of Universities

The reputation of the higher education system will be influenced by the nature of administration associated with it. The attention to streamlining the academic administration for efficiency and effectiveness is as important as the care towards maintaining the academic standards. In fact poor administrative practices will steadily erode the confidence in the academic quality of the institution. In general very little attention has been devoted to improving the university and college administration since their inception, when the general governmental procedures were adopted. Even as the size of the higher educational institutions grew very large, the same practices continue to be followed increasing the level of inefficiency, at a higher cost of administration with considerably greater degree of harassment and dissatisfaction to the students and the public.

From the time an announcement is made calling for application to the time when a student leaves the institutions, there is a large number of administrative requirements to be fulfilled. Each step involves uncertainty, delay, hassle, corruption and dissatisfaction. For each step, such as procuring an application form for admission, filing in the application, waiting for admission with uncertain feeling, registration, payment of various kinds of fees for tuition, residential accommodation, examination, library, sports etc. obtaining the mark sheets, and provisional certificate, until awaiting the uncertain date for convocation, the student has to go through a grueling experience, eating into the precious academic time.

The colleges and universities should be required to streamline their administration practices to serve the best academic interests of student community. Given the advances in Information Technology, these tasks could be introduced rapidly and at considerable savings in time and money to the institutions. Such simple practices as standardised dates for opening and closing of institutions, the period of examinations and vacations, the dates of convocations and the dates of other special events are not beyond realisation. The use of Internet for announcing the college catalogues with courses offered, fees prescribed, as also the standard application for admission would help the students in making the right choices. The tendency to fleece the students many times over with exorbitant application fees by several institutions is tantamount to mental cruelty. Adding to this trend is the practice of every college and university holding entrance examination for most courses straining the financial capacities of students to unbearable levels.

Evolving enforceable norms for the whole range of administrative practices of higher educational institutions will be a great humanitarian service besides setting higher standards of education. The right to information and the code of transparency should be effectively insisted upon in the higher education sector. The marking and grading systems adopted for undergraduate courses in the colleges and universities require drastic revision. The present system is known to have major deficiencies of reliability of the marks and grades obtained by students. Innumerable cases of careless marking of answer scripts are rampant. The least that could be done is to provide the student with a right to see the copy of the graded answer script as is done in some of the colleges and universities in Tamil Nadu to prevent the erosion of confidence of students in the education system as a whole.

College Education

Nearly seventy five per cent of the students in higher education in Tamil Nadu are studying in the various colleges of the universities. The colleges are affiliated to the universities. Some of the colleges have been given the autonomous status by joint evaluation by the State and the UGC so that they could adopt greater innovation in introduction of new courses, updating the curriculum, adopt better teaching and learning practices and conduct examinations and evaluations with high degree of credibility. The status of arts and science colleges in Tamil Nadu as also of the engineering colleges is discussed in this section.

Arts and Science Colleges

Presently in Tamil Nadu, there are 440 arts and science colleges, 22 colleges of education, nine oriental colleges, four colleges of physical education and two colleges of social work. The management categories of these institutions are shown in Table 10.17.

TABLE 10.17

Arts, Science and Special Colleges in Tamil Nadu (Management-wise) (2001-02)

Type of College	*Govt.*	*Aided*	*Self-Finance*	*Total*
Arts and Science	60	133	247	440
Education	7	14	1	22
Oriental	—	9	—	9
Physical Edn.	—	3	1	4
Social Work	—	2	—	2
Total	**67**	**161**	**249**	**477**

Source: Policy Note, Higher Education (2002-03). Demand No. 19, Govt. of Tamil Nadu (2002).

The number of arts, science and other colleges (shown in Table 10.17) affiliated to the various universities is given in Table 10.18.

TABLE 10.18

Number of Arts, Science and Special Colleges Affiliated to Universities in Tamil Nadu (2001-02)

S. No.	*University*	*No. of Colleges*
1	University of Madras	146
2	Madurai Kamaraj University	85
3	Bharathiar University	76
4	Bharathidasan University	75
5	Manonmaniam Sundaranar University	55
6	Periar University	40
	Total	**477**

Source: Policy Note, Higher Education (2002-03). Demand No. 19, Govt. of Tamil Nadu (2002).

Growth Pattern

The growth of the arts and science colleges in the past along with the enrolment trend and strength of teachers is shown in Table 10.19.

The growth of Indian higher education system during the last 15 years has been predominantly in the private sector. Following the pattern set by the States in Southern and South Western Region (Andhra Pradesh, Karnataka, Maharashtra, and Tamil Nadu) this trend is gaining momentum in other regions of India. For example, in Tamil Nadu, the number of arts and science colleges has increased rapidly during the last six years mostly through self-financing (Table 10.20). The number of government and aided colleges has remained stagnant. The percentage of women students

TABLE 10.19

Growth of Enrolment in Arts and Science Colleges in Tamil Nadu

Year	*No. of Colleges*	*Enrolment*				*No. of Teachers*		
		Boys	*Girls*	*Total*	*% of Girls*	*Men*	*Women*	*Total*
1978-79	188	136,229	65,331	201,560	32.4	8,501	3,795	12,296
1980-81	187	102,437	54,224	156,661	34.6	8,695	3,881	12,576
1984-85	193	119,022	73,039	192,061	38.0	9,408	4,479	13,887
1988-89	187	118,888	77,714	196,602	39.5	9,928	4,980	14,908
1992-93	223	145,778	113,758	259,536	43.8	10,758	5,872	16,630
1995-96	280	173,074	145,137	318,211	45.6	10,991	6,279	17,270
1996-97	304	159,942	157,771	317,713	49.7	11,286	6,799	18,085
1997-98	340	155,914	166,671	322,585	51.7	12,105	7,534	19,639
1998-99	365	163,479	177,193	340,672	52.0	11,915	8,264	20,179
1999-00	384	189,453	202,254	391,707	51.6	11,516	8,704	20,220
2000-01	440	201,482	209,026	410,508	50.9	12,418	9,310	21,728

Source: Tamil Nadu: An Economic Appraisal. Govt. of Tamil Nadu and Manivannan, I.V. (2002).

in the arts and science colleges has shown remarkable increase during the last two decades from 32.4 per cent in 1978-79 to nearly 51 per cent in recent years.

TABLE 10.20

Growth in Arts and Science Colleges in Tamil Nadu (Management-Wise) (1993-2001)

Year	*Government*	*Aided*	*Self-Finance*	*Total*	*Enrolment*	*% of Women*
1993-94	56	132	54	242	280658	42.89
1994-95	57	132	72	261	304201	45.50
1995-96	58	132	90	280	318211	45.60
1996-97	58	132	114	304	317713	49.70
1997-98	58	132	150	340	322585	51.70
1998-99	60	133	172	365	340672	52.00
1999-00	60	133	192	385	391707	51.60
2000-01	60	133	247	440	410508	50.90

Source: Policy Note, Education (1998-89). Demand No. 17, Govt. of Tamil Nadu (1998) and subsequent Policy Notes.

TABLE 10.21

Enrolment in Colleges Vs. Universities (1997-98)

Type of Courses	*All Colleges*	*All University Departments*
UG Courses	288446	88334
PG Courses	31106	11809
M.Phil	1430	824
Ph.D	209	1877
Diploma & Others	10809	2255
Total	332000 (76%)	105099 (24%)

Source: Policy Note, Education(1998-99). Demand No.17, Government of Tamil Nadu (1998).

The number of students studying in the university departments of all the universities in Tamil Nadu as against the number in all colleges in 1997-98 for which comparable data is available is shown in Table 10.21. It is seen that three-quarters of the student population in higher education are in the college system. The need to give greater attention to the teaching and learning processes in the colleges deserves greater attention than so far.

Technical Education

Engineering Colleges

The number of engineering colleges in Tamil Nadu has shown a phenomenal growth reaching a total of 222 institutions in 2001-02 with an intake capacity of over 55000 students, accounting for about 25 per cent of the All-India capacity. Nearly half the increase has taken place during the last three years. Most of the increase has been in the category of self-financing colleges with insignificant growth in government and aided institutions (Table 10.22).

The implications of this growth require a careful analysis and development of future strategies to maximise this advantage. The severe imbalance between government and aided institutions on the one hand and the self-financing institutions on the other, has introduced unbearable distortions in the accessibility and affordability of engineering degree to vast sections of rural and underprivileged sections of the society. The fee structure approved by the government is flouted with impunity through many unauthorised and forced levies on helpless students. The existing laws and regulations, even if implemented diligently, seem inadequate to the magnitude of the problem

TABLE 10.22

Growth of Engineering Colleges in Tamil Nadu

Year	*Government*	*Aided*	*Self-Finance*	*Total*	*Intake*
1985-86	4	3	22	29	
1987-88	4	3	26	33	
1989-90	4	3	29	36	
1991-92	5	3	30	38	
1993-94	7	3	34	44	
1995-96	7	3	62	72	
1996-97	7	3	71	81	20250
1997-98	7	3	76	86	21500
1998-99	7	3	106	116	28500
1999-00	7	3	119	129	30750
2000-01	7	3	143	153	40491
2001-02	7	3	207+5*	222	55500

* indicates Deemed Universities.

Source. Manivannan I.V. (2002) and Policy Note, Higher Education (2002-03). Demand No. 19, Govt. of Tamil Nadu (2002).

TABLE 10.23

Distribution of Engineering Branches in Tamil Nadu (2001-02)

Engineering Branches	*No. of Colleges*	*Intake Capacity*
BIOTECHNOLOGY (including Aquaculture, Pharmaceutical)	4	240
CIVIL	33	1060
CHEMICAL (including Polymer, Rubber, Leather, Textiles, Ceramics, Food Processing, and Petro-chemicals	39	2400
MECHANICAL (including Industrial, Production, Auto, Aero, Marine, and Metallurgy)	116	7840
ELECTRICAL (including Electronics, Communication, and Instrumentation)	220	21080
COMPUTER (including Information Technology)	217	23340

Source: AICTE Annual Report 2002.

There is considerable skew in the engineering disciplines available now (Table 10.23). Any dislocation of the job market, as has happened in the Information Technology industry recently, would create frustration among the graduates three or four years from now.

Most of the increase in seats has taken place in the electronics, communications and IT disciplines within a short span of three years. The colleges find it impossible to find suitable teachers in these disciplines. Because of the under-qualified and inexperienced teachers manning these courses, the competence of the students is low thereby bringing down the reputation of the engineering graduates of Tamil Nadu in India and abroad. The proliferation of same courses in a large number of colleges has led to fragmentation of the available resources, facilities and faculty thinly distributed among them leading to under performance. There is an urgent need to develop a consolidation strategy by redistributing and networking of the courses and facilities instead of permitting opening of new institutions, except in emerging specialsed areas of technology. The increase has also deprived the arts and science colleges of the relatively bright students in several important areas of natural and social sciences as well as in agricultural and veterinary sciences.

Polytechnics

The growth of polytechnics in Tamil Nadu was significant during 1995-96 to 1998-99 and thereafter has shown only a slight increase (Table 10.24). The demand for polytechnic education steeply declined after the large-scale increase in the engineering colleges. The job market for the diploma holders was also not very bright and many of them started entering engineering colleges after finishing their diploma through various means. Under normal situation the ratio between polytechnic and degree intake should have been about two. In Tamil Nadu the enrolments are nearly equal especially after the spurt in demand for candidates with IT related qualifications at degree and diploma levels. Similar to the engineering colleges, the development of polytechnics was also through self-financing and the managements found them financially unviable. There was no increase in the number of government and aided polytechnic.

In due course the value and utility of polytechnics will be questionable unless their programmes are restructured to meet the market demand for specialised skills and on the job training. They should be reorganised as skill development institutes in all trades. There should be sufficient incentives for skilled diploma holders to obtain a degree in technical skills rather than being attracted by classical engineering degrees. Unless a bold decision on revamping polytechnic education is taken soon the huge financial investments in this area will deteriorate. Since the AICTE has delegated all responsibilities in respect of polytechnic education to the State Governments, there is sufficient scope for Tamil Nadu to set a new direction for polytechnic education. The importance of skill development has long been recognised. In India, the policy framework for its promotion needs further strengthening in the present context to attract trainees in large numbers to various economically valuable trades. There is a need to reorient and restructure the present training institutions and their training schemes to make them respond to the changing requirements of skills. The schemes should devote attention not only to the tools and techniques but also to issues of quality, diversity and market assessment capabilities.

TABLE 10.24

Growth of Polytechnics in Tamil Nadu

Year	*Govern-ment*	*Aided*	*Self-Finance*	*Total*	*Intake*		
					Government	*Aided & Self-Finance*	*Total*
1985-86	23	34	69	126			
1987-88	23	35	74	132			
1989-90	23	35	75	133			
1991-92	24	35	72	131			
1993-94	21	35	75	131	9453	48157	57610
1995-96	21	35	84	130	9372	49292	58664
1996-97	21	35	98	154	9870	45787	55657
1997-98	21	35	112	168	10248	48179	58427
1998-99	21	35	143	199	10362	48429	58791
1999-00	22	35	145	202	9635	58384	68019
2000-01	22	35	148	205	11685	53574	65259
2001-02	22	35	149	206	11685	54830	66515

Source: I.V. Manivannan (2002) and Policy Note, Higher Education (2002-03). Demand No. 19, Govt. of Tamil Nadu (2002).

Management Education

During the recent decades, there has been a general trend on the part of the firms and industries to induct professionalism in their management practices. The liberalisation of economy has also changed the attitudes of governmental establishments in favour of seeking outside professional help in their undertakings. The size of management consultancies has been growing.

In response to this trend, there has been a rush to increase the number of educational institutions offering management education. Initially the management education programmes were limited to Indian Institutes of Management (IIM), some university departments and a few autonomous private institutions. During the last two decades, Master of Business Administration (MBA) and Post-Graduate Diploma in Business Management (PGDBM) are offered in a large number of technical institutions as well as in colleges of arts and sciences. The National growth trend in Management Education is shown in the following Table.

Growth of in MBA Programme in India

Year	*Number of Institutions*	*Annual Intake*
1994	259	26494
1995	411	39484
1996	508	45288
1997	584	50318
1999	647	53544
2002	872	69540

Source: AICTE Annual Reports.

The entry requirement for the two-year MBA programmes is a degree in any discipline, except in some institutions such as Anna University which admits only engineering graduates for its MBA. The desire to seek admission is next only to medicine and engineering. For graduates in arts and sciences, acquiring a management degree offer better career prospects. There are also specialsed Management Education programmes at the Master's level such as Banking Management, Financial Management, Tourism Management, and Hospital Management etc., which are not under the purview of the AICTE.

There is also a sizeable distance education programmes through correspondence courses, open universities and virtual universities, besides some offshore campuses of foreign universities. These would add approximately another 20000 to the intake capacity shown in the above Table. Some institutions also offer the Bachelor of Business Administration (BBA).

The size of the MBA programme in Tamil Nadu consists of 130 institutions with an intake capacity of 9595 in 2002. In 1999 the MBA programme was offered in 105 institutions with an intake of 7565. This does not include the distance education programmes in MBA offered by most of the universities in the State. Tamil Nadu has the distinction of having the largest number of Management Institutions followed by Maharastra and UP.

It is generally agreed that there are extreme variations in the quality of Management Education among these institutions. Even if they are not able to reach the level of quality of the IIMs and some of the better institutions such as the Bharathidasan Institute of Management in Trichirappalli, the students expect a reasonable degree of preparation to compete in the job market. While the graduates of the better institutions are sought after with high salaries by reputed firms, the students from the less endowed institutions struggle to obtain even a low salaried job in ordinary companies. The spot surveys carried out by different organisations indicate that nearly 65 per cent of these institutions are below the market expectations, even though they charge exorbitantly high fees.

The management education programme continues to expand without adequate guidelines on the size, curriculum, teaching and learning methods, evaluation of quality and scope for assimilation in the market.

The following policy initiatives will help to restore the reputation of the Management Graduates from the institutions in Tamil Nadu:

- The State establishes a projection for the size and rate of growth of Management Education in the State. It also should specify the criteria for expansion in terms of consolidation of existing programmes rather than starting of new ones. From the present level of nearly 10000 intake a growth rate of about 5 per cent per year may be desirable until the quality aspects especially the faculty shortages and programme contents are attended to.
- There should be greater level of quality checks on the existing programmes, especially those offered under the distance education mode. These checks should be devised as multilevel monitoring processes with the advice of independent professional bodies such as Madras Management Association, rather than as routine bureaucratic exercises.

Community Colleges

During the last two decades the role of private entrepreneurs in education has steeply increased. But their interest has been concentrated on the type of education which can bring to them high return on investment with low levels of input. The establishment of vocational education centres is not considered profitable. The demand for such education has been declining due to distorted perception on the value of skill development. In recent years there has been a spurt in the vocational training programme limited to a few high-volume demand areas such as Hotel Management, Travel Services, Medical Laboratory Technologies and Information Technology. There are many other skill related areas such as construction sector, appliances industry, manufacturing processes, building maintenance, food-processing, office management, advertising, communications, journalism etc., which have not witnessed sufficient development. These areas do not need a polytechnic or an engineering college.

The efforts towards vocational education at school level have not produced the expected level of skill-based output partly because of lack of facilities and partly due to low level of motivation in the school age group. At this stage, it will be of substantial social and economic benefit if the approach to skill-based education is reviewed in the context of emerging demand structure for skills and changing technology environment. The community college system offers several advantages for this purpose.

Even though there has been occasional interest in Tamil Nadu developing the community college system, the progress in establishing them has not been significant. The concept of community colleges, derived from countries such as USA and Canada, is to provide opportunities for completing part of the higher education, after higher secondary education, in and around their hometown. This helps to reduce the cost of university education since the students can transfer some or all of the credits obtained in the community college to complete the university degree.

Another important aspect of the community college is the flexibility in the choice of subjects, especially for foundation courses and in skill oriented subjects. The community colleges are well equipped with facilities and staff to offer a wide range of subjects and at varying hours of the day and evening. In our country, every major educational commission has emphasised the importance of skill-based vocational education since our independence. Yet the degree of attention to vocational training has been relatively low compared to the value attached to academic programmes. In spite of several ministries and departments of Central and State governments being mandated with vocational education, its growth has been marginal and in fact there has been a marked decline.

Since the conditions that have given rise to community colleges in the western countries are not obtainable in India, attempts have been made, mostly in Tamil Nadu, by interested groups to initiate the community college system. The primary emphasis in the development of the community college system in Tamil Nadu is to give importance to vocational education to those who have completed 12th standard education. The type of skills associated with these institutions is generally on non-technical subjects such as accountancy, tourism, computer operation etc., as distinct from those offered in the community polytechnics.

There are about 30 institutions in India offering courses in the community college mode either for those could not continue college education or those who are registered in the distance education programmes or those studying for a first degree. The universities in Tamil Nadu have not taken notice of these initiatives except Manonmaniam Sundaranar University (Tirunelveli), which gave recognition to a few community colleges in its area.

The following aspects should be resolved as early as possible to enable the community college system to play a useful role in the development of Tamil Nadu.

- The curricular framework for persons with different entry qualifications should be spelled out by the State in consultation with State Council for Higher Education.
- The credit system for courses with different durations and varying vocational content should be streamlined.
- The policy for transfer of credits for obtaining higher qualification should be evolved.
- The quality of teaching and learning should be monitored with the help of professional and industry association to ensure that the students are able to get the maximum benefit.

Distance Education

The demand for distance education though has been growing significantly from those who could not avail the opportunities of formal higher education system for reasons such as qualification norms, economic constraints and geographic and domestic limitations. It also provides opportunities to those who wish to upgrade their qualification while working. The distance education programmes are offered by all the general universities, some professional universities, and a few autonomous colleges. The programmes offered by Tamil Nadu institutions cater to candidates all over India and some even abroad. These programmes as of now are in the classical correspondence mode rather than by the Open University system. Some of them have begun to experiment offering a few of the courses through the internet. The growth in enrolment in distance education for three of the major universities in Tamil Nadu is shown in Table 10.25.

The correspondence courses are a source of substantial revenue to the universities. However in the coming years they have to compete effectively with the Indira Gandhi National Open University and various State Open Universities in India besides the Virtual Universities from abroad. This would require restructuring their courses, offering greater flexibility in the course combinations, greater managerial efficiency and adoption of modern technological tools for developing and delivering the contents and for effective interactivity between the learner and the course instructor. If not many of them will be forced to wind up sooner or later.

TABLE 10.25

Growth in Distance Education in Tamil Nadu Universities (1981-2001)

Year	*Universities*		
	Annamalai	*Madras*	*Madurai Kamaraj*
1981-82	21052	20775	68320
1985-86	37049	51081	76578
1989-90	37238	49302	43729
1995-96	103077	32778	70608
1996-97	84927	39094	68072
1997-98	90143	54741	85763
1998-99	208049	138968	107635
1999-00	238600	137276	117954
2000-01	250686	139329	114283

Source: Manivannan, I.V. (2002).

Growth Strategy for Higher Education

Planning for Growth

There are several key issues to be considered in arriving at the growth strategy for the near future and for long term. Looking at the fast changing demands for higher education in nearly all disciplines it would be prudent to design a growth scenario for the period until 2010. Letting the educational development take its own course may create a situation in which damage control at a later stage may be impossible. The following issues may be kept in view in the planning process:

- the enrolment capacity in different types of institutions;
- the number of institutions in the various categories;
- the desirable balance among the disciplines;
- mechanism to ensure efficiency and quality.

Enrolment Capacity

The basic consideration in arriving at the increase in the enrolment capacity is the extent to which the desire for higher education can be met through the various types of supply in relation to the rise in demand. It is seen that various types of competing systems of post-secondary education will come into existence other than the formal system. Perhaps some of the newer modes of educational supply may be beyond the planning process. In this section only those system where some degree of direct or indirect intervention may be desirable and possible is considered.

There are two ways of looking at the enrolment capacity. One is based on the output at the Plus Two stage and the other based on age group coverage.

School Output Basis

By the output based approach, the intake capacity at the first degree level may be determined by providing for formal higher educational opportunities to at least 90 per cent of those successfully completing their secondary school with first class (Above 60 per cent marks). The number of students who appeared, passed and with first class from 1995 to 2000 in Tamil Nadu is shown in Table 10.26. In the year 2000, about 85 per cent of 3.5 lakh of higher secondary school students passed Plus Two examination. About two lakh candidates (57 per cent) secured first class. The rate of growth of candidates appearing for Plus Two examination may be assumed as 5 per cent (similar to the recent trends) per year until 2010. The pass percentage may be assumed as 85 per cent and the percentage of first class may be taken as 60 per cent.

Accordingly the estimated school output by 2010 is as follows:

- Number estimated to appear in +2 in 2010: 5.60 lakh
- Number estimated to pass +2: 4.76 lakh
- Number estimated to secure first class: 3.36 lakh

To provide formal higher education for 90 per cent of those securing first class, the intake capacity at the first degree level in the State should be increased from 1.2 lakh to at least 3 lakh in 2010. The PG intake may be correspondingly increased from 0.93 lakh at present to 1.5 lakh in 2010. Thus the enrolment at UG level will be about 9 lakh and at PG level 3 lakh with a total enrolment in higher education at 12 lakh.

Age Group Coverage Basis

An empirical target may be set to provide opportunities for higher education to a proportion of the eligible age group likely to be benefitted. There is an emerging consensus among educationists in India that at least 15 per cent of the age group of 18 to 22 should be enrolled in the higher system as against the present level of 7.5 per cent. This target is much less than what is available in many of the more developed countries. However increasing the capacity to higher levels may add to the problem of educated unemployment.

In Tamil Nadu 10.6 per cent of this age group is presently in the higher education system. Raising the intake capacity at the first-degree level in Tamil Nadu

TABLE 10.26

Higher Secondary Output in Tamil Nadu (1995-2000)

Details	*Student Category*	*1995*	*1996*	*1997*	*1998*	*1999*	*2000*	*2001*	*2002*
No. of Regd. Students	Regular + Private	353834	372069	345546	357749	402930	414524	463955	497560
Through Schools	Regular	276960	288803	282928	301017	329127	343798	389443	429867
	Boys	145987	149394	142325	151442	163801	171055		
	Girls	130973	139409	140603	149575	165326	172743		
General Stream	Total	231953	240966	237475	251978	277605	295431		
	Boys				123589	135556	144018		
	Girls				128389	142049	151413		
Vocational Stream	Total	45007	47837	45453	49039	51522	48367		
	Boys				27853	28245	27037		
	Girls				21186	23277	21330		
Pass Per cent	Total	64.8	64.2	78.6	83.4	76.7	83.3	83.29	84.55
	Boys	59.5	58.8	74.1	79.3	74.9	78.7		
	Girls	70.8	70.1	83.2	87.6	84.4	88.7		
First Class	Number (lakh)	110067	113268	152858	176346	174453	195301	2.2	2.66
	Percent	39.7	39.2	54.1	58.6	53	56.81	57	61.9

Source: Policy Note School Education (2002-2003). Demand No. 41. Govt. of Tamil Nadu (2002) and Policy Notes of Previous Years.

from the present level of 1.2 lakh to 3 lakh and at PG level from 0.93 lakh to 1.5 lakh by 2010, will result in UG enrolment of 9 lakh and PG enrolment of 3 lakh. Thus it is estimated that 15.7 per cent of this age group will be enrolled in the formal system of higher education comparable to the national goal. This means that the average annual rate of increase in the intake capacity will be 17500 seats in UG and 16500 in PG courses. The other non-formal modes will further enhance the proportion by a significant amount.

The anticipated increase in enrolment should best be accommodated by increasing the intake in the existing institutions rather than starting of new colleges, whether by the government or in private sector. The mushrooming of new colleges is leading to rapid deterioration of educational standards mainly on account of paucity of qualified and competent teachers and poor teaching facilities. The growth in intake should be encouraged in well established and accredited colleges including organising shift system in some of them to maximise the use of the infrastructure already developed. This will facilitate better utilisation of available capacity at marginally additional investment. Flexible curriculum should be developed for cross migration among disciplines; and between regular and distance mode education availing modern information and communication technologies.

Institutional Growth

There is a great deal of reluctance on the part of governments to start new educational institutions mainly due to financial reasons whereas the private sector has shown more than ordinary enthusiasm to invest in new colleges. The government on its part may evolve a policy to upgrade the existing government colleges with sufficient addition to their infrastructure and staff strength in such a way that at least 25 per cent of enrolment capacity in the State is available in them. They may also permit them liberally to offer self-supporting courses as a means of generating revenue. This will have salient effect on the runaway levels of fee structure in the State besides giving an options to students from weaker sections to pursue higher education.

The problem of inequities is growing more acute with the lopsided growth in self-financing institutions. The strategy should identify areas for investment in higher education catering to the needs of rural population, weaker and disadvantaged sections and an affordable higher education with potential for economic opportunities. With nearly 40 per cent of students passing out of higher secondary schools being first generation learners special support for this population in counselling and guidance will be necessary. The higher education policy of the State should cater to this objective.

The State may consider a policy for reducing the number of aided colleges many of which are functioning more as self-financing colleges than as publicly supported institutions. There are several aided colleges with creditable records. They should be encouraged to expand their enrolment capacity by offering self-supporting courses and shift system. The existing regulatory mechanism on aided colleges need liberalisation for them to perform effectively in meeting the growing needs.

In increasing the enrolment levels the government as well as aided colleges should endeavour to offer career-oriented courses of contemporary interest, eliminate courses with poor intake, and maintain high quality to attract better students.

There should be clearly enforceable policy to discourage starting of new colleges by private sector except under special circumstances justifiable by academic and professional reasons. In any case the rate of growth of new colleges should not be greater than one per cent. This policy should be strictly enforced in case of arts, science and engineering colleges. The requirements of other professions such as law and medicine may be assessed separately.

On account of central government policies, there is a recent trend to create deemed universities by converting colleges, mostly in the private sector. Similarly there are demands for creating new state universities by redistributing colleges under existing universities. The existing guidelines are too vague to be of any value in guiding this process. The State should assess the implications of this trend to arrive at transparent norms for establishing new universities. The university education should not be allowed to be devalued. Its primary role in generating knowledge and producing scholars and professionals of high competence should not be lost sight of. The justification for new university level institutions should also be to strengthen the national capacity for high quality post-graduate education. The establishment of a Central University in Tamil Nadu will be a positive step in this direction.

Balancing Disciplinary Knowledge

The investment in higher education should be governed by an objective to maintain a balanced development of different disciplines keeping in view the longer term perspectives of national interest. At the same time there should be enough scope for supporting those disciplines which have a higher market demand at a particular point of time. The case of Tamil Nadu is examined from this perspective.

The enrolment in different disciplines at the undergraduate (UG) and postgraduate (PG) levels in Tamil Nadu institutions is shown in Tables 10.27 and 10.28.

TABLE 10.27

Growth in Enrolment in UG Disciplines in Tamil Nadu (1997 - 2001)

Discipline	*1997-98*	*2000-01*	*% incr./yr*
B.A	86364	97431	4.27
B.Sc	113536	169038	16.30
B.Com	56797	73333	9.70
BBA/BBM/BCA	11530	22881	32.80
ENGG.	95960	113000	5.92
Others	12000	15000	8.30
Total	376187	490683	10.15

TABLE 10.28

Growth in Enrolment in PG Disciplines in Tamil Nadu (1997 - 2001)

Discipline	*1997-98*	*2000-01*	*% incr./yr*
M.A	8544	11136	10.11
M.Sc	11741	17942	17.72
M.Com	2853	4410	18.19
MCA	5519	9371	23.27
MBA	1733	3193	28.08
M.Phil	1427	1768	9.97
Ph.D	209	261	8.29
ENGG	7600	10000	10.5
Others	1200	2000	22.00
TOTAL	40826	60081	15.72

Source: Policy Note, Education (1998-99). Demand No. 17 Govt. of Tamil Nadu (1998) and subsequent Policy Notes on Higher Education.

Tamil Nadu may determine the disciplinary distribution of the projected increase in the intake capacities of 17500 at the UG and 16500 at PG level (7500 in colleges and 9000 in Universities) for the period upto 2010. A suggested distribution is as follows:

Suggested UG Courses Distribution	Per cent
Arts, Humanities and Social Sciences:	5
Natural Sciences:	15
Commerce, Management, and Business:	25
Engineering:	5
Other Professional Disciplines:	25
Skill & Career oriented/New and Emerging Disciplines:	25

Suggested PG Courses Distribution	Per cent
Arts, Humanities and Social Sciences:	10
Natural Sciences:	20
Commerce, Management, and Business:	25
Engineering:	10
Other Professional Disciplines:	25
Skill & Career oriented/New and Emerging Disciplines:	10

Explicit goals for disciplinary balance similar to the suggested rates above will enable colleges and universities to plan ahead of time in creating facilities and recruiting staff and deploy financial resources in a calculated manner.

Mobilising Finances

Having set out the objectives for the development of higher education, it is necessary to mobilise the financial resources to attain the objectives. It will be necessary to seek the support of the traditional sources of funding indicated earlier such as the Central and State Governments and internal revenues. In view of the current trend of declining support to higher education it will also be necessary to explore non-traditional sources of funds

India's premier higher educational institutions such as the Indian Institute of Science, the IITs, the IIMs, some of the Regional Engineering Colleges, several of the Central and State Universities, and a number of government and aided colleges have earned high acclaim by offering prestigious programmes on account of their predictable financial resource base. Thereby they have devised their goals and strategies so as to supplement their resources through private support. The symbolism of availability of public funds to higher educational institutions should not be minimised in the Indian context.

The privately funded institutions, despite their enormous facilities have not yet attained the level of credibility and reputation anywhere near ordinarily equipped governmental and aided institutions. Most of the self-financing higher educational institutions are as yet beyond the public scrutiny in respect of their practices in generating their resources and deploying them. Many private institutions charge exorbitant fees (beyond prescribed norms) in the form of many kinds of levy (not accounted by vouchers and receipts) and are able to provide very modern facilities and (sometimes) even competent faculty strength. The non-affordability of the programmes of such institutions to a vast majority of eligible students is a matter of public concern. This dilemma needs to be reconciled in the interest of harmonious growth of higher education system in the country.

Compulsions for Fund Raising

Universities are struggling to survive in the face of increasing enrollment and growing complexities of new types of academic programmes. There are many different kinds of expectations from the universities by the students, parents, business sector and public at large. Ironically the investment in higher education is sharply declining at the Central level while they are expressed to show world-class performance. The situation is comparable to the expectations to win gold medals in all Olympic events from players who are kept on starvation diets. Tamil Nadu has endeavoured to provide reasonable support for higher education within its meager resources but this is also showing inconsistent trends.

Central Education Expenditure

The Plan allocation for higher education in the Central Plans has been declining sharply (Table 10.29 and 10.30). The centrally funded institutions are struggling to cope with this reduction resulting in deterioration of infrastructure and lack of resources for new developments.. The state funded institutions, in any case, get a very small part of the Central Plan fund and they depend heavily on state support and their own devices to meet the fund requirements.

TABLE 10.29

Share of Higher Education in Total Education Expenditure

(Per cent)

Year	*Centre*	*States*	*Centre + States*
1989-90	32.2	12.7	14.7
1990-91	28.7	11.8	13.4
1991-92	28.9	11.4	13.0
1996-97	15.7	10.9	11.5

Source: Anandakrishnan (2002).

The non-plan expenditure by the central government on education is shown in Table 10.31 and Figure 10.7. The allocation under non-plan has been increasing mainly to meet the commitment to the salary and operating expenditure. Very little of this is available for development expenditure.

TABLE 10.30

Central Plan Allocation for Higher Education

Plan	*Period*	*Amount (Rs. Crore)*	*Per cent*
I	1951-56	14	9
II	1956-61	48	18
III	1961-66	87	15
Plan Hol.	1966-69	77	24
IV	1969-74	195	25
V	1974-79	205	22
VI	1980-85	559	22
VII	1985-90	1201	16
Plan Hol.	1990-92	588	12
VIII	1992-97	1516	8
IX	1997-00	2500	7

Source: Anandakrishnan (2002).

TABLE 10.31

Non-Plan Expenditure by Central Government on Education, Art, Culture and Youth Affairs

Year	*Amount (Rs. Crore)*
1990-91	1686
1991-92	1755
1992-93	1878
1993-94	2376
1994-95	2799
1995-96	3630
1996-97	3988
1997-98	5134
1998-99	6535

Source: Economic Survey, 1998-99 Govt. of India. P.42.

FIGURE 10.7

Education Expenditure of the Centre (Non-Plan)

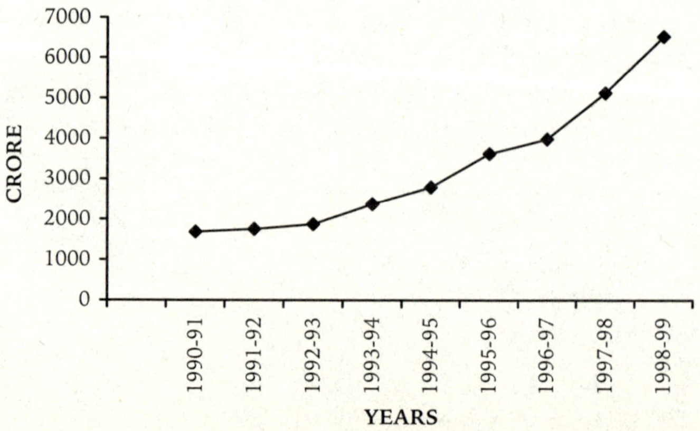

Tamil Nadu Education Expenditure

The expenditure on education from revenue and capital accounts by Tamil Nadu is shown in Table 10.32 and Figure 10.8 and 10.9. There has been an increasing allocation under revenue expenditure for education but this is flattening out recently. The capital allocation for education has been erratic making it difficult to make any anticipatory development planning for education.

TABLE 10.32

Expenditure on Education between Revenue and Capital Accounts in Tamil Nadu 1978-79 to 2002-03

Year	Revenue Account			Capital Account		
	Total	Education		Total	Education	
	Rs. Crore	Rs. Crore	%	Rs. Crore	Rs. Crore	%
1978-79	753.51	183.41	21.7	58.34	3.46	5.96
1980-81	1152.25	235.46	20.4	85.05	4.27	5.02
1984-85	2210.33	439.90	19.9	155.64	4.04	2.61
1988-89	4730.79	1051.60	22.2	190.29	7.23	3.81
1990-91	7255.27	1322.24	18.2	222.49	9.34	4.21
1992-93	8542.52	1548.05	18.1	322.93	5.58	1.73
1994-95	9634.95	1920.34	19.9	679.95	14.57	2.14
1995-96	10910.57	2180.59	20.0	590.94	15.22	2.57
1996-97	13064.88	2516.87	19.3	919.94	19.32	2.10
1997-98	14950.84	2889.57	19.3	1467.80	35.05	2.38
1998-99	17697.4	3853.03	21.8	1153.32	72.43	6.28
1999-00	20727.83	4348.72	21.0	1644.93	63.10	3.83
2000-01	21952.45	4396.00	20.0	1546.89	13.67	0.88
2002-03	26861.64	5859.28	21.8			

Source: Tamil Nadu: An Economic Appraisal. Govt. of Tamil Nadu and Manivannan, I.V (2002) and Policy Note on Education, 2002-03.

FIGURE 10.8

Education Expenditure in Tamil Nadu (Revenue Account)

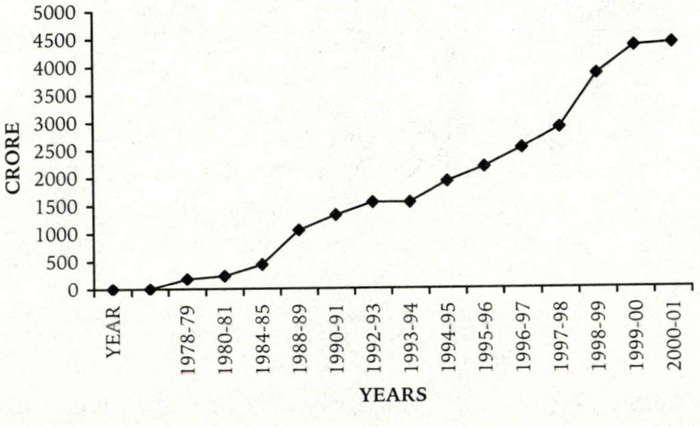

FIGURE 10.9

Education Expenditure in Tamil Nadu (Capital Account)

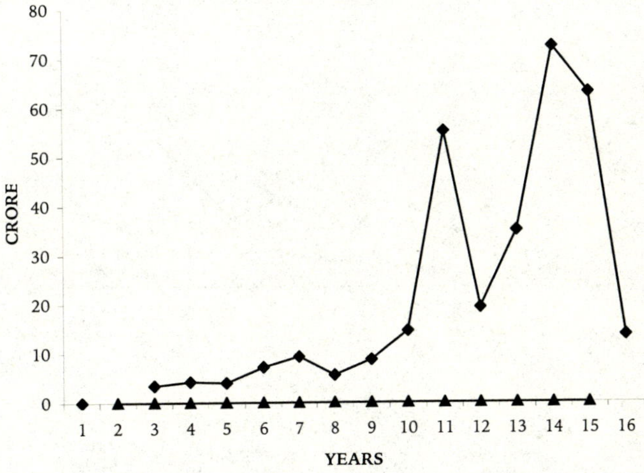

This needs a review in order to make the Plan funds predictable. The distribution of funds for different levels of education in Tamil Nadu is shown in Table 10.33 and Figure 10.10. The growth rate of funds for all levels of education in Tamil Nadu is decreasing in recent years.

TABLE 10.33

Expenditure on Different Levels of Education

(Rs. Crore)

Year	Primary	Secondary	University & Higher Education
1984-85	214.04	119.93	44.18
1986-87	295.98	161.72	58.69
1988-89	373.71	277.04	77.08
1990-91	515.41	357.14	129.94
1992-93	731.98	555.97	207.48
1993-94	808.79	617.53	234.94
1994-95	887.30	685.39	249.78
1995-96	997.30	786.58	321.83
1996-97	1158.95	621.32	312.50
1997-98	1351.22	1056.15	334.14
1998-99	1831.52	1462.20	413.35
1999-00	1967.89	1624.86	644.05
2000-01	1997.13	1631.98	734.84

Source: Government of Tamil Nadu:Various Budget Documents and Manivannan, I.V.(2002).

The allocation as a proportion of the Net State Domestic Product (NSDP) at current prices is shown in Table 10.34. From a high of 5.36 per cent in 1988-89 it has been reduced to less than 4 per cent in the last decade.

FIGURE 10.10

Expenditure on Different Levels of Education in Tamil Nadu

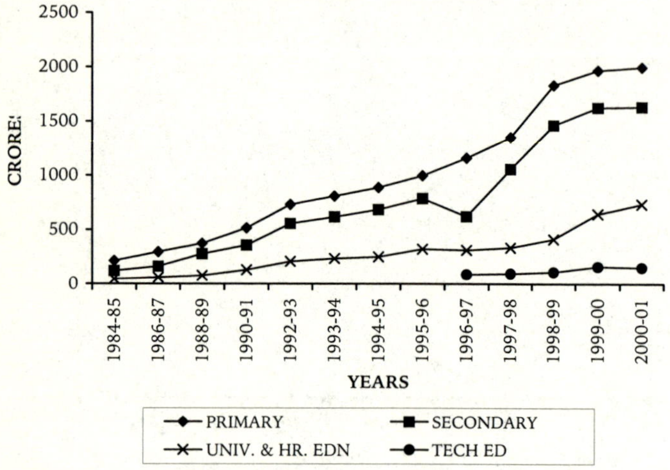

TABLE 10.34

Share of Education in Net State Domestic Product (at Current Prices)

Year	*NSDP (Rs. Crore)*	*Expenditure on Education (Rs. Crore)*	*% Share in NSDP*	*Per Captia Income (Rs.)*
1978-79	5023.02	183.41	3.65	1069
1980-81	6381.02	235.46	3.69	1324
1984-85	12027.75	439.90	3.66	2128
1988-89	19631.55	1051.60	5.36	3594
1990-91	25915.65	1322.24	5.10	3594
1992-93	37822.32	1569.96	4.15	4619
1993-94	51641.69	1749.67	3.39	8952
1994-95	61450.53	1934.92	3.35	10520
1995-96	70329.48	2235.80	3.18	11891
1996-97	80062.03	2536.19	3.17	13382
1997-98	92850.38	2924.62	3.15	15361
1998-99	106955.69	3925.46	3.67	17528
1999-00	117825.43	4257.92	3.61	19141
2000-01	131730.56	4627.79	3.51	21229

Source: Tamil Nadu: An Economic Appraisal. Government of Tamil Nadu and I. V. Manivannan, (2002).

The share of higher education in the total education expenditure (plan + non-plan) has been slightly improving (Table 10.35, 10.36 and 10.37) though the plan allocation has been declining (Table 10.38).

Allocation Norms

The allocation for all education should be 6 per cent of the GDP in the Central Budget and 6 per cent of the NSDP in the State Budget. Presently it is around 3.2 per cent at the Centre and 3.5 per cent in Tamil Nadu (Table 10.34).

TABLE 10.35

Allocation for Higher Education in Tamil Nadu (Rs. Crore) (Plan + Non-Plan)

Education Sector	*1996-97*	*1997-98*	*1998-99*	*1999-00*	*2000-01*	*2002-03*
All Education (Total)	2536.19	2924.62	3925.46	4257.93	4627.79	5859.28
Hr. Education	312.50	384.14	413.35	644.06	734.84	629.82
As % of Total	12.32	13.13	10.53	15.15	15.88	10.74
Tech. Education	88.11	95.89	109.55	159.84	151.98	143.77
As % of Total	3.47	3.28	2.79	3.75	3.28	2.45

Source: Derived from Tables 10.34 to 10.36.

TABLE 10.36

Share of Higher Education in Tamil Nadu (Plan + Non-Plan)

	1996-97	*1997-98*	*1998-99*	*1999-00*	*2000-01*
As % of NSDP	0.39	0.41	0.39	0.55	0.56
As % of Rev. Exp	2.39	2.57	2.34	3.11	3.35

Source: Derived from Tables 10.34 to 10.36.

TABLE 10.37

Share of Technical Education in Tamil Nadu (Plan + Non-Plan)

	1996-97	*1997-98*	*1998-99*	*1999-00*	*2000-01*
As % of NSDP	0.11	0.10	0.10	0.14	0.12
As % of Rev. Exp	0.67	0.64	0.62	0.77	0.69

Source: Derived from Tables 10.34 to 10.36.

TABLE 10.38

Plan Allocation in Tamil Nadu for Higher Education and Technical Education

	1996-97	*1997-98*	*1998-99*	*1999-00*	*2000-01*
Hr. Edn. (Rs. Crore)	4.50	4.64	12.38	13.20	8.32
Tech. Edn. (Rs. Crore)	21.79	23.86	22.62	20.50	3.43

Source: Derived from Tables 10.34 to 10.36.

- The share of the Higher Education should be 1 per cent of GDP in the Central Budget and 1 per cent of NSDP in the State Budget. Presently it is 0.1 per cent in the Centre and 0.56 per cent in Tamil Nadu (Table 10.36).
- The share of Higher Education in the Total State Education Budget (Plan and Non-Plan) should be 20 per cent. Presently it is 15.5 per cent and declining.

- The share of Higher Education (Plan and non-Plan) as proportion of the State revenue expenditure should be 5 per cent compared to 3.35 per cent in Tamil Nadu at present.
- The share of the Technical Education may be kept at 0.1 per cent of the NSDP and 0.75 per cent of revenue expenditure as at present.
- Any combination of the above norms may be adopted as long as it is adopted as a standing policy.

Implications of Financing Trends

Fund raising is becoming the major pre-occupation of heads of higher educational institutions in India. In the recent past their efforts were devoted mainly to raise additional resources for new development programmes over and above the basic Plan grants for capital expenses and annual grants for running expenses. In recent years, they are driven to raise resources even for their basic needs. These compulsions are strong mostly in case of institutions that are publicly accountable. By and large they are either institutions that are fully or partly funded by the government of the State or the Centre.

Financial Requirement

The university finances are required partly for development purposes and partly for running expenses. Every university has to plan on continuous and upward growth to reach newer levels of competence. Older buildings and equipments have to be revamped or replaced. Newer courses and academic programmes have to be developed and nurtured. A respectable level of research activities should be promoted both for enriching the teaching programmes as well as for contributions to new knowledge and greater productivity. They have to link up with reputable institutions within and outside the country. They are expected to organise and participate in intellectual and academic events of eminence and undertake exchange of ideas and knowledge. They are responsible for world-class publications of articles, monograms, books and journals. Among all these responsibilities, they are also expected to exhibit a keen sense of social responsibility in their varied operations such as admission norms, scholarship support, social development functions, employment generation efforts and many such public interest activities.

They are also expected to recruit and maintain adequate levels of teaching, research and support staff and pay them at prescribed rates of emoluments. They need to maintain their academic and residential buildings and their surroundings in a clean and elegant form. They are required to provide the stationeries and consumables for hassle-free functioning. They need a variety of computing devices, display and presentation equipments, copying machines, scanners, communication equipments like telephones, e-mail, fax, internet and so on. They have to conduct many mandated meets relating to governing and academic bodies, sports events, convocations, professional society events, student body activities, public relation activities and many such activities which involve considerable expenses. The colleges, which are affiliated to the universities, are also expected to perform similar activities to a significant but lesser degree. Whatever be the level of funding which the governments can afford to set apart for education, the quantum has to be predictable to enable institutions to plan in advance. *Ad-hoc* allocations have resulted in wastages of scare resources spent without long term goals.

Financing Models

The Plan allocation is meant for longer term development purposes in improving facilities and infrastructure of the institution to fulfill the strategic objectives. Too small of Plan allocation is counter productive. An ideal ratio between capital and recurring expenditure would be 40 to 60. This is perhaps not attainable in most higher educational institution in India at present. However the higher education policy should aim at a ratio of at least 25 (capital) to 75 (Recurring).

The Plan expenditure should be shared between the institution, the State and the Centre in a proportion of 20:30:50. At present the Plan allocation of the Centre is mostly spent on the centrally sponsored institutions and very little is available to the state supported universities and colleges. This distortion should be remedied for the future. The institutional share could be generated by various non-traditional approaches and there should be sufficient freedom to the institutions to achieve their targets. The State share should be indicated as a policy norm to enable institutions to prepare their schemes in advance.

Institutions should be encouraged to maintain Corpus Fund for development expenditure by apportioning part of the income from the traditional as well as the non-traditional sources to be utilised for seed money for new initiatives and for supporting the educational goals of deserving students.

The total Non-Plan (recurring) expenditure of the institution should be generated as follows: Tuition and other Fees–15 per cent; Internally Generated Resources–20 per cent and State Support–65 per cent. The individual institutions could raise substantial resources by raising the tuition fees to meet the recurring expenditure to the extent of 15 per cent from the present level of 5 per cent. The State should abandon the system of 'Deficit Financing' which acts as damper on the publicly funded institution to undertake any kind of resource generation effort. On the other hand the State should reward the institutions for raising additional resources and for efficiency in resource utilisation by reducing wastages and non-productive expenses. The uncontrolled expansion of the non-teaching staff strength should be discouraged.

Traditional Sources

Until about fifteen years ago, the traditional sources of financing higher education consisted of budgetary allocation by the government supplemented by different types of fees collected from students for tuition, examination, diplomas and certificates, special fees and rents. For capital expenses, allocation were made during each Plan period and running expenses covered in the annual budgets. These provisions were barely sufficient to maintain on-going activities. In recent years these supports have either remained frozen or substantially declined forcing higher educational institution to down grade their programmes or abandon some of them. Some of them managed to survive by running correspondence courses. Some State governments took a cut in this resource also. Some States resort to 'deficit financing' methods which hardly provide any incentives for universities (and colleges) to try and improve their financial situation.

The tuition and other fees collected from students hardly contribute to 5 per cent of the running expenditures. Raising the fee levels have helped to a small extent while at the same time overburdening some students. There is certainly justification for upward revision of fee levels, which have remained unaltered over decades. But raising them to astronomical level, comparable to the levels charged by self-financing institutions, has created public resentment on the one-hand and encouraging governments to withdraw their traditional commitments on the other. There should be a justifiable relationship between cost and price of education. Under such circumstances what are the possible policy norms, which could help institutions to embark on anticipatory development?

- Every institution should aim to provide for development *vs.* running expenses in the ratio of 25 to 75 at the minimum. At present most institutions operate with a ratio of 5 to 95, hardly leaving any scope for development and growth and consequently diminishing competence and efficiency in the use of resources.
- Some of the departments, centres and institutions manage to secure large scale sponsored research and consultancy projects. About 15 per cent of the value of such projects is available as overheads to the university budget. Excepting for a few nationally prominent institutions, this source of income is not very significant for most universities and colleges. Lack of support for major research and consultancy encourages migration of high-level talents to move on to other organisations in India or abroad, contributing to further deterioration of the university. Under such circumstances, it will be prudent to encourage such institutions at least to develop strong and innovative teaching programmes to maintain its special reputation in a few selected areas as an outstanding teaching institution. In a large country like ours, there is no need for high caliber R & D activity (sometimes artificially propped) in every one of the higher education institutions, unless they develop and demonstrate their inherent capacity to manage them.
- The Central and State governments should share the capital as well as running expenditures of publicly funded institutions in the ratio of 80 to 20. As a basis for predictability, the support should be on a per capita student expenditure for the approved enrolment level as is done in most European Countries. The institutions should raise funds above this assured level of support based on its capabilities. The government should abandon the primitive "deficit financing" system in favour of per-capita support.
- These institutions should be free from micro level interferences from the government and allow them to formulate their own strategies to raise additional resources within a normative framework. The government should allocate for education 6 per cent of GDP (as promised by several Prime Ministers) as against 3.2 per cent now, of which 1 per cent of GDP should be assigned to higher education against 0.1 per cent now. This is necessary both to enable creation

and strengthening the Indian knowledge society but also to enlarge the enrolment level in higher education from the present 7.5 per cent of eligible age group to 15 per cent of the group.

- The National or State Level Education Fund established by governmental and non-governmental subscriptions and managed professionally as a revolving fund could help to lessen the budgetary pressures on the governments and enable institutions to undertake hassle-free development schemes. This has been mooted for several years at high levels but has not been implemented for unknown reasons.

Non-Traditional Resources

In recent years the publicly funded institutions, whether they are at the university or college level, are resorting to very many forms of resource mobilisation from non-traditional sources. There are differing viewpoints on the validity and acceptability of these approaches. Even as debates proceed on the imperatives of these developments, it will be necessary to move towards those forms of non-traditional resources, which do not affect the credibility of these institutions, nor should they lead to decline in academic standards. Some of the prevalent forms of non-traditional resources are outlined below:

- Floating of self-supporting courses distinct from publicly funded programmes, offer scope for substantial revenue generation. It is however necessary to formulate these courses as academic endeavors to fulfill the felt needs and at the same time cost-effective.
- Adopting new forms of distance learning programmes combining conventional methods with different degrees of e-learning techniques could provide additional resources while meeting the special demands in the society.
- Developing and marketing of academic programmes to be offered off-campus within and outside the country is becoming possible. Some of these are also offered as franchised programmes. There is an understandable degree of concern on the worth of these programmes. The concerns could be eliminated by strict control over the content, delivery and evaluation through effective monitoring procedures.
- All these programmes will gain widespread acceptance if they are open to valid accreditation process similar to those in vogue for regular programmes.
- Development of separate organisational entities within the universities and colleges to offer vocational, career-oriented, skill-based courses of different degrees of sophistication have proved to be of substantial source of income. These could be offered in fields of arts, sciences, humanities, technology, medicine and so on. They also contribute towards employment generation and continued upgradation of knowledge and skills needed in the changing competitive environment.
- Many institutions have effectively rented out the excess capacity of their physical and academic infrastructure in many different ways adding to their revenue and at the same time maximising the utilisation of available capacities.
- Some have offered to share their expensive instruments and research facilities for development and testing of new products and processes of high value and mutual benefits through sustained interactions.
- The physical facilities such as the play fields, auditoriums, lecture halls and residential complexes that become available at periodic intervals over and above the institutional needs, may be made available to reliable users at a reasonable cost adding to a steady level of income.
- Many different forms of co-operation and joint ventures with outside organisation to utilise the special competence of the partners for mutual financial gains have been tried out.
- Development of copyrighted and patented products and publications of special value is a source of revenue if managed properly while adding to the image building of the institution.
- The ability to borrow from financial institutions, whenever it is prudent, could be a substantial source of non-traditional income. This could help institutions to overcome the financial constraints in undertaking bold development ventures. They should in any case endeavour to build corpus funds for future development out of the non-traditional income to offer long-term financial security and viability.

Sliding Quality of Higher Education

There is sufficient justification for the concerns frequently voiced in India for the deterioration in the quality of higher education. While the quantitative growth has been impressive, qualitative improvements have not matched the increase in numbers. In a sense it is this massive increase that is contributing to the decline in quality. With the onslaught of foreign institutions in India, the reputation of the Indian higher education in its present condition will be eroded. That there should be a change in the system has been widely acknowledged but no concrete initiate has been forthcoming.

One of the main causes of the slide is the increasing level of political and bureaucratic interference in the affairs of the publicly funded universities and colleges. The governing structure of these higher educational institutions spend all their time on pedestrian and sectarian issues and have hardly time, interest or competence to dwell on long term goals and strategies. The heads of these institutions are chosen more for their political and sectarian loyalties and less for their competence to provide leadership and good governance. The entrenched vested interests in these institutions have made the administration of student and faculty functions archaic at the cost of transparency, efficiency and ethics. The enunciation of national policy guidelines for the structure and composition of these high level bodies and the criteria for appointment of heads of academic institution could save many of them from rapid deterioration.

The highly reputed institutions in the State and the country, whether at the level of colleges or universities, are free from such interferences. Some of the best colleges in the State are autonomous. The board of governors of IITs is least political. The deterioration of the well-endowed Regional Engineering Colleges can be directly attributed to the unseemly political and bureaucratic control. This proves the point that financial resources alone cannot make a quality institution.

The growth of self-financing colleges has been useful to absorb the growing pressures for higher education. All the same, the mushrooming growth has brought in unscrupulous persons mostly with political and bureaucratic clouts and connections to engage in educational endeavour with no interest in quality of education other than quick profit and illicit collections and conversions of money. The latest trend is the proliferation of deemed universities run by such persons. These are literally private universities with official sanctions. In this process those institutions and foundations with better academic and ethical credibility but without comparable political and bureaucratic connections have been edged out of the educational enterprises. Unfortunately the regulatory bodies meant to establish credible norms and standards have also been playing second fiddle to the political biddings. Some of them have capitalised on this chaos by large-scale corrupt practices to enrich themselves by approving institutions of known substandard quality.

The dignity of teaching profession has been totally lost due to the treatment of the teachers like bonded labour by many self-financing colleges and deemed universities. In the publicly supported institutions, in spite of attractive salaries and service conditions, the behaviour of teachers has rapidly tended to be more akin to that of the trade unions than of the academics. Even the academic bodies intended to set curricular standards and norms have become unwieldy and ineffective.

The saving grace in this sad saga is the existence of a few institutions and managements striving to resist the interferences and maintain international quality of education. It is not certain if they will survive for long. The urgent need of the time is to establish a high power committee by the parliament with membership of persons free from political orientation with one key agenda — what should be done to save the fast sliding quality of our higher education system.

Enhancing Educational Quality

Investment in higher education will not yield the expected social and economic returns until the quality of teaching and learning is substantially enhanced. The deterioration in educational quality is taking place for many reasons.

The government colleges suffer from inadequate financial resources to provide even the minimal academic facilities. In addition they suffer from excessive administrative controls from the university and the government departments. The policy of transfers and new appointments of teachers has reduced their morale and academic loyalty to the institution and the community. The academic capability of teachers is on the downslide and there is very little sustained effort to provide opportunities to upgrade their knowledge and methodologies. In spite of sufficient enhancement in the salary levels of government college teachers, the code of conduct suggested for teachers is hardly followed.

The formal system for assessment of quality has been introduced in India through the National

Assessment and Accreditation Council (NAAC) under the UGC for colleges and universities while the National Board of Assessment (NBA) is engaged in assessing the Engineering disciplines. The operation of this has introduced an awareness of the quality requirements. In due course of time it is expected that these systems will help to improve the educational qualities of at least a substantial number of institutions. The State should actively support all the academic institutions to submit for assessment. No academic institution, whether in government or in private sector should be given any support for increasing their enrolment or becoming autonomous or deemed university or seeking grants or subsidies unless they have been assessed and rated better than average.

Conclusions

There is an urgent need to make a deliberate departure from the educational processes that existed until now in Tamil Nadu over the past 150 years. Whether the centre takes the initiative or not Tamil Nadu can set the new directions for higher education in tune with its past reputation and future needs. Since there is substantial scope and responsibility for innovations in higher education on the part of the State, the new directions in higher education will help to meet the social and economic goals of the State.

The broad directions for change will comprise of increasing the supply capacity for higher education in arts, science, engineering and other professional disciplines to meet the anticipated growth. This may be accomplished not by increasing the number of colleges in private or public sector as in the past but by enlarging the available facilities and maximising their utilisation efficiency. Consolidation of existing programmes whether in arts and sciences or in engineering and other professions should be the core objective instead of unplanned fragmentation of institutions and disciplines leading sub-critical facilities and faculties.

The State could set a new trend for the country in enlarging the number of autonomous and accredited institutions by continuing to maintain its past record in this effort. The undesirable academic influence of the outdated affiliation system should be progressively eliminated by adopting the suggestions of eminent national educational commissions. The scope for networking of institutions to decentralise the teaching and learning processes and to share the valuable educational infrastructure exists in Tamil Nadu and this should be supported by new educational policies.

The publicly funded institutions in higher education will continue to deteriorate if they depend only on the State and Central Government finances whose allocations are showing severely declining trends. At the same time it will be a short sighted approach if the governments abandon their role in long term development of the higher education system on a sustained and balanced basis to establish the core competence of the society in knowledge sectors.

The partnership approach between the institution, government and the society in the growth of the higher education would be necessary by raising resources through various traditional and non-traditional means. The respective responsibilities should be spelled out on a normative and predictable basis to enable institutions to develop strategies based on specific objectives and targets. The norms indicated in this paper are easily attainable with marginal adjustments to the patterns of resource allocation on the one hand and the incentives to the institutions for managing their resources efficiently on the other.

Our country is endowed with strong core competence in academic performance built over many decades by scholars, visionaries and philanthropists. The new financial compulsions should not let this competence whither away leading to a state of dependence on external support.

References

Albrecht, D. and Adnan Ziderman (1991). "Deferred Cost Recovery for Higher Education," *World Bank Discussion Paper 137.*

————. (1992). "Funding Mechanisms for Higher Education," *World Bank Discussion Paper 153.*

Ambani, Mukesh D. (2001). "A Competitive India for Global Leadership," in *Building Sustainable Competitive Strength*, AIMA, New Delhi.

————. (March 2000). Reform in Education in India: A Position Paper prepared for Prime Minister's Advisory Council.

Anandakrishnan, M. (June 2001). "Higher Education in Tamil Nadu and Future Developments" in *Higher Education During 10th Five Year Plan – A Proposal.* NIEPA.

————. (2002). "Predictability of Financing for Higher Education: Suggested Funding Models," Keynote Address at the National Conference on Management of Higher Education, *21st Century Challenges*, Jamia Milia Islamia, New Delhi.

————. (2002). "Predictability of Financing for Higher Education: Suggested Funding Models," *National Conference on Management of Higher Education*, Jamia Milia Islamia, New Delhi.

Census of India, (2001). Government of India.

Delhi University (1993). *The Gathering Storm: Resource Crisis for Universities.*

DTERT (1993). *Strategy Plan of Action to Achieve Universal Primary Education in Tamil Nadu* by 2000 A.D, Chennai, Government of Tamil Nadu.

FICCI (21 Aug. 1996). Background Paper for Seminar on Higher Education, Chennai.

Government of India (1986). Ministry of Human Resources Development, *National Policy on Education*, Programme of Action.

Government of India, *New Education Policy*, 1986 (revised in 1992).

Government of India, *Education For All - The Indian Scene*, Dec. 1993.

Government of India, *Ninth Five Year Plan 1997-2002*.

Government of India, Ministry of Education, *Report of Education Commission, 1964-66* (1966).

Government of India, *Report of the University Education Commission, 1948-49*.

Government of India, *Tenth Five Year Plan 2002-07*.

Government of Tamil Nadu, *Ninth Five Year Plan*, State Planning Commission, (1998).

Government of Tamil Nadu, *Policy Note(s), Demand No.17*, Education Department For the Years 1997-98 to 2002-03.

Government of Tamil Nadu, *Eighth Five Year Plan, 1992-1997*.

Government of Tamil Nadu, *Ninth Five Year Plan, 1997-2002*.

Government of Tamil Nadu, School Education Department, *Policy Notes on Education*, Chennai.

Government of Tamil Nadu, *Statistical Statements from the Education Department*, Chennai.

Government of Tamil Nadu, *Tamil Nadu – An Economic Appraisal 1997-98*, Department of Evaluation and Applied Research.

Government of Tamil Nadu (2000). *District Primary Education Programme 2000-2001*.

Haq, M. and Haq, K. (1998). *Human Development in South Asia*, Oxford, Oxford University Press.

India Development Report (1999). Kirit Parikh (ed) New Delhi, Oxford University Press.

Indian National Commission for Co-operation with UNESCO. *Higher Education in India: Vision and Action*. Country Paper (Oct. 1998).

Manivannan, I.V. (2002). *A Study of Public Expenditure on Education and Human Resource Development in Tamil Nadu*, Ph.D Thesis submitted to Madras University.

Manivannan, I.V., (2002). *A Study of Public Expenditure on Education and Human Resources Development in Tamil Nadu*, Thesis submitted for Ph.D degree of Madras University.

Naik, J.P., *History of Education in India, During the British Period*, (1951).

NCAER (1992). *"Non–enrolment, Dropout and Private Expenditure on Elementary Education": A Comparison Across States and Population Groups*, New Delhi.

NIEPA. *Higher Education During 10th Five Year Plan – A Proposal* (June 2001).

NIEPA. *Policy Recommendations on Financing of Higher Education* (May 2000).

Powar, K.B. (1997). "Higher Education in India Since Independence: Retrospect and Future Options," AIU Occasional Papers 97/1.

Radhakrishnan, P. and Akila, R. (2000). "Progress Towards Education For All: The Case of Tamil Nadu," in Govinda, R. (ed) *India Education Report, New Delhi*. OUP for NIEPA and UNESCO.

Tilak, J. (2000). "Financing Elementary Education in India" in Govinda (ed) *India Education Report*, New Delhi. OUP for NIEPA and UNESCO.

Tilak, J.B.G. (1989). "Education and its Relation to Economic Growth, Poverty and Income Distribution," World Bank Discussion Paper 46.

Tilak, J.B.G. (1997). "Lessons from Cost Recovery in Education" in *Marketising Education and Health in Developing Countries: Miracle or Mirage*, Clarendon Press, Oxford.

UGC. (1993). *Report of Justice Dr. K. Punnayya Committee (1992-93) on UGC Funding of Institutions of Higher Education.*

UGC. (1990). *Report of the UGC Committee Towards New Educational Management – Gnanam Committee Report.*

UGC. (March 1996). *Report of the Group on Modalities to Provide Educational Opportunities to Foreign Students and to Generate Resources for Higher Education.*

World Bank (1986). *Financing Education in Developing Countries. An Exploration of Policy Options.*

Abbreviations

CABE	Central Advisory Board on Education
DIET	District Institute of Education and Training
DPEP	District Primary Education Programme
EFA	Education For All
GER	Gross Enrolment Ratio
MHRD	Ministry of Human Resources Development
NER	Net Enrolment Ratio
NPE	National Policy on Education
PoA	Programme of Action
UEE	Universal Elementary Education
UPE	Universal Primary Education

Chapter 11

Social Security

Introduction

The concept of social security has been largely associated with developed countries, where the term has been used to denote measures for protecting workers from fall in income due to various contingencies such as death, old age, sickness, unemployment etc. Such a definition is highly inadequate in the Indian context where more than 90 per cent of the workforce is engaged in the informal sector, and more than 35 per cent of the population lives below the poverty line.

In its broadest connotation, "social security" involves the "maintenance of incomes so as not to fall below a basic minimum which is considered to be necessary for a living without want". Such a definition would encompass two fundamental types of social security measures - "promotional" measures that aim at improving incomes and Ameliorating poverty and "protective" measures that provide minimum entitlements to those affected by specific contingencies such as old age, widowhood, maternity etc.

This paper attempts to study the performance of the State of Tamil Nadu in the provision of an overall package of social security for its citizens. Following this introduction, Section-II of the paper discusses the various classifications of "social security" which help to define the strengths and weaknesses of the State in each of these areas. Section-III focuses on the schemes designed to provide protective social security, their history, coverage and impact. Section IV looks at the special initiatives of the State in the areas of nutrition and women's livelihood security. The last section summarises the challenges facing the State in providing social security for its citizens, as well as policy gaps and implementation issues that need to be addressed to put in place a sustainable long term social safety net.

Social Security - Protective and Promotional

In developed countries, provision of basic social security, though largely within the government ambit, has definite contributions from households, employers and communities. In the context of this paper, we will examine only state sponsored initiatives to ensure basic entitlements to the people. Further, since workers in the organised sector have already been granted a minimum level of social protection in our country, the focus will be on implementation of schemes to ensure social security for the informal sector.

As already discussed, social security measures can be divided into two basic types, promotional and protective. A further interesting classification of the types of social security made by Guhan (1994) and further elaborated by Prabhu and Iyer (2001), define "three sets of measures that proceed like a set of three concentric circles from wider to narrower domains of specificity while recognising that all three measures are called for". The outer circle of promotional measures (Level I) includes macroeconomic and institutional measures that provide social infrastructure to improve the standard of living of the public. These include interventions in areas such as primary education, primary health and nutrition which are directed towards the poor but not confined to them. The second circle (Level II) consists of promotional measures which are more directly targeted at the poor. Examples include poverty alleviation and employment generation schemes, which are largely individual oriented. Further, these schemes directly impact the incomes of the poor, and thereby reduce their level of vulnerability. The inner circle (Level III) contains specific measures aimed at providing relief to individuals from deprivation arising out of specific contingencies such as old age, death of the bread-winner etc. These are almost always means tested schemes aimed to relieve the most destitute from economic distress arising out of a specific situation. It is necessary to clarify that the three levels of measures are not mutually exclusive - they complement each other. Further, the efficacy of schemes in the inner circle tend to depend largely on the implementation and success of the schemes in the outer circles.

Studies on the priority given by Tamil Nadu towards various social security schemes show that the State has maintained an overall level of expenditure and performance in Level-I measures such as education, health and nutrition, resulting in a well developed social infrastructure (Prabhu and Iyer, 2001). Most of these areas are already covered in detail in the respective chapters. However, the coming sections will examine the State's noon-meal programme, in terms of its history and evolution as well as its cost and impact. This unique scheme straddles the boundary between Level-I (provision of nutrition) and Level-II (provision of food security) objectives. The main area of focus of the paper will be on Tamil Nadu's initiative in Level III Schemes - social insurance schemes for provision of relief to those in specific vulnerable situations. This social assistance package basically consisting of old age pensions, survivor benefits and maternity benefit schemes was promoted by Tamil Nadu much before the Central Government introduced similar schemes under the National Social Assistance Programme. While the State's performance in these schemes is no doubt impressive, it is obvious that the State has not given much priority to Level-II schemes for income and employment generation. Except for faithfully implementing the schemes funded by the Central Government, Tamil Nadu has not implemented any major State sponsored schemes in this area. This is a policy gap that needs to be addressed to build synergy with the existing initiatives of the State in Level I and Level III social security measures. The highly innovative scheme of the State to form self help groups of women to help them acquire economic empowerment through micro credit is also discussed in this paper. Though the primary objective in setting up the women's group was not promotional social security, income enhancement and poverty reduction have turned out to be the logical outcomes of the scheme's successful implementation. This scheme also has characteristics of a Level III measure, in as much as the group savings guard against various contingencies, and as a Level I measure, in as much as it contributes to the overall empowerment of women in the rural community.

Protective Social Security

Pension Schemes

The basic old age pension scheme was introduced in Tamil Nadu with effect from 1st April 1962 to provide monthly pension to persons above the age of sixty subject to certain destitution criteria (see Table 11.1). This scheme was extended in different stages to physically handicapped persons (1974), destitute widows (1975), destitute agricultural labourers (1981) and deserted wives, with the age limit being modified for each of these categories.

The quantum of pensions has always been the same for all types of pensions. Table 11.2 shows how the monthly pension has increased from Rs. 20/- a month in 1962 to Rs. 200/- a month from the year 2000-01.

TABLE 11.1

Eligibility for Various Pension Schemes in Tamil Nadu

Sl. No.	*Categories of Pension Scheme*	*Eligibility to Get Assistance*
1.	Old Age Pension (Normal Scheme)	1. The minimum age limit is 60 years in case of destitutes (who are incapacitated to earn their livelihood due to blindness, leprosy, insanity, paralysis or loss of limb). For others – the minimum age limit is 65 years.
		2. No source of Income.
		3. No habitual beggars.
		4. Do not have a son of the age of 20 or above and not supported by son or grandson.
		5. Do not own any property, value of which is more than Rs. 1,000/-.Could not work and earn livelihood.
2.	Destitute Physically Handicapped	1. The age limit initially prescribed was 55 years and it was reduced to 45 years during 1975 (G.O.Ms.No. 972, Finance Deptt. dt: 6-10-1975)
		2. Physically handicapped destitute persons, whose disability is 50 per cent or more are eligible for the pension.
		The Government have constituted a District level committee as per G.O.Ms.No. 964, Social Welfare Deptt. dt. 19-12-80 in each district with the Collectors, the District Medical Officers and District Social Welfare Officers as members to examine the applications received from physically handicapped persons and sanction pension to them, considering the individual hardship without reference to age rules.
		The scheme has been extended to leprosy patients also vide Govt. letter No. G2/16369/82, Dt. 22.7.82.

Contd..

...Contd...

Sl. No.	*Categories of Pension Scheme*	*Eligibility to Get Assistance*
3.	Destitute Widows	1. The age limit initially prescribed was 45 years as per G.O.No. 391, Finance (T&A) Deptt. dated 27.4.78 and it was reduced to 40 years. However, the age limit was removed as per G.O.Ms.No. 257, Social Welfare Deptt. dated 24.5.90. 2. The destitute widows who have not remarried and who are having legal heirs of 18 years of age also eligible for pension under this scheme (as per G.O.Ms. No. 92, Social Welfare Deptt. dated 2.6.98) 3. The other conditions under the scheme are the same as those applicable in the case of OAP (Normal) scheme.
4.	Destitute Agricultural Labourers	1. The minimum age limit is 60 years. 2. The conditions under the scheme are the same as those applicable in the case of OAP (Normal) Scheme.
5.	Deserted Wives	1. The minimum age limit is 30 years. 2. The wife deserted by her husband, should obtain legal separation certificate from the competent court of law w.e.f 25.4.86 (as per G.O.Ms. No.1465, Social Welfare Deptt. Dt.3.5.84) 3. The marriage should be legal one, she should not have correspondence with her husband for a period not less than 5 years, deserted should satisfy the rule. 5 of OAP rules and have permanent residence at Tamil Nadu to be eligible for assistance under the scheme. 4. If the deserted wives get remarried or rejoin her husband, get employment opportunities, get any assistance from her deserted husband, the pension will be stopped.The deserted wives are eligible for pension though they are having legal heirs who have completed 18 years of age and above.

Under this scheme, the pension amount has been increased to all five categories year after year as detailed below:

TABLE. 11.2

Monthly Assistance Under Various Pension Schemes (Year-wise)

Sl. No.	*Period of the Year*	*Assistance (in Rs.)*	*Government Order*
1.	1.4.62 to 31.3.79	20	G.O.Ms.No. 73, Finance Deptt. 22.1.62
2.	1.4.79 to 31.3.82	25	G.O.Ms.No. 805, Finance Deptt. 11.6.79
3.	1.4.82 to 30.4.89	35	G.O.Ms.No. 1412, Social Welfare, Dt.13.5.82
4.	1.5.89 to 31.1.92	50	G.O.Ms.No. 440, SW & NMP Deptt. Dt.8.5.89
5.	1.2.92 to 30.6.95	75	G.O.Ms.No.225, SW & NMP Deptt. Dt.1.4.92
6.	1.7.95 to 31.3.98	100	G.O.Ms.No.187, SW & NMP Deptt. Dt:4.7.95
7.	1.4.98 to 31.3.2000	150	G.O.Ms.No. 67, SW & NMP Dept. Dt:21.4.98
8.	1.4.2000 to till date	200	In the year 2000-2001, the amount of pension has been enhanced from Rs. 150/- to Rs. 200-/ The pension amount has been sanctioned to Fisherman also.

In addition to the monthly pension, beneficiaries under the scheme are also eligible for one *saree* and one *dhoti,* twice a year since 1979. Presently, the *saree/dhoti* are distributed on *Pongal* and *Deepavali* days

The scheme has also had a food security component from 1980. Starting with a provision of 1 kg. rice per week since 1980, the present scheme provides for the option of a free noon-meal under the existing programme and a free supply of two kg. of rice a month. Those who do not opt for the noon-meal get four kg. of rice free per month.

Administration of the Scheme

The scheme is operated through the Revenue Department. The authority competent to sanction the pension is the Special *Tahsildar* (Distress Relief Scheme), an officer available at the *Taluk* level exclusively for the purpose. The applications are sanctioned based on the verification of eligibility by the field level functionaries of the Revenue department.

Coverage Under the Scheme

Table 11.3 shows the coverage under various pension schemes over the past decade. A look at the Table shows the rapid growth in numbers from 1988-89 to 1990-91, an increase of almost 40 per cent in one year. This can be explained by the fact that prior to 1989, pensions in all categories were regulated by financial ceilings in each district. Once the ceilings were reached and the budgets exhausted, eligible individuals were left out but kept on a waiting list. They were sanctioned the pension as and when a vacancy arose mainly due to death of an existing pensioner. The ceilings were occasionally raised on an *ad hoc* basis. Subsequent to 1989, the ceilings were scrapped and pensions were allowed to be sanctioned to all those on the waiting list.

Beyond 1990, there is a growth of 94.93 per cent over the decade, which though not uniform shows a consistent increase in coverage. The sudden increase in numbers in the year 1999-2000 is due to a liberalisation in the destitution criteria under the destitute widow pension scheme by making the widow eligible for pension irrespective of the age of her living children.

An Estimation of State and District Level Coverage

An attempt has been made to estimate the district wise total number of persons above 60 using the National Sample Survey date (NSSO, 50th Round 93-94) extrapolated to the year 2000 and corrected to the

TABLE 11.3

Number of Beneficiaries Under Various Pension Schemes (2002)

Sl.No.	Scheme	1988-89	1990-91	1995-96	1996-97	1997-98	1998-99	1999-2000	2000-01	2001-02
1	Old Age Pension (Normal)	169386	222082	281835	302649	336207	349796	415399	449016	481390
2	Destitute Physically Handicapped	20698	26128	44783	57240	34554	39015	39847	41381	58159
3	Destitute Widows	122193	179452	225704	225035	281073	329247	397850	437768	462802
4	Deserted Wives	12747	20807	33778	36906	50896	51291	70489	86298	93230
5	Destitute Agricultural Labourers	47665	66960	69788	60948	70001	73946	78572	70897	79149
	Total	372689	515429	655888	682778	772731	843295	1002157	1085360	1174730

Source: Statistics Department Report on Old Age Pension Performance Budget 2002-2003.

TABLE 11.4

Study of Coverage in 1999-2000 - Districtwise

Sl. No.	Districts	*No. of beneficiaries > 60*				Rural Population	Urban Population (*)	Rural Population > 60	Urban Population > 60 (*)	Total Population	Corrected Population > 60	Total Population > 60 (**)	Percentage of Coverage Under Pension Scheme
		Old Age Pensioners	Destitute Agricultural Labourers	Destitute Widows	Total								
		(1)	(2)	(3)	(4)	(5)	(6)	(7)	(8)	(9)	(10)	(11)	(12)
1	Chennai	44419	10	14954	59383	0	4275178	0	287497	4275178	287497	322859	18.39
2	Chengai MGR	38328	6477	11277	56082	3155453	2236338	207572	156129	5391791	363701	408436	13.73
3	North Arcot	31598	10177	10946	52721	2320769	1204370	190634	67911	3525139	258545	290346	18.16
4	South Arcot	28817	7969	10276	47062	4830762	1051437	297800	66965	5882199	364765	409631	11.49
5	Thiruvannamalai	22719	7120	8328	38167	1938710	246790	136563	17457	2185500	154020	172964	22.07
6	Nagapattinam	7984	1278	3187	12449	1182809	433427	72939	36853	1616236	109792	123296	10.10
7	Thanjavur	26044	2863	6535	35442	948767	706805	79258	53613	1655572	132871	149214	23.75
8	Salem	33821	4506	7577	45904	3153938	1394558	221927	101818	4548496	323745	363566	12.63
9	Dharmapuri	16353	3188	2412	21953	2200539	268073	139055	19792	2468612	158847	178385	12.31
10	Periyar	13229	923	1610	15762	1654895	540775	152041	45425	2195670	197466	221754	7.11
11	Coimbatore	17935	1438	2408	21781	2078671	1829797	157527	128624	3908468	286151	321348	6.78
12	The Nilgiris	2050	432	391	2873	399833	287454	26209	16669	687287	42878	48152	5.97
13	Tiruchirapalli	27643	11827	11941	51411	6353853	1122719	489067	73099	7476572	562166	631312	8.14
14	Madurai	29545	3235	8440	41220	2268884	2021962	127237	151103	4290846	278340	312576	13.19
15	Dindigul	8855	1249	2027	12131	1349355	402581	98388	23162	1751936	121550	136501	8.89
16	Pudukkottai	9569	1376	2539	13484	1122324	242938	88996	20929	1365262	109925	123446	10.92
17	Pasumpon	8246	1221	2112	11579	792845	355644	83526	24170	1148489	107696	120943	9.57
18	Ramanathapuram	6919	1421	1631	9971	859280	293192	58811	26944	1152472	85755	96303	10.35
19	Kamarajar	9879	1731	2453	14063	987321	628786	101367	48815	1616107	150182	168654	8.34
20	Tirunelveli	13475	1333	2190	16998	926970	921614	81563	77639	1848584	159202	178784	9.51
21	Chidambaranar	8886	1312	1411	11609	860701	684098	88630	55515	1544799	144145	161875	7.17
22	Kanyakumari	4269	654	853	5776	1294868	272079	116693	25593	1566947	142286	159787	3.61
	Total	**410583**	**71740**	**115498**	**597821**	**40681547**	**21420615**	**3015803**	**1525722**	**62102162**	**4541525**	**5100132**	**11.72**

Source: Statistics Department Report on OAP & other pension schemes.

(*) After correction to expect group on population projection.

(**) After second correction to age groupwise population figures.

State level age group estimates of the expert group on population. The total number of beneficiaries in this age group under existing pension schemes has been calculated assuming that those covered under Old Age Pension, DALP and one third of the widow pensioners (based on a sample survey by Directorate of Economics and Statistics) would come under this category. This method ignores the pensioners in this age group under the physically handicapped and deserted women categories as they are assumed to be insignificant.

The coverage ratio have been worked out for the 22 districts in existence in 1994 using this Data.(Table 11.4) The purpose of the study is to arrive at the level of coverage in this age group under the old age pension scheme. The level of coverage is estimated to be 11.7 per cent of the total 60+ population. Though it is quite difficult to estimate a poverty ratio among this age group, we may assume it to be around 40 per cent, marginally higher than the general earning population. It is, therefore, clear that the State's present coverage extends to only about 30 per cent of the target group of eligible old age destitutes. The exclusion could be due to various features—the most important of which are lack of access to the government system and very stringent destitute criteria.

It may be safe to assume that some of those who are excluded are probably worse off than those who have managed to enter the safety net.

An earlier study by Guhan (1990) estimated the coverage level under the OAP and DALP schemes to be 13.5 per cent. However as the assumptions for projection of the eligible population were different, and older widows were not brought under the scope of the earlier study, the two assessments cannot be strictly compared. Using the present set of assumptions, the coverage level in 1990 works out to 7 per cent, showing that there has been a marked increase in percentage coverage over the decade.

Another interesting pattern that emerges is the pattern of coverage of old age pension across districts. A comparison with Guhan's study (1990) shows that while Thanjavur showed the highest coverage in both cases, and Kanyakumari and Nilgiris occupied the lowest positions, the relative position of the other districts has changed. Significantly, the coverage in Chennai and the combined district of North Arcot (Vellore and Tiruvannamalai) has increased substantially. The variation across districts has also increased considerably, which is an area of concern.

As regards the other pension schemes, district-wise analysis is very difficult due to the non-availability of reliable Data on projected population. However, an assessment on the widow pension scheme by the Directorate of Economics and Statistics (2001), shows the State level coverage to be around 10.04 per cent of the eligible target group which is marginally better than the coverage of 9.5 per cent estimated in the earlier study. The same study (Directorate of Economics and Statistics, 2001), shows a 31.64 per cent coverage of deserted women and a coverage of 18.21 per cent of physically handicapped persons. The relatively high coverage levels especially for deserted women have to be interpreted along with the fact that the Data on estimated eligible population is not very reliable.

Study on Impact of Pension Scheme

A sample survey was conducted by the Directorate of Economics and Statistics (DES 2001), (n=10246), under various pension schemes in the State. The survey found that 82.81 per cent of the beneficiaries are women. Though this is largely due to the fact that beneficiaries under the widows and deserted wives schemes are fully women, it is interesting to note that 70.5 per cent of the beneficiaries under normal OAP and 75.21 per cent under the destitute agricultural labourer pension schemes are also women, showing that the scheme is favourably biased towards women.

A further analysis of the two major pension schemes shows that under the old age pension scheme, the eligibility criteria were met rather well with 64.69 per cent having no other income other than the pension. Before getting the assistance, the pensioners mainly worked as agricultural labourers (37.64 per cent) and casual workers (21.73 per cent). After receiving the pension, the percentage of pensioners with no activity increased from 18.98 per cent to 71.49 per cent. This substantial change in the activity status of pensioners needs to be studied further as it could be interpreted in many alternate ways. On the one hand, it could imply that the quantum of pension though small was enough to cover the basic needs of the pensioners, thus making it unnecessary for them to work. It may also suggest some level of family support for many of the pensioners. Alternatively, it may show that given the health and skills status of most of the destitute pensioners, at present wage levels there was not much marginal benefit in seeking employment.

It is also noticed that most pensioners preferred to chose the 4 kg. rice option (63.33 per cent) while only 9.43 per cent availed the free meal, 27.25 per cent of old age pensioners did not avail either of these benefits. This outcome of the sample survey shows that the pensioners in spite of their vulnerable condition are still exercising an element of choice in this area, clearly preferring the take home ration to the noon-meal. Another interesting observation is that a quarter of the pensioners are not availing the food security component of this scheme, which again seems to indicate that some of the pensioners still have support from extended family systems. However further detailed study needs to be made before any clear conclusion can be drawn on this subject.

The sample study of destitute widows shows a similar pattern. (DES, 2001). However, though 43.94 per cent of the beneficiaries reported no activity after becoming pensioners, nearly 23.86 per cent continued to work as agricultural labourers and 14.67 per cent as casual labourers. Wages constituted 35.25 per cent of their income, while other sources of income such as small trade constitute 17.7 per cent, that is, more than 50 per cent of the beneficiaries continued to have an alternate source of income based on employment.

The other feature noticed is that only 30.02 per cent of the beneficiaries are above 60 years of age and nearly 38.49 per cent are less than 50 years of age. This has major implications on the possible duration of coverage under the widows pension scheme which is bound to be quite long, given the age profile of the beneficiaries. Both the above observations bring out the possibility of covering the younger groups of widows with alternative promotional social security schemes to enhance their wage earning potential rather than address the problem by giving them long term pensions.

Survivor Benefit Schemes

Unlike old age pensions, the concept of survivor benefits for poor households did not attract the attention of policymakers till the eighties. The initial schemes were only designed for providing relief to accident victims. In Tamil Nadu, a scheme for providing a survivor benefit of Rs. 5000/- to the families of those who died while engaged in certain specified hazardous occupations was introduced in 1977. In the same period (1978), cash relief was provided for families of road accident victims.

The earliest scheme to provide distress relief to families due to the death of the breadwinner was designed to cover weavers in the cooperative sector. Introduced as early as 1975, this scheme is an innovative one that links savings to insurance cover, and is jointly financed by the beneficiaries and the Government. Though its coverage is limited, the scheme has been sustained till today using the interest on the corpus fund jointly built up by the beneficiaries and the government. The only other early initiative in this regard was a life insurance scheme for agricultural labour households introduced in 1986-87. The scheme, operated through the Life Insurance Corporation, was limited in its benefit (Rs.1000) and coverage.

The year 1989-90 marked the beginning of comprehensive schemes both for family distress relief and relief to families of accident relief victims funded totally by the State government.

Family Distress Relief Schemes (FDRS)

This scheme, launched in 1989 provided a grant of Rs. 2,000/- to the bereaved families of all 'poor' households who suffer a loss of income on account of the death of the breadwinner. The quantum of financial assistance has now increased to Rs. 10,000/- (Table 11.5). Further, the scheme which was completely State funded, has now been brought under the Central Government sponsored National Family Benefit Scheme.

The eligibility criteria under the scheme is given in Box 11.1a. It may be seen that the scheme coverage is very broad, covering all landless agricultural labourers.

TABLE 11.5

Quantum of Assistance Under FDRS & ARS

Name of the Scheme	*State Funds*		*Central Funds*		*Total Amount Provided (Rupees)*
	From	*Quantum (Rupees)*	*From*	*Quantum (Rupees)*	
Tamil Nadu Family	23-05-1985	2000	—	—	2000
Distress Relief Scheme	01-04-1990	3000	—	—	3000
	23-06-1992	5000	—	—	5000
	02-10-1995	5000	02-10-1995	2500	7500
	28-08-1996	2500	28-08-1996	5000	7500
	01-08-1998	Nil	01-08-1998	10000	10000
Integrated Accident	23-05-1989	10000	—	—	10000
Relief Scheme	02-10-1995	5000	02-10-1995	5000	10000
	28-08-1996	5000	28-08-1996	5000	10000
	01-08-1998	5000	01-08-1998	10000	

In addition, small and marginal farmers as well as non-agricultural households whose annual income is less than Rs. 7,200/- (originally Rs. 5,000/-) per annum are covered under the scheme. The head of the family, whether male or female is treated as the breadwinner unless old or incapacitated.

The survivor benefit which represents more than a year's income to the poor family, after meeting funeral expenses, is meant to help the family subsist as it recovers from the death of the bread winner.

BOX 11.1(a)

Eligibility Criteria Under FDRS

The scheme is intended to benefit poor families and for this purpose the criteria adopted are as follows:

a. In the case of families which are solely dependent on agriculture for their livelihood, 'poor families' are those
   (i) of agricultural labourers without land in which all earning members in the family are solely dependent on wage income;
   (ii) of small and marginal farmers where the ownership of land holding of the family is less than 2.5 acres of irrigated land or 5 acres of unirrigated land. For this purpose, one acre of irrigated land is treated as 2 acres of unirrigated land. Leased in lands will be clubbed with own lands for arriving at ownership holding of small and marginal farmers by taking one acre of land taken on lease as equivalent to 0.5 acre of land owned under the same category of irrigated or unirrigated land. These guidelines on ownership of land relate to land on which cereals are grown. In cases where remunerative cash crops are raised, the total income is taken into consideration and it should not exceed Rs. 5000/- per annum.
b. In case of families which are wholly or partly dependent on non-agricultural income, the annual income earned from all the sources should not exceed Rs. 5000/- per annum

The eligibility income level was enhanced from Rs. 5000/- to Rs. 7200/- in G.O. Ms. No. 726, Revenue (SI) Department, dated 5.8.96.

Accident Relief Scheme (ARS)

As already mentioned, accident relief schemes covering various occupations and households were merged in 1989-90 into a single scheme known as the Accident Relief Scheme. The quantum of death benefit provided under the scheme has increased from Rs.10,000/- in 1989 to Rs.15,000/- since 1999. (See Box 11.1b). Of this, Rs.10,000/- is met under the Central government Schemes while Rs. 5,000/- is funded by the State government.

BOX 11.1(b)

Eligibility Criteria Under ARS

There is no income ceiling fixed for claiming the assistance, but the victim should be employed in any one of the occupational categories are given below:

1. *Dhobies*
2. Cobblers
3. Carpenters, Cart-builders
4. Drivers of animal drawn vehicles
5. Blacksmiths, Hammersmith
6. Goldsmiths, Silversmiths
7. Basket Weavers
8. Stone-cutters, Stone Carvers, Masons
9. Tile Workers
10. Brick layers
11. Well Constructors
12. Well Diggers
13. Agricultural Labourers, Small and Marginal Farmers
14. Neera Tappers
15. Swearage Workers
16. Pesticide Sprayers
17. Palmyrah/Coconut Tree Climbers
18. Fishermen (not members of co-operative society)
19. Building and Construction Workers
20. Truck Drivers
21. Autorickshaw Drivers
22. Drivers of Private Cars, Taxis and Buses
23. Barbers
24. Cart Pullers
25. Cyclerickshaw Drivers
26. Handloom Weavers in the Private Sector
27. Mud Pot Makers and Mud Toy Makers
28. House Servants Working in Houses
29. Snake Catcher whose regular profession is snake catching
30. All workers in the cinema industry excepting cinema actor/actresses
31. Loading and unloading workers of lorries and Tamil Nadu warehouse
32. White Washers, Painters and Electricians
33. All brick workers who are employed as daily wages
34. Tailors
35. Poor occupational category of Gramiya Nadanam and Naiyandi Mela Artists

Contd...

...*Contd*...

36. Poor occupational category of cooks engaged in the marriage and other functions
37. The workers engaged in the flour mills unregistered under the Factories Act 1948
38. Conductors engaged in the private buses
39. Category of workers involved in the work of erection of pandal and stage, *mandapa* work, decorative arches for conferences and marriages etc. and the workers connected with the provision of light and sound.
40. Persons engaged in the collection of honey, gallnut, etc. of hill and forest products.
41. The persons engaged as full time cleaners in private cars, lorry, truck and van.
42. The persons engaged as full time plumbers
43. Full time employees of match works and Fire Work Industries
44. Snake bite or bite of other poisonous insects. etc.,

There is no income criteria under the scheme but the victim should have been employed in any of a wide range of occupations, mainly involving manual labour, ranging from agricultural labour to the construction and cinema industry.

Administration of the FDRS/ARS Schemes

Both the schemes are implemented through the Revenue department with the application being received at the *Taluk* level, by the special *Tahsildar* (DRS). The *Tahsildar* sanctions the applications based on eligibility after enquiry by the field level staff and his own personal verification of 10 per cent of the cases.

Coverage Under the Scheme

The year-wise break up of number of beneficiaries under both the FDRS and ARS schemes may be seen in Table 11.6.

It is observed that the number of beneficiaries, under the FDRS showed an increase in spurts reaching the level of 61755 families in 1996-97. Following this year, there has been a steady fall to an unprecedented low of 18,632 in 2000-01 and 7929. Though the trend is not so marked in the early years under the ARS scheme, the two years 1995-96 and 1996-97 show the highest coverage. The fall in coverage in 2002 is very pronounced, falling below the 1989-90 level. In view of the erratic fall in coverage, no attempt is being made to assess the percentage of coverage. However, it may be noted that in Guhan's study (1990), the coverage of 20,900 cases in that year under Family Distress Relief Scheme was assessed to have achieved a coverage of roughly 25.2 per cent of the possible death of male workers in the 20-59 age groups.

TABLE 11.6

Physical and Financial Performance of Family Distress Relief Scheme(FDRS) and Accident Relief Scheme (ARS)

Sl. No.	*Year*	*FDRS* Number of Families Benefitted	*FDRS* Expenditure Incurred	*ARS* Number of Families Benefitted	*ARS* Expenditure Incurred
1	1989-90	13281	294.15	550	49.76
2	1990-91	22154	636.65	998	88.65
3	1991-92	22161	669.56	1081	91.36
4	1992-93	39087	1266.39	961	70.00
5	1993-94	36835	1562.00	991	66.06
6	1994-95	19296	1148.90	1024	89.74
7	1995-96	54762	2456.39	1836	200.89
8	1996-97	61755	3088.62	1548	133.41
9	1997-98	40034	2618.70	992	120.29
10	1998-1999	37214	3591.91	1578	236.73
11	1999-2000	22574	1884.46	1166	95.05
12	2000-2001	18632	1791.38	684	61.52
13	2001-2002 (Upto Feb 2002)	7929	792.90	392	39.20

Source: Policy Note of Revenue Department 2002-2003.

The reasons for the fall in coverage seem to lie in the financial administration of the scheme. The Central component of the assistance was introduced on 2nd October 1995, and the quantum of Central assistance under FDRS was increased in August 1996. During these two years the scheme showed a massive increase in budgetary outlay, though a substantial portion of the increase was met through Central grant. From 1997-98, overall expenditure outlays started to decrease. Further, the Central assistance was maintained at Rs. 16-17 crore, while State funding for the scheme practically withered away. The financial management of the scheme was moved to the district level with the Collector being made responsible for directly availing funds from the Central government.

However, it is obvious that unless corrective measures are taken quickly, the damage to the existing social security framework may be irretrievable.

Study of the Quality and Performance of the FDRS/ARS Schemes

A study was undertaken by the Directorate of Evaluation and Applied Research (1999) to assess the quality and performance of the FDRS/ARS schemes under various parameters. The study observed that both the schemes were pro-poor and the eligibility criteria were met in almost all the cases. However, only 64 per cent of the FDRS beneficiaries and 52 per cent of ARS beneficiaries were able to receive the benefits within six months.(Table 11.7) Considering that the application is normally submitted between three and six months of death, the assistance does not seem to be timely enough to serve as an efficient social security measure.

TABLE 11.7

Gap Between Application and Receipt of Assistance (FDRS/ARS)

Sl. No.	Gap	FDRS		ARS	
		Number	%	Number	%
1	3 months	195	32.5	30	30
2	6 months	190	31.7	22	22
3	9 months	80	13.3	14	14
4	1 year	64	10.7	16	16
5	> 1 year	71	11.8	18	18
	Total	**600**	**100**	**100**	**100**

Source: DEAR Field study.

The utilisation of the expenditure also showed interesting features (Table 11.8). A substantial portion of the assistance under both schemes was used for repayment of debts. Consumption expenditure also claimed 13 per cent of the money under FDRS and 15.4 per cent in the case of ARS. Thus a very small portion of the money could be used for future planning or asset creation. One could argue that the survivor benefit cannot be used as an asset creation scheme - by its very definition. There seems a need to tie up such bereaved families into a comprehensive promotional social security scheme to ensure that their income level is restored at least to its earlier level prior to the death of the breadwinners.

TABLE 11.8

Utilisation of Assistance : FDRS and ARS

Sl. No.	Utilisation	FDRS		ARS	
		Amount	%	Amount	%
1	Clear old debts	1147450	26.2	330000	24.5
2	Clear medical expenses debts	730950	16.7	73700	5.5
3	Clear debts (funeral expenses)	497350	11.4	137000	10.2
4	Consumption expenditure	575250	13.1	207200	15.4
5	Creation of assets	125800	2.9	63800	4.7
6	Deposits in banks	690600	15.8	337000	25.1
7	Education and marriage of children	348500	8.0	94000	7.0
8	Others	220100	5.0	101500	7.6
9	If not fully utilised future plans	44500	1.0	0	0.0
	Total	**4380500**	**100**	**1344200**	**100**

Maternity Benefit Scheme

Maternity benefits have formed part of the social security package in the developed countries and to some extent in the organised sector in our country. However, the first attempt to introduce it in the informal sector was made by Tamil Nadu in 1989. The scheme covers all working women belonging to "poor" households, with the definition of such households being the same as under the survivor benefit scheme. The scheme provides a monthly cash assistance for four months, the two months preceding and two months following delivery. It covers only the first two children and is available only to those mothers whose age at marriage was twenty years or more.

Initially the amount was disbursed in two equal instalments but the scheme was later modified to pay the entire amount in one lump sum before delivery. From 1992-93, the cash support was enhanced to Rs. 300/- and subsequently to Rs. 500/- from September 1996, when the scheme was brought under the National Social Assistance Programme. Initially, the State government was bearing Rs. 200/- out of the Rs. 500/- grant. Since August 1998, the entire amount is available as a grant from the Central government, and disbursed directly to the district.

Administration of the Scheme

From its inception, the scheme was implemented by the Social Welfare Department. The eligible pregnant women had to submit their applications to the District Social Welfare Officer (for rural areas) and the Municipal Commissioners (for urban areas). The identification at the field level was done through the health and nutrition staff. However, in the current year, the schemes have been transferred to the Health department. Now the Deputy Director, Health Services releases the funds through the Primary Health Centre doctors, based on the recommendations of the Village Health Nurses. This is expected to expedite disbursal of benefits under the scheme.

Coverage Under the Scheme

Table 11.9 shows the year wise coverage of beneficiaries under the Maternity Benefit Scheme.

It may be seen that the coverage under the scheme which was covering under two lakh has started falling drastically in the last three years. The reasons for this fall are mostly administrative in nature, due to changes in implementation procedure. This is supported by the fact that the pendency of applications at any point is nearly equal to two lakh, which is roughly one years coverage. Further the pendency is not evenly distributed throughout the districts, showing that there are administrative lacunae that need to be addressed in certain districts.

TABLE 11.9

Target and Achievements Under Maternity Benefit Scheme

Year	*Physical (in Nos.)*		*Financial (Rs. in lakh)*		*Percentage*
	Target	*Achievement*	*Target*	*Achievement*	
1989-90	200000	191625	400.00	383.25	95.81
1990-91	225000	224987	450.00	449.97	99.99
1991-92	200000	177250	400.00	354.50	88.63
1992-93	200000	187580	400.00	375.16	93.79
1993-94	141700	149650	425.10	448.95	105.61
1994-95	200000	199554	600.00	598.67	99.78
1995-96	200000	194949	600.00	584.95	97.49
1996-97	290500	219355	581.00	438.71	75.51
1997-98	290500	235220	581.00	470.44	80.97
1998-99		104402	610.05	522.01	85.57
1999-2000					
2000-2001		196716		1061.76	
2001-2002		91366		471.35	

Source: DEAR, Jan 2001 and Performance Budget of SW Dept.

With the erratic fall in coverage and pattern of pendency, district level coverage cannot be studied. At the State level, the total number of births is estimated to be 11.4 lakh, of which 24.5 per cent relate to higher order births, which are not eligible under the scheme. Assuming the poverty level to be around 30 per cent the estimated target population of eligible beneficiaries under the scheme would be around 2.5 lakh beneficiaries. This shows that if the scheme performance is restored to its earlier level, by ironing out the administrative lacunae, the coverage level could be considered satisfactory.

Study of the Performance of the Scheme

The Department of Evaluation and Applied Research (1999), has carried out a study regarding the performance of the scheme, in quantitative and qualitative terms. The study found that more than 90 per cent of beneficiaries assisted under the scheme satisfied the eligibility criteria and were able to use the money to supplement their meagre household income. However, nearly 49.8 per cent of the beneficiaries were not engaged in any economic activity (Table 11.10). In these cases, the scheme was more a poverty alleviation scheme rather than an income supplement to forego lost wages during the delivery period. Of those women who were engaged in economic activity, nearly 60 per cent reported a loss of earning of above Rs. 1000 in the four month period before and after delivery. The present quantum of assistance compensated 42 per cent of the average loss of earnings.

Another important finding was that the disbursement of assistance was delayed (i.e. received after the third month) in nearly 81 per cent of the cases Table 11.11). With the money being received well after childbirth, beneficiaries reported that the money was mainly used for general consumption expenditure and day to day expenses. (Table 11.12) It is doubtful that the amount claimed to have been spent on medicine and special diet for the month, was actually spent for that purpose.

TABLE 11.10

Occupational Status of Sample Beneficiaries Under Maternity Benefit Schemes

Sl. No	*Occupational Status*	*Total*	*%*
1	Cultivator	26	8.3
2	Agricultural Labourer	69	21.9
3	Non-agricultural Labourer	46	14.6
4	Village Artisan	1	0.3
5	Business/Petty Shop	1	0.3
6	Working in Central/State Government/Undertaking	1	0.3
7	Working in Private Sector	14	4.4
8	Not Working	157	49.8
	Total	**315**	**100.0**

TABLE 11.11

Timeliness in Disbursement of Assistance (Maternity Benefit Scheme)

(in Months)

GAP for Receiving Assistance	*No. of Beneficiaries*	*%*
1. Before Delivery	7	2.2
2. After Delivery		
a. One months	5	1.6
b. Two months	13	4.1
c. Three months	35	11.1
d. Four months	20	6.3
e. Five months & above	235	74.6
Total	**315**	**100**

In the overall situation of chronic poverty, pregnant and lactating women are definitely in need of special attention. Hence though this scheme does not serve as an income replacement scheme in nearly half the beneficiaries, it serves the purpose of supplementing the income of poor families at a critical period. The coverage of the scheme may also be nearly adequate. The main requirement seems to be a need to streamline the implementation so that the money reaches the women's hands in the last trimester of her pregnancy.

TABLE 11.12

Utilisation of Assistance Under Maternity Benefit Scheme

Category	*Total*	
	Amount	*%*
General Consumption	25220	16.1
Medicine	36500	23.2
Special Diet	19780	12.6
Delivery Assistance	4750	3.0
Old Debts	4050	2.6
Others	66700	42.5
Total	**157000**	**100.0**

Occupation Specific Schemes of the State Government for Providing Social Security

The Table 11.13 below gives the various schemes of the State Government for providing social security to the poor employed in various occupations in the informal sector:

The last initiative of the State Government deserves mention. The Tamil Nadu Manual Workers' Social Security and Welfare Board was meant to cover workers in 67 categories. The scheme was originally designed as a savings scheme with the worker's contributing Rs. 20/- per month. The employer's contribution was fixed at 3 per cent was also meant to be added to this corpus to make the scheme a self-sustaining one. In addition to the death, educational, marriage and

TABLE 11.13

Various Schemes of the State Govt. for Providing Social Security to the Poor

Occupation	*Benefits under the Scheme*	*Eligibility & Coverage*	*Method of Funding*
1. Weavers Scheme			
a) Pension	1) OAP of Rs. 200/- per month after the age of 60 years. 2) Family pension of Rs. 250/- per month for 10 years to families of those died before 60 years.	Handloom weavers enrolled in Primary Co-operative Societies 86,211 weavers enrolled 7711 getting OAP 407 families getting family pension	Members contribute 8p for each rupee of wages matched by 4p from Central Government. Out of 12 per cent interest sanctioned for the fund 7 per cent is credited to beneficiary account and 5 per cent is used for pension schemes.
b) Survivor Benefit	Rs. 60,000 to the families of those who die before the age of 60		Death benefit funded by State Govt. (Rs. 50000) and Co-optex (Rs. 10000) as a self insurance scheme delinked from LIC. Central Government contribution to premium of Rs. 40/ beneficiary incorporated into this scheme.
2. Fishermen			
a) Savings cum Relief Scheme	Assistance of Rs. 300 per month disbursed to the participants during the four lean months.	1.86 lakh fishermen covered at a cost of Rs.13.25 crore in 2000-01	A sum of Rs. 50/-per fisherman collected from fishermen for eight months a State Government contribution of Rs. 500/- Central Government to Rs. 300/-
b) Group Insurance	Survivor benefit of Rs. 50,000/- for death and Rs. 25,000 for partial disablement	Fishermen who are members of co-operative societies 2.97 lakh fishermen covered	Premium of Rs. 14 paid to National Federation of Fishermen Cooperatives by State and Central Government
	Survivor benefit of Rs. 15,000/- for death and Rs. 7,500/-for partial disablement	Fishermen who are members of co-operative societies 2.97 lakh fishermen covered Extended on 14.12.2000 to 66,027 fisher women	A premium of Rs. 4 per annum paid by State Government
3. Construction Workers			
	Group Accident Insurance scheme Rs. 1 lakh paid to the survivor in the event of accidental death. Natural death Rs. 10,000 paid as survivor benefit Maternity assistance Rs. 2000 is paid to a registered construction worker for two pregnancies Marriage and education assistance also given.	Any worker involved in construction activity the identified by any agencies engaged in construction and registered with the Construction Worker's Welfare Board. 3,94,462 workers registered under the scheme.	3 per cent of construction project cost collected from construction agencies at the time of building plan approval.
4. Tamil Nadu Manual Workers Social Security and Welfare Board (9 other boards now existing to be merged)			
	Accidental death Survivor benefit of Rs.1 lakh Natural death benefit Rs. 10,000 Maternity Assistance Rs. 2000, twice in the lifetime Educational and Marriage assistance	5.96 lakh workers registered	For employees in Auto and taxi employment 1 per cent of Motor Vehicle tax to be paid which will be transferred to the Board. Employers' contribution of other categories fixed at 3 per cent of wages but not yet collected

maternity benefits, the savings were to be returned with interest and gratuity to the worker when he left the scheme. The savings component of the scheme was scrapped based on worker resistance and the benefits were made comparable to those under the Construction Labour Welfare Board.

This scheme found unworkable for two reasons.

a) Administratively, worker's savings were found to be difficult to manage. The contribution from workers was also resisted by the workers themselves, who compared themselves to construction workers where the benefits were similar but no such payment was required.

b) The provisions for collecting employers contribution except for the mandatory 1 per cent from motor vehicle tax was not implemented.

Thus, though the scheme saw a relatively high registration of nearly six lakh manual workers, time will have to tell if any real measure of social security can be achieved through this programme.

Promotional Social Security

Noon-Meal Programme

School meal programmes have been used throughout the world for targeting food towards nutritionally vulnerable sections of the population, while at the same time achieving positive synergy through increased enrolment and better school performance. The State introduced this scheme as far back as 1956. Through the next three decades the scheme underwent many transformations in design and funding. Starting as a voluntary contributory scheme, it evolved into a fully State funded programme. Many implementation models were tried till the pattern of cooking the meals at each school premises became the practice.

It was against the background that the "Nutritious Noon-Meal Programme" was announced on July 1, 1982 by the then Hon'ble Chief Minister, M.G. Ramachandran. The massive populist programme was launched as a frontal attack against hunger - its aim being to provide a hot meal daily to all children between the ages of 2 to 15. The programme was initially started as an attempt to cover the highly inaccessible pre-school age group, by setting up a new network of nearly 25000 pre-school centres in the rural areas. Another interesting feature is that these centres were manned by local women, especially widows. Hence the programme indirectly served as a major employment promotion measure for rural womenfolk.

During the same year, the programme was expanded first to cover urban pre-school children, then rural and urban primary school children and finally older school children up to the age of 15, in rural schools. In 1983, old age pensioners were brought under the programme, which was finally expanded in 1984 to cover urban school children up to Class X. Since December 1995, pregnant women can also enjoy the benefit of a noon-meal for four months under this programme. Thus, the scheme has acquired the character of both a promotional as well as protective social security initiative not only for children - but for destitute pensioners and pregnant women as well.

The school children eat their noon-meal at school while all the other categories are provided their meal at the pre-school centres. Though there is an income criteria for coverage under the scheme, the scheme is intrinsically self selecting in operation, as culturally, only the relatively poor avail themselves of the benefits under the programme. One estimate indicates that around 33 per cent of the pre-school age group are covered under the programme.

If we consider school age children, the coverage almost corresponds with school attendance in the State funded schools. Hence coverage is almost universal in the primary sections and falls off as we reach the higher classes where the drops out rates are significant (Table 11.14).

TABLE 11.14

Direct Nutrition Coverage in Tamil Nadu 2002-2003

Scheme	*No. of Centres*	*Beneficiaries* *Children*	*Adults*	*Total*
A Pre-School Centres				
ICDS (Standard)	10420	440050	104586	544636
WB-ICDS-III (TINP)	19500	787247	293334	1080581
Other Urban Pre-school	718	30096	3105	33201
Total - A - All Pre-school Children	30638	1257393	401025	1658418
B School Centres				
Rural	38925	6015252	Nil	6015252
Urban	2087	476410	Nil	476410
Total - B - All School Children	41012	6491662	Nil	6491662
Total - (A+B) - All Children	71650	7749055	401025	8150080

Source: Policy Note of Social Welfare 2002-2003.

Integration with Other Child Development Schemes

Integrated Child Development Scheme (ICDS)

The other interesting feature of the scheme in Tamil Nadu is the way in which other child development schemes have been integrated into the noon-meal scheme.

The centrally sponsored ICDS Scheme was introduced in Tamil Nadu in 1975, starting with two rural and one urban project. At present, there are 113 standard ICDS projects (67 in rural areas 41 in urban areas and 2 in tribal areas). The programme covers children under six and women in the reproductive age group with a specific focus on pregnant and lactating women. A comprehensive package of five services are provided under the scheme through an "anganwadi", a centre which covers about 1000 population. In addition to supplementary nutrition and pre-school education, the centre level services include health check-ups immunisation, referral and nutrition and health education. The Central government bears all the costs except supplementary nutrition which is met by the State government. Since 1982, this nutrition consists of the noon-meal, which is provided under the State noon-meal programme.

Tamil Nadu Integrated Nutrition Project

In 1980, the Tamil Nadu Integrated Nutrition Project was started with funding from the World Bank. This was a more focused, scientifically designed scheme targeting the most vulnerable age group of children up to 36 months. The project attempted universal growth monitoring and selective feeding of those children who were undernourished or whose growth was faltering. The effort was to educate the community, especially mothers, about the child's nutritional status and need for food supplementation. The project had a smaller food bias, focusing instead on health education and change in family feeding practices.

By 1989, TINP covered 173 rural blocks in the State. It was succeeded by TINP-II, which eventually covered all the 316 non-ICDS blocks. Unlike TINP-I, this project was designed around the existing noon-meal scheme, which covered all pre-school children. So TINP-II was designed on the lines of ICDS, adding pre school and health services to the existing noon-meal centres along with growth monitoring of children under 36 months as provided under TINP-I.

By 1998, the TINP-II programme was renamed as WBICDS-III in keeping with the standard nomenclature for child development services in the country as well as to indicate the source of funding for the programme activities received from the World Bank. In August 2000, the State Government has attempted to standardise the feeding methodology under all pre-school programmes and bring the principles of selective feeding into the standard ICDS areas also.

The merger of all the pre school programmes at the field level has led to comprehensive direct nutrition coverage for this age group. There are further attempts

TABLE 11.15

Prevalance of Malnutrition Among Children Aged 1-4 Years in India and Selected States, 1992-93

Country/State	*Underweight (weight-for-age below 2SD of median)*			*Stunted (height-for-age below 2SD of median)*			*Wasted (weight-for-height below 2SD of median)*		
	Rural	*Urban*	*Total*	*Rural*	*Urban*	*Total*	*Rural*	*Urban*	*Total*
India	59.9	45.2	53.21	54.1	44.8	52	18	15.8	17.5
Andhra Pradesh	52.1	40	49.31	—	—	—	—	—	—
Assam	51.8	37.3	50.41	53.5	39.6	52.5	11.4	5.6	10.8
Bihar	64.1	53.8	62.51	61.8	55.2	60.9	22.7	16.3	21.8
Gujarat	45.8	40.5	44.31	44.6	41.6	43.6	20.3	16.1	18.9
Haryana	39.4	33	37.3	48	42.4	46.7	5.7	6.4	5.9
Himachala Pradesh	48.3	30.2		—	—	—	—	—	—
Jammu & Kashmir	—	—	44.5	—	—	40.8	—	—	14.8
Karnataka	—	—	54.3	—	—	47.6	—	—	17.4
Kerala	30.6	22.9	25.51	29.6	21.5	27.4	11.5	12	11.6
Madhya Pradesh	59.4	50.1	57.41	—	—	—	—	—	—
Maharashtra	57.5	45.5	52.5	50.8	39.1	46	21.5	18.3	20.2
Orissa	—	—	53.3	—	—	48.2	—	—	21.3
Punjab	47.4	40	45.3	40.4	38.4	40	21.4	14.3	19.9
Rajasthan	41.1	43	41.5	43	43.5	43.1	17.7	29.1	19.5
Tamil Nadu	**52.1**	**37.3**	**46.6**	—	—	—	—	—	—
Uttar Pradesh	—	—	48.5	—	—	49.2	—	—	16.2
West Bengal	—	—	56.5	—	—	43.2	—	—	11.9

to integrate the ICDS programme with the WB-ICDS-III at the State level to streamline the administration and implementation of the scheme. The State plans to use these nutrition centres as nodes for implementing various programmes for disability detection, empowerment of adolescent girls etc. To some extent it can be observed that the populist food-centred noon-meal programme seems to have overwhelmed the focus on allied services such as nutrition, education, health services and pre-school education. It is for the State government to re-establish the priorities of the programme so that maximum benefit can be achieved for the vulnerable age group of pre-school children.

Extent of Nutritional Impact

A detailed analysis of the levels and trend in nutrition indicators in the State done by Rajivan (2001) helps to place the value of the direct nutrition programmes in ensuring different levels of social security. Data from the National Family Health Survey shows that in Tamil Nadu around 46.6 per cent of the children below five years are underweight (Table 11.15). The data, pertaining to 1992-93, shows that this percentage was higher in rural areas (52.1 per cent) compared with urban areas (37.3 per cent). While these figures are better than the corresponding All-India situation of 53 per cent overall, Kerala, Haryana and even Rajasthan seem to be doing better than Tamil Nadu. Similar figures are found in baseline and evaluation data from the ongoing nutrition programmes in the State, which show that less than 50 per cent of the children under thirty six months were classified as normal during this period (except for one study in 1995) (Table 11.16).

TABLE 11.16

Percentage Distribution By Nutritional Status of 0-36 Month Old Children in Tamil Nadu Integrated Nutrition Project, 1992-93 To 1997

		Normal	*Grade I*	*Grade II*	*Grades III & IV*
1	Baseline (Phase I-III) Survey (1992-93)	41.4	34.9	18.8	4.9
2	National Family Health Survey (1992-93)	43.8	33.0	19.1	4.1
3	Baseline (Phase IV & V) Survey (1995)	54.6	29.6	13.1	2.8
4	Monitoring Data (December 1995)	40.0	39.4	16.8	3.8
5	Mid-term Survey (April/May 1996)	44.7	26.5	19.0	9.8
6	Monitoring data (December 1996)	45.4	40.0	13.5	1.1
7	Endline Survey (October 1997)	48.4	35.2	13.4	3.0

Though the level of malnutrition is quite high, a trend analysis shows a distinct improvement of the nutrition status of pre-school children over the last two decades. Though the figures do not correspond exactly, the positive trends are borne out both by project and independent data. (Table 11.17)

TABLE 11.17

Percentage Distribution of Children Aged 1-5 years by Nutritional Status in Rural Areas of Selected Indian States, 1975-79, 1988-90 and 1994

State	*Period*	*Normal*	*Mild*	*Moderate*	*Severe*
Andhra Pradesh	1975-79	6.10	32.40	46.10	15.40
	1988-90	8.70	39.50	44.30	7.50
	1994	4.80	46.10	41.70	7.40
Gujarat	1975-79	3.80	28.10	54.30	13.80
	1988-90	7.30	33.90	45.80	13.00
	1994	4.80	28.00	55.10	12.10
Karnataka	1975-79	4.60	31.10	50.00	14.30
	1988-90	4.80	38.10	48.80	8.30
	1994	6.20	40.60	46.00	7.20
Kerala	1975-79	7.50	35.70	46.50	10.30
	1988-90	17.70	47.40	32.90	2.00
	1994	15.10	50.60	32.60	1.70
Madhya Pradesh	1975-79	8.40	30.30	45.10	16.20
	1988-90	17.70	27.40	38.90	16.00
	1994	10.20	36.10	42.10	11.60
Maharashtra	1975-79	3.20	25.40	49.50	21.90
	1988-90	6.70	38.00	47.50	7.80
	1994	8.60	37.20	43.70	10.50
Orissa	1975-79	7.50	35.90	41.70	14.90
	1988-90	8.10	34.60	46.60	10.70
	1994	6.30	40.40	47.90	5.40
Tamil Nadu	**1975-79**	**6.20**	**34.20**	**47.00**	**12.60**
	1988-90	**8.00**	**42.00**	**45.80**	**4.20**
	1994	**13.20**	**46.70**	**36.80**	**3.30**
All Eight States		5.90	31.60	47.50	15.00
		9.90	37.60	43.80	8.90
		8.50	40.40	47.90	5.40

Source: NIN (1999a).

Note: Nutritional grades are based on Gomez Classification using NCHS standards.

The Tamil Nadu trend shows that it is similar to All-India figures, with normal and mildly malnourished (>75 per cent reference weight) children in the 1-5 age group increasing from 40.4 per cent to 63.6 per cent, a percentage increase which is however nearly double that of the All-India rate of increase. Similarly, the percentage of severely malnourished children dropped from 12 per cent to 2.9 per cent, while the all India figure decreased from 15.0 per cent to 6.2 per cent. A comparison with eight other States over the same period shows that only three States, Kerala, Maharashtra and Tamil Nadu showed a doubling of the percentage of normal children. The same three States also show more than a halving of children in the severely malnourished category. Though Kerala's performance is spectacular on all counts, there is no doubt that Tamil Nadu is one of the top three performers among States in this sector.

It is a matter of debate as to what extent these improvements in nutritional status of this age group is directly attributable to the nutrition programmes prevailing in the State, and how much is associated with general improvement in society. A comparison with all India performance, shows that while a portion of the benefits come from all round development, the consistent priority given by the State to this sector has played a part in its level of nutritional attainment.

If we attempt to analyse the success of the noon-meal scheme as a social security scheme, in terms of coverage and utility, we have to acknowledge that the noon meal largely operates as a substitute meal rather than a nutrition supplement. This may be the reason why the gains in the nutrition sector are not as significant as expected. The programme therefore operates as a Level-II scheme directly targeting nutrition to the most vulnerable, effectively supplementing the income of the poor family.

There are also questions raised as to the administrative leakages in the scheme as well as to the improvements in the nutrition sector as a function of the cost of the scheme. The scheme has to be viewed in its totality - as the pre-school nutrition centres continue to be used to support nutrition and health efforts as well as other programmes for reaching benefits to the vulnerable sections of society. Hence, the true benefits of the programme in developing social infrastructure are difficult to estimate, and will have to be studied in the long run.

Tamil Nadu Women's Development Project - *Mahalir Thittam*

The early pioneering effort for the creation of self help groups to improve the social and economic condition of poor women was started with the help of funding from International Fund for Agricultural Development in the Dharmapuri district of Tamil Nadu in 1989-90. Implemented with the active assistance of NGOs, the project was supported by the banking system especially the Indian Bank and NABARD. The project expanded to the Salem and South Arcot districts in 1991-92, followed immediately by Madurai and Ramanathapuram Districts in 1993.

By 1995-96, the project was well established and evaluations showed that the women's groups were not only inculcating financial discipline in the rural community, but also acting as agents of social empowerment. The success of this project led to its becoming a growth model for a State wide project—the Tamil Nadu Women's Development Project or *Mahalir Thittam* - covering all 28 districts of the State including Chennai Corporation.

Administration of the Scheme

The project is implemented through the Tamil Nadu Women's Developments Corporation at the State level, a public sector unit under the Social Welfare department. At the district level, the Project Implementation Unit (PIU) is headed by a Project Officer (drawn from any of the development departments) assisted by six assistant project officers, including a banker, in various functional areas. At both the State and district level, there are committees headed by the Chief Secretary and Collector respectively, to provide policy inputs and monitor the programme.

Each village group has an animator, a village women who is responsible for the smooth functioning of the self group at the village level. There are also two representatives for each Self Help Group from among the group members who assist the anemator in achievement of the programme goals. The groups are supervised by a cluster coordinator, a NGO representative who covers five village *panchayats* or about 20 Self Help Groups. The NGO also has district/block level coordinators, depending on the area of coverage, to provide overall supervision for the cluster level coordinators.

Unique Features of the Project

One of the unique features in the programme is threeway partnership between the government, the bankers and the NGO in order to benefit the community. The NGO is associated with the group formation exercise right from the outset, being responsible for training and motivation inputs. The NGO also monitors and guides the group on its path to self reliance as well as serving as a link to the banking system as well as government departments.

Group Formation

The project, since its inception has placed great emphasis on the empowerment of women. The groups

TABLE 11.18

Progress Report of *Mahalir Thittam* as on 31.03.2002

Sl.No.	Districts	Rural Panchayats									Urban Local Bodies			Grand Total		
		Total No. of Blocks	Blocks Covered	No. of Panchayats	No. of Panchayats Allotted	No. of Panchayats Covered		Groups Formed	No. of Women Enrolled	Total Savings Rs. in Lakh	Groups formed	No. of Women Enrolled	Groups Savings Rs. in Lakh	Groups Formed	Women Enrolled	Total Savings Rs. in Lakh
1	2	3	4	5	6	7		8	9	10	11	12	13	14	15	16
PHASE - I - 1997-98																
1	Villupuram	22	22	1104	1104	1097	99%	5251	102242	1340.2	505	9767	53.37	5756	112009	1393.57
2	Dharmapuri	18	18	588	588	526	89%	4911	91197	2158.84	301	5800	103.12	5212	96997	2261.96
3	Namakkal	15	15	331	331	331	100%	2774	49408	769.9	623	10454	122.3	3397	59862	892.2
4	Cuddalore	13	13	682	682	682	100%	4327	83598	919.37	796	15574	123.59	5123	99172	1042.96
5	Ramnad	11	11	429	429	429	100%	2925	56766	905.75	267	5128	67.31	3192	61894	973.06
6	Thiruvarur	10	10	430	430	430	100%	3758	66951	649.02	355	6138	57.46	4113	73089	706.48
7	Vellore	20	20	753	753	666	88%	2922	48967	380.28	456	7414	22.1	3378	56381	402.38
8	Madurai	13	13	431	431	431	100%	2804	57594	696.61	502	9608	74.32	3306	67202	770.93
9	Thiruvallur	14	14	539	539	533	99%	3270	51798	523.03	458	6975	24.61	3728	58773	547.64
10	Salem	20	20	385	385	385	100%	3294	55186	674.53	813	13265	87.14	4107	68451	761.67
11	Karur	8	8	158	158	158	100%	2318	33346	290.54	253	3593	24.34	2571	36939	314.88
12	Thoothukudi	12	12	408	408	408	100%	2896	50269	388.37	509	9189	80.78	3405	59458	469.15
13	Theni	8	8	130	130	130	100%	1349	22427	247.66	570	8755	63.95	1919	31182	311.61
14	Virudhunagar	11	11	450	450	450	100%	2565	46634	363.74	597	10909	54.68	3162	57543	418.42
PHASE-II-1998-99																
15	Sivagangai	12	12	445	445	445	100%	2510	43120	448.39	283	5272	32.65	2793	48392	481.04
16	T.Veli	19	19	425	425	425	100%	3338	59917	452.3	1228	22803	128.41	4566	82720	580.71
17	Trichy	14	14	408	385	385	94%	3709	61436	453.68	950	15243	93.97	4659	76679	547.65
18	T.V.Malai	18	18	860	860	860	100%	2714	46259	269.39	215	5950	21.31	2929	52209	290.7
19	Pudukottai	13	13	498	498	498	100%	3816	61988	408.07	221	3536	24.05	4037	65524	432.12
20	Nilgiris	4	4	35	35	35	100%	1132	17269	150.59	844	12343	130.66	1976	29612	281.25
21	Erode	20	20	343	343	343	100%	3504	49682	338.93	1064	15815	82.25	4568	65497	421.18
PHASE - III - 1999-2000																
22	Coimbatore	19	19	389	389	389	100%	3033	42842	368.11	1511	22721	149.13	4544	65563	517.24
23	Kancheepuram	13	13	648	614	614	95%	3223	53738	319.28	533	8552	49.81	3756	62290	369.09
24	Kanyakumari	9	9	99	99	99	100%	2297	43165	446.35	2185	41573	341.32	4482	84738	787.67
25	Perambalur	10	10	322	322	322	100%	2633	44477	238.59	150	2516	13.03	2783	46993	251.62
26	Thanjavur	14	14	589	589	580	98%	3727	62376	442.33	445	7350	48.17	4172	69726	490.5
27	Nagapattinam	11	11	434	434	434	100%	4186	70236	478.35	531	8417	72.68	4717	78653	551.03
28	Dindigul	14	14	306	306	306	100%	2935	44795	267.49	540	8431	49.24	3475	53226	316.73
	TOTAL	**385**	**385**	**12619**	**12562**	**12391**	**0.98**	**88121**	**1517683**	**15389.69**	**17705**	**303091**	**2195.75**	**105826**	**2000000**	**17585.44**

are formed in the poorest habitations with members generally between the ages of eighteen and sixty. The group size generally does not exceed twenty, and the present project guidelines mandate that all members should be below the poverty line.

The group meets every week to ensure regular savings and repayment of loans from the group members. The members are encouraged to save as much as each can without fixing a ceiling. A minimum saving is generally fixed, but groups are allowed flexibility to decide the quantum of saving. A common group fund is created which is rotated among the members at a rate of interest to be decided by the group, usually varying between 2 per cent and 3 per cent per month. The group loans or 'Sangha loans', as they are called are used by members to meet their small consumption and emergency needs without going to a moneylender.

Once the group has stabilised, by showing its capacity to generate and rotate internal savings, the group is considered for economic assistance under any available government scheme. Presently, the *Swaranajayanthi Gram Sevarojgar Yojana* (SGSY) scheme of the Rural Development department has been dovetailed under this scheme, making the Self Help Groups eligible for subsidised loan funding for asset creation. Other sources include loans meant for scheduled and backward classes, *Rashtriya Mahila Kosh* loans or loans from NABARD or banks directly. While the source of subsidised loans is flexible, all release of loans and repayments have to be done through the group account. Any subsidy has to be "back ended" that is, the subsidy is given as an incentive after repayment of the loan and it has to be administered through the group account only.

These guidelines have made it possible to inculcate fiscal discipline and the repayment ethic among SHGs. The concept of cluster level federations (CLFs) is also emerging now, where a federation of SHGs is being formed to take over the role of social intermediary when the NGO withdrawn from the project.

Coverage Under the Scheme

The growth of self help group under the project has been phenomenal - as may be seen from the Table 11.18 original project target to form 60,000 groups to cover 10 lakh women has been exceeded. It is also encouraging to find that out of the total membership of 20 lakh women, nearly 5.54 lakh women have been linked to bank credit with a total financial outlay of Rs. 255.8 crore as on 31.3.02 (Table 11.19). The recovery rate for the loans, which have basically been given for rural based activities is quite high at 85 per cent though there is variation in recovery between the weaker and stronger groups. However, the success of the project lies in the fact that bankers today recognise women's self help groups as more credit worthy than the general population.

Evaluation of the Project

Various independent evaluation of the IFAD assisted project are available on the impact of self help group formation on the rural community. The terminal evaluation of the IFAD project found that the major benefit observed in the village was social empowerment with women's self confidence increasing considerably. The group members came together to work for the community and for social causes such as literacy and women's health. The evil practice of taking consumption loans from moneylenders has almost come to a close whenever the SHGs have stabilised. Though the asset based activities undertaken by the women were basically traditional and low risk, 64.24 per cent of the beneficiary families had succeeded in crossing the poverty line.

The role of NGOs in the project has also been significant. As the NGOs had been selected based on their past credentials, their vision fitted in with the programme's mission of social empowerment of women, which was achieved in no mean measure. The NGOs were also largely responsible for the environment of fiscal discipline and repayment culture that characterised the SHGs. The study however, found that the NGOs did not pay as much attention to the economic activities taken up using bank credit as some of them did not have much experience in this regard.

A smaller study using the methodology of participatory rural appraisal (PRA) came up with some interesting findings on various aspects of the project. In the original IFAD funded project, there was some measure of targeting with 68 per cent of the members studied being below the poverty line. This finding has been incorporated into the guidelines of the present project where there is a clearer focus on targeting the poorest and most vulnerable households.

On the issue of economic impact, the study revealed a positive but slightly lesser impact than that registered by the terminal evaluation referred to earlier. 35 per cent of SHG member households had witnessed a significant improvement in status, whereas the control group of non-members, only 7.5 per cent had registered an improvement. Where the groups had accessed bank credit, the figure was even higher with 52 per cent of member households having shown improvement over their original condition. This shows that the ultimate strength of the SHG approach lies in dovetailing the group formation with access to bank credit.

The study also looked at the effect of group formation on deterioration in status of the rural households due to sudden social and environmental calamities. While only 4 per cent of SHG members witnessed such a dip in status, the figure in case of non-members was as high as 10 per cent This clearly shows that the self help groups act as a buffer against various causes of contingent poverty, basically due to the internal lending mechanism which saves women from the clutches of moneylenders.

The study also addressed another concern, whether compulsory savings would create an adverse impact on the availability of food in the household, especially for women and children. It was revealed that not only had general household consumption increased, (partly due to increased household income), intra family food distribution had shifted in favour of women.

TABLE 11.19

Tamil Nadu Women's Development Project (*Mahalir Thittam*)
Total External Credit Linkage-Progress as on 31.03.2002 From All Sources

Sl. No.	*District*	*No. of SHGs*	*No. of SHGs More than 6 Months*	*Total No. Rate as Per the Credit Guidelines*	*No. of SHGs Eligible from the Rated List*	*Total No. of SHGs Sanctioned Loan*	*Amount of Loan Sanctioned Rs. in Lakh*	*Total No. of SHGs Disbursed Loan*	*Total Amount of Loan Disbursed Rs. in Lakh*
PHASE -I - 1997-98 (RURAL)									
	PHASE - IV - 2000-01 (URBAN)								
1	Villupuram	5756	4633	4016	2324	3077	1366.86	2999	1224.06
2	Dharmapuri	5212	4373	3966	3716	5082	4293.39	5005	4051.02
3	Namakkal	3397	3089	2810	2571	1723	735.96	1536	472.96
4	Cuddalore	5123	4029	3542	2778	1887	652.45	1707	507.72
5	Ramnad	3192	2816	2669	2131	2235	1947.72	2181	1893.85
6	Thiruvarur	4113	3574	2879	2358	2309	533.96	2133	435.36
7	Vellore	3378	2782	2750	2042	1784	859.87	1543	604.66
8	Madurai	3306	2505	1931	1731	2647	2186	2637	2161
9	Thiruvallur	3728	2006	2006	1407	1382	390.36	1069	286.61
10	Salem	4107	3340	2942	2702	2703	2295.56	2307	2058.03
11	Karur	2571	2303	2272	1803	1785	1007	1733	636.73
12	Thoothukudi	3405	2889	2429	2429	2651	1159.32	2626	1154.07
13	Theni	1919	1887	1257	884	858	519.42	763	391.63
14	Virudhunagar	3162	2562	1934	1888	1825	891.04	1775	852.5
	PHASE -II -1998-99 (RURAL)								
	PHASE - IV - 2000-01 (URBAN)								
15	Sivagangai	2793	2566	2315	1899	1444	458.41	1444	458.41
16	T. Veli	4566	4117	3160	2783	2351	537.43	1731	383.68
17	Trichy	4659	4105	4105	2463	2364	545.12	2065	480.61
18	T.V. Malai	2929	2929	2874	1528	1301	530.93	869	197.24
19	Pudukottai	4037	3952	3121	2972	1401	381.46	1348	333.26
20	Nilgiris	1976	1213	889	762	627	396.95	627	396.95
21	Erode	4568	3739	2636	2240	1213	355.62	1032	293.72
	PHASE - III - 1999-2000								
	PHASE - IV - 2000-01 (URBAN)								
22	Coimbatore	4544	4491	4172	2953	2613	1430.66	1672	718.35
23	Kancheepuram	3756	2275	1773	1259	959	223.31	946	218.78
24	Kanyakumari	4482	2566	2430	2136	1868	528.68	1868	528.68
25	Perambalur	2783	2595	2001	1392	1121	145.63	861	106.92
26	Thanjavur	4172	3529	2442	2358	1558	354.88	1499	334.04
27	Nagapattinam	4717	3943	3763	3467	2434	512.72	2156	443.01
28	Dindigul	3475	2846	2377	1928	904	343.5	649	197.14
	TOTAL	**105826**	**87654**	**75461**	**60904**	**54106**	**25584.21**	**48781**	**21820.99**

There is no doubt that the formation of SHGs has indeed strengthened the hands of poor women in the State in their struggles against poverty and social discrimination. The SHGs have also served as an effective channel of credit for the existing income generation programmes.

The caveat to be observed is that self help groups by themselves cannot be regarded as a panacea for poverty reduction and income enhancement in the rural community. The project should not lose its focus on group capacity building and training as it expands throughout the State. There should be continued emphasis on the group formation process and social empowerment of women to make sure that the positive impact made by the project is not lost.

Providing Social Security for All - Constraints and Issues

The preceding sections establish the fact that Tamil Nadu has made some headway in providing social security for its citizens, especially in the area of protective social security. Yet, the scenario is far from perfect. Some of the issues and constraints to be tackled in order to improve the performance of the State are discussed below.

Lack of a Comprehensive Social Security Framework

In spite of Tamil Nadu's reasonable success in implementing certain social security schemes, these are merely "add-on components" and do not fit into a comprehensive framework (Prabhu, 2001). Unlike in the case of formal sector workers, no attempt has been made to spell out a clear package of minimum entitlements for all citizens to ensure their social security. The two major constraints in adopting this approach are lack of an adequate data base and shortage of funds. Both these will have to be addressed if the state's role in providing a safety net for its citizens is to be achieved.

Lack of Adequate Coverage

Coverage under social security schemes can be defined in many ways. While the State has placed a high priority on protective social security and nutrition schemes there is practically no State-led initiative for income and employment generation. This lopsided priority has made it difficult to obtain maximum positive effects from the existing schemes, especially in the context of a developing economy where there is chronic poverty. Without income enhancement, there can practically be no exit criteria from the existing protective schemes, thus increasing the financial burden on the State Government with no tangible results.

Among the protective social security schemes, the coverage observed is not universal for all eligible beneficiaries. The old age pension schemes, show wide variation in district level coverage, with the highest coverage being observed in districts with proximity to power centres. It has further been observed that in times of fiscal stress, the State has found it difficult to protect the current levels of coverage, even in its flagship schemes in this sector.

Implementation Issues

Targeting entitlements to the most vulnerable sections has always presented a challenge - especially when their access to government mechanisms is very poor. Changes also need to be made, on the design side to dovetail existing schemes, so as to achieve long term objectives. For example, groups like young widows have to be provided a linkage to training/employment schemes as a mere survivor benefit scheme or minimum pension cannot provide an answer to the bereaved family's economic needs.

The major focus area in implementation will have to be on timely and automatic delivery of benefits. In many existing schemes, this has been difficult to accomplish. The whole purpose of providing immediate support to the vulnerable will be defeated unless a breakthrough is made in simplifying the procedures.

An important issue to be addressed in this area is the streamlining of financial administration after the introduction of the National Social Assistance Programme. Though the Central government has ploughed in additional funds directly to the social security sector, it is observed that these funds have been used to substitute State government funds rather than supplement them. As a matter of fact, coverage levels have dropped in two of the three schemes after the change in administration of the scheme. It is also observed that not much flexibility has been given to State governments under this scheme, with targets up to the district level being fixed by the Central government itself. This has acted against the interests of progressive States like Tamil Nadu, where existing implementation mechanisms through the State budget had to be dismantled. The State and Central government will have to jointly sort out these issues so that maximum coverage and benefit can be achieved under the schemes coming under NSAP.

Changing Demography and Emerging Areas of Concern

With the fall in birth rates in the last two decades and increasing longevity, the demography of the entire country, especially States like Tamil Nadu are undergoing drastic changes. It is anticipated that in Tamil Nadu, the proportion of population over 60 years will go up from 6.45 per cent in 1981 to 11.43 per cent in 2011. Studies also show that dependency ratios, especially in urban areas are bound to become adverse in the coming years. Further, the implications of breakdown in the joint family system will have to be taken into account. The State will have to plan for providing some form of minimum social security for the aged in the years to come. With higher levels of morbidity among the aged, inability of government health care system to cope with the demand and rising costs of tertiary health care, some provision for health insurance will also have to be devised. Such a comprehensive scheme will have to be partly funded by the beneficiary's contribution, which will have to start during his working years. The Central government is planning some steps in this direction, but it is for Tamil Nadu, playing its usual pioneering role to look for an innovative solution to this problem.

Decentralisation and Public Participation

It seems obvious that schemes for protective or promotional social security can best be implemented if identification of beneficiaries can be decentralised at least to the village *panchayat* level. The schemes could be accepted and owned by the public which will not only improve their effectiveness but will strengthen the government's hands by augmenting the resource availability. Providing social security cannot be the responsibility of the State alone. Awareness has to be built among the public regarding the need for future planning and methodologies for tapping public savings have to be put into place. These are the challenges before the State and the country in coming years.

Other Social Welfare Programmes

The Directorate of Social Welfare is the nodal agency for coordinating the implementation of the 18 point programme for women and children. Each of these indicators are further subdivided and targets have been set against each of the indicators given below and it is reviewed on a monthly basis.

18 Point Programme for Women and Children

Point No. *Thrust Areas*

1. Improving the health of adolescents especially of adolescent girls.
2. To liberate women from the shackles of early and frequent child bearing.
3. Eradication of female foeticide and female infanticide.
4. Reduction of low birth weight.
5. Elimination of vaccine preventable diseases.
6. Prevention of disability in early childhood and early detection and intervention.
7. Early childhood care and development - Focus on parenting role and responsibilities during the first three years of life.
8. Reduction of IMR.
9. Reduction of severe and moderate malnutrition among 0-3 years children.
10. Elimination of deficiencies.

10.a. Elimination of Vit.A deficiency

10.b. Elimination of iodine deficiency disorders.

10.c. Reduction of Anemia in children, adolescent girls and pregnant women.

11. Popularising girl child protection scheme and improving the status of the girl child.
12. Make all hospitals and maternity centres women and child friendly.
13. Prevention of Early child identification of heart diseases and free open heart surgeries for children.
14. Elimination of child labour.
15. Ensuring 8 years of Schooling for every child.
16. Safe drinking water supply and better access to sanitary facilities at all schools, child care centres.
17. Raising women's literacy and status.
18. Empowerment of women through Self Help Groups.

Convergence of Services

Convergence of services of all departments under Social Welfare at the block and village level are a vital component of the empowerment of the poor as part of the linkage building process for the poor. It is well known that strengthening existing "connections" and building new connections would bring in a sustainable growth process. This will be given top priority under X Plan.

Gender Equity

Under Tenth Plan barriers to gender equity on the demand side also need to be addressed. This includes sensitization of men on reproductive and sexual rights of women and their responsibility in this regard, changing public attitudes towards inequalities in distribution of food and health care, strengthening knowledge on infertility and sex-determination, and promoting health insurance or credit for poor women through better convergence between health and village-level community based organisations.

Institutional Structures for Addressing Violence Against Women

Several institutional structures that exist for addressing violence against women needs to be sensitised and strengthened through all women Police stations, free legal aid board, Family Counselling

Centres, as well as State Commission for Women which have been established in Tamil Nadu.

Elimination of Child Abuse and Child Prostitutes

A comprehensive approach will be followed for elimination of child abuse and child prostitutes will be identified and rehabilitated. Based on the need, setting up of creches, homes for abandoned children, crisis intervention centres, short stay homes for mothers and children will be taken up. Adoption procedure will be simplified and adoption will be promoted. With a view to preventing female infanticide in the districts, cradle baby scheme and girl child assistance scheme will be continued. For the welfare of juveniles, the new Juvenile Justice Care and Protection Act 2000 will be implemented in its spirit. The children on the streets will be ensured their rights and rehabilitated properly with the objective of ensuring that no child is left on the streets during Tenth Plan. Institutionalisation of children in childcare institutions will be reduced and the child right to family will be ensured.

Unmet Needs of the Aged

In order to overcome the vulnerability of the aged, a range of service provisions will be established to fulfil the unmet needs of the growing ageing population. Hence focus will be on income, health, peer support, accommodation, community education and recreational programmes to ameliorate the existing circumstances of the aged. The existing scheme of provision of noon-meal will be continued, old age pension scheme will be continued, new old age homes and day care centres will be started, community based programmes will be encouraged, more service schemes will be launched in rural areas, health care needs will be taken care of, dental and eye camps will be conducted, vocational training will be given for income-earning and Dying Destitute Homes will be set up in big districts to take care of dying old destitutes.

Rehabilitation of the Disabled

For the rehabilitation of the disabled, thrust will be given on early detection of disabilities, immunisation of girls against Rubella, awareness creation on prevention of disabilities, training to personnel at different levels, provision of educational facilities, setting up of special schools in the districts where there are no special schools at present, introduction of new courses, new techniques and teaching materials, integrated education with resource rooms and resource teachers, supportive facilities like scholarships, transport, hostels, aids and appliances, vocational training, employment and self-employment opportunities, on-job training to visually handicapped and hearing impaired persons, awareness creation through mass media, strengthening of the existing schools, provision of environment friendly access facilities such as ramps, toilets etc., in public places, community based rehabilitation, issue of National disability identity card and surgical correction to orthopaedically handicapped persons / spinal cord injured persons. Monitoring and periodical evaluation will be built-in in all the welfare programmes.

Conclusion

Comparison With Other States

Easwara Prasad in his quick review of the position of Social Security Schemes in 1993, (prior to the introduction of the National Social Assistance Programme), observed that Tamil Nadu was one among the few States where pension schemes extended not only to the aged, but to agricultural labourers, widows and physically handicapped. In 1993, maternity benefits to poor women to compensate for loss of wages were being implemented in Gujarat, Karnataka, Kerala and Tamil Nadu only. However, Tamil Nadu did not have a strong employment guarantee scheme, as found in Maharashtra, but only an unemployment relief scheme (which was also gradually phased out). Another significant observation was that while the rest of the country had welfare schemes aimed at the general population below the poverty line, in Gujarat, Tamil Nadu and Maharashtra, these schemes were generally focussed more towards women and children.

Subsequent comparison of the relative performance of 15 major States in expenditure on Social Security Schemes between 1991-95 by Prabhu and Iyer (1999), confirm the same observations. Tables 11.20 and 11.21 shows that the total expenditure on social security for all the States constituted 2.63 per cent of SDP and 16.63 per cent of Revenue expenditure respectively. In this study, Elementary education, rural and public health, family welfare and nutrition are classified as Level I programmes, while asset and employment generation programmes are classified as level II. Level III consists of expenditure on protective social security such as pension and survivor benefit. Tamil Nadu shows a level of 3.45 per cent on SDP and 18.25 per cent of the Revenue expenditure being spent on social security in the period under review.

While the State ranks fourth among the fifteen States on the basis of these figures, all other States

TABLE 11.20

Study of Coverage in 1999-2000

Sl. No.	Districts	No. of Beneficiaries > 60: Old Age Pensioners	Destitute Agricultural Labourers	Destitute Widows	Total	Uncorrected: Rural Population	Urban Population	Rural Population >60	Urban Population >60	Corrected Urban Population	Corrected Urban Population >60	Total Population	Corrected Population >60	Total Corrected Population >60	To be Coverage
		(1)	(2)	(3)	(4)	(5)	(6)	(7)	(8)	(9)	(10)	(11)	(12)	(13)	(14)
					(1)+(2)+(3)					(6)* 1.298	(8)* 1.298	(5)+(9)	(7)+(10)	(12)* 1.123	(4)/(13)
1	Chennai	44419	10	14954	59383		3293666		221492	4275178	287497	4275178	287497	322859	18.39
2	Chengai MGR	38328	6477	11277	56082	3155453	1722911	207572	120284	2236338	156129	5391791	363701	408436	13.73
3	North Arcot	31598	10177	10946	52721	2320769	927866	190634	52320	1204370	67911	3525139	258545	290346	18.16
4	South Arcot	28817	7969	10276	47062	4830762	810044	297800	51591	1051437	66965	5882199	364765	409631	11.49
5	Thiruvannamalai	22719	7120	8328	38167	1938710	190131	136563	13449	246790	17457	2185500	154020	172964	22.07
6	Nagapattinam	7984	1278	3187	12449	1182809	333919	72939	28392	433427	36853	1616236	109792	123296	10.1
7	Thanjavur	26044	2863	6535	35442	948767	544534	79258	41304	706805	53613	1655572	132871	149214	23.75
8	Salem	33821	4506	7577	45904	3153938	1074390	221927	78442	1394558	101818	4548496	323745	363566	12.63
9	Dharmapuri	16353	3188	2412	21953	2200539	206528	139055	15248	268073	19792	2468612	158847	178385	12.31
10	Periyar	13229	923	1610	15762	1654895	416622	152041	34996	540775	45425	2195670	197466	221754	7.11
11	Coimbatore	17935	1438	2408	21781	2078671	1409705	157527	99094	1829797	128624	3908468	286151	321348	6.78
12	The Nilgiris	2050	432	391	2873	399833	221459	26209	12842	287454	16669	687287	42878	48152	5.97
13	Tiruchirapalli	27643	11827	11941	51411	6353853	864961	489067	56317	1122719	73099	7476572	562166	631312	8.14
14	Madurai	29545	3235	8440	41220	2268884	1557752	127237	116412	2021962	151103	4290846	278340	312576	13.19
15	Dindigul	8855	1249	2027	12131	1349355	310155	98388	17844	402581	23162	1751936	121550	136501	8.89
16	Pudukkottai	9569	1376	2539	13484	1122324	187163	88996	16124	242938	20929	1365262	109925	123446	10.92
17	Pasumpon	8246	1221	2112	11579	792845	273994	83526	18621	355644	24170	1148489	107696	120943	9.57
18	Ramanathapuram	6919	1421	1631	9971	859280	225880	58811	20758	293192	26944	1152472	85755	96303	10.35
19	Kamarajar	9879	1731	2453	14063	987321	484427	101367	37608	628786	48815	1616107	150182	168654	8.34
20	Tirunelveli	13475	1333	2190	16998	926970	710026	81563	59814	921614	77639	1848584	159202	178784	9.51
21	Chidambaranar	8886	1312	1411	11609	860701	527040	88630	42770	684098	55515	1544799	144145	161875	7.17
22	Kanyakumari	4269	654	853	5776	1294868	209614	116693	19717	272079	25593	1566947	142286	159787	3.61
	Total	**410583**	**71740**	**115498**	**597821**	**40681547**	**16502787**	**3015803**	**1175439**	**21420615**	**1525722**	**62102162**	**4541525**	**5100132**	**11.72**

TABLE 11.21

State-Wise Proportion of Government Expenditure on Social Security in NSDP, 1991-95

(per cent)

Sl. No.	State	Ele. Edu.	Level I Rl.&Ph.	F.W.	Nutrition	Total	Assets	Level II Emplt.	Total	Level I+II Promotional	Level III Protective	LevelI+II+III Total
(1)	(2)	(3)	(4)	(5)	(6)	(7=3+4+5+6)	(8)	(9)	(10=8+9)	(11)	(12)	(13=11+12)
1	Andhra Pradesh	1.19	0.15	0.18	0.04	1.56	0.29	0.29	0.58	2.14	0.19	2.33
2	Assam	2.92	0.22	0.20	0.04	3.38	0.23	0.07	0.30	3.68	0.20	3.88
3	Bihar	2.16	0.18	0.23	0.03	2.60	0.22	0.81	1.04	3.64	0.51	4.15
4	Gujarat	1.60	0.14	0.13	0.25	2.13	0.18	0.21	0.39	2.52	0.10	2.62
5	Haryana	0.99	0.11	0.11	0.08	1.29	0.07	0.10	0.17	1.46	0.63	2.09
6	Karnataka	1.59	0.04	0.17	0.16	1.95	0.22	0.21	0.43	2.39	0.44	2.83
7	Kerala	2.37	0.16	0.21	0.04	2.77	0.12	0.27	0.39	3.16	0.39	3.55
8	Maharashtra	0.73	0.10	0.09	0.04	0.95	0.04	0.29	0.33	1.28	0.15	1.44
9	Madhya Pradesh	1.81	0.18	0.17	0.06	2.22	0.12	0.49	0.61	2.83	0.21	3.04
10	Orissa	1.53	0.16	0.24	0.12	2.05	0.15	0.55	0.70	2.75	0.48	3.24
11	Punjab	0.72	0.16	0.10	0.00	0.98	0.02	0.07	0.09	1.07	0.26	1.33
12	Rajasthan	2.09	0.24	0.24	0.08	2.65	0.28	0.33	0.62	3.27	0.14	3.41
13	**Tamil Nadu**	**1.71**	**0.12**	**0.19**	**0.62**	**2.64**	**0.11**	**0.31**	**0.42**	**3.06**	**0.38**	**3.45**
14	Uttar Pradesh	1.67	0.22	0.25	0.02	2.16	0.22	0.43	0.65	2.82	0.23	3.04
15	West Bengal	1.16	0.14	0.13	0.02	1.45	0.10	0.31	0.41	1.86	0.21	2.07
16	Mean	1.46	0.15	0.17	0.11	1.89	0.15	0.33	0.48	2.37	0.26	2.63
17	Centre	0.02	0.00	0.01	0.00	0.03	0.02	0.04	0.07	0.10	0.05	0.15

Source: Computed from NIPFP Data Bank & Reserve Bank of India (1998), Report on Currency and Finance: 1997-98, Vol. II. Statistical Statements, p.6.

TABLE 11.22

State-Wise Proportion of Government Expenditure on Social Security in Total Revenue Expenditure, 1991-95

(per cent)

Sl. No.	*State*	*Level I* Ele. Edu.	*Level I* Rl.&Ph.	*Level I* F.W.	*Level I* Nutrition	*Level I* Total	*Level II* Assets	*Level II* Emplt.	*Level II* Total	*Level I+II* Promotional	*Level III* Protective	*Level I+II+III* Total
(1)	(2)	(3)	(4)	(5)	(6)	(7=3+4+5+6)	(8)	(9)	(10=8+9)	(11)	(12)	(13=11+12)
1	Andhra Pradesh	7.84	0.97	1.20	0.25	10.26	1.91	1.94	3.84	14.11	1.25	15.36
2	Assam	15.47	1.18	1.05	0.23	17.93	1.21	0.37	1.58	19.51	1.08	20.59
3	Bihar	11.48	0.98	1.20	0.15	13.81	1.18	4.32	5.50	19.31	2.73	22.04
4	Gujarat	10.55	0.95	0.86	1.68	14.04	1.19	1.35	2.54	16.58	0.64	17.22
5	Haryana	6.98	0.76	0.75	0.55	9.05	0.51	0.70	1.22	10.26	4.46	14.73
6	Karnataka	9.88	0.25	1.03	0.98	12.14	1.36	1.32	2.69	14.82	2.75	17.57
7	Kerala	12.57	0.84	1.09	0.20	14.71	0.64	1.43	2.07	16.77	2.05	18.82
8	Maharashtra	5.99	0.80	0.73	0.30	7.81	0.36	2.40	2.75	10.57	1.25	11.82
9	Madhya Pradesh	10.56	1.08	0.99	0.33	12.96	0.71	2.85	3.56	16.52	1.25	17.77
10	Orissa	8.04	0.85	1.26	0.63	10.77	0.79	2.88	3.67	14.44	2.54	16.98
11	Punjab	5.20	1.18	0.70	0.02	7.10	0.13	0.49	0.63	7.73	1.90	9.63
12	Rajasthan	11.20	1.26	1.30	0.44	14.21	1.52	1.79	3.32	17.52	0.76	18.28
13	**Tamil Nadu**	**9.05**	**0.64**	**1.03**	**3.26**	**13.99**	**0.60**	**1.63**	**2.23**	**16.22**	**2.03**	**18.25**
14	Uttar Pradesh	9.75	1.28	1.48	0.11	12.62	1.29	2.53	3.82	16.44	1.33	17.77
15	West Bengal	8.71	1.06	1.02	0.12	10.90	0.78	2.33	3.11	14.01	1.55	15.57
16	Mean	9.23	0.94	1.06	0.67	11.91	0.97	2.08	3.05	14.96	1.67	16.63
17	Centre	0.10	0.03	0.07	0.01	0.21	0.13	0.28	0.40	0.62	0.30	0.91

Source: Computed from NIPFP Data Bank.

with performance above 3 per cent of the SDP except for Kerala fall among the low income States. Comparisons of the performance of these States like Bihar, Orissa and Rajasthan with Tamil Nadu may not be meaningful. We can however, reasonably observe that the best performers are the middle income States of Kerala, Tamil Nadu and Karnataka in the same order.

A look at the break up of expenditure, component wise shows that Tamil Nadu's percentage expenditure on elementary education, rural public health and family welfare however around the average of the 15 States (Table 11.22). The States expenditure on nutrition at 0.62 per cent of NSDP and 3.26 per cent of Revenue expenditure is far ahead of average figures, confirming the State's priority in the area.

The proportion of expenditure on asset creation and employment generation schemes in Tamil Nadu are considerably less than the mean performance. Even discounting the higher percentages of the low income States, the performance of Tamil Nadu in these areas is very poor, ranking 11th among the 15 States studied. As regards protective schemes, Tamil Nadu again leads the group, ranking fifth in performance with three out of the higher four States being low income States. The performance of Haryana in this category is remarkable and will need further analysis.

The same study came to conclusion that there seems to be a trade off between the various types of social security expenditure among the States, "with not much evidence of a balanced package of promotional and protective measures being implemented in any of the States".

Yet among the major States, it is clear that Tamil Nadu has done well in the area of protective social security. In the area of nutrition and women's micro credit, the State has become a model for the country to replicate. But its efforts in the area of asset creation and employment generation are inadequate even according to Indian standards.

The Path Forward

The State has to evolve a comprehensive social security policy, spelling out a minimum entitlement for its 'citizens'. This policy will have to specifically address the needs of the poor subjected to sudden changes in their lifestyle due to natural and man made causes. A database will have to be created regarding all those who live below the poverty line and all those who have a danger of falling beneath it. A very strong rural income generation scheme, in the lines of an Employment Guarantee Scheme will have to be put in place - which will automatically provide succour to

TABLE 11.23

State-Wise Share of Government on Components of Social Security in Total Social Security Expenditure, 1991-95

(per cent)

Sl. No.	*State*	*Level I*					*Level II*			*Level I+II*	*Level III*	*Level I+II+III*
		Ele. Edu.	*Rl.&Ph.*	*F.W.*	*Nutrition*	*Total*	*Assets*	*Emplt.*	*Total*	*Promotional*	*Protective*	*Total*
(1)	(2)	(3)	(4)	(5)	(6)	(7=3+4+5+6)	(8)	(9)	(10=8+9)	(11)	(12)	(13=11+12)
1	Andhra Pradesh	51.76	6.29	7.80	1.63	66.79	12.42	12.61	25.03	91.81	8.19	15.36
2	Assam	75.11	5.74	5.10	1.14	87.09	5.87	1.79	7.67	94.75	5.25	20.59
3	Bihar	52.09	4.44	5.43	0.70	62.65	5.37	19.58	24.95	87.60	12.40	22.04
4	Gujarat	61.28	5.53	4.97	9.75	81.53	6.91	7.86	14.76	96.29	3.71	17.22
5	Haryana	47.42	5.13	5.12	3.77	61.44	3.48	4.77	8.25	69.69	30.31	14.73
6	Karnataka	56.23	1.42	5.85	5.58	69.08	2.76	7.54	10.29	84.37	10.63	17.57
7	Kerala	66.78	4.47	5.82	1.08	78.14	3.39	7.58	10.97	89.12	10.88	18.82
8	Maharashtra	50.62	6.74	6.15	2.54	66.10	3.03	20.27	23.30	89.40	10.60	11.82
9	Madhya Pradesh	59.43	6.06	5.55	1.88	72.92	4.02	16.03	20.05	92.97	7.03	17.77
10	Orissa	47.31	4.99	7.43	3.70	63.43	4.66	16.95	21.61	85.04	14.96	16.98
11	Punjab	54.02	12.23	7.32	0.16	73.73	1.36	5.14	6.49	80.22	19.78	9.63
12	Rajasthan	61.28	6.89	7.11	2.42	77.71	8.34	9.79	18.13	95.84	4.16	18.28
13	**Tamil Nadu**	**49.60**	**3.53**	**5.62**	**17.88**	**76.63**	**3.30**	**8.94**	**12.24**	**88.87**	**11.13**	**18.25**
14	Uttar Pradesh	54.87	7.22	8.30	0.63	71.03	7.26	14.23	21.49	92.52	7.48	17.77
15	West Bengal	55.99	6.78	6.53	0.77	70.06	4.98	14.98	19.96	90.02	9.98	15.57
16	Mean	55.52	5.66	6.40	4.05	71.63	5.81	12.51	18.32	89.94	10.06	16.63
17	Centre	11.44	3.14	7.46	1.26	23.30	14.07	30.17	44.24	67.54	32.46	0.91

Source: Social Security Expenditure from NIPFP Data Bank.

those who are placed in vulnerable situations. As regards the aged, a contributory model pension scheme can be thought of, so that the increasing needs can be met. The State will also have to put in place a health insurance system at reasonable cost for its middle class in order to support the existing services provided in the public sector.

Today's technological advances make it possible to think of innovative solutions for successful contributory pension and health insurance schemes. At the same time, the State cannot absolve itself of its liability towards the poorest and the destitute. A need based assessment will have to be done of the coverage required under the existing schemes and funds provided wherever required. The quantum of pension should be constantly upgraded to see that minimum basic needs are met. Last, a special effort must be made to make the administration of the schemes more transparent and simple to see that the benefits reach those for whom they were intended. NGOs and CBOs should be used to the maximum extent possible to see that this exercise is a success.

With a little forethought and financial investment Tamil Nadu can hope to become the first State to put in place a comprehensive social safety net for its people.

Chapter 12

Financial Services Sector of Tamil Nadu

Financial Services Sector

With the opening up of the economy and the advances in communication and information technology (IT), the financial services sector has seen rapid changes in recent times. With increasing globalisation, the distinction between different segments of financial intermediaries is gradually getting blurred, which has resulted in the need for prudent financial practices so as to ensure financial stability. This chapter describes the various constituents and the recent developments of the financial services sector.

Banks

As in any developing economy like that of India, the mainstay of financial intermediation has been the banking sector. The scheduled banking structure in India consists of banks that are listed in the Second Schedule of the Reserve Bank of India Act, 1934. These scheduled banks comprise of both public and private commercial banks, regional rural banks, urban co-operative banks and State co-operative banks.

During the decade 1991-2001, the Indian banking sector has witnessed several changes in the nature of banking activity, regulation and use of technology. As a response to these changes, the Indian banking sector responded to the emerging challenges of increased competition and uncertainties. While the prudential and supervisory norms are being brought in conformity with international best practices to further strengthen the Indian banking system, the ongoing reforms provide greater operational flexibility to commercial banks. In their business strategy, commercial banks have put more emphasis on product diversification, customer orientation, thrust towards retail banking, adoption of IT for improved service, better management information systems (MIS) and risk management, and strategic mergers and acquisitions, across bank groups.

Recent Developments in Commercial Banking

Thrust on Retail Banking

The retail banking portfolio encompasses deposit and asset-linked products as well as other financial services offered to individuals for personal consumption. Retail banking is, increasingly, viewed by banks as an attractive market segment with opportunities for growth with profits. The products offered in the retail banking segment are mostly in the personal finance segment such as housing loans, consumer durable loans, auto loans, credit cards and educational loans. The loan amounts could, typically, range between Rs. 2 lakh and Rs. 100 lakh. The loans are generally for a duration of three years to seven years, with housing loans granted for a longer duration of 15 years. Credit card is another rapidly growing sub-segment of this product group.

The growth in retail banking has been facilitated by growth in banking technology and automation of banking processes to enable extension of reach and rationalisation of costs. Automatic Teller Machines (ATMs) have emerged as an alternative banking channel, which facilitate low-cost transaction *vis-à-vis* traditional branches. It also has the advantage of reducing the branch traffic and enables banks with small networks to offset the traditional disadvantages by increasing their reach and spread. The increased use of ATMs by foreign banks and private sector banks has helped these banks to compete with Public Sector Banks (PSBs) by enabling them to expand their reach and to contain costs. The use of ATM technology is quite low in the case of PSBs and the old private sector banks. Given the fact that the PSBs are in the process of rationalisation of staff strength (especially in the light of the VRS, which closed in March 2001), introduction of ATMs would help facilitate improved customer service by these banks. Some of the factors, which inhibit the rapid growth of the ATMs, are the absence of a shared payments network, the high cost of ATM cards and machines and poor telecommunication infrastructure.

Entry into Insurance

The Government of India Notification specifying insurance as a permissible form of business under Section 6(1)(O) of the Banking Regulation Act, 1949, was issued on August 3, 2000. Based on this, detailed guidelines were issued by RBI on August 9, 2000. Since then, State Bank of India has been permitted to set up a life insurance subsidiary, on a risk participation basis with 74 per cent equity holding. Jammu & Kashmir Bank Ltd. and Vysya Bank Ltd. have been accorded approval to contribute 25 per cent and 49 per cent, respectively, to the equity of insurance joint ventures on risk participation basis. Punjab National Bank and Vijaya Bank have been permitted to make strategic investment to the extent of 15 per cent and 8 per cent, respectively, in the life and non-life insurance joint venture and in a distribution and services company. Citibank, American Express, Standard Chartered Bank, HSBC, ABN-Amro, HDFC Bank and Deutsche Bank have been given 'in principle' approval to act as corporate agents of insurance companies for distribution of insurance products on fee basis. All these approvals have been granted, subject to the banks obtaining necessary clearance from the Insurance Regulatory and Development Authority (IRDA). In addition, Banks have also been permitted to act as a distribution channel for insurance products.

Co-operative Banking

Co-operative credit institutions occupy an important position in the financial system of the economy in terms of their reach, volume of operations and the purpose they serve. Rural co-operative banks play a pivotal role in the rural credit delivery system with credit co-operatives forming almost 70 per cent of the rural credit outlets. Urban co-operative banks (UCBs), on the other hand, aim at mobilisation of savings from the middle-and low-income urban groups and purvey credit towards the weaker sections. The majority of credit from UCBs is channeled towards the priority sector segments.

The objective of co-operative banking is to create enduring and sustainable financial institutions, which remain responsive to the credit needs of the weaker sections. Concerns have been expressed that the financial health of a large number of co-operative credit institutions is extremely fragile. Keeping in view the primacy of the role of the credit co-operatives and the need to review and improve the functioning of the credit co-operatives, various groups and committees have been constituted from time to time.

Some of the common financial problems faced by the co-operative credit institutions, which have been identified by these committees, include the following:

- Low capital base
- Low levels of diversification in business operations
- Inadequate loan appraisal systems and credit planning
- Mounting over-dues and non-performing assets (NPAs) and
- Poor recovery performance.

In order to address these problems, the Committees have made several recommendations that indicate:

- Functioning of co-operative credit institutions should be member-driven and democratic;
- Making the co-operative credit system sustainable and the underlying institutions viable, requires the introduction of professionalism in the operations of these institutions, and they need to be run on the basis of sound business principles. Co-operative banks need to be more competitive and devise ways to adapt to the new business ambience which has arisen out of the financial reform process;
- Revamping and streamlining the regulation and supervision mechanisms of the co-operative credit institutions need urgent attention. There is need to explore possibilities of establishing a suitable unified agency to supervise the co-operative credit institutions; and
- Healthy and transparent functioning of the financial system requires prudential norms. Compared to the commercial banks, the applicability of such principles for the co-operative banks remains rather limited, especially in the context of rural co-operative credit institutions. Over time, the co-operative credit

system also has to be brought under the purview of the prudential norms.

The government is considering these measures and necessary action needs to be initiated by amending the various Statutes concerned.

Non-Banking Financial Companies (NBFCs)

NBFCs have been the subject of focused attention during the nineties. In particular, the rapid growth of NBFCs, especially in the ninenties, has led to a gradual blurring of dividing lines between banks and NBFCs, with the exception of the exclusive privilege that commercial banks enjoy in the issuance of cheques. Simplified sanction procedures, orientation towards customers, attractive rates of return on deposits and flexibility and timeliness in meeting the credit needs of specified sectors (like equipment leasing and hire purchase), are some of the factors enhancing the attractiveness of this sector.

Owing to certain disquieting developments in the NBFC sector, the RBI Act was amended in 1997, providing for a comprehensive regulatory framework for NBFCs. A new concept of "public deposits" (meaning deposits received from public including shareholders in the case of public limited companies and unsecured debentures/bonds other than those issued to companies, banks and financial institutions) was introduced for the purpose of focused supervision of NBFCs accepting such deposits.

The RBI (Amendment) Act, 1997 has provisions for compulsory registration of all NBFCs with the RBI, irrespective of their holding of public deposits, for commencing and carrying on business, minimum entry point norms, maintenance of a portion of deposits in liquid assets, creation of a Reserve Fund and transfer 20 per cent of profit after tax (PAT), annually, to the Reserve Fund. The Amendment Act also conferred powers on RBI to issue directions to companies and its auditors, prohibit deposit acceptance and alienation of assets by companies and effect winding up of companies. The registration is compulsory for all NBFCs, irrespective of their holding of public deposits.

Supervision of NBFCs

The supervisory framework for NBFCs is based on three criteria:

(a) the size of the NBFC;

(b) the type of activity performed; and

(c) the acceptance or otherwise of public deposits.

Towards this end, the RBI has put in place, a four-pronged supervisory strategy comprising:

- on-site inspection, based on the CAMELS (capital, assets, management, earnings, liquidity, systems and procedures) methodology;
- computerised off-site surveillance through periodic control returns;
- an effective market intelligence network; and
- a system of submission of exception reports by auditors of NBFCs.

The regulation and supervision is comprehensive for companies accepting or holding public deposits to ensure protection of interests of depositors. Companies holding or accepting public deposits are required to comply with all the directions on acceptance of public deposits, prudential norms and liquid assets, and should submit periodic returns to the RBI.

NBFCs, not holding or accepting public deposits, are regulated and supervised in a limited manner. They are required to comply only with prudential norms relating to income recognition, accounting standards, asset classification and provisioning against bad and doubtful debts. They are less frequently inspected. Such companies are presently not required to submit any returns to the RBI. Thus, market intelligence and auditors' inspection reports constitute important supervisory tools in respect of these companies.

Financial Institutions (FIs)

All-India financial institutions (FIs) constitute an important segment of the financial system, which cater for the medium, long-term financing and, of late, working capital requirements, of varied sectors in the economy. The RBI regulates and supervises these institutions, keeping in view the need for enhancing the transparency in their performance and maintaining systemic stability. The supervision of All-India FIs by the RBI is of recent origin. It may be emphasised that the scope and coverage of the FIs inspection are very limited, unlike that of NBFCs and are not as rigorous as that of banks.

FIs could be broadly categorised into All-India level financial institutions (AIFIs), state-level institutions and other institutions, with the AIFIs being the most dominant in terms of assets and range of operations. The progressive deregulation of financial markets, the disintermediation pressures arising therefrom and the diversification in portfolio preferences of investors have warranted growing sophistication and innovation in financial services. These developments have necessitated introduction of policy measures for greater transparency in operations, better monitoring and more comprehensive regulation. In response to the same, the extant guidelines in respect of prudential supervision and regulation of FIs have been reviewed and new guidelines have been introduced by the RBI in various areas of operations of FIs.

Housing Finance Companies (HFCs)

In India, investment in housing is financed mainly by own sources or from informal credit market. The formal housing finance institutions contribute only 15 per cent to 20 per cent of housing investments in the country (NSS, 44th Round, 1988-89). However, within the formal housing finance sector, the conventional sources of housing finance in India have been the public sector institutions. Over the years, they were found to be grossly inadequate to meet the requirements of the new investments and maintenance of housing and habitat systems. Accordingly, since the mid-eighties, efforts have been directed at the development of housing finance institutions to meet the large resource gap that exists for housing finance in the country.

The formal segment of housing finance includes funding provided by the Central and State governments and funds from financial institutions like GIC, LIC, commercial banks and specialised housing finance institutions and cooperative banks. HUDCO was set up in April 1970 as an apex techno-finance organisation in order to provide loans and technical support to State and city-level organisations. Almost all the States have set up Housing Boards in order to facilitate the implementation of the social housing schemes.

The second formal tier of housing finance consists of insurance corporations, commercial banks and housing finance companies. In 1976, the RBI issued its first set of housing finance guidelines to scheduled commercial banks for the benefit of weaker sections of the society. At present, banks are required to extend up to 3 per cent of incremental deposits for housing finance in a financial year. This apart, the financial market for housing includes HFCs, which provide the bulk of housing finance. Although there are around 400 HFCs in operation, the market is dominated by a few big players. In recognition of the need for developing a network of specialised housing finance institutions in the country, the National Housing Bank (NHB) was set up in July, 1988 as a wholly-owned subsidiary of the RBI under the National Housing Bank Act, 1987, to function as an apex bank for housing finance. NHB regulates HFCs, refinances their operations and expands the spread of housing finance to different income groups all over the country, while functioning within the overall framework of the housing policy. More than 95 per cent of disbursements are accounted for by only 29 leading HFCs having refinance facility from the National Housing Bank (NHB).

Venture Capital (VC)

With the onset of new economy companies in the areas of Information Technology, communication and entertainment, there emerged another stream of specialised finance companies, which invested in start-up ventures. The VCs invest in the early stage of the enterprise and solely aim at making huge capital gains on the securities in which they have invested once the early-stage companies establish themselves and grow to achieve sufficient market and business size. In addition to the financial assistance, the VCs provide management expertise to the entrepreneurs in establishing their start-up ventures.

VCs are primarily promoted by FIs and High Networth Individuals (HNIs). The VCs have a corpus fund through which they invest in different ventures. The objective is to have a balanced portfolio of investments that would yield high capital gains in short periods of time.

There are several foreign VCs that have a presence in India and have made investments in several ventures. However, the main Indian VCs are the ones promoted by ICICI and IFCI, namely, ICICI Ventures and IVCF. Some of the other Indian VCs include Canbank Venture Capital Fund, IL&FS Venture Capital Fund, and SIDBI Venture Capital Fund. In addition to these, there are several state level VCs, promoted by State Finance Corporations

Performance of the Financial Services Sector of Tamil Nadu

An overview of the past performance of the various segments of the financial services sector is presented in this chapter.

Contribution of Financial Services Sector to State Income

The contribution of the Services Sector to the State Income (Net State Domestic Product - NSDP) has been more than 40 per cent during the years 1993-94 to

1999-2000 (Table 12.1). The share of the services sector in NSDP has grown from 41.5 per cent in 1993-94 to 51.2 per cent in 1999-2000. The share of banking and insurance services in the total services sector which, primarily, represents the financial services sector has also steadily increased from 14 per cent in 1993-94 to 19.2 per cent in 1999-2000, registering a Compounded Annual Growth Rate (CAGR) of 24.85 per cent.

TABLE 12.1

Banking and Insurance Services Contribution to State Income

(Rs. Crore)

	1993-94	*1994-95*	*1995-96*	*1996-97*	*1997-98*	*1998-99*	*1999-2000*
Banking & Insurance*	3010	3830	5264	7771	8863	10042	11397
Services Sector*	21447	26097	31550	37986	45884	53023	59308
NSDP*	51648	61495	70343	79781	93308	105862	115644
Banking & Insurance as per cent of NSDP	5.83%	6.23%	7.48%	9.74%	9.50%	9.49%	9.86%

Source: Department of Economics & Statistics, Chennai
(*All figures at current prices).

As seen from Table 12.1, the contribution of the banking and insurance sector to the NSDP has risen from 5.83 per cent in 1993-94 to 9.86 per cent in 1999-2000.

Employment Potential

The employment that is provided by the financial services sector is quite substantial. Though sufficient data are not available for the whole of the sector, the number of people employed by the commercial banks alone was 80,886 in 1990-91 and 85,228 in 2000-01.

Tamil Nadu accounts for about 8.3 per cent to 8.5 per cent of the employment provided by this segment at the national level. Considering the other financial services segments like FIs, NBFCs, chit funds, nidhis and insurance companies, this sector is one of the major employment providers in the State.

Banks

Scheduled Commercial Banks (SCBs)

In Tamil Nadu, at the end of December 2001, there were 68 SCBs, including 27 public sector banks, 25 private sector banks, 13 foreign banks and 3 Regional Rural Banks (RRBs). Over the period 1990-91 to 2000-01, the number of bank branches of SCBs has gone up from 4283 to 4946. The proportion of these branches in terms of their location was 37 per cent in the rural areas, 25 per cent in semi-urban, 17 per cent in urban areas and 21 per cent in metropolitan areas.

During the period 1990-91 to 2000-01, the aggregate deposit of these SCBs has grown from Rs. 11231 crore to Rs. 63488 crore, registering a CAGR of 18.91 per cent (Table 12.2). This amounts to 6.7 per cent of the all India aggregate deposits. Term deposit forms the major chunk of aggregate deposit, at 64 per cent, followed by savings deposit, at 24 per cent and current deposit, at 12 per cent.

The total bank credit disbursed during the same period has grown at a CAGR of 17.81 per cent from Rs. 11169 crore to Rs. 57518 crore. This accounts for 10.5 per cent of the total bank credit disbursed at the national level. Industry accounts for about 50 per cent of the total bank credit followed by trade and personal loans. Agriculture accounts for 9 per cent of the total credit advanced. The composition of the total bank credit in terms of sectoral distribution, during the year 1999-2000 is as indicated in Figure 12.1.

FIGURE 12.1

Sectoral Distribution of Total Bank Credit in Tamil Nadu (1999-2000)

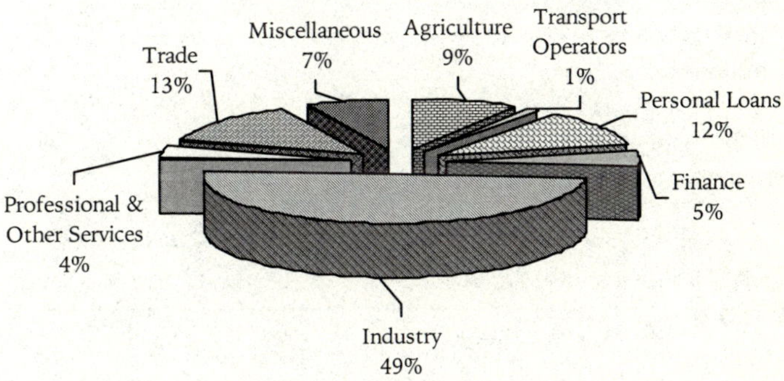

Source: RBI Banking Statistics

As indicated in Table 12.2, Tamil Nadu is one of the States that have the highest credit-deposit ratio, of over 90 per cent.

TABLE 12.2

Scheduled Commercial Banks – Credit and Deposits

(Rs. Crore)

	1990-91	*1995-96*	*1996-97*	*1997-98*	*1998-99*	*1999-2000*	*2000-01*
Deposits	11231.1	29096.4	33266.0	39975.3	45857.2	55174.0	63488.0
Credit	11168.9	27469.3	32040.3	37036.2	41390.5	48252.1	57518.0
C-D Ratio	99.44%	94.41%	96.32%	92.65%	90.26%	87.45%	90.60%

Source: RBI Banking Statistics.

The investments of SCBs in State government securities and other government instruments that partially fund the developmental expenditure of the State has registered a CAGR of 18 per cent during the period 1990-91 to 2000-01. The details of the investments are indicated in Table 12.3. However, these investments as a percentage of the total investments made by SCB's at the national level, has fallen from 7.22 per cent in 1990-91 to 6.2 per cent in 1999-2000.

TABLE 12.3

Investments by SCB's in State Government and Related Instruments

(Rs. Crore)

Instruments	*1991*	*1996*	*1997*	*1998*	*1999*	*2000*
State Govt. Securities	889.9	1843.0	2020.0	2256.4	2404.2	2738.1
Regional Rural Banks	0.5	0.9	1.1	3.6	5.9	5.2
Co-operative Institutions	18.6	13.1	13.0	12.9	13.6	14.5
State Electricity Boards	515.3	597.0	548.8	520.4	531.0	589.1
Municipalities, Mun. Corps & Port Trust	30.4	33.4	33.7	32.9	20.3	15.2
State Financial Corporations	131.8	213.1	208.1	208.8	174.4	179.7
Housing Boards	38.4	56.3	53.3	53.6	37.9	39.2
State Industrial Dev. Corpn.	55.8	77.4	86.0	92.9	130.6	154.4
Road Transport	0.0	0.1	0.0	0.0	0.0	0.0
Other Govt. & Quasi Govt. Orgns	14.2	19.7	15.0	28.4	90.8	150.1
Tamil Nadu Total	**1694.9**	**2853.9**	**2979.0**	**3209.9**	**3408.7**	**3885.4**
All-India Total	**23491.2**	**39401.0**	**42752.5**	**49296.8**	**53754.3**	**62642.0**

Source: RBI Banking Statistics.

As seen from Table 12.3, the investments of SCB's has increased only in State Government Securities and has shown a declining trend in most of the other state entities. This clearly reflects the weak performance of these State entities, resulting in the SCBs shying away from them. Also, the increase in the SCBs' investments in State Government Securities is partially due to the statutory requirements as prescribed by the RBI, proportional to the increase in the business of the SCBs.

With increased competition from the private sector banks and the computerisation of processes therein, the SCB's are currently in the phase of consolidation of their branch networks. In the recent times, the private banks segment has also seen some mergers and acquisitions (ICICI Bank – Bank of Madura, Standard Chartered – ANZ Grindlays Bank). These banks are now moving towards universal banking so as to act as a one-stop shop for all the financial needs of their customers.

Urban Co-operative Banks (UCBs)

Tamil Nadu has been one of the pioneer States of the co-operative movement. The first Urban Cooperative Credit Society was established in Kancheepuram in 1902. During the period 1990-91 to 2000-01, the number of branches of UCBs has grown from 329 to 451 (Table 12.4). However, the number of new banks opened, in this segment, has been negligible compared with the other southern states.

During the last couple of years, the UCBs have witnessed a spurt in the deposits, which can be attributed to the diversion of deposits from the NBFCs. However, due to regulatory limitations and the dual control of RBI and the State government, the performance of the UCBs has not been impressive.

TABLE 12.4

Performance of UCBs in Tamil Nadu

	1990-91	*1996-97*	*1997-98*	*1998-99*	*1999-2000*	*2000-01*
No. of Branches	329	394	368	386	431	451
Deposits (Rs. Crore)	386.0	882.9	1058.2	1502.1	2008.5	2673.3
Loans & Advances (Rs. Crore)	328.8	694.5	827.1	955.3	1319.0	1714.9
Credit-Deposit Ratio	85.18%	78.65%	78.16%	63.59%	65.67%	64.15%

Source: RBI Banking Statistics.

This is also reflected in the drop in credit-deposit ratio among these banks. In addition, factors like poor governance, lack of professionalism in managing funds and training opportunities have resulted in the under-performance of these banks.

State and District Co-operative Banks

The number of branches of State and District co-operative banks in the State of Tamil Nadu has grown at a CAGR of 4 per cent, from 623 in 1994-95 to 757 in 1999-2000. As per the latest data available from RBI for these banks, the trend has been a decline in the credit to deposit ratio among both the State Co-operative Banks and District Central Co-operative Banks. The credit and deposit figures are indicated in Table 12.5.

TABLE 12.5

Performance of State and District Co-operative Banks in Tamil Nadu

(Rs. Crore)

	State Co-op Banks		*District Co-op Banks*	
	1998-99	1999-2000	1998-99	1999-2000
Credit	1261.6	1199.7	4471.8	5013.6
Deposits	2239.6	2676.1	4839.3	6029.9
Credit-Deposit Ratio	56.33%	44.83%	92.41%	83.15%

Source: RBI Banking Statistics.

Non Banking Financial Companies

During the last five years, the NBFCs have witnessed major changes due to the enforcement of strict regulations by the RBI to curb unscrupulous operators in this segment. In order to protect the interests of depositors and also to quell fly-by-night operators, the RBI has put in place prudential norms for this sector. However, some of the good NBFCs have had to face the brunt of the new regulations, primarily in pruning the deposit levels and this has drastically affected their performance. In spite of the shake out in this segment, Tamil Nadu has to its credit some of the best NBFCs operating in the country such as Sundaram Finance Ltd., and Cholamandalam Investment and Finance Company Ltd.

At present, there are about 2650 finance companies in Tamil Nadu that are under the control of Department of Non-Banking Supervision at RBI office at Chennai. The enforcement of prudential norms for the NBFCs has led to a decline in the number of NBFCs operating in the State and also the quantum of deposits held by them. The recent trend in the number of reporting NBFCs at RBI, Chennai and the public deposits held by them is given in Table 12.6.

TABLE 12.6

Public Deposits & Number of NBFCs in Tamil Nadu

	1997-98	*1998-99*	*1999-2000*
Number of Reporting NBFCs	466	408	340
Public Deposits Held (Rs. crore)	4715	3843	2577

Source: Report on Trend & Progress of Banking in India, RBI.

In order to safeguard the interests of depositors, the Tamil Nadu State Government has enacted the Tamil Nadu Protection of Interest of Depositors (in Financial Establishments) Act, 1997 and a Special Court, as required by the Act has been constituted, which is in operation since 1998.

Chit Funds

Tamil Nadu has been the seat of traditional finance companies like Chit Funds, Nidhis and Benefit Funds. Chit funds fall under the RBI classification of Miscellaneous Non-Banking Companies (MNBCs). There were 4225 Chit Fund Companies doing chit business in Tamil Nadu as on December 31, 1996. The number of chit groups conducted by them were 37,598 with the security deposit value of Rs.318.15 crore. The current numbers are estimated at more than 5,000 registered companies, conducting over 50,000 chit groups and the turnover is expected to be in the region of Rs.12,000 crore to Rs.15,000 crore. These companies are governed by the Tamil Nadu Chit Fund Act, 1984.

The State Government has put a comprehensive mechanism in place to administer this segment. The Inspector General of Registration is the Registrar of Chits. One Additional Registrar of Chits and one personal assistant (Chits) are in the headquarters to assist the Registrar of Chits. The Deputy Inspectors General of Registration, under the Registration Act, 1908 are appointed as Joint Registrar of Chits in their respective jurisdiction, under Chit Funds Act, 1982. Further, there are 47 Sub-Registrars working as Inspector of Chits to attend to the chit fund work in the districts. There are four Special Chit Arbitrators at Madras (North), Madras (South) and Madras (Central) and Coimbatore for chit arbitration cases.

Nidhis

Tamil Nadu has been the pioneer of Nidhi companies, classified by RBI as Mutual Benefit Financial Company (MBFCs). These companies are regulated by the Department of Company Affairs (DCA) and are registered under the Companies Act but with some exemptions considering the nature of their business.

Traditionally, these companies have been very conservative in their lending norms and credit is advanced only against jewellery and mortgages. There are several Nidhi companies in the State that are more than a century old. However, in this segment a number of companies had mushroomed during the second half of the ninenties. The current number of Nidhi and Mutual Benefit Companies in Tamil Nadu is estimated at more than 800. The size of the operations of these companies is estimated to be about Rs.1,200 crore to

TABLE 12.7

Assistance by All Financial Institutions Sanctioned and Disbursed in Tamil Nadu

	Sanctions						*Disbursements*					
	1995-96	*1996-97*	*1997-98*	*1998-99*	*1999-2000*	*2000-01*	*1995-96*	*1996-97*	*1997-98*	*1998-99*	*1999-2000*	*2000-01*
ICICI	2085.8	1213.85	1980.9	3573.2	3801.9	2928.8	667.3	1030.24	858.2	1470.4	1922.4	2135.6
IFCI	630.8	513.05	525.6	510.9	54.6	51.5	421.9	481.23	474.5	423.2	157.4	94.2
IDBI	1413.2	1181.87	2839.6	2532	3368.1	2381.2	1281	1002.56	1001.6	1407.4	1213.5	1201.1
SIDBI	595.6	571.58	532.7	509.4	557.1	432	503.2	468.91	451.3	363.3	439.1	257.4
IIBI	63.3	57.73	151.1	228.1	349.6	326.9	49.1	44.48	44.6	126.5	138.6	208.1
SFCs	632.7	426.8	235.7	151.5	244.3	279.9	320.7	341.1	192.9	117.7	172.8	200.2
SIDCs	104.5	110	41.1	39.8	28.3	0.7	63.2	68.1	40.7	27.5	10.3	11.5
EXIM	60.7	20.48	64.1	55.5	166.7	33.1	58.3	32.2	42.7	22.3	67.4	50.5
Total	5586.5	4095.36	6370.8	7600.4	8570.6	6434.2	3364.7	3468.82	3106.5	3958.3	4121.6	4158.7
All INDIA	**58242.8**	**43381.89**	**73268**	**79524.8**	**98245.4**	**110642.4**	**37454.9**	**36772.05**	**52517.9**	**55564.8**	**64402.6**	**72307.5**

Source: Development Banking Report 2000-01.

Rs. 1,400 crore, covering about 10 million members/ subscribers.

During the late-ninenties, several of the Nidhi companies who did not follow conservative lending norms defaulted on their public deposit, resulting in the government clamping stringent regulations to check the unscrupulous elements. The DCA had constituted the Sabhanayagam Committee to look into the regulatory framework. The Committee had tabled its Report and the latest regulatory norms have been notified by the DCA in July 2001.

Accordingly, strict measures in terms of asset portfolio composition, net-owned funds, minimum equity from members', etc., along with prudential norms for asset classification and NPA recognition have been imposed. The timeframe for compliance of these norms has been extended to the maximum of two years for the existing companies, but is to be with immediate effect for the new entrants.

However, the Nidhi companies that have been around for many years are of the opinion that the regulations should not be imposed on them with such a short time frame for compliance. As these companies have substantial deposits and outstanding credit, they feel that sufficient time should be given to them in order to comply with these regulations, as it would be impossible for them to make changes in their asset portfolio, equity base, etc., within a short time.

Institutional Finance

During the last decade, the assistance disbursed by the FIs saw a declining trend and reached the lowest during the years 1996-97 to 1998-99. This may reflect the rather subdued industrial activity of the State during the late-ninenties. However, the disbursements have improved from 1998-99 and have seen a growth of 27 per cent, year-on-year (yoy) during 1998-99 and about 8 per cent yoy during 1999-2000. The details of assistance sanctioned and disbursed by various FIs are given in Table 12.7.

As seen from Table 12.7, the State's share of the total disbursements by the FIs has decreased from 9.1 per cent in 1995-96 to 5.8 per cent in 2000-01, reflecting a decline in the number of new industrial projects financed by them.

The disbursements have declined in the years 1995-96 to 1997-98 during which period, the implementation rate of investment projects has also been low. The details of the investments sanctioned and the implementation percentages for Tamil Nadu are given in Appendix III. However, the disbursements have shown an increase during the years 1999-2000 and 2000-01 during which years, the implementation of projects has improved.

Insurance

Tamil Nadu has 261 offices of Life Insurance Corporation of India (LIC). At present there are about 95,000 LIC agents in the State. LIC has issued 24.32 lakh policies during 1999-2000 with the sum assured being Rs. 13,242.32 crore.

The General Insurance Company United India Insurance Company Ltd. (UII), a subsidiary of General Insurance Corporation of India, is headquartered in

Chennai and has a network of three regional offices, 50 divisional offices and 90 branch offices in Tamil Nadu. The number of policies sold and the premium collected is given in Table 12.8. The premium collected has grown at a CAGR of 10.11 per cent during the period 1991-92 to 2000-01.

TABLE 12.8

Performance of UII in Tamil Nadu

	1991-92	1995-96	1996-97	1997-98	1998-99	1999-2000	2000-01
Premium (Rs. Crore)	134.79	231.35	264.67	282.9	319.12	326.22	320.7
Policies Sold	846384	807691	1090340	972454	998261	1087691	1136637

Source: UII Head Office, Chennai.

In addition to the resource mobilisation, both LIC, and GIC and its subsidiaries have invested in the corporate sector in the State. The sanctions and disbursements made by LIC and GIC are indicated in Table 12.9. The disbursements have registered a CAGR of 64 per cent, during the period 1995-96 to 2000-01.

With the deregulation of the insurance sector, Tamil Nadu has also witnessed the entry of private players in the insurance area and Chennai has been the base for the insurance venture of Sundaram Finance in tie-up with Royal Sun of the UK, Royal Sundaram Alliance Insurance.

Venture Capital

The two main Indian Venture Capital firms, IVCF and ICICI Ventures, have made investments in several ventures in Tamil Nadu. The details of the sanctions and disbursements made by the two VCs are indicated in Table 12.10.

As seen from the above Table, the sanctions and disbursements of IVCF have fallen, over the period, due to the financial problems of the promoter IFCI. However, the disbursements of ICICI Ventures in Tamil Nadu have grown at a CAGR of 46 per cent during the period 1995-96 to 2000-01. The share of Tamil Nadu in the total disbursements made by these VCs has increased from 9.7 per cent in 1995-96 to 21.5 per cent in 2000-01, indicating that the State has been able to attract more new economy companies to set up their operations in Tamil Nadu.

Housing Finance

As per the report on Trend and Progress in Housing in India, June 1999, published by NHB, there were 368 housing finance companies in India, of which 100 HFCs reported to the National Housing Bank. Among these 100 HFCs, 29 are refinanced by the NHB and the

TABLE 12.9

Financial Assistance Sanctioned and Disbursed by LIC & GIC in Tamil Nadu

(Rs. Crore)

	Sanctions						*Disbursements*					
	1995-96	*1996-97*	*1997-98*	*1998-99*	*1999-2000*	*2000-01*	*1995-96*	*1996-97*	*1997-98*	*1998-99*	*1999-2000*	*2000-01*
LIC	116.4	129.41	120.2	554.4	195.0	188.2	19.3	135.44	23.4	36.7	187.3	386.9
GIC	65.6	64.45	40.4	75.6	75.0	19.9	15.0	71.50	34.0	16.4	22.9	22.1
Total	181.9	193.86	160.5	629.9	270.0	208.2	34.3	206.94	57.4	53.1	210.2	409.0

Source: Development Banking Report 2000-01.

TABLE 12.10

Financial Assistance Sanctioned and Disbursed in Tamil Nadu by Venture Capital Funds

(Rs. Crore)

	Sanctions						*Disbursements*					
	1995-96	*1996-97*	*1997-98*	*1998-99*	*1999-2000*	*2000-01*	*1995-96*	*1996-97*	*1997-98*	*1998-99*	*1999-2000*	*2000-01*
ICICI	10.7	0.85	2.0	7.8	20.6	43.1	6.0	7.18	1.6	5.9	17.3	40.4
IVCF	1.0	2.50	0.0	0.0	0.0	0.0	0.0	0.75	1.1	0.3	0.0	0.0
Total	11.7	3.35	2.0	7.8	20.6	43.1	6.0	7.93	2.7	6.1	17.3	40.4
All INDIA	**64.4**	**33.30**	**28.7**	**21.1**	**185.4**	**207.3**	**62.3**	**45.33**	**37.8**	**19.5**	**132.9**	**188.2**

Source: Development Banking Report 2000-01.

loans advanced by these 29 HFCs accounts for more than 90 per cent of the total housing loans disbursed in India.

Tamil Nadu has 44 branches of these NHB-approved HFCs in the State. In addition to the HFCs, housing is also financed by the Apex Co-operative Housing Federations (ACHFs). During the years 1997-98 and 1998-99, Tamil Nadu ranked first in terms of the number of units constructed and loans disbursed by ACHFs, with more than 50 per cent share. The details are highlighted in Table 12.11.

TABLE 12.11

Housing Finance by ACHFs for Tamil Nadu

	1997-98	*1998-99*
No. of Units Constructed	43,907	1,20,311
Housing Loans disbursed by ACHFs (Rs. Crore)	283.91	456.62

Source: NHB Report on Trend & Progress of Housing in India, June 1999.

Capital Markets

The capital markets in Tamil Nadu are, primarily, represented by the two stock exchanges in Chennai and Coimbatore. Both the stock exchanges are under the purview and regulation of Securities and Exchange Board of India (SEBI).

The Madras Stock Exchange had a membership of 171 as on June 2000. The Coimbatore Stock Exchange, at present, has 136 individual members and 57 corporate members. The annual turnover on these stock exchanges is given in Table 12.12.

TABLE 12.12

Annual Turnover of Stock Exchanges

(Rs. crore)

	1995-96	*1996-97*	*1997-98*	*1998-99*	*1999-2000*
Madras Stock Exchange	1,594	2,315	1,228	370	250
Coimbatore Stock Exchange	2,503	2,398	2,136	395	39

Source: SEBI Annual Reports.

Now, since most of the brokers have membership of Bombay Stock Exchange (BSE) and National Stock Exchange (NSE), and can trade online at these exchanges, the volume and value of transactions on Chennai and Coimbatore stock exchanges have declined substantially.

Performance Summary

The Financial Services Sector has had a positive impact on the economy of Tamil Nadu. The contribution of this sector to the NSDP (at current prices) of the State has shown a growing trend with a CAGR of 24.85 per cent during the period 1993-94 to 2000-01. At the national level too, Tamil Nadu is one of the prominent States in financial services sector. The State figures among the top ten in several parameters of the banking and financial services and also has to its credit some of the leading institutions and companies in the financial services sector. With proper facilitation and support initiatives from the State Government, Tamil Nadu can achieve further growth in this sector.

Tamil Nadu vis-à-vis other States

Some of the statistics that indicate the position of Tamil Nadu *vis-à-vis* other states as of 2000-01, are presented below*:

- Tamil Nadu has the highest credit-deposit ratio, among all the states;
- The State ranks 4th and accounts for 8.5 per cent of the total employment provided by SCBs;
- In terms of the number of bank offices of SCBs, Tamil Nadu ranks 7th in the country, accounting for 6.9 per cent of the total number of bank centres and offices in the country;
- The State ranks 4th with, 451 Urban Co-operative Bank branches, accounting for a 5.3 per cent share of the total number of UCB branches in the Country
- Tamil Nadu has 757 State and District Co-operative Bank branches in the State and ranks 6th among all the States.
- Tamil Nadu ranks 3rd among all the states with a share of 7.8 per cent of the cumulative assistance disbursed by all FIs.

Changing Dynamics of the Sector

The financial services sector has witnessed several disquieting events over the past decade resulting in changes in the regulatory mechanisms, players in the industry and also the preferences of the investors. In addition, changes in the macroeconomic environment, like falling interest rates, have further resulted in

* The details of the above statistics for the top ten States is given in Appendix 12A.3.

realignment of the various players in this sector. These events have resulted in blurring of the distinction between various constituents of the financial services sector.

The majority of the changes have adversely affected the NBFCs. With Tamil Nadu being one of the States with a large presence of NBFCs, these changes have had a larger impact on the State, compared with the other States. Some of the key changes are listed below:

- The entry of banks into the areas of operations earlier dominated by NBFCs like hire-purchase and leasing, consumer finance, etc.;
- Entry of large multinationals into the financial services business has brought in higher levels of competition and has changed the basic structure of delivering financial products and services to the customers;
- Some of the areas of operations like leasing is no longer an attractive business proposition due to changes in the business and regulatory conditions;
- Entry of unscrupulous and fraudulent players in the early and mid-nineties and their unceremonious exit have put tremendous pressure on the established and upright NBFCs with flight of deposits from NBFCs to commercial and co-operative banks;
- With the regulatory authorities imposing stringent prudential norms on smaller and traditional players like nidhis, benefit funds and chit funds, the survival of the older players in these segments which form a major source of finance for the economically weaker sections of the society in the State is under threat.

However, some of the players from the financial services sector of Tamil Nadu have shown initiative in utilising the opportunities that the liberalisation and deregulation of the various segments of this sector has provided. Few instances that demonstrate this are the establishment of private mutual funds and insurance companies by players from this State, *viz.* Shriram Asset Management, Sundaram-Newton and Cholamandalam-Cazenove in the mutual funds area, and Royal Sundaram Alliance and AMP Sanmar Assurance in the insurance segment.

State Initiatives

This chapter highlights the various steps that the State government could initiate in order to accelerate the growth of the financial services in the State of Tamil Nadu. The suggestions made in this chapter are based on the interaction with members from various segments of the sector and also our analysis of the financial services sector.

The majority of regulations governing the Financial Services Sector are controlled by central apex bodies, viz., the RBI, DCA and SEBI. In view of this, the initiatives of the State Government would primarily be towards creating the necessary infrastructure for the growth and development of this sector.

Ensuring Growth in Trade and Industrial Activity

The financial services sector is a support sector in the economy and in order to grow, it would require growth in trade and industrial activity of the State. To ensure that there is growth in the industrial sector and also that the State is attractive for investments, the Government should concentrate its efforts in making Tamil Nadu a desired destination for making investments.

Tamil Nadu ranks 3rd among all states, only behind Maharastra and Delhi, in attracting Foreign Direct Investment (FDI). The cumulative FDI approved in the state during the period August 1991 to September 2001, was Rs.22492.5 crore, accounting for 8.35 per cent of the total FDI approvals at the national level.*

In order to continue its good performance and meet the challenges posed by other progressive States like Karnataka, Gujarat and Andhra Pradesh, the Tamil Nadu Government should play an active role by facilitating and encouraging:

- Pro-business attitudes;
- Prudent and minimal government regulations;
- Local availability of professionals;
- Technology/telecom infrastructure;
- Entrepreneurial activity;
- Moderate taxes;
- Transportation/land use for easy commute;
- Affordable quality housing;
- Attract professionals from inside the country;
- Research/innovation activities; and
- Good colleges and universities

* *Source*: Secretariat for Industrial Assistance (SIA) Statistics.

Promotion of Chennai as a Financial Centre

Chennai has been the headquarters for banks like Indian Bank, Indian Overseas Bank, insurance companies like United India Insurance Company Ltd., Royal-Sundaram Insurance, premier NBFCs like Cholamandalam Investment & Finance Co., Sundaram Finance Ltd., and financial institutions like IDFC.

In the recent past, the city has been able to attract several financial services companies including global majors like the World Bank to set up back-office operations. The availability of quality infrastructure and manpower has attracted these companies to set up their operations here.

In addition to these, Chennai is a port city and is very well connected by all means of transport, *viz.*, road, rail, sea and air to important international destinations like Singapore, South and South-East Asian countries and also to the Middle-East countries. The city has a prevailing good and peaceful law and order history.

In the light of these advantages enjoyed by the city and the recent developments, the State Government should work towards making Chennai an international financial centre by providing the necessary policy and infrastructure support. The State government should move fast and take advantage of the fact that there is no major financial centre in Southern India.

The recent Exim Policy announced by the Central government that allows offshore banking centres in Special Economic Zones (SEZs) provides the right fillip to the State government to pursue this project at the earliest.

Proactive Changes in Regulation to Fuel Growth

The majority of the regulations governing the financial services sector are driven by Central apex bodies and only a couple of segments are under the State regulatory purview. The segments of the financial services sector that are governed by the State regulations are the Chit Funds and Co-operative Banks.

As seen from Chapter 3, the performance of the co-operative banks in the State has been deteriorating in the recent past. This is partially due to the dual regulatory mechanism involving both the RBI and the State government co-operation department, resulting in lower efficiencies. The RBI, on its part, has proposed to set up an independent regulatory authority for the co-operative banking segment including UCBs. The Tamil Nadu Government should play a proactive role in putting the new mechanism in place at the earliest to facilitate growth and improve the performance of this segment in the State.

With reference to Chit funds, the State has fully implemented to the Central Chit Funds Act. The players in this segment feel that there are several archaic Statutory requirements in the Act that have resulted in a drop in the performance of this segment and has forced the exit of many players. Some of these Statutory provisions that could be corrected to keep pace with time include:

- Sanction of State government for commencement of each and every chit group;
- Separate bank deposit or security for each and every chit group;
- Declaration filed with the Registrar on full subscription of each and every chit group;
- Manual formats for maintaining books of accounts and submission of financial statements to the registrar of chits; and
- Impounding of 100 per cent of first month's subscription by the government till all the subscribers are fully paid.

These provisions have made the compliance to regulations a very cumbersome and tedious exercise. These issues get compounded in cases of bigger chit companies who run several chit groups. Suitable changes could be made to correct these aberrations such as:

- Acceptance of computerised formats for filing of financial statement and books of accounts;
- Based on the performance of the chit fund and the size of operations, suitable changes to the provisions be made towards filing of declarations; sanction of commencement and security deposits, wherein it could be done for a defined set of groups instead of each and every chit group; and
- Partial impounding of first month's subscription (50 per cent) instead of 100 per cent that would provide the necessary working capital to the foreman to manage any delays by some of the subscribers. This need is strongly felt, since the RBI has restricted Commercial Banks from lending to Chit funds to meet their working capital needs.

Such changes have been successfully implemented by neighbouring States like Andhra Pradesh where the performance of the Chit fund industry has been superior compared with Tamil Nadu.

Support for Enforcement of Contract/Court Orders

As the financial services sector deals with public deposits and savings, any illegal and fraudulent practices can even take away the lifetime savings of people. There have been many instances, in the past, wherein people have lost huge sums of money to fly-by-night operators.

However, the regulatory authorities have clamped stringent regulations in order to avoid occurrences of such events in the future. One such move has been the enactment of the Tamil Nadu Protection of Interests of Depositors Act, 1997, by the State government. The State government has also set up a special court to deal with such offences. The government should now concentrate on efficient expediting of pending cases in the special court so that the offenders are punished. This will act as a strong deterrent for any unscrupulous elements entering the financial services sector.

There is a positive feedback from the vehicle-financing segment wherein the State Police has actively supported the recovery of vehicles from defaulting borrowers. The Hire Purchase and Leasing companies strongly feel that such support should also be extended by the State Police to deal with asset financing cases to enforce the court orders towards recovery of assets from defaulters.

APPENDIX 12A.1

List of Documents Referred

1. RBI Annual Reports
2. RBI- Reports on Trend and Progress of Banking in India 1996 - 2001
3. RBI - Banking Statistics 1991-2001
4. CMIE - EIS - Money & Banking
5. Tamil Nadu Chit Funds Act
6. Tamil Nadu Protection of Interests of Depositors Act 1997
7. Development Banking Report 2000 & 2001

APPENDIX 12A.2

List of People Contacted/Met

1. Dr. Lakshmanan, AGM Planning & Economic Research, Indian Bank
2. Prof. Radhakrishnan, Member, Sabhanayagam Committee on Nidhis
3. Mr. R Thyagarajan, Chairman, Shriram Group
4. Mr. Vaidyalingam, Zonal Manager, LIC, Chennai
5. Mr. Pattabhiraman, GM, Madras Stock Exchange
6. Mr. S Vaidhyanathan, AGM, United India Insurance
7. Mr. H K Sharma, Regional Mgr, National Insurance
8. Mr. J Chacko, Regional Mgr, Oriental Insurance
9. Mr. Madhusudan, Secretary, Chamber of Nidhis
10. Mr. A M Balakrishnan, GM, Dept of NBS, RBI Chennai
11. Mr. V Devaraju, ED, Coimbatore Stock Exchange

APPENDIX 12A.3

Banking Statistics For Top Ten States
SCB's Credit-Deposit Ratio

Rank	*State/Union Territory*	*Credit-Deposit Ratio (%)*
1	**Tamil Nadu**	**90.25**
2	Chandigarh	78.45
3	Maharashtra	77.80
4	Andhra Pradesh	67.58
5	Karnataka	65.45
6	Delhi	60.00
7	Gujarat	52.75
8	Madhya Pradesh	52.43
9	Haryana	51.28
10	Rajasthan	49.83

Source: RBI Banking Statistics.

Employment Provided by SCBs

Rank	*State*	*No. of People Employed*	*All -India Share*
1	Maharashtra	142392	14.1%
2	Uttar Pradesh	104440	10.4%
3	West Bengal	86690	8.6%
4	**Tamil Nadu**	**85228**	**8.5%**
5	Karnataka	74943	7.4%
6	Andhra Pradesh	71504	7.1%
7	Gujarat	60137	6.0%
8	Delhi	52672	5.2%
9	Bihar	50419	5.0%
10	Madhya Pradesh	49818	4.9%

Source: RBI Banking Statistics.

Number of SCB Centers and Offices in the State

Rank	*State*	*No. of Centres*	*No. of Offices*	*Total*	*All-India Share*
1	Uttar Pradesh	5598	9100	14698	14.2%
2	Maharashtra	2619	6510	9129	8.8%
3	Bihar	3680	5085	8765	8.5%
4	Andhra Pradesh	2805	5261	8066	7.8%
5	Madhya Pradesh	2670	4592	7262	7.0%
6	Karnataka	2373	4870	7243	7.0%
7	**Tamil Nadu**	**2206**	**4941**	**7147**	**6.9%**
8	West Bengal	2473	4549	7022	6.8%
9	Gujarat	1725	3768	5493	5.3%
10	Rajasthan	2001	3375	5376	5.2%

Source: RBI Banking Statistics.

Number of UCB Branches in the State

Rank	*State*	*No. of Centres*	*No. of Offices*	*Total*	*All-India Share*
1	Maharashtra	549	3184	3733	44.2%
2	Gujarat	222	1059	1281	15.2%
3	Karnataka	246	807	1053	12.5%
4	**Tamil Nadu**	**151**	**300**	**451**	**5.3%**
5	Andhra Pradesh	79	295	374	4.4%
6	Kerala	55	310	365	4.3%
7	Uttar Pradesh	41	187	228	2.7%
8	Madhya Pradesh	83	127	210	2.5%
9	West Bengal	101	107	208	2.5%
10	Rajasthan	42	114	156	1.8%

Source: RBI Banking Statistics.

Number of State and District Co-operative Bank Branches

Rank	*State*	*State Coop Banks*	*District Coop Banks*	*Total*	*All-India Share*
1	Maharashtra	46	3648	3694	27.9%
2	Uttar Pradesh	29	1463	1492	11.3%
3	Gujarat	0	1087	1087	8.2%
4	Madhya Pradesh	22	1049	1071	8.1%
5	Punjab	21	779	800	6.0%
6	**Tamil Nadu**	**41**	**716**	**757**	**5.7%**
7	Karnataka	28	626	654	4.9%
8	Andhra Pradesh	24	578	602	4.6%
9	Bihar	14	481	495	3.7%
10	Kerala	20	447	467	3.5%

Source: RBI Banking Statistics.

Cumulative Disbursements by All Financial Institutions

Rank	*State*	*Rupees in Crore*	*All-India Share*
1	Maharashtra	97579	23.4%
2	Gujarat	57977	13.9%
3	**Tamil Nadu**	**32381**	**7.8%**
4	Karnataka	27060	6.5%
5	Uttar Pradesh	26969	6.5%
6	Andhra Pradesh	26855	6.4%
7	Delhi	19090	4.6%
8	West Bengal	18106	4.3%
9	Madhya Pradesh	16709	4.0%
10	Rajasthan	14899	3.6%

Source: Development Banking Report – 2001.

Investments Sanctioned and Implemented

	1996	*1998*	*1999*	*2000*	*2001*
Sanctioned Investments (Rs. Crore)	90650	121467	138562	155985	157884
Implementation	23.9%	20.3%	18.5%	27.0%	21.6%

Source: CMIE, Statistical Handbook – Tata Services Ltd.

Chapter 13

Information Technology in Tamil Nadu

Introduction

There has been spectacular growth of the information technology industry in Tamil Nadu in the last decade. Software exports crossed $ 1 billion in 2000-01, and Tamil Nadu stands second only to Karnataka in terms of exports. Despite the global recession, software exports continue to do well. However, information technology related education which took off in a big way in the nineties has begun to slow down in Tamil Nadu reflecting the tightness in the overseas job market. Nevertheless, the information technology industry has grown substantially in the state and accounted for roughly 2 per cent of GSDP in 1999-2000. About 40,000 professionals are employed in the information technology sector. Reputed organisations like the World Bank, ABN-AMRO, and EDS have established their back offices and Global Development Centres in Chennai. Bharati Enterprises, a telecom service provider has started operations in Tamil Nadu, and is constructing the world's biggest submarine Optical Fibre Cable project connecting Chennai and Singapore. The telecommunications backbone of the State is also being strengthened by providing an Optical Fibre Cable (OFC) network. Private communication providers are laying the network throughout the State, so that even villages will have internet access.

The Government of Tamil Nadu has taken various initiatives to promote the growth of the industry by providing the necessary infrastructure, initiating e-governance activities, and supporting information technology education. Tamil Nadu was the first State to announce an information technology policy in 1997. The present government announced a new information technology policy in 2002 with the objective of making Tamil Nadu a preferred destination for IT investments.

Data on the information technology sector in Tamil Nadu are sketchy and not as comprehensive as the other industrial sectors. The web-sites of Software Technology Parks of India (STPI), and Tamil Nadu Industrial Development Corporation (TIDCO) are major sources of the data. Output is expressed in sales turnover and not in terms of value addition as in other industrial sectors. However, the general contours of the growth of the industry can be observed from the available information. We discuss the information technology policy, the stated objectives, the degree of achievement of the objectives, and conclude with a brief discussion of the issues for the future.

Information Technology Policy Initiatives

Tamil Nadu has comparative advantage in skilled and educated manpower, good educational institutions, reasonably good infrastructure, and lower costs of operation. The presence of an international airport and seaport has helped the growth of the information technology industry in Tamil Nadu. Tamil Nadu was the first Indian State to announce a comprehensive information technology policy and later set up a task force with representatives from government, industry and academia to oversee its implementation. It was also the first State to establish an information technology department within the government.

The main objectives of the information technology policy of 1997 are as follows:

1. To encourage and accelerate the growth of hardware and software industries and associated sources in the State and to remove the bottlenecks for starting and running such units in Tamil Nadu.
2. To increase both domestic and export earnings of software and hardware sectors in the State.

3. To upgrade and develop manpower skills required for the information technology industry by facilitating training, to accelerate the use of information technology in schools, colleges and educational institutions with a view of providing skills and knowledge to the youth to make them fit for employment in this sector.
4. To upgrade the quality of life of the citizens of the State by facilitating access to consumer application of information technology.

The policy also mentions the existing incentives (tax concessions and subsidies) as well as the new infrastructure initiatives such as information technology parks, telecom services/information backbone and the venture capital fund for development of the information technology industry in the State. With respect to human resource development, the policy initiatives include the setting up of training institutions, computer training in schools, etc. The present government announced a new information technology policy in 2002. The major objectives of the new policy are as follows:

1. To establish Tamil Nadu as the Destination of choice for IT investments, particularly with regard to IT enabled services and business process outsourcing.
2. To upgrade the quality of life for the citizen through e-governance and IT application in government.
3. To empower people in the rural areas so as to bridge the digital divide.
4. To develop research and development initiatives.
5. To promote the use of Tamil in Information Technology.

The government also announced several fiscal, administrative, and physical incentives as part of the policy. The list of the 2002 policy is given in Annexure I.

Growth of the Information Technology Industry in Tamil Nadu

Software

There has been a phenomenal growth in this sector since 1993-94 and particularly in the last five years. The number of companies has increased from 10 in 1993-94 to 866 in 2001-02 representing a compound growth rate of 79 per cent in the number of companies (Table 13.1). The value of exports (in current prices) has mushroomed from Rs. 2 crore in 1993-94 to Rs. 5223 crore in 2001-02.

The increase of 67.8 per cent from Rs. 3116 crore ($677 million) in 2000-01 to Rs. 5223 crore ($1.1 billion) in 2001-02 occurred despite the worldwide recession in the information technology sector. Tamil Nadu is now second behind Karnataka with regard to software exports. There are 558 software export companies in the State, most of them are Software Technology Park (STP) units. Tata Consultancy Services is the top exporter, followed by Hindustan Computers Technologies, Pentasoft, Infosys and WIPRO. Although there are 75 multinational companies in Tamil Nadu, their contribution to exports is only Rs. 604 crore (12 per cent).

TABLE 13.1

Growth of Export Turnover of Software Companies in Tamil Nadu

	No. of Companies	*Exports (Rs. Crore)*
1993-94	10	2
1994-95	23	12
1995-96	34	37
1996-97	69	161
1997-98	108	393
1998-99	166	1246
1999-00	596	1914
2000-01	766	3116
2001-02	866	5223

Source: STPI – www.stpc.soft.net

Within the software export field, the areas of expertise of the STPI units in Tamil Nadu in 2000-01 are given in the following Table 13.2:

TABLE 13.2

Areas of Expertise of STPI Units (2000-2001)

Area	*Export (Rs. Crore)*	*Per cent of Total*	*No. of Units*	*Per cent of Total*
Application Software	1167	39.5	138	39.2
On-Site Consultancy	739	25.0	30	8.5
System Software	626	21.2	32	9.1
Information Technology Enabled Services (ITES)	260	8.8	71	20.2
Web Applications	121	4.1	56	15.9
Product Packages	43	1.4	25	7.1
Total	**2956**	**100.0**	**352**	**100.0**

Source: STPI – www.stpc.soft.net

Note: Information Technology Enabled Services include data processing, medical transcription, CAD/CAM, GIS Applications and Call Centres.

Application software, on-site consultancy, and system software make up the large proportion in terms of exports (85.7 per cent) and in terms of units (56.8 per cent). However, information technology enabled services (ITES), web applications, and product packages are gradually gaining strength, particularly in terms of units although their export turnover is small compared to software applications.

The breakdown of number of the STPI units by export turnover is given in Table 13.3.

TABLE 13.3

Export Turnover of Software Units

(Current prices)

Export Turnover (Rs. Crore)	*No. of Units* 1998-99	1999-2000	2000-2001
400-500	—	—	2
200-300	2	2	1
100-200	2	2	5
50-100	1	2	1
10-50	9	17	18
1-10	37	70	97
Total	51	93	125

Source: STPI - www.stpc.soft.net

Eight units exceeded export turnover of Rs. 100 crore and two units exceeded Rs. 400 crore in 2000-01, which represents a quantum jump from the previous year. However, nearly 100 units (78 per cent) are small units with turnover of Rs. 1-10 crore per year. The next largest segment are 18 units with turnover between Rs. 10–50 crore per year.

TABLE 13.4

Geographical Distribution of Software Units

Place	*STP Units*	*Others*	*Total*	*Per cent*
Chennai	591	85	676	89.3
Coimbatore	63	3	66	8.7
Madurai	3	2	5	0.7
Trichy	2	0	2	0.3
Tirupur	2	0	2	0.3
Tirunelveli	2	0	2	0.3
Others	4	0	4	0.5
Total	**667**	**90**	**757**	**100.0**

Source: STPI – www.stpc.soft.net

Chennai accounts for the lion's share of software units (89 per cent) followed by Coimbatore (9 per cent) (Table 13.4). The turnover in these secondary centers is as follows: Coimbatore (Rs. 42.55 crore), Trichy (Rs. 5.24 crore), Tirunelveli (Rs. 1.59 crore), Vellore (Rs. 0.67 crore), Thanjavur (Rs. 0.65 crore) and Madurai (Rs. 0.26 crore).

Hardware

The liberalisation policies such as easing of foreign investment norms, allowance of 100 per cent foreign equity, and reduction in customs tariff have encouraged growth of the electronics industry. The sales of personal computers has been increasing due to the popularity of the Internet. Thus, there is tremendous potential for the growth of the hardware industry. Significant export opportunities also exist for components, embedded systems, wireless telecom systems according to a recent study. Contract manufacturing involving the production of printed circuit boards, sub-assemblies and other product lines may also provide opportunities for the hardware industry.

The rapid growth of the software sector has not been matched by an equally fast growth of hardware. The EXIM policy has provided for Electronic Hardware Technology Park (EHTP) scheme for the hardware sector. It allows sale into the domestic market at much lower customs duties. The performance of the EHTP units from Tamil Nadu is given in Table 13.5.

TABLE 13.5

The Performance of the EHTP Units from Tamil Nadu

No.	*Year*	*Export in Rs. Crore*
1.	1998-1999	351.34
2.	1999-2000	399.81
3.	2000-2001	575.65
4.	2001-2002	482.43
5.	2002-2003	291.49

Source: STPI

Hardware exports grew steadily till 2000-2001 but have been declining due to the downturn in the world economy. Areas of expertise include automatic test equipment, integrated circuits, chip resistors, multimedia services, and telecommunication hardware. The Union Ministry of Information Technology and Communications is setting up a taskforce to stimulate the growth of the Indian hardware industry to complement the software sector.

Information Technology Infrastructure

- Optical Fibre Cables (OFC) – Six agencies have been permitted on a non-exclusive basis to create high bandwidth OFC networks to cover every district of the State. Internet access will then be available throughout the State.
- Software Technology Parks of India (STPI) has been given financial assistance to set up international data links at Madurai, Trichy, Tirunelveli and Chennai. This is in addition to the STPI and VSNL facilities at Coimbatore. This will facilitate the spread of the information technology industry, including software and ITES and create employment opportunities throughout the State.
- Information Technology Corridor – The Tirupur Information Technology Corridor along the Old Mahabalipuram Road will be provided with world class infrastructure and Knowledge Industry Townships (KITs) aimed at Knowledge Oriented Industries.

Telecom Infrastructure

The telephone density in Tamil Nadu is one of the highest in the country second only to Kerala in the Southern States (Table 13.6)

TABLE 13.6

Telephone Density in Southern States

(as on March 31, 2000)

States	*Area in '000 sq.km.*	*No. '000 of Telephones*	*No. Per sq. km.*	*No. Per 100 Population*
Andhra Pradesh	275	2333	8.5	3.1
Karnataka	192	1957	10.2	3.8
Kerala	39	1812	46.5	5.6
Tamil Nadu	**130**	**2840**	**21.8**	**4.5**
All-India	**3287**	**28396**	**8.7**	**2.9**

Source: Indian Telecommunication Statistics (2000), Ministry of Communication.

TABLE 13.7

Rural Coverage – Telecom

(as on March 31, 2001)

States	*No. of Villages*	*No. of VPTs*	*% Coverage*
Andhra Pradesh	29460	23383	79
Karnataka	27066	27056	100
Kerala	1530	1530	100
Tamil Nadu	**17991**	**17898**	**99**
All-India	**607491**	**408922**	**67**

Source: www.bsnl.con.in

Tamil Nadu like the other southern states has nearly 100 per cent rural connectivity in terms of village phone terminals (VPT) compared to the All-India average of 67 per cent (Table 13.7).

Information Technology Parks

- TIDEL Park, a one million square feet information technology park is now functioning in Taramani. Reliable power supply and communication/uplink facilities are critical requirements of software companies which are provided at TIDEL Park. TIDEL-II with a floor space of two million square feet is being planned.
- Elnet City – Elnet is a joint sector company of the Electronics Corporation of Tamil Nadu (ELCOT) with the objective of constructing and maintaining the first private sector software technology park in the country. Elnet City has a built up area of 140,000 sq.ft. and is part of the Cyber Corridor in Taramani.
- SIPCOT has developed a 1000 acre information technology park in Siruseri village, 20 km. South of Chennai, for allotment of land to information technology companies. There has been good response from large companies like TCS.
- The 1700 acre Mahindra Park a joint venture of TIDCO, ILFS and Mahindras is being developed South of Chennai near the Airport.
- Tex City – A Software Park with 90,000 sq. ft. space is located close to the Coimbatore Airport to encourage prospective software developers to locate their office space.

Role of National Informatics Centre (NIC)

NIC Tamil Nadu functions in close coordination with the Government of Tamil Nadu in promoting IT applications.

- *Taluk* Information System has been implemented in 206 *taluks* in the State.
- Registration System has been implemented in 125 offices. Use of Tamil is a feature of this package.
- Guideline values are provided in the six Municipal Corporations.
- Treasury System is implemented in the Sub-Treasuries and District Treasuries
- Chief Minister's Special Cell handles more than 1000 petitions per day.

- NIC maintains the Secretariat LAN which has 250 nodes and hosts the Tamil Nadu Government Website.
- Block level version of "Rural Soft" for use at the Block and Village *Panchayat* offices.
- Tamil Nadu Maps site provides district, *taluk*, and block boundaries with list of villages, towns and municipalities.
- NIC has been actively supporting the State government during elections.

The District Centres of NIC assist in promoting IT culture at the grassroots level. Apart from implementation of the systems, they are actively involved in developing systems which are horizontally used in other districts. NIC Tamil Nadu has been working in close coordination with various divisions at headquarters and has taken up the responsibility for development and implementation of some national level projects as well. Training is an important activity in all NIC centres in Tamil Nadu.

Information Technology Enabled Services (ITES)

The Tamil Nadu Government is exploring the possibility of setting up a special purpose vehicle to develop and promote Coimbatore, Madurai and Trichy as preferred hubs for ITES. ITES is one of the fastest growing segments of the information technology industry worldwide. Tamil Nadu is well placed to develop the ITES sector because of its better educational and overall infrastructure.

Tamil Nadu is emerging as a key hub for ITES and Business Process Outsourcing in the country particularly in the banking, financial services, and insurance sectors. Many institutions are scaling up their operations from Chennai. A draft ITES policy has been announced by the Government of Tamil Nadu. The draft policy mentions various employment and promotional incentives and human resource development initiatives.

The ITES sector faces certain problems. There is high turnover in many of the firms since personnel have to be available at all hours. Upward mobility may also be restricted. There is also need for proper training and certification in ITES related activities. The draft ITES policy encourages ITES industries to obtain ISO 9000 and other process certifications of quality.

E-Governance Initiatives

The Government of Tamil Nadu has introduced computerisation in several departments to make them more user friendly. A Government to Citizen website was developed with inputs from District and *Taluk* officials called MIN-ARASU. Information on government schemes, forms for issue of certificates etc. will be available on-line. Other initiatives taken by various government departments include:

1. Computerisation of The Revenue Department

Touch screen kiosks have been installed in 30 model *taluk* offices. The public can view the details of land *patta*, birth and death details, guidance value and get printouts of certificates/details. Kiosk systems will be implemented in all the *taluks* of the State.

2. Computerisation of Registration Department

350 sub-registrar/district registrar offices are being computerised in a phased manner. Land record computerisation using Tamil software will be taken up at all the *taluks*.

3. Computerisation of Transport Department

Transport department has initiated Computerisation. Laminated driving licenses are now issued in all the 82 RTO offices. 45 lakh driving license cards have been issued since 1996.

4. Secretariat Facilities

- Videoconferencing linking all the District Collectors offices with the Chief Minister
- 100 ISDN exchange for intercom facility for Ministers and Secretaries

5. Computerisation of Agricultural Marketing

Electronic display boards are available in nine regulated markets to enable the farmers to get the best price for their produce.

6. Geographical Information Systems

Development of Geographical Information Systems are underway at the Institute of Remote Sensing, Anna University and Bharatidasan University, Trichy. The maps will have information on natural resources, socioeconomic information and infrastructure.

E-governance activities will also help to stimulate domestic demand for the products of the information technology industry. Development of local on-line information in Tamil will spur application of information technology in many government departments and provide a good interface with the public.

Although several e-governance projects have been implemented in Tamil Nadu, there are some difficulties which need to be highlighted. IT vendors often underestimate the complexity and scope of the projects. Pilot approaches and small projects may be better in the initial stages. To a large extent, e-governance has not been interactive and is mostly one-way communication since the websites are still first generation sites. The majority of web-sites display static information such as statutory forms, policies, rules and regulations. The projects have not fully capitalised on the relational power of the internet medium.

The major reasons for the low effectiveness of e-governance projects include:

- Poor requirement gathering.
- Non-involvement of end users during the process.
- Low I.T. awareness among decision makers.
- Non compatibility between I.T. projects and business processes.
- Poor risk management and choice of technology
- Over ambitious projects.

For e-governance projects to succeed, there is a crucial need for training of functionaries and proper documentation. Attitudinal change is also necessary to work with a different medium. Andhra Pradesh has set up an Institute of e-governance to monitor the projects and make recommendations. This approach could be adopted in Tamil Nadu. Tamil Nadu has allocated Rs. 12.50 crore out of a total I.T. budget of Rs. 50 crore in the Tenth Plan for e-governance activities. E-governance issues are also discussed in the final chapter on Governance.

Sustainable Access in Rural India (SARI)

SARI seeks to show that viable markets exist for information and communication services in rural areas by inventing and deploying innovative technologies, assessments and business models. The ultimate goal is to link these activities to sustainable human development objectives. SARI has a diverse partnership of universities, non-profit organisations, and the private sector which will ultimately link one thousand neighbouring villages in two Indian districts. The project in Tamil Nadu proposes to cover all the villages and towns in Madurai District except for the city of Madurai. Connections will be provided in every village or town. The objectives of the project are:

- To bridge the digital divide between the rural and urban areas.
- To establish rural connectivity.
- To transfer the benefits of information technology to reach rural areas.
- To facilitate dissemination of information on various aspects of human development.

A pilot project has been undertaken in Melur *Taluk* of Madurai District covering two *Panchayat* Unions of Melur and Kottampatti. An access centre has been established and will cover every village and small town with 25 km. of the *Taluk* headquarters. Kiosks have been set up in the villages around the access centre. These are run by a variety of STD-PCO operators who have upgraded their services, self help groups, etc. Connections are provided to various government offices, private schools and colleges, hospitals and private sector companies. The Government of Tamil Nadu has decided to scale up the SARI project. It has been redesignated as RASI- "Rural Access to Services through Internet" and will ultimately be extended to the whole State.

RASI is to cover all districts in a phased manner, starting with 10 districts. Rural internet kiosks have opened up new channels of communications. On-line application for birth, death, income, community and nativity certificates has been made possible. Information on canal timings, weekly rainfall, civic complaints and market price information is now available. Agriculture extension services and veterinary services are also provided through the internet. The Government of Tamil Nadu can also coordinate with the *Samadhan Kendras* set up by the Rural Electronics Division of the Department of Information Technology at the Centre.

Wireless Local Loop Services (WLL)

WLL based on cordless digitally enhanced telephony was developed by Prof. Ashok Jhunjhunwalla of IIT Madras. The technology provides wireless access to more than 1000 systems within a radius of 25 km. The kiosks have been established by individuals who have invested Rs. 50,000 in computers and other accessories. The owners who have installed the user friendly Tamil software make an average income of Rs. 2500 per month. Villagers in about 30 villages have e-mail identities which they use to get assistance from the government under various schemes.

Information Villages

The M.S. Swaminathan Research Foundation has connected ten villages near Pondicherry by a hybrid wired and wireless network consisting of personal computers, telephones, VHF radio duplex devices, and e-mail connectivity through dial-up telephone lines. The purpose of the project is to encourage collective action for spread of technology. The exercise involves local volunteers to gather information, feed it into an Intranet, and provide access through nodes in different villages. Use of Tamil, multimedia, and participation by local people are the noteworthy features of the project. The project began in 1998 in the village of Villianur, 20 km from Pondicherry, but is currently *not* operational in Tamil Nadu. However, the concept of "Information Village" could be later extended to Tamil Nadu.

Murugappa Group

EID Parry, a major business house in the Murugappa Group in partnership with n-Logue is implementing an information technology project in Nellikuppam, Cuddalore District, Tamil Nadu. The project will cover 271 villages in the Nellikuppam region. Internet business will be run in these villages through an access centre. The primary clients are the sugar farmers who are the raw material suppliers to EID Parry.

Information Technology Education

The Tamil Nadu Government has taken several initiatives to propagate information technology education in schools and colleges.

- The Computer Science syllabus for Classes 11 and 12 of the State Higher Secondary Board has been revised and updated.
- Computer Science is now available as an option in all Government Schools. 1197 schools producing 40,000 students per year have been covered. Teachers are also being trained in computer literacy skills.
- One year computer literacy programme for all students in 60 Government Arts and Science Colleges, 11 Medical Colleges, 1 Dental College and 5 Law Colleges has been launched. This programme will cover 30,000 students per year.
- Tamil Nadu has about 250 engineering colleges with an intake capacity of about 60,000 seats. 30,000 seats are available in computer and information technology related disciplines but of late enrolment has declined. Ways and means have to be explored to redesign these courses with anticipated changes in the information technology industry.
- ELCOT has given training to 5000 BC/MBC/DNC candidates for a one-year period.

Tamil Virtual University (TVU)

The Tamil Nadu Government established the Tamil Virtual University to provide Internet based resources and opportunities for the Tamil communities living in different parts of the globe as well as others interested in learning Tamil and acquiring knowledge of the history, art, literature and culture of Tamil Nadu. TVU has developed a large digital library with literature, dictionaries, video and pictone galleries. A massive exercise of converting all government websites in bilingual form for dissemination of information to the public in rural areas is being undertaken jointly by TVU and ELCOT.

Issues for the Future

Continuity of Information Technology Policy

Tamil Nadu was the first State to develop an information technology policy and to set up an information technology department with the government. Many initiatives were taken with regard to infrastructure, e-governance, information technology in education, and the use of Tamil. The Government of Tamil Nadu announced a new IT policy in 2002. Continuity of information technology policy is very important for the sustained growth of this nascent sector. The use of information technology applications in many industries will have to be promoted. The policy encourages information technology units not only in Chennai but in the secondary cities to improve the geographical coverage of the industry. Most important, the best talent from all sectors—industry, academic, and government—should work together to develop and implement the policy in Tamil Nadu.

Information Technology Education

Tamil Nadu has witnessed a mushrooming growth of private training institutes in information technology in the large cities and towns. They offer a wide variety of training ranging from basic skills to advanced programming languages, but the training offered is unstructured. Enrolment has declined even in prestigious institutes like NIIT. Hence these institutes will have to restructure their courses to take advantage of other business opportunities both in India and aboard. Specialisation is needed to provide the right type of information technology courses for engineering, communications, and other applications. The information technology education provided should be relevant to the needs of industries. NASSCOM and other specialised agencies can give guidance on the nature of information technology education, particularly differentiation in course structure for different purposes.

Information Technology Institute of Tamil Nadu (TANITEC)

The Government of Tamil Nadu set up an Information Technology Institute of Tamil Nadu (TANITEC) as a centre of excellence which was to take care of the training and technology upgradation aspects of information technology in the State. But TANITEC faced start up problems and has now been merged with Anna University. Since it has not taken off like the Indian Institute of Information Technology (IIITs) in some other States, it may be necessary to review and redesign the structure of TANITEC.

Information Technology in School Education

Although Tamil Nadu has been a pioneer in introducing information technology in schools, it is restricted to the higher secondary level. Other States are introducing computer education even at the primary level. Children can become computer literate even at a young age. The government will have to take the necessary steps to introduce the use of computers at the elementary and middle school levels.

Infrastructure

While information technology infrastructure such as telecom facilities and software parks are important for the growth of the industry, it is crucial that social infrastructure like housing, roads, schools, hospitals and other facilities are provided for the growth of the information technology sector. While Tamil Nadu generally has good physical infrastructure, there is growing need to meet the requirements of the information technology professionals in the various ST Parks who now reside in the State.

E-Governance

The government has taken various steps to promote e-governance. However, many more applications/areas are possible. For example, the payment of utility bills has been facilitated through a single location at shopping centres in Kerala. Education related information from colleges and universities could also be put on the web, apart from admissions/marks alone.

Linkage with Other Industries

Information Technology has grown rapidly due to the export market, and it may continue to do so in the future. However, it is important that both industries and government utilise the information technology expertise available locally for a wide variety of services. The sustained growth of the information technology sector is possible only if there is domestic demand for information technology. Policies have to be initiated to promote demand in various sectors of the economy for the application of information technology, information technology enabled services, etc.

Increasing Competition

All the Southern States including Pondicherry are promoting the information technology sector. Incentives like investment subsidy, sales tax holidays, and venture capital finance are being provided. Tamil Nadu cannot afford to be complacent given the stiff competition from the neighbouring States to attract information technology business. The good pool of human resources as well as the physical infrastructure will have to be maintained and strengthened to make Tamil Nadu an attractive destination for information technology.

Localisation of Content and Language

Wide coverage of information technology within the State can take place only if Tamil is used in communication. The government has successfully developed an encoding standard and keyboard for Tamil. On-line content and software development in Tamil is now possible. Extensive use particularly in rural areas can now be promoted using local information in Tamil.

Promoting Hardware

Tamil Nadu like the other Southern States has tended to focus on software. Pondicherry on the other hand has offered tax concessions, and has managed to get IBM, WIPRO, HCL and ACER to set up manufacturing plants there. Tamil Nadu may consider diversifying to hardware which has the potential to employ a large number of people of varying educational and skill levels, and which will have better linkages with other manufacturing industries. It may be necessary to upgrade and orient the educational and research system to meet the needs of the hardware industry.

Chapter 14

Tamil Nadu Tourism

Tourism and Global Economy

Global economy has been showing a shift in its orientation from the primary and secondary sectors to the tertiary sector in the last few decades. This trend is highlighted by the increasing contribution of the tertiary sector to the GDP in almost all of the developed world and in a number of developing countries including India.

Within the tertiary sector, tourism with an annual rate of growth of 5 per cent has emerged as a significant player accounting for 11 per cent of global GDP and 8 per cent of world trade employment (Table 14.1).

TABLE 14.1

World Travel and Tourism (T&T) 2000 A.D.

Global Index	*Share of T &T (%)*
GDP	11.0
Employment	8.0
Exports	7.9
Capital Investment	9.4

Source: Ministry of Tourism, Government of India.

In the year 2000, international tourism flows across frontiers touched 698 millions accounting for receipts of US$ 595.00 billion. Domestic tourism flows were reportedly, at least, ten times more. The World Tourism and Travel Council has estimated that in the decade 2001-11, global tourism related exports will go up from US$ 1063.80 billion to US $ 2538.30 billion which would account for 12.8 per cent of global export value. Global Capital investment in tourism is forecast to escalate from the present US$ 657.7 billion to US$ 1434.00 billion which would be 9.3 per cent of total global investments.

The main beneficiaries of the phenomenal increases in global tourism investments and receipts would be the developing countries. Projections based on the latest Tourism Satellite Accounting Research (TSAR, 2001) identify the emergence of India as "one of the foremost growth centres in the world in the coming decade". Estimates made by the Department of Tourism, GoI place the employment generation potential of tourism in India (full time/part time/casuals) at 42 million jobs. In India, tourism currently accounts for 16.5 million direct and 22.4 million indirect jobs.

Tamil Nadu Economy – Role of Tourism

Tamil Nadu's economy is no exception to the global and national phenomenon of a higher rate of growth of the tertiary sector compared to the primary and secondary sectors. Figures of the changing composition of the State's GSDP (New Series) (CSO, GoI) since 1993-94 reflect this trend. In 1993-94, the share of the primary and secondary sectors to the GSDP was 24.32 per cent and 32.40 per cent respectively. In 1998-99, their shares fell to 20.06 per cent and 28.94 per cent respectively whereas the share of the tertiary sector jumped to 51.01 per cent from 43.27 per cent in the same period. This has been largely due to the emphasis placed by the State government and private enterprise on the spread of human development related services, notably, health, education, housing, and economic activity related services like transport, financial services and Information Technology. Of the latter group, 'Trade, Hotels and Restaurants' recorded an impressive growth in their contribution to the GSDP from 13.75 per cent in 1993-94 to 17.52 per cent in 1998-99. A part of this contribution can, doubtless, be ascribed to tourism.

Tamil Nadu's economy is also marked by the declining relative share of agriculture in the NSDP over the years. This factor coupled with the less than significant fall in population dependent on agriculture from 56.94 per cent in 1997-98 to 50.00 per cent in 2000-01, would suggest an economic policy correction aimed at shifting a part of this population out of agriculture to other sectors. It is worth noting that real per capita income in the agricultural sector recorded only a marginal rise in 38 years from Rs. 3907 in 1960-61 to Rs. 4398 in 1997-98 despite doubling of agricultural output over the period.

In Tamil Nadu where the need for employment generation is paramount the services sector has emerged as the instrument of choice in development. Among the many avenues available to the state in this sector for promotion, tourism holds out much promise at relatively low levels of investment. Department of Tourism, GoI has estimated that an investment of Rs.10 lakh in tourism creates 47.5 jobs as against 44.7 in agriculture and only 12.6 in manufacturing industry.

TABLE 14.2

Tourist Arrivals in Tamil Nadu

Year	*Domestic (Lakh)*	*%Change from Previous Year*	*Foreign (Lakh)*	*% Change from Previous Year*	*Total (Lakh)*	*% Change from Previous Year*
1990	92.5	—	3.0	—	95.5	—
1991	110.4	18.9	3.3	9.9	113.7	18.7
1992	131.1	18.7	4.0	20.8	135.1	18.8
1993	211.37	3.55	72.24	13.52	218.59	3.85
1994	160.3	12.8	4.9	14.4	165.2	12.8
1995	172.1	7.4	5.9	17.6	178.0	7.7
1996	182.1	5.7	6.1	4.8	188.2	5.7
1997	189.3	4.0	6.4	3.9	210.5	7.7
1998	204.1	7.8	6.4	(–)0.3	195.7	4.0
1999	211.4	3.5	7.2	13.5	218.6	3.8
2000	229.8	8.7	7.9	8.8	237.7	8.7
2001	238.1	3.6	7.7	–1.6	245.8	3.4
2002	246.62	3.6	8.0	3.9	254.66	3.6

Source: Department of Tourism, Tamil Nadu.

Tamil Nadu attracted nearly 30 per cent of the foreign tourists to India in the year 2000 (Table 14.2). The 7.90 lakh foreign tourists who visited the State for an average of 4.7 days spent foreign exchange equivalent to Rs. 4320 crore, a truly impressive figure. If the average length of stay could be enhanced by two days, then even without any increase in tourist arrivals, foreign tourist expenditure in Tamil Nadu can cross Rs. 6000 crore. On an average, a foreign tourist spends Rs. 2080 per day in Tamil Nadu of which 35.5 per cent is spent on shopping, 19.5 per cent on accommodation and 12.5 per cent on intercity transport.

Domestic tourist arrivals in the State stood at 230 lakh in the year 2000. During their average stay of 9 days, they spent Rs. 1250 crore. Their average spending per day worked out to Rs. 545 of which shopping accounted for 24 per cent, accommodation 17.9 per cent and transportation 17.7 per cent.

Tourism Trends in Tamil Nadu

Table 14.3 gives the category-wise (activity-wise) distribution of tourist arrivals in Tamil Nadu in the years 1998, 1999 and 2000. Tables 14.4 and 14.5 show centre-wise break up of tourist arrivals during the years 1998 to 2002. Figures on tourism generated by various countries and average lengths of stay of tourists in Tamil Nadu can be seen in Tables 14.6-14.7 and 14.8 respectively.

The activity-wise distribution is interesting and is also quite revealing of the touristic strengths of the State and revealed consumer preference on which a tourism promotion policy should be based. Business and industry related tourism is seen to be gaining ground, followed by the traditional pilgrimage tourism, visits to already well frequented hill stations and historical places. Numbers of tourists visiting areas of scenic interest and wild life reserves seem to be recording slow or poor rates of growth.

TABLE 14.3

Category-wise (Activity-wise) Distribution of Tourist Arrivals During 1998, 1999, 2000

(Per cent)

Category	*1998*			*1999*			*2000*		
	Domestic	*Foreign*	*Total*	*Domestic*	*Foreign*	*Total*	*Domestic*	*Foreign*	*Total*
Business and Industrial Centres	29.0	48.2	38.60	29.2	47.9	38.55	30.1	48.0	39.05
Pilgrim Centres	31.2	10.1	20.65	31.1	10.4	20.75	29.4	10.6	20
Hill Stations	15.5	13.8	14.65	15.7	13.3	14.50	15.2	13.4	14.30
Historical Places	15.5	19.8	17.65	15.4	20.4	17.90	15.7	19.8	17.75
Natural and Sightseeing Areas	8.7	7.5	8.1	8.5	7.4	7.95	8.6	7.5	8.05
Wild Life Sancturies	0.1	0.6	0.35	0.1	0.6	0.35	1.0	0.7	0.85

Source: Department of Tourism, Tamil Nadu.

TABLE 14.4

Centre-wise Break up of Domestic and Foreign Annual Tourist Arrivals in Tamil Nadu

Sl. No.	Destination	1998			1999			2000		
		Domestic	Foreign	Total	Domestic	Foreign	Total	Domestic	Foreign	Total
1.	Chennai	3959596	258875	4218471	3962108	287698	4249806	4230709	309178	4539887
2.	Elagiri	25225	594	258109	26805	783	27588	28912	857	29769
3.	Mamallapuram	601962	62420	664382	629301	70644	699945	679170	73296	752466
4.	Kancheepuram	638882	30564	669446	668414	36403	704817	691633	38028	729661
5.	Tiruthani	609888	5281	615169	633922	5517	639439	701026	5855	706881
6.	Chidambaram	236428	5492	241920	259350	6549	265899	284723	7418	292141
7.	Pitchavaram	2806	409	3215	3110	421	3531	3207	457	3664
8.	Udhagamandalam	1565330	45107	1610437	1647254	50209	1697463	1657642	56185	1713827
9.	Coonnoor	89545	1549	91094	101203	1825	103028	107406	2018	109424
10.	Mudumalai	21051	3812	24863	25568	4124	29692	23293	4043	27336
11.	Thanjavur	388260	13655	401915	431175	17682	448857	496485	22153	518638
12.	Velankanni	322668	1945	324613	360636	2360	362996	396764	2572	399336
13.	Nagore	107588	740	108328	118731	872	119603	236536	959	237495
14.	Poompuhar	6395	446	6841	6922	605	7527	7306	663	7969
15.	Madurai	2155115	49795	2204910	2182150	58565	2240715	2255662	65115	2320777
16.	Kodaikanal	1490895	40724	1531619	1532985	43357	1576342	1522802	45694	1568496
17.	Palani	1046888	3980	1050868	1123032	4618	1127650	1360444	5018	1365462
18.	Rameswaram	1345805	3505	1349310	1383322	4202	1387524	1483915	4781	1488696
19.	Courtalam	454270	3141	457411	463816	3361	467177	474662	3417	478079
20.	Panchalankurichi	3825	00	3825	3721	00	3721	3753	00	3753
21.	Kannyakumari	1145910	42644	1185554	1174212	47724	1221936	1379192	52979	1432171
22.	Trichy	1005755	41260	1047015	1005414	46948	1053262	1114965	52604	1167569
23.	Salem	367990	486	368476	393189	697	393886	437944	867	438811
24.	Yercaud	124615	935	125550	141061	1081	142142	157048	1211	158259
25.	Hogenakkal	39645	389	40034	42368	523	42891	45183	583	45766
26.	Tiruchendur	1140486	6845	1147331	1123507	7477	1130984	12368517	8077	1276594
27.	Coimbatore	605877	6110	611987	784340	8980	793320	955395	12386	967781
28.	Kumbakonam	311039	3773	314812	350151	4395	354546	383209	4713	387922
29.	Thiruvannamalai	599454	1924	601378	559174	4822	563996	594379	5038	599417
	Tamil Nadu	**20413193**	**636400**	**21049593**	**21136941**	**722442**	**21859383**	**22981882**	**786165**	**23768047**

Source: Department of Tourism, Tamil Nadu.

TABLE 14.5

Centre-wise Break up of Domestic and Foreign Annual Tourist Arrivals in Tamil Nadu

Sl. No.	Destination	2001			2002		
		Domestic	Foreign	Total	Domestic	Foreign	Total
1.	Chennai	4361559	300979	4662538	4635278	310198	494576
2.	Elagiri	30514	2442	32956	33041	4846	37887
3.	Mamallapuram	688821	71447	760268	723526	72302	795828
4.	Kancheepuram	693085	37942	731027	718958	38922	757880
5.	Tiruthani	663914	7433	671347	631364	7685	639049
6.	Chidambaram	258998	7380	266378	228115	7512	235627
7.	Pitchavaram	3311	468	3779	3511	507	4018
8.	Udhagamandalam	1695706	57371	1753077	1806969	67014	1873983
9.	Coonnoor	116936	2122	119058	140735	2645	143380
10.	Mudumalai	24043	3465	27508	24601	3935	28536
11.	Thanjavur	562091	24911	587002	613622	26416	640038

Contd...

...Contd...

Sl. No.	Destination	2001 Domestic	2001 Foreign	2001 Total	2002 Domestic	2002 Foreign	2002 Total
12.	Velankanni	390368	3034	393402	409358	6674	416032
13.	Nagore	225308	816	226124	230042	884	230926
14.	Poompuhar	9109	597	9706	10444	547	10991
15.	Madurai	2323432	63685	2387117	2380408	60899	2441307
16.	Kodaikanal	1547184	45697	1592881	1662616	50906	1713522
17.	Palani	1461935	4844	1466779	1455314	4504	1450093
18.	Rameswaram	1553784	5421	1559205	1424817	5276	1430093
19.	Courtalam	481934	2844	484778	396264	2146	398410
20.	Panchalankurichi	3538	0	3538	3571	0	3571
21.	Kannyakumari	1423195	51209	1474404	1496416	50065	1546481
22.	Trichy	1177074	47508	1224582	1223861	48998	1272859
23.	Salem	485337	1059	486396	550641	1080	551721
24.	Yercaud	206859	1261	208120	289267	1373	290640
25.	Hogenakkal	45942	520	46462	51230	569	51799
26.	Tiruchendur	1324918	7173	1332091	1397508	6648	1404156
27.	Coimbatore	1002593	12594	1015187	1007301	13017	1020318
28.	Kumbakonam	426518	4490	431008	447956	4455	452411
29.	Thiruvannamalai	624037	4361	628398	665020	4618	669638
	Tamil Nadu	**23812043**	**773073**	**24585116**	**24661754**	**804641**	**25466395**

TABLE 14.6

Nationality-wise Tourist Arrivals in Chennai, Airport

Country	*1993*	*1994*	*1995*	*1996*	*1997*
USA	14853	16295	18364	19442	20735
Canada	2566	2807	3855	4616	4563
France	8211	10181	12523	13813	12398
Germany	3018	5123	7152	8206	8472
Italy	1682	2288	3651	3256	5110
U.K.	7927	8792	11851	13411	13466
Srilanka	49011	60414	84656	82509	84445
Malaysia	25698	28051	35722	37514	37302
Singapore	21051	20786	22996	23379	24079
Japan	3158	4211	6229	7334	6507
Australia	6109	7240	7898	8965	7071
Others	13350	19511	23298	26156	30443
Total	**156598**	**185699**	**238195**	**248604**	**254591**

TABLE 14.7

Nationality-wise Tourist Arrivals in Chennai, Airport

Country	*1998*	*1999*	*2000*	*2001*	*2002*
USA	232554	27925	32774	30536	30810
Canada	5553	6305	6788	7162	7769
France	16641	19175	20801	22965	22533
Germany	8731	9097	9444	9256	7270
Italy	3190	2934	4011	3875	3722
U.K.	13770	15917	17156	17537	17984
Srilanka	77354	86310	92044	81217	74344
Malaysia	30687	35989	37961	37820	31532
Singapore	23189	22047	22230	31987	20818
Japan	5998	6251	11576	6581	5941
Australia	7896	8438	9464	9073	8977
Others	34901	35138	32880	25858	47315
Total	**251164**	**275526**	**297129**	**283867**	**279015**

TABLE 14.8

Average Lengths of Stay in Tamil Nadu From Major Tourists Generating Countries During 1998, 1999 and 2000

Name of the Countries	*No. of Days 1998*	*1999*	*2000*
United Kingdom	5.1	4.3	5.00
USA	4.6	4.7	4.5
Srilanka	3.7	2.9	4.0
France	4.8	4.7	4.6
Germany	5.2	4.4	5.1
Japan	5.3	4.6	3.0
Italy	5.4	6.4	6.0
Malaysia	6.2	5.1	5.6
Canada	4.1	4.5	4.6
Australia	5.1	4.5	4.9
Singapore	6.8	6.1	7.4
All Countries	5.0	4.7	5.4

Source: Department of Tourism, Tamil Nadu.

Business and Industrial Tourism

Tourism, a term once applied to visits to places of worship and scenic interest, is now understood in a wider context. It includes tours undertaken in pursuit of business, trade, commercial and professional interests and visits to scientific and technical gatherings. This class of tourism now accounts for the biggest share (39.05 per cent) of overall tourism activity in Tamil Nadu. 30.1 per cent of domestic and a high 48.0 per cent of foreign tourists to Tamil Nadu visited the State on business and industry related work in the year 2000.

The reasons for the rapid growth of business and industry related tourism are easy to understand. The head start which Tamil Nadu has had as an industrial, business and export hub in Southern India is the outcome of its geographical location and human capital. These endowments, particularly human capital in the form of abundant availability of highly skilled manpower in areas of Information Technology, banking, business accounting, engineering and medicine have, in recent years, made Tamil Nadu a location of choice for national and multinational corporate entities and financial institutions to base their Indian offices and global back-offices. As an investment centre, Tamil Nadu ranks high with corporates, Indian and foreign.

Business and industry related tourism has a high spin-off in generating demand for upmarket hotel accommodation, fashionable shopping centers, restaurants and entertainment and hence its contribution to the State's economy and employment generation efforts would be very significant. In the hotel industry, an investment of Rs. 10 lakh is estimated to give direct employment to 12 persons and five rooms in a five star hotel provide direct employment to eight persons. Creation of more indirect employment is an inevitable adjunct.

Religious and Cultural Centres – Pilgrimage Tourism

Few regions in the world can boast of such a rich and ancient cultural heritage as Tamil Nadu. Tamil is the world's most ancient language in current day to day use. Its rich literature and the cultural tapestry that it has helped to weave over millennia have an everlasting appeal. The ancient and sacred Sanskrit, the oldest known member of the Indo-European family of languages, find its efflorescence in Tamil Nadu. The richness of these two languages is embodied in the temples and pilgrimage centres with which the State abounds and in the highly stylised music and dance forms like Carnatic music and Bharatanatyam.

Tamil Nadu is a colourful and tranquil mosaic of several religions faiths. St. Thomas attained his martyrdom in Chennai in the first century AD. The San Thome Church on the seashore in Chennai is consecrated to him. The Church of our Lady of Health, Velankanni, near the port town of Nagapattinam (250 miles South of Chennai) attracts pilgrims of all faiths throughout the year. Likewise, worship is offered by the public regardless of their religions following at the hallowed shrine of Hazrat Meera Sultan Syed Hameedi in Nagore near Nagapattinam.

The innumerable religious shrines dotting the State, big and small, are the staple of tourism. The bigger of these like the Brihadeeswarar temple in Thanjavur, the Meenakshi temple in Madurai, the Ranganatha temple in Srirangam (Thiruchirapalli), the shore temples in Mamallapuram and the Siva temple in Rameswaram with the largest colonnade of any temple in the world, have a global appeal for their enormity and surpassing architectural beauty. Two of these, the Brihadeeswarar temple and the Mamallapuram complex have been declared as World Heritage sites by the UNESCO. 38 towns have been recognised as cultural and historical towns by the State government (Table 14.10).

TABLE 14.9

Pilgrimage Tourists to Tamil Nadu

Year	*Domestic Tourists (lakh)*	*Foreign Tourists (lakh)*	*Total*	*% Share in Total Number of Tourists*
1997	53.62	0.61	54.23	27.6
1998	63.59	0.64	64.23	30.5
1999	65.80	0.75	66.55	30.7
2000	67.99	0.76	68.75	28.9

Source: Department of Tourism, Tamil Nadu.

TABLE 14.10

Identified Cultural and Historical Towns (As per G.O.Ms.No.163, MA&WS Department Dt.6.7.1993 are G.O.Ms.No.191, MA&WS Department Dt.18.7.1994)

1. Kancheepuram	20. Tranquebar (Tharangambadi)
2. Chidambaram	21. Nagore
3. Srirangam	22. Velankanni
4. Rameswaram	23. Courtallam
5. Srivilliputhur	24. Sriperambuthur
6. Mahabalipuram	25. Tirunelveli
7. Thanjavur	26. Tiruchengode
8. Kumbakonam	27. Karaikudi
9. Gangaikondacholapuram	28. Perur
10. Poompuhar	29. Bhavani
11. Madurai	30. Pichavaram
12. Palani	31. Marudhur
13. Tiruchendur	32. Kurinjippadi (Birth place of Vallalar)
14. Thiruthani	33. Thirumayam
15. Kanyakumari	34. Chittannavasal
16. Thiruvannamalai	35. Avudayarkoil
17. Gingee	36. Padmanabhapuram
18. Chettinad	37. Kolachel (Kanyakumari Distrct)
19. Valivallam	38. Marakkanam

An interesting index of the popularity of some of Tamil Nadu's temples is provided by the ranking of temples all over India in terms of their annual earnings. The Palani devasthanam (Dindigul district) earned Rs. 80 crore, the Meenakshi temple in Madurai Rs. 7 crore and the Rameswaram temple Rs. 4 crore which puts them in the top 20 temples of the country. (Source: "Cymbals of Wealth"-Economic Times, Chennai, 6 January, 2003)

It can be said with justification that the temples and other religious centres of Tamil Nadu have been and shall continue to be prime attractions for tourists, both domestic and foreign. In any strategy for promoting tourism in Tamil Nadu, the anchor role of pilgrimage tourism should, therefore, be recognised.

Historical and Heritage Tourism

The rulers of the kingdoms that flourished in different parts of Tamil Nadu during the ancient and middle ages had left their impress in the form of monumental temples which are invaluable historical and heritage sites (Table 14.11 below). But nothing remains of their other historical monuments except the Rockfort in Tiruchirapally built by the Pallava king, Mahendravarman I (7th Century A.D.). The forts and palaces that attract tourists today were built by the Naiks who were chieftains of the Vijaynagar empire and other local rulers before and after the advent of the British (Table 14.12). These historical sites continue to record significant tourist arrivals which stood at 35 lakh in the year 2000. This accounted for 17.75 per cent of all tourist arrivals in Tamil Nadu and 19.8 per cent of foreign tourists (Table 14.10). Provision of sound and light shows which bring alive the glory of the history embedded in these monuments has added to their appeal. Museums and Art Galleries have also proved quite popular with foreign and domestic tourists (Table 14.13).

TABLE 14.11

Visitor Statistics of Select Places in Tamil Nadu – 1998-2000

Monument Centres	*No. of Tourists*		
	1998	*1999*	*2000*
Sri Brahadeeswarar Temple, Thanjavur	6354747 (93.3 %)	6468883 (92.8 %)	6553500 (90.9 %)
Monument at Mamallapuram	461525 (6.8 %)	505388 (7.2 %)	656536 (9.1 %)
Total	**6816272** (100 %)	**6974271** (100 %)	**7210036** (100 %)

Source: Department of Tourism, Tamil Nadu.

Imaginatively conceived events linked with 'heritage towns' giving the tourists a taste of life of the bygone era like the one being attempted by the Indian National Trust for Art and Cultural heritage with its throwback to Tamil Nadu's connection with ancient Rome would prove vastly successful with foreign tourists.

TABLE 14.12

Forts and Palaces

	No. of Tourists		
	1998	*1999*	*2000*
Circular Fort, Vattakkottai & King Marthanda Varma Palace	108099 (4.1%)	507598 (17.5%)	884683 (25.4%)
Padmanabapuram Palace	313847 (11.8%)	352574 (12.2%)	571359 (16.4%)
Thirumalai Naicker Palace, Madurai	214977 (8.1%)	231074 (8.0%)	252661 (7.3%)
Kattabomman Fort, Panchalankurichi	92741 (3.4%)	103880 (5.4%)	121907 (5.5%)
Rajagiri and Krishnagiri Fort, Gingee	91137 (3.4%)	156167 (5.4%)	191774 (5.5%)
Danishburg Fort, Tranquebar	19928 (0.8%)	39731 (1.4%)	16548 (0.5%)
Ramalingavilasam Palace, Ramanathapuram	5010 (0.2%)	5882 (0.2%)	6516 (0.2%)
Rockfort, Trichy	1809420 (68.1%)	1496473 (51.7%)	1436912 (41.2%)
Total	**2655159 (100 %)**	**2893379 (100 %)**	**3482360 (100 %)**

Source: Department of Tourism, Tamil Nadu.

TABLE 14.13

Museums and Art Galleries

	No. of Tourists		
	1998	*1999*	*2000*
Government Musuem, Chennai	415433 (38.0%)	331289 (32.7%)	342407 (30.3 %)
Government Art Galley, Thanjavur	160017 (14.6 %)	199057 (19.6 %)	140481 (12.4%)
Government Museum, Vellore	34738 (3.2%)	37173 (3.7%)	57181 (5.1%)
Government Museum, Trichy	27409 (2.5 %)	32696 (3.2 %)	62740 (5.5 %)
Government Museum, Pudukottai	55100 (5.1 %)	51792 (5.1 %)	78995 (7.0 %)
Government Museum, Udhagamandalam	3207 (0.3 %)	3177 (0.3 %)	3051 (0.3 %)
Government Museum, Salem	8913 (0.8%)	9895 (1.0%)	10893 (1.0%)
Government Museum, Erode	8675 (0.8%)	8721 (0.9%)	10789 (1.0 %)
Archaeological Museum, Dharmapuri	2957 (0.3 %)	37435 (0.7%)	52970 (4.6 %)
Silappathikara Kalaikoodam, Poompuhar.	368754 (33.8%)	301270 (29.7 %)	370606 (32.7 %)
Archaeological Museum, Rameswaram	7074 (0.6 %)	1267 (0.1 %)	1624 (0.1%)
Total	**1092277 (100 %)**	**1013772 (100 %)**	**1131737 (100 %)**

Source: Department of Tourism, Tamil Nadu.

TABLE 14.14

Wild Life Sanctuaries and National Parks

Sl. No.	Name of Sanctuary	Wild Life Sanctuaries Area in ha.	National Parks Area in ha	Location (District)	Best Season
1.	Mudumalai Wildlife Sanctuary and National Park	21778	10324	Nilgiris	Throughout the year (except June and August)
2.	Kalaka-Kundanthrai Tiger Reserve	79096	—	Tirunelveli	October to March
3.	Vedanthangal Sanctuary	30	—	Kancheepuram	November to February
4.	Point Calimere Sanctuary	1726	—	Nagapattinam	Birds-Novermber to February. Animals-Throughout the year.
5.	Guindy National Park	—	282	Chennai	Throughout the year.
6.	Indira Gandhi Wildlife Sanctuary & National Park	84149	11711	Coimbatore	Throughout the year (except June to August)
7.	Vettangudi Birds Sanctuary	38	—	Sivaganga	November to February
8.	Mukurthi National Park	—	7846	Nilgiris	February to May
9.	Public Lake Birds Sanctuary	153667	—	Virudhunagar	Throughout the year
10.	Srivilliputhur Grizzled Squirrel Wildlife Sanctuary	48520	—	Virudhunagar	Throughout the year
11.	Chitrangudi Birds Sanctuary	48	—	Ramanathapuram	October to April
12	Karikili Birds Sanctuary	61	—	Kancheepuram	November to February
13.	Kanjirankulam Birds Sanctuary	104	—	Ramanathapuram	October to April
14.	Vallanadu Black-buck Sanctuary	1641	—	Tuticorin	Throughout the year
15.	Gulf of Mannar Bio-spere Reserve and National Park	—	623	Gulf of Mannar in Tuticorin and Ramanathapuram	Throughout the year.
16.	Udhayamarthandapuram Wildlife Sanctuary	45	—	Tiruvarur	November to February
17.	Veduvoor Birds Sanctuary	128	—	Tiruvarur	November to February
18.	Karaivetti Birds Sanctuary	77	—	Perambalur	November to February
19.	Vellode Birds Sanctuary	129	—	Erode	November to February
20.	Kuthakulam, Kudankulam Birds Sanctuary	129	—	Tirunelveli	November to February
21.	Melsevanar, Keelselvanar Birds Sanctuary	593	—	Ramanathapuram	November to February
22.	Arignar Anna Zoological Park (510ha Reserved Forest Area)	—	—	Kancheepuram (Vandalur- 32 km from Chennai)	Throughout the year
	Total	**253808**	**30786**		

Source: Department of Tourism, Tamil Nadu.

Hill Stations

Tamil Nadu has several hill resorts but of these Udhagamandalam (Ooty) and Kodaikanal (Kodai) are preferred to others overwhelmingly by tourists, domestic and foreign. Besides being well developed to handle heavy tourist inflows, the two stations have exquisite botanical gardens and scenic lakes and are climatically agreeable enough to visit throughout the year. As a result, they receive around 15.5 per cent of domestic and 13.5 per cent of foreign tourists to the State. There are other hill stations like Elagiri (Salem district) and Valparai (Pollachi district) which can be developed into more popular resorts than they are today.

Nature and Wildlife Tourism

Despite its low average rainfall and prevailing high temperatures for a better part of the year, Tamil Nadu is fairly rich in its floral and faunal wealth. The State has five National Parks (including the Gulf of Mannar and the Mudumalai Sanctuary and National Park which have been declared as 'biosphere reserves' by the Ministry of Environment and Forests, GoI) and 17 game sanctuaries including the Kalakkad-Mundanthurai Tiger Reserve in Tirunelveli district (Table 14.14). Eight of these 22 nature reserves can be visited throughout the year and the remaining are best seen from late autumn to spring.

Despite their appeal and easy accessibility, *in-situ* wildlife conservation centres in Tamil Nadu have been able to attract only a miniscule percentage of both foreign and domestic tourists. This may well be due to better known reserves being available elsewhere in India for the tourists, particularly foreigners, to visit. The Gulf of Mannar would certainly be an exception as it is the biggest of the available marine parks in India with rich coral formations.

In contrast to wildlife reserves, *ex-situ* conservation sites like zoological and botanical gardens and safari parks seem to have caught the imagination of tourists (Tables 14.14, 14.15 and 14.16). A strong reason for this could be the fact that they are located within or close to large urban centres.

TABLE 14.15

Botanical Gardens

Botanical Garden	*No. of Tourists*		
	1998	*1999*	*2000*
Botanical Garden, Udhagamandalam	1945977 (71.0 %)	1911691 (72.9 %)	1631151 (67.2 %)
Sim's Park, Coonoor	417747 (15.3 %)	303240 (11.6 %)	342396 (14.1 %)
Bryant Park, Kodaikanal	374064 (13.7 %)	404928 (15.5 %)	452581 (18.7 %)
Total	2737788 (100 %)	2619859 (100 %)	2426128 (100 %)

Source: Department of Tourism, Tamil Nadu.

TABLE 14.16

Wildlife Tourism

Wildlife Sanctuary	*No. of Tourists*		
	1998	*1999*	*2000*
Zoological Park, Point Calimere	2450 (0.2%)	7595 (0.5%)	8807 (0.5%)
Vandalur Zoo, Chennai	676630 (53.9 %)	1009246 (60.1 %)	1295343 (67.2%)
Zoological Park, Karumpapatty (Salem district)	24457 (2.0 %)	24250 (1.4 %)	47697 (2.4 %)
Crocodile Bank, Mamallapuram	306917 (24.4 %)	370168 (22.0 %)	300815 (15.6 %)
Wild Life Sanctuary, Mudumalai	12615 (1.0 %)	40659 (2.4%)	75213 (3.9 %)
Tiger Sanctuary, Mundanthurai	232733 (18.5%)	227142 (13.5%)	200583 (10.4 %)
Total	**1255802 (100 %)**	**1679060 (100 %)**	**1928458 (100 %)**

Source: Department of Tourism, Tamil Nadu.

"Fruits to Roots" Tourism

The South Indian diaspora to South and South-east Asia is more than hundred years old. A sizeable percentage of population in Malaysia, Singapore and Sri Lanka is of Indian origin speaking the Tamil language. These ethnic connections account for tourist arrivals from these countries far outnumbering arrivals from all other countries put together. Happily, Tamil Nadu's tourism strategy recognises the tourism potential of such cultural and sentimental connections.

Coastal and Beach Tourism

Tamil Nadu's unbroken 960 km long coastline with vast stretches of sandy beaches, lagoons and coral formations could well be converted into a tourist's paradise. Unfortunately, there has been little effort to harness this natural endowment to promote tourism. Leisure tourism in its variegated forms ranging from surfing and other water sports to health and fitness regimes and relaxed entertainment could be promoted. The Tenth Five Year Plan proposals of the Department of Tourism, Tamil Nadu include development and beautification of six beach stretches.

Health Care and Nature Cure Tourism

Healthcare based on ancient systems of indigenous medicine is a speciality of Tamil Nadu. The State is the home of Siddha School of Medicine and also of practitioners steeped in Ayurveda. The efficacy of naturopathy and these traditional systems of medicine in the treatment of ailments not amenable to modern medicine is now recognised the world over. Tamil Nadu should mount an aggressive compaign in publicising its strengths in traditional medicine.

Tamil Nadu is a leader in the country in having modern institutions of excellence in medical disciplines like Oncology, Cardiology, Neurology, Diabetology and Ophthalmology. This human capital can help attract large numbers of patients from within the country and abroad. An attractive feature of healthcare facilities in Tamil Nadu is their high quality delivered at relatively low cost.

Tourism Strategy for Tamil Nadu

The tourism strategy of Tamil Nadu should be built on the revealed preferences of tourists as seen in the previous paragraphs. In practice this would translate into:-

(i) Creating greater opportunities for business and trade related visits and gatherings including healthcare related tourist arrivals;

(ii) Creating better infrastructural facilities at religious and pilgrimage centres and at historical places;

(iii) Development of selected minor hill stations and according them special publicity;

(iv) Preference to be given to the development of *ex-situ* plant and wildlife conservation sites over *in-situ* sites;

(v) Promoting visits of ethnic Tamil speaking Indian community abroad particularly in South and South-east Asia; and

(vi) Launching a vigorous and sustained publicity campaign in India and abroad through electronic and print media of the special features of Tamil Nadu; this would include making available extensive and uptodate information through an interactive website. This would obviate the expensive alternative of settings up tourism promotion offices abroad.

(vii) Involving private enterprise closely in tourism development activities.

Tamil Nadu's Tourism Policy (1992)

In May, 1992, Department of Tourism, Tamil Nadu came out with a Tourism Policy 'handbook' with clear objectives and strategies.

The eight elements of the policy were:-

(i) "Area Development Approach, keeping foreign tourist in mind.

(ii) Encouraging private sector investment in tourism.

(iii) Promotion of local and domestic tourism.

(iv) Manpower development in the hotel and tourism industry.

(v) Adequate publicity for tourism promotion in India and abroad.

(vi) Promotion of cultural tourism – Fairs and Festivals.

(vii) Developing facilities for tented tourism, adventure tourism and beach tourism.

(viii) Using a growth centre approach and integrating tourism development with the overall development of the place and its people".

Under the Policy, tourism was given the status of an industry, and incentives in the form of soft loans, capital investment subsidy, deferral of sales tax on restaurant sales for five years, waiver of 50 per cent of Luxury Tax on rooms, elasticity tariff concession and capital subsidy for purchase of generators were announced. Three Special Tourism Areas, namely the stretch from Muttukadu to Pondicherry, Tharangambadi (a settlement founded by the Dutch) and Kancheepuram were identified for focussed development. 12 towns were declared 'heritage towns' deserving of orderly town planning, beautification and presentation of their archaeological and architectural heritage. To promote cultural tourism, a dozen festivals were to be given publicity. Criteria for approval of hotels for giving them star ratings were also prescribed.

There appears to be a fair degree of implementation of the 1992 policy, Tourist arrivals, both foreign and domestic, registered an increase. Modest pricing of tourist facilities created both by the State government and private sector seem to have helped the budget tourist. In December 2002, the State government provided a further reduction in Luxury Tax on hotel rents, thus meeting a longstanding demand of the hospitality industry. This should make accommodation in hotels enjoying star status more affordable than before which in turn will generate greater demand for hotels, result in extended stay of tourists and more spending.

The new rates of Luxury Tax are :

Rate of charge for accommodation per day	Rate of Luxury Tax (as % of rate of charge for accommodation)
Rs. 200 upto less than Rs. 500	5
Rs. 500 upto less than Rs. 1000	10
Rs. 1000 or more	12.5

(Tamil Nadu Government Gazette Extraordinary No. 842 dated 31.12.2002)

The 1992 Tourism Policy has been revisited by the state government and a new policy is on the anvil.

Ninth Five Year Plan (1997–2002)

Details of actual expenditure during the Ninth Five Year Plan were as below (Table 14.17):

The sources of funding during the Ninth Plan were as below (Table 14.18):

Some of the important achievements recorded during the Ninth Plan were:

(i) Setting up of Tourist Information Centres at Thiruvananthapuram, Bangalore and Hyderabad to give greater publicity to Tamil Nadu;

(ii) Upgradation of the Food Craft Institute, Tiruchirapally to a State Level Institute of Hotel Management and Catering Technology;

(iii) Provision of infrastructure facilities at Heritage Centres and other tourist centres;

TABLE 14.17

Expenditure

(Rs. Lakh)

Scheme Name	*1997-98*	*1998-99*	*1999-2000*	*2000-01*	*2001-02*	*2002-03*
Promotion and Publicity of Tourism, Advertisement and Printing	71.81	53.75	43.28	38.06	389.20	537.99
Fairs and Festivals	30.48	37.45	31.80	27.79	74.71	99.94
Capital Subsidy for Hotel Projects and Generator Subsidy	28.81	29.29	17.29	00.00	00.00	00.00
Schemes	261.16	477.75	207.75	220.78	791.24	349.36
Non-Plan	148.84	207.44	435.68	225.76	220.33	231.37
Total	**541.10**	**805.68**	**735.80**	**512.39**	**1475.48**	**1218.66**

Source: Department of Tourism, Tamil Nadu.

TABLE 14.18

Sources of Funding

(Rs. Lakh)

Sub Head	*1997-98*	*1998-99*	*1999-2000*	*2000-01*	*2001-02*	*2002-03*
Non - Plan	148.84	207.44	435.68	225.76	220.33	869.30
State-Plan	235.30	452.88	217.25	162.80	531.91	62.00
Centrally Sponsored Schemes	81.50	60.31	52.25	14.41	15.87	40.80
Schemes Shared Between the State and the Centre	75.46	85.05	30.50	115.72	707.37	246.56
Total	541.10	805.68	735.68	518.69	1475.48	1218.66

Source: Department of Tourism, Tamil Nadu.

(iv) Grant of incentives for construction of hotels and encouraging joint venture schemes;

(v) Development of Tharangambadi and Marina beach (Chennai) and Guindy park (Chennai)

(vi) Establishment of a tourist complex at the Omanthurar government estate in Chennai to serve as a premier information centre; and

(vii) Participation in Travel Marts in Berlin and Singapore (March – April, 1999) to give publicity overseas.

Tenth Five Year Plan (2002–07)

A Plan outlay of Rs. 210.00 crore is envisaged for the Tenth Plan (Table 14.19).

The Tenth Five Year Plan of the Tamil Nadu Department of Tourism, envisages a cumulative annual growth of 12 per cent in domestic and foreign tourist arrivals to the state. The average length of stay of domestic tourists is sought to be extended from the present nine days to twelve days and of foreign tourists from 4.7 to 6.8 days.

Towards achieving the above goals, the following activities, among others, have been proposed:

(i) Development of at least two centres in each district as District Tourist Centres provided with adequate infrastructure for accommodating tourists;

(ii) Development of the historical moments in Pulicat (North of Chennai) and in Tranquebar (Tharangambadi), the latter with Dutch Government assistance;

(iii) Setting up of new boat houses and upgradation of existing boat houses;

(iv) Beautification of six beaches, Marina (Chennai), Elliots (Chennai), Nagapattinam, Kannyakumari, Rameswaram and Tiruchendur;

(v) Development of ten national parks and game sanctuaries,

(vi) Promotion of "Village Tourism", Adventure Tourism, and Eco-tourism,

(vii) Setting up a spacious convention centre at a location between Chennai and Mamallapuram capable of hosting National and International conferences and complete with a 1000 roomed hotel, a shopping arcade and entertainment centres; and

TABLE 14.19

Financial Outlay for Tenth Five Year Plan

(Rs. crore)

Year	*Infrastructure*	*Publicity*	*Incentives*	*Fairs & Festivals*	*Others*	*Total*
	a. Development of Infrastructure Facilities at Tourist Spots b. Development of Pulicat/Tranquebar c. Setting up of New Boat Houses and Upgradation of Existing Boat Houses d. Improvement of Minor Dams e. Beautification of Beaches f. Development of National Parks/Sanctuaries g. Village Tourism h. Adventure Tourism i. Eco-Tourism j. Government of India Assisted Schemes k. Convention Centre	a. Publicity Measures b. Participationin International Tourism Marts c. Mobile Audiovisual Publicity System d. Fam Tour				
2002-2003	13	15.00	0	1	3.64	32.64
2003-2004	21	15.00	1	1	4.00	42.00
2004-2005	22	15.00	1	2	4.00	44.00
2005-2006	23	15.00	1	2	4.00	45.00
2006-2007	24	15.36	1	2	4.00	46.36
Total	103	75.36	4	8	19.64	210.00

Source: Department of Tourism, Tamil Nadu.

(viii) Extending capital subsidy upto Rs. 10.00 lakh for one, two and three star hotel projects and grant of generator subsidy.

A Critique of the Tenth Plan

A look at the activities envisaged above and the sites which are proposed to be taken up raises several questions. Foremost, the potential of private participation in promoting tourism in the State has not been spelt out, though this was given prominence in the 1992 Policy. With assistance available from banks and financial institutions, one should expect private enterprise to play a substantial role in taking up many of the activities that were once the responsibility of the government.

Direct cash subsidies from the government may be substituted by greater facilitation by the State in the form of assignment or long lease of government land on concessional terms to hotels and other projects. This will reduce substantially the capital cost of such projects and help avoid delays involved in negotiations between individual landholders and entrepreneurs. This route will be found particularly useful in establishing hotels and related projects in hill stations and near nature reserves.

In developing adventure or eco-tourism, government should play only a regulatory and facilitating role like identifying sites, prescribing minimum facilities, including safety measures to be provided, and leasing out government land for constructing accommodation instead of taking upon itself the entire responsibility. Well qualified specialist agencies have came up in the country which can take on activities like organising wild life safaris or running adventure clubs for people of all ages. Similarly, it is advisable to give away the 10 boathouses, three restaurants and four canteens to private bodies on lease. A beginning has been made to privatise the operation and maintenance of the Ooty Lake in April, 2003.

The above suggestion that the Department of Tourism or a governmental agency like Tamil Nadu Tourism Development Corporation (TTDC) should keep out of activities which can be better entrusted to private enterprise is reinforced by the experience of Youth Hostels in Tamil Nadu. A well intentioned scheme to provide in expensive accommodation to the budget tourist, Youth Hostels, some of which were run privately and by NGOs, were once profit centres. But, over the years, they could not sustain themselves and had to be merged with Tamil Nadu Hotels promoted by TTDC.

The TTDC today runs 54 hotels/restaurants out of which government approval has been obtained to enfranchise 30 hotels and seven restaurants. Out of these 30 hotels, nine have been enfranchise so far and action is afoot to enfranchise the other 21 also. With this experience, it would be advisable to let private enterprise run hotels and for the government and its public enterprises to exit.

The entry of private enterprises into areas which had been the preserve of the State Government hitherto is seen in the entrustment of the conduct of the Mamallapuram Dance Festival (December 2002–January 2003) to a private Event Manager. Promotional and marketing activities in the tourism sector would now have the benefit of assistance of a professional consultant.

A Consultancy Wing has been established within the TTDC to advise the corporation and the Department of Tourism of the State government in identifying private agencies for preparing master plans and technoeconomic feasibility studies and exploring availability of private funding and implementing agencies.

To provide land to private entrepreneurs in setting up tourist facilities a new initiative has begun in the form of creating a Land Bank at the Tourism Commissioner's office. The Land Bank is the data source on all vacant government lands in the State which could be made available to prospective entrepreneurs on long lease. Identification of such lands has already been completed in the districts of Namakkal and Kannyakumari.

Private sector investment in tourism in Tamil Nadu in the coming years is expected to be around Rs. 2000 crore. Investment of that order can and should take care of many of the activities now envisaged to be taken up by the government.

Tamil Nadu Tourism Development Corporation (TTDC)

TTDC, started in the year 1971, has been the prime mover in providing tourist infrastructure in Tamil Nadu. The profits of TTDC are showing a falling trend from Rs. 16.25 lakh in 1999-2000 to Rs. 2.95 lakh in 2000-01. This has been due mainly to the need to make adjustments of Rs. 29.44 lakh towards losses incurred in the past. Still the accumulated losses of TTDC run to Rs. 223.05 lakh. To turn itself into a profit making organisation, TTDC should divest itself of some of its present activities.

Role of Other Departments in Tourism Promotion

Tourism promotion is a cross-cutting activity involving, besides the nodal department of Tourism, many other wings of the State government like the departments dealing with Town and Country Planning, Urban and Rural Development, Transport, Highways, Culture, Religion endowments, Forests and Wildlife. Their plans and programmes need to be dovetailed with the activities of the Department of Tourism.

Tourist Centres in Tamil Nadu are marked by haphazard growth and lack of civic amenities which offend hygiene, sanitation and aesthetics. The local bodies, whether they be municipal corporations, municipal committees or village *panchayats*, can play an effective role in improving conditions in tourist centres. In fact, local bodies can be said to be under an obligation to do so because the local economy is the main beneficiary of tourist arrivals. Likewise, the Hindu Religions Endowment Board and Wakqf Boards can extend their interest from within the temples or mosques to the environment outside.

Tamil Nadu's Tourism Policy of 1992 sought to establish Special Tourism Development Authorities (SDA) in Mamallapuram to cover the coastal stretch from Muttukadu to Pondicherry, in Tharangambadi covering an area of 10 km radius, and in Kancheepuram. Such authorities were also sought to be set up in the 'heritage towns'. Barring the three SDAs at Mamallapuram, Tharangambadi and Kancheepuram, such authorities could not be set up at other centres for want of funds.

Tamil Nadu's Capacity to Handle Greater Tourist Arrivals

Tamil Nadu's capacity to handle the envisaged higher tourist influx is contingent on its infrastructure for accommodation and transportation. On both these counts, the situation is bright indeed.

Tourist Accommodation

Besides the 54 hotels owned by TTDC, there are 151 private hotels approved by the Department of Tourism enjoying star rating and 18 others which have not earned any classification. Two of the approved hotels are recognised as 'heritage hotels'. The approved private hotels have 9170 rooms. In addition, the 1800 unapproved hotels in the State have a total room strength of 5000. This accommodation is augmented by the Youth Hostels run by the State government, private organisations and Sports Authority of India (SAI) and located at hill resorts (Ooty, Kodaikanal and Yercaud) wildlife sanctuary (Mudumalai), pilgrimage centres (Rameswaram, Chennai, Chidambaram) and cultural centres (Mamallapuram).

At an average occupancy of 60 per cent, there's sufficient hotel accommodation in the State to handle the present levels of 7.9 lakh foreign and 230 lakh domestic visitors. Department of Tourism, Tamil Nadu is confident that the projected increases in tourist arrivals in coming years can well be handled by the existing accommodation capacity operating at higher occupancy rates. This comfortable accommodation position coupled with moderate pricing of facilities is an attractive feature that sets Tamil Nadu's tourism centres apart from those in many other States.

Transportation Facilities

Tamil Nadu is well served with a rail and road network, airports and seaports. The 4181 km long rail network (2044 km of Broad Gauge and 2137 km of Metre Gauge) crisscrosses the length and breadth of the State. The 150647 km. length of roads, translated into a road density of 539.69 km per lakh of population and 74.90 km per 100 km^2 of area, places the State well above the national level.

The five airports at Chennai, Madurai, Coimbatore, Tiruchirapally and Salem are located strategically to serve tourism interests.

Tamil Nadu enjoys the distinction of having a well-run public road transportation system catering to the needs of urban and rural commuters. This is well augmented by private transport. Together they complement and compete with the railways. The TTDC operates tours with a fleet of 27 coaches including air-conditioned luxury coaches. A conjunctive use of the facilities offered by the public and private transport operators and the railways will synergise and optimise their operations thereby conferring greater benefits on the travelling public, particularly tourists for whom time and expenditure are important considerations. Statistics gathered by the Department of Tourism, Tamil Nadu for the year 1999–2000 show that intercity transport accounted for the 12.5 per cent (Rs. 260.00) of a foreign tourist's average daily expenditure of Rs. 2080.00 in Tamil Nadu. The corresponding figures for a domestic tourist was a relatively high 17.7 per cent (about Rs. 100.00) out of his daily average expenditure of Rs. 545.00. Less travel cost and less commuting time would make for greater overall spending.

To conclude, Tamil Nadu is well poised to extend its hospitality to tourists, domestic and foreign, in the coming years. Tamil Nadu needs tourism for its economic development and Indian tourism needs Tamil Nadu, the 'most-Indian' part of India.

Chapter 15

Finances of Tamil Nadu Government

Introduction

Tamil Nadu has traditionally been a financially well-administered State, but in more recent years, the government finances have been under stress. It is essential to trace the causes that have led to the difficult financial situation in which Tamil Nadu is now placed. This financial crisis is standing in the way of the development of the State and if not solved quickly, it may lead to great financial instability and social tensions in the State. In this chapter, we attempt to trace and analyse the developments in the financial position of the Tamil Nadu Government during 1980-81 to 2000-01.

Broadly, our objective in this chapter is to review and analyse the following:

(i) the overall trends in revenues, expenditures and fiscal balances;

(ii) the trends in the level and composition of revenue receipts and expenditures;

(iii) the composition and trends in own tax and own non-tax revenues;

(iv) the trends and composition of capital receipts and expenditures; and

(v) the ways of restructuring the State finances.

In making the above analysis, we compare the financial performance and tax structure of Tamil Nadu with those of the major State governments in the country. On the basis of the results of our analysis, we suggest the lines of reform and improvement in the fiscal and tax policy of the Government of Tamil Nadu.

Fiscal Trends: An Overview

Budget expenditure of Tamil Nadu as a ratio of its GSDP stood around 17 per cent generally in years since 1980-81 to 1990-91 (Table 15.1).[1] Within this total, the ratio of revenue expenditure went up. While revenue receipt-GSDP ratio decreased from 13.9 per cent in 1980-81 to 12.5 per cent in 2000-01, revenue expenditure increased from 12.5 per cent to 14.8 per cent during the same period.

Growth rate estimates show that during 1990-91 to 1999-00, the GSDP grew at the annual rate of 6.67 per cent in real terms. Since the economy was growing fairly fast, one could expect an equally fast growth of the government sector. However, revenue receipts grew only at the rate of 4.35 per cent per annum and revenue expenditures at 4.61 per cent. That is, the growth of revenue receipts and revenue expenditures in the nineties was relatively low as compared to that in the eighties. The causes for this low growth are analysed later in this chapter.

The revenue account registered a surplus up to 1985-86 and after that it showed a deficit in all the years shown in Table 15.1.

The revenue deficit-GSDP was 1.6 per cent in 1990-91 and 0.4 per cent in 1995-96. But it increased to 3.4 per cent in 1999-00. Thus, it seems that the financial situation deteriorated during second half of the nineties. It is noted that while revenue receipts as a percentage of GSDP decreased from 14.8 in 1985-86 to 13.5 per cent in 1995-96 and further to 12.7 in 1999-00, revenue expenditure kept increasing as a percentage of GSDP from 1980-81 (except for 1995-96) and reached

1. Since the GSDP figures in the old series (up to 1992-93) are not comparable with those in new series (from 1993-94 onwards), we have adjusted the old series figures in such a way that they are comparable with new series figures. It is noted that among the major states Tamil Nadu (Rs. 20899) ranked fifth in the per capita income in 1999-00. Therefore, we can infer that the potential tax base of Tamil Nadu (as measured in terms of per capita GSDP) is larger than those in several states in the country.

TABLE 15.1

Overall Fiscal Trends in Tamil Nadu

(Rs. Crore)

	1980-81	1985-86	1990-91	1995-96	1999-00	2000-01	2003-04 (BE)
Revenue Receipts	1280 (13.9)	2638 (14.8)	5088 (14.3)	10599 (13.5)	16328 (12.7)	18317 (12.5)	22666
Revenue Expenditure	1152 (12.5)	2450 (13.7)	5641 (15.8)	10911 (13.9)	20728 (16.1)	21752 (14.8)	26599
Capital Expenditure of Which,	470 (5.1)	657 (3.7)	700 (2.0)	1351 (1.7)	1296 (1.0)	2000 (1.4)	3011
Capital Outlays	8.5 (0.9)	152 (0.9)	222 (0.6)	591 (0.8)	645 (0.5)	1547 (1.1)	2557
(Net) Loans and Advances	254 (2.8)	400 (2.2)	350 (1.0)	353 (0.4)	337 (0.3)	95 (0.1)	454
Total Expenditure	1622 (17.6)	3107 (17.4)	6341 (17.8)	12262 (15.6)	22024 (17.1)	23752 (16.1)	29610
Revenue Deficit*	–128 (–1.4)	–189 (–1.1)	553 (1.6)	311 (0.4)	4400 (3.4)	3435 (2.3)	3933
Fiscal Deficit	211 (2.3)	363 (2.0)	1126 (3.2)	1256 (1.6)	5382 (4.2)	5077 (3.5)	6944
Public Debt	1964 (21.3)	2907 (16.3)	5501 (15.4)	12552 (15.9)	23232 (18.1)	27641 (18.8)	40947^
GSDP#	9203	17823	35662	78767	128646	147093^	

Source: Government of Tamil Nadu (Various Years), RBI (2002), EPW (2001) and CSO (1999 & 2000)-Diskettes.

Figures in parentheses indicate the percentages of GSDP. BE-Budget Estimates.

#- Up to 1990-91, the old series data were adjusted to be comparable with new series (the adjustment factor is 0.878); * Minus sign indicates a surplus. ^ Provisional figures.

16.1 in 1999-00, raising the revenue deficit to 3.4 per cent.[2] On the other hand, capital expenditure declined steadily as per cent of GSDP, reaching 1 per cent in 1999-00. It is also noted that capital expenditure accounted for 29 per cent of total expenditure in 1980-81, but declined to only 5.9 per cent in 1999-00.

The fiscal deficit (=net borrowing) as a per cent of GSDP increased from 2.3 per cent in the beginning of the eighties to 3.2 per cent at beginning of the nineties. By the end of the nineties, the fiscal deficit ratio had gone up to 4.2 per cent. There was a drop in the ratio in 1995-96; the main reason for the fall in fiscal deficit ratio in the year seems to be the decrease in the revenue expenditure GSDP ratio, which was more than the fall in the revenue receipts-GSDP ratio. After that the fiscal deficit-GSDP ratio started rising again.[3]

2. However, the revenue receipts-GSDP ratio declined to 12.5 per cent and revenue expenditure-GSDP ratio to 14.8 per cent in 2000-01, reducing the revenue deficit to 2.3 per cent.

3. It is noted that the revenue deficit as a percentage of fiscal deficit (which measures the extent to which the borrowings of the government are used to finance its revenue expenditure) increased (from 25 per cent in 1995-96) to 82 per cent in 1999-00 (68 per cent in 2000-01). This means that out of every rupee of net loan that it borrowed in 1999-00, the government spent 82 paise on non-revenue yielding expenditure items and only 18 paise on capital (development) expenditure. It is also noted that the fiscal deficit-GSDP ratio declined to 3.5 per cent in 2000-01.

Continuing increases in fiscal deficits have led to a mounting interest burden of the State. Interest payment accounted for nearly 13 per cent of revenue expenditure in 2000-01 (shown later). Thus, the key fiscal ratios discussed above reflect increased borrowing to finance public expenditures in Tamil Nadu, rising revenue deficit and fall in the capital expenditure. Table 15.1 also shows the stock of public debt in Tamil Nadu over the years. From 1980-81 to 2000-01, the stock of debt in absolute terms increased from Rs. 1964 crore to Rs. 27641 crore, but fell as a percentage of GSDP. As against 21.3 per cent in 1980-81, the Debt-GSDP was 18.8 per cent in 2000-01. Although this ratio is still within limits and compares well with those of many other states, it is a matter of concern that a large part of net borrowing, about 80 per cent, is used to finance revenue expenditures. From the above analysis, it is clear that in recent years the finances of the Tamil Nadu Government have been under stress.

Trends and Composition of Revenue Receipts

Tamil Nadu's revenue receipts were 12.5 per cent of GSDP in 2000-01, lower than the ratio of 14.3 per cent in 1990-91. This decline was mainly due to the lower

TABLE 15.2

Trends in Current Revenues of Tamil Nadu

(Rs. Crore)

Year	*Own Tax*	*Own Non-Tax*	*Shared Taxes*	*Grants*	*Revenue Receipts*	*Per Capita Revenue (Rs.)*
1980-81	639 (49.9) [6.9]	232 (18.1) [2.5]	292 (22.8) [3.2]	117 (9.1) [1.3]	1280 (100) [13.9]	266 {266}
1985-86	1548 (58.7) [8.7]	239 (9.1) [1.3]	517 (19.6) [2.9]	335 (12.7) [1.9]	2638 (100) [14.8]	505 {338}
1990-91	3124 (61.4) [8.8]	381 (7.5) [1.1]	1003 (19.7) [2.8]	579 (11.4) [1.6]	5088 (100) [14.3]	916 {407}
1995-96	7151 (67.5) [9.1]	858 (8.1) [1.1]	1806 (17.0) [2.3]	784 (7.4) [1.0]	10599 (100) [13.5]	1814 {495}
1999-00	10919 (67) [8.5]	1357 (8.2) [1.0]	2667 (16.3) [2.1]	1385 (8.5) [1.1]	16328 (100) [12.7]	2652 {561}
2000-01	12282 (62.1) [8.3]	1711 (9.3) [1.2]	2784 (15.2) [1.9]	1540 (8.4) [1.0]	18317 (100) [12.5]	2949
2003-04 (BE)	15833 (69.9)	1506 (6.6)	3435 (15.2)	1892 (8.3)	22666 (100)	
Annual Growth Rates (Constant Prices) in per cent						
1980-81 to 1989-90	6.14	1.11	4.86	8.47	5.42	3.88
1990-91 to 1999-00	6.27	1.15	2.97	–1.29	4.35	3.27
1980-81 to 1999-00	6.57	3.41	4.22	4.13	5.54	4.27

Source: Government of Tamil Nadu (Various Years) and CSO (1999 & 2000)-Diskettes.

Figures in parentheses indicate the percentages of total revenues. Figures in brackets indicate the percentages of GSDP and figures in {} are the per capita revenues in 1980-81 prices. BE-Budget Estimates.

rate of growth of the central transfers as shown above. Table 15.2 shows that the revenue receipts (at 1980-81 prices) grew at the rate of 5.42 per cent per annum during the eighties. During the nineties, the rate was 4.35 per cent.

Own tax revenues constituted the largest single revenue source of Tamil Nadu (62 per cent) in 2000-01. In fact, the share of own tax revenues increased over the years since 1980-81. But the share in total of own non-tax revenues fell over the same period from 18 per cent in 1980-81 to around 9 per cent in 2000-01. However, the share of total own revenues (own tax + own non-tax) increased from 68 per cent to 72 per cent. As a per cent of GSDP the share of own total revenues remained the same at about 9.5 per cent. The share of devolution and grants fell from 32 per cent to 23.6 per cent in the same period.

In constant prices, own revenues grew at almost the same rate as GSDP in the period 1980-81 to 1999-00 (6.1 per cent). In the period 1990-91 to 1999-00, the growth was slightly lower (5.47), but significantly lower than the GSDP growth rate (6.67 per cent). On the other hand, in the latter period, shared taxes grew only at about 3 per cent while the growth rate of grants was negative. That is the reason why the total revenues of the government could not grow as fast or nearly as fast as GSDP. In the nineties, as against the real rate of growth of GSDP of 6.7 per cent per annum, total revenues could grow only at 4.4 per cent, resulting in a fall in the revenue-GSDP ratio from 14.3 per cent to 12.7 per cent. It is clear that in the nineties, the reduction in rate of growth of Central transfers (from 4.2 per cent during the eighties to 1.5 per cent) far below the growth rate of GSDP considerably added to the financial difficulties of the state government.

Some Comparisons with Other States

Tamil Nadu's revenue performance compares well with those of other major States. In 1999-00, per capita own revenues of Tamil Nadu at Rs. 1998 was lower than those of only Gujarat, Haryana, Himachal Pradesh, Maharastra and Punjab; that is, Tamil Nadu occupied the sixth rank (Table 15.3). However, in terms of per capita own tax revenues, Tamil Nadu (with Rs. 1777)

TABLE 15.3

Revenue Receipts in Selected States in 1999-2000

States	*Per Capita*				*As a % of GSDP*			
	Revenue (Rs.)	*Own Tax Revenue (Rs.)*	*Own Revenue (Rs.)*	*Transfer from Centre (Rs.)*	*Revenue Receipts*	*Own Tax Revenue*	*Own Non-Tax Revenue*	*Own Total Revenue*
Andhra Pradesh	2248	1205	1532	716	13.8	7.4	2.0	9.4
Assam	1855	469	640	1215	17.2	4.3	1.6	5.9
Bihar	1511	437	648	863	17.4	5.0	2.4	7.5
Gujarat	2804	1646	2235	569	12.9	7.6	2.7	10.3
Haryana	2804	1710	2322	481	12.2	7.5	2.7	10.1
Himachal Pradesh	5716	954	2579	3137	32.9	5.5	9.3	14.8
Karnataka	2487	1492	1803	684	13.6	8.2	1.7	9.8
Kerala	2517	1646	1814	703	12.3	8.0	0.8	8.8
Madhya Pradesh	2167	951	1356	811	13.3	5.8	2.5	8.3
Maharashtra	2665	1821	2236	429	10.5	7.2	1.6	8.8
Orissa	1627	471	669	958	15.5	4.5	1.9	6.4
Punjab	3130	1655	2645	486	11.9	6.3	3.8	10.1
Rajasthan	1777	823	1108	669	13.0	6.0	2.1	8.1
Tamil Nadu	**2657**	**1777**	**1998**	**659**	**12.7**	**8.5**	**1.0**	**9.5**
Uttar Pradesh	1318	576	700	618	11.5	5.0	1.1	6.1
West Bengal	1294	646	721	573	7.7	3.8	0.4	4.3

Source: Computed from Reserve Bank of India (2000) "State Finances—A Study of Budget of 2000-2001" and GSDP (advanced estimates for 1999-00) Data provided by EPW Research Foundation-2002 (diskettes).

TABLE 15.4

Composition of Revenue Receipts and Revenue Expenditures for Selected States in India (1999-2000)

States	*Composition of Revenue Receipts (%)*				*Composition of Revenue Expenditure (%)*		
	Own Tax	*Own Non-Tax*	*Shared Tax*	*Grants*	*General Services*	*Social Services*	*Economic Services*
Andhra Pradesh	53.6	14.5	19.9	12.0	37.3	40.6	21.3
Assam	25.3	9.2	29.9	35.6	42.1	40.7	17.1
Bihar	28.9	14.0	40.5	16.6	42.3	38.6	19.0
Gujarat	58.7	21.0	12.0	8.3	32.8	35.6	31.3
Haryana	61.0	21.8	9.1	8.1	41.8	32.5	25.8
Himachal Pradesh	16.7	28.4	24.8	30.1	37.9	36.0	25.6
Karnataka	60.0	12.5	16.5	11.0	35.0	36.0	26.3
Kerala	65.4	6.7	19.3	8.6	43.0	36.4	19.9
Madhya Pradesh	43.9	18.7	24.7	12.7	32.5	38.5	25.0
Maharashtra	68.3	15.6	10.3	5.8	42.4	37.9	17.8
Orissa	29.0	12.2	29.7	29.2	34.1	47.3	18.3
Punjab	52.9	31.6	8.6	7.0	54.8	26.6	18.1
Rajasthan	46.3	16.1	22.3	15.3	42.3	40.9	16.7
Tamil Nadu	**66.9**	**8.2**	**16.3**	**8.5**	**37.4**	**36.9**	**20.8**
Uttar Pradesh	43.7	9.4	34.8	12.1	46.8	30.2	20.0
West Bengal	50.0	5.8	29.2	15.1	41.2	42.0	15.5

Source: Computed from RBI (2002).

had the second rank after Maharastra (Rs. 1821). In respect of own tax revenue as per cent of GSDP, Tamil Nadu occupied the first rank with a ratio of 8.5 per cent. However, own non-tax revenues as per cent of GSDP was only 1 and Tamil Nadu compared poorly with most States.

As can be seen in Table 15.4, the share of own revenues in Tamil Nadu constitutes about 75 per cent of total revenues. The corresponding figures for Andhra Pradesh, Karnataka and Kerala are 68 per cent, 72.5 per cent, and 72 per cent, respectively. States such as Gujarat (80 per cent), Haryana (83 per cent),

TABLE 15.5

Compositions of Tax Revenues

(Rs. Crore)

Year	*Total Sales Tax*	*General Sales Tax*	*State Excise*	*Taxes on Vehicles*	*Land Revenue*	*Stamp and Registration Fees*	*Total Own Tax Revenue*
1980-81	457 (71.5) [5.0]	371 (58.1) [4.0]	13 (2.0) [0.1]	81 (12.7) [0.9]	-4 (-0.7) [0.0]	45 (7.0) [0.5]	639 (100.0) [6.9]
1985-86	992 (64.1) [5.6]	846 (54.6) [4.7]	242 (15.6) [1.4]	111 (7.1) [0.6]	16 (1.1) [0.1]	95 (6.1) [0.5]	1548 (100.0) [8.7]
1990-91	2066 (66.1) [5.8]	1787.9 (57.2) [5.01]	435 (13.9) [1.2]	227 (7.3) [0.6]	14 (0.5) [0.0]	226 (7.2) [0.6]	3124 (100.0) [8.8]
1995-96	4689 (65.6) [6.0]	3988 (55.8) [5.1]	935 (13.1) [1.2]	392 (5.5) [0.5]	25 (0.4) [0.0]	613 (8.6) [0.8]	7151 (100.0) [9.1]
1998-99	6113 (63.5) [5.2]	5398 (56.1) [4.6]	1710 (17.8) [1.5]	518 (5.4) [0.4]	29 (0.3) [0.0]	673 (7.0) [0.6]	9625 (100.0) [8.2]
1999-00	7024 (64.3) [5.5]	6194 (56.7) [4.8]	1834 (16.8) [1.4]	578 (5.3) [0.4]	47 (0.4) [0.0]	818 (7.5) [0.6]	10919 (100.0) [8.5]
2000-01	8197 (66.7) [5.6]	6013 (49.0) [4.1]	1869 (15.2) [1.3]	590 (4.8) [0.4]	56 (0.5) [0.04]	910 (7.4) [0.6]	12282 (100) [.3]
2003-04 BE	10476 (66.2)	9369 (59.2)	2264 (14.3)	878 (5.5)	21 (0.1)	1279 (8.1)	15833 (100.0)
				Annual Growth Rates (%)			
1980-81 to 1989-90	6.49	7.03	11.4	3.57	-1.06	9.46	6.05
1990-91 to 1999-00	5.82	5.84	9.44	2.14	0.93	5.77	6.27
1980-81 to 1999-00	6.51	6.78	9.70	3.20	-0.50	7.73	6.50

Source: Government of Tamil Nadu (Various Years), and CSO (1999 & 2000)-Diskettes.

Figures in (.) parentheses indicate the percentages of total while the figures in [.] brackets indicate taxes as percentages of GSDP. BE-Budget Estimates.

Maharastra (84 per cent), and Punjab (84.5 per cent) have relatively a high proportion of own revenues because of larger share of non-tax revenues. It is noted that Tamil Nadu (8 per cent) was the third lowest in terms of percentage share of non-tax revenues, next after West Bengal (5.8 per cent) and Kerala (6.7 per cent) in 1999-00.

Thus, Tamil Nadu had the largest per capita revenue and own revenue among the Southern States.

Own Tax Revenues

As mentioned earlier, own tax revenue is the largest single revenue source of Tamil Nadu Government. It may be noted that during the nineties, the own tax revenues of Tamil Nadu grew at the annual rate of 6.3 per cent (6 per cent in the eighties), which was slightly lower than that of GSDP in the same period (6.67 per cent).[4]

Composition of Own Tax Revenues

Among the State taxes, sales tax is by far the most important own tax revenue source (Table 15.5). Its relative share declined from about 72 per cent in 1980-81 to 67 per cent in 2000-01. The State general sales tax accounts for the major part—49 per cent (in 2000-01). What is noteworthy is also that the sales tax as percentage of GSDP remained stable around 5-6 per cent over the years. In real terms, the sales tax revenue grew at the rate of 6.5 per cent per annum during the eighties and at 5.8 per cent during the nineties.

Next comes State Excise.[5] Its relative importance has increased steadily over the years. Its percentage share increased from 2 per cent in 1980-81 to 14 per cent in 1990-91. In 2000-01, it was about 15 per cent. The

4. This rate of growth is slightly higher than that in Kerala (5.4 per cent), and Andhra Pradesh (5.5 per cent). But in Karnataka, the rate was 7.5 per cent.

5. State Excise is levied on liquors, spirits and narcotic drugs. Besides, the State levies a sales tax on liquor. However, the sales tax revenue from liquor is included in the general sales tax revenue of the State. States like Andhra Pradesh also levy a sales tax on liquor in addition to the Excise Tax on liquor. The sales tax revenue from liquor in Tamil Nadu was Rs. 491 crore in 1995-96 and Rs.1173 crore in 1999-00. We don't have the details of other states that levy a sales tax on liquor.

growth rate estimates show that the State Excise (in real term) increased about 9.5 per cent in both eighties and nineties. However, the State Excise as percentage of GSDP ranged between 1.2 and 1.5 per cent since 1985-86.

On the other hand, the share of the tax on motor vehicles declined steeply from 12.7 per cent of the total in 1980-81 to 7.3 per cent in 1990-91. In 2000-01, it was only 4.8 per cent. The share of stamps and registration remained more or less the same (between 7-8.7 per cent except in 1985-86). To sum up, the combined share of stamp and registration and the motor vehicle tax has fallen from about 20 per cent to 12 per cent over the study period. They together constitute less than one per cent of GSDP in recent years. Thus, almost 82 per cent of the own tax revenues of the State are derived from two taxes (Sales and State Excise).

It is also interesting to note that Tamil Nadu ranks second in terms of per capita sales tax (Rs.1143) and sales tax-GSDP ratio (i.e., 5.5 per cent) next only to Kerala among the major States. It ranks third in the ratio of State Excise to GSDP (at 1.4 per cent), next to Punjab (at 2 per cent), and Haryana (1.6 per cent). It also ranks third in the per capita State Excise revenue (Rs. 298), next to Haryana (Rs. 372) and Punjab (Rs. 516) in 1999-00 (not shown).

The tax buoyancy was more than one for sales tax (1.08) and State Excise (1.5) in Tamil Nadu during 1980-81 to 1989-90 (not shown). The own tax buoyancy was about one. However, during 1990-91 to 1998-99, the buoyancy was more than one only for State Excise (1.2).[6] The own tax revenue buoyancy was 0.9. It may be noted that Tamil Nadu compared badly with most states in sales tax buoyancy during 1990-91 to 1998-99, but compared well in the case of State Excise buoyancy (Table 15.6).[7] While efforts must be made to maintain a high rate of growth of revenue from sales tax and State Excise at about the existing rates (i.e. around 6 per cent and 9 per cent in real terms respectively), one has to closely examine why receipts from stamps and registration, land revenue and taxes on motor vehicles have been growing slowly and initiate proper steps to increase the buoyancy of these taxes.[8]

TABLE 15.6

Own Tax Buoyancies in Selected States (1990-91 to 1998-99)

States	*Sales Tax*	*State Excise*	*Total Own Tax Revenue*
Assam	0.690	5.248	1.511
Bihar	0.025	0.112	–0.107
Gujarat	1.475	0.252	0.894
Haryana	2.521	–4.169	0.676
Himachal Pradesh	1.646	1.238	1.427
Karnataka	1.414	0.284	0.845
Kerala	0.981	0.708	0.698
Madhya Pradesh	2.084	1.238	1.166
Maharashtra	1.295	0.823	0.629
Orissa	1.111	0.418	0.459
Punjab	1.944	1.054	0.661
Tamil Nadu	**0.840**	**1.175**	**0.879**
Uttar Pradesh	1.718	0.488	0.982
West Bengal	1.189	0.419	0.454

Computed Using data from CMIE (1996 & 2001) and CSO (1999 & 2000) diskettes.

Own Non-Tax Revenues[9]

The share of own non-tax revenues in total revenue receipts declined from 18.1 per cent in 1980-81 to 8.2 per cent in 1999-00 (Table 15.2).[10] This 8.2 per cent was the third lowest among the major States (Table 15.4). In spite of the fact that non-tax revenues cannot normally increase as fast as tax revenues, augmenting own non-tax revenues should be considered an important means for improving Tamil Nadu State's finances.[11] What is noteworthy is also that Tamil Nadu

6. The buoyancy for stamps and registration was –0.85 and motor vehicle tax was –0.28 during the nineties while the buoyancy for stamps and registration was 1.57 and for motor vehicle tax was 0.64 during the eighties.

7. Strictly speaking, the buoyancies of sales tax and State Excise in different states are not comparable as some states like Tamil Nadu levy a sales tax on liquor and the general sales tax of those states includes the revenue from sales tax on liquor. An exercise shows that the tax buoyancy of sales tax in Tamil Nadu during 1991-92 to 1998-99 was 0.84 with sales tax on liquor and 0.69 without sales tax on liquor. The buoyancy of State Excise alone was 1.41 and that of Excise including the sale tax on liquor was 1.55 during the same period.

8. Annual growth rate of motor vehicle tax declined from 3.6 per cent during the eighties to 2 per cent during the nineties while that of stamps and registration declined from 9.5 per cent to 5.8 per cent. Land revenue registered a negative growth of about 1 per cent during the eighties and registered a positive growth of about 1 per cent during the nineties.

9. The own non-tax revenues consist of interest receipts and dividend, royalty receipts, forestry receipts from sale of sandalwood and timber, cost recoveries on account of various services provided by the government, licence fees and fines.

10. The contribution of own non-tax revenues has fallen from 2.5 per cent of GSDP in 1980-81 to 1.2 per cent in 2000-01. This is mainly due to the non-revision of rates and fees for services provided by the government.

11. For instance, the Water Resource Organisation wing of PWD of the State government spends about Rs. 275.61 crore (according to 2001-02 RE) on major and medium irrigation systems in the State. This includes actual cost of maintenance, salaries and other allowances for engineers and other staffs working in the irrigation systems and interest payment. But the staffs of PWD carry out both operation & maintenance and capital works. If we assume that 30 per cent of this amount could be accounted for expenditure on general administration and capital works and some subsidy that government would like to give to farmers, the rest of Rs.193.11 crore accounted for actual cost of supply of water through the irrigation projects (excluding depreciation). But the revenue from this sector covers less than one-fifth of this amount as water rates are fixed at low levels. Therefore, there is a clear restructuring of water charges in Tamil Nadu for resource mobilisation.

TABLE 15.7

Structure of Own Non-Tax Revenues (%)

Details	*1980-81*	*1985-86*	*1990-91*	*1995-96*	*1999-00*	*2000-01*	*2003-04 BE*
Own Non-Tax Revenue (Rs. crore)	233 (100)	239 (100)	381 (100)	858 (100)	1357 (100)	1711 (100)	1506
1. ***Interest Receipts***	57.7	27.8	23.5	39.9	25.6	23.6	27.5
2. ***Dividends and Profits***	0.5	0.9	0.9	3.3	3.1	2.1	1.7
3. ***General Services***	8.9	12.3	19.6	13	20.7	18.5	15.5
Public Service Commission	0.1	0.1	0.2	0.1	0.2	0.1	0
Police	0.9	1.8	3.3	2.2	2.1	1.7	5.5
Jails	0.6	0.6	0.7	0	0	0	0.2
Stationery and Printing	0.2	0.5	0.4	0.3	0.3	0.1	0.3
Public Works	0.5	0.9	1.1	0.6	0.5	0.6	0.4
Other Administrative Works	3.1	3.8	5.9	5.6	5.9	3.3	4.9
Contribution & Recovery (Pension, Retirement Benefits)	1.2	1	1.5	0.7	0.9	0.6	0.9
Miscellaneous General Services	2.4	3.6	6.5	3.6	10.8	12.1	3.4
4. ***Social Services***	11.5	18.2	4	13.3	16.9	13.3	19.0
Education, Sports, Art & Culture	5.2	5.1	5	3.5	3.3	3.1	5.9
Medical, Health, Family Welfare, Water Supply and Sanitation	3.9	6.1	6	4.2	5.7	4.0	6.3
Housing	0.6	1.4	1.6	1.2	1.9	1.5	1.9
Urban Development	0.1	0	0.2	0.1	0	0.1	0
Labour and Employment	0.4	0.8	0.9	0.9	1.5	1.4	1.5
Social Security and Welfare	0.7	3.2	-10.5	2.5	4.1	2.9	2.7
Others	0.8	1.5	0.8	0.9	0.4	0.4	0.6
5. ***Fiscal Services***	0	0	0	0	0	0	0
6. ***Economic Services***	21.3	40.8	51.9	30.4	33.8	42.4	36.3
Agriculture & Crop Husbandry	6.3	14.9	12.1	7.3	5.5	3.8	5.2
Animal Husbandry	0.5	0.6	0.5	0.7	0.9	0.5	0.6
Fisheries	0.2	0.7	0.5	0.2	0.1	0.9	1
Forestry and Wild Life	6.3	11.4	11.6	6.8	9.6	7.7	9.7
Co-operation	0.9	1.9	2.6	1.7	1.7	1.0	1.2
Other Agricultural Programmes	0	1	0.3	1.2	1.4	1.2	1.6
Major and Medium Irrigation	0.8	0.5	0.6	0.4	0.7	0.5	0.8
Minor Irrigation	0.5	0.9	0.6	0.4	0.2	0.2	0.2
Power Projects	0	0.1	0	0	0	0	0
Village and Small Industries	0.6	2.3	1.8	0.6	1	1	1.5
Industries	2.7	2.7	16.3	7.9	8.4	22.8	11.2
Ports and Light Houses	0.1	0.2	0.1	0.1	0	0	0
Tourism	0	0.2	0.1	0.1	0.1	0.1	0.1
Others	2.5	3.3	4.7	3	4.1	2.7	3.3

has the lowest annual growth rate of own non-tax revenues (1.15 per cent) during the nineties among the southern states (not shown).

Table 15.7 shows the changing structure of non-tax revenues over time. The proportion of revenue from economic services steadily went up from 21 per cent in 1980-81 to 52 per cent in 1990-91. After that year, there has been a decline; in 1999-00, the share was only 34 per cent. The main reason for this is the decline in the shares of the agriculture and crop husbandry, forestry, irrigation and wild life and industry. The proportion of revenue from general services increased up to 1990-91 and in 1999-00 it maintained more or less the same level as in 1990-91. This increase was mainly due to increased contributions from police and other miscellaneous general services.

The share of the social sector showed ups and downs. But its share increased from 11.5 in 1980-81 to 17 per cent in 1999-00. This was due to the rise in the shares of medical, health and water supply and social security and welfare schemes during this period. In 2000-01, the share of the social sector declined to 13.3 per cent, due to fall in the shares of medical, health and water supply and social security and welfare schemes.

It is also noteworthy that the share of almost all economic services declined during the nineties. The possibility of raising fees and service charges in line with inflation needs to be examined.[12]

The interest receipts accounted for 58 per cent of total own non tax revenue of the State in 1980-81. Its share declined to 40 per cent in 1995-96 and 25 per cent in 1999-00 (23 per cent in 2000-01). The fall in the share of interest receipts during the nineties was due to the reasons that (i) the public sector undertakings and cooperative societies have not been repaying their loans taken from the government because of their poor financial position (and poor performance) and (ii) loans given by the government have not been rising.

Resource Transfers from the Centre

As shown in Table 15.2, the shared tax is the second largest single source of revenue of the State. Currently, it forms approximately 15 per cent of the total receipts. The grants-in aid forms about 8 per cent.[13] The combined share of shared tax and grants declined from 32 per cent in 1980-81 to 23 per cent in 2000-01. This decline is partly due to the changes in the successive Finance Commission's recommendations and modified Gadgil Formula for allotting state plan assistance by the centre and partly as a result of states own effort in resource mobilisation.[14]

Growth and Composition of Expenditures

As mentioned earlier, the total expenditure of Government of Tamil Nadu stood around 17 per cent of GSDP in all years shown in Table 15.1, except in 1995-96. The revenue expenditure accounted for nearly 70 per cent of the total expenditure in 1980-81, 89 per cent in 1990-91 and in 1995-96 and 92 per cent in 2000-01. Thus, the share of capital expenditure declined from 29 per cent in 1980-81 to only 8 per cent in 2000-01 (Table 15.8).

TABLE 15.8

Composition of Expenditures (%)

Details	*1980-81*	*1985-86*	*1990-91*	*1995-96*	*1999-00*	*2000-01*	*2003-04 BE*
Revenue Expenditure	71.0	78.9	89.0	89.0	94.1	91.6	89.8
Capital Expenditure	29.0	21.1	11.0	11.0	5.9	8.4	10.2

Computed using Table 15.1.

The per capita revenue expenditure of Tamil Nadu in 1980-81 prices was Rs. 712 in 1999-00. This had steadily risen from Rs. 239 in 1980-81 over the years to Rs. 451 in 1990-91 and then to Rs. 510 in 1995-96 (Table 15.9). It is to be noted that in the later half of the nineties, the per capita revenue expenditure increased by nearly 40 per cent in constant prices.

An interstate comparison reveals that in 2000-01 Tamil Nadu (Rs. 3502) ranked fifth, next only to Gujarat (Rs. 4356), Kerala (Rs. 3731), Maharastra (Rs. 3866) and Punjab (Rs. 4822) in terms of per capita revenue expenditure (in current prices) among the major States (not shown).

It is noteworthy that during the nineties the revenue expenditures grew at the rate of 4.6 per cent as against the revenue growth of 4.4 per cent and GSDP growth of 6.6 per cent during the same period.

Composition of Revenue Expenditures

Table 15.9 shows that about 57 per cent of Tamil Nadu's total revenue outlay was on development services in 2000-01. This ratio is lower than in the eighties (more than 70 per cent) and early-nineties. The decline in proportion has taken place under economic services (from 34 per cent in 1980-81 to 21 per cent in 2000-01), particularly under agriculture (and allied services), irrigation, transport and communication.

As in other states, the proportion of non-development revenue expenditure has risen significantly (i.e., from 24 per cent in 1985-86 to 38 per cent in 2000-01). In fact the major part of the increase has taken place only since 1990-91. The main cause of this is the increase in the proportions spent on grants to local bodies, pension and miscellaneous services and interest (their share increased substantially from 17 per cent to 33 per cent since 1990-91).

Table 15.10 shows the economic classification of revenue expenditures from 1991-92 to 2000-01. Salaries

12. In an analysis, we find the growth rates of all major sources of own non-tax revenues during 1995-96 to 2000-01. Revenues from interest receipts, stationery and printing, sports, archives and museums, medical education, training and research, public health, family welfare, urban water supply, urban and rural housing, information and publicity, nutrition, crop husbandry, cattle and buffalo development, poultry development and sheep and wool development, dairy development, social and farm forestry, agriculture research and education, major irrigation, all minor schemes, industries, inland water transport, tourism, port, lighthouses registered negative growths. Revenues from dividends, police, other administrative services, contribution from pension, general education, urban development, cooperation, power, petroleum, and road grew at less than 6 per cent per annum during this period. These items need policy attention.

13. The share of plan grants declined from 88 per cent in 1990-91 to 84 per cent in 1999-00 and 71 per cent in 2000-01 (not shown).

14. A major system constraining that the State is facing in the horizontal sharing of Central taxes amongst the States is the increasing weight given to redistribution criteria in the successive Finance Commission recommendations. As a prudent State, Tamil Nadu has not qualified for gap grants. At the same time, Tamil Nadu's high per capita income rules out any additional central financial assistance on the ground of equity.

TABLE 15.9

Composition of Revenue Expenditures

(% Shares)

Details	*1980-81*	*1985-86*	*1990-91*	*1995-96*	*1999-00*	*2000-01*	*2003-04BE*
Revenue Expenditure (Rs. Crore)	1152 (12.5)	2450 (13.7)	5641 (15.8)	10911 (13.9)	20728 (16.1)	21752 (14.8)	26599
1. Development Expenditure	71.8	72.7	72.3	66.8	57.7	57.1	49.5
a) Social Services	37.5 (4.7)	48.8 (6.7)	44.2 (7.0)	39.7 (5.5)	36.9 (5.9)	35.8 (5.3)	34.9
Education,, Art and Culture	20.7	22.9	22.8	20.0	21.0	20.2	19.0
Medical, Family Welfare, Health, Water and Sanitation	9.1	10.7	9.2	8.6	6.8	6.2	6.2
Housing	0.7	0.5	0.5	0.4	0.1	0.1	0.3
Urban Development	0.3	0.7	1.2	0.6	0.6	0.6	0.7
Welfare of SCs, STs and BCs	0.0	0.0	2.3	2.9	2.3	2.3	2.0
Labour and Labour Welfare	0.6	0.8	0.8	0.6	0.5	0.5	0.5
Social Security and Welfare	5.0	6.5	2.5	2.2	2.8	3.1	2.6
Food and Nutrition	0.0	3.8	4.2	3.3	2.5	2.5	2.4
Relief (natural calamities)	0.7	2.5	0.5	0.6	0.1	0.0	1.0
Others	0.4	0.4	0.3	0.5	0.2	0.3	0.1
b) Economic Services	34.3 (4.3)	23.8 (3.3)	28.1 (4.5)	27.1 (3.8)	20.8 (16.1)	22.3 (3.1)	14.7
Agriculture & Allied Service	13.0	7.4	9.4	8.8	9.7	6.1	4.3
Rural Development	0.0	6.8	5.7	3.0	2.7	3.0	2.9
Special Areas Programme	0.0	0.0	0.2	0.1	0.1	0.1	0.1
Irrigation, Flood and Energy	12.2	3.6	2.9	2.0	1.9	2.0	2.2
Industry and Minerals	1.8	2.6	2.2	2.6	0.9	1.1	1.1
Transport & Communication	5.8	3.0	2.5	2.8	1.6	1.2	1.4
Science, Tech. & Environment	0.0	0.1	0.0	0.1	0.0	0.1	0.0
General Economic Services	1.6	0.3	5.1	7.8	3.9	7.6	2.7
2. Non-Development Expenditure	25.6 (3.2)	23.7 (3.3)	25.8 (4.1)	31.2 (4.3)	37.4 (6.0)	38.4 (5.7)	44.2
Organs of States	1.1	0.9	0.8	1.0	1.1	0.9	0.8
Fiscal Services	1.7	2.1	1.7	1.8	1.6	1.6	2.4
Interest	9.8	7.5	8.6	12.6	13.1	14.4	17.1
Administrative Services	10.3	9.5	8.2	8.4	8.1	7.7	7.8
Pensions and Miscellaneous	2.8	3.7	6.4	7.5	13.6	13.9	16.0
Grants to Local Bodies	2.5	3.7	1.9	1.9	4.9	4.5	6.3
Per Capita Revenue Expenditure (in Rs.)*	**239 [239]**	**469 [314]**	**1016 [451]**	**1867 [510]**	**3367 [712]**	**3502**	

Source: Government of Tamil Nadu (Various Years), RBI (2002) and CSO (1999 & 2000)—Diskettes.

*Figures in parentheses are the ratios to GSDP (in %) and figures in brackets are per capita revenue expenditures in 1980-81 prices.

TABLE 15.10

Economic Classification of Revenue Expenditures (%)

Year	*Salary*	*Pension*	*Administrative Overheads*	*Interest*	*Subsidies*	*Others*
1991-92	30	5	5	6	7	47
1992-93	34	6	6	8	14	32
1993-94	38	6	6	11	12	27
1994-95	38	7	7	11	13	24
1995-96	39	7	7	12	14	21
1996-97	38	8	6	11	14	23
1997-98	38	9	6	12	13	22
1998-99	43	10	6	12	10	19
1999-00	41	13	5	13	10	18
2000-01	39	13	5	13	13	18

Source: Government of Tamil Nadu (2001).

and pensions amounted to 35 per cent of total revenue expenditure in 1991-92. In 1999-00, its share was 54 per cent. It is noteworthy that there was a big jump in 1998-99. This rapid rise was the consequence of implementation of the Central Fifth Pay Commission's recommendations. With the State having little control over the existing levels of wages and pensions immediately (or in the medium term), the government should attempt to bring down the rate of growth of employment and formulate a more realistic wage increase policies. In this regard, the Tenth Plan Document suggests that the staff strength needs to be reduced through a policy of net attrition and a contributory pension plan to make terminal benefit self-financing.[15] Recently, the State has constituted the Swaminathan's staff and expenditure review committee, which in its interim report provide suggestions in respect of reorganising the departments in the secretariat and measures to control administrative expenditures. The government has instructed all departments to undertake a zero-base budgeting. Besides, the Finance Minister has announced a new pension plan that is similar to the Centre's Contributory Pension Scheme.

Interest payments continuously increased from 6 per cent in 1991-92 to 13 per cent in 1999-00. The figures for subsidies given in the Tamil Nadu government account (Table 15.10) are misleading.[16] First, subsidies in respect of school education have been included. Strictly speaking, they should be shown as a part of expenditure on public good. Second, only subsidies actually paid to Tamil Nadu Electricity Board (TNEB) are included, not the amounts that the government owes the Board. Other book adjustments were also made. Hence, the burden of subsidies, which the government has to pay according to its policies are not revealed.

We have a detailed breakdown of subsidies for one year (Table 15.11). The interpretation of the figures in this Table is subject to the limitations pointed out above. It is seen that food subsidy is the largest component of the subsidies in 2000-01(RE), amounting to Rs. 1719 crore and forming 67 per cent of total subsidies. The food subsidy comprises the supply of subsidised rice to poor people through the public distribution system (PDS) and price support to paddy producing farmers of the delta region for selling paddy to Tamil Nadu Civil Supplies Corporation (TNCSC). The State government purchases the BPL allotment of rice from the Food Corporation of India at Rs. 5.65 per kg. and purchase the rest from farmers of Cauvery delta at Rs. 11.90 per kg.[17] But the issue price of rice under PDS is Rs. 3.50 per kg. only.

TABLE 15.11

Details of Major Subsidies in 2000-01(RE)

Details	*Rs. Crore (%)*
1. Public Distribution System	
Food Subsidy - Reimbursement of Losses to TNCSC	1700 (66.2)
Subsidy to Fair Price Shops	15 (0.6)
Supply of Essential Commodities to Police at Subsidised Rates	4 (0.2)
2. Agriculture	
Subsidy to TNEB for Free Supply of Power to Farmers Cash only	250 (9.7)
Production Incentives to farmers	50 (1.9)
Other Subsidies to Agriculture	21 (0.8)
3. Handlooms	
Free *Sarees* and *Dhoties* Scheme	95 (3.7)
Rebate on the Sale of Cloth	78 (3.0)
Free *Sarees* and *Dhoties* to Old Age Pensioners	14 (0.5)
Weavers Housing Scheme	3 (0.1)
4. Industrial Sector	
Capital Subsidy to Industries	30 (1.2)
Power and Generator Subsidies to Industries	8 (0.3)
5. Transport- Free Bus Pass for Students	165 (6.4)
6. Milk Subsidy	30 (1.2)
7. Diesel Subsidy for Fishermen	3 (0.1)
8. Housing Sector	
Free House-site Scheme and Construction of Houses	96 (3.7)
Credit-cum-subsidy Scheme for Rural Housing	7 (0.3)
Total	**2569 (100.0)**

Source: Government of Tamil Nadu (2001) White Paper on Tamil Nadu Government Finances (with modified categories); RE-Revised Estimates.

Besides, the government sells kerosene and sugar at lower prices than the issue prices fixed by the Union Government. There is considerable evidence to suggest

15. As of 1998, of the total employee compensation, 92 per cent was accounted for by C and B groups and the number of employees in these two groups formed 88.3 per cent of the total number of government employees (not shown). As, the combined compensation share of Groups B and C employees was higher than their employment share, an appropriate policy of net attrition should reduce the staff strength in these categories by at least 15 per cent in the next 5 years. By doing so, it would be possible for the government to reduce the salary-GSDP ratio by 0.5 percentage point in the next five years. We suggest an effective wage policy for Government employees in the concluding section.

16. Subsidies refer to the difference between the cost of goods and services provided publicly and the actual recoveries made from those using them. However, these differences in respect of school education are not generally treated as subsidy.

17. Besides, the government provides Rs. 40 per quintal as incidental charge over and above the minimum support price fixed by the government of India.

that urban consumers are the major beneficiaries of PDS. Since the ration-card holders are not properly classified by the recent poverty line estimates, there is enough potential to rationalise the subsidy structure (under PDS).

Power subsidy to farmers is the second single major component, amounting to Rs. 250 crore and constituting 10 per cent of total subsidies. But as stated above, this only the subsidy actually paid, not what is owed.[18] The State government started giving free power to agricultural consumers from 1990-91. The agriculture sector consumes roughly 25-27 per cent of power distributed by the Tamil Nadu Electricity Board. Since the State is facing a financial crisis with a large fiscal deficit, it is necessary to remove or at least reduce the quantum of power subsidy to farmers. The third single major component of the subsidy is transport-free pass to students. Its share is about 6 per cent. The handloom sector also receives a considerable amount of subsidy due to rebate on sale and the free *sarees* and *dhoties* scheme.

Indirect Subsidies

In addition to the above direct subsidies, there are indirect subsidies due to non-recovery of user charges for the services provided by the government. For instances, revenues realised from five major and 47 medium irrigation schemes was only 20 per cent of the revenue expenditure incurred on these systems. The government should revise water charges to cover at least 50 per cent of the actual cost immediately and to cover 75 per cent within five years.

Public Sector Undertakings (PSUs)

At present, there are about 60 PSUs (including State Transport Corporations, TANSI and TANCEM) in the State. The aggregate government investments in these organisations in the form of share capital assistance/ loans increased from about Rs. 790 crore in 1990-91 to Rs. 1992 crore in 1999-00. But their performance and contribution to the State finances were negative. The ratio of earnings to capital employed by the government in PSUs was only 1.6 per cent in 1999-00. The government constituted the Raghavan Committee in 2001, which in its Report suggested a radical restructuring of many PSUs and immediate closure of PSUs, which are beyond redemption.

Government Guarantees

The State government provides guarantees (as opposed to direct budgetary provisions) to the lending agencies for loans taken by the statutory corporations, government companies and cooperative institutions. The total outstanding guarantees of the government as on March 2001 was Rs. 12,388 crore, constituting around 70 per cent of total revenue receipts of the government in 2000-01.[19] This much of guarantee liabilities of the government is a cause for serious concern.

Cash Reserves of the Government

The government meets its day-to-day expenditures from its cash reserves. When reserves are not available, it uses the ways and means advance (WMA) from RBI (up to a limit of Rs. 436 crore). When the ways and means advance limit falls short of expenditure commitments, the government takes recourse to an overdraft (OD) facility/additional loan from RBI. Recourse to WMA/OD means a mismatch between receipts and expenditures and reflects the poor financial management of the government. Table 15.12 depicts the cash position as on the last working day of the financial year during 1995-96 to 2000-01. It is noteworthy that the cash reserves have been completely depleted over the years and the government is using the overdraft facilities of the RBI.

TABLE 15.12

Cash Position of the State Government

(Rs. Crore)

Year	*1995-96*	*1996-97*	*1997-98*	*1998-99*	*1999-00*	*2000-01*
Cash Position	649	846	964	74	-412	-242

Notes: Negative figures indicate the availability of ways and means and overdraft.

Source: Government of Tamil Nadu (2001).

TABLE 15.13

Ways and Means Advance and Overdraft From RBI

(Rs. Crore)

Year	1985-86	1995-96	1996-97	1997-98	1998-99	1999-00	2000-01
WMA	85	57	0	0	742	3761	5152
OD	53	0	0	0	0	1486	1713

Source: Budget Memorandum (Various Years).

18. Since the State government is unable to meet the actual liability to the TNEB for free supply of electricity of Rs. 3208 crore, the TNEB has been borrowing heavily to finance its deficits.

19. Of these, 33 per cent was accounted for by the TNEB, 15 per cent by TN Co-operative Housing Federation Ltd., 12 per cent by TIDCO and 8 per cent each by TWAD and TN co-operative State Agriculture and Rural Development Bank Ltd.

Table 15.13 shows that after 1997-98, the amount of WMA and OD increased significantly over the years.

Composition of Capital Outlays

Table 15.14 provides the details of composition of capital outlays in Tamil Nadu overtime. The share of capital outlays on general services was quite low up to 1995-96 (around 5 per cent) and in 1999-00 its share suddenly increased to 24 per cent, due to the increase in the proportion spent on public works. In 2000-01, the share of general services declined to around 10 per cent. The share of economic services decreased drastically from 80 per cent in 1985-86 to 55.7 per cent in 1995-96. The main reason of this decrease is the decrease in the proportions spent on irrigation and flood control, agriculture and allied works, industry and minerals and other economic services. In 2000-01, it declined further to 50 per cent due to decreases in the capital outlays on industry and transport.

The share of social services was 15 per cent in 1985-86 and increased to 41 per cent in 2000-01. The main cause of this increase is the increase in the proportions spent on water supply, sanitation, housing and urban development in 1999-00.

Concluding Observations

Our study of the evolution of Tamil Nadu Government's Finances during the last two decades shows:

- Tamil Nadu's record of resource mobilisation is one of the best among the States in the country. It ranks first in terms of own tax-GSDP ratio and it has the highest per capita revenue and own

TABLE 15.14

Details of Capital Outlays

(% Share)

Details	*1980-81*	*1985-86*	*1990-91*	*1995-96*	*1999-2000*	*2000-01*	*2003-04(BE)*
Capital Expenditure (Rs. Crore)	85 (0.92)	152 (0.86)	222 (0.62)	591 (0.75)	645 (0.50)	1547 (1.05)	2557
General Services	*3.74 (0.03)*	5.79 (0.05)	6.33 (0.04)	5.49 (0.04)	24.18 (0.12)	9.83 (0.10)	11.87
Police	—	—	0.00	0.00	9.59	4.75	5.98
Stationery and Printing	0.00	0.00	0.29	0.02	0.09	0.03	0.00
Public Works	3.64	5.72	5.87	4.69	14.31	5.03	3.58
Other Administrative Services	0.09	0.07	0.16	0.78	0.19	0.02	2.31
Social Services	23.20 (0.21)	14.71 (0.13)	22.18 (0.14)	38.82 (0.29)	41.91 (0.21)	41.00 (0.43)	32.81
Education, Sports, Art & Culture	5.02	2.37	4.20	9.34	9.63	0.88	1.25
Health & Family Welfare	6.84	5.18	4.72	3.40	10.47	1.74	3.19
Water, Sanitations Housing, and Urban	4.28	4.59	7.81	21.60	15.64	36.92	24.85
Information and Publicity	0.01	0.04	0.59	1.78	0.35	0.17	0.04
Welfare of SC's, ST's and OBC's	6.79	2.31	3.95	2.04	5.24	1.05	3.35
Social Welfare and Nutrition			0.29	0.12	0.20	0.27	0.06
Other Social Services	0.26	0.24	0.62	0.54	0.39	-0.05	0.06
Economic Services	73.07 (0.68)	79.49 (0.68)	71.49 (0.45)	55.69 (0.42)	33.90 (0.17)	49.18 (0.52)	55.32
Agriculture & Allied Activities	18.48	13.72	14.96	8.65	16.33	6.50	4.68
Rural Development	0.36	0.09	1.21	0.08	0.08	12.58	0.06
Special Areas Programme	2.73	1.34	3.73	1.22	2.24	0.86	0.57
Irrigation & Flood Control	22.56	31.63	21.73	11.59	56.01	18.87	14.00
Energy	–0.89	0.00	0.00	0.00	–112.58	–14.19	0.98
Industry & Minerals	9.23	8.73	13.13	4.61	0.16	0.02	0.08
Transport	13.00	13.30	16.36	29.00	71.34	24.44	34.93
Other Economic Services	7.58	10.69	0.37	0.54	0.32	0.11	0.02

Source: Government of Tamil Nadu (Various Years) and CSO (1999 & 2000)—Diskettes.

*Figures in parentheses are the ratios to GSDP (in %); BE-Budget Estimates.

revenue among the Southern States. However, the own non-tax revenues are fairly low.

- The government sector has not been growing as fast as the economy during the nineties.
- Wages (and pensions), interest payments and subsidy accounted for about 80 per cent of current revenue, reflecting a high degree of rigidity in the revenue budget.
- Considerable increase in revenue deficit especially after 1995-96 is one of the major structural problems in the Tamil Nadu budget and this leads to a large fiscal deficit and interest burden.
- High salaries and pension component and subsidies are the major causes of the present crisis.

During the nineties, the revenue-GSDP ratio fell from 14.3 per cent in 1990-91 to 12.7 per cent in 1999-00, whereas the revenue expenditure GSDP ratio rose from 15.8 per cent to 16.1 per cent in the same period. Given that the revenues were falling as a proportion of GSDP, efforts should have been made to curtail the rate of growth of revenue expenditure. Instead, revenue expenditures were allowed to grow fast. One of the main causes of the large increase in revenue expenditure was the implementation of the Fifth Pay Commission's recommendations. Generous increases in subsidies, including payments to TNEB to compensate the Board for free supply of power to farmers etc., also played a significant role in increasing the gap between revenues and expenditures.

On the revenue side, the main cause for the fall in the revenue GSDP ratio was the low growth of Central transfers relatively to GSDP growth. Own tax revenues grow more or less at the same rate as GSDP. But the performance of own non-tax revenues in terms of growth was quite poor.

The record of revenue mobilisation by the Tamil Nadu State Government has been good. The State has the highest own tax revenue to GSDP ratio at about 9 per cent among the major States in 1999-00. Tamil Nadu has sixth (fifth) rank in the per capita revenue (own revenue) among the major States. As for the coming decade, while rates of taxes cannot perhaps be raised, a rationalisation of the tax structure and improvement in administration must be undertaken urgently. Also ways of raising non-tax revenues must be explored so as to make such revenues grow as fast as GSDP. Besides, Tamil Nadu must, jointly with some of the other States represent to the Government of India and the 12th Finance Commission that the principles and the basis on which Central devolution of taxes and grants are given must be examined and changed so that the transfers to well-performing States do not continually decline as per cent of their total revenues and as per cent of their respective GSDPs.

In order to put the finances of the State back on the rails, apart from revenue-side measures, the State government should undertake some substantial or even radical reform measures.[20] First of all, the State government should address the problem of the very unsound financial position of the TNEB. As it is, the revenue deficit of the government is understated, because instead of fully compensating the Board for the loss suffered due to the free supply of power to the farmers, the government is giving a subsidy of only Rs. 250 crore, and hence TNEB is incurring and building up debt to meet current expenses and no proper depreciation can be provided for. Since the State government has to ultimately bear the responsibility for meeting the liabilities of the TNEB, the State government's finances cannot be made sound, without a thorough reform of the power sector, particularly of the tariff structure.

Second, this is in a way an aspect of the power tariff reform—the government must drastically reduce subsidies and target the remaining subsidies towards deserving groups and economically justifiable objectives. Of course, subsidies have to be met out of taxes and charges. The limit of total subsidies is determined by the willingness and ability to raise taxes.

Third, it is recommended that the State government should introduce two major changes in expenditure policy. First, the government should introduce a 3-year medium term expenditure plan. Under this plan, major targets would be set for the budget for the 3rd year and the budgets for the two years preceding should be derived from the 3rd year figures. And the receipts and expenditures of the first (initial year) will be so determined that their repercussions in the 3rd year will be consistent with the targets set for that year.[21]

Another change in expenditure policy that is absolutely necessary is that the appointment of Pay

---

20. In 2002, the State government constituted a Tax Reforms and Revenue Augmentation Commissions headed by Dr. Raja J. Chelliah to study and recommend measures for tax reforms and revenue augmentation for the Government of Tamil Nadu. The Commission has submitted its Report.

21. Recently, the Government has prepared a Medium Term Fiscal Plan (MTFP). The details of MTFP and our assessments on MTFP are discussed in the Appendix.

Commissions at intervals of 10 years or somewhere around must be given up. Instead, adjustments in real incomes to be effected should be commensurate with the increase in the per capita GSDP of the State. The percentage increase in real income (wage) should be equal to a fraction of the per capita GSDP, say 1/4th of the increase in per capita GSDP (The entire increase in GSDP does not translate into increase in per capita income of individuals because part of the increase would go towards investment and for government expenditure on goods and services. Besides, there are poorer sections whose real incomes must grow faster). Thus, if the per capita GSDP of the State grows by 15 per cent in three years, the real salary level of a government servant would grow by a minimum of 3.75 per cent at the end of the period. Over and above this, some increases could be granted to attract highly qualified individuals. The methodology and the proportions could be varied, but the real increase in salaries must be linked to the growth in the GSDP of the State.

APPENDIX

Medium Term Fiscal Plan

In 2003, the Government enacted the Tamil Nadu Fiscal Responsibility Act 2003. The Government also prepared a Medium Term Fiscal Plan (MTFP).[22] The salient features of the MTFP are:

i. to wipe out the revenue deficit by 2008-09 by controlling unproductive revenue expenditures and by ensuring enhanced revenue receipts through various reform measures; and to bring down the fiscal deficit to 3 per cent of GSDP;

ii. to ensure a continuous step up in the capital outlay from Rs. 1892 crore in 2002-03 and to ensure proper maintenance of assets created;

iii. to provide a comprehensive social safety net;

iv. to ensure that public utilities are self sufficient; and

v. to ensure greater fiscal transparency and better accountability.

The projections of revenues, expenditures, deficits etc., of MTPF during 2003-04 to 2008-09 are shown in Table I.

The MTFP assumes 8 per cent growth of GSDP (in 2002-03 prices) for two initial years of projection (2003-04 and 2004-05); 8.5 per cent growth for 2005-06 and 9 per cent for 2006-07; and finally 9.5 per cent growth for the last two years (i.e., about 9 per cent average annual growth). The estimates of revenue growth are made with existing tax rates/structure and tax devolution formula. For the period 2003-04 to 2008-09, the projection assumes 9.6 per cent average annual growth of revenues and 6.2 per cent growth of revenue expenditure (in 2002-03 prices). With these growth rates in revenues and revenue expenditures, the revenue deficit would be reduced below zero by 2008-09 (as shown in Table I).

It is noted that in 2001-02, the revenues (in current prices) increased only by 2.74 per cent (exponential growth rate) and revenue expenditure declined by 0.9 per cent over the previous year. However, in 2002-03, the revenues (in current prices) increased by 8.7 per cent and revenue expenditure increased by 16.5 per cent.

During the first year of the Plan (2003-04 RE), the revenue receipts exceeded the projected figure by more than Rs. 400 crore (registering 10.3 per cent growth over the last year). It was achieved through implementing the additional revenue measures recommended by the Tax Reform and Revenue Augmentation Commission: rates of agricultural income tax, stamps and registration, and motor vehicle tax were increased; power charges were raised; tax on electricity consumption was levied; free power scheme was given up; and rates of fees charged for government services were raised.

At the same time, the growth of revenue expenditures was also controlled to 3.8 per cent through the following measures: all government departments adopted a zero-based budgeting; perquisites given to the government servants have been curtailed to some extent; attempts have been made to reduce staff strength; and the distribution of commodities under PDS is restricted only to low income group with a monthly income below Rs. 5000 and issue prices of rice, sugar etc., under PDS are raised.

In 2004-05 also, the revenues are expected to exceed the projected level for the year in the Plan by about Rs. 500 crore. Although several concessions amounting to Rs. 140 crore are given for the fiscal 2004-05 (including waiving of land revenue and agricultural income tax, resale tax exemption to co-operatives, sales tax exemption to 10 AIDS drugs and musical instruments, and reduction in sales tax on computer peripherals and handicraft articles), it is expected that take over of IMFL retail trade by the government will bring an additional excise revenue of Rs. 700

TABLE I

Medium Term Fiscal Plan

(Rs. Crore)

Details		Projections						2003-04*	2004-05*
	2002-03	2003-04	2004-05	2005-06	2006-07	2007-08	2008-09	(RE)	(BE)
Revenue Receipts	20456 (13.31)	22148 (13.34)	24039 (13.41)	26609 (13.68)	29096 (13.72)	31893 (13.73)	34944 (13.74)	22567 (13.59)	24538 (13.68)
Own tax	14342	15833	17159	18788	20609	22734	25083	15942	17439
Non-Tax	1480	1220	1426	1495	1618	1697	1756	1529	1646
Central Transfer	4634	5096	5454	6326	6870	7462	8105	5097	5454
Revenue Expenditure	25106 (16.33)	25881 (15.59)	27434 (15.30)	29505 (15.17)	30667 (14.46)	32738 (14.10)	34903 (13.73)	26084 (15.71)	27688 (15.44)
Primary Deficit	2859 (1.86)	2143 (1.29)	1493 (0.83)	643 (0.33)	–577 (–0.27)	–1245 (0.54)	–2309 (–0.91)	1419 (0.85)	1508 (0.84)
Interest Payment	4107	4649	5271	5798	6427	7070	7673	4672	5227
Revenue Deficit	4650 (3.02)	3732 (2.25)	3395 (1.89)	2897 (1.49)	1570 (0.74)	845 (0.36)	–40 (–0.02)	3517 (2.12)	3150 (1.76)
Fiscal Deficit	6966 (4.53)	6792 (4.09)	6764 (3.77)	6441 (3.31)	5850 (2.76)	5825 (2.51)	5364 (2.11)	6091 (3.67)	6735 (3.76)
GSDP	153729	166027	179309	194550	212060	232206	254265	166027	179309
GSDP Growth	3.50%	8.00%	8.00%	8.50%	9.00%	9.50%	9.50%	8.00%	8.00%

Source: Budget Speech of Finance Minister (2004-05). Figures in parentheses are percentages of GSDP; negative means surplus. *Figures are slightly adjusted.

22. The details of MTFP are given in an appendix of the budget speech of Finance Minister of Tamil Nadu in February 2004.

crore over the previous year. At the same time, the revenue expenditures are expected to exceed the projected level by about Rs. 250 crore.

Thus, for the initial two years of projections (2003-04 and 2004-05), the revenue receipts exceed the projected values by more than Rs. 400 crore. Although the revenue expenditures slightly exceed the projected levels, both revenue deficit and fiscal deficit are considerably less than the projection levels in these two years (despite the present drought situation in the State). As the targets for first two years are met, we can hope that targets for other years would be met provided that the government makes adequate effort in mobilising additional resources and cutting non-productive expenditures.

Chapter 16

Governance

Local Governance

Governance has become all over the world a much more difficult and complex task in recent years. In the developing countries the expectations and aspirations of the governed have almost become something beyond the capacity of the governments to handle. The process of Globalisation and the force unleashed by it have aggravated the problem. In this situation National governments were not able to satisfy even the basic needs of the poorer and weaker sections of society. Taking India in particular, a nation of a billion people was represented by about 700 MPs and about 5000 Members of Legislature. Government in the process became remote from the governed, resulting in a huge gap which was filled up by power brokers.

In this scenario the best option appeared to be strengthening the governance at the local levels to satisfy at least the basic needs of the people by authorities located at closer quarters. Though such authorities were in position in various states there was no continuity, certainty or strength in them. It is to rectify the situation that the Indian Constitution was sought to be amended. The statement of objects and reasons spelt out in the amendment bill makes it clear as indicated below:

"Though the Panchayat Raj Institutions have been in existence for a long time, it has been observed that these Institutions have not been able to acquire the status and dignity of viable and responsive peoples bodies due to a number of reasons including absence of regular elections, prolonged supersessions, insufficient representation of weaker sections, inadequate devolution of powers and lack of financial resources"

"Article 40 of the Constitution lays down that the State shall take steps to organise village *Panchayats* and endow them with such powers and authority as may be necessary to enable them to function as units of self government (emphasis supplied). In the light of the experience in the last 40 years and in view of the shortcomings which have been observed it is considered that there is an imperative need to enshrine in the Constitution certain basic and essential features of Panchayat Raj Institutions to impart certainty, continuity and strength to them"

After the amendment to the Constitution in 1992 the situation obtained in different states is also different depending upon each state's past history and experience in local self governance. Hence, to understand and appreciate the present stage of decentralised local governance we will have to study the past history of local governance in the State.

Past History of Local Governance in Tamil Nadu

Rural, Local Governance

Pre-Independence Period

Tamil Nadu generally boasts of a long tradition of local self governance and as evidence for it cites the local governance prevalent at the time of the later *Cholas* as enshrined in the Uttiramerur Temple inscriptions. But what is of relevance today is the immediate past. In this way the beginning of decentralised local government can be traced during the British Rule to the Constitution of District Road Funds in 1854. The first piece of legislation in this regard was the Madras District Road Cess Act enacted in 1866 which enabled the government to levy a cess for construction, repair and maintenance of district roads.

The earliest attempt to create local bodies was the passing of Madras Local Funds Act 1871 which empowered the Governor to set up Local Fund Boards to construct, maintain, and repair schools, hospitals and roads. The Board comprised of members appointed by the Governor in Council with the Collector of the District as the *ex officio* President of all local fund Boards in his district.

The Madras Local Boards Act of 1884 enacted as a result of Lord Rippon's Local Self Governance Resolution of 1882 ushered a three tier local self government at the District, *Taluk* and Union of villages levels. The District Collector was the *Ex Officio* President of the District Board, the Revenue officer in charge of the Division in which the *taluk* was situated became the *ex officio* President of the *Taluk* Board. This legislation for the first time introduced non-official participation in local self-government with the members being partly elected and partly appointed/nominated in the ratio of 3:1 in District Boards and 2:1 in *Taluk* Boards. However, the franchise was restricted to taxpayers only.

The next major piece of legislation was the enactment in 1920 of Madras Local Boards Act and the Madras Village Panchayat Act. The Madras Village Panchayat Act 1920 extended the structure of Self Governance below the Union of villages to single revenue village or groups of contiguous villages. All the members of the village *Panchayat* were elected. For the first time this Act provided for universal adult suffrage to the local governance system by extending it wherever it was applicable. Still the franchise was confined only to male residents of 25 years of age and above.

It should also be remembered that under this Act *Panchayats* were formed for only about 10 per cent of the villages of the entire Presidency comprising more than 50000 villages. In 1934 the *taluk* boards were abolished and there were only two tiers of local governance. Also in 1930 by an amendment universal male suffrage provided under the Village *Panchayat* Act 1920 was reverted to the more restricted basis of the Local Boards Act 1920. This amendment also for the first time identified the functions of the local agencies and classified them as those Statutorily entrusted to them (mandatory) and those Statutorily permitted to be undertaken by them (discretionary).

The Madras Village Panchayat Act 1941 gave the government powers to supercede the village *Panchayats* and the District Boards.

Post-Independence Period

The first enactment in this period was the Madras Village Panchayat Act 1950. While piloting the Bill the Minister for Local Administration said:

"In a country like ours which is predominantly rural in character and where there is still in our villages, a live sense of corporate unity, the village must be the basic administrative unit. The next step is to make every village a self contained unit managing its own affairs and meeting as far as possible all its needs in the matter of food and clothing by local production and providing on its own initiative for all the social economic and cultural necessities of the people".

Under this Act a two-tier structure of village *Panchayats* at the grassroot level and district boards at the district level came into existence with no linkages between the tiers. The Act provided for universal adult franchise and also for covering the entire State with village *Panchayats*. The Act further assigned to the *Panchayats* judicial power by which the *Panchayats* could administer civil and criminal justice within the area of jurisdiction. The District Boards maintained medical and public health services, high schools and primary schools. In 1955-56 following was the position in the State:

Position in the State

Activity	*Maintained by District Board*		*State Total*
	No.	*Per cent*	
1. Medical Institutions	634	76.85	825
2. High Schools	304	31.54	964
3. Primary Schools	12748	51.52	24741

It may be seen that the District Board's share is substantial in the Health and Education Sector.

The Village *Panchayats* also undertook many activities like education, public health, road works, public markets, car stands, maintenance of parks, gardens etc.

In the meantime the Government of India launched the Community Development and National Extension Service Scheme in 1952 with the aim of area development through development block and participation by the people. The Government of India also appointed a committee under the Chairmanship of Thiru.Balwantrai Mehta which recommended that development programmes undertaken in a local area should be implemented through local elected bodies. Against this background the Tamil Nadu Government passed the Madras Panchayat Act 1958 and the Madras District Development Council Act 1958. Prior to this enactment the government placed a White Paper on "Reform of Local Administration" which was discussed at length both in the Legislative Assembly and

Legislative Council. These enactments created Panchayat Unions co-terminus with the development blocks, abolished the district boards and created a District Development Council as an Advisory Body with Collector as the Chairman. This two-tier system continued for more than three decades.

An amendment to the 1958 Act in 1981 sought to provide for reservation of 18 per cent of seats for Scheduled Castes and Tribes and 15 per cent of seats for the women for the Post of Panchayat Union Chairman. But this provision was repealed by another amendment in 1985. The two tier system operated on democratic lines till 1975 through elections. The tenure of the Panchayats Unions was extended for some time and thereafter special officers were appointed to the local bodies till 1986 when elections were held. Again the tenure was extended upto March 1991 when special officers were appointed till new elections were held in October 1996 under the New Tamil Nadu Panchayat Act 1994.

From 1989 onwards the Government of India sought to amend the Constitution to include a separate part relating to *Panchayats*. This was construed by many State governments including the Government of Tamil Nadu as an attempt to by pass the State governments and maintain direct contact with the local agencies. The bill was defeated in the Rajya Sabha. Finally in 1992 the 73rd and 74th Constitutional amendments were carried out and the State governments were required to carry out amendments or to enact new legislations by 24th April 1994 in tune with the Constitutional Amendments.

Post-Constitutional Amendment Phase

The Government of Tamil Nadu did not bring any legislation to amend the existing Act or to enact a new Act immediately after the Constitutional amendment. There was no serious attempt to study the implication of the Constitution amendment by way of bringing a White Paper as was done in 1957. In fact, the draft bill for the new Panchayat Act was introduced on 18th April 1994 and was passed on 19th April 1994 without any discussion with major opposition parties boycotting the Assembly. The bill received assent of the Governor on 22nd April 1994 and was notified on the Gazette on the same day. It looks as if the Act was passed more out of compulsion brought about by the Constitution amendment and not out of any conviction. It looks as though all political parties have the same mind set when it comes to the question of local self-governance.

However, the objects and reasons for the enactment were lofty and laudable *viz.* "for greater participation of the people so as to make the *Panchayats* institutions of self government and for more effective implementation of rural development programmes.

Even after passing the Act elections were not held immediately. Elections were held only after a new government took over after Assembly elections in 1996.

After the elections the following *panchayats* were constituted.

- Village *Panchyats* – 12619
- *Panchyat* Unions – 384
- District *Panchayats* – 28

Urban Local Governance

The major legislation in urban governance in Tamil Nadu was the Madras City Municipal Corporation Act 1919 and the Madras District Municipalities Act 1920. When five other municipalities (Madurai, Coimbatore, Tirunelveli, Tiruchirappalli and Salem) were upgraded and constituted as city Municipal Corporations a separate Act was enacted for each Corporation.

Realising the need for a comprehensive Act the Government of Tamil Nadu enacted the Tamil Nadu Urban Local Bodies Act 1988 repealing the other Acts and incorporating the provisions of the Constitutional amendments. Necessary rules were also framed and the Act came into effect from 1st August 2000. However, due to representations received from the elected representatives the Act has been kept in abeyance from 23.8.2000. Only the earlier Acts are now in force.

The major changes brought about in Urban Local Governance after the Constitutional amendments are:

Town *Panchayats*, which earlier came under the Tamil Nadu *Panchayat* Act, have now been treated as transitional areas and have been brought under the District Municipalities Act.

Earlier reservation for scheduled caste and scheduled tribes and women was made applicable only for councilors of Municipalities. Now reservation is made for the office of Chairpersons of Municipalities as well.

The Constitutional obligation has also been cast on the State government for holding periodic elections that too before the expiry of the term of office of the earlier body.

At present there are 611 town *Panchayats* with 9794 Wards, 102 Municipalities with 3392 Wards and six Municipal Corporations with 474 Wards.

Powers and Functions Entrusted to the Local Bodies

As per article 243G of the Constitution "subject to the provisions of the Constitution the legislature of a State may by law endow the *Panchayat* with such powers and the authority as may be necessary to enable them to function as institutions of self-government and such law may contain provisions for the devolution of the powers and responsibilities of *Panchayats* at the appropriate levels subject to such conditions as may be specified there in with respect to:

- the preparation of plans for the economic development and social justice
- implementation of schemes for economic development and social justice as may be entrusted to them including those in relation to matters listed in the 11th Schedule".

The 11th Schedule listed out 29 items. To enable the government to take a view on the entrustment of the responsibilities indicated above to different levels of the *Panchayats* the State government constituted in September 1996 a working group of the State Planning Commission under the Chairmanship of Sri L.C. Jain, Member State Planning Commission. The group presented its Report to government in April 1997.

The main principle adopted by the group for bifurcation of functions between State departments and *Panchayats* was:

"What can be done by the *Panchayats* and where the *Panchayats* have greater stake and better access to requisite local information and knowledge necessary for development, that matter be assigned to the *Panchayats*. Similarly, as between the three tiers of Panchayat Raj Institutions, the functions to be allocated to each tier should be assigned on the basis of what it can best do and where it is better placed and only that which cannot be assigned to the higher tier that is Panchayat Union and/or District *Panchayats*".

With the above principle in mind the group indicated the various functions and activities which can be entrusted to the three levels of *Panchayats* at Village, Union and District level out of the 29 items indicated in the Schedule. It is not possible to furnish all the recommendations made by the group, as it is voluminous. Taking the two sectors which were traditionally under the control of local governments namely Primary Education and Public Health the recommendations of the group were as follows:

"Elementary education was largely the responsibility of local self governments when these institutions came into existence in Tamil Nadu during the early part of the century. The local boards and district boards established and managed primary schools, middle schools and high schools. With the abolition of the district boards in Tamil Nadu in 1958 and the establishment of Panchayat Raj Institutions at the village and block levels the secondary education was taken over by the government and the elementary education was transferred to Panchayat Union Councils. Between 1958 and 1981 opening of new primary and elementary schools, recruitment and transfer of teachers, supervision of schools etc., were the responsibilities of the Panchayat Union and elected representatives of Panchayat Raj Institutions who played a key role in promoting elementary education in the State.

Between 1981-1994 elementary education underwent three major structural and organisational changes *vis-à-vis* (a) creation of a separate directorate at State Level, b) conversion of supervisory network at the district level, and c) conversion of all Panchayat Union teachers as government servants.

The primary and elementary school teachers numbered about 1.75 lakh. They are government servants and should continue as government servants. The pay and privileges enjoyed by the existing teachers, as government servants should be protected. At the same time they should be responsible to the democratically elected Panchayat Raj Institution at the block and village level. The Assistant Elementary Education officers should attend the review meeting convened by the Panchayat Union. At the District Level the District Elementary Education Officers should advise the District Panchayats in all matters of elementary education."

The State Planning Commission finally recommended that the Panchayat Raj Institutions shall be vested with the power to review and supervise the functioning of primary/elementary schools.

Health and sanitation is an important item in Schedule 11 of the Constitution and the Constitutional amendments envisage entrustment of power and responsibilities in respect of this item to Panchayat Raj Institutions. The State Planning Commission accordingly made the following recommendations:

Decentralisation should be based on the principle of accountability and to fulfil this the health personnel from village level upto district level should be accountable through reporting system. The Primary Health Centres, Health Sub Centres, Community Health Centres, will be brought under the control of local bodies. The Panchayat Union should be entrusted with the powers to look after primary health care.

The State Planning Commission Group was of the view that the personnel working in the Panchayat Raj Institutions should be fully and wholly accountable to the local self-government. In order to achieve this objective, the commission suggested designing a personnel policy by which over a stipulated period of time a separate cadre of professionals committed to the *Panchayat Raj* system would emerge. The emoluments, service conditions and promotions of the health personnel already protected as government servants will be governed as per government rules.

Government did not fully accept the recommendations of the State Planning Commission Group. However, government constituted a committee with the Minister for Rural Development and Local Administration as Chairman and members of Legislative Assembly as members. This Committee submitted its Report in January 1999. The Committee made 1008 recommendations and 718 of its recommendations were accepted. However qualitatively these recommendations were of not much significance, in increasing the powers and functions of the Panchayat Raj Institutions. Taking again as illustrations the education and health sector the powers given to the village Panchayats under education was generally in the nature of assisting the existing functionaries in executing the schemes. In respect of Panchayat Unions, which earlier had a substantial role in elementary education, the powers given were again such as supervision and recommendation or giving complaints against personnel. However the power to take action was retained with the education department. The district *panchayats* were also not given any effective power of control or supervision of personnel engaged in elementary education.

The same is the case with respect to health and sanitation. Most of the powers are in the nature of assisting the existing personnel. At the level of Panchayat Union also the same was the case.

This is not surprising since the committee constituted by the government did not include representatives from Panchayat Raj Institutions but consisted only of members of the legislature who perhaps were not keen to entrust substantial and real powers to the Panchayat Raj Institutions fearing that such a step may well curtail their own functions and powers. In fact, the Panchayat Raj Institutions under the 1994 Act appear to have less functions and powers in such crucial sectors like primary education and primary health than what they had earlier.

The main problem for the government in entrusting substantial powers of control over the staff to the PRI was the opposition from the personnel working at these levels. They are also large in number. There are nearly 1.75 lakh teachers who form a powerful unionised body enjoying the support almost of all political parties. The parties are also not keen to entrust power of control and supervision over the staff to the Panchayat Raj Institutions at the cost of foregoing the support of these powerful unions. At the same time, the elected members of the Panchayat Raj Institutions are not able to bring an unified countervailing pressure on the government for entrustment of real and substantial powers in view of conflicting party loyalties of the members of the Panchayat Raj Institutions.

The role and functions of the three-tier PRI are shown below:

Functions of Panchayat Raj Institutions

Village Panchayat	*Intermediate Level Panchayat*	*District Level Panchayat*
• Provision and maintenance of civic services	• It has to instill among people within its jurisdiction a spirit of self-help and initiative and work for raising standard of living	• Advisory and funds distributing bodies
• Public hygiene	• Providing support for implementation of development programmes	• Secondary education
• Maintenance of public work	• Execution of welfare and development activities in the fields of agriculture, animal husbandry, health, sanitation elementary education, cottage industries and social welfare	• Advice government in all matters relating to rural development in the district
• Primary education • Providing inputs for agricultural production • Rural industries, primary health care and women and child welfare	• Utilising village housing project funds and loans	• Review the progress made under various schemes in all blocks.

Source: Tamil Nadu Economic Appraisal 1999-2000.

The Tamil Nadu Panchayat Act 1994 specifies that the Village *Panchayats* should identify the gap in provision of basic amenities and draw up a shelf of projects at village level. These schemes will be operationalised on a priority basis. The Panchayat Unions aggregate this shelf of projects at the Block level and the District *Panchayat* will consolidate these scheme proposals at the district level. This kind of exercise will help to map up quantum of resources needed at the district level and take up the schemes on a priority basis.

The ultimate objective of the above planning exercise is to optimise the benefits reaching the people who are underprivileged and deprived of the enjoyment of the benefits of the scheme. The District Planning Committee is expected to do such a planning exercise at the district level on a continuous basis. To realise the above objectives, the District Planning Committee does evolve suitable planning strategy with the co-ordination of the State Planning Commission and impart effective training to those who are involved in preparation of the district plans.

The State planning commission group which considered the entrustment of powers to *panchayats* also considered the entrustment of powers to urban local bodies regarding the 18 items mentioned in Scheduled 12 of the Constitution. The principle that the group adopted for the delegation of functions by the State government to urban local bodies was that "what can be done by the urban local bodies and have greater stake and better access to requisite local information and knowledge necessary for development that matter be assigned to them".

Unlike in the case of Panchayat Raj Institutions government did not appoint any high level committee to consider the report of the Planning Commission. No additional powers or functions appear to have been entrusted to the urban local bodies.

This is both surprising and disappointing in view of the steady growth in the urban population in Tamil Nadu. As per Census 2001 the proportion of urban population to the total population has risen to 43.9 per cent from 34.2 per cent. The decadal growth (1991-2001) rate for urban population is 42.79 per cent compared – 5.20 per cent for rural population. Tamil Nadu is certainly on the path of rapid urbanisation and hence the better and efficient functioning of urban local bodies will be crucial to the overall future development of the State.

District Planning Committees (DPC)

The constitutional amendments provide for Constitution of a District Planning Committee. In accordance with the above provisions District Planning Committees have been constituted in all the 28 Districts. The main function of the committee is to

Financial Resources of Local Bodies in Tamil Nadu

Own Taxes	*Assigned Revenues*	*Grants*	*Other Revenues*
		I. Village Panchayats	
1. House Tax	1. Local Cess	1. House Tax Matching Grant	1. Non-tax Revenues like Income from Properties such as Shops, Bus Stands, Guest House etc.
2. Professional Tax	2. Entertainment Tax	2. Water Supply Grant	2. License Fees on D&O Trade
3. Vehicle Tax	3. Stamp Duty Surcharge	3. Lighting Grant	3. License Fees on Building Regulations
4. Tax on Agricultural Land	4. Surcharge on Sales Tax	4. Rural Development Programmes Grant (1-statutory 2 & 3 *ad hoc*)	4. User Charges
	5. Minor Minerals		5. Misc. Revenues.
		II. Panchayat Unions	
Local Cess Surcharge on Land Revenue	1. Local Cess	1. Local Cess Surcharge Matching Grant	Income from Properties & Misc. Revenues.
	2. Entertainment Tax	2. Local Roads Grant	
		3. Discretionary Grants for Entrusted Functions like Dispensary, Maternity Centers, Minor Irrigation (all on *ad hoc* basis)	
		4. Agency Function Grant	
		III. District Panchayat	
		Nil	

Source: 'Report' of the State Finance Commission for Local bodies, Government of Tamil Nadu, November 1996.

consolidate the plans prepared by the *Panchayats* and Municipalities in the District and to prepare a comprehensive draft district development plan for the district as a whole.

Initially government appointed the District Collector as the Chairman of the District Planning Committee. Subsequently, government has appointed the Chairperson of the District *Panchayat* as the Chairman of the Committee and the collector as its Vice-Chairman.

The DPCs have been operationalised and made functional only recently. The first meeting of the DPCs was held only on 4.2.2002. To assist the District Planning Committee government has created a District Planning Cell in each District with District Panchayat Secretary as the District Planning Officer with a minimum supporting staff.

Financial Health of the Rural Local Bodies:

The Rural Local Bodies are empowered to raise their own resources by way of collecting house tax, professional tax and other resources. They are also entitled to receive funds from the State government as a Statutory right. Before the enactment of Tamil Nadu Panchayat Act, 1994, the financial position of most of the *Panchayats* and Panchayat Unions was very weak. Following the recommendations of the First State Finance Commission, the Rural Local Bodies were receiving grants from the government based on certain norms. The PRIs are also encouraged to mobilise their resources through incentive matching grants. Still across the *Panchayats*, there are vast differences in potential available for tapping their resources.

Devolution of Funds to Local Bodies

Article 243 I and 243 Y of the Constitution of India introduced by the 73rd and 74th amendment provide for the constitution of a State Finance Commission within one year from the commencement of the Constitution 73rd amendment Act 1992 initially and thereafter at the expiry of every fifth year. The First State Finance Commission was accordingly constituted in April 1994 and it gave its Report to government in 1996 covering the period of April 1997 to March 2002.

The First State Finance Commission (FSFC) suggested creation of two pools as indicated below:

Pool A: This contains taxes which belong to local bodies, but collected by the government. However, this does not form part of State taxes, except for entertainment tax. This pool is to be distributed among the local bodies concerned.

Pool B: This is the divisible pool containing all State taxes excluding entertainment tax in pool A. a) Sales Tax, b) Motor Vehicle Tax, c) State Excise Revenue, and d) all others. The FSFC proposed a progressive devolution from pool B as indicated below.

1997-98 – 8 per cent

1998-99 – 9 per cent

1999-2000 – 10 per cent

2000-01 – 11 per cent

2001-02 – 12 per cent

However, the government froze the percentage of devolution at 8 per cent for all the five years owing to resource crunch.

The FSFC recommended the distribution of funds between rural and urban local bodies in the ratio of 60:40. However government revised it as 55:45.

The devolution of funds led to a steady increase in the fund flow to local bodies as may be seen from the following statements indicating the position prior to and after devolution furnished in the report of the Second State Finance Commission.

Devolution of funds prior to devolution by First State Finance Commission (1996-97)

(Rs. crore)

	Grants	*Assigned Revenue*	*Total*
Rural	105.87	66.99	172.86
Urban	179.51	235.88	415.39
Total	285.38	302.87	**588.25

** This does not include commitment of government on Local Bodies pension, which was about Rs. 60 crore for that year.

Statement showing devolution of funds under pool A (Assigned Revenue) and pool B (Global Sharing)

(Rs. crore)

Year	*Pool A*	*Pool B*	*Total*
1997-98	295.10	612.56	907.85
1998-99	364.91	792.94	1157.85
1999-2000 (Actuals)	391.96	805.19	1197.15
2000-01 (Budget Estimate)	298.09	1036.41	**1334.50

** This includes commitment of government on Local Bodies Pension.

Source: State Budget Documents.

The Tenth Finance Commission of the Centre also recommended grant of Rs. 402.86 crores during the award period as capital grant to the local bodies. The Eleventh Finance Commission has recommended that Rs. 132 crore per annum be provided as revenue grants to these institutions for maintenance of assets during 2000-05. With all these the fund flow from both Centre and State government to local bodies has considerably increased—more than 10 times during the last 10 years. It was Rs. 108 crore in 1981 and it went up to Rs. 1130 crore in 2000-01.

The White Paper on government's finances placed before the Assembly on 18th August 2001 has observed:

"In spite of substantial increase in these grants over the years the finances of local bodies continue to remain strained. Internal resource mobilisation of the local bodies has not been commensurate with the increase in the cost of varied services being provided by them. The most worrisome issue is the low and declining contributions of user charges and other sources of non-tax revenue to that total receipt".

The following Table 16.1 shows the pattern of the resource utilisation by the local bodies in the State for the period 1997-98 to 2001-02.

TABLE 16.1

Comparative Statement of Revenue Income and Utilisation by the Local Bodies (1997-1998 to 2001-02)

Local Body	*Revenue Income – Rs. crore*				
	Own Revenue	*Assigned Revenue*	*Devolution through State Finance Commission*	*Total (Rs. crore)*	*% of Salary & O&M in Total Revenue Income*
Village Panchayats	453	477	1318	2248	67
Panchayat Unions	482	26	997	1505	63
District Panchayats	—	—	177	177	11
Town Panchayats	616	337	498	1451	69
Municipalities	1288	441	369	2098	84
Municipal Corporations	2067	688	544	3299	70
Total	4906	1969	3903	10778	61 (Average)

Source: White Paper on Government Finances.

As per the Constitutional provision the Second State Finance Commission (SSFC) was constituted in December 1999 to make its recommendations for the five year period commencing from 1st April 2002. The Commission presented its Report in May 2001. The Commission maintained equi-distant stance *vis-à-vis* Government and Local Bodies similar approach as between local bodies and line agencies. According to the Commission "the three components of meaningful decentralisation are functions, funds and functionaries in that order. Therefore functions precede finance. Presently, the affairs of both the local bodies and the State government are inextricably intertwined and their respective roles are not clearly defined."

The Commission further observed that "over a period of time the local bodies have come to excessively dependent on the State government for discharging their functions in a satisfactory manner. This dependency syndrome needs to be gradually and steadily replaced by a self-reliance index and the local bodies will have to be helped to stand on their own legs".

The Commission suggested that during the award period (2002-2007) the own income of local bodies as share of total income needs to be closely monitored and consciously increased. The Commission has suggested the following level to be achieved for the middle of the award period for the various types of local bodies.

S. No.	*Type of Local Body*	*Self Reliance Index at Present*	*Self-reliance Index for the Middle of the Award Period*
		Average	Average
1.	Municipal Corporations	54.7 %	65 %
2.	Municipalities	52.57 %	60 %
3.	Town Panchayats	39.86 %	45 %
4.	Village Panchayats	21 %	25 %

The government accepted most of the recommendations of the SSFC. The Commission recommended devolution from State's own tax revenue to local bodies as follows.

2002 - 03	8 per cent
2003 – 04	8 per cent
2004 – 05	9 per cent
2005 – 06	9 per cent
2006 - 07	10 per cent

However, government decided to freeze the transfer at the same 8 per cent for the entire five year period. The Commission also recommended that 5 per cent of Central devolution also be passed on to the local bodies; but the government has not accepted this recommendation.

Government has accepted the recommendations of the Commission for sharing 87 per cent of the recommended devolution between Panchayat Raj Institutions and Urban Local Bodies in the ratio of 58:42. The Commission recommended that after allocating the salary requirements of district *panchayats*, the balance funds shall be distributed between village *panchayats* and Panchayat Unions in the ratio of 60:40 respectively. Government has decided to continue to adopt the existing ratio of 47:45:8 for village *Panchayats*, panchayats unions and district *Panchayats* respectively for the distribution of funds. The Commission recommended the vertical sharing of devolution among corporations, municipalities and town *panchayats* in the ratio of 33:32:35 respectively. Government has decided to adopt the ratio 31:34:35.

In view of the acute financial crisis that the Government of Tamilnadu is facing there is not much hope of any larger outflow of funds from the government to local bodies. Hence, it is for the local bodies to tap their own local resources. The White Paper has also concluded "if the cherished objectives of democratic decentralisation through the Panchayati Raj Institutions are to be achieved, the local bodies may have to augment own sources of revenue through rationalisation of taxes, improvement in tax collection and revision of user charges for services being provided by them".. But this is easier said than done.

As the SSFC has observed "the dependency syndrome of local bodies is embedded so deeply leading to the agitation of the local body staff seeking release of devolution grants from State government for paying their salary arrears". The Commission then has drawn attention to the observation of Dr. P.V. Rajamannar, Chairman of the Committee on Centre-State Relations 1971 that chronic indebtedness and dependence on the Centre's charity gradually make the States ineffective and they develop a tendency not to take any responsibility but to throw the blame on the Centre for their default. The Commission has wryly commented "these remarks are equally applicable to State-local bodies financial relations also"

Elections to Local Bodies

As already stated, one of the major aims of the Constitutional amendments is to ensure democratic continuity of the local bodies. It is no longer possible for State governments not to hold elections to the local bodies and run these bodies through special officers appointed by them. The Constitution itself has provided for constituting a State Election Commission for conducting elections to the local bodies.

In Tamil Nadu, elections were held under the new Panchayat Act in October 1996 for all the three tiers. There are direct elections for President and Ward Member of the village *Panchayats* and for Ward Members of *Panchayat* Union and District *Panchayats*. Elections for Chairman of *Panchayat* Union and President of District *Panchayat* is done by the Ward Members of the Union and District *Panchayats* respectively. At the *Panchayat* Union level there is one Ward Member for a population of 5000 and at the District Level one member for a population of 50000. However, in village *panchayats* there may be one to three members per ward. There are 12619 Village *Panchayats* and in them 41086 Wards and 97446 Ward Members.

Election at the Village *Panchayat* Level is not held on Party basis. The party symbols are frozen and candidates are allotted different symbols. However, at all other level elections are held on party basis.

There is reservation for women and scheduled castes and scheduled tribes for village *Panchayat* presidents, village ward members, *Panchayat* president ward members, district *Panchayat* ward members, *Panchayat* union Chairman and President of District *Panchayat*. Reservation for women is to the extent of 1/3rd of the total number and that for SC/ST is in proportion to their population. In the first election, there were 24148 representatives from SC, ST and 38391 women at various levels.

Elections to Panchayat Raj Institutions were held by and large peacefully. However, in certain village *panchayats* there was opposition to the reservation for SC, ST. In a few villages elections could not be held at all in view of the strong opposition from the dominant caste which also resulted in no representative from Scheduled Caste coming forward to file the nomination.

Initially, the women presidents and members of *Panchayat* Bodies were not very active and in a few cases were just acting as *benamies* of their husbands or fathers. The situation is changing slowly and the women representatives are becoming active and assertive.

Elections to the *Panchayats* were again held in October 2001. In these elections of the 97374 village *panchayat* members 20660 were elected unopposed. Where elections were held the over all percentage of poll was about 74. However, the problem of not being able to hold election for President in *panchayats* reserved for scheduled caste persisted in two villages. The concept of rotating the reserved wards and *panchayats* has not been seriously considered at *Panchayat* level. Perhaps one reason could be it has not been considered even for assembly and parliamentary elections.

Elections were held for Urban Local Bodies also in October 2001 for the post of 609 town *panchayat*

Chairmen, 9794 Ward members of Town *Panchayats*, 102 Chairpersons of Municipalities, 3392 Municipal Councilors, Mayor of six corporations and 477 Councilors.

Elections in urban area were less smooth, compared to rural areas with election in Chennai City Corporation topping the list with allegations of booth capturing and tampering with counting of votes in certain areas.

Some Major Issues in Local Governance

The most striking feature of the study of local governance in Tamil Nadu is perhaps the guarded and cautious approach of the government both prior to and after independence in entrusting the local bodies with adequate powers and functions. Any progress in this field has generally been as pointed out by the State Planning Commission's Report due largely to the impetus from developments outside the State at an All-India level. After independence also the government preferred to retain the Collector of the District as a king pin of all development efforts in the district. The State was reluctant to allow strong democratically elected leadership at the district level. The abolition of district boards in the mid-fifties ensured that democratically elected Panchayat Union Councils were in position till the late-seventies. During the eighties and nineties elections were not held and either tenure of the existing elected bodies were extended or special officers were appointed. Generally there was lack of political will to make the Panchayat Raj Institutions, units of self-government even though it was proclaimed as the aim in various legislations.

The government also has an overwhelming presence even at the village level, with governments staff far out numbering the village *panchayat* staff. The SSFC has indicated that the following employees are typically found in any village *panchayat* in the State and has pointed out that both the *panchayat* and the government staff do not have a full days work.

Local Body Staff	Government Staff
1. Panchayat Assistant	1. Village Librarian
2. Over Head Tank Operators	2. Village Health Nurse
3. Sanitary Workers	3. Health Inspector
4. Makkal Nala Paniyalargal	4. Village Administrative Officer
	Live Stock Inspector
	PDS Salesmen
	PDS Packer
	Noon-Meal Organiser
	Noon-Meal Cook
	Noon-Meal Assistant
	Anganwadi Workers
	Helper

The SSFC has also pointed out that the role envisaged for Panchayat Raj Institutions is invariably advisory in character and has suggested that with Local Bodies firmly in position, the line departments and agencies could avail themselves of the opportunity and entrust village level functions to Panchayat Raj Institutions as agency functions where local knowledge would be critical for proper implementation of the schemes. It has also been pointed out that there will be considerable savings to the tune of about Rs.1,00,000 if the two staffs for integrated and rationally deployed. The government and the line departments so far has been very reluctant to entrust village level functions to village *panchayats*.

Corresponding to the reluctance of the government there has also been no effective and sustained demand from the representatives of the local bodies for the needed powers and functions to make the institutions as units of self-government. The members of the local bodies at various levels appeared to be more loyal to the political parties rather than to their local institutions. Even though elections at the village level are not held on party lines still the elected members though elected at least on paper not on party lines were still not able to set aside their party loyalties. Thus, even though there are nearly a lakh of ward members of the village *panchayats*, they could not become a powerful unified force for asserting the rights of village *panchayats* as units of self government. Thus, the government even if they want to entrust certain functions and the functionaries to the *panchayats* find it more expedient and convenient not to do so in view of the reluctance and opposition from the functionaries. This is particularly so in respect of the key sectors of primary education and primary health.

An additional factor is the lack of close linkage between the tiers. Under the 1958 Act the Presidents of village *panchayats* automatically became the members of the *panchayat* unions and Chairman of *Panchayat* Unions automatically became a member of the District

Development Council. Under the new Act there is no such linkage. Now for about the population of 50000 in a locality there is a ward member of the district *panchayat*, about 10 ward members of *panchayat* union, and about 75 ward members of village *panchayats* and perhaps about 5 village *panchayat* presidents. In addition of course there is the Member of Legislature and Member of Parliament representing the locality. There appear to be too many representatives with no clearly demarcated functions and responsibilities.

Initially as per the 1994 Act MLAs and MPs could participate in *Panchayat* Union Councils. By an amendment in 1996 this was removed. However, it was not removed in the district *panchayats*. In 1997, MLAs and MPs were given the right to vote in district *panchayats*. This needs to be changed. Just as Members of Parliament have no voting right in the State Legislatures, Members of State Legislatures should not have voting rights in the Local Bodies.

The local bodies also do not appear to be keen to get away from the dependency syndrome under which they depend heavily on government grants for maintaining core civic services. There doesn't seem to be much urge to be truly self dependent and self governing institution. They seem to be content with pleading their inability to meet the demands of the local people citing lack of resources as the reason and throw the blame on the State government.

The elections to the local bodies reveal that voters participation progressively declines as the degree of urbanisation increases. While the participation at the village level is good it gradually declines as we proceed to Town *Panchayats*, then to Municipalities to Municipal Corporations and finally to the Chennai Corporation.

The percentage of votes polled during the local body elections held in October 2001 in various types of local bodies is furnished below.

Figure 16.1 Showing the percentage of votes polled in the Local Bodies Election 2001 in different local areas.

Village Panchayats	–	74.04 per cent
Town Panchayats	–	64.59 per cent
Municipalities	–	55.63 per cent
Municipal Corporations	–	40.24 per cent
Chennai Corporation	–	34.54 per cent

This is a serious and sad situation; more so when we take note of the trend of rapid urbanisation in the State.

FIGURE 16.1

Percentage of Votes Polled in the Local Bodies Election 2001 in Different Local Areas

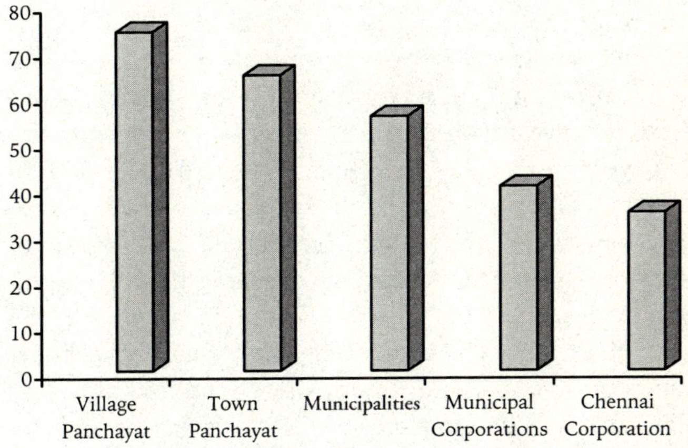

The above state of affairs also indicates a major trend in elections in our country. Generally only the poor people seem to participate in the elections using their voting right to obtain for them basic services like water, road and electricity. Those who already enjoy these facilities in the urban areas do not appear to bother about participation in elections. As a result provision of basic facilities becomes extremely important for political parties to win the elections at all levels. Hence, even MLAs and MPs have to cater to these expectations of the voting sections. This has given rise to the Special Area Development schemes sponsored by to the MPs and MLAs. This has further affected the self-governing nature of the local bodies. This has also resulted in municipalisation of Parliamentary and Assembly elections.

The local bodies are not able to maintain their status as self-governing institutions from a lack of interest from both the government and the local people. Neither of them appear to be keen that these should be self-governing units. This lack of interest on the part of government is best expressed in the report of the State Planning Commission on the entrustment of powers to *panchayats* as follows;

"At the very start the group had requested in writing all departments running schemes which are implemented at rural local bodies level to advise as to which of such schemes they considered necessary to be retained at the State level and to state the reasons thereof. In spite of reminders no departments responded except very few. The group was keen to have direct discussions with selected *panchayat* office bearers to gauge their views. But for reasons beyond the control of the group such meetings could not be organised."

The lack of interest of the people is very well demonstrated in the low voter turn out in urban local body elections.

In the end the success of local bodies as self-governing institutions will depend upon the people of the locality and their representatives. Both should seriously strive to transform their local government into self-government. The representatives of the people in the local body should go beyond party loyalties in achieving this. The people also should take pride in their local governance and give strength and extend their support to the representatives in achieving the above objectives. There are signs that this can happen. Public spirited young men, independent of party affiliation have become presidents of *panchayats* and are striving hard to make their *panchayats* a truly self-governing republic as in the case of *Kuthambakkam* Village Panchayat in Thiruvallur District. They are few right now but one hopes, their numbers increase in the future. With such independent dedicated leaders in local bodies Good Governance perhaps will be ushered through Local Governance.

Capacity Building Through Training

Strengthening participatory democracy in *panchayats* and long-tern sustainability depends on developing human capital. Efforts therefore need to be made in developing the capacity of elected representatives who have a responsible role to play in ensuring transparency and accountability. Capacity is a multi-dimensional and complex attribute. Some of the attributes are awareness, knowledge, skill and self-confidence. Capacity building is a gradual process and needs to be integrated with the functioning of the *panchayats*. Capacity building can take the form of structured training, field exposure, information dissemination, etc.

Training is a planned and systematic effort to modify or develop knowledge/skills/attitudes through learning experience. Its purpose is to enable an individual to acquire abilities in order to perform a given task. Training needs to be provided to improve the technical capabilities, managerial and administrative abilities and also behaviour for improving interpersonnel relations and leadership qualities. After the enactment of the 73rd & 74th Constitutional Amendment Acts and Tamil Nadu *Panchayat* Act 1994, three tier *Panchayat* Raj System has been introduced in the rural local bodies and as per Tamil Nadu District Municipalities Act 1994, Town *Panchayats*, Municipalities, and Corporation in the urban local bodies. This has resulted in the election of more than 1.2 lakh representatives representing the 12618 Village *Panchayats*, 6499 representatives of 385 *Panchayat* unions and 648 representatives of 29 District *Panchayats*. These local bodies are entrusted with a large number of responsibilities to strengthen the democratic decentralisation and make these Institutions of self-government. Most of the elected representatives are first timers. They need to be aware familiar with the administration of Panchayat Raj Institutions. They are expected to be involved in the preparation of local level plans. In the planning process, a variety of functionaries *viz.*, planners, administrators, sectoral functionaries, elected representatives, NGOs, social beneficiaries and voluntary groups, people in their individual capacity are involved in respect of the 29 items to the Village *Panchayats*, *Panchayat* Unions and District *Panchayats* in the State. Each of these groups has specific roles or functions to perform in the local planning with multiplicity of interests and without skill. Herein lies the importance of capacity building through training. It involves formulation of a strategy for training by assessing training needs and evolving suitable training modules in a systematic and time bound manner. Training will be effective in promoting the participatory approach if it is extended to the Panchayat Raj Institutions; Community based organisations and Self-help groups.

The multi-level planning exercise involves assessing of the financial and other resources for the plan and allocation of funds to rural/urban local bodies in the district, integration of rural/urban plan in the district plan, credit plan in the district plan, to decide on matters of common interest between the rural/urban local bodies including spatial planning, sharing of water and other physical and natural resources, integrated development of infrastructure and environmental conservation and to establish co-ordination between various departments in the district. Taking into account all these aspects, it has been proposed to organise capacity building training programmes to all the chairpersons of the rural/urban local bodies, by involving training institutions like State Institute of Rural Development, Rural Extension Training Centres, Tamil Nadu Institute Urban Studies, Coimbatore, Gandhigram Rural University, Avinasilingam Deemed University, Coimbatore and also reputed NGOs and voluntary ogranisations.

Towards Better Governance

The last years of the 20th Century were marked by widespread awareness among the people of the country of the need for greater transparency in government, at all levels. The major factors that triggered the movement for reform in the manner in which government works came from the growth of corruption in government departments and government funded programmes, the failure of development programmes to deliver results to the people and the deterioration of services provided by government departments and utilities. There was also general disillusionment with the adverse impact of many major government projects on peoples lives, the absence of consultation of people in decision making and the total lack of accountability of public servants for the results of the massive expenditures incurred by them, ostensibly for the benefit of the people

The first initiatives were taken in Rajasthan in 1995 by social activists working in rural areas revolving round the issue of social audit of development expenditure. After a long struggle and mass movement conducted by peoples organisation, the Government of Rajasthan conceded the demand for easy access to any person of all information pertaining to Block and *Panchayat* works, including financial matters and muster rolls. This was followed by initiatives in Madhya Pradesh, prompted by a segment of enlightened bureaucracy. A couple of years later, several States, including Goa, Karnataka, Tamil Nadu and Maharashtra passed legislation on the subject. In some States it took the form of administrative measures and orders. The latest law was the one passed by Parliament in December 2002, called the Freedom of Information Act.

Governments have tried to respond to the widespread demand for greater transparency and accountability in several ways. The cornerstone of the response has been to enshrine into law the right of every citizen to demand and obtain information on the working of public authorities, particularly when it concerns him and the public interest. This right is also translated into Citizens Charters issued by public authorities having public dealings and substantial interface with the citizens. New technologies have enabled governments to make life easier for citizens, providing immediate access to information through computers and facilitating the interface between citizen and government through fast, painless, corrupt free electronic methods. E-Governance is growing at a fast pace and also includes a variety of mechanisms to increase the speed and efficiency of decision making in government.

Right to Information

Government of Tamil Nadu enacted the Right to Information Act in May 1997. Under this Act any bonafide person requiring information may have access to such information in accordance with the procedure specified under the Act. Under the rules enacted by the government, the form in which information can be asked for and the name of the competent authority are prescribed. The Act provides for an appeal against the order of the competent authority. Section 3 (2) of the Act has a list of 22 kinds of information which will not be given to any person. Although it is five years since the Act was passed, there is not much information as to the extent to which citizens have made use of the provisions and to what results. A brief critique of the working of the legislation was made by the Citizen, Consumer and Civic Action Group, a Chennai based NGO. Of the 27 cases in which CAG asked for information under the Act, only 12 replies were received from the concerned organisations. In most cases, information was not provided inspite of reminders. None of the appeal cases have been disposed off.

A number of comments on the shortcomings of the Tamil Nadu Right to Information Act have appeared in the newspapers ever since 1997. A few meetings have also been organised by rights activists. The main points of criticism of the legislation are:

1) The need for bringing entities which are funded by the government or executing programmes or works on behalf of the government within the purview of the Act.
2) The need to reduce the classes of information which will not be made available to the citizens. It has been pointed out that the Constitution provides for reasonable restrictions to freedom guaranteed in the Article 19 (1) (a) for specific reasons. The Tamil Nadu Act goes much beyond these provisions.
3) The appeal provision does not prescribe any time limit for the disposal of appeals.
4) The Appellate Authority is not specified in the Act or in the Rules and is merely stated as "the Government".
5) The Act has no provision for providing information within 48 hours where it relates to life or liberty of the individual.
6) The Act does not have a penalty clause to punish errant officials for not furnishing information within the specified time or supplying false information.
7) The Act should make it obligatory for government departments to establish systems

for maintaining, indexing and retrieval of records.

8) It is felt that the Public Records Act of 1993 should be reviewed so that the classification of records of the government is amended to make old records more accessible to the public.

9) There is widespread feeling in the country that the Official Secrets Act is a major obstacle to freedom of information and it needs to be reviewed, if not scrapped.

10) There is need for pro-active dissemination of information by the government, particularly in the matter of projects, programmes, policies and legislations likely to have an impact on citizens.

11) The Act should provide for public hearings in respect of major projects planned to be implemented by government organisations.

12) It has been suggested that the Act could also cast duties on the State government to disseminate information to the local bodies in the light of the 73rd and 74th Amendments to the Constitution.

13) The Act should provide for the Ministers to publish, at least once a year, a document describing the functions of his department, description of all classes of records under its control, description of procedures, manuals, rules and regulations and an assessment of the working of the Right to Information Act.

The most progressive initiative on the right to information is reported to be the Maharastra Government Ordinance of September 2002. This is amply exemplified by Section 4 which says "Every Competent Authority shall, —

a) maintain all its records, in such a manner and form, as is consistent with its operational requirements duly catalogued and indexed;

b) publish in the manner prescribed, from time to time,—

   i) the particulars of its organisation, functions and duties;

   ii) the powers and duties of its officers and employees and the procedure to be followed by them in decision making process;

   iii) the norms set by the public authority for the discharge of its functions;

   iv) the rules, regulations, instructions, manuals, government resolutions, orders and guidelines and the list of record in the office, which can be made available to the citizens;

   v) the details of facilities available to citizens for obtaining information;

   vi) the name, designation and other particulars of the Public Information Officer; and

   vii) such additional information as may be prescribed by the competent authority concerned, from time to time;

c) publish all relevant facts concerning important decisions whether administrative or quasi-judicial and policies that affect the public while announcing such decisions and policies;

d) before initiating any project, publish or communicate to the public generally and to the persons affected by the project in particular, the facts available to it or to which it has reasonable access and which in its opinion should be known to the affected persons."

The Ordinance provides for two appeals, the second to the *Lokayucta*. It provides for councils, with non-governmental participation, to monitor the working of the Act. It provides for a Commission of Records to advise the government on release of old records to the public. It provides for information to be supplied within 24 hours in cases involving the life and liberty of a person. The most progressive section is the one which provides for a fine of Rs. 250 per day for each day of delay in furnishing information to be recovered from the salary of the official concerned.

However, with change in government, the Ordinance lapsed. It is reported that very recently a draft bill incorporating the same provisions as the Ordinance of September 2002 has been sent to the Central Government for their assent before introducing the same in the Legislative Assembly.

Citizen's Charters

What is a Citizen's Charter?

A Citizen's Charter is a document written for citizens and it takes into account their needs. In it, a service provider describes the steps taken by them to provide quality service, and thereby provide customer satisfaction. The Charter sets standards and ensures the accountability, openness and transparency of the provider. Ideally, it should also state the responsibilities of the provider towards the citizen, and the steps that a citizen could take if the standards of the service are not met. A Charter must also necessarily contain contact information, details of the various schemes and services that the provider offers, and a detailed complaint redressal procedure. In short, the Charter while being *for* the citizen and *because* of the citizen, should also be a source of information about the service provider.

A report produced by the Citizen, Consumer and Civic Action Group states that the service provider would be expected to:

1. Set standards for their various services, indicating the reasonable minimum and maximum response time, or frequency of providing services, as the case may be, as far as possible in consultation with the users of the services to suit their convenience.
2. Such standards are to be well displayed and readily available to the public.
3. Standards to be scrupulously adhered to. Officials to be answerable.
4. Standards to be frequently improved and reviewed (with simplification of procedures, if possible).
5. Grievance Redressal procedure to be prescribed (indicating response time for replies to complaints).
6. Should be fully transparent and information should be easily available, with well defined display, saying who to approach for what information.
7. Should be a single window disposal instead of the citizen being pushed around.

The common citizen should gain the following from a Charter:

1. The common citizen should gain confidence that he would be heard by the man behind the counter.
2. The common citizen would know he can expect and demand courteous and effective service.
3. If things go wrong, the citizen knows whom to approach.
4. The citizen can shed his/her fear, and finally raise his/her voice.

Tamil Nadu

In G.O.Ms.No.263, P & A.R. (T) Department, dated 4.11.1997, orders were issued for the formulation of Citizen's Charter for each Department of Government. The intention behind the Citizen's Charter is to ensure accountability and transparency in regard to the services available to the people. Further, the Charter increases the general public awareness of their rights and of the standards that public services aim to achieve. Citizen's Charter helps the department to update the principles of good public service underlying the programme.

Guidelines were prepared by P & A.R. (AR) Department for preparation a Citizen's Charter and a booklet viz. "Guide" has been sent to all departments of Secretariat. 27 departments of Secretariat and certain government organisations have prepared Citizen's Charter and placed them on the table of the Legislative Assembly.

The Citizen's Charters have been made available through NICNET/INTERNET in Website – www.tn.gov.in.

In G.O.Ms.No.252, P & A.R. (T) department, dated 22.10.97, orders were issued that all departments of government have to ensure that the public has access to the details of government welfare schemes and procedures on the computer through the NIC and therefore opened ten information-cum-facilitation counters in the following places at Chennai:-

i) Collectorate
ii) High Court
iii) Secretariat
iv) Central Library (LLA Building)
v) I.G. of Registration
vi) DMS Complex
vii) Ezhilagam Complex
viii) Metro Water
ix) SIDCO and
x) Connemara Public Library

In G.O.Ms.No.308, P & A.R. (T) department, dated 22.12.1997 all Departments of Secretariat and Collectors were instructed to open information-cum-facilitation counters, so that "administration will be effective, responsive and people friendly".

Further, all departments of Secretariat have been directed to review and assess the impact of Citizen's Charter for better public service and better departmental functioning. They have also been directed to send a report on various points including the response of the public regarding the implementation of the Charters as well as the awareness of the staff and consumers and their satisfaction. The departments of Secretariat are expected to conduct periodical reviews on the implementation of Citizen's Charter introduced by them.

Government orders stated that "the procedures regarding public oriented schemes should be given to public in a manner that public can understand easily. For instance, the public should be given opportunities to understand easily the government procedures regarding the day to day affairs relating to the registration and purchases and sale of land, permission for construction of house from the Municipalities, getting family card under Public Distribution System, obtaining of electricity and drinking water connection, payment of charges, getting driving licence, registration of vehicles and registration of voters. Without these opportunities and facilities, the public have to secure these facilities only through the touts.

The government desired that Citizen's Charters specify the standard and quality of services to the public and the time limit that the public reasonably expect formalities should be completed.

"The government is of the view that it is possible to give transparent and people friendly administration by way of revising a Citizen's Charter and bringing it to the use of public with sufficient publication. With the view to implement the Citizen's Charter, the government have decided that each department should place before the Legislative Assembly in the Budget session, a hand book, along with the policy note, containing the details of welfare scheme benefiting directly with the public, how the services can be availed by the public and the related procedures and rules and regulations, the forms to be used for applying for the benefits, the officers to be approached for availing the benefits and the realistic time limit and then sell the hand book to the public at the cost prices".

According to the P & AR department, as of January 2003, the following departments have prepared Citizen's Charter:

1. Agriculture
2. Animal Husbandry & Fisheries
3. Adi-Dravidar and Tribal Welfare
4. Backward Classes, Most Backward Classes and Minorities Welfare
5. Commercial Taxes
6. Co-operation, Food and Consumer Protection
7. Higher Education
8. Finance
9. Environment and Forest
10. Energy
11. Housing and Urban Development
12. Handlooms, Handicrafts, Textiles and *Khadi*
13. Health and Family Welfare
14. Information and Tourism
15. Industries
16. Labour and Employment
17. Municipal Administration and Water Supply
18. Public Works
19. Revenue
20. Small Industries
21. Social Welfare & Nutritious Meal Programme
22. Tamil Development Culture & Religious Endowments
23. Transport
24. Highways
25. School Education
26. Rural Development, and
27. Home

According to a report and critique brought out by the Citizen, Consumer and Civic Action Group in May 1999, the Citizen's Charter in India, and with particular reference to Tamil Nadu, is yet to prove it's effectiveness. "We are still at a stage where departments have to be coaxed into forming Charters, let alone implementing them."

The report states: "Upon visits to the Secretariat, it was found that government departments are given a relaxable time of three months to formulate Charters. Some have made Charters, but are still 'fine-tuning' them for release within another two months. According to some of them, no official notice has been received asking them to 'speed it up'. Departments like Tamil Development are even planning to bring out their Charter within six months 'if it is ready by then'. There is no perceptible mood of urgency in formulating a Charter. Many of those that had brought them out have no idea if the Charter is being implemented, or what purpose it's creation has served. The general attitude seemed to be 'The Charter has been published because it had to be published'. The front office of every State Department, which is the interface between the public and the Department, also displayed a lack of knowledge of the Citizen's Charter. Few of the officials in the reception of all departments visited knew what a Charter was. They all had to contact either the Joint Secretary or the Under Secretary inside to know what a Charter was, if it was available, and if it could be distributed to a member of the public.

Such a reaction calls for a need for government officials to educate themselves on the Citizen's Charter. Only then will the entire concept prove useful and valid. In Britain, the Charter concept is vigorously advertised on billboards, pamphlets, newsletters and stickers. Members of the public are thus aware of their rights, and what course of action is open to them lest something go wrong. This is exactly the purpose that a Charter serves, and citizens of India need information that such a concept actually exists. By and large, the percentage of the Indian Population that know of the existence of Citizen's Charters in India, or what it means, is abysmally low. This is starkly evident not only among the uneducated but even among the educated masses.

"If the entire project was approached with a sense of urgency, commitment, and an honest need to be a good service provider, the success of the Citizen's Charter in India would be well within our reach."

The Citizen's Charter of the Chennai Metropolitan Water Supply and Sewerage Board was seen by consultants appointed by the ODA, U.K. in the year 2000, to recommend "Strategy for Institutional Options" for CMWSSB. The "Stakeholder Analysis" segment of their report states that out of over 50 Focus Groups of citizens/consumers interviewed in April-May 2000, less than half a dozen persons said that they had heard of the Citizen's Charter of Metrowater. Even Metrowater employees said that they had not seen it!

It may be mentioned that a study conducted by Transparency International India in 2002 of Citizen's Charters of 11 departments of the Government of Delhi and 2 departments of the Central Government found similar serious shortcomings in most departments. They include lack of awareness among the public, lack of confidence among "service seekers", lack of infrastructure, untrained and unmotivated staff, complex rules and procedures and insensitivity of officials.

Model Charter

The CAG has formulated a list of parameters for complete evaluation of any Charter. By themselves, these parameters indicate the contents of a model charter, i.e. a blueprint that every published charter should conform to.

The Parameters are:

1. *Date of Charter,* including revision if any.
2. *Statement of Service*
   a) Stated functions of department
   b) Hierarchy of persons authorised to interact with public
   c) Daily Department Information:
      - for office personnel
      - for public interaction
3. *Documents*

   Documents to be made mandatorily available for public –

   a) Written procedure for application
   b) Rules/Guidelines
   c) Rights of the consumer *vis-à-vis* the department
   d) Responsibilities of the consumer
   e) Charter
   f) Frequently Asked Questions (FAQs):

   Do you have a document providing these?
4. *Applications*
   a) Are costs for sanction/connection indicated?
   b) Are there any clearances to be obtained from other government departments?
   c) Designation of personnel to whom application is to be submitted.
   d) Designation of personnel authorised to give clarifications/where complaints can be lodged.
   e) Timeframe for acknowledging receipt of application.
   f) Timeframe for process/sanction/connection.
5. *Information Cell*
   a) Details of the functioning of the Information Cell.
   b) Designation of personnel to contact to obtain information.

c) Timeframe for receipt of information.

6. *Information of senior officers* with whom complaints can be registered after office hours:

Name/official phone number/residence phone number/fax no./email address.

7. *Complaint Redressal Procedures*

a) How to complain

b) Who to complain to

c) Time frames

d) Rights of the citizen

e) Time for refund of dues/deposit

f) Grievance redressal day.

8. *Charter Review*

a) Is there a periodical review of the Charter

b) Names of members of public/organisations, who will be invited, including their address.

c) Method of evaluating their suggestions including timeframes.

d) Consumer interaction day to improve services/ review charters.

9. *Overall clarity of charter*

a) Readability

b) Openness and transparency.

E-Governance

The new government in Tamil Nadu announced it's IT Policy in 2002. It states, among other things, that "Government will use Information Technology to empower the people with knowledge and participation in the decision making process, through a Public-Private Partnership programme to take the fruits of technology to the masses".

To upgrade the quality of life for the citizens through e-Governance and IT applications in government.

To empower people in the rural areas so as to bridge the Digital Divide.

To promote use of Tamil in Information Technology.

Various computerisation projects executed in government departments like Transport, Registration, Sales Tax and Education need to be integrated to effectively deliver the services needed by the citizens. Hence plans are made to introduce Electronic Delivery of Services (EDS).

"Steps towards conversion of the domain knowledge available in Secretariat and Government offices all over the State in key areas will be digitised and made available for all departments to facilitate a knowledge-based decision making process.

Suitable innovative schemes will be devised in consultation with government employees to upgrade the levels of IT usage in government departments up to the Section Officer level. Specific need based syllabus will be drawn up to remove the techno-phobia in rural and semi-urban offices.

IT Act 2000 of Government of India, Chapter III, Section 4 provides for recognition of electronic records. Section 5 deals with legal recognition of Digital signatures. Government will come out with guidelines for e-signature and electronic records as per Section 6 of the Act.

"Government of Tamil Nadu will set a specific annual target in order to ensure that e-governance activities of each department are completed within the next four years and will pass directives to take the following action:

"Launch and ensure wide participation of existing staff in computer literacy programmes".

The role and responsibility of the IT cell in each department/government body will be:

To prepare an overall IT vision or strategy for a four year period for the department.

Identify the areas which have maximum citizen interface, and which can be electronically delivered.

Implementation, maintenance and frequent upgradation of the applications.

"Tamil Nadu Government will encourage the development of IT applications that benefit under privileged people in the State. For instance, IT can help hill tribal people in Tamil Nadu to sell their products through the Internet".

"Government will encourage setting up of Internet Kiosk and Online libraries in existing infrastructure like public libraries/public government offices throughout the State.

"The government emphasis will be on governance with transparency. This policy is aimed at removing illiteracy and promoting technocracy, creating opportunities specially targeting rural areas. Tamil will be given a prominent place not only in the IT world but also in the commercial world."

Progress in e-Governance

In a handout issued by the Department of IT entitled "Achievements of Tamil Nadu in IT Sector", the progress made in the application of Information Technologies in various sectors has been reported. In the matter of rural connectivity, it states that the power of IT has reached the villages, signalling a new dawn of an easier and faster communication access for the rural people. It is stated that rural Internet has become a reality and has got potential for creating employment opportunities and wealth. Rural Internet Kiosks have set the pace of new dimension in the rural areas. These Kiosks, according to the handout, provide a wealth of information like canal timings, weekly rainfall etc. and can also be used for civic complaints like street lamp burning, water pump repairs etc. A Project called Rural Access to Services through Internet (RASI) has recently been launched, as an experimental project, to cover 10 districts to begin with.

The handout states that under the computerisation of land records programme (Tamil Nilam), all the 206 *taluk* offices have been fully computerised and Data digitised. With Tamil Nilam, the citizens access to land records has become easier and faster, according to the official handout. The Touch Screen Kiosks at the 30 Model *Taluk* offices will enable the public to view details like land, *patta*, guideline value, birth details etc., at one touch. Among the other departments reported upon, the handout mentions the computerised issue of laminated driving licences at all the RTO offices in the State, a website with virtual tour of government museum galleries, a Touch Screen Kiosk for information, promotion and publicity in the Tourism Department and online registration and issue of Provisional SSI Registration Certificates to entrepreneurs.

The handout mentions an ambitious programme to impart computer literacy and education in all the government higher secondary schools. It is reported that a total of 1,197 schools have been covered so far. All the government Arts, Science and Law Colleges numbering 65 have also been covered by this programme. The handout mentions that 140 out of 323 Assessment Circles of the Commercial Taxes Department have been computerised, which will benefit the tax payers. Other initiatives in IT application to improve governance include a video conferencing facility at the Secretariat to maintain contact with the District Collectors, computerisation for Low Tension Billing in the Electricity Department, GIS System introduced in the Forest Department and the computerisation of the operations of Agriculture Regulated Markets in Tamil Nadu.

A major programme, according to the handout, is the comprehensive computerisation of the Registration Department under which all 650 offices of Sub-Registrars and District Registrars will be covered. The handout states that the issue of encumbrance certificate, document registration, guideline value information etc., would then be easily accessible to the people. The handout also states that a massive programme for computerisation of the Urban Local Bodies with World Bank assistance is being undertaken.

Scope for Reform

Since many of the initiatives in e-governance are of recent origin, it is too early to evaluate the progress, the extent of public use of these services, the quality of the services and citizens satisfaction. However, taken together with such initiatives as Citizen's Charters and Right to Information Legislation there is no doubt that these are powerful instruments for improving services to the citizens and reducing the scope and opportunity for corruption which exists in most departments. Unfortunately, till recent years, the need for interface between the citizen and the government has been all pervasive, right from buying airline/railway tickets to purchasing a kilo of rice or sugar. It is only during the last decade that the reform process has set in, and although in fits and starts, considerable progress has been made in liberalisation, competition, privatisation and reduction in the bureaucratic hold on entities providing services to the citizens. The State government should in future quantify the results of E-Governance and publicise them widely. An example of this is available in a recent handout of the Government of Andhra Pradesh where the progress of the Computer aided Administration of Registration Department is reported: "The CARD Project has registered more than 2.5 million documents in two years."

The real test of improved governance in Tamil Nadu through the use of such legislative, administrative and technological instruments will lie in the satisfaction of citizens and consumers, and would happen only when they can rightfully claim and obtain services provided by the government without harassment and payment of bribes. This is possible only through sincere open government, complete transparency, participative decision making, accountability of government functionaries and responsiveness of the administration to the real needs of the people. All this cannot happen just through technological innovations. A whole new mindset is needed, which must permeate from Fort St. George right down to the Districts, *Taluks* and the *Panchayats*.

References

Report of the State Finance Commission for Local Bodies 1996 – Government of Tamil Nadu.

Report on the Entrust of Powers to Panchayats – April 1997 – State Planning Commission, Government of Tamil Nadu.

Report on the Entrustment of Power to Urban Local Bodies – November 1997 – State Planning Commission, Government of Tamil Nadu.

Report of the High Power Committee for Examining the Means for Entrusting Rights, Responsibilities and Powers to the Three Tier Panchayati Raj Institutions, December 1998 – Government of Tamil Nadu (in Tamil).

Report on the Action taken on the Recommendations of the High Power Committee – May 1999 – Government of Tamil Nadu (in Tamil).

Democratic Decentralisation – Power Entrusted to Panchayat Raj Institutions – October 1999 – Rural Development Department, Government of Tamil Nadu.

Report of the Second State Finance Commission, May 2001 – Government of Tamil Nadu.

White Paper on Tamil Nadu Government's Finances – August 2001 – Finance Department, Government of Tamil Nadu.

Decentralised Governance and Planning – A Comparative Study in Three South India States. Abdul Aziz and Others, Macmillan India Ltd, 2002.

Experience of Tamil Nadu First Panchayat Raj Institutions – A Survey (in Tamil) – People Governance Cell, Information Bulletin No. 22 – May, June 2001.